Very Young Children with Special Needs

A Foundation for Educators, Families, and Service Providers

Fifth Edition

Vikki F. Howard

University of Montana Western

Betty Fry Williams

Whitworth University

Denielle Miller

Montana Office of Public Instruction

Estee Aiken

University of Montana Western

PEARSON

Boston   Columbus   Indianapolis   New York   San Francisco   Upper Saddle River
Amsterdam   Cape Town   Dubai   London   Madrid   Milan   Munich   Paris   Montréal   Toronto
Delhi   Mexico City   São Paulo   Sydney   Hong Kong   Seoul   Singapore   Taipei   Tokyo

Vice President and Editor in Chief: Jeffery W. Johnston
Executive Editor and Publisher: Stephen D. Dragin
Editorial Assistant: Anne-Marie Bono
Marketing Manager: Joanna Sabella
Production Editor: Annette Joseph
Production Coordination and Electronic Composition: Shylaja Gattupalli/Jouve India Private Limited
Operations Specialist: Michelle Klein
Cover Design: Suzanne Behnke
Cover Image: Dave Clark Digital Photo/Shutterstock

Credits and acknowledgments borrowed from other sources and reproduced, with permission, in the textbook appear here or on the appropriate page within text.

Close-Up image: Amenic181/Fotolia

Library of Congress Cataloging-in-Publication Data
Howard, Vikki F.
 Very young children with special needs : A foundation for educators, families, and service providers / Vikki F. Howard, University of Montana Western, Betty Fry Williams, Whitworth University, Denielle Miller, Montana Office of Public Instruction, Estee Aiken, University of Montana Western. — Fifth edition.
     pages cm.
  ISBN-13: 978-0-13-311215-3
  ISBN-10: 0-13-311215-2
 1. Children with disabilities—Education (Early childhood)   2. Child development.   3. Special education.   I. Title.
  LC4019.3.V47 2014
  371.9—dc23

2013014671

18 2023

ISBN 10: 0-13-311215-2
ISBN 13: 978-0-13-311215-3

In Memory of Pat Port,
a beloved friend to us
and to children everywhere

This book is dedicated to the many children, students, colleagues, parents, and family members who have taught us well throughout our personal and professional lives. They set high standards for themselves and others, respected individual differences and needs, and committed themselves unselfishly to advocate for the care and education of children. It is their lessons we have tried to share in this text and from which we continue to learn.

About the Authors

Vikki F. Howard began her career working with families with infants and toddlers in Eastern Ohio. Later she served as a Peace Corps volunteer in Jamaica, serving families with very young children and school aged children with disabilities. As a professor at Gonzaga University, Dr. Howard collaborated with Dr. Williams to develop an ECSE program. She is author of many articles, chapters, and funded grants associated with infants, toddlers and preschoolers with disabilities and their families. Currently, she teaches at the University of Montana Western, where she directs the special education program and collaborates with tribal colleges in Montana to deliver special education pre-service education.

Betty Fry Williams has over 30 years teaching in schools with very young children with disabilities and in higher education. She is professor of education at Whitworth University in Spokane, Washington, where she chairs the Special Education program and teaches courses in early childhood special education. Her body of professional work reflects her interests in behavior analysis and in methods of teaching infants, toddlers, and preschoolers with disabilities and autism.

Denielle Miller retired from public school teaching after 25 years of serving children with special needs. She taught students ages 3-21. Denielle received her BS and MA from Montana State University–Billings. She is currently working for Side-by-Side K-12 Consulting and for the Montana Office of Public Instruction as a consultant for the Montana Behavior Initiative (MBI) and Response to Intervention (RTI). In addition, she provides professional development to Head Start teachers on several of Montana's Native American reservations. Denielle trains and assists schools in setting up school-wide positive behavior interventions and supports and creating literacy-rich environments. She is an adjunct professor in the special education department at the U of M Western.

Estee Aiken has worked in early childhood education for more than a decade across numerous states. She has spent the last five years educating pre-service teachers, predominantly in preparation for careers in the field of early childhood. In addition to her interest in the education of very young children, she also works with and conducts research with gifted children. Estee currently teaches in the Education Department at the University of Montana Western.

Brief Contents

Contents

Part 2   Human Development, Typical and Atypical

Chapter 3   Principles of Human Development   83

Part 3   Educational Programs and Services

Chapter 9   Discretionary Programs for Infants and Toddlers with Special Needs   329

Chapter 10   Mandated Services for Young Children   365

Preface

This text is a collaborative effort, not only on the part of the authors, but also because of the contributions of the many parents, professionals, researchers, and students who have added to the growing body of knowledge about how to best serve very young children with disabilities and their families. It was our intention to synthesize perspectives and information from the fields of medicine, education, intervention, psychology, law, sociology, and family life for use by those who will work with infants, toddlers, and preschoolers with special needs. It was also our goal to challenge our readers to consider the future of early intervention and their role in shaping the field of early childhood special education. We hope this text is a relevant and long-lasting resource.

The purpose of this text is to provide an introduction to early childhood professionals who plan to engage in providing services and intervention to very young children with disabilities. It is not intended as a methods text, but rather as a foundation regarding the philosophy, history, family impact, legal issues, medical concerns, and educational contexts that are most relevant for early services to children with exceptional needs. Though early childhood special education teachers may make up the majority of readers who use this text, the term *early childhood professional* is also used to include individuals from many disciplines, including health care, social work, physical and occupational therapy, childcare, and those who are involved in interagency services to young children and their families.

Part 1 articulates a philosophy that is foundational for early childhood professionals. Chapter 1 presents an overview of the guiding philosophies of the text, which will be applied and reiterated throughout the chapters. Chapter 2 focuses on the growth of special services for those with disabilities and their families. Part 2 considers the biological and environmental factors that influence development. Chapters 3 through 8 provide details on normal development and the etiology of disabling conditions that affect the very young child with exceptional needs. Part 3 describes the educational programs and services that are available to very young children with special needs. Chapters 9 and 10 address how intervention and support are provided to young children and their families. Very young children with special needs are the focus of this text, but to thoroughly understand and serve a child with disabilities, one must be knowledgeable about typical development, understand how health and genetics affect potential, and recognize the influence of the child's family and environment on realizing that potential. Throughout the book, special issues will be identified through Close Ups in order to highlight important contextual factors associated with serving children and their families. The text is interdisciplinary, inclusive, and family-focused.

New in This Edition

- Updated demographics reflecting the 2010 census
- Updated information on autism
- New content on neuroscience-based learning
- Information about improvements in the viability of extremely and very low birth weight infants
- New discussion of advances in research and treatment for children with genetic disorders
- Results of CDC's Early Hearing Detection and Intervention program
- New evidence of the impact of the Great Recession and poverty on early childhood
- Updates on IDEIA Part C Regulations
- New information on working with children with challenging behaviors
- Updated guidelines for writing IEPs

Acknowledgments

The authors extend their deepest gratitude to those who provided insight, inspiration, and encouragement. Though everybody listed was extremely busy, they all gave generously of their time and talents. There are no words that can adequately express our thanks.

We thank the many individuals at Pearson who shepherded us through this process, now and in the past; the photographers, Brian Price, Randy Williams, and the parents who shared their children's photos; and the reviewers who kindly read our manuscript and provided constructive comments: Douglas E. Carothers, Florida Gulf Coast University; Hsin-Yuan Chen, Millersville University; Darbi Haynes-Lawrence, Western Kentucky University; Kathleen Winterman, Xavier University.

We are especially grateful to Pat Port, our dear deceased friend, collaborator, and coauthor of the original text.

1 Philosophy of Early Education

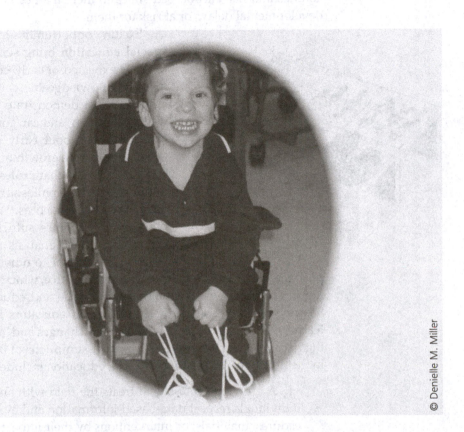

© Denielle M. Miller

With the first cry in the delivery room, there is a sudden pause in what has been a growing frenzy of action and emotion, like a long exhalation of relief and joy, and a baby is born. Parents beam, laugh, and cry; attendants share smiles and swing into action; and baby, bewildered and naked, draws in the first breath of life. Whatever this little one's life will become later, it is begun totally dependent on family, caregivers, educators, and the community. A new life, whose potential is determined not only by genetics, environment, and accidents of fate, but also by the larger value and support society provides, begins its journey.

For children born with disabilities and those whose conditions place them at developmental risk, the journey has built-in roadblocks. At the same time, these children and their families can expect far greater support than has been the case in the past. Early education for infants and children with special needs offers both promise and challenge. Although the field is relatively young, its knowledge base is established enough to be considered a necessary and important part of the educational system. Today, to a much greater degree than in the past, society acknowledges the need for early childhood services, and it values the quality of care and education provided for young children. Professional educators recognize the legitimacy and importance of education and treatment during early development. Consequently, Congress has mandated the provision of services to preschool-age children with disabilities and has encouraged states to meet the needs of infants and toddlers with developmental delays or at risk for them.

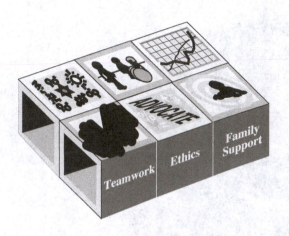

Exciting opportunities in the field of **early childhood special education** bring serious responsibilities as well. Much is expected of early educators today. Professionals must be knowledgeable concerning issues important to families, must demonstrate skill in providing direct services to children, and can contribute to the growing body of knowledge about early development and care. The recent, impressive growth of early childhood special education is a legacy that professionals can advance only by understanding the philosophy and knowledge base of the discipline's best practices. When a practice (a method or philosophy) becomes sufficiently tested through application and critical analysis that professionals accept the practice as superior to other approaches used to accomplish the same goal, it qualifies as a **best practice,** which is a dynamic concept, changing in content as the technologies of service and education are extended through research and application. Early childhood educators should expect to be lifelong learners, keeping abreast of evolutionary changes and, at the same time, actively taking part in these changes. The current assumptions of best practices most important in the field of early childhood special education include the following:

1. A growing professional treats the field with an **attitude of science.** That is, individuals respect data-based information and evaluate the effects of new procedures, materials, or interventions by their impact on the children and families being served.

2. An early childhood professional **personalizes** services to children with disabilities across a continuum of placements, recognizing the value of treatment in natural settings while respecting the specific treatment needs of individuals and the desires of their families. Early intervention is comprehensive care, not a predetermined method or place.

3. An effective professional is **culturally sensitive,** prepared to work with various populations and cultures in respectful and supportive ways.

4. A professional in early childhood education recognizes that very young children are a part of their larger family support systems and the environments that surround them. Such a professional may provide direct services to children but only within the context of family needs and environmental demands and in ways that will **empower** families.

5. An early childhood professional works in **collaboration** with families as well as experts from other disciplines to develop and provide the comprehensive services very young children need.

6. Finally, early childhood special educators must practice their profession with the highest **ethical standards for conduct.** Moreover, professionals must serve as advocates for parents and children, politically and professionally as well as through service to their communities.

Professionals now entering early childhood special education are in the position of launching their careers equipped with skills and attitudes others have taken decades to identify and develop. Other texts address methodological best practices; this chapter explores key philosophical concepts in terms of their value to professionals. These concepts also will be woven throughout the content of the text.

The Importance of an Attitude of Science

Many professionals consider teaching to be an art; that is, it is a natural aptitude or ability granted a person at birth, which flowers with opportunity and experience. Some of this may be true; certainly, most professionals in early childhood education were drawn into the field by the pleasure they found in working with young children and their families. Some gifted individuals possess talents that seem especially suited to working with infants, toddlers, and preschoolers. They display tolerance, playfulness, and a keen intuition for teaching. Others may be adept at communicating with children and parents, may be more sensitive to others' needs, or may be more skilled at working with diverse personalities and backgrounds. However, in all fields, the factor separating hobby artists from professional artists is the quality of study and effort put into developing their natural gifts, whether they are in painting, dance, drama, or teaching. Inspiration comes not from spontaneity but from a combination of knowledge, talent, and experience.

Professional artists enhance their talents by reflectively studying the work of other artists. They strive to identify principles that will improve their craft and advance the field for others. An artful teacher who relies on raw ability alone may take years to become skillful in working with and helping a variety of students. Another artful teacher who reads the professional literature, experiments with and evaluates recommended materials and procedures, and holds an attitude of science builds on natural talent to efficiently become a versatile and effective teacher.

What Is an Attitude of Science?

An attitude of science deals with what is parsimonious and empirical. **Parsimony** is the adoption of the simplest assumption in the formulation of a theory or in the interpretation of data. That is, one would look for a simple explanation before investigating more complicated possibilities. For example, if a small infant awakens crying in the middle of the night, one would first see whether the child is hungry or wet. One would not immediately jump to the conclusion that the child is suffering from separation anxiety or is ill with an intestinal infection.

Parsimony does not guarantee correctness—because the simplest explanation may not always be the correct one—but it prevents our being so imaginative as to lose touch with the reality of observed data. (Alberto & Troutman, 2009, p. 4)

Often, what is simplest is not the most interesting. For years, psychologists blamed autism specifically on mothers who were accused of being cold and rejecting toward their infants. This was an intriguing theory that grew from a complicated Freudian explanation based on psychotherapy with verbal adults, but it was not the most parsimonious. A great deal of mental suffering on the part of mothers, as well as misspent therapy, might have been saved if a parsimonious explanation had been investigated earlier. Although there is still no explanation for the etiology of autism, parsimony might have led professionals to investigate biochemical or physical causes earlier if complex theories of attribution had not been so appealing to earlier psychologists.

In special education, many methods of intervention have evolved from complicated theories. Some theories, because they make assumptions about activities in the brain that can neither be seen nor measured easily, are not testable. One example of such a method is patterning or neural training developed by Doman and Delacato. *Patterning* was a regimen that prescribed physical exercises that were purported to retrain the brain in a "normal" neural pattern that could cure motor, language, and cognitive disabilities. Thousands of parents were trained to use patterning techniques for several hours every day, often using a team of volunteers to guide precise movement exercises. Later, this method was declared to be ineffective and a distraction from more practical and effective methods (Novella, 1996). In fact, recent research suggests that much of early education, including physical movement exercises, should be conducted within the context of natural daily routines (McWilliam, 2010). The latter offers a more parsimonious solution to families and children.

An attitude of science is also a "disposition to deal with the facts rather than with what someone has said about them. . . . Science is a willingness to accept facts even when they are opposed to wishes" (Skinner, 1953, p. 6). An attitude of science requires one to be **empirical** (that is, to rely on observation or experimentation) and to be guided by practical experience rather than theory alone. A professional who is empirical tries new materials and procedures with careful observation to determine their effects on children or families using them. Based on the outcomes of such experiments, professionals decide to continue or discontinue the use of individual procedures. For example, theory (or trend) may indicate that pastel colors have a warm and calming effect on infants, encouraging their attention. To evaluate this suggestion, an empirical professional might place an infant in a plain crib with a pastel yellow, pink, and blue mobile and observe carefully to see how much the infant vocalizes, kicks, looks at the mobile, and so on. This professional would then compare the same infant's behavior when the baby is placed in the same crib and room with a mobile of contrasting white and black. Scientific professionals experiment to find out whether a theory really applies in a particular situation rather than accepting a theory without a verifiable demonstration.

Of course, a professional cannot function efficiently if every piece of advice must be directly tested or experienced before it is adopted. Fortunately, "science is more than the mere description of events as they occur. Rather, empiricism is an attempt to discover order, to show that certain events stand in lawful relations to other events" (Skinner, 1953, p. 6). Other professionals and researchers work to **replicate** results, that is, to demonstrate the same results with other children and in other settings. A scientific professional can then review research to identify data-based procedures that have been verified repeatedly through experimentation and that are likely to work, with and without adaptation, in the professional's own situation.

When the same results can be replicated consistently and when there is a well-documented literature base, the theory or principle has **predictive utility.** Such a theory provides accurate forecasts regarding how a child might respond in certain circumstances, thereby giving professionals a useful tool for supporting or modifying a child's behavior. This is not to say the data-based method selected will work with all children. However, the likelihood is increased that this method will work more often or effectively than an untested or unverified method. For example, the principle of **reinforcement** states that if a stimulus is a reinforcer, the behavior it follows is likely to increase in frequency. A professional might find that giving requested items (a music box, for example) to Amy when she says "please" increases the rate of her saying "please." The professional might then use those items as consequences for Amy when she takes a step independently, predicting with some confidence that the music box (for example) will act as a reinforcer to increase Amy's independent walking.

When a body of knowledge is advanced enough to provide a set of principles based on extensive research and experimentation, it becomes a conceptual system. A **conceptual system** shows researchers and professionals how similar procedures may be derived from basic principles.

> This can have the effect of making a body of technology into a discipline rather than a collection of tricks. Collections of tricks historically have been difficult to expand systematically, and when they were extensive, difficult to learn and teach. (Baer, Wolf, & Risley, 1968, p. 97)

Look again at the example of Amy's saying "please." Using the music box as a consequence seems like a pretty good trick to Ms. Johnson, who is visiting that day. When she returns to her classroom, she tries the music box as a consequence for Joey to see if it will increase his babbling. Nothing happens. Ms. Johnson would have been more successful if she had understood the principle behind the use of the music box. If she had had the *concept* of reinforcement in her repertoire, she would have looked for some consequence that was already effective in increasing the rate of Joey's behavior. A brief observation might show that Joey reaches for a toy more frequently when the toy is squeezed to make a noise after each reaching motion. Squeezing the toy as a consequence to increase Joey's babbling has a higher probability of success than playing the music box. Or if Ms. Johnson recognized the concept that a child's frequently chosen activities or materials often act as reinforcers, she might have found that marshmallows, bouncing, or clapping could also be predictable reinforcers. Ms. Johnson's skills would have been much improved if she had a data-based conceptual system from which to work, not just a set of tricks. Applied behavior analysis offers one data-based conceptual system that is of great value to educators. Behavioral approaches are parsimonious because they deal with observable relationships between environmental stimuli, behavioral responses, and contingent consequences.

> For a behaviorist, all learning principles are defined on the basis of what actually happens, not what we think is happening. (Alberto & Troutman, 2009, p. 23)

The basic principles of behavior analysis were developed through extensive empirical testing and were replicated in thousands of classroom, clinic, and home applications. Therefore, the principles and procedures have a high degree of predictive utility, and many successful interventions have been developed based on this conceptual system. Although it is not within the scope of this text to teach the principles of behavior analysis, a few behavioral examples will help to illustrate elements of a conceptual system (see Table 1–1). The basic principles of behavior analysis include reinforcement, punishment, and extinction, although these simple principles have been extended to dozens of procedures that help children learn. Yet this conceptual system, like all others, must be challenged by scientific educators to build on and improve their abilities to match intervention to the needs of the children and families served. The scientific professional builds on natural talent for working with children, families, and professionals by drawing from a knowledge base of concepts that work because they are parsimonious, empirically derived, and replicable.

The purpose of research in education is to explain phenomena, to predict what will happen to behavior under given circumstances and to use that knowledge to control the conditions that affect behavior. To be considered scientific, we must aspire to achieve two things: (1) to identify generalizations that allow us to explain, predict, and control the outcomes of our interventions and (2) to advance progressively, that is, to lay some questions to rest as we work to solve others. Gallagher (1998) cautioned that science must never replace values as a part of the professional conversation. We hasten to add, however, that values must also not replace

Table 1–1 Basic Principles of Applied Behavior Analysis

Basic Principle	Contingent Consequence	Effect on Future Rate of Behavior	Example
Reinforcement	When a stimulus is presented (positive) or removed (negative) contingent upon a response,	the future probability of that response *increases*.	A child who chews a carrot carefully before swallowing is given ice cream immediately after and in the future chews carefully more often (positive reinforcement).
Punishment	When a stimulus is presented or removed contingent upon a response,	the future probability of that response *decreases*.	A child who hits a play partner is removed from the play activity and told to watch for 5 minutes before being returned to the play activity and in the future hits less often.
Extinction	When the contingent stimulus for a previously reinforced response is no longer presented,	the future probability of the behavior *decreases*.	A child who takes toys away from others has in the past been allowed to keep playing with the stolen toys, and the rate of stealing toys increased. Now the teacher makes sure the child returns any toy taken from another child, and the rate of stealing decreases.

empiricism; it is essential that professionals balance the two. We must embrace a philosophy of moral advocacy that also determines, explains, and makes effective our course of action.

The History of Disability Rights

Disability rights have been a part of the larger civil rights movement in the United States and in many ways mirrored or echoed the history, actions, and achievements of better-known activists who fought for racial equality in the United States (see Figure 1–1). During the 18th and 19th centuries, the exclusion and segregation of people both of color and with disabilities predominated. It took a civil war to eliminate slavery, but even into the mid-20th century, people of color were still not guaranteed the right to vote, the right to an education, or access to political office or economic security. At the same time, people with disabilities were locked away from society in asylums, hospitals, workhouses, and prisons and were often abused in these restrictive settings (Stubblefield, 2007).

At the end of the 1880s, rates of institutionalization actually increased, and the growth of social Darwinism and the eugenics movement brought forced sterilization of persons with disabilities. Tens of thousands of women in the United States who were classified as "feebleminded" or morons, were involuntarily sterilized during

Figure 1–1   Phases in the Development of Disability Rights, an Echo of the Civil Rights Movement and the Bridges That Led to Progress

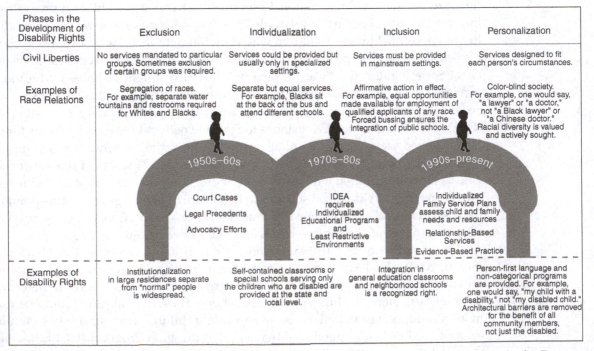

Source: Information taken from *Enabling and Empowering Families: Principles and Guidelines for Practice*, by Dunst, Trivette, and Deal, 1988, Cambridge, MA: Brookline.

the 20th century (Stubblefield, 2007). In fact, most of the ideas for extermination used by Hitler were borrowed from the eugenics movement in the United States. The Nazis murdered hundreds of thousands of persons with disabilities by lethal injection, starvation, withholding of treatment, and poisoning.

Individualization

Following World War II, years of fighting racial segregation in public schools resulted in victory in 1954 as Special Counsel Thurgood Marshall and the National Association for the Advancement of Colored People (NAACP) won in the case of *Brown v. the Board of Education,* ensuring that no children could be excluded from receiving an education in their local schools, regardless of race. This case had the effect of ending the separate education of children in schools that respectively served children based on the color of their skin. The Supreme Court stated: ". . . in these days it is doubtful that any child may reasonably be expected to succeed in life if he is denied access to education. Such an opportunity, where a state has undertaken to provide it, is a right which must be available to all on equal terms . . . equal facilities are inherently unequal." In determining that exclusion from education violated the due process clause of the 14th Amendment of the Constitution, the court established the right to an equal opportunity to education.

This victory was a catalyst for the African American civil rights movement and a major inspiration to the disability rights movement at a time when the political climate was equally supportive. Former presidents John F. Kennedy and Lyndon B. Johnson, both strong forces for progress in civil rights and racial equality, also were essential in increasing federal involvement in the care and treatment of people with disabilities. Kennedy had a personal interest, because his sister had been institutionalized with mental retardation. Consequently, Kennedy established programs to improve the care of persons with disabilities. It was Kennedy who proposed funding to train personnel to serve children with disabilities, to increase research in the area of disabilities, and to provide incentives for community-based services. Johnson's Great Society initiated a "war on poverty" that also sought improved educational services for all children. During his administration, Title I of the Elementary and Secondary Education Act of 1965, the Elementary and Secondary Education Act (ESA) of 1966, and Federal Assistance to State Owned and Operated Schools for the Handicapped were passed. Paralleling the desegregation of schools based on race after *Brown v. Board of Education,* the ESA spelled the end of an era of separate or private facilities for children with disabilities. Segregation gave way to state and federal provisions for individualized services in less restrictive settings. From this point on, the roles of federal agencies in early childhood special education and early intervention were to provide access to services and to improve the quality of services.

One example of this federal vision is seen in the development of Head Start (Smith, 2000). Head Start was begun in the mid-1960s to provide early education for children in poverty, but in 1972, the program specifically set aside 10 percent of its enrollment slots for children with disabilities. Thus, federal funds could be used in local communities to initiate services to young children with disabilities. Another example is the Handicapped Children's Early Education Program (HCEEP), which was established in 1968 and for 30 years promoted research and development efforts aimed at improving assessment, instruction, and service delivery for preschoolers with disabilities. In this way, the federal government was able to generate a knowledge base that supported state and local programs (Smith, 2000).

Parent groups and professional associations united in advocating for children with disabilities at a time when many of these children were totally excluded from any educational services. From 1972 through 1974, court cases regarding the right to education were heard in 28 states (Crockett & Kauffman, 1998). When Congress was finally persuaded to act, it approved the original 1975 legislation that would later be named Individuals with Disabilities Education Act (IDEA); it called for the free, appropriate education of children in the **least restrictive environment (LRE).** Prior to IDEA's passage, a million children had been excluded from public school because of their disabilities. Those who attended public school often received inadequate services in isolated settings.

The LRE is the legal term used to define the rights of children with disabilities to be educated in settings where they are not segregated from children without disabilities. The Education for All Handicapped Children's Act of 1975 states:

> 1. To the maximum extent appropriate, children with disabilities are educated with children who are nondisabled; and 2. Special classes, separate schooling, or other removal of children with disabilities from the regular educational environment occurs only when the nature or severity of the disability is such that education in regular classes with the use of supplementary aids and services cannot be achieved satisfactorily. (Section 34 C.F.R. 300.550([b]))

The legal provisions for the LRE supported no immutable rule of placement but a preference for including children in regular classrooms and allowing specialized (separated) services as needed by individuals. When asked if placement of a child with a disability in the regular classroom clearly constituted the LRE, the courts responded ambiguously. The placement decision must consider how well a child progresses in a regular setting, parents' preferences, availability and need for special **related services,** and other highly individualized factors.

Inclusion

When children with special needs are served in settings that were designed for and primarily serve children without disabilities, this practice is referred to as *inclusion*. Since the passage of IDEA in 1975, public programs serving children with special needs ascribed to a **continuum of services** model that depended on the regular classroom and a variety of increasingly segregated options in terms of special education placements and related services. Until recently, the more challenges a child had, the more segregated was the placement, which also implied more specialized and intensive intervention.

Despite federal incentives for states to serve very young children with disabilities, many states did not take advantage of the funding to begin providing comprehensive programs. Advocates, discouraged by this lack of universal response, convinced Congress to extend IDEA through mandated services for 3- to 5-year-olds; additional incentives were added for providing services to very young children from newborn to age 3 with disabilities. By 1994, all states had mandated services for preschoolers and established early intervention policies.

Natural Environments

In the 1997 amendments to IDEA, early intervention regulations stressed a preference for **natural environments** for providing services to very young children within an inclusion model. This meant that as much as is appropriate, given individual child and family needs, infants and toddlers should be served in homes, day-care centers, and preschools where children without disabilities would be naturally present. Inclusion philosophy, therefore, rests on the assumption that special education with its related therapies should be thought of as a service, not a place.

Preschool programs, due to their ecology, may provide an ideal context for inclusion. Most early childhood programs are language- and social-skills based and have multiple daily activities in which children are encouraged to learn from contextually relevant and problem-based curricula. Inclusion is not simply a placement; it also has to do with the integrity of a placement. When a child with a disability is placed in a regular setting, personnel and resources should be capable of meeting the child's developmental, behavioral, social, family, and health needs. At the same time, such limitations should not be used as an excuse for exclusion of children when it is feasible to secure the necessary training and resources.

Challenges for Inclusion and the Natural Environments Approach

Now, decades after a philosophy of inclusion in special education, resistance to and capacity for implementing inclusive programs with integrity remain frustratingly common. Specific challenges in natural settings include professional specialization, intensity of service delivery, appropriate response to individual needs, respect for family needs and priorities, and a lack of quality settings, community resources, and support.

Professional specialization. There is considerable overlap in the preparation needed for professionals serving infants, toddlers, and preschoolers with or without special needs. Both require strong grounding in developmental growth, relationship building with caregivers, and effective methods of facilitating development across domains. Yet, early childhood preparation for children without disabilities does not concentrate on the skills needed to design and implement services for children with special needs. This gap in training is more pronounced in professionals working with this very young population because children identified for services before school age tend to have significant developmental disabilities. Children with disabilities (even those enrolled in natural environments) require specialized services that can be provided only by specialists in early childhood special education. Likewise, therapists in physical and occupational therapy, speech and language development, mental health, and other related services struggle with immersion treatments in settings that have not been designed for specialized services.

Intensity of service delivery. Natural environment practice at the preschool level is an acknowledged best practice, even if it is not universally implemented. However, debate continues around early intervention for children from birth to 3 years of age (Shelden & Rush, 2001). The early detection of problems and the provision of appropriate intervention can improve outcomes for an infant or toddler with disabilities, but the quality of the intervention that is actually delivered is of fundamental importance (Fenichel, 2001). The ultimate impact of any intervention depends on both the expertise of the persons delivering intervention and the personal relationships those persons establish with each child's family (Fenichel). An intensive and individualized approach that works toward well-defined goals related to the specific needs and resources of children and their families may be more important than the configuration of a service delivery model.

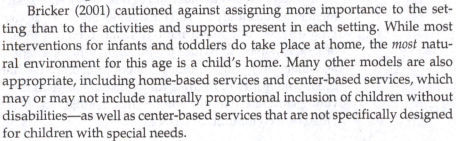

Bricker (2001) cautioned against assigning more importance to the setting than to the activities and supports present in each setting. While most interventions for infants and toddlers do take place at home, the *most* natural environment for this age is a child's home. Many other models are also appropriate, including home-based services and center-based services, which may or may not include naturally proportional inclusion of children without disabilities—as well as center-based services that are not specifically designed for children with special needs.

Appropriate response to individual needs. Education law—based on educational best practices—has always required that intervention be based on individual needs. Such a perspective may be particularly important for children from birth to 3 years of age, because these children tend to represent those children with the most severe disabilities (Table 1–2). Approximately 343,000 infants and toddlers received early intervention in 2011 (National Early Childhood Technical Assistance Center, 2012). This number represented only 2.8% of all children from birth to 3 years of age, whereas nearly 13% of school-age children were served in special education. Mild disabilities such as learning disabilities, mild intellectual disabilities, and mild behavior disabilities, representing over 80% of children in special education in schools, are usually not identified until school age. Many infants and toddlers with serious developmental delays also have significant medical, physical, and family adjustment needs. Service delivery models that cannot provide support for these and other high maintenance needs, even if they might be considered as provided in a more natural environment,

Table 1–2 Characteristics of Children from Birth to 5 Years with Developmental Delays

Proportion of Population	Area of Delay
46%	Were reported as having a lot of trouble with communication
26%	Described as having developmental delays
70%	Were male
19%	Could not pay attention and stay focused
25%	Startled easily
39%	Were very active and excitable
11%	Were often aggressive

would be less suitable in the very early years than a program that provides high-quality, comprehensive services.

Respect for family needs and priorities. As mentioned, some families of infants and toddlers receiving early intervention also present factors that may place their children at risk (see Table 1–3). Unfortunately, as state agencies change the way personnel deliver services, particularly when the agencies move toward fee-for-service structures often tied to Medicaid or other insurance systems, services tend to be fragmented at the family level. This fragmentation tends to reduce collaboration among professionals, to make it more difficult to embed interventions within the context of families' lives, to reduce the integration of interventions with those of other professionals, and to make it much more difficult to be "family-centered" (McCollum, 2000). The reality of funding may cause agencies to limit choices to families of very young children with disabilities; thus, families lose the options that might be provided by a continuum of services.

Lack of community settings, resources, and support. While advocates were striving for early intervention services and inclusion in typical environments, communities simultaneously experienced a decline in the availability of quality childcare. At the same time, there appeared to be an increased need for services as more children with disabilities were being identified (Table 1–4) at an earlier age (National Center for Special Education Research, 2012). The percentage of preschool children served under IDEA increased in 48 states (excluding Texas and Idaho); 46 states saw increases (excluding Delaware, Florida, Mississippi, and Ohio) in infants and toddlers served

Table 1–3 Characteristics of Families of Children Receiving Early Intervention and Preschool Services

Approximate Proportion of Children	Risk Factors of Families
1/4	Had incomes of less than $20,000 a year Fathers with some college education
1/5	Mothers with some college education
1/3	Received welfare or food stamps in the previous year
1/3	Were in households that did not include the child's biological or adoptive father (given that these children were under 3 years of age, this number was likely to increase over time)
<5%	Were born to teenage mothers
<5%	Were born to mothers over age 40

Source: Preschoolers with Disabilities: Characteristics, Services, and Results, National Center for Special Education Research, Institute of Educational Sciences, 2008. From *http://ies.ed.gov/ncser/pubs/20063003/summ_a.asp*

Table 1–4   Demographic Changes in the Percentages of Children Served in Early Childhood from 1997 to 2006

Demographic	1997 Percentage of Children Identified	2006 Percentage of Children Identified
5 yr old	6.27	7.41
4 yr old	4.89	6.07
3 yr old	2.88	4.01
2 yr old	2.49	3.91
0–2 yr old	1.65	2.40
White preschoolers/infants and toddlers	4.86/1.41	6.45/2.55
Black preschoolers/infants and toddlers	4.43/1.66	5.93/2.32
Asian preschoolers/infants and toddlers	2.28/1.18	3.59/1.95
American Indian preschoolers/infants and toddlers	6.31/1.81	8.14/2.45

Source: Preschoolers with Disabilities: Characteristics, Services, and Results, National Center for Special Education Research, Institute of Educational Sciences, 2012. From *http://ies.ed.gov/ncser/pubs/20063003/summ_a.asp*

under IDEA. Obviously, a dilemma arises when professionals advocate for including children in childcare programs but most services available are of poor quality, or there are simply too few high-quality natural environments for very young children. Bricker (2001) recommended that "when possible and appropriate, services should be delivered to children in their natural environment; however, the individual needs of some children may supersede blanket policy and require that other placements be considered. The bottom line is that services should meet the individual needs of children and families" (p. 2). In other words, the priority for infants and toddlers with special needs is for high-quality services first and natural environments second—and the best of all possible models is when these two priorities coincide.

Personalization

Personalization is a new term used to capture a philosophy of care that recognizes the multiple, comprehensive services that very young children with disabilities often need while the diverse priorities and needs of their families are also accommodated. Personalization emphasizes the "person-first" attitude of advocates for the disabled who serve *children* with intellectual disabilities rather than *mentally retarded* children. The latter language places more value on category than person. Moreover, personalization seeks to create a community where services are tailored to fit the goals and aspirations of each child and that child's family and to provide support so that each child can reach her or his full potential.

Personalization is a logical progression in the development of rights and services related to disabilities, moving beyond the recent prevailing philosophy of **inclusion,** which is generally applied to educating students with and without disabilities together within regular classes in neighborhood schools. To understand how personalization differs from inclusion, we must return to the roots of inclusion: the political struggle for establishing rights for those with disabilities.

Many gains for people with disabilities were made through civil rights–based strategies that resulted in state and federal laws providing entitlement programs for those with disabilities. At the same time, these entitlements were contingent on being able to define an individual as disabled. This meant that although opportunities were guaranteed, persons had to identify themselves as "abnormal" and apart from their peer communities to take advantage of such programs (Clapton & Fitzgerald, 2002). Today, advances in genetic technology and reproductive science further emphasize the differences of those with diagnosed disabilities. Therefore, it becomes increasingly critical that society embrace a new conception of disability. We need to understand disability as part of the gradient of the human condition that can affect any of us any time in our lives, that can be a part of any family, and that is a natural condition found in any community. We need to value disability as we have come to value diversity of race, religion, culture, age, sexual orientation, and other human differences (Clapton & Fitzgerald).

It is the responsibility of professionals to advance high-quality, effective early childhood special education and early intervention in two ways. Recent international and national economic austerity decisions continue to erode a once robust social safety net that included expansion of services for very young children with special needs. Therefore, professionals in this field must first act to protect and even expand the tremendous federal gains made in the 1980s and 1990s, and then they must act to strengthen state—and perhaps more important—local commitment. In addition to the shrinking of the pie, there is an ever-present threat that federal measures may be rescinded altogether. When former president Ronald Reagan tried to repeal IDEA in 1980, a groundswell of protest stopped his attempt, yet the Early Education Program for Children with Disabilities (formerly HCEEP) was repealed in 1997, to reduce the federal bureaucracy despite 30 years of proven effectiveness (Groark, Eidelman, Kazmarek, & Maude, 2011). Before it was repealed, HCEEP provided $25 million annually to research and development in early childhood education and services. The unlimited numbers of public needs currently vying for limited public resources make the job of adequately funding early childhood services more difficult.

It would be wise at this time in our history to rebuild a sense of local community and its responsibilities in providing services to young children with special needs (Smith, 2000). All citizens need to understand that, as we fight for early intervention services, we also need to ensure high-quality services for all young children and their families. The real change in how young children are cared for in our society relies on what is in the hearts and minds of individual citizens (Smith). This change is best accomplished by building communities that are family friendly and that care enough about children to increase taxes, to restructure jobs so families can spend more time at home, to value early childhood professionals, and to attract the best and brightest for serving young children.

What Is Meant by Personalization in Early Education and Intervention?

Personalized intervention is based on several important principles (Williams, 2003):

1. *Each child's abilities and needs are unique and specific to that individual.* A child's program of goals and treatment should depend on that child's developmental progress, the therapeutic needs related to the type and severity of the disabling condition, risk factors and supports present within the environment, and family strengths and concerns. Planning requires comprehensive, interdisciplinary assessment and planning. No child should be treated based solely on age, economic level, or type of diagnosis. The individual outcomes identified for a child must drive what supports are provided, and all eligible children must have access to the most comprehensive services available.

2. *Each child's success depends on the quality of interaction, therapy, and education provided by caregivers, family, and professionals.* The level of care must be consistent with the level of need of the child and the family. "The ultimate impact of any intervention is dependent on both staff expertise and the quality and continuity of the personal relationship established between the service provider and the family that is being served" (National Research Council and Institute of Medicine, 2000, p. 365). High standards for professional training and delivery of services must be met and positive relationships established. Of most importance is the quality of parent–child transactions, which should reflect sensitivity, reciprocity, affective warmth, and other positive traits (Guralnick, 2001). Also of great importance are the relationships among all members of the service team, the professionals, and the family. Finally, it is especially meaningful when families have the opportunity to connect to each other.

3. *A full spectrum of services and placement options must be available in order to appropriately serve each child's needs.* IDEA, Part C, stipulated that services may encompass a wide range of options, including family training; counseling; home visits; special instruction; speech, language, and audiology services; occupational and physical therapy; psychological services; medical services; health services; social work services; vision services; assistive technology; transportation; and other supports. Early intervention may be provided in a range of locations including hospitals, homes, childcare centers, special schools, clinics, and other settings. Only rarely is a single entity capable of providing all necessary early intervention services for a family. Types of services needed and delivered change within and across children. When appropriate, all children should have the opportunity to interact with peers who are nondisabled and disabled, but service providers should be able to customize services and placements to meet individual needs.

4. *The focus of intervention must be on achieving goals identified for each individual child and family, by maximizing all learning opportunities.* Research-based practices are determined to be most likely to benefit each child. Intervention should be designed around authentic, meaningful, and functional therapeutic activities. Even so, not every child benefits from even the most validated procedures. Therefore, a child's progress must be evaluated on an ongoing basis. After a child's goals and expected outcomes are defined, a review of relevant research

should identify treatments most likely to be effective. As the selected interventions are implemented, data should reveal if and to what extent treatment needs to be changed or modified to further enhance progress.

5. *The primacy of parent decisions must be respected and the family's values, priorities, and needs honored.* Parents are the most important factor in the service equation. Without a relationship between caregivers and professionals that values families where they are at—emotionally, culturally, and economically—even the highest quality intervention will not matter. Information should be fully disclosed and a range of community resources offered so that families can make good choices for their children. In addition, practices that allow families to become more knowledgeable and confident should be used to assist each family's growth and self-determination. Stressors that affect the quality of family interaction and effectiveness, such as unmet information needs, interpersonal distress, lack of resources, and confidence threats, should be assessed and addressed to ensure that each family functions optimally (Havens, 2005).

6. *Comprehensive care requires full community commitment.* In order to provide a full spectrum of options for families and their very young children with disabilities, the whole community must be aware of local needs and must participate in providing the resources necessary for support. Childcare providers who are capable and willing to accept children with disabilities, neighbors and extended family who are supportive and understanding, and employers who recognize legitimate family demands on an employee's time should be available. There should also be a range of professionals and treatment settings available to provide alternatives that most closely meet the needs of children and families. A collaborative spirit among these professionals and a sense of responsibility throughout the community provides a powerful net surrounding and supporting families and children with special needs. A commitment to provide the best possible services to all children raises the standard of care and education of all children.

The Implications of Personalization

A professional commitment to a philosophy of personalization requires a good deal of groundwork to be effectively operationalized. A number of baseline conditions optimize the possibility that practices can be personalized:

1. Services to very young children with disabilities require *full funding*. It is incumbent on Congress to finally and immediately commit funds promised to IDEA (Diament, 2011). By creating a federal safety net to support service providers who educate children with extraordinary needs that require more resources, states would have adequate funds to implement services for preschoolers and the mandate to provide early intervention to those from birth to 3 years.

2. Priorities must be set for *personnel training* in order to fill positions with highly qualified personnel who are in short supply. Boe and Cook (2006) found that only 44 percent of first-time special education teachers were fully certified. Further shortages in pediatric therapies abound and make it difficult to provide alternative placements and comprehensive services to children.

3. Well-documented, evidence-based best practices in early intervention should be implemented on a wider, more regular basis. In addition, information about advancements in the technology of early intervention areas must be developed and disseminated to make it easier to access information and plan treatments. The process is complicated by the lack of time available to professionals and families who are directly involved in child intervention. Resources that will allow speedy response to immediate needs must be made available.

4. *Advocacy* on behalf of individuals with disabilities must continue. Membership in advocacy groups such as the Council for Exceptional Children has decreased in recent years (Smith, 2000). Vigilance is required to protect rights that have been hard won, or we risk losing them. We also must find ways to impassion grassroots groups who have always achieved the greatest gains for the disabled, to seek higher quality services now. It is critical that advocates recognize that real change in how young children are viewed and cared for in this society should not rest on federal or even state laws but must be founded on local citizens' concern for the children within their midst. "You can't mandate everything that matters!" (Smith, p.13).

The Importance of Being Culturally Sensitive

The United States is one of the most ethnically diverse countries in the world, with at least a hundred racial, ethnic, and cultural groups. In recent years, however, trends in birthrates, immigration, family structures, and economics have greatly altered national **demographics** and will continue to do so in the future. Those trends continue to change the face of America and to affect the national dialogue and relationships between citizens. In the 2010 census, individuals of Spanish/Latino or Hispanic origin accounted for 16.3% of the population (43% increase from 2000), those of African American descent made up 12.6% (12% increase from 2000), Asians composed 4.8% (43% increase from 2000), American Indian and Alaska Natives made up 0.9%, and 2.9% reported mixed-race origins. Caucasians made up 72.4% of the population (5.7% decrease from 2000). In 2008, the population of the United States broke a 300 million benchmark (U.S. Census Bureau, 2008). The proportion of children under the age of 5 increased more for African American, American Indian, Native Hawaiian, and Hispanic groups than for Asians or Caucasians. In the 2010 census, nearly half of children under age 18 were from racial minorities. In fact, minority children accounted for 92% of the growth in the child population from 2000 through 2010, with Hispanic children accounting for nearly half of that increase.

Such diversity has often led to conflict because of a lack of receptiveness to differences (Taylor, 1998). Negative interpersonal reactions to others may result from a number of factors:

1. *Assumed similarity.* We assume our beliefs and values are the same as others'.

2. *Ethnocentrism/denigration of differences.* We hold the attitude that our own culture or origin is superior.

3. *Anxiety/tension.* We are uncomfortable when our basic values are opposed.

© Ruth Jenkinson/DK Images

4. *Prejudice.* We hold a hostile attitude toward people who belong to a different group.

5. *Stereotyping.* We make assumptions about people based on their ethnic or cultural group.

6. *Comfort with the familiar.* We are drawn to people who share similar interests and values and exclude others.

Effective early childhood educators overcome the tendency to ignore the importance of a child's home language and culture. These educators respect and preserve diversity, celebrate shared beliefs and traditions, and honor what is distinctive in the many groups that make up this nation. That is, professionalism includes cultural competence or an ability to transform knowledge and cultural awareness into interventions that support healthy relationships within the appropriate cultural context (King, Sims, & Osher, 2000). Elements of cultural competency include a respect for diversity in every form, an understanding of one's own culture and of how personal cultural practices affect those with other values, and the regular practice of embedding cultural knowledge into all aspects of a program (King et al., 2000).

The challenge of becoming culturally competent begins with an honest assessment of how one relates to those who are different (Vincent, Randall, Artledge, Tobin & Swain-Bradway, 2011). Questions to be asked include the following: How much time do I spend with people who are culturally different from me? How comfortable am I in immersion experiences? What is my commitment to being culturally competent? Negative answers to these questions help identify new experiences that should be sought out to improve **cultural competence.**

Population Trends

In the first census of the 21st century, Hispanic Americans overtook African Americans to become the country's largest ethnic minority (U.S. Census Bureau, March 2001) and grew by another 43 percent by the second census of the 21st century (U.S. Census Bureau, 2011). People of Hispanic origin include immigrants from many countries and cultures connected to Spain, Mexico, Central and South America, and the Caribbean. Asian Americans encompass an astounding variety of people, languages, religions, and cultures with many differences among them. Although relatively small, the Asian American population too grew by 43 percent between 2000 and 2010 (U.S. Census Bureau, 2011). While the overall rate of population growth slowed in the 21st century, the rate of growth was disproportionately comprised of people of color. By the year 2050, it is expected that there will be no clear majority race. Six states now have majority minorities, with California and then Texas having the largest percentage of students of color (U.S. Census Bureau, 2011).

A major factor influencing ethnic demographics is immigration. As compared to historic waves of immigration to the United States, today's immigrants are less educated, poorer, and more likely to be unemployed than those from past eras. Nearly two-thirds of Hispanic immigrants live and work in the United States illegally before being granted legal status. Other factors contributing to demographic shifts are birthrates, which are slightly higher in foreign-born families than in native-born ones, and the fact that the average age of immigrant females is younger than the average age of native-born women. Nearly one-third of Hispanic individuals are under age 18.

Hispanics, like most recent immigrant groups throughout history, suffer from the highest rates of poverty, have the highest school dropout rates, and are educated in mostly urban, impoverished, and highly segregated schools. In 2010, 37% of Hispanic families were headed by a female (up from 23% in 1993). Over 20% of Hispanics were at or below poverty in the 2010 census, with more than half of that group children who were 5 years old or younger; 72% of Hispanics held unskilled or semiskilled jobs. About 50% of Hispanics will not finish high school, 38% are held back at least one grade, and 50% are overage at grade 12. Hispanic children were placed in special education six times more often than were children in the general population.

Though the African American population increased 12% from 2000 to 2010, African American enrollment in public schools decreased, dropping from 17% to 15% from 1990 through 2010 (National Center for Education Statistics, 2012). The percentage of Caucasian students also decreased during the same period, from 67% to 54% (National Center for Education Statistics). In 2010, 27% of African Americans reported living below the poverty level (U.S. Census Bureau, 2010). Nearly half (48%) of the nation's students are students of color, yet teachers of color represent only 16% of the teaching force (Boser, 2011). Moreover, this gap is expected to widen; by 2020, it is predicted that the percentage of children of color will continue rise to over 50%, while the percentage of teachers of color will drop to 5% (Boser). This disparate statistic suggests two immediate needs: (1) Those that teach must be well prepared for diversity, and (2) there is a need for enhanced recruitment and training opportunities for minority educators.

Special education services are not proportionately representative of minority populations (U.S. Commission on Civil Rights, 2009). Hispanics, African Americans, and American Indians tend to be overrepresented in special education. For example, during the 2001–2002 school year, African American students accounted for 14.8% of the general population of students but made up nearly 20% of the special education population (U.S. Commission on Civil Rights, 2002). In addition, African American students were diagnosed as mentally retarded at a rate more than twice their national proportion in the general population, and their representation in the categories of developmental delay and emotional disturbance were nearly two-thirds higher (U.S. Commission on Civil Rights). African American students are also more likely than Caucasian students to be placed outside the regular classroom in residential facilities, separate schools, and correctional facilities.

These racial discrepancies are probably due to many confounding factors that tend to correlate with minority status: low educational attainment, language differences, lack of economic resources, and lack of health insurance, all of which may contribute to an endless cycle of educational disadvantage (Smart & Smart, 1997). Although difficult to estimate precisely, the discriminating impact of institutional biases in testing, curriculum, social expectations, and teaching strategies on the appropriate education of minority children is also apparent. Adding to the problem are poor-quality "regular" education that triggers more referrals, poorly trained teachers and diagnosticians, lack of adequate school resources, and use of special education as a form of discipline (U.S. Commission on Civil Rights, 2002).

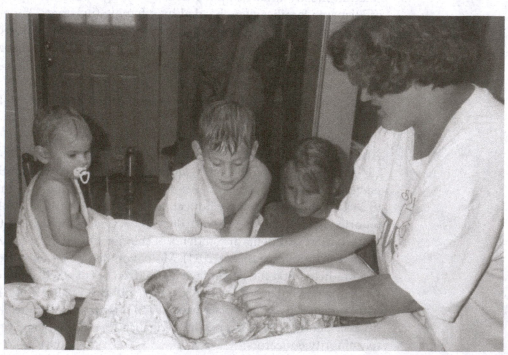

© Denielle M. Miller

Economics

From 1912 until 1979, the average family's economic situation gradually improved; the poverty rate for children dropped to a low of 14%, while the middle class grew. In the 1980s, the number of children living in poverty in the United States dramatically increased; by the early 1990s, about 20% of all children lived below the poverty line; and by 1993, the figure for children under age 6 who lived in poverty reached 26% (Guo, 1998). After the "Great Recession" of the late 2000s, a worrying trend emerged in the spatial and ethnic concentration of poverty (Lichter, Parisi, & Taquino, 2012). Lichter and colleagues found that the economic decline of the late 2000s tended to isolate and ghettoize poor people, who have become even poorer as a result of a collapsed economy. This economic, geographic, and social isolation increases the stranglehold on economic progress that was much tighter for persons of color, who were disproportionately affected by the economic downturn.

Very young children were the most likely to be poor; the poverty rate for American children under age 3 (2.1 million in poverty in 2000) was about 80% higher than the rate for adults or the elderly (Song & Lu, 2002). Another 2.6 million children under age 3 lived in near poverty (calculated at 200% of the federal poverty level), which made them eligible for Medicaid and State Child Health Insurance (Song & Lu). In those states (Mississippi, Louisiana, New Mexico, Alabama) with the highest poverty rates and in Washington, D.C., the poorest citizens were babies and preschoolers (O'Brien & Dervarics, 2007).

The consequences of childhood poverty are multiple. Poor children are more likely to have a low birth weight, to die in the first year, and to suffer hunger or abuse but less likely to have adequate medical care. Children from poor homes start off at a disadvantage with less access to prenatal and early health care, quality day care as infants, and quality early childhood programs (Slavin, 1998).

Since 1990, the number of children born to single mothers has increased from 26% to 40% (Center for Public Education, 2007). In 1950, approximately 28% of mothers worked outside the home. In 2012, 68% of mothers worked outside the home, a number that is even higher for mothers of children under 18 (71%) (Park & Wang, 2013). The great number of children who spend a significant amount of each day in professional care places greater responsibility on early educators to provide appropriate experiences for these children and their families.

The likelihood that a child will live in poverty tends to parallel the data on children from minority families. Although 18% of Caucasian children are poor, 46% of African American children live in poverty; the latter proportion has not been lower than 40% since 1959 when the Census Bureau first started measuring childhood poverty (Mitchell, 1995). More than two of three African American children in single-mother households are poor (Montgomery, Kiely, & Pappas, 1996). As with other trends, a disproportionate percentage of African Americans and people of Hispanic origin are among the homeless (Williams & DeSander, 1999). Of children under age 3, young African American and Hispanic children are three times more likely than Caucasian children to live in poverty (Song & Lu, 2002). For children under age 3 who lived with single mothers, the poverty rate was 52% for African American children and 45% for Hispanic children (Song & Lu, 2002).

Children also make up the fastest growing segment of the homeless population (Williams & DeSander, 1999). As proof, families with children represented 36% of those in homeless shelters (Children's Defense Fund, 1998). By 1997, more than a million American children were homeless; 250,000 of those were below school age (Nunez & Collignon, 1997). Homeless children displayed a wide range of social, emotional, and academic difficulties typically seen in children who qualify for special education (Walther-Thomas, Korinek, McLaughlin, & Williams, 1996). These deficiencies include poor personal/emotional development, reduced gross motor and fine motor skills, and underdeveloped interaction skills. Poor children also have significantly higher rates of lead poisoning, which contributes to neurological damage and long-term behavior problems (Dugbatey, Croskey, Evans, Narayan, & Osamudiamen, 2005).

Early educators must be especially sensitive to the needs of poor and homeless children when designing programs. For example, programs for young homeless children must be maximally flexible about scheduling, opening at earlier times and closing later, and should provide respite care for parents. Programs should provide transportation or funds to cover transportation expenses. They should provide social and case-management services and emphasize special attention for specific developmental delays and emotional problems that poor and homeless children may exhibit. Staff of such programs must be sensitive to the support and encouragement parents need.

Family Composition

Most people recognize that the traditional nuclear family of the stay-at-home mother, full-time employed father, and three healthy children neither predominates today, nor did it ever truly exist; but perhaps many people do not fully comprehend how much diversity exists. In 1992, of every 100 children born, 58 entered a broken family (Fagan & Coontz, 1997). By 1993, the proportion of young children living with one parent in the home was 21% for Caucasians, 66% for African Americans, and 34% for Hispanics (Hernandez, 1995). These statistics are significant, because research indicates that children in families headed by both parents, biological or adoptive, tend to do better in terms of social adjustment and academic performance than children in either **blended families** or those headed by a single parent. The single-parent family is a much riskier place for a child (Fagan & Coontz). Being born out of wedlock increases the risk of infant mortality and of ill health in early infancy; and the rates of abuse are 13 times higher in single-mother families and 20 times higher in single-father families (Fagan & Coontz).

Most of the differences in children's outcomes are, however, explained by economic disadvantage. In other words, adoptive families and those headed by two biological parents tend to be more economically stable, and it is the lack of resources, not the family configuration, that place children at social and academic risk. Parental childrearing behaviors may have much less to do with children's outcomes than family income and parents' educational levels. Unfortunately, among very poor families making less than $15,000 a year, marriage has all but disappeared, and among working class families with incomes between $15,000 and $30,000 a year, families are as likely to be headed by one adult as they are by two adults.

The sharp rise in childhood poverty since the mid-1970s is accounted for in large part by the increased proportion of children living in families headed by single mothers (Montgomery et al., 1996). Between 1970 and 1994, the percentage of children living in single-mother households rose from about 13% to about 31% (Florsheim, Tolan, & Gorman-Smith, 1998). There is substantial evidence that children growing up in single-mother families are at higher risk for developing achievement-related problems that may be the consequences of being financially disadvantaged (Florsheim et al.). The poverty rate for children in single-mother families is five times higher than that for children in two-parent families. More than 55% of children in single female-headed families live in poverty. The majority of these single mothers are divorced or separated, but the number who never married is increasing.

Adolescents in single-parent families are more likely to become adolescent parents (Moore, Manlove, Glei, & Morrison, 1998). Birthrates among teenagers in the United States are substantially higher than in other Western industrialized countries (Atkins & Wilkins, 2013). Nevertheless, the rate of teen pregnancies dropped dramatically over recent decades, falling 40% between 1990 and 2008 to an unprecedented low of 70/1000 girls aged 15-19 (Ventura, Curtin, Abma, & Henshaw, 2012). Low **socioeconomic** status for the family has also been correlated with higher risk of adolescent childbearing.

Divorce, remarriage, and never-married parenting have greatly affected the composition of American families. The term *stepfamily* is now used to include households in which there is an adult couple, at least one of whom has a child from a previous relationship (Kelley, 1996). According to Kelley, by 1990, 20% (about 5.3 million) of married-couple households cared for at least one stepchild, and children in stepfamilies tended to have higher rates of behavioral, health, and education problems.

Divorce, however, does not account for all family diversity. Children may be living with grandparents, in foster care, or in residential facilities. Since the late 1980s, foster care in the United States has been overwhelmed by the number of children who need assistance. This is partly because the total number of foster families has dropped significantly. Many infants and young children spend the early part of their lives in "boarder" nurseries, temporary shelters where shift changes and high ratios of children to caretakers decrease the possibility of healthy attachments. Children lucky enough to be placed in foster care may find untrained foster parents overwhelmed by the demands of, and unwilling to accept or keep, children with special needs.

© Denielle M. Miller

An emerging family option, developed out of necessity, is **kinship care**. Defined broadly, **kin** may include extended family, such as grandmothers and aunts, as well as other members of a community who are close to a family. This type of informal care is also referred to as "kith & kin" care and accounts for about 30% of out-of-home placements (Brown-Lyons, Robertson, & Layzer, 2001). Parents using kinship care are more likely to be less educated than individuals in the general population, to have lower income, and to tend toward having larger families. For example, high rates of kinship care are more common in families receiving Aid to

Families with Dependent Children funds than in other families (Brown-Lyons et al.). Minority families are also most likely to use kinship care. Parents tend to choose kinship care because of its affordability, safety, flexible scheduling, lack of other available care, and the special needs of a child. However, the primary reasons for full-time kinship care are parental drug abuse and neglect.

Full-time living arrangements with kin tend to have significant advantages over traditional foster care options, however. Children who stay with kin tend to be more stable, with fewer associated behavioral problems than for those placed in foster care, even though most kinship caregivers live in poverty themselves (Metzger, 2008). Additionally, biological parents are more likely to visit their children when placed in kinship homes, possibly explaining why these children tend to have better self-concept and greater resiliency (Metzger). Multigenerational family relationships, the sharing of childrearing and economic relationships across household boundaries, and the use of unrelated household members and parent surrogates have added greatly to the complexity of children's lives.

What can professionals do to assist families whose lives are complicated by divorce or separation or whose lives in some other way no longer fit the "traditional" image? Although research is limited, there are some useful strategies that can help build and sustain relationships. Teachers should modify their language and actions to match existing family patterns—inviting a grandparent to open house and speaking with foster parents at child conferences. Professionals need to make special efforts to keep communication open with both parents and other appropriate guardians. This may mean adjusting conference times, making evening telephone calls when working parents are home, or sending out multiple copies of announcements. Finally, professionals can extend the safety net of consistency and support as children go through transitions in family situations. Still, none of these expectations are as simple as they might appear; solutions are complex and require persistent, coordinated efforts.

Summary on Diversity

This nation is rapidly becoming a people of color with significant growth in minority populations who, in every region of the country, are disproportionately poor and more likely to be single-parent families. Although the United States has moved forward in defining equity, justice, and diversity, the country has done a poor job of addressing the academic achievement gap that contributes to social and economic inequities for minority families (Leach & Williams, 2007). Minority children, who receive fewer resources, continue to be vulnerable to poverty, discrimination, social disadvantage, and institutional barriers.

To conclude that educational underachievement and other social problems are caused by racial characteristics would be inaccurate and dangerous. The correlation between race and educational disadvantage is far more complicated because multiple factors influence members of racial minorities in this country. Educators need more preparation in working with families who are at risk. Family service planning and case management must become a natural part of all educational planning. Early childhood professionals need to be familiar with local resources and be able to empower families to identify and access community services. Special service delivery must reach beyond the traditional services of the school building to locations on the streets, in shelters, and within community centers. Traditionally delivered services are unlikely to reach those in greatest need if they are offered only within the agency setting. Likewise, such services provide only part of what is needed unless they are given in conjunction with social services support. Team management and social support should include family counseling, financial assistance, job training, family planning, and housing.

As educators address the needs of increasing numbers of children who are at risk, more comparisons will be made between minority children and children of the dominant culture. Because race is certain to be emphasized, these comparisons may inaccurately foster a view that minority students are inferior and incompetent, particularly when cultural differences are viewed as deficits. Early childhood professionals must be careful to document the ways in which minority children achieve educationally and find methods to promote the ecological, situational, and cultural factors that encourage success. Professionals must also collaborate with other service providers to work constantly to eliminate bigotry and discrimination, which may limit opportunities available to all children and families within this diverse population.

Slavin (1998) suggested a process to reduce the social inequity of education. First, we need to constantly remind ourselves to think of all children as being a promise. We help fulfill that promise when, as educators, we identify and build on our own cultural and personal strengths and accept nothing less from ourselves than outstanding performance so that we design high-quality education that is sensitive to students' needs from the beginning. Second, we start early by providing early childhood programs that enhance children's preparation for elementary school while children are highly motivated and confident in their abilities to learn. Finally, we determine success by working on many fronts at once—addressing the multitude of needs children in poverty face.

The Importance of Serving Children in the Context of a Family

Empowerment is a term widely used in social science fields. Empowerment means increasing one's control over one's life and taking action to get what one wants (Turnbull & Turnbull, 1997). For families of children with special needs, empowerment can be viewed as having been usurped by the special circumstances of needing the support and services of external entities. On the other hand, empowerment is a goal of early intervention and preschool service, whereby organizations can help families claim their voices in making choices, in planning for and receiving care, in accessing resources, and in advocacy for their child and other children with disabilities.

Effective professionals who work with children with disabilities recognize their ability to enhance not only a child's life but also the lives of the child's entire family (Van Haren & Fiedler, 2008). Empowerment promotes family strength, competence, and decision making. Professionals are sometimes motivated more by "political correctness" than by sound pedagogical practice in giving lip service to empowerment. For example, culturally diverse families often feel helpless because their values are not respected and their needs are not met (Xu, 2007). If not careful, parents may also view the empowerment principles as paternalistic, rejecting the notion that professionals have the right to "grant" them the power that belongs to them in the first place.

In the last 30 years since the implementation of the first national special education laws, a shift has occurred—from targeting intervention to close gaps created by family deficits to planning intervention to take advantage of family strength and resilience (Xu, 2007). Empowering families allows them to acquire a sense of control and to create opportunities for themselves to become more competent in meeting their needs and attaining goals. Practices that are empowering include families in decision making, serve the whole family, not just the child, are guided by family priorities, and offer respectful choices to families (Van Haren & Fiedler, 2008).

What Is a Family?

One of the most significant shifts in special education, particularly in early childhood, is the move from focusing on the child to focusing more broadly on the child within the family system. This model recognizes that each family member is affected by other family members and events that influence one another. For example, if a child with a disability requires extraordinary medical attention, other siblings may be affected by loss of parental attention, perhaps loss of financial support once available for activities or things, and by having more responsibilities around the home. Similarly, the amount of involvement in programs associated with a child with a disability is affected when caregivers are required to work extra hours to make rent payments, when they lose a job because they need to take time off to provide extraordinary care, or if they experience marital conflict. Professionals, naïve or neglectful of the family system, are likely to become frustrated if they concentrate solely on the needs of a child while ignoring forces that affect family dynamics.

A child-centered model (see Figure 1–2), although convenient and compatible with most professionals' training, has not been terribly effective for families whose members do not already possess considerable self-efficacy.

Definitions of family are influenced by culture, politics, economics, and religion. Consequently, among early childhood professionals, there is no consensus on criteria for membership in families. Yet the issue is not moot; the scope of services relies on such a definition. For example, a broad definition of family (e.g., parents, siblings, grandparents, childcare providers, involved relatives, and close friends of the family—all of whom influence the development of the child in question) would require that all of these persons be considered in the development of a family service plan. A more narrow definition (e.g., blood relatives who live in the child's dwelling) reduces the scope of intervention required but may also limit possible benefits for children with special needs.

Clearly, the traditional definition of family as a nuclear construct will not suffice. For the purposes of early childhood special education, a family might be any group of interdependent relatives and nonrelatives with a head of household who assume the responsibility of caring for each other. This simply stated definition is consistent with the *family systems model*, which acknowledges every important influence on individuals within families. Still, society struggles with "moral" issues related to the "correctness" of diverse family structures. However, early childhood educators can little afford to be exclusive or judgmental when defining families. Family

Figure 1–2 Ecological Mapping of the Child and Family

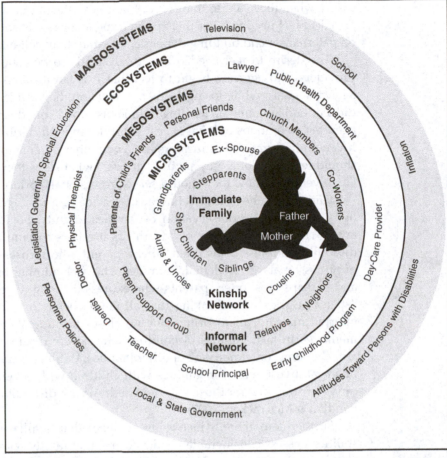

Source: Information taken *Enabling and Empowering Families: Principles and Guidelines for Practice,* by Dunst, Trivette, and Deal, 1988, Cambridge, MA: Brookline

configurations include foster families, adoptive families, nuclear biological families, single-parent families, extended families, and same-gender-parents families.

Although it is difficult to define families to everyone's satisfaction, the next step—involvement of all family members in early intervention—is even more difficult. For example, the "parent" in parent–professional interactions has almost exclusively referred to mothers. While more fathers are attempting to engage more equally in parenting responsibilities, a number of maternal beliefs and behaviors perpetuate the mother's power in childrearing (Allen & Hawkins, 1999). Again, early educators can be most effective when they move beyond popular opinion in interactions with families. A true "family-centered" approach to early childhood intervention compels professionals to find ways to encourage fathers to be involved in decision making and childcare.

Empowerment

Families are empowered when their needs are met, and most of the credit for progress goes to the families themselves. When a professional can boast, "Look, they don't need me to make decisions, locate information, or access services," a family is empowered.

Fostering empowerment requires that educators practice in a way that they never have before. Social service professionals, in particular, feel useful, wanted, even necessary when they can do things "for" families. It is not unusual for professionals to "need to feel needed," yet this apparent benevolence is counterproductive—based on paternalism and building dependency rather than self-efficacy.

The desire to feel needed eventually leads to behavior that supports service providers, and agencies begin to feel that it is families' responsibility to serve the agencies' goals, while losing focus on needs on the families. Agencies can become didactic and judgmental, labeling families as "good" or "dysfunctional" based on the agencies' definitions of what is best for children with disabilities and their families. It is not uncommon for educators and even other parents to prescribe how families should feel, how long they should "grieve," what steps they should take to become "involved," and how they should serve professionals' priorities.

Changes in the verbal behavior of service providers can reflect a new philosophy based on the preservation of families' dignity. For example, one might do away with the psychology of "death" as it relates to families with members with disabilities. Professionals often label a parent who refuses to accept the opinions of professionals as "in denial," families who seek another opinion as "bargainers," and perhaps most often, parents who express their rights as "angry." Learning the "stages of grief" and thinking that all family behavior can fit into this model of inferred maladjustment brings one no closer to understanding individual family members. In fact, families of children with severe disabilities face problems that are "the same, only more so" of other families. While this may be true, the time and financial investments for families with children with severe disabilities is significantly greater than for those without children with disabilities (Flanders, Engelhart, Pandina & McCracken, 2007).

Furthermore, there is increasing evidence that families with children with disabilities possess considerable resilience and that family resources quickly compensate for their new stress (Heiman, 2002). Treating families as if they were disabled because their child is disabled runs counter to the principle of family-centered services. Krausse (1991) proposed an alternative view of families, which he refers to as the "family adaptation hypothesis." This hypothesis rejects the concept of pathological maladaptation associated with the presence of a child with a disability (grief model) and acknowledges the hardiness of families who find ways to cope both initially and over time. The fundamental assumption of empowerment is that families are the center. All decisions move from the center outward; all action by the periphery is to serve the center (see Figure 1–2).

The goal of empowerment is to enable families to make decisions and take action serving their self-selected needs. When professionals ignore the principle of family empowerment, they are likely to overrate their effectiveness by providing noncontingent helping. Lack of scaffolding for empowerment fails to advance the needs of families in becoming more effective agents of long-term change.

Noncontingent helping is defined as providing services or support for families while expecting no proactive behavior on the part of families. While seemingly "helping" families, professionals actually usurp opportunities for empowerment when family members are given no responsibility. Dunst and colleagues (1988) defined empowerment as fulfillment of three criteria:

1. Taking a **proactive stance;** enabling experiences and attribution of change to help the seeker. A proactive stance is one in which professionals assume that families are either competent or capable of becoming competent. Assuming that some families are incompetent and unable to change renders a professional useless for those children and their families.

2. Creating opportunities for families to display their strengths in order to gain new competencies is the responsibility of helping systems. "A failure to display competencies is not due to deficits within the person but rather failure of the social system to create opportunities" (p. 4).

3. Enabling families to acquire a sense of personal control over family affairs. "It is not simply a matter of whether or not family needs are met, but rather the manner in which needs are met that is likely to be both enabling and empowering" (p. 4).

Building a climate for authentic parent–professional partnerships is, perhaps, the field's greatest challenge; much is still unknown. There is an inherent imbalance between families who have the most "skin in the game" and service providers who reign over resources, knowledge, and professional pedigree. Because of this imbalance, some professionals seize control, whereas some parents forfeit their equal place at the table. Most discouraging is the fact that those families who may benefit the most from family empowerment (i.e., minorities and low-income families) are the least likely to receive empowering services (Balcazar, Keys, & Suarez-Balcazar, 2001). Research efforts in the 21st century should be devoted to identifying methods of supporting the philosophy of empowerment and the spirit, finally, of IDEA.

The Importance of Working Collaboratively

An infant or toddler whose medical condition, developmental delay, or physical disability is so severe that she or he comes to the attention of caregivers and service providers at an early age is likely to present more complex needs than a child who does not demonstrate a disability until reaching school age. Very young children with medical, cognitive, or physical complications are typically at risk for developing disabilities in related developmental areas. For example, a child with abnormal muscle tone may have trouble learning to walk, may have motor problems related to eating difficulties, may not develop necessary motor movements to produce intelligible speech, and, with poor tools for communication, may be unable to demonstrate cognitive abilities. This child has one primary disabling condition, poor muscle tone, yet the intervention services of a physical therapist, occupational therapist, speech therapist, special educator, and parents are all necessary.

Although a single professional working with a child was common practice in the past, it is unlikely that any one professional could serve very young children with special needs well. Consequently, teams of specialists attending to different aspects of children's care and development are now considered best practice. An **interdisciplinary approach** combines expertise from many disciplines to scrutinize a child's various aspects of development and bring together assessment, planning, and practices to promote a child's overall development.

The 2011 Annual Report of the Children's Defense Fund

The Children's Defense Fund was established in 1973 with the mission of being a strong, effective, political voice for all children in America, especially poor, minority, and disabled children. This private advocacy group functions to raise national consciousness and to work on behalf of children and families. Its 2011 annual report provides an important statistical picture of the status of young children and their families.

The Children's Defense Fund has identified five major program objectives that would ensure all children a healthy and fair start on their lives. The first is to obtain comprehensive physical and mental health coverage for all children in America. This objective is in response to the fact that of the 8.3 million children in America who were uninsured in 2009, almost 90 percent lived in working households. The second objective is to promote increased availability of high-quality early childhood education through community services such as Head Start, Freedom Schools, and Supporting Partnerships to Assure Ready Kids (SPARK). The third objective is to lift families from poverty; this concern grows from the enormous impact poverty has on child survival, health, safety, and capacity to learn and

grow. In 2009, 15.5 million children lived in poverty in the United States (nearly 4 million more than in 2000), even though nearly 70 percent of these live in families with at least one working parent. The fourth major objective is to promote safe and permanent families. Currently, 1.7 million children have a parent in jail or prison, and more than 1 million children are homeless. This objective works to prevent families from losing their children to the child welfare system and foster care: One-third of children in foster care are five or younger. The fifth objective is to work with faith communities to give children a moral start by inspiring hope, compassion, and strength for overcoming life's obstacles. All of these objectives feed into the purpose of helping children make successful passages to adulthood by supporting local, state, and national leadership to provide better community care for young children and youth.

Source: State of America's Children 2011 Report by Author, 2011, Washington, DC, Children's Defense Fund. Retrieved June 18, 2012, from *http://www.childrensdefense.org/child-research-data-publications/data/state-of-americas-children-2011-report.html*

When a number of professionals collaborate with a family, close teamwork becomes absolutely necessary. Without careful coordination, there might be unnecessary duplication of services and paperwork, lack of communication with important parties, an increase in confusion and contradiction, and resultant poor services to children and their families. A successful team approach must be organized to produce timely and accurate assessment, comprehensive and effective intervention, clear and inclusive communication, and regular evaluation and review. An effective team approach is reached only through mutual trust and respect, practice, and hard work.

Several approaches to teaming have worked well as long as fundamental guidelines are respected. First, **consensus building** is more effective than an authoritative structure. When various professionals gather with parents, each comes with differing levels of professional status and biases. It is hard to set priorities unless all participants are willing to listen carefully to all parties and to "give and take" in regard to their particular area of expertise. In situations with a breakdown of give and take, team coordination is at an impasse.

Sharing knowledge and priorities requires mutual support. For example, during a planning meeting, a parent requests that the team include toilet training on his son's Individualized Education Program (IEP). The teacher reports to the team that the boy, who has been identified with autism, has not had any "accidents" at school for months. The parent, acknowledging this observation, contends that his son continues to have difficulty at home and needs to have his toileting routine continued at school. If the other team members refuse to listen to the father's request, the IEP process may eventually reach an impasse. This conflict would be avoided if members of the team valued the input of all members and tried to accommodate as many priorities as possible from each member.

Each professional must be flexible and willing to share roles as well as information. Consider a child who presents a language delay; the teacher, the physical therapist, and the parents must all work to develop the child's language whether that is within that person's area of expertise or not. This team approach requires that each member have some working understanding of other disciplines or at least a willingness to implement suggestions made by other professionals. For example, both speech therapist and teacher should learn how to position a child with physical disabilities in the most appropriate way during all aspects of the child's home or school day. This requires some cross-disciplinary instruction and modeling by a physical therapist.

Finally, effective **group process** is essential for ensuring a positive team experience. Group process includes making all participants comfortable in sharing their concerns and desires, listening carefully to all team members, valuing the input of each member, and making decisions based on consensus. For example, parents are often intimidated when meeting with a large group of professionals and may hesitate to speak honestly and clearly regarding their priorities. If coerced into silence by intimidation or lack of opportunity, parents may leave a meeting unhappy with the planning and uncommitted to the work a plan involves. To decrease anxiety, parents should be greeted when they arrive, perhaps offered refreshments and comfortable seating, and introduced to all members of the team. These practices may seem overly zealous to some. As one educator put it, "This is not a social gathering! Do you get refreshments when you go to a law office or a dental office?" This objection has no merit—for the goal of legal and dental services is hardly one of shared responsibility; the goals of early childhood special education are incompatible with the client–expert hierarchy of many other professions. To enhance communication, professionals should refrain from using technical jargon or should take care to explain critical terminology carefully to other members of the team. Written plans should never be formally completed ahead of time, nor should parents be expected to sign an Individualized Family Service Plan (IFSP is the planning document for families of infants and toddlers with disabilities up to age 3) or IEP at the time of the meeting. Soliciting parent suggestions and input before decisions are made is a necessary (and legally required) component of the group process. One person should act as a facilitator, to make sure a meeting begins promptly, to keep the discussion on task, to see that all members have a chance to give input or to object when appropriate, and to restate or summarize when agreement has been reached. Before a meeting ends, everyone present should know what will happen next, who is responsible for each part of a plan, and when the team will meet again to review progress.

Teaming Models

There are three basic team models, or arrangements, and they vary in the degree to which team members are able to work together. **Multidisciplinary** teams are made up of members who work independently in providing assessment and direct services to a child and meet to share their goals and progress reports, although there is little direct coordination of efforts. For example, the psychologist may meet with a child to test intelligence and achievement levels and then meet with the team to report the results and make recommendations for treatment. Members in an **interdisciplinary** model may conduct their assessments and plan goals together but continue to provide direct services on an independent basis. For example, the speech therapist may observe while the psychologist is testing a child and check off speech sounds, or phonemes, that the child can say rather than duplicating the testing in a separate speech session. In a **transdisciplinary** model, professionals share roles and may combine their assessments and treatment tasks so that any one individual may be carrying out the responsibilities of a different professional. For example, the classroom teacher may use a phoneme check-off instrument to obtain information for the speech therapist or may carry out a language program the speech therapist has recommended.

Of particular benefit to a child served by a team approach is that each team member sees the child's problem from that member's own perspective. Sometimes a teacher may be intimidated by the knowledge of other specialized team members; however, the generalist perspective that a teacher brings is a necessary part of team dynamics. Specialists have in-depth knowledge of their discipline, but teachers are better prepared to see the whole child functioning in a variety of settings, both socially and physically.

The team configuration used in a particular situation depends on the administrative policy of the school and service agencies involved and on the comfort and cohesiveness of the professionals serving a particular child. There is no question, however, that teaming across disciplines is a necessary part of services to young children. The greater the ability of the team to interact, to share roles, and to inform each other across disciplines, the more unified and complete a child's services are likely to be. Table 1–5 summarizes the strengths and weaknesses of each of these models.

Collaboration in Early Intervention

Collaboration with other professionals is not as easy as it might appear. In fact, many teachers report that their jobs are made most difficult by lack of cooperation among their peers and themselves. Teachers who feel the most confident about their teaching are more amenable to collaborative problem-solving. Moreover, collaboration is actually increased by one's sense of efficacy (Shachar & Shmuelevitz, 1997). In other words, collaboration fosters efficacy and efficacy fosters collaboration. One might conclude from research that two important barriers to collaboration are a lack of self-confidence and distrust in the work of others, yet collaboration by all professionals with other professionals as well as with parents is a necessary prerequisite to program effectiveness.

In early intervention, the challenge of integrating services for families demands the most of collaborative efforts. As family needs increase, need for services increase—as does the need for more coordination of disciplines (see Figure 1–2). For example,

Table 1–5 Team Models

Team Model	Strengths	Weaknesses
Multidisciplinary team	• Involves more than one discipline in planning and services • Pools expertise for decision making • Reduces mistakes and biases	• May not promote a unified approach to intervention • May lack team cohesion and commitment
Interdisciplinary team	• Allows activities and goals to complement and support other disciplines • Allows commitment to a unified service plan • Allows a case manager to coordinate information flow	• May threaten professional "turf" • May reduce efficiency due to professionals' inflexibility • May allow case manager to become autocratic if role is ambiguous
Transdisciplinary team	• Encourages interaction within many disciplines • Encourages role sharing • Provides a unified, holistic plan for intervention • Allows a more complete understanding of the child • Leads to professional enhancement and increased knowledge and skill	• Requires participation by many experts • Places largest responsibility on the teacher as case manager • Requires a high degree of coordination and interaction • Requires more time for communication and planning

families with multiple needs cannot be well served by autonomous narrowly defined programs. Consider the following real story:

Barry's mom and dad never married, though they had two children, including Barry's older sister, Gloria. Barry also has a younger sister, Gretchen, who has a different dad. Mom drank and smoked when she was pregnant with her children, and Gretchen has several health problems. Both Barry and Gretchen have conduct disorders associated with attention deficit hyperactivity disorder (ADHD).

Although Barry did not know his own father well, he talks about killing his dad. He remembers his father holding a knife to his mom's throat. After that, the family left Barry's father and moved into a very small apartment. Mom had a lot of boyfriends, and often locked the children in their bedroom when boyfriends visited the apartment. Mom also worked at a bar, but did not get a babysitter while at work. Her friends came by after work to party and often visited even when mom was not at home. These friends frightened the children. While mom was away, the children watched TV.

Barry hated when mom was home because she frequently yelled at and hit him. Her boyfriends hit Barry too if mom was mad. Barry and Gloria would hide in the closet, though Gloria often cried uncontrollably.

Even though Barry was enrolled in preschool, his mom did not let him go all the time. One day, grandma and grandpa came to pick up Gloria and Barry for a vacation on their grandparents' ranch. They stayed more than a year.

"We were going to go to their ranch and vacation for a few weeks. I was so excited because I am good with horses and now I have two. We stayed for a long time, more than a year. I went to school by grandma and grandpa's."

Even though the children liked staying on the ranch with their grandparents, Barry had many social problems. After this long "vacation," Barry's mom showed up to take the children. Mom told them they were going to have a baby, and the children would need to babysit. They went back to Billings with her.

Mom's new boyfriend was mean, and with Mom he would smoke and drink and rarely went to work. The boyfriend did not hit the children, but he was not nice to Mom even though she was pregnant. "I hated him," said Barry. "The boyfriend also had friends, and his friends would take Gloria into another room and hurt her." "When Gretchen was born, she could fit into grandma's hand! Gretchen finally came home from the hospital, but mom didn't seem to want her around." Mom often disappeared, leaving Gloria and Barry to take care of the baby. Again, the children seldom went to school. One day, Gretchen's dad came home and began hitting Barry, who grabbed Gretchen and ran to the bedroom, locking the door. "He then started fighting with my mom who began screaming. The police came and took Gretchen's dad away. They took mom too."

Now, all the children live on their grandparents' ranch. Their mother is in jail. This incarceration took place after her children were removed from her custody. "She became involved with a new boyfriend but was convicted for hurting his children. That is why she is in jail. I hate her." The children are preparing to testify that their dad tried to hurt their mom, because their dad now wants his children back. Barry continues to experience difficulty in preschool, even though his grandparents are working closely with his teachers.

This family's issues may be viewed from an ecological systems model described by Bronfenbrenner (1986). The most immediate needs, schooling for Gloria and Barry and early intervention for Gretchen, are at the **microsystem** level. At the **mesosystem** level, there is a linkage between microsystems, such as a linkage between the grandparents and the schools or between the schools and the child welfare system. The **exosystems** are those affecting families but with no direct relationship with agencies, such as church and neighbors. Finally, families are influenced by **macrosystems,** broad social values and belief systems of cultures and subcultures, such as political support for social safety nets for families or drug rehabilitation. The interdependency of agencies serving families from these multiple perspectives is a crucial philosophy. A service coordinator creates a formal link between other professionals and agencies and early childhood programs serving Barry and his family. This person is responsible for assessing family and child needs, coordinating the planning for intervention and delivery of services, and monitoring the services delivered.

Infants and Toddlers with Disabilities: Relationship-Based Approaches

Traditional team models were based on child deficits with some consideration of family strengths.

In contrast, the recent emphasis on family-centered service delivery emphasizes the need for families to be major planners in treatment and for professionals to operate using transdisciplinary approaches. This goes beyond simple collaboration and requires all members of a planning and treatment team to share their expertise. To do so requires a high level of communication among disciplines assessing and treating young children. Collaboration, as a philosophy, is possible only when professionals are able to separate their own needs from those of clients and are nonjudgmental, open minded, and committed to providing families with the very best services possible. Relationships become very important, and relationship-based approaches are a new organizing principle in early intervention.

One outcome of this perspective is new attention to parent–child relationships and their important effects on the development of children (Atkins-Burnett & Meares, 2000). It appears that increases in maternal–child responsivity have as many positive effects on child outcomes as does the presence of an intervention itself. Three components are key: (1) sensitivity to a child's interests and engagement in the child's interests, (2) consistency and appropriateness of parental responses to a child, and (3) how well the parent engages a child in turn taking.

A second important relationship is the one between the parents and the service providers. Rather than dwelling on deficits, good relationships focus on family strengths and respect parents as experts on their child. Service providers highlight the family's strengths and assist in identifying and locating necessary supports to make the most of those. Professionals join parents in creative problem-solving to design services that meet a family's needs and desires while relieving identified stressors.

Families consistently identify competent and caring, supportive, and trustworthy professionals as the most essential part of successful early intervention. Respectful, responsive listening is highly valued. But professionals need help in balancing a friendly relationship with boundary issues, paying attention to their own and the parents' emotional needs, and dealing with conflict. Diversity of cultural backgrounds also represents a challenge in relationship-based approaches. It is also important for service providers to reflect on how interventions can be congruent with family beliefs and values.

Early childhood professionals need to understand basic principles of infant mental health:

- The baby's primary relationships need to support developmental needs—that is, the core of a baby's capacity to love well and grow well.
- Each parent and each baby is unique in many ways, including temperament, interaction style, and emotional makeup. This affects the "goodness of fit" of any relationship.
- The particular environmental context in which a baby and parent reside deeply affects functioning.
  - Service providers can understand parents' behavior only by trying to walk in parents' shoes. They need to know about parents' feelings, dreams, desires, and perceptions.
  - Service providers must be aware of their own feelings and how their behavior affects their relationships with parents. Supported parents are more likely to nurture and support their children.

• The perfect relationship-based organization does not exist. It is the ongoing striving toward that ideal that distinguishes quality organizations.

Programs that are successful at integrating these services are correlated with such broad-based family benefits as decreased birthrates in adolescents, lower incidences of low birth weight babies, increased school participation by parents, decreased drug abuse and behavior problems, increased financial self-sufficiency, and higher IQ and test scores. Clearly, one professional or agency cannot possibly address all of these areas.

The Importance of Ethical Conduct and Advocacy

What do **ethical conduct** and **advocacy** have to do with philosophy? Many decisions that educators make, including their daily activities in a classroom, are based on a set of personal ethics or personal philosophy. Charged with working with families of very young children with disabilities, professionals are held to the highest ethical standards. First, educators should know and follow the ethical standards of their profession. Second, educators should actively advocate for issues that will encourage society to respond to the needs of families and children with disabilities in an ethical fashion.

Ethical professional behavior means that one will be the best early childhood professional that one can be and will support others in providing high-quality services. Professional organizations serving children have already articulated high ethical and accreditation standards for those who provide services to young children. A prime example is the Code of Ethical Conduct developed by the National Association for the Education of Young Children (NAEYC) (2011). These standards for ethical behavior in early childhood education describe professional responsibilities in regard to children, families, colleagues, the community, and society. The first principle presented in the NAEYC Code expresses its ideals well:

> Above all, we shall not harm children. We shall not participate in practices that are emotionally damaging, physically harmful, disrespectful, degrading, dangerous, exploitative, or intimidating to children. This principle has precedence over all others in this Code.

Advocacy Issues

An *advocate* is someone who takes up another person's cause. For what should one advocate? Simply, one should advocate for something one believes in and is willing to work for (Matt & Morrison, 2008). For an early childhood professional that may mean working and playing with children or helping others working to meet the needs of children. It may mean voting regularly and from an informed position, writing one's Congressional representatives (state or national), or participating on state councils or research projects. Children's Defense Fund (2011) identified national priorities for children that few could argue against. These goals included the following:

1. End child poverty;

2. Guarantee every child and pregnant woman comprehensive health and mental health coverage and services;

3. Protect every child from abuse and neglect and connect each one to caring permanent families;

4. Provide high-quality early childhood care and development programs for all children;

5. Ensure every child can read at grade level by fourth grade and guarantee quality education through high school graduation; and

6. Stop the criminalization of children at increasingly younger ages and invest in prevention and early intervention.

Obtaining good childcare is a nationwide problem due to two main factors: affordability and quality (Clark, 2007). The National Association of Child Care Resource and Referral Agencies (NACCRRA) in the United States reports that nearly 11 million children under the age of 5 years are in some kind of childcare (NACCRRA, 2011). The average number of hours per week children of working mothers under age 5 spend in childcare is 35. Two-thirds of parents assumed their caregivers had been trained to work with children, but only 15 states require early childhood education for caregivers. While 67 percent of parents assumed their childcare programs were inspected regularly, 20 states conduct inspections once a year or less frequently.

Although the federal government sets standards for many aspects of daily life, the regulation of childcare is minimal and primarily left to state governments. Consequently, tremendous variability exists among state laws and enforcement levels (NACCRRA, 2011). Even when states have regulations on the books, many are not able to properly inspect centers and enforce these regulations. In no cases do states require an inspection before licensing and/or allowing child care providers to operate when six or fewer children are served. Consequently, many children are cared for in unlicensed settings. Yet, even a license on the wall does not guarantee that appropriate care is being provided. Bowing to the pressure resulting from complaints broadcast on the Internet, 26 states now post inspections results. But, who should monitor the quality of childcare provided? Who should insist on high standards for programs for young children, and who should enforce these standards? Parents are often ill equipped to do so because they are victims of a provider's market; the short supply of openings available and the high cost of quality day care tend to make parents settle for availability and affordability (NACCRRA, 2011). It is absolutely essential that early childhood professionals advocate for appropriate, high-quality services to very young children. Professionals have the education, the commitment, and the voice to insist that standards for childcare be adequate and that society contribute to the health, safety, and education of all children regardless of race, disabling condition, or economic status. This is not a new role or futile use of energy because educators have accomplished (hand-in-hand with parents) extraordinary changes in legal, pedagogical, financial, practical, and ethical practices in the past few decades.

Another area that will have an impact on early childhood special education is the reform of public assistance policies at state and federal levels that require single mothers (and families) on public assistance to work and that limit the length of time for which families are eligible for assistance. Such policies will most assuredly increase the need for low-cost childcare and place a further burden on a system already in crisis.

To date, policymakers have not addressed this need. Therefore, it is possible that the lack of childcare will result in higher rates of child neglect and homelessness and a greater need for special services. The prolonged economic crisis in the United States and abroad has resulted in a political enthusiasm for austerity measures. Consequently, the weak safety net is being severely threatened. The most vulnerable citizens are targets for a politic that is unsympathetic to a "shared responsibility" ethos. Early childhood services, including those for children and families with children with disabilities, face a return to church basements and bake sales if citizens fail to muster sustained and loud advocacy for a standard of care that we once considered a good beginning. A professional should be an informed citizen and advocate for families by voting, writing articles or blogs, using social media such as Twitter or Facebook, contacting Congressional representatives, sending letters to the editor of the local newspaper, and using other effective ways to inform the public of issues important to families of young children with disabilities.

How to Get Involved in Advocacy

Advocacy is a dynamic and continuous process that begins with the recognition of an unmet need and does not end until that need is met. An advocate's work progresses in two directions at once as the advocate supports and obtains services for an individual and works to promote changes across the system that eventually could apply to large numbers of children. Effective advocacy can begin within a family, a classroom, or a community.

Parents of children with disabilities need healthy communication to take place between the many professionals with whom they deal as well as emotional support, economic support, respite care, legal protection, and information about the future. Your advocacy may begin by connecting parents with each other, or providing informational brochures.

On a broader level, a person can become involved in child advocacy in numerous ways. Many community organizations, from parent–teacher associations to Kiwanis Clubs, Junior Leagues, and religious charities, have an interest in child issues. Every state now has at least one organization devoted to child advocacy. These organizations may track state legislation, monitor the voting records of elected officials, lobby for child issues, and fund research and education aimed at improving children's circumstances. A phone call or letter will put one in contact with a number of national organizations working on behalf of children.

A number of national professional, parent, and citizen organizations specialize in advocacy for young children and those with disabilities. Information about membership, missions, activities, and goals for most of these can be found easily on the Internet, and many have local groups that meet regularly. Among these are

- The ARC for People with Intellectual and Developmental Disabilities
- American Occupational Therapy Association
- American Speech–Language–Hearing Association
- Child Welfare League of America

- Council for Exceptional Children
- Disability Rights Education and Defense Fund Inc.
- Division for Early Childhood of the Council for Exceptional Children
- National Down Syndrome Congress
- Easter Seals Society
- National Association for the Education of Young Children
- National Association of School Psychologists
- TASH (formerly The Association for the Severely Handicapped)
- The Neuro-Developmental Treatment Association
- Tourette Syndrome Association
- U.S. International Council on Disabilities
- Zero to Three

A profession is more than a job; it requires a long-term commitment to the field. In early childhood education, that commitment is to the well-being of children, and that well-being cannot be ensured if efforts are confined to one's classroom, playground, or home. The health, safety, and education of children depend on society and its efforts to protect children from discrimination, poverty, disease, abuse, violence, and ignorance. Marian Wright Edelman, president of the Children's Defense Fund, gave this advice on life: "Hang in with your advocacy for children and the poor. The tide is going to turn . . . Don't think you have to be a big dog to make a difference. You just need to be a persistent flea . . . Enough committed fleas biting strategically can make even the biggest dog uncomfortable and transform even the biggest nation, as we will transform America . . ." (Edelman, 1991).

IN CONCLUSION

This chapter has summarized the major assumptions of early childhood special education. Over the past three decades, since early childhood education seriously began its business of serving children with special needs and their families, an increasingly liberal philosophy has evolved in sharp contrast with the social changes in an increasingly conservative society. Already, this change in cultural values has meant the closure of many early intervention programs and the reduction of funds for preschool special education programs. Cuts are being made, despite decades of research establishing the benefit to children and society when effort is invested early in a child's life (O'Brien & Dervarics, 2007). This is especially true of children with mild delays or those who are at risk for delays. An analogy to automobile maintenance can be made. If a problem is detected early and repaired quickly, the cost and effort are small. However, if the problem is allowed to persist, the automobile will suffer extensive damage that will subsequently be more costly and difficult to repair.

Professionals in early intervention are at a crossroads where resources are diminishing at the same time the need for services is increasing. How can society be made to recognize the considerable benefits that may be gained by early investment in our children? We think it is up to those professionals who know the research best to advocate for very young children with special needs and their families.

STUDY GUIDE QUESTIONS

1. What are the two important elements of an attitude of science? Give an example from your experience when you had to demonstrate an attitude of science.

2. What is the value of a conceptual system? How does the use of a conceptual system help you in your work?

3. In what ways does applied behavior analysis meet the criteria for a good conceptual system? What other conceptual systems dominate in early childhood?

4. What does personalization of intervention mean? What are its basic premises? Which of these do you believe you will be able to achieve first?

5. What is needed to make the philosophy of personalization a reality? Which of these do you believe will be the most difficult to achieve?

6. How has the racial distribution in the population of the United States changed? What changes have you observed in your own lifetime?

7. State two reasons why sensitivity to cultural differences is important in early childhood education. What cultural challenge is most difficult for you personally?

8. What impact do changing demographics have on education? What trends have you seen in your own community?

9. What are the detrimental effects of childhood poverty? Which of these have you seen in your work?

10. How have families changed in recent years? Give an example of how those changes will affect your interaction with families.

11. What can early childhood professionals do to support children from nontraditional families? What have you done in this effort?

12. What problems accompany a philosophy of empowerment? How do these problems affect your work with families?

13. How is family defined within a family systems model? What components make up your family?

14. Why is noncontingent helping not helpful? Give an example of this from your work or your life.

15. What can professionals do to ensure that a team works well together? Give an example of an effective strategy you have observed that helped a team work together.

16. What are two ways in which each of the three primary team models differs from the others?

17. Give examples of ways you could relate to the single mother of a child with Down syndrome that would contribute to a successful collaborative team.

2 Relationship-Based Teaming with Families

© Brian Price

The poet Maya Angelou captured the social importance of family, "At our best level of existence, we are parts of a family, and at our highest level of achievement, we work to keep the family alive." In recent years, federal education legislation passed by Congress has provided legal mandates to strengthen a commitment to collaboration. Perhaps the most extraordinary outcome of legislation supporting services for very young children with disabilities and their families has been the requirement of interdisciplinary and interagency cooperation with families. Our nation has matured considerably from the days, in the not too distant past, when parents were shamefully considered the cause of their children's disabilities to a point now at which families are viewed as partners and collaborators in the decision making and treatment of their children's special needs.

Family-centered practice and philosophy embrace the following key concepts (Beach Center on Families and Disability, 2012):

1. Keep families intact, by preserving family unity and integrity.

2. Protect a families' right to autonomy, to make their own choices about raising their children, seeking and accepting services, and other personal business.

3. Empower families to participate in making decisions about what and how services are delivered.

4. Provide flexible programming to meet the cultural, ethnic, and linguistic character of the family.

5. Be family centered: Services should be family directed because when one member of a family has a disability, all family members are affected.

Family-centered principles encourage delivering services in natural, least restrictive settings while honoring child needs and family preferences. They encourage identifying, both formal and informal, family supports in the home and in the community. In delivering these services, professionals should be sensitive to the cost to families both in terms of time and resources. Finally, to be "family first" is to speak people-first language that refers to the person before the disability (e.g. an *infant* with Down syndrome or a *child* with autism). In short, these principles increase the power of families to navigate their own destiny.

Family empowerment is succinctly prescribed by law as the delivery of support to families to "enhance their capacity." Those who foster empowerment promote family self-efficacy by partnering to access resources and simultaneously transferring decision making. Central to empowerment is an assumption of equality and reciprocity between partners. One of the most important functions of empowerment is to provide skills that promote relative self-sufficiency. This is not a pejorative view of family independence, in which families who express needs are made to feel insufficient or deficient. Rather families, even those with the most severe challenges, are provided choices that help them climb the scaffolding offered by professionals to become as self-determined as they may desire. Empowerment philosophy has five primary outcomes (Bailey et al., 2006):

1. Families can articulate their child's abilities and special needs

2. Families are clear about their rights and can advocate for their child by using these rights

3. Families acquire and implement strategies to facilitate their child's development

4. Families have and use support systems

5. Families access desired services and programs in their communities

To say that family-centered intervention is built on a partnership between professionals and family members is only the beginning. One prerequisite that may be necessary is a synchrony between the emotional needs of a professional and those of a family (Brotherson et al., 2010). For example, if a family does not have a sense of urgency about intervention activities and a professional is anxious to move quickly on those activities, a mismatch will occur. While families cannot be expected to align their needs to those of professionals, only when both needs are addressed can a supportive family-centered partnership develop. It has been found that taking advantage of natural learning environments and using everyday activities and places is a noninvasive approach to family capacity building that increases the likelihood of improving caregiver competence and confidence (Swanson, Raab & Dunst, 2011). A parent will find it more natural to take turns making facial expressions to build communication skills while giving a baby a bath than he or she would if asked to set aside 30 minutes a day to "teach imitation skills."

There is more to family empowerment than a virtuous philosophy. There are also measurable benefits. When early intervention focuses on capacity building, by providing support, access to resources, and building on the strengths of families, parents develop greater self-efficacy and well-being (Friend, Summers, & Turnbull, 2009; Trivette, Dunst, & Hamby, 2010). Additionally, these parents have improved relationships with their children with disabilities, and the children themselves benefit developmentally. Effective practices used to achieve family empowerment were summarized by Friend and colleagues (2009):

1. *Less is more:* Fewer rather than frequent (> 16) family–professional sessions are more beneficial.

2. *Adjustment period:* Prenatal intervention that occurs after 6 months is more effective than intervention during the first 6 months after birth.

3. *Relationship building:* Intervention that focuses on the relationship between child and family improves both family cohesion and communication.

4. *Comprehensive services:* Programs that can address multiple family–child needs improve family wellness and cohesion.

5. *Natural environments:* Use of responsive teaching methods improve family well-being.

6. *Support groups:* Family support groups improve family well-being.

7. *Peer-to-peer:* Peer support provides a medium for families in similar circumstances to share information and emotional support.

8. *Family as center:* A two-generational program that offers a comprehensive array of services focusing simultaneously on child and family enhances family outcomes.

9. *Respite:* Quality respite care, utilized frequently, increases family well-being.

Paraeducators in Special Education Programs

Special education programs employ more paraeducators than any other employer, and the numbers of paraeducators increased by 48 percent during the 1990s. These

assistants work alongside professional teachers and therapists to provide vital support to students with disabilities, including supplementary aids and services that make participation in inclusive settings effective. Many parents request that a dedicated paraeducator accompany their child throughout the school day. The use of paraeducators may also have increased because of greater focus on high standards for student achievement, which has emphasized the need for individualized instructional support. In addition, shortages of fully qualified professionals who can provide related services have required the employment of more paraeducators (or paratherapists) under the professionals' direction, to assist in the delivery of such services as special education, speech–language therapy, physical therapy, and occupational therapy so that more students can be treated.

The benefits of employing paraeducators include improved student behavior, higher academic engagement, and more positive attitudes toward learning and school. Many parents feel paraeducators are indispensable for successful inclusion because they ensure the child's health and safety as well as increased socialization and learning. Teachers report improved morale, reduced stress, and better home and school relationships when paraeducators are assigned to students with disabilities. There is also evidence that paraeducators assist families in their communities outside of the school environment.

With so much responsibility resting on paraeducators, it is important that their work be as effective as possible. The roles of paraeducators need to have clearly defined appropriate and inappropriate tasks and duties. Paraeducators should never be solely responsible for any student; ultimate responsibility for planning, scheduling, assessing, and addressing IEP goals and directing and delegating tasks should continue to lie with the teacher or therapist in charge. This means that teachers and therapists need specific training in how to supervise and evaluate staff who assist them. Face-to-face contact is critical, and scheduled meetings are important. Paraeducators also need appropriate training because program integrity is based on the qualifications of those who deliver services. Hiring standards are generally low, and training budgets are often inadequate.

Paraeducators should be knowledgeable of

- Specific disabilities
- Ways to follow team plans
- Behavior management
- Communication with children
- Social, emotional, physical, and communication development
- Ways people learn
- Instructional techniques
- Inclusion rationales and strategies
- Assistive technology
- Ways to promote social acceptance
- Individual and small group instruction
- Ways to work with other adults
- Special education process and laws
- Specific information about individual children to whom they are assigned

The training that paraeducators receive must be well developed and comprehensive. Training should be designed to count toward higher degrees since many paraeducators eventually move into professional programs.

Source: From "Paraeducators in Special Education Programs," by N. K. French, 2003, *Focus on Exceptional Children, 36*(2).

Relationship-Based Services to Families

To be genuinely "family friendly," early intervention and preschool practitioners need to pay attention to the emotional experience of family members (Brotherson et al., 2010). A capacity for empathy is especially essential when helping families facing multiple challenges, such as dealing with a child's medical condition, obtaining funding for needed treatment, finding respite care so a family member can continue to work, and providing support to siblings who are not disabled. Although empowerment requires a focus on a family's strengths, it does not mean professionals should ignore a family's vulnerability and pain. Frequently, there are barriers to a family's effective use of the help offered by early intervention and special education professionals due to a complex mix of attitudes, feelings, expectations, and behavior. Effective collaboration in serving a child with a disability is most likely to occur when the parents and professionals involved have established a trusting relationship.

Fraiberg (1996) described the importance of family relationships across four modalities: concrete assistance, emotional support, developmental guidance, and insight-oriented psychotherapy. Each term indicates increasing levels of psychological support and can be thought of as points along a continuum. The first point concerns helping parents identify basic needs (**concrete assistance**), such as housing, childcare, and transportation, for which a team could provide direct assistance or offer referrals to appropriate providers. For example, for a family that is homeless, the first priority may be to find affordable, decent housing. Once the family has a stable home base where therapists can visit, then the parents may more readily build their skills for interacting with their child who is disabled. **Emotional support** involves encouraging, eliciting, listening to, and thinking about parents' descriptions of their experiences. Is a parent afraid about the future, exhausted by the demands of caring for the child, or feeling guilty about causing a disabling condition? For example, a therapist may want to ask why a parent is reluctant to hire a caregiver who can provide some respite time so the parent can have a break. If the parent expresses fear that the child may be physically or sexually abused by another person, the parent and the therapist may want to discuss ways they could reduce the risk of this happening. Perhaps the therapist could talk to the parent about how a criminal check could be done, how references could be gathered for a possible caregiver, or how the child might be able to stay in a well-staffed group setting and not be left alone with any one person. This would show respect for the parent's concern by suggesting solutions that might alleviate the parent's fear and provide needed respite.

> Shepherding a child through infancy and toddlerhood is a process that shakes all parents to the core at certain moments, no matter how many resources and how much support they have. The simple act of someone else knowing, bearing witness to, and normalizing this fact can make the difference between a parent feeling like the most horrible person on earth at such a moment, and feeling like one in the number of parents populating the planet. (St. John & Pawl, 2000, p. 4)

Developmental guidance involves providing information about age-appropriate behaviors, interests, concerns, and conflicts and suggesting positive parental responses based on the parents' understanding of the development of their child. For example, a typical 2-year-old might explore the environment by opening doors, banging toys, and making messes around the house. A suggestion for parents of a 2-year-old with a disability might be for them to find ways for their nonmobile child to also explore, encouraging and even celebrating the resulting messes rather than getting angry when they occur.

Psychotherapy, on the other hand, involves understanding a parent's reactions to the child in the context of that parent's own early experience, current circumstances, or psychological conflicts. For example, the parent of a child with Down syndrome may remember having an uncle with Down syndrome who was institutionalized and who frightened the parent as a young child on one of the rare occasions when the uncle joined a family get together. That early experience may make the parent feel unaccountably sad and pessimistic about the child's future. The level of psychological support that might be appropriate in this situation would be the specialty of a mental health professional, such as a social worker or counselor, and would be explored only in those cases when there are complicated emotional needs. An early interventionist or special education preschool provider who has an empathetic relationship with a parent should recognize when a referral for such services is needed.

A relationship-based approach seeks to establish and maintain partnership, attention, and connectedness between a parent and child as well as between the professional and the parent (St. John & Pawl, 2000). Professionals are required to be flexible and active in noticing and responding to new information coming from parents and their children about their experiences. Noticing the unique way a parent and child interact, helping parents find their own solutions to problems, and being comfortable with the results are other aspects of such relationships. Relationships can be instruments for change and growth. Early intervention and special education professionals should share observations about an infant's or preschooler's growth and development, offer anticipatory guidance to the parent that is specific to the child, alert the parent to the child's individual accomplishments and needs, and help the parent find pleasure in the relationship with his or her child (Weatherston, 2000).

An early childhood professional's role in this relationship is to offer parents multiple opportunities to nurture, protect, steady, and enhance their understanding about their very young child. Team members can use spontaneous events as "teachable moments" to provide information that should help parents understand their child's temperament, behavior, and development (Childress, 2011). A **teachable moment** is a spontaneously occurring interaction that provides the context for modeling new skills, praising parents for their insight, adapting a technique to be slightly more effective, or exploring emotions related to the event. Observing parents and children together, noticing what is happening, inviting the parent's comments, and reinforcing what is going well help a team make useful suggestions. As professionals and parents grow comfortable with each other, it becomes possible to discuss both pleasurable and painful aspects of the parent–child relationship. Professionals need to allow parents to take the lead in interacting with the child, and determining what to talk about, to enhance the capabilities that each parent brings to the care of the child.

As advocates, professionals should help parents voice their feelings about their relationships with their children and understand these feelings. This may mean identifying and discussing early negative as well as positive parenting experiences the parent has had with the child. This will require listening, allowing emotions and conflicts to be expressed, attending to and responding to parent concerns, and collaborating with others if needed to provide treatment in those situations where there may be serious family dysfunction, such as drug abuse, mental illness, or violence (Weatherston, 2000).

The Early Start Denver Model (ESDM) provides an example of an early childhood program using relationship-based strategies (Dawson et al., 2010). ESDM is based on integrated behavior analysis procedures and behavior analysis and developmental procedures for intervening with preschoolers with autism spectrum disorder (ASD). This approach is paired with relationship-based intervention delivered by therapists and parents. This approach is used in natural environments during normal daily activities (e.g., eating meals, playing, and bathing), and parent roles are designed around each family's unique characteristics. Parents select the activities and objectives they believe are of the highest priority. Multiple professionals also collaborate to provide speech therapy, physical therapy, and medical and psychotherapy services. When Dawson and colleagues compared ESDM to community-based services available to children with ASD, they found that children's gains in adaptive behavior were significantly higher and autistic behaviors declined and were significantly lower than those children in the comparison group.

Facts Related to Understanding Families

In order to establish a trusting relationship between families and professionals, early childhood providers may need first to calibrate their own attitudes and perspectives. Special education services have a history of stereotyping parents in ways that have not been productive. Stereotyping or generalizing about families is not confined to educators, but this practice creates an especially serious barrier to meeting treatment objectives in early childhood services. The challenge for practitioners is to overcome these tendencies. From 1960 through 1980, a large body of research was compiled indicating that families of children with disabilities, as compared to families of children without disabilities, were at increased risk for stress, depression, family chaos and strain, and greater social isolation. Subsequently, both researchers and theorists assumed that these families had an increased risk of family dysfunction. Research in the 1990s focused less on the pathology of deficiency and found that many of the early research assumptions had to be questioned. It is now clear that the psychosocial functioning of families of children with disabilities is more similar to that of families of children without disabilities than it is different. Although extensive needs are expressed by all families, those with children who

have disabilities face different, but not necessarily extraordinary, obstacles.

Like other families facing crises, the impact of a disability may be negative or positive, but more likely the impact will vary across family members and over time. The results of studies investigating the impact of disability on marriage have been mixed. Early studies found that divorce or disruption of marriage was disproportionately high when there was an exceptional child in the family. More recent studies indicated that the divorce rate is not higher for these families (Hatton, Emerson, Graham, Blacher, & Llewellyn, 2009) and that these marriages are sometimes strengthened because of a shared commitment to the child. A number of factors may contribute to the likelihood of marital stress. For example, parents of children with autism are twice as likely to divorce during the child's early years, but if their marriage survives those years, the likelihood decreases (Hartley et al., 2010). Although Hatton and colleagues (2009) found that family composition changed more in the first five years after the birth of a child with disabilities than it did for families with children without disabilities, nearly all this change was attributed to differences in socioeconomic status. In other words, the more important stressor to family integrity was economic.

One mother shared how her daughter's disability changed her life:

> In my house there is an eight-by-ten picture of me taken on my wedding day. It is just my face, looking somewhat seriously into the camera. When I am in a particularly melancholy frame of mind, it is sad for me to see it, for the woman in that picture is gone. . . . I was 23, my husband Jim had just turned 22, and we knew little about anything then. Eleven months later, . . . Maggie was born. She was not a planned child, and I do not think much else in my life has been since that day. As my husband peered into the nursery, he saw Maggie turn, in his words, "navy blue." He came running into my room yelling, "There's something wrong with the baby!" and my life changed forever. . . . I wish that the woman in that picture could have left me less suddenly, less painfully. But the person she left behind is smarter, wiser, more confident. . . . She has tested the love of her family and friends and has found it to be strong and enduring. She knows there is little life can put in her path that she will not be able to face and conquer head on. (Klemm & Schimanski, 1999, pp. 109–110)

As with children without disabilities, mothers typically assume the primary responsibility for caring for their family's needs, including the special needs of a child with a disability. In fact, fathers are typically viewed by practitioners and researchers in early childhood as the shadow parent to children with disabilities, resulting in unintentional exclusion and a feeling of disenfranchisement by fathers (McDonald & Hastings, 2010). Fathers tend to spend about the same amount of time providing childcare regardless of whether their children have disabilities or not. When dads do engage with children, their interactions tend to be more playful and active and less authoritative than mothers. Yet, both parents measure their sense of family balance by their assessment of the amount of "quality time" spent with their child (Milkie, Kendig, Nomaguchi, & Denny, 2010). Both parents tend to view their experience with a child with a disability as transformational. It is important, therefore, that efforts to empower a family be directed to both parents. The more fathers take an active role in intervention, the more confident they become as change agents in their childs' lives (Bauman & Wasserman, 2010).

Research is similarly mixed on siblings in families with children who are disabled. For example, there tends to be a higher incidence of emotional and behavioral problems, such as higher rates of depression, in siblings of children with autism as well as a negative impact on siblings of children with severe behavior problems (Neece, Blacher, & Baker, 2010) and on siblings of students with intellectual disabilities (Labato et al., 2011). Siblings of children with autism have identified both challenges and growth opportunities (Mandleco, Roper, Freeborn, Ward, & Dyches, 2012). Difficulties experienced by siblings include less parental attention, extra responsibilities, dealing with intrusive behaviors (hitting, screaming, tantrums, destructive behaviors), and interrupted communication with the sibling with a disability. At the same time, siblings acknowledged the following rewards: valuing time spent together as a family, development of empathy, and love and understanding of their sibling with autism. While siblings in this study reported that they would prefer that the behavior problems related to autism could be changed, they did not wish that the disability itself could be changed. As with parents, siblings of children with disabilities tend to be left out of the process, even though they tend to want more information about the disability (Kresak, Gallagher, & Rhodes, 2009). Moyson and Roeyers (2011) asked siblings of children with disabilities to assess their perceived quality of life according to nine domains. The following sibling responses, in their own words, provide a window into the lives of their families: (Moyson & Roeyers, 2011, p. 94).

Domain 1: Joint activities

"I can play with my brother, but only on his level—you understand? Without his disability, I could really play with him, like games I also like to play. Because, last week, I played dominoes with him, but then I have to say to him which card he needs to lay down, so we play without winning and losing." (Diewke, 12 years old)

Domain 2: Mutual understanding

"Sometimes, I want to be just like him, because I want to know what he wants, how he feels, what he thinks. So, I will be more considerate with him." (Nell, 9 years old)

Domain 3: Private time

"Every school day, I come home at four o'clock and my brother is only at home at six o'clock. So, every day, there are two hours I can do the things I want and I don't have to show consideration for him. That's really good!" (Nell, 9 years old)

Domain 4: Acceptance

"One day, I said to myself: Come on Marie, it is sad to have a sister with a disability, but that's the way she is and always will be. She is different, she has other capacities and that's so nice! I really learned to appreciate the things she can do!" (Marie, 11 years old)

Domain 5: Forbearance

"Once, I was away during one week on a school camp and my mother sent me a letter, saying that my brother was well-behaved. I remember I felt happy and proud!" (David, 12 years old)

Domain 6: Concern about well-being of sibling with disability

"There are a lot of things I can do, but my brother can't. Sometimes we play a game and he asks if he can play with us. But then we have to say: No you can't, because it's too difficult. I think it is hard for him to see us doing things he can't." (Chris, 9 years old)

Domain 7: Exchanging experiences with like-minded peers

"When I'm at school, I am just Diewke, I don't think about Emiel. When I go out shopping with Emiel and people are staring at him because of his behavior, then I feel I am a sibling and I feel a lot of stress. But when I go to the activities of the parent group, I can be his sister, because I know that all people there are experiencing the same things. So, then I can relax and even enjoy Emiel's behavior." (Diewke, 12 years old)

Domain 8: Social Support

"It's hard for my parents to handle my brother, day after day. So, in the evening, when my brother is in bed, they're just happy that they can sit down and relax. I don't want to disturb them then with my worries or problems!" (Diewke, 12 years old)

Domain 9: Dealing with the outside world

"When we go out for a walk with her, I just want to show everybody, um, I don't know how to say it, um, I just want to say to everybody that we really love her!" (Rosie, 12 years old)

Extended-family members may also be an important part of the family unit as well as a source of support; this is more so in some cultures than in others. Grandparents often participate in a wide range of everyday tasks related to family care. In African American families, for example, grandmothers are commonly the family matriarchs who provide shelter, care, and advice on a daily basis. When there is a child with a disability, the whole family may be called into action; the grandmother may accompany the parents to planning meetings and doctors' visits, an aunt may arrange transportation, and cousins may babysit siblings left at home. This kind of support makes economic sense and encourages the well-being of the parents and the child with a disability; more people care and advocate for the child with special needs. While social opportunities for families of children with disabilities are restricted, parents have reported creating a community of support that includes family and enclaves of "wise" persons (Green, Barnhill, Green, Hawken, Humphrey, & Sanderson, 2011). As members of these self-constructed villages, grandparents may provide lifelong enrichment for children with disabilities and their families.

Whether discussion focuses on families of children with disabilities or families of children without disabilities, the reality is that many family units are not composed of two parents. Although statistics vary, it is now probable that professionals supporting families will be working with many families that consist of one parent (either a mother or father) with one or two children. Furthermore, in two-parent households, it is likely that families will consist of a blend of children from at least one previous marriage and will consequently include multiple family systems. Other family configurations include the following:

- Extended family members as primary caregivers (grandmother, grandfather, aunt, or uncle)
- Same-sex parenting partners
- Families without homes
- Families built through adoption or foster care

Each of these family configurations changes the dynamics and presents new challenges to professionals. Table 2–1 highlights some of the factors that may be involved in diverse family structures and the impact of these variations on family relationships with professionals.

Although family service programs have historically been based on a traditional, albeit somewhat fictional, family model, it is realistic to define families more broadly today. Dettmer and colleagues (1999) recommend an inclusive definition of family that was articulated at the Second Family Leadership Conference:

Table 2–1 Variables That Make Family–Professional Interaction Challenging

Situation	Impact
Family structure	Loyalties, power, complex and varying rules under similar conditions, transitions between dwellings, availability of equipment
Childcare requirements	Availability of childcare for infants, toddlers, and young children with disabilities; debates with childcare providers about the realities of serving children with disabilities; financial burdens
Single-parent families	Time and resource management, single-parent income, transportation issues, ill-child responsibilities, possible conflict with personal goals, increased need for respite care
Nontraditional partnerships	Prejudice of service providers and local community, debates over "proper parenting authority," legal authority issues
Poverty	Prejudice of service providers toward poor persons, lack of transportation to get to and from services, possible lack of phone services, possible lack of a permanent address
Substance abuse	Immediate impact on the person suffering the abuse, subsequent impact on immediate and extended family members, inability to keep priorities in desired order, secondary health issues, guilt, shame
Foster care	No long-term goals or personal authority, lack of accurate history

A family is a group of people who are important to each other and offer each other love and support, especially in times of crisis. In order to be sensitive to the wide range of life styles, living arrangements, and cultural variations that exist today, family . . . can no longer be limited to just parent/child relationships. Family involvement . . . must reach out to include mothers, fathers, grandparents, sisters, brothers, neighbors, and other persons who have important roles in the lives of people with disabilities. (Family and Integration Resources, 1991, p. 37, as cited in Dettmer et al., 1999)

Census data support such an inclusive definition. For the first time in the history of the U.S. Census, in 2010, the percentage of nuclear-family households dropped below 50 percent. Factors related to this drop include choices by adults to have children at a later age, high rates of divorce, and births outside marriage that have contributed to a rise in single-parent families. While single-women-headed households still outnumbered single-men-headed households, the rise in male-headed households significantly outpaced the rise in female-headed households between 2000 and 2010. Cohabitation has become so commonplace that 40 percent of all children will spend some time in such an arrangement before age 16. A survey of gay and lesbian adults who considered themselves unmarried partners revealed that as many as 27 percent of these partners cared for children in a family situation.

The 2010 census showed that multigenerational families have been growing in number since the 1970s, with a sharp rise taking place after 2007 and the Great Recession. These changes have occurred as a result of social and economic factors. In a majority of cases where there are two generations of adults, it is the older adult who takes the role of head of household. One in ten children in the U.S. lives with one or more grandparents who are the primary caregivers (U.S. Census Bureau, 2010).

Presenting a unique challenge to early childhood special education professionals are homeless families, 85 percent of which are headed by single mothers (Waldman & Perlman, 2008). Understandably, the children in these families, who spend an average of 10 months a year homeless, are at very high risk of disability. In fact, preschoolers who are homeless are twice as likely to have learning disabilities and three times as likely to have social and/or emotional disabilities as children who are not homeless (Waldman & Perlman, 2008).

Morin (2011) conducted a study that evaluated the extent to which sweeping demographic changes in family structure over the past 50 years are perceived to be acceptable to the American population. The study found that about one-third of the public self-selects into one of three groups: accepters, rejecters, and skeptics. Accepters, who are disproportionately represented by women, Hispanics, East Coast residents, and secular respondents, said that current trends make no difference to society or are good for society. Rejecters, on the other hand, who are disproportionately white, older, Republican, married, and religious, said that most trends are bad for society (except for interracial marriage and fewer women having children). Finally, skeptics tended to be more like accepters than rejecters, but had more concern about the effects of women having children without a male partner. The skeptics, who were overrepresented by young, Democrat or independent, and minority respondents, thought that the other trends had either no impact on society or no positive impacts. These findings illustrate the diverse viewpoints and the personal beliefs about change held by Americans. The various viewpoints have no impact on either the demographic trends themselves or the effects of these trends on society. However, it is useful for professionals to understand their own biases and to use this knowledge to understand families they serve.

Parental Responses to the Diagnosis of a Disability

For many families, life becomes more difficult from the first moments a child's disability is diagnosed. After a review of the literature, Moore, Howard, and McLaughlin (2002) concluded that all families have needs; it just so happens that for families of children with disabilities, the challenges are those of a child with special needs. Other families must deal with issues such as poverty, mental illness, child abuse, divorce, drugs, or death of family members, but not of a child with a disability. According to Moore and colleagues, these factors do not make families special, unusual, dysfunctional, or, least of all, homogeneous. However, some shared reactions to crisis should be recognized.

Parents unexpectedly faced with the loss of "typical child" hopes and expectations often proceed through several common stages, ranging from total disbelief and bewilderment to the ability to grasp and control the situation. Even so, every parent or couple responds to the diagnosis of a disability in accord with their own external and internal resources. Dr. Elizabeth Kubler-Ross, in her classic research with cancer patients (Kubler-Ross, 1969), first identified the general progression people in grief follow; these stages are referred to as the *grief cycle*.

Professionals working with parents of infants who are at risk or infants in crisis recognized that many, although not all, parents of children with disabilities proceed through the same or similar phases. Today, many early childhood professionals refer to Kubler-Ross's reaction cycle as **stage theory response.**

Stage theory response is useful primarily to parents who find that naming their complex emotions helps them to understand their emotions and facilitates communication with others who have similar experiences. Knowledge of stage theory response also helps professionals validate parental emotions. However, when used to label parents or to associate a pathology with a particular stage, stage theory response is potentially harmful.

Consider two conversations as samples of appropriate and inappropriate use of grief stage theory. A parent may say, "Sometimes when I'm told about all my child's problems, I get so angry I feel like throwing things." A professional conscious of stage theory may appropriately respond, "That's not unusual. I've known other parents who felt the same way. Do you suppose your anger is a part of how you are coping emotionally?" On the other hand, if a parent says, "I feel like screaming sometimes, because I am treated like a bystander and no one asks my opinion about my child's treatment!" and the professional inappropriately thinks, "That woman is clearly in the anger stage and just needs to get over it!" and ignores the parent's perception of the relationship, the stage theory is being applied inappropriately. Professionals need to realize that passage through grief, like any other life passage, is not a sign of dysfunction but of normalcy.

The stages, or phases, described are neither sequential nor of equal duration, intensity, or frequency of recurrence, either within or across families. Parents often report that the stages overlap and almost always recur, often at periods of significant transition. A "stage" may last one day or one year. What is important to know and remember about the grief or adjustment process is that knowledge of the process often helps parents to understand that many others in similar circumstances share these common emotions. The key components of the stage theory, or grief process, as described by Kubler-Ross and subsequent researchers, are shock and denial, anger and frustration, volatile emotions (hope, isolation, depression), bargaining, and, finally, acceptance or reestablishment.

Anderegg, Vergason, and Smith (1992) studied the grief process with 130 parents. Their work led to the development of a slightly different model, although it still supports earlier work. This research indicated that parents and extended family members pass through three phases:

1. Confronting (denial, blame and/or guilt, shock)

2. Adjusting (depression, anger, bargaining)

3. Adapting (life-cycle changes, realistic planning, adjusting expectations)

A number of factors account for a family's ability to reach a point of adjustment and acceptance. Among the most significant factors are the characteristics of a child's exceptionality, the degree of exceptionality, and, in particular, the behavioral demands of a child with an exceptionality. Although demographic characteristics such as family size and family configuration may play some part in adjustment, access to resources, social and environmental support, and parental problem-solving abilities were found to be of greater importance than other factors in parents' well-being (Aaron, Benz, & Elliott, 2012). In fact, these factors along with parents' ability to appraise threats and problem-solve, outweighed the severity of a child's disability and the parental demographics variable in determining the well-being of families (Aaron et al., 2012).

The passage from diagnosis to adaptation is cyclical and complex. Some parents feel they never really move out of a low-grade sadness that seems to permeate their lives. However, shifts usually do take place. The early panic that follows a diagnosis of an infant in crisis usually changes and develops according to healthy patterns of adaptation.

Stage theory response has a distinct psychiatric flavor, which may imply that parents are maladjusted and need counseling when, in fact, they are responding normally. Therefore, caution should be used in applying stage theory response to any particular parent or family. Parents arrive at adjustment in many ways, and the sequence and time needed are different for every parent. In fact, families often tend to face crises, including adjustment to a child with a disability, with resiliency (Benzies & Mychasiuk, 2009). Families that possess or develop protective factors emerge from this challenge stronger. These protective factors fall into three categories that include individual, family, and community strengths (Table 2–2).

Family Hardiness

In addition to the basic needs and desires of all families, researchers have identified stressors that may be prominent in families of children with disabilities. **Acute stressors** are periodic incidents related to a child's disability; **chronic stressors** include concerns about the future, financial limitations, and society's acceptance of human differences; and, last, **transition stressors** are linked to significant milestones, such as entry into school, that occur throughout a child's lifespan. Based on these unique stressors, there is a need for **family hardiness,** defined as a constellation of three dimensions that include viewing the events of life as challenges not threats, thinking they have control over how they respond to stress, and having a commitment to and involvement with each other (Sheppard, Mandleco, Roper, Dyches & Freeborn, 2012). Hardiness can be described as a family's sense of control over events that provides a means of coping with stress. Families that possess greater hardiness see crises as an opportunity or challenge to be met rather than a threat to security.

Throughout the course of a child's life, services and providers will come and go. The primary functions and needs of a family may change. Cultural and community norms may expand or contract, and society's acceptance of persons with special needs may be uncertain. Funding and research in the area of early childhood education and intervention will undoubtedly pass through emotional and practical troughs and peaks. How families experience these fluctuations will depend upon the resiliency built in or developed through supportive community services including early childhood programs.

Connections with other parents who have had similar experiences may be one of the most powerful mechanisms for strengthening family hardiness. These parents can teach others about professionals they never knew existed, words and acronyms that are unfamiliar, and reactions from friends and families that cannot be anticipated (Klemm & Schimanski, 1999). Other parents provide information and emotional support as a family learns about a disability and what it will mean. Following the table are a small subset of important resources that help connect parents to each other and to supportive resources:

Table 2–2 Factors Related to Family Resiliency

Individual Factors
- Those with an internal locus of control feel that they can control their own future and have the ability to create and change their circumstances
- Those with the power to modulate their emotions are able to regulate impulse control and think clearly during stressful conditions
- Those with a positive outlook on life and who possess spiritual beliefs have a greater ability to develop a sense of meaning during adverse conditions
- People who possess relatively high levels of self-efficacy believe in their own ability to reach goals and are self reliant and able to think independently
- Resilient family members use coping skills to buffer stress by recognizing available resources
- Parents' education levels are associated with financial stability, adaptability, and ability to facilitate child growth
- Easy temperaments in children with disabilities elicit positive responses and more warmth from parents and reduce parental anxiety
- Being female is associated with lower levels of aggressive behavior, which is believed to be related to the harsher punishment associated with being male

Family Protective Factors
- Certain family structures, such as small families and those with an older, mature mother, are more likely to be resilient to stressors
- In two-parent families, a stable, warm relationship with effective communication is predictive of ability to cope
- The ability of a family to face challenges by mutually supporting each other is an indication of cohesion, a protective barrier
- Warm and nurturing interactions between parents and children that promote cognitive development through joint activities help protect families and children from negative outcomes
- When parents provide stimulating activities with appropriate scaffolding, their children develop problem-solving skills and favorable behavioral outcomes
- Families with social supports they feel they can depend on in times of crisis are more able to face those crises confidently
- Children in families that possess strong protective factors are more likely to acquire and use those same protective factors as they develop
- Stable employment and adequate income protect children from uncertainty and provide a protective barrier under challenging conditions
- Whereas housing instability and frequent moving are related to low school performance, adequate, reliable housing is a protective barrier

Community Protective Factors
- Involvement in community activities gives families a sense of belonging and access to social support networks as well as personally rewarding activities
- Acceptance of children with disabilities by their peers is a very strong protective factor
- When children with disabilities establish relationships with nonfamilial mentors who express belief in a child's potential and have high expectations, these children are more able to adapt to challenges than children who do not
- Families that live in safe neighborhoods have a greater ability to reliably provide for core needs than families that live in toxic neighborhoods
- Quality childcare and schools boost resiliency by helping children and families overcome deficits in areas other than the child's disability
- Access to quality health care reduces stress in families, especially when that health care is affordable

Source: From "Fostering Family Resiliency: A Review of the Key Protective Factors," adapted from Benzies, K., & R. Mychasiuk, 2009, *Child and Family Social Work, 14,* 103–114.

- Beach Center on Disability: http://www.beachcenter.org
- National Dissemination Center for Children with Disabilities (NICHCY): http://www.nichcy.org
- Fathers Network: http://www.fathersnetwork.org
- Parent to Parent USA (P2P USA): http://www.p2pusa.org

Barriers to Relationships

Though it may not be strictly true, it is most productive to assume that all families love their children and want what is best. In many cases, parents' (and often professionals') own skill deficits create barriers to collaboration that have to be overcome before an empowering relationship can flower. Many parents fear and mistrust school and agency personnel because of their own negative experiences in school or prior disagreeable interactions with other professionals. Overburdened by economic and personal hardships that create work-schedule, transportation, and childcare distress, parents may find early childhood services to be one more challenge in their overtaxed lives. Some parents fear being blamed for their child's condition or being judged for their cultural, lifestyle, or educational choices. Cultural differences can make parents feel ill at ease or misunderstood. Establishing conditions to mitigate existing barriers requires respect, trust, and cooperation, and it is a professional's responsibility to acknowledge and value differences. Dettmer and colleagues (1999) advise the following mind-set for working in this sensitive field:

1. Remember that a professional's place is on a parent's side as a team member working toward the common goal of each child's success.

2. Be aware of feelings of defensiveness, take a deep breath, and put those feelings aside.

© Randy Lee Williams

3. Remember that the focus is on the needs and interests of families and their children, not their values—attack the problem, not the person.

4. Accept people as they are and stop wishing they were different.

5. Remember that most families are doing the best they can.

6. Respect family rights to their values and opinions—even when they differ from yours.

7. Demonstrate open-mindedness and flexibility.

As with all human relations, relational practices exercised by families and professionals are both challenging and rewarding. Family members experience growth in self-efficacy, greater internal locus of control, competence as family-centered help givers, and enjoyment (Dunst & Trivette, 2009). This family-based growth has the secondary effect of improving how children behave and function. Finally, professionals learn more about the children in their care and improve communication and advocacy in their communities.

While relational interactions are considered fundamental to effective parent–professional interactions, the highest level of synchrony is achieved when interactions are also participative (Dunst & Trivette, 2009). In fact, according to Dunst and Trivette, the dimension that matters most in the family-capacity building is the element that is least used—participative help giving. Both relational and participative help giving are considered enabling practices in that each facilitates the engagement of others in decisions and actions that build new competencies. Relational practices are those interpersonal behaviors considered good clinical practice, such as active listening, empathy, respect, and compassion, whereas participatory help giving is individualized in such a way that information provided to families enables family members to make choices, formulate plans, and execute plans to achieve the family's expressed outcomes. After analyzing early childhood special education frameworks and practices, Dunst and Trivette concluded that participative help-giving practices—the most important indicators of family-centered capacity building—are largely absent. Davis and Gavidia-Payne (2009) found that, as whole, family-centered professional support for parents of children with disabilities was perceived as the strongest predictor of the family's quality of life. Therefore, the goal of empowering families requires that professionals learn how to use both relational and participative practices in interactions with families.

Communication between Parents and Professionals

Communication, in its most basic form, is the ability of two or more people to send and receive messages. Of all the skills expected of early childhood professionals, communication skills rank among the most necessary. When Linda Davern (1996) interviewed parents regarding their suggestions for improving the quality of home–school relationships, they recommended the following:

1. Convey a clear, consistent message about the value of a child. View the child in different ways, not just in terms of academic achievement, and focus on the child's progress rather than on comparisons to other children.

2. Walk in the parents' shoes. Try to understand what it is like to have a child with a disability. Understand their frustration.

3. Expand awareness of cultural diversity. Be aware of the cultural lenses through which judgments about children and families are made.

4. See individuals, and challenge stereotypes. Do not make assumptions about parents and their skills just because their child has a disability. Don't lump all parents together.

5. Persevere in building partnerships. Consider this a long-term commitment that takes time and flexibility.

6. Demonstrate an authentic interest in the parent's goals for the child. Work to diminish distance between professionals and parents while establishing connections. Avoid sending the message that professionals are the experts and parents know nothing.

7. Talk with parents about how they want to share information. Ask parents which school person they want to communicate with, how often, and through what means.

8. Use everyday language. Avoid jargon that is confusing.

9. Create effective forums for planning and problem-solving. Formal meetings can be very intimidating, so schedule regular, less formal meetings at which parents can be more comfortable.

Several basic communication concepts and skills can enhance relationships between parents and professionals. These involve active listening, checks, and ways to accurately state needs.

Active Listening

Active listening means that listeners (receivers of information) are attentive to a speaker on multiple levels: hearing, interpreting, sorting, and analyzing (see Table 2–3). It is the opposite of passive listening, in which the recipient hears without understanding the intended message and without responding appropriately to the speaker. Table 2–4 illustrates the problems that can develop when one listener is active and the other is passive and, ultimately, the effect this has on communication and learning.

When active listening is done well, relationships develop between the sender and the listener: Partners hear and can respond to what their counterpart is saying, parents and children learn that what they have to say is important and respected, and professionals increase the probability that the right supports will be given to parents. Unlike passive listening, which involves only one sender, active listening is

Table 2–3 Active Listening

Skills	Description
Hearing	Understands and comprehends the words (spoken or written)
Interpreting	Is attentive to nuances, the larger context of the statement, and the political, cultural, and emotional dimensions of comments
Sorting	Categorizes information with other like information to increase the meaning or clarify intent
Analyzing	Compares information with other knowledge about the topic and draws conclusions

Table 2–4   Example of Interaction When Only One Party Is Actively Listening

Actively Listening Parent	Passively Listening Preschool Teacher
"I would very much like to have my child use his communication board on a more regular basis. Currently, he becomes very frustrated because he can't tell us what he needs." The parent frowns and looks sad.	"All the students in my class are able to speak. We will have the speech–language pathologist work with Andy so that he can speak as well." The teacher is fiddling with papers she needs for her next parent conference.
"Perhaps you didn't read Andy's file carefully. His cerebral palsy is so involved that he is not able to make any understandable speech sounds. We have already had him evaluated by a speech therapist at St. Luke's and they created the communication board for him so he could develop his language skills." The parent shakes her head and pushes a catalogue of language devices toward the childcare provider.	(Still looking at her other papers.) "We have an excellent speech–language pathologist. She will have Andy talking in no time. Andy can work with her during circle time since that is oral and Andy wouldn't be able to participate."
"We don't want Andy to miss out on circle time. He loves to be a part of the group. We can choose appropriate pictures to put on his communication board so he can respond with the rest of the children. He gets very frustrated when he is not allowed to be with the rest of the students." The parent's shoulders tighten and she leans forward, thumping the catalogue of language devices to emphasize the use of the communication board.	"Oh, we don't let the children bring toys to the circle. He has to be able to speak up like everyone else. Also, I've been meaning to talk to you about his behavior. He has been refusing to cooperate with our group activities. I'd like to send him to time out when this happens."
(She gives a big sigh.) "As I said, he gets very frustrated when he isn't able to communicate and when he isn't a part of the group. I don't think time out would be the right answer for this problem."	"Well, if you don't allow us to control his behavior, I don't know how Andy is ever going to be able to be a part of our class." She looks at her watch, ready to end the meeting.
"We seem to have a different understanding of Andy's problems. Perhaps we need to meet as a team again, so the speech–language pathologist can also be involved. I'm concerned that you are not addressing Andy's communication needs." The parent's face is red, her hands are shaking as she pulls the catalogue back to her bag. The parent takes a deep breath, pulls her bag over her shoulder, and leaves, shaking her head as she goes.	"That would be fine, because I have another parent coming now and can't talk any longer. It has been a pleasure meeting with you today." The childcare provider smiles and shakes the parent's hand as she shuffles her papers together and heads toward the door to greet the next parent.

an inclusive engagement between and among people. Table 2–5 presents an example in which both parties are actively listening.

Communicating Well

The following strategies can help make a professional a more effective communicator, and they may help improve relationships with other professionals and with family members:

Avoid Binding Statements   Binding communications are habits of interaction that generally close or diminish the probability of continued conversation. By contrast, freeing communications are those habits of interaction that actually encourage

Table 2–5   Example of Interaction When Both Parties Are Actively Listening

Actively Listening Preschool Teacher	Actively Listening Parent
"We didn't address this in our last IEP meeting, but I think Cherise has matured in her language and self-help skills enough that she is ready to start toilet training. What do you think about this?" The teacher leans forward, looking the parent directly in the eye.	"Do you really think she could learn to go by herself? It would be such a relief to not have her in diapers, now that we are expecting another child." The parent smiles.
The teacher nods enthusiastically. "I just want to explain what this would involve and make sure we can work on this at both home and school. I'd like to check her every 15 minutes to see if there is a pattern to when she is wet and then start putting her on the potty at those most likely times each day. Can you do the same thing when she is at home with you in the afternoon and evening?" The teacher watches the parent's face and notices that her mouth falls a little.	"I don't think I could check every 15 minutes. We have the two older ones you know, so I'm always driving them to soccer or dance lessons, and Cherise's therapy sessions usually run at least 45 minutes and I don't like to disturb her once she is started in those." The parent sits back in her chair, pushing away from the table.
"Of course, you are probably on the go so much there isn't a lot of downtime during which you could stop and do this every 15 minutes. Is there any period of time, like maybe the hour just before bed that you could work on this? I find kids learn toileting so much faster when we work on it at school and at home." The teacher raises her eyebrows in a hopeful gesture.	"Maybe I could ask my husband to watch Cherise when I take her older sister off to dance. That way she'd be home for the two hours before bed. Would that be enough to make a difference?" The parent leans on the table.
"I appreciate you rearranging your hectic schedule. I think that could make a big difference, and once Cherise is out of diapers, you'll have a little more free time with the new baby."	"I'm so glad you think we can do this. It would make a huge difference not to have two in diapers. Cherise will be happier too if she can be like the big girls." She hesitates. "But what if I can't carry through at home? What if she doesn't learn?"
"I know it's harder to do these things at home when your hands are full. We'll keep working on it at school, and we might brainstorm another way to accomplish it at home. Cherise might not learn right away, but I've got some ways to motivate her. Perhaps we could use a buzzer that will let us know when she starts to wet, so we don't have to watch the clock. You just let me know if you don't think it's going well at home and we'll go back to the drawing board."	"Thank you for being so understanding. I'll give it my best shot." She rises and extends her hand. "I'm so glad you thought to work on this. It's like you read my mind."

expanded dialogue. The following examples illustrate a few habits that often lead to binding communications:

- Giving overly enthusiastic responses that are generally based on what would be best for the professional
- Changing the subject without explanation
- Explaining others' behavior by interpreting their history ("You act this way because your mother acted this way")
- Providing direct advice and even persuasion ("If I were you, this is what I would do")

- Setting up expectations that bind the speaker to the past, which disallows change and innovation ("You've never acted this way before; what's wrong?")

- Communicating expectations that bind the speaker to the future ("I'm sure you'll figure this out and do such and such")

- Denying feelings ("You really don't mean that!" Or, "You really don't feel that way, do you?")

- Overgeneralizing ("Everyone feels that way"), diminishing the other, making one feel like one's feelings or experiences really do not matter much

- Approving on personal grounds: praising the other for thinking, feeling, or acting in ways that agree with or that conform to a professional's standards

- Disapproving on personal grounds: blaming or censuring the other for thinking, feeling, or acting in ways you do not like

- Commanding and ordering: telling the other what to do (including "Tell me what to do.")

- Obligating emotionally: controlling through arousing feelings of shame and inferiority ("How can you do this to me when I have done so much for you?")

In summary, binding statements are those comments that diminish the listener's desire to continue the conversation.

Use Freeing Statements   Freeing statements, such as "go on," "tell me more," and "how do you feel about that?", actually increase the speaker's desire to continue and increase both personal autonomy and power. As a note of caution, professionals must use these statements sincerely and avoid assuming a therapeutic tone.

Avoid Killer Phrases   Killer phrases range from those comments that discourage further comment to those that break a person's spirit. Appropriately named for the effect they have on communication, killer phrases are generally (though not always) uttered in moments of frustration, anger, or depression. Examples are "It won't work," or "It's all right in theory, but can you put it into practice?" Early childhood professionals should recognize killer phrases and attribute no more to them than indications of weariness. As for the language of professionals, to the greatest extent possible, it should be void of killer phrases. Table 2–6 gives more examples of killer phrases to avoid.

It is much easier for a professional to hurt a parent than vice versa because professionals are generally supported in several ways by the power vested in them through training, social norms, and organizational structure. Therefore, the playing field is never level. In consideration of this relationship, professionals should prepare to weather killer phrases aimed at them without bowing to the temptation to respond in kind.

Allow and Respect "No"   Most novice professionals find themselves eager to pass on what they know and to support parents' decisions. Professionals simply do not set out to be offensive or to get in a family's way; yet it happens. It happens, against all intentions, because service providers fail to recognize the more basic needs of families, one of which is not to need a professional support person! In the course of each family or family system, there comes a time when parents and other members

Table 2–6 Examples of Killer Phrases

- That's a swell idea, but . . .
- Good idea, but your family is different.
- It's too academic (or it's too medical).
- We're rural (or we're too large).
- It's too simplistic.
- It needs more study.
- We've never done it that way.
- I haven't the time.
- I'm not ready for it. (You're not ready for it.)
- There are better ways than that!
- You haven't considered . . .
- Let's not step on anyone's toes.
- Why start anything now?
- The agency won't understand.

of the family wish to be left alone. Families may grow weary of professional conversations and interactions; they may well have priorities that professional support persons do not share.

Not wanting to discourage or seem ungrateful, parents will find various and subtle ways to say, "Stay away for now." For a shy parent, avoidance may begin by simply canceling meetings or calling in ill. Others will tell a professional that the timing is bad and reschedule for some distant date. In such situations, it is the professional's responsibility to analyze the communication as carefully as possible and to draw and confirm a conclusion. When it becomes apparent that a parent is asking for some free space from professionals, support for that request needs to be forthcoming. If professionals are unclear about a parent's actual intent, they need only ask parents directly "Would you like my assistance? Please feel free to say no." If the parent answers "no," that answer must be accepted with the same dignity afforded the opposite response. In short, parents and caregivers need to be allowed to say "no" to support or services (after all, it is their legal right to do so) and then be respected for saying it.

Use Perception Checks Sometimes, despite best efforts, it is difficult to draw an accurate conclusion about a speaker's intent. When this happens, it is possible to draw on a communication skill called a **perception check,** which means that listeners check their perception or understanding of what was said (e.g., the parent doesn't want to waste the specialist's Saturday morning) against what the speaker was actually thinking (e.g., "My oldest child was sick all night, and I'm exhausted. Please leave me alone!"). A perception check is performed not by asking the speaker to repeat what was just said but by saying, "This is what I understand you to mean. . . ." This pattern allows the initial speaker to confirm or deny the perception.

Perception checks are especially important to use when more than two people are engaged in an interaction. During assessment sessions, in planning meetings, or in family consultations, early childhood professionals may find a good deal of confusion about the intent or content of transactions or interactions. By using any of the following phrases, professionals can help keep the communication lines clear and open.

- I was listening to what you just said. Is (give explanation) what you mean?
- So many people have been offering comments. I'm a bit unsure of your position on (name the issue). Is (give explanation) what you meant?
- You just said, "No." Are you trying to accommodate my schedule, or is there really a better time for us to get together?

These three statements ask for clarification without judging the speaker's effectiveness or ability.

Use Paraphrasing   Paraphrasing is another way to confirm what has been stated. It involves restating the essence of the comment or conversation. In paraphrasing, listeners put into words what they think they have just heard. Although a perception check seeks clarification ("Is this what you meant?"), paraphrasing seeks the right direction. Using the latter technique, the listener accepts responsibility for interpretation (e.g., "Another way to say what you just said is . . ." or "So what you just said is . . ."). Paraphrasing conclusions or using paraphrasing to confirm what is to be done next are the two most commonly used and highly productive forms of paraphrasing.

Use Descriptions of Behavior Rather Than Descriptions of Feelings   Parents, siblings, and professionals avoid participating in difficult or sensitive conversations in a number of ways. On one end of a continuum, people avoid engaging in difficult topics by withdrawing. On the other end of the continuum, people avoid a topic by engaging in unrelated conversations or behaviors. Although these postures are perhaps admirable during a poker game, they generally complicate family discussions, interdisciplinary work, and most social interactions. When behaviors ranging from withdrawal to unrelated engagement occur, listeners must confront two issues. First, what is the person indicating through actions and words or lack of action or words? Second, what is the parent, sibling, or professional really feeling?

Early childhood professionals working with parents and family members need to be especially aware of words, communication styles, and the feelings that ought to correspond to those words or gestures. For example, it is not uncommon to find a parent or professional colleague nodding "Yes" only to find out later that the parent did not agree at all. Because human beings sometimes experience a dissonance between their logical conclusions and their actual feelings, professionals must be aware of discrepancies between descriptions of behaviors and descriptions of feelings.

Someone wishing to make clear the intent of a participant who suddenly pushes her chair back and withdraws from a discussion can interject, "I've noticed that you pulled out of the conversation [description of behavior]. Would you like to talk about what's going on for you at this time [asking for description of feelings]?" The person may well choose to say nothing because his feelings are still too close to the surface. In this case, the professional may return to the individual after a short while and ask again. It is more productive to rest comfortably with a description of behavior (which is something that can be seen, touched, or heard) and refrain from making assumptions about feelings based on behavior (which are only an interpretation). An accurate description of behavior can come from an observer; an accurate description of feelings can come only from the person experiencing those feelings.

Special Skills for Communicating with Parents at the Time of Diagnosis

One of the most difficult and bewildering times for families of children with disabilities is learning the diagnosis of their child. Watson, Hayes, and Radford-Paz (2011) described the occasional obtuseness with which medical professionals deliver a child's diagnosis; that is, parents are commonly informed over the phone by a consultant who delivers the information pessimistically, with cold indifference and a lack of respect. In some cases, families have reported not being informed at all, but learning about their child's disability from a third party (i.e., social services disability workers or local housing authority) or from reading their child's medical records.

The manner in which a diagnosis is delivered to a family has long-lasting effects on parents (Kisler & McConachie, 2010). Parents are clear about the manner in which they prefer to be treated by professionals (Watson, Hayes, & Radford-Paz, 2011). Professionals perceived by families as being warm, honest, and sympathetic during disclosure of a diagnosis generate the greatest satisfaction. In addition, parents expect to be empowered by professionals, who build a sense of collaboration by treating parents as experts about their child. The following guidelines are suggested for effectively delivering unhappy diagnoses to parents.

- Provide complete and honest information about the condition of the child.
- Repeat information in many different ways and at many different times.
- Try to tell both parents at the same time.
- Be careful not to overwhelm parents by the number of professionals present.
- Recognize parents as the experts on their child and invite them to be partners in the process.
- Provide parents with time to filter the information. Always schedule a follow-up meeting.
- Be prepared to be empathetic and supportive; expect an emotional impact, and invite parents to express their emotions.
- Understand that parents may respond with anger. The anger is about the diagnosis—not about the informant.
- Think culturally about language interpretation, meaning assigned to a diagnosis, and treatment or educational preferences.
- Discuss and practice strategies for informing brothers, sisters, and other family members.

Conferencing with Parents

Formal conferences between families and professionals are often structured around a child's IEP or arise from a particular concern on the part of the parent, the school, or the agency. Meetings such as these can be a source of considerable apprehension, especially for parents, if they are viewed as an unpleasant obligation rather than an opportunity to strengthen the cooperative ties between home and school. As a professional, the important objective is to bring out the best in people—to empower them, not to be overly directive or to "do for" them. Monitoring reactions to parents and learning to communicate a genuine caring for families and their children by displaying sincere warmth and caring supports parent empowerment.

Building rapport is essential to conferencing. Parents may be put at ease when a meeting begins with pleasant informal conversation—"small talk" and an offer of coffee, a soft drink, or other refreshment. Holding the meeting around a table rather than on opposite sides of a desk also relaxes the participants. Using "door-opening statements" helps to encourage the parents to talk and to promote one's own listening. Encouraging parents to express concerns and make suggestions, even to "blow off steam" if they are upset or angry is appropriate.

Empathizing with a parent's situation and reflecting the affect that is behind another person's words encourages communication. Restating a parent's feelings in words or with facial expressions conveys understanding. Clarifying a parent's statement to ensure it is understood and noticing nonverbal cues help demonstrate careful listening. Responding to and acting on the concerns that are expressed are essential.

More important than any of the factors described above is the ability of professionals to learn as much as possible about the needs of children. Parents are often frustrated by professionals' weak knowledge and understanding of their child's disability and failure to provide parents with useful information and support services (Novak, Lingam, Coad, & Emond, 2011). Often these parents become the default expert and primary advocate in schools. This responsibility is costly to families who may already be exhausted and guilt ridden—unable to meet the needs of other family members due to time spent advocating for their child. Professionals can restore the balance by becoming informed and supporting families.

Responses to Family Priorities

Although a professional's role in the past may have been one of dispensing expertise, today's professional is responsive to the family's priorities. Above all, families and professionals join in a partnership that is truly collaborative in nature. In its best form, members are mutually engaged in the work to be accomplished and recognize the constraints placed on each other.

Constraints and Conflicts

An area that can cause considerable constraints and a possible area for conflict between families and professionals that deserves special attention involves the level of stress that time demands place on a family. Researchers have found that the greater the time demands of children with disabilities, the greater the risk of psychological problems for mothers (Sawyer et al., 2011). Indeed, the amount of time demanded by caregiving responsibilities was the stressor most often mentioned by parents of children with disabilities. Brotherson and Goldstein (1992) described the availability of time within families:

> Time is an example of a fundamental resource to family well-being that families can only partially generate and control themselves. To a large extent, a family's time is

controlled externally by people, institutions, and events that impose expectations and requirements on the family. Time is a resource when it is available and when it can be negotiated and used; as with other resources, its absence often redefines time as a constraint. (p. 509)

Although issues of time literally cross thousands of activities, three overarching characteristics of families with respect to time emerged from a review of research conducted by McCann, Bull, and Winzenberg (2012). First, parents with children who have complex needs have excess responsibilities that do not diminish as their children get older. Second, vigilance, a term that describes supervisory childcare, is uniquely burdensome for parents of children with complex needs. Finally, health-care-related needs demand time, which is sometimes extraordinary and outside typical parenting roles.

Parents noted four supports that would help them in their use of time. The first of these is a need to fit therapy and education activities into the family's daily routine and environment. Obviously, time is used more efficiently when therapists integrate activities into the family's daily routines in the home environment. For professionals to know how to truly integrate activities into home life, professionals may need to spend time in families' homes. No single prescription can fit different family demands. Some parents also use time to frame the issue of transfer of knowledge from clinic to home. In part, this is a time issue, but it is also an issue of effective transferability of skills to the home environment and the material conditions of families' lives. Brotherson and Goldstein quoted a parent on this issue:

> In the past, the therapist would show me how to do this exercise on a nice round ball and wedges and then she turns around and says, "But you can do this with a dish towel and a beach ball." How am I going to get this together when I go home and try to do the exercises she's just told me about? This year we have been getting home PT and that has been very helpful, because they've got what you've got to work with and can show me how to work on the living room floor between the TV and stereo. (pp. 515–516)

It is also critical that professionals listen to what parents know about their child and family. Perhaps the most common frustration of parents is when professionals "discover" what families have already told them. Having to repeat information or wait for the results of clinical assessments only to confirm what families already know frustrates parents and undermines professional legitimacy. Parents feel (whether it is true or not) that they were not taken seriously and the information they offered was less than credible. This frustration frames the broader questions: (1) What information, provided by parents, needs to be reaffirmed by a professional, and what can be assumed to be factual? and (2) How can both parents and professionals learn to share information that results in the best use of time by both parties?

Today, professionals must learn to use technology for therapy and education activities as a way to work more efficiently. The Internet, Skype, conference-call capabilities, cell phones, faxes, e-mail, 800-number phone lines, and social media forums (e.g., Twitter, Facebook, and YouTube) provide ways of communicating with families that were not possible in the past. Early childhood educators can help parents by teaching them how to access and use those technologies that will free up time and lead to more consistent and less stressful communication.

Professionals must devote adequate time and be consistent to develop trusting relationships with parents. Professionals who believe they can quickly meet with a family, assess their needs, and immediately participate in the development of an appropriate Individualized Family Service Plan (IFSP) or IEP are badly mistaken. Time must be invested to develop and to maintain a relationship, even though an IFSP or IEP cannot be delayed beyond legal time limits. Services may begin while the process of association continues and a partnership is built.

Parents have also reported at least four common impositions on their time: (1) a lack of coordination among professionals, (2) being overwhelmed with therapy and educational activities, (3) trying to access services not available in the community, and (4) a lack of flexible and family-centered scheduling. In order to respond to these complaints, professionals need to address the lack of flexibility within the structures of their organizations and the inherent difficulty in meeting all the needs of an entire family.

Cultural Constraints

Early childhood special education and intervention are envisioned as partnerships between professionals and families for serving young children with special needs and their families. This partnership means both professionals and families bring their culture to the table as they develop and deliver services. The challenge is to provide child and family programs that are consistent with best practices based on research while respecting the culture of the families who are served.

Anne and Rutherford Turnbull (1996) offer a definition of culture that is especially relevant to professional relationships with families:

> Culture refers to many different factors that shape one's sense of group identity, including race, ethnicity, religion, geographical location, income status, gender, sexual orientation, disability status, and occupation. It is the framework within which individuals, families, or groups interpret their experiences and develop their visions of how they want to live their lives. (p. 56)

It is important that professionals be aware of their own cultural perceptions so that these do not unduly affect the way they interact with diverse families. A key element of professional development is becoming knowledgeable about others' cultural values so that the professional can understand the basis on which family decisions are made. Professionals must deal with stereotyping by recognizing that their cultural preferences are not superior and that making assumptions based on ethnicity can be quite misleading. Early educators must be sensitive to cultural differences that may be of concern to specific culturally diverse groups. Consider these examples of cultural tendencies (but be careful not to stereotype):

- Caucasian educators generally place a high value on eye contact when talking with a student, but many African Americans engage in conversation without making eye contact at all times; some may participate in unrelated activities while still paying attention to a conversation.

- Hispanic children may be reluctant to ask for help because they are accustomed to families that respond to nonverbal cues when help is needed. Hispanic children may work well in group projects but may not be motivated to strive for individual gain.

- Asian American parents may be reluctant to seek help for a child with disabilities, preferring instead to handle a child's abnormal development within the family.

- American Indian children with disabilities may be so absorbed by family and community that it is difficult to identify and provide services to these children and their families.

To enhance a professional's understanding of the family and promote successful communication between the school or agency and the home, early educators need to work hard to learn about a child's culture and customs. However, responding to family members as individuals and making no assumptions, but allowing each to "be himself or herself," is the most productive approach. Whether a family is culturally different from a professional or not, personalization is the key to successful interaction. A professional should never expect a family to fit into a particular cultural "box."

Hispanic Families   For many Hispanics or Latinos (a broad ethnic group that can include people whose families originally came from South and Central America, Mexico, Spain, and the Caribbean), children are the most important and valued assets, even when the family is in poor economic straits (Gonzales-Alvarez, 1998). Having many children is considered a blessing, but having a child with a disability (as in most cultures) is very difficult. That child may always be viewed as sick and, if the disability is severe, may always be considered a child. Parents tend to feel sad about these children. Religion, often a strong influence within this culture, affects the parents' view of a disability. Sometimes a child with a disability is seen as a punishment or curse from God, in which case the family may feel it is pointless to seek out services because doing so would go against God's will. A growing number of Hispanic families view a disability as fate, something that happened for a purpose. Mothers are more likely to seek services because they are the main caretakers. But fathers are the decision makers and often must be consulted on setting appointments and agreeing to intervention (Gonzales-Alvarez).

Hispanic families typically include extended-family members and have a great deal of respect for their elderly members. Interpersonal relationships, interdependence, and cooperation are emphasized. Family structure is patriarchal, and it is courteous to speak to the husband before speaking to the wife when both are present. A father's decisions regarding recommendations should be acknowledged even when the father is not present.

To work effectively with Hispanic families, service providers must become close to the family. Hospitality is important, and home visits may begin with food and conversation. Providers must be open to family invitations and become someone the family learns to trust. Speaking Spanish helps, but Spanish differs depending on the country of origin, so one should recognize there may be difficulties communicating. Hispanics tend to respect authority and may say they agree with recommendations when in fact they are not comfortable with the suggestions (Gonzales-Alvarez, 1998). Therefore, it is especially useful to be open about various ways you can help and encourage families to contribute their own ideas to foster collaboration.

Hispanic families may be reluctant to send their children to preschool because school is not believed to be more beneficial than home (Bauer & Shea, 2003). Because an extended and nurturing family is often involved, parents may hesitate to turn over caregiving to a school. Hispanic families rely on nuclear and extended family for support, loyalty, and solidarity. School services tend to be less satisfying for Hispanic families because of language barriers and the uninviting formal nature of school relationships.

Asian Families   Asian (another broad and varied ethnic group encompassing Chinese, Japanese, Korean, Vietnamese, Thai, Indonesian, and often other Pacific Islanders) families may consider matters involving a child with a disability to be private. This preference for privacy may be exaggerated by a long-standing stigma associated with disabilities in most Asian cultures. On the other hand, Asian parents of children with disabilities tend to be treated as if they are incapable of understanding and/or caring about information related to services for their children (Chu & Wu, 2012). For this reason, choosing an interpreter, when needed, can be a critical, although difficult, decision, because the interpreter must be trusted and respected by the family; a community leader or clergyman, for example, may be a wise choice as an interpreter. Unlike Hispanic families, who may dislike formality, an Asian family should be treated formally; for example, adults appreciate the use of Mr., Mrs., or Miss with the family name, simple greeting words in the family's native language, and written materials prepared in the family's language. Many Asian families convey information through nonverbal communication such as silence or eye contact. Silence may mean respect or disagreement, and direct eye contact is viewed as disrespectful. Encourage Asian families to bring people who are important to them to conferences and to choose a setting that is comfortable for them. It is usually common courtesy when making a home visit to remove one's shoes upon entering. Greet older persons with a slight bow, and avoid sitting with legs crossed. It is likely that food will be offered. If a meeting is in a public place, try to choose a private, quiet area.

Families with Asian roots may place great value on group welfare, family cohesion and responsibility, obligation, interdependence, educational achievement, and reverence for their elders. Status centers around birthright, inheritance, family name, age, gender, and role rigidity; the roles of men and women are clearly defined. The parent–child bond is very important, and children are viewed as extensions of their parents. However, parents provide authority and make decisions for their children. Asians may be perceived as more formal and emotionally controlled than people from other cultures. Some may be so polite and respectful as to be perceived as overly submissive (Bauer & Shea, 2003).

In planning interventions, differing Asian child-rearing practices may require that approaches and goals be altered. For example, often young children do not self-feed but are assisted during mealtime. Infants rarely sleep alone, and children under school age often sleep with their parents. Because teachers are often revered, parents may feel it is appropriate to be dependent rather than active partners. Sometimes, families may use shame to achieve behavioral control. At the same time, Asian origins are very diverse; each family is different, and one must never assume something about a family based on cultural stereotype. Many Asians are newly immigrated and may be additionally challenged if they are refugees (Bauer & Shea, 2003). Educators will be most effective if they are willing to learn about people and their individual as well as cultural uniqueness each time they meet a new family.

African American Families   African American families also have great diversity in their family living arrangements. Kinship is highly valued, and extended families are supportive. Educators might find multigenerational family relationships, sharing of child rearing, economic relationships across household boundaries, and a much greater role for fictive kin and parent surrogates (such as a friend who lives with the family). As with Asian and Hispanic cultures, a great deal of respect is given to the elderly and their role in the family. Grandparents, particularly grandmothers, are more likely to be actively involved in parenting children than in Anglo cultures. Extended kin and nonrelatives play a significant role in childcare, child management, rule setting, and discipline. When planning services, it is important to ask, how do parents and other caregivers organize childcare and parenting tasks? Who participates in the provision of care? What is the role of parenting agents inside and outside the household?

African American families may also place more value on communal and movement-expressive attitudes and practices. Dubbed as "verve," this quality emphasizes liveliness, variability, and stimulation (Bauer & Shea, 2003). These families may prefer group activities that allow for music, movement, and high energy. An emphasis on time management, quietness, and low-energy activities (typical in school settings) may not be compatible with family values.

Native American (American Indian) Families   Native Americans also value group life and respect their elders, experts, and spiritual leaders (Belmonte, 1996). Grandparents may be viewed as the primary parents, and other family members as the disciplinarians. Customs and traditions are very important, and service providers need to be careful not to infringe on these social mores. Children with special needs may have fewer demands placed on them because these children are believed to suffer enough challenges. Native American families tend to accept "what is" and seek harmony with their situations. As with any ethnic group name, the term *Native American* encompasses many different Indian nations and customs that vary greatly; there are more than 600 officially recognized and unrecognized tribal groups and more than 300 indigenous languages in the United States (Stubben, 2001). Further, Native Americans living on reservations or in rural areas face different stressors than those in urban areas who are more isolated from their traditional communities. Urbanization of Native Americans has often disrupted extended family supports (Stubben).

Although cultural pride remains strong in most American Indian families, many also have suffered a long history of challenges: loss of tribal identities, removal to boarding schools and foster homes, high rates of alcohol and drug abuse, high incidence of suicide, and poverty (Bauer & Shea, 2003; Stubben, 2001). They may feel alienated from school settings and service providers and may respond defensively. Some American Indians consider themselves bicultural, which can create dissonance in either a traditional or a mainstream way of life; others observe that those who try to be bicultural seem stranded between two cultures (Stubben).

When possible, a service provider should become known to the tribal community and should work to understand the particular tribal community that is being served: its values, history, and even language (Stubben, 2001). Most Native American families prefer a Native American service provider; such a person can be useful in communicating with elders and sharing personal information. Spirituality is a key factor in American Indian life and can be applied to help resolve family problems.

For example, a medical doctor may work with a tribal healer prior to treating a member of the family (Stubben).

Caucasian (Anglo) Families   The majority of professionals providing services in early intervention and early childhood special education (and many of the families they serve) have Anglo-European (Caucasian) roots. This culture values personal control over the environment, human equality, individualism, self-efficacy, and competition. Clearly, these values conflict with those of many other cultures. Anglos tend to be oriented toward the future and act more directly, openly, and informally. Time management is valued, and punctuality is highly regarded. It is customary to treat men and women with equal respect and courtesy.

Cultural differences also abound even within "mainstream" America. For example, a rural family may have different traditions and resources than an inner-city or suburban family. The way people relate family matters to professionals may also vary in different regions of the United States. Northeasterners may have different expectations than families from the deep South, for example.

In fact, low income levels may create more cultural differences than ethnic origin (Harry, 2002). Researchers have found that families of low socioeconomic status tend to (1) be less verbal, (2) use more coercive discipline, (3) hold less positive beliefs regarding the effectiveness of early education, and (4) have access to fewer resources, such as space, transportation, and childcare. These challenges may require additional resources and interaction with the family to ensure its access to and comfort with a plan for quality child services and support.

Each Family Is Unique   Despite these examples of cultural differences among various ethnic groups, one must always be aware that in the United States each family comes with its own unique experience and distance from traditional beliefs and practices. A family's educational level, history within the mainstream culture, socioeconomic status, and geographic location make a great deal of difference in how closely or how differently the family mirrors a particular cultural profile (Harry, 2002). Rather than generalizing from what a given ethnic culture is supposed to look like, it is better to consider each family within its personal "activity setting." That is, the family context is the basis for consideration: Who is present? What is the physical setting for the family's daily routines? What is the script for conduct within this family? (Harry). Such questions, with careful listening to parents, permit one to work within a family's "zone" and identify goals for a child and the family's preferences for services. It is always critical to get to know the heritage of each individual family and its immediate circumstances.

When working with families, it is important to consider the context for the family, which may create different needs that vary with the child's type of disability and the family's resources. For example, families with more cohesion tend to have less stress, as do families with higher incomes, whereas single-parent families are the most stressed regardless of income. Sometimes, the needs of other family members take precedence over the specific needs of the child with a disability, for example, when a parent becomes sick or loses a job. Often, educational needs may be a lower priority for families compared to needs for such basics as food, housing, childcare, and health care.

Financial needs can be a significant concern. In addition to hospitalization expenses, families may also accumulate expenses for specialized equipment, transportation, time off from work, therapy services, medications, and dietary supplements. Sometimes private and public insurance coverage, such as Medicaid or the Supplemental Security Income program, helps, but there are many gaps. Even relatively small out-of-pocket expenses can create a significant burden if a family has few resources to spare. In fact, families with children who are disabled tend to be economically worse off than families with healthy children even before the extra costs associated with the disability are taken into account. Families caring for children with special needs were 2% to 8% more likely to be living in poverty. Because of extraordinary medical and therapy costs, families with severely affected children are particularly hard hit.

Young children with disabilities often have unusual or special caregiving needs that demand significant time and energy from their parents and that contribute to fatigue. Feeding difficulties or behavioral disturbances can add significant stress. A lack of communication skills, difficult temperaments, or the need for constant supervision adds to the strain. This creates stress on the usual routines of family life and makes finding respite difficult.

Emotional needs, including grieving and reactions to stress, are also important to consider. Not all parents react in the same way, and their reactions may change as the family life cycle changes. Often sadness reappears when developmental milestones are missed, and the sadness can be more intense than the impact of the original diagnosis (Bosch, 1996). As mentioned earlier, cultural values may inhibit a family from discussing personal issues with "outsiders" or prevent reliance on help outside the family.

Parents' greatest perceived need is for information (Bosch, 1996). When a diagnosis is made, families face an immediate "crisis of information" in regard to their child's current and anticipated health and development (Guralnick, 1998). Parents of very young children with disabilities seek medical and diagnostic information. Those with older children want to know how to teach them, what services are currently available, and what their children might need in the future.

Parents need to establish their own priorities and choose the appropriate level and type of intervention that suits their family's needs. However, the following must always be considered in planning for family needs: (1) adequate economic and institutional supports should be available to help families provide for their children with disabilities, (2) access to appropriate services should be facilitated through coordination among agencies, (3) informal supports may be as important as formal support, and (4) extended family, friends, neighbors, and community should be assessed as possible resources. Professionals must behave competently as a team of individuals with different expertise who are available to provide information, resources, and support.

Close Up   The Journey to Accepting Support

Advances in medical technology and treatment have extended the lives of more children with severe and multiple disabilities. Because these children continue to require complex and specialized services, their families often find themselves depending on others who provide support in caring for their children. Parents of these children often report loneliness, isolation, and difficulty coping, but accepting support from others, as vital as it may be, can be also be difficult.

Interviews with parents about receiving such support reveal their conflicting and confusing emotions. Acknowledging the need for support is the first part of the journey to accepting support. Parents reach a "point of change" at a time when they admit they cannot go on alone. "I felt absolutely worn out and for the good of everyone I realized that the time had come when I had to say 'yes, I need help.'" Parents sometimes find it difficult to admit a need for help because society holds a negative attitude toward their children, seeing them as burdens or tragedies when the parents do not see them this way. The everyday life of the family may have to break down because of the parent's own exhaustion and distress before the parent recognizes that the disruption has led to a turning point. Parents may feel that asking for support is an admission of failure: "People might think I can't cope. . . . I wouldn't want anyone to think I was letting her down." Support can be seen as a form of loss in which the parent's autonomy in making decisions for a child is compromised and the responsibility for care must be shared with others. "I felt embarrassed and vulnerable. . . . I had been proud of the way I had coped and now that was taken from me." Professionals need to help parents not view their choice to request support as a sign of being powerless; rather, they should see that they are putting themselves in control of their situation. It helps parents to see their choice as a "moment of vision" for which they can feel better. Parents should be recognized as experts and partners in support experiences.

Source: From "The Journey to Accepting Support: How Parents of Profoundly Disabled Children Experience Support in Their Lives," by Jane Brett, 2004, *Pediatric Nursing, 16*(8), 14–18.

Formation of Collaborative Teams

Clearly, parental involvement in the education of children with disabilities results in academic, developmental, and social benefits, yet professionals have not been especially successful in facilitating such involvement or in promoting collaboration as much as possible. Parents are an essential source of information about their children because of their firsthand knowledge of their children's physical, social, emotional, and cognitive traits. By working together, everyone—parents, professionals, and children—benefits, and programs comply with the spirit of the federal law, not just the letter of the law. Specific steps can be taken to strengthen partnerships with families, such as increasing communication, using parent networks, and learning to understand family views and strengths in shared decision making. Collaborative strategies such as home visits and parent forums are useful, but the most important strategy may be the use of an effective collaborative team for planning, carrying out, and monitoring programs for young children.

Collaborative teams should be made up of all those who are essential in serving a young child with disabilities. This includes parents (and extended family as appropriate); teachers (both regular and special educators); specialists and therapists who work directly with a child, such as occupational or physical therapists; a family advocate, if desired; an administrator or designee who can commit to program services; and someone who can interpret evaluation results as needed. Others who might be invited could include an interpreter, if needed, paraprofessionals, and perhaps medical personnel, such as a visiting nurse or pediatrician. Families may also wish to include support persons of their choosing, such as a disability advocate or friend.

Collaborative teaming has been implemented and researched in both regular and special education since the early 1970s. "Teamwork is not magic, and simply 'getting along' or communicating information to one another does not constitute collaboration" (Hinojosa et al., 2001). Although researchers do not agree on the essential components of collaborative teaming, at least five elements, or attributes, are common to most models of collaborative, or cooperative, teaming:

1. There is a *common goal* or set of goals to which all parties agree. The first order of business in team conduct is to determine the primary goal of the team. All other decisions, personal and team, should be measured against this fundamental intent.

2. There is an *agreed upon strategy* for achieving each goal or set of goals (responsibilities). Members of a team collectively determine the most efficacious method or methods. Even when the goal is quite clear, however, finding common ground on a method for achieving the goal can be a challenge.

3. There is a *commitment to dignified and meaningful interactions,* individual skill development, and task completion. In short, professional conduct is fundamental to team success.

4. There is a *commitment to dependence on each other.* In other words, teamwork cannot be completed if any one member fails in his or her responsibility. On the other hand, the entire team celebrates together when success is achieved because it was achieved collectively.

5. Individuals *commit to a shared system of decision making and accountability.* Decisions about leadership, role assignments, agendas, and evaluation are made together.

Several other factors, which have been discussed in the literature, are believed necessary if a team is to function and collaborate successfully. Trust building is essential. Teams must have a way of building and maintaining trust. This trust is generated only over a period of time and, once developed, is the basis for mutual respect and security (Friend & Cook, 2009). In the absence of trust, members feel vulnerable and essential collaborative elements degrade, namely open communication, necessary for decision making, including the willingness to admit errors and uncertainty, and reliance on other team members to perform their roles in accomplishing objectives. Ultimately, competition will prevail over cooperation for recognition and resources and commitment to team goals will be replaced by self-interest. A team may recognize the absence of trust when they see the following signs: an active and inaccurate grapevine, with members expressing intolerance of each other, quiet meetings where members are reluctant to give input, and a culture where members avoid unnecessary interactions with each other.

Regular face-to-face interactions must occur, even in the 21st century. It is relatively simple today to communicate ideas without actually seeing our colleagues. One can usually e-mail, fax, phone, and voice mail ideas more quickly than scheduling and attending a meeting. Though these media can become a meaningful bridge to real contact, these types of "interactions" are not as effective as a primary means of communicating. The sacrifice of time and effort made in order to meet will be rewarded by increased understanding and relationship building. Misunderstandings that may arise from digital communication may be averted or resolved when individuals sit in the same room and have the opportunity to make use of communication skills discussed earlier in this chapter. Prolonged engagement with one another is essential for bonding, reflecting, and carrying on in-depth discussions (Hinojosa et al., 2001).

Team members must acquire, refine, and practice small-group interpersonal skills. Most professional educators would agree that committee work can be torturous if decision makers lack the basic skills to conduct small-group work. Although individuals can be mandated through policy to work together, collaboration cannot be coerced (Friend & Cook, 2009). Persons who feel that the conditions necessary for effective team work are absent can and will opt out of group decision making. For example, collaboration requires equity among participants: Each member of a team must be equally valued even though certain members may become more pivotal at different points in the process (Friend & Cook). With collaboration, all members of a team are considered uniquely qualified "experts" and may serve as consultants or consultees at different points in time.

The following strategies can be helpful to early interventionists and preschool providers seeking to become vital and reliable members of teams:

1. Be clear about what is known and what is not known. One professional is not expected to know other professional orientations, philosophies, and content as well as his or her own and should not pretend otherwise.

2. Listen. And listen some more. Think carefully about what has been heard and be careful to analyze it correctly. Do not screen out information at an early stage based on past experiences or personal biases.

3. Consider both the short- and long-term consequences of a position and the short- and long-term consequences of the other possibilities placed before the group.

4. Insist on clarification. If a goal statement is ambiguous or unclear to one person, it may be unclear to others.

5. Check all assumptions underlying a goal before agreeing to support or reject it.

6. In setting goals on behalf of an infant or young child, be creative. Develop habits of conscience and imagination in order to move beyond personal experiences or the limits of one's education.

Haroutunian-Gordon (1991) identified four rules of conversation that need to be understood and practiced in group problem-solving:

1. Offer ideas that are supported by data (research or experience).

2. Ensure that individuals are listening carefully to one another.

3. Uncover and discuss contradictory evidence.

4. Allow members to build on one another's knowledge and comments and to validate new associations of information.

These skills require individual members to find value in collaboration itself. If collaborative teams are truly going to serve well, a practice of personal responsibility within a culture of shared and mutual responsibility must be developed. For example, members of teams must not let minor issues, which they find contrary to their own thinking or judgment, go unresolved. These differences should be addressed at the time the differences are first identified. At the same time, team members must allow the long ramblings and dominating behaviors of certain members. Similarly, members should confront, with compassion, those individual or group behaviors that obstruct the work and direction of the group. Likewise, feedback about tasks or responsibilities done well is equally necessary. Finally, when members acknowledge the source of their input—whether they are speaking from opinion, fact, experience, intuition, or research—the team will have a basis for judging the merit of their contributions.

Despite an almost universal acceptance of the importance of collaborative teaming in relationship-based, family-centered early intervention and special education, collaborative teaming is not easy. Those in early intervention and special education need to be aware of pitfalls and be prepared to work around them. Among these are conflicts in philosophy and practice among different disciplines, conflicts with family values, system boundaries such as lack of space and time in a schedule to have formal and informal exchanges, and determination of who gives and who takes advice. Therapists and educators may profess to value collaborative decision making but seem most comfortable with their own autonomy. "The one thing I love about my job is that I have a lot of freedom, and I can do what I want and it helps build my confidence, and it helps build my communication. It helps me build my little world" (Hinojosa et al., 2001). People tend to define themselves by their roles, even though this tendency is counterproductive to teamwork and collaboration. Team collaboration and trust are difficult to achieve in many early intervention environments that operationally limit time together and reduce communication opportunities. Planning, organizing, and training teams to address these factors needs to be done before and during team work to successfully collaborate in a mutually satisfying manner.

Collaboration is much easier for individuals who remain flexible, retain a sense of humor, communicate effectively, demonstrate tolerance for ambiguity, respect others' input, and have confidence in their own professional ability and the integrity of other team members. Such an atmosphere encourages a "trusting team" not only in planning but also in providing services, solving problems, and managing programs.

Teaming and the Individuals with Disabilities Education Improvement Act (IDEIA)

Federal law requires that early intervention and preschool special education services provided to children with disabilities or who are at risk be coordinated by a team of professionals and parents. Team members are expected to assist a child eligible for early intervention or school services and the child's family in receiving the rights, procedural safeguards, and services that are authorized. The team must draw together relevant professionals from various disciplines to share their expertise, decision making, and intervention skills with parents. To do so successfully requires team members to have confidence in the abilities of each other, to value the opinions of each member of the team, and to accept the roles assigned to them. Such attitudes do not develop magically; they require that a great deal of time and energy be devoted to working collaboratively.

In practice, this progression toward increased collaboration requires a number of regular activities. Stump and Wilson (1996) identified the following few guidelines for working on collaborative teams:

1. Set a clear team purpose and identify what each individual brings to the team. Identify talents and abilities and ways they can best be used collaboratively. Set expectations for each team member.

2. Establish schedules. Be consistent in when meetings are held, and set a specific amount of time for meetings. Plan to spend a lot of time when first working collaboratively.

3. Conduct meetings. Set a specific purpose for each meeting and stick to it until a plan is developed. List who is going to do what and set dates for completing tasks.

4. Share workload and responsibilities. Vary assignments so that members are not always doing the same thing. Be flexible about each member's time demands.

5. Share expertise. Identify shared and unique expertise. Share knowledge and skills.

6. Follow through. Check in to be sure that agreed on tasks have been completed.

7. Celebrate successes and shoulder failures together.

8. Keep the lines of communication open.

Early intervention and preschool teams coordinate several important components necessary for serving very young children with disabilities and their families; these include resource supports, social supports, and information and services (Guralnick, 1998). Resource supports include providing awareness of, access to, and coordination of services. Providing supplemental supports, such as financial assistance or respite care, are additional components. Social supports involve parent-to-parent groups, family counseling, and mobilization of family, friend, and community networks. Information and services include the formal intervention program (in home or center), parent–professional relationships (problem-solving, decision making), and individual therapies.

If early intervention and special education systems are working well, then services will be individually matched to the needs of the child and family (Guralnick, 1998). Some children and their families will require only surveillance or minimal supports, whereas others will require highly intensive, long-term programs. This diversity of need implies that professionals must have a great deal of knowledge and the will to use that expertise flexibly, according to the needs of individual families.

Responsibilities of Collaborative Teams

The following tasks, detailed in later chapters, are the primary responsibilities for which collaborative teams must be prepared because of the special skills required at each stage in a family's adjustment to having a child with a disability. These stages include points at which a team determines eligibility for special services, informs parents of their rights, plans and provides treatment and education across a continuum of settings, evaluates outcomes of these services, and prepares for transitions to other educational placements.

Interacting at Diagnosis or Determination of Eligibility Guralnick (2001) asserted that a child's developmental outcomes are governed by the quality of a family's interactions, the relationship between parents and child, the kind of child experiences a family can orchestrate for its child, and the level of health and safety a family can provide. It makes sense, then, for collaborative teams to begin interacting with a family as soon as possible after the family receives a diagnosis of a disability or a determination that a child is eligible for special services. Early interaction supports positive family adaptation to having a member with a disability (Bauer & Shea, 2003). Among the initial tasks the team performs are providing information the family needs to understand the disability and the child's unique development; responding to interpersonal distress experienced as the family adjusts its expectations toward the child; identifying resources that might reduce family stressors, such as respite care; and promoting confidence in the family's ability to carry out its new parenting roles under atypical circumstances (Guralnick).

Informing Parents of Their Rights It is critical that collaborative teams inform families of young children with disabilities of all their legal rights. A large majority of parents of children with special needs said their children lost out because their families were "in the dark about the services they are entitled to" (Public Agenda, 2002, p. 11). Families reported that information about how special education works, what it offers, and what their child was entitled to was difficult to obtain. More than half of families surveyed by Public Agenda said they had to find out on their own what was available to their children because the school would not volunteer the information.

Families need their legal rights explained in simple language rather than jargon and in their dominant language if it is not English. Important rights parents should be familiar with are these:

- A wide range of special services, from audiology to transportation, are to be provided if the child's assessment indicates they are necessary.
- A family's records are to be kept confidential but are open to the family's inspection.
- The intervention or educational plan is developed by the team including the parents and other persons the parents would like to include.
- Meetings should be held at a time and place convenient to the family and in its native language or mode of communication; if the parents choose not to attend, written parental consent is still required before a program can begin.
- A service coordinator or school staff responsible for implementing the plan must be identified.
- The educational or treatment plan must be developed within 45 days of referral and reviewed regularly (every six months for children from birth to age 3 or every year for children from 3 to 21 years of age).
- A family may disagree with a team's educational or treatment plan and appeal for mediation or a hearing to review the appropriateness of the plan.

Planning and Providing Treatment and Education across a Continuum of Settings
After assessing both a child's and family's needs, a plan for intervention or education is developed. Early intervention can be provided across a wide range of settings, including a hospital, special center, childcare setting, the home, or elsewhere (Hanson & Bruder, 2001). Not all services have to be provided in the same location, and services may change over time as needs change. A wide breadth of professionals may be involved, and all should be a part of the collaborative team as long as a family does not feel overwhelmed by dealing with too many individuals. It is helpful if parents are allowed to choose their service coordinator or main contact person. Parent choice should also be honored in terms of the model for services they desire for their child; such services should fit into the routines and demands of the family's life. Likewise, parents tend to be more engaged in their child's education if they are actively involved in developing the objectives targeted, are able to prioritize objectives they feel need immediate attention, and can make an informed decision about the best way to provide treatment and education (Bauer & Shea, 2003).

In an open discussion of the services needed, objectives should be identified that include how intense the services should be, who would deliver the services, and what the family's role would be; all of this should be recorded in a family-friendly document (Guralnick, 2001). The information most helpful to families surveyed regarded methods they could use to help a child meet the next milestone (McWilliam & Scott, 2001). Talking with a family about their daily routines and identifying where difficulties arise can help determine which skills are most important for the child to work to develop.

Family constraints should also be recognized and plans made to build on family strengths. The team should consider what a family needs in the way of material support—such as resources to meet basic needs and adaptive materials or equipment for their child—and financial support (often through state and federal assistance programs). Emotional support, whether through professionals or other parents, is one of the most important factors in reducing family stress and promoting well-being (McWilliam & Scott, 2001). Connections to parent groups and information about how to build support networks with friends and extended family are important.

Evaluating Outcomes   Although a family service plan or individualized education plan should be reviewed to determine whether goals, outcomes, and specific objectives for the child are being realized, other outcomes are also important to families and should be considered. Priorities for early intervention include not only improved child development and functioning but also a better quality of life for the child and enhanced parenting competence and confidence (Dunst & Bruder, 2002). All of those involved should know how a child and family are progressing and what should be adjusted. From time to time, stressors will also change as major life events occur or because of a child's transitions, and these events may require that a plan be adjusted (Guralnick, 2001).

Planning for Transitions   Transitions occur at several different points in the early life of a child with a disability. The move from a hospital to home, entry into an early intervention program, transition to a preschool special education program, and then graduation into the primary grades of an elementary program disrupt a family's routines and create turmoil (Guralnick, 2001). These transitions cause stress for parents, often renewing anxieties about adjusting to new patterns and expectations. The importance of advanced team planning for transitions has been long underestimated; such planning can help both the child and family make these moves smoothly. The team must make a conscious effort to communicate to staff in the new program, to share information about the child's progress, program, and priorities. A visit to the new environment can help allay fears and may allow for planning needed accommodations ahead of time.

IN CONCLUSION

Collaboration is the future (Dettmer et al., 1999). It is essential for achieving school reform, for responding to changing student needs, and for ensuring the development of global, economic, and technological productivity. The work each professional does as a part of a collaborative team adds to the framework for continued collaboration throughout the global village (Dettmer et al.). A personal plan for today's small collaborative efforts may have an impact on the future. Consider the following suggestions for ways you can encourage collaboration on a wider scale (Dettmer et al.):

1. Be a guest speaker about collaboration at community clubs and service organizations.

2. Develop a networking system that delivers positive "strokes" to school staff and families.

3. Inform colleagues of legislative and judicial activity.

4. Host sessions at conferences for school policymakers and administrators.

5. Have an open house and invite school board members.

6. Send summer postcards to school personnel saying, "I am looking forward to working with you this year."

7. Serve as an officer and committee member to organizations that support valued goals.

Bringing together all the team members of a student's special education program takes considerable effort and time, but it is necessary and ultimately rewarding (Marks, Schrader, & Levine, 1999). However, collaboration is more than just meeting together; a group's power lies in a team's capacity to merge its members' unique skills, to foster feelings of positive interdependence, to develop creative problem-solving skills, and to hold one another accountable for a student's success (Wood, 1998). It is only when individual members open themselves to each other's influence that the behaviors and attitudes necessary for collaboration can emerge. Those who effectively serve young children with disabilities and their families must be informed, caring, skilled, and flexible. Early intervention service providers must believe in diversity, meeting individual needs, and supporting shared decision making. Finally, early intervention professionals must seek to strengthen alliances with parents and peers rather than achieving professional status by insulating themselves from those they serve (O'Shea, Williams, & Sattler, 1999). In short, effective teaming requires a commitment to children and families first, using multiple resources and skills to support the best efforts to help the children achieve success.

STUDY GUIDE QUESTIONS

1. How would you describe family-centered practice to someone who is not in early intervention or preschool special education?

2. What would be the final measure of whether a family was empowered? What might you see that family doing?

3. Describe the different levels of relationship-based teaming. What kind of assistance is given at each level?

4. What common negative assumptions about families of children with disabilities have grown from past research on these families? How has that changed in more recent years?

5. In your own words, how would you define *family*?

6. Describe the typical stages of the grief process and how professionals might misuse them.

7. What is meant by *family hardiness*, and what are its three dimensions?

8. Give examples of specific communication skills that should be used and pitfalls that must be avoided when working with families.

9. How should one deliver difficult diagnostic information to families?

10. What have researchers learned about time as a family resource? What are the implications for early childhood professionals?

11. Give an example of how a family's ethnic culture might affect the way it treats a child with a disability.

12. What are some of the unique needs faced by families of children with disabilities?

13. What are five elements that are desirable, if not key, in collaborative teaming? State them in your own words.

14. What guidelines should direct the regular activities of a collaborative team?

3 Principles of Human Development

© Denielle M. Miller

Nature, which is responsible for the changes that take place between human conception and the first years of school, largely awaits scientific explanation. Our understanding of human development is confined to describing the surprisingly predictable processes and stages through which the human species matures. Psychologists, linguists, biologists, geneticists, sociologists, educators, and other researchers continue to study this fascinating phenomenon. Even without complete answers, however, our present knowledge of human growth is vital to fields serving families with very young children.

Importance and use of Knowledge of Human Development

A thorough understanding of human development is fundamental to the competency of early childhood professionals. Without basic knowledge of the principles and stages through which infants and preschoolers pass, educators would be unable to communicate with parents, identify anomalies and assess children's relative progress, design instruction, set expectations, select intervention strategies, or evaluate child progress and program efficacy. Parents turn to early childhood professionals for information and assistance, expecting them to be experts in normal development. To satisfy this need, educators must have at least a basic knowledge of developmental patterns for physical, cognitive, language, and social and emotional growth.

Perhaps the most important use of our knowledge of human development is in pinpointing appropriate intervention objectives and selecting related intervention strategies. Because human development is largely predictable, it is possible to note a child's present behavior and identify the probable emerging behavior. Selecting a target behavior that is too simple or too difficult for a child would constrain that child's success and, consequently, lessen the professional's effectiveness.

Intervention strategies must also be appropriate for a child's developmental capabilities. Professionals should be capable of matching and adapting materials to a child's cognitive levels, giving instructions to match a child's understanding of language, determining how long a child can be expected to pay attention, and knowing the degree of social interaction that can be expected from a child.

Knowledge of normal human development paired with knowledge of conditions that may lead to developmental disabilities enables professionals to estimate the potential effects of a particular disability on a child. For example, an educator might anticipate that a child with a moderate degree of athetoid cerebral palsy will experience difficulties in expressive language and motor development. The probability of such problems should prompt this child's team to focus on intensive communication intervention and physical and occupational therapy as well as to consider assistive devices as the child matures.

The fact that for millennia the human species has largely navigated the course of human development with little effort is astonishing given the complexity of the process. It often takes professionals years to master the little knowledge thus far acquired. Fortunately, many resources on development are available to assist in making day-to-day and long-term decisions. While these resources are no substitute for mastery, they provide a useful supplement to a soundly established basic understanding of human development. Some basic principles of development are well established in the literature, and knowledge of these guidelines assists professionals in making daily decisions.

Prenatal Growth and Development

At birth, infants have undergone an average of 38 weeks of the most miraculous development. This period is divided into three stages: ovum, embryo, and fetus. For 2 weeks following the time of conception, the ovum, or fertilized egg, travels down one of the fallopian tubes and eventually attaches to the wall of the uterus, completing the **ovum stage;** it remains here throughout the prenatal period.

Figure 3–1   Developing Fetus in Prenatal Environment

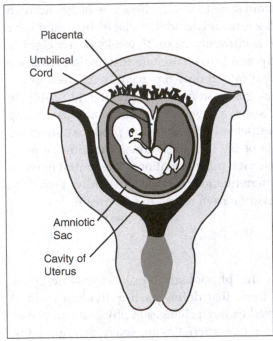

Placenta

Umbilical Cord

Amniotic Sac

Cavity of Uterus

The **embryonic stage** begins in the 3rd week when cell differentiation permits the emergence of a central nervous system and a circulatory system. The stage is completed by the end of the 8th week when ossification of the bones begins. During the embryonic phase, the heart, lungs, digestive system, and brain develop from unspecified cells to well-defined structures. Muscular and nervous-system development accompanies these structural changes. At the extremities, hands, feet, fingers, and toes are formed, as are facial features such as eyelids and ears.

The embryonic period is the most vulnerable stage of pregnancy. Because many women are unaware of their pregnancy at this point, they may inadvertently cause harm to the fragile embryo. Many embryos spontaneously abort when they detach from the uterine wall and are expelled. During this early period, harmful substances (e.g., cigarette smoke, radiation) or trauma can be especially potent and can disrupt the structural development taking place in an embryo. Hence, embryonic damage may result in spontaneous abortion, miscarriage, or development of a birth defect.

Supporting the developing embryo and later the fetus are the **placenta,** umbilical cord, and **amniotic sac** (see Figure 3–1). The placenta is a fleshy mass made up of villi, or projectiles that insert themselves into the lining of the uterus. The largest and most important of these is the **umbilical cord,** which joins the bloodstream of the embryo at the site of the child's abdomen to the bloodstream of the mother via the uterine lining. This connection permits the exchange of life-sustaining substances between the maternal bloodstream and the fetus. Although the fetal and maternal blood do not mix, the passage of nutrients, oxygen, and other gases through the umbilical cord to the fetus sustains the unborn baby. At the same time, fetal waste products such as carbon dioxide and other metabolites pass back through the umbilical cord to be excreted by the mother. The placenta also serves as a barrier to large molecules and potentially harmful substances; however, it is not infallible. The placenta, unable to differentiate healthy from damaging chemicals, permits some dangerous drugs (including alcohol), hormones, and bacterial and viral organisms to cross into the bloodstream of the developing human.

Another important fetal structure is the amniotic sac, which contains liquid amniotic fluid and surrounds the embryo. This sac, made pliable by the encapsulated fluid, protects the vulnerable embryo from physical shocks a mother might experience and maintains a constant temperature for the fetus.

The final and longest stage of development is the **fetal stage,** which begins in the 9th week and lasts through the 9th month. While each system was primitively developed during the embryonic stage, these systems undergo rapid growth and increase in complexity through differentiation during the final period. At 12 weeks, a fetus resembles a human figure, and spontaneous movement of the limbs may be observed. By 16 weeks, a mother can usually feel movement by the infant, referred to as "the quickening." Concurrently, a fetus can also open and close its mouth and eyes and grows fingernails and hair.

Legally, the age of viability ranges from state to state, with a low of 19 and high of 28 weeks. Medically, the age at which a fetus is considered viable, or would have the potential to live outside the womb, is currently 22 to 23 weeks or a weight of 400 g (Arzuaga & Lee, 2011). While it is possible to resuscitate extremely premature infants, a recent study reported a survival rate of only 6 percent of 22-week gestation newborns and 26 percent of 23-week gestation newborns (Stoll et al., 2010). To permit independent survival, a fetus must have developed reflexes such as sucking and swallowing, and its lungs must be sufficiently developed to produce surfactant, which allows breathing without collapse of the lungs. The final 2 months of pregnancy feature more subtle but nonetheless vital transformations. The central nervous system, including the brain, continues differentiation, and the fetus grows rapidly in height and weight, preparing for the transition from womb to first breath.

Child Growth and Development

After birth, development continues as the physiological process just described evolves into biological and behavioral traits that define each individual child. A child's genetic inheritance may be observed through changes in physical and behavioral characteristics. Although a number of characteristics are solely determined by genetic code (e.g., eye color), others are influenced to some as yet unknown degree by other factors. Attributes that are determined by both genetic and environmental factors tend to progress, although varying in rate, in a continuous and predictable pattern.

Maturation is the universally observed sequence of biological changes that take place as individuals age. Maturation permits the development of psychological functions. For example, as the brain develops in the early months of life and becomes capable of understanding and producing language, infants who are exposed to language gradually develop linguistic abilities. If an interruption in either exposure to language stimulation *or* neurological growth occurs, language cannot develop normally. Along with physical development is a maturation of perceptual abilities including sight, hearing, and balance (see Table 3–1). Each of these senses interacts with the other and with other developmental areas to foster normal patterns and rates of development.

Normal development refers to a sequence of physical and psychological changes that are very similar for all children. Zigler and Stevenson (1993) coined the term **range of reaction** in describing the extent to which environment is likely to influence this sequence or the extent to which individuals will realize their potential. Favorable conditions (again, both genetic and environmental) enable children to reach the high end of their potential, and unfavorable conditions can depress development.

Major indexes of developmental accomplishments, such as "Casey just took his first step yesterday" or "Alice just learned to say 'mama'!" are used to measure developmental progress. These indexes, which are identified across developmental areas (e.g., language and social skills) and across years, are referred to as **developmental milestones.** Established milestones are based on the average age at which children acquire skills or pass through stages. For example, an average child begins to take

Table 3–1 Patterns of Perceptual Development

Sense	Ability at Birth	Patterns of Development
Vision	Estimated at 20/600 at birth; blue/red color discrimination; preference for large, bold patterns	20/100 at 8 mo; approximately 20/20 at 1 year; 180 visual arc at 3 months; 3-dimensional focus at 3 months; age and gender discrimination at 5 1/2 months
Hearing	At 20 weeks gestation, fetus hears music, mother's voice; at birth, hears 40 dB threshold; startle response; habituation to sound; soothing to rhythmic music	Limited auditory responsiveness 0–4 mo; speech sounds (ba/pa) discrimination at 4–14 weeks; 20 dB threshold at 3–8 months; localization to sound and preference for female voices at 4–6 months
Gustatory	Different responses to different stimuli: i.e., sweet, sour; dislike salty taste	Begin to prefer salty tastes at 4 mo
Olfactory	Preference for different smells at birth	
Intermodal	Newborns have ability to connect incoming sensory information	In first 6 mo, ability to respond to multimodal information is difficult; increased ease of intermodal perception at 6–12 mo
Tactile	Reflexive responses to touch; pain felt; discrimination of warm and cold; individual preference for type of touching, holding, stroking	Decreased response threshold across first 5 days; by third day, ability to habituate to tactile stimulation; body adjusts to temperature changes by 10–12 days; knows objects by touch at 10–12 mo

Close Up

The Effect of War on Children in Iraq

Half of Iraq's population is under 18 years of age.

Iraq is not unique in its persistent state of warfare and oppression but is recent history's most salient battleground. For those concerned about the harmful effects of war on the growth and development of the most innocent victims, the children, Iraq offers a lens through which to understand the suffering of many, many others across the planet. Once considered among the most developed countries in the Middle East, with a sophisticated infrastructure, high literacy rate, and free health care and education, Iraq's downward spiral to preindustrial status began with the Iran–Iraq war in the 1980s. The first Iraq War in 1991 was followed by 13 years of suffocating sanctions, which strangled domestic systems and greatly exacerbated the suffering. If living conditions for families prior to 2003 were poor, the invasion of U.S. and coalition forces in that year rendered the lives of children especially dire.

Obviously, the most direct effect of these wars has been the loss of lives and the injuries—both temporary and life altering. Death and injury have been a consequence of the nearly universal absence of the primary element of civilization—safety. "Survivors" must cope with severe shortages in the other essential elements of life: food, water, and shelter. One-fourth of Iraqi children between 6 months and 5 years are chronically or acutely malnourished. The water-treatment capacity was intentionally targeted and disrupted in the 1991 campaign—a condition gradually worsened by sanctions and the even more destructive second military campaign. In addition to 450,000 families made homeless by the most recent war, as many as 1.5 to 5.0 million orphans, mostly street dwellers, are estimated to live in Iraq. Further intentional bombing has degraded other parts of Iraq's infrastructure: 63% of Iraqis are not connected to the sewage system, the health care system has collapsed, and almost 50% of children do not attend school; a vast majority of those unable to attend are girls.

The indirect effects of the collateral damage of war are many and have long-term, if not permanent, effects on the development of very young children. The constant violence experienced by children has multiple observed consequences: *fear*—nearly two-thirds of children interviewed believed they would not survive to adulthood; *psychological damage*—it has been estimated that 50% of Iraqi children suffer from post-traumatic stress syndrome; *behavioral problems*—feelings of revenge and anger may be behind the fact that 50% of soldiers are under 18 years of age; and *anxiety and depression*—children as young as 4 years have clear ideas of the effect of war; 40% of those interviewed believe that life is not worth living.

Sanctions alone have been cited as causing hundreds of thousands of childhood deaths in Iraq from lack of sufficient food. Those who survive malnourishment are at high risk for stunted physical growth and arrested development of mental and cognitive skills. Lack of potable water has resulted in an increase in disease as well as infant and childhood mortality. The combined effect of food shortages, contaminated water, lack of sanitation, and disrupted health care has been the return of diseases that were controlled under the rule of Saddam Hussein: cholera, hepatitis, meningitis, and polio. The lack of basic medicines and inability to provide regular immunization

services further places young children at risk for preventable disease and disability.

The bombing, which began in 1991, leaves a lethal by-product that is suspected of killing hundreds of thousands of children in Iraq. The culprit is depleted and undepleted uranium, which was used on the tips of munitions for the first time in 1991 and declared by the U.S. Department of Defense to be "irreplaceable." Hundreds of tons of undepleted uranium debris are spread across Iraq with no cleanup effort attempted during the 15 or more years of polluting. The radiation emitted from these munitions is believed to be responsible for a fivefold increase in cancer in children and a threefold increase in birth defects and leukemia.

These statistics of war do not tell the whole story; for example, sweeping poverty has led to a dramatic increase in child labor as every family member is counted on to support dwindling resources. Children, especially girls, are targets of child abuse and neglect. Children are kidnapped or sometimes sold by their desperate families into the lucrative sex trade. Illicit drug use and trafficking by children has increased. A pediatrician from Basra provided a compelling summary of the condition of children in this war-torn region of the world. He reported a 30% increase in child mortality since the Saddam Hussein era. The primary causes of this high infant mortality are unsafe water, malnutrition, diarrhea, infectious disease, maternal stress, and poverty.

Source: From "The Cost of War: The Children of Iraq," by S. T. Ismael, 2007, *Journal of Comparative Family Studies,* 337–357.

first steps at 12 months and begins to say "mama" at 9 months. The milestones at which children are expected to achieve skills are determined by taking a representative sample of children and calculating the average age at which they acquire those skills.

Norms are statistically determined standard (normal) age levels for developmental milestones. For example, the norm for independent sitting is 6 months. Some children sit earlier, and others take longer than 6 months to acquire this skill, but on the average, infants learn to sit by themselves about midway through their first year. It is important to stress, however, that norms are simply averages around which there is a **range of normalcy.** For example, slight deviations in motor development are known to be related to infants' sleeping posture. Since the early 1990s, parents have been advised to place sleeping infants on their sides or backs to reduce the possibility of sudden infant death syndrome. Research indicated that 6-month-old infants who slept face down developed some motor and other skills earlier than infants who slept on their backs or side (Lung & Shu, 2011). However, by the time infants reached 18 months, there were no developmental differences regardless of early sleep posture. This research shows how prevailing is nature's pattern on child development (Carmeli, Marmur, Cohen, & Tirosh, 2009). Moreover, since the mid-1990s parents have been discouraged from putting their child to bed in either the prone (face down) or side lying positions to prevent the incidence of sudden infant death syndrome (Sperhake, Zimmerman, & Püschel, 2009).

Typically developing children who acquire developmental skills earlier or later than the norm but within the range of normalcy are still considered normal. It is when the acquisition of developmental milestones occurs some time beyond the range of normalcy that parents and educators should be concerned about a child's progress. For example, if a child is not sitting independently (norm is 6 months; range is 4–8 months) by 10 months of age, parents should seek professional advice. Children who exceed the norms in several areas or the expected ranges in a few areas may be **at risk** for **developmental delays.** Significant delays in reaching milestones in one or more developmental areas indicate eligibility for early childhood special education.

Patterns of Growth

From conception throughout early adulthood, humans experience physical growth. The most obvious index of growth is size as measured by changes in height and weight. Height and weight increase rapidly during fetal development and early childhood. An increase in weight of 300 percent is expected between birth and the time a child is 12 months of age, and height is expected to increase 200 percent by 24 months of age. This rate of growth slows after the first year to an almost linear rate until adolescence. While some children grow in spurts, others appear to grow steadily throughout childhood. In addition to individual genetic differences in rate and pattern of development, factors such as nutrition and health influence growth outcomes. Children from families who are economically advantaged tend to grow faster than children from families who are economically disadvantaged, and they tend to have poorer nutrition and more frequent illnesses.

Size

Body proportion changes as a children age. At birth, a child's head accounts for approximately one fourth of the total body height and weight. Gradually, the proportion of the head to the body decreases while the proportion of the legs gradually increases. Ossification, or hardening of the bones, is another function of growth beginning during the prenatal period. This skeletal development is necessary for posture and strength. During early infancy, the bones of the legs and arms are fragile and unable to support an infant's weight. As hardening of the bones takes place, the extremities straighten, and 1-year-olds are able to bear weight in standing and walking.

Developmental Patterns

Three universal patterns of physical growth govern motor development. **Cephalocaudal** growth is the sequence in which growth and development of motor skills occurs progressively downward from head and neck to the trunk, hips, and legs, and finally to the feet and toes. Infants first gain head and neck control, which enables them to hold their heads steady and look around; then they gain trunk control, which allows them to turn from back to tummy, to sit, and so on. A second principle, **proximo-distal** sequencing, refers to development that progresses from the center of the body outward toward the extremities. Legs and arms, being closer to the midline of the body, can be controlled earlier than toes and fingers, as seen by gross movements of extremities in the play of young infants. A child reaches (arm movement) before grasping because the hands are farther from the center of the body; finger control comes later.

   Refinement is a third principle that is also referred to as *simple-to-complex* or *gross-to-fine development*. A child's motor development is initially concentrated on large muscle groups for sitting and walking and then on small muscle group control for such things as scribbling and writing with a crayon. Understanding these three principles helps adults predict a child's development so that intervention is appropriately concentrated on present and emerging stages of development.

Physical Growth

At birth, an infant should be capable of independent functioning that is separate from its mother. Even though organ systems are not all fully developed, they should function well enough to permit growth and development. Deviations from the normal progression of growth may indicate a health problem, but more often they are normal variations that relate to genetic predisposition. Again, although the normal sequence of growth and development is known, the individual timing of certain milestones is not always predictable.

   Physical growth implies a biological change in the structure and mass of a person through increases in weight and size. In each of us, growth is a reaction to a predetermined but idiosyncratic plan. Events and relationships influence growth, although they rarely stop advancement completely. Finally, because of the nature of human growth, behavior observed and accepted during one stage of development may be considered abnormal during another stage of development.

   Major organ systems develop at different rates and at different times. All of the major systems are established during fetal life, and by birth have developed to the point at which their adaptation to extrauterine life can occur. Major organ systems include the respiratory, cardiovascular, gastrointestinal, renal, neurological, skeletal, and integumentary. Each of these systems controls different activities of normal physiological functions that are critical to a normal life.

   The **respiratory system** is made of many complex structures that enable human beings to both take in oxygen, essential for cellular life, and give off carbon dioxide (a by-product of cellular function). The lungs are the main organs of the respiratory system, although healthy cardiovascular functioning is critical to normal functioning of the lungs. Adequate nutrition is necessary for normal lung growth.

© Denielle M. Miller

This factor can be very important when dealing with certain infants and children, such as those with cerebral palsy who suffer from diseases that affect either the lungs themselves or the ability to sustain adequate caloric intake.

The **cardiovascular system** is comprised of the heart and the blood vessels that extend throughout the body connecting all cells to their source of nutrition. A fetal heart begins to beat at approximately 4 weeks of gestation. This development provides the link necessary for the placenta to adequately provide oxygen and nutrition to a fetus. The fetal circulatory system then carries these nutritional elements (oxygen, glucose, etc.) to the fetus and circulates them throughout the body.

After birth, the act of independent respiration changes the normal blood flow. This transition occurs when the lungs expand, changing the pathway of blood to the lungs for oxygenation. Newborns consequently become physiologically self-reliant in the exchange of oxygen and carbon dioxide. Deviations in development of heart structure or the pathways for blood flow can significantly affect the growth of a child.

The **gastrointestinal (GI) system** both processes and absorbs nutrients taken in with food, to maintain metabolism and to support growth. The system includes the mouth, esophagus, stomach, and small and large intestines. The GI system also is involved with excretion of both digestive residue and waste products absorbed from the blood as it passes through the intestinal tract. A functioning GI system is essential for life. Failure to develop this system or a GI malformation can produce serious problems related to malnutrition and failure to thrive.

Prior to birth, the **neurological system** is the fastest growing system. Rapid brain growth occurs between 18 and 20 weeks of gestation and between 30 weeks gestation through the first 12 months of postnatal life. Typically, the size of the head changes rapidly during the first year of life and then slows down during subsequent years.

During the first 6 months of life, the brain cortex increases in size and function as **neurons** (cells responsible for receiving and sending messages) of the brain increase in number and connectedness to other neurons. Immediately after birth, the brain's cortex has little control over neonates' activities. Primitive reflexes controlled by peripheral nerves and the brain stem generally guide the activity of very young infants. As growth and development occur, the brain, through its developing pathways, exerts increasing control over the reflex activity of infants, facilitating the acquisition of more complex abilities. Cortical control requires the development of a **myelin sheath** on the nerves. This sheath permits electrical impulses to move quickly along the nerve fiber or axon (see Figure 3–2). That is, the more myelinization there is, the more efficient or rapid the nervous system becomes at sending and receiving messages. Hence, myelinization of the nervous system is required before complex motor skills can be developed. Immature myelinization or damage to the myelin sheath leads to motor disorders such as cerebral palsy. Myelinization is also required before visual discrimination can occur.

Figure 3–2   Neural Transmission of Myelinated Axon

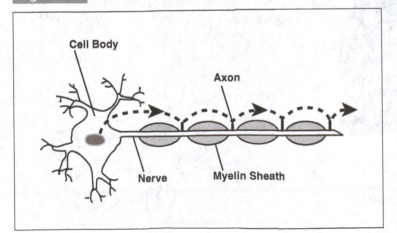

Increases in body size require both new bone growth and the maturation of existing bone structures. The development of new skeletal cells and connective tissue leads to this linear growth. Through maturation, tissues consolidate into a permanent shape that provides structure for the body. Constantly being self-constructed, broken down, and rebuilt, bones grow, mend themselves, and retain their strength. Bone growth follows a genetic plan that continues for up to 20 years after birth. Many diseases that affect children may affect bone growth. For example, chronic lung disease in premature infants increases the possibility for decreased food intake, leading to poor nutrition that can adversely affect bone growth.

Muscle growth also has a role in childhood development. Muscle fibers, which were laid down in fetal life, remain constant in number throughout the lifespan but increase in size at varying times. Growth periods are probably most apparent during adolescence when hormonal changes in puberty stimulate the muscle fibers to increase in size. By contrast, muscles that are unused in childhood will shrink in size, ultimately leading to atrophy with eventual loss of muscle function.

Dentition (tooth formation) is another process of growth. Primary and secondary tooth formation can be categorized into stages that consist of growth, calcification, eruption, and tooth loss. Ages at which teeth erupt are inconsistent among children, but the order in which they erupt is fairly constant (see Figure 3–3). With the exception of the first molar, the teeth erupt from the incisors, or front teeth, backward in order to the molars. Still, significant delays in eruption may indicate the effect of nutritional factors or other health problems.

Weight is a growth variable that is influenced by many factors. Heredity, gestational age, maternal conditions, and environmental influences all affect weight.

Figure 3–3 Sequence of Eruption and Loss of Primary Teeth and Permanent Teeth

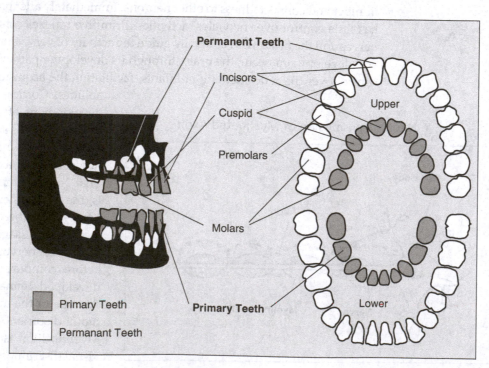

Permanent Teeth

Incisors

Cuspid

Upper

Premolars

Molars

Primary Teeth

Lower

Primary Teeth

Permanant Teeth

Weight and height in combination make it possible to determine normal ranges of growth for different populations. Periodic measurements of weight and height are monitored using standard charts to determine an individual child's rate of growth according to the norm. This information is useful in comparing growth in relation to that of other children of the same age. Children who deviate from the norm are categorized as "large for age" or "small for age." In addition to marking normal individual differences related to heredity, these deviations give information related to a particular child's overall health and indicate potential or real problems.

Growth parameters follow age-related guidelines. However, age stages are arbitrarily determined and do not generally take into account individual differences. Therefore, it is more important to follow the weight gain in a particular child than to make assumptions about health based solely on where a child lies on the standard growth curve.

Typical stages of growth include the **prenatal** period (from conception to birth), the **neonatal** period (from birth to 30 days of age), the **infancy** period (from 30 days to 12 months), the **toddler stage** (from 1 to 3 years), the **early childhood stage** (from 3 to 6 years), the **middle childhood stage** (from 6 to 12 years), and the **adolescent stage** (from 13 to 18 years). As mentioned, the prenatal growth period consists of the embryonic and the fetal stages of development. When providing prenatal care, obstetricians can determine whether growth complications that may lead to problems during the neonatal period are present. During the neonatal period, babies attain the stability that allows them to go from intrauterine to extrauterine life. Infants must transition completely from fetal circulation patterns, during which they relied on their mothers for all of their metabolic needs, to assuming much of the responsibility for meeting their own needs.

An average newborn weighs 7.4 lb; 95 percent of all newborns in the United States weigh between 5.5 and 10 lb (Donahue, Kleinman, Gillman, & Oken, 2010). Conventional wisdom suggests that the statistical reduction in risk factors that has occurred over recent decades, including associated increased maternal weight, reduction in smoking, and older maternal age, should result in fewer preterm births and higher birth weights. Yet, both average birth weight and gestational age have been declining in the United States (Donahue et al., 2010). Researchers have not been able to explain this decline, though the trend is significant. At the same time, an infant's height normally ranges between 45 and 55 cm—slightly taller for males than females (National Center for Health Statistics, 2002a, 2002b). Newborns generally lose about 7% to 10% of their body weight during the first 5 days of life but gradually regain that weight and stabilize gains to approximately an ounce per day. **Neonates** have poor temperature control and require external heat management, such as with extra blankets, to maintain a normal temperature of 98.6°F (37°C). Poor heat control is related to the insufficient fat stores under the skin that produce fuel for maintaining body temperature. Neonates also have a rapid heart rate and a fast but somewhat inconsistent breathing pattern. Because of their small stomach size, neonates eat small amounts frequently. Breastfed infants may eat as often as every hour.

The infancy period (from 30 days to 12 months) is also a time of very rapid physical growth. By 1 year, normally progressing infants have tripled their birth weight and are approximately 1.5 times their birth height. The head and chest circumferences have become proportional. The heart rate continues to be elevated but is less rapid, and the respiratory pattern is well established. Infants can maintain temperature stability, and fat stores are sufficient to preserve heat. Skeletal and muscle growth has also occurred, enabling infants to progress through the developmental tasks that are appropriate for this age, especially those related to gross motor skills. Primary tooth eruption usually occurs, and by 12 months, infants have an established pattern of three meals a day with an additional feeding before going to bed for the night. Most infants sleep approximately 12 hours each day.

Toddlers (from 12 to 36 months) generally weigh 4 times their birth weight (26–32 pounds) and are about 32 to 33 inches tall at the end of this stage. Head circumference is increasing, although more slowly now, and primary dentition is usually complete by 30 to 36 weeks. Toddlers have food preferences and may not exhibit much of an appetite. In spite of this, many toddlers' abdomens protrude, and their extremities appear to have an excess of fat. Toddlers' heart rates may continue to be slightly elevated and average about 100 beats per minute. The respiratory rate continues at about 25 breaths per minute with use of the abdominal muscles. Many toddlers have inconsistent sleep patterns and are reluctant to go to bed.

Theories of Development

A spectrum of theories regarding human development lends direction to research and practice in the fields of early intervention and preschool education. Some developmental theories are so broad they are disciplines in themselves. Although others may be less weighty, it would be difficult to fully comprehend the elements of each theory in the brief space allowed in this text. Nevertheless, it is useful to review the dominant models. These systems fall into general categories that are often associated directly with a dominant theorist: psychodynamic, psychosocial, maturationist, environmental/behavioral, cognitive, social developmental, and attachment/ethological.

Sigmund Freud was perhaps the first psychologist to acknowledge the relationship between childhood and adult behavior. Specifically, his theory suggested explanations for anomalies of early childhood that led directly to adult mental illnesses. According to Freud, individual personality develops from three aspects of the psyche. The "id" directs a person's need for pleasure, is present at birth, and is unconsciously responsible for all individual energy. Much later in childhood, between 3 and 6 years of age, a child begins to develop a "superego." As children internalize the moral teaching of their parents and culture, the superego drives individuals unrealistically to seek perfection. At the awareness level and developing in early infancy is a person's "ego," or sense of reality. In other words, the ego balances an individual's competing drives for pleasure and perfection. Prominent in Freud's theory of childhood experiences are psychosocial stages in which too much or too little gratification by parents can lead to "fixation" deviancy. For example, adults who act compulsively may have an "anal fixation" that can be blamed on an overly rigid toilet training regimen; premature weaning can lead to an "oral fixation" in the form of compulsive smoking or overeating.

Like Freud, *Erik Erikson*'s psychosocial theory of child development provided a hypothesis for understanding the genesis of adult mental health problems (Erikson, 1963, 1968, 1980). According to this theory, all babies are born with basic capabilities and temperaments that are gradually and differentially shaped through eight stages of development. Each stage is characterized by a different psychological "crisis" that must be resolved before moving on to the next stage; failure to resolve each crisis leads to specific social maladaptation in adulthood. The following is a brief description of the first four stages of Erickson's theory, which cover the first 12 years of life.

1. Between birth and 12 months, infants must resolve the basic **trust/mistrust crisis.** If infants are provided essential food, security, and affection, they should develop secure attachment and become trusting children and adults. If not, infants will become distrustful of others' behavior.

2. The **autonomy/doubt crisis** is normally resolved between 1 and 2 years of age when the issues surround walking and toilet training—each of which requires a degree of self-control. Parents who encourage initiative will foster confidence, self-control, and independence. On the other hand, if parents are too overprotective and/or disapproving, their children will develop self-doubt, shame, and a sense of dependency.

3. The remaining preschool years (2–6 years of age) are devoted to resolving the **initiative/guilt crisis.** A child needs to be provided a balance of adventure and responsibility. Encouraging risk taking with limits helps children self-manage at the same time they are learning to push the boundaries of their imagination. Again, discouraging parents will cause their children to be plagued by guilt and to be overly dependent.

4. Elementary-age youth are challenged by the **competence/inferiority crisis,** a crucial stage in which an individual acquires the skills necessary to become a worker or provider. Success in school leads to enjoyment of learning and consequently competence, whereas failure will lead to an enduring sense of inferiority.

The key maturationist theorist was *Arnold Gesell,* who explained development as a biological process that occurs across time and along a predictable—and sequential—timeline (Gesell & Thompson, 1934). Developmental milestones are based on this prominent description of childhood. Gesell theorized that skills are acquired naturally and automatically with little deviation unless a child has some serious biological interruption.

By contrast, environmental/behavioral theory credits a child's environment with playing a key role in the rate and direction of development. Broadly explained by prominent behaviorist *B.F. Skinner,* a child's biological endowment is gradually influenced by differential consequences for behavior. Through rigorously controlled laboratory and clinical research, Skinner developed principles of human behavior resulting from repeatedly observed phenomenon. This scientific approach was based on the contention that what is unobservable, and therefore unmeasurable, cannot be known and therefore is not helpful in developing methods of teaching that might be relied on to work. Two key behavioral principles of learning, reinforcement and punishment, shape behavior across time—gradually developing a child's repertoire of behavior (Skinner, 1953). Reinforcing consequences increase the likelihood that a behavior will be repeated under similar circumstances. Conversely, punishing consequences decrease the likelihood that the behavior will be produced again. The strength or predictability of a behavior is determined by both the conditions under which a behavior is learned and the schedule, timing, and type of consequences delivered. Of special interest to Skinner was the development of language; his book, *Verbal Behavior,* led to a great deal of research and intervention practices for children with language delays (Skinner, 1957).

Albert Bandura, categorized variously as a behaviorist, a cognitivist, and a social learning theorist, began his research with aggressive adolescents in the 1950s. Bandura suggested that the relationship between behavior and one's environment were interrelated—not unidirectional (Bandura, 1971). This theory of reciprocal determinism holds that a person's psychological processes—specifically language and imagery—interact with the person's environment and behavior. Bandura's most significant theoretical contribution was the importance of modeling to learning. Through observation of children, he defined steps for learning through modeling:

1. **Attention:** Factors that heighten (e.g., attractiveness or prestigiousness of the model) or diminish (e.g., tiredness, sickness, or distraction) a person's ability to attend to a model will influence a child's ability to learn from that model.

2. **Retention:** Imagery and/or language are the mediums through which incoming information is converted to memory.

3. **Motor reproduction:** Physically replicating a model's behavior and being able to judge the accuracy of the reproduction are necessary to learning.

4. **Motivation:** External and vicarious reinforcement as well as self-reinforcement provide both motivation and consequences that maintain behavior.

Russian theorist *Lev Vygotsky* authored a social/development theory (Vygotsky, 1962, 1978). Positing that social and cultural indicators play key roles in cognitive development, Vygotsky believed that every human function is first exercised and learned in the context of an interpersonal interaction. That is, all higher functions of language and cognition (attention, memory, logic, conceptual formation, etc.) originate from actual relationships between individuals. Furthermore, the limits of cognitive development are determined by the integrity of social interactions during critical time periods that are associated with maximal learning. In early childhood, teaching children "what" and "how" to use cognitive skills evolves from problem-solving *with* someone else. Gradually, the responsibility for problem-solving transfers from others to a child. Placing particular emphasis on the role of language in socialization, Vygotsky explained that a child's internal tool for self-directed behavior is through the medium of language. As children age, intellectual development constantly depends on the integrity of social interactions.

One of the most influential developmental theorists was French psychologist *Jean Piaget* (Piaget, 1963). A biologist, philosopher, and psychologist, Piaget was perhaps the first psychologist to suggest that children think and process information differently than adults. Simply put, his theory provided a description of intellectual stages of child development (sensorimotor, preoperational, concrete operations, formal operations). Piaget created his theory by intensively observing the learning patterns of his own children over a number of years. He viewed intelligence as the ability to assimilate (take in new information and mentally organize the new data within an already existing framework of related knowledge) and accommodate (incorporate new information within an existing cognitive framework or scheme modified to adjust to new elements). Therefore, child development is viewed as an increasingly complex ability to process information based on primitive foundations laid in earlier stages of development. Piaget was one of the first theorists to place special emphasis on the active role that children have in their own intellectual development. That is, he noted that a child may neither be prematurely "taught" out of one stage into another nor develop increasingly complex schemes without interacting with the environment. Accordingly, nature and nurture are interdependent forces on development.

Bridging social learning theory and psychoanalysis were *John Bowlby*'s important contributions regarding attachment or ethnological theory (Bowlby, 1958, 1960, 1969). Attachment, it seemed to him, serves a biological purpose in providing a child with physical security necessary for exploring the environment. The quality of a child's early separation events with the mother may have long-term consequences. Bowlby identified three phases of separation response that represent important transitions: protest (separation anxiety), despair (grief and mourning), and detachment/denial (defense mechanism). Bowlby stressed the importance of early and active mother-and-infant bonding relationships. Repeated or prolonged separation might lead to feelings of abandonment or rejection. The consequences of disturbances to attachment would be psychological maladjustment. In sum, he posited, separation angst occurs when attachment is breached and cannot be alleviated until reunion is restored.

This brief description of the array of theories of child development does not do justice to the great effort made by the aforementioned theorists and the many important corollary contributions of devotees to the respective bodies of knowledge. Theories range from unverifiable (psychoanalytic) to completely dependent on scientific verification (behavioral). While contemporary psychologists and practitioners place less confidence in some of these theories than in others, each has had an important role in our current understanding of child development. Still, much is not known. In fact, none of these theories, either alone or put together, adequately explains the mechanisms of child development. It is possible that emerging biological research will provide the missing links. What seems increasingly clear is the important role of human relationships to cognitive, linguistic, and social development, now supported by neurophysical research. For example, when infants respond to their parents' initiatives in positive ways, a hormone is released in the adult's brain that influences those adults' future interactions. Other research shows that fetal and infant brains are endowed with excessive neurological structures (e.g., dendrites, neurons). Those that are unused are sloughed off while those that are repeatedly used grow, forming the "hardwiring," or structure of the brain. In short, the "soft" science of developmental psychology is about to collide with the "hard" sciences of neurology and endocrinology—leading to ever-evolving theories of child development.

Principles and Patterns of Development

Several principles of normal development have been derived from decades of observation of infants and young children. These principles represent our current knowledge and beliefs about human patterns of physical and behavioral development. These principles probably will be revised or replaced in the future as our understanding of very young children grows. Still, what we now know allows early childhood professionals to plan interventions and to advise parents. Assessment tools, instructional strategies, and curricular materials are based on the principles of development that follow.

© Estee Aiken

Infants Are Highly Competent Organisms

As research on child development emerges, the bar keeps rising as the complex ability of infants continues to astound observers. Even newborn infants are capable of learning new behaviors, solving problems, and adapting to changes in their environment. Early researchers were unaware of neonatal abilities to use perceptual and cognitive abilities to acquire vast knowledge. For example, a windup mobile was once thought to be appropriate stimulation for a "passive" infant. Now mobiles that jingle or turn only when the infant touches them are considered appropriate because they help infants establish cause-and-effect and encourage them to take control of their environments.

Infants Are Socially Interactive

Recently, educators have recognized that social interaction is not only a critical area of development but also influences development in intellectual growth. In fact, it is possible that social competencies may more accurately predict later abilities than many measures of cognitive abilities. Evidence suggests that the need for social attachment is a biological drive. For example, positive social interactions stimulate the release of endorphins in a baby's brain, eliciting pleasure and excitement (Lipari, 2000).

According to MacDonald (1992), human affection motivates children to be compliant and accepting, and it correspondingly encourages adults to invest in their children. For example, in the past, parents were sometimes advised to feed a child on a fixed schedule of 3-hour intervals. Considering the interactive nature of development, parents are now trained to respond to a child's cues, such as facial expressions, vocalizations, or activity levels, to continue to feed or stop feeding. Parents try to read a child's intent and respect the child's social communication. A child who has not experienced such interactions on a regular basis may learn to be a passive participant.

Infants Are Active Learners

Developmentalists believe infants are not merely passively modified by the goings-on around them but also play an active, if not always intentional, role in their own development. Early give-and-take interactions between infants and caregivers provide the context for a child to learn control over the environment. In fact, a child may be biologically programmed to engage in behaviors (e.g., cooing, smiling) that elicit parental responses (e.g., communication, proximity, smiling) that are optimal for brain development (Reis, Collins, & Berscheid, 2000).

Infant Development Is Multidimensional

The process by which infants' skills become more complex and integrated is a non-arbitrary sequence. Rather, this highly organized process unfolds predictably as children simultaneously grow physically and develop cognitively and socially. Behaviors in each area have an impact on behaviors in other domains as skills develop across domains at the same time. The following example illustrates the interdependency of developmental domains. Children with Down syndrome often have cognitive delays. Their ability to problem-solve is complicated by poor language development, which is also typically delayed. Articulation difficulties may further compound the communication problems. Consequently, when these children need help in solving a problem, they may not be able to request it in an understandable way. As a consequence, social interactions are affected.

Developmental Sequencing Is Universal

Developmental milestones describe a universal sequence of steps through which children progress. Although not all children progress through the steps at precisely the same age, the pattern of development is very reliable. Significant deviations in this pattern place a child at risk of developmental disability.

Skills Become More Specialized

As children develop, they are able to integrate more refined skills in one area with newly acquired skills in another to perform coordinated behaviors. For example, infants learn to recognize an adult's voice as their auditory discrimination improves. At the same time, facial muscle control increases to the point that a child can smile voluntarily. The result is a specialized ability to smile at mom when she is speaking. This acts to enhance social relationships. In early childhood, children scribble non-discriminately. Gradually, they refine this skill so that they can copy lines and circles. As children near school age, they integrate their emerging cognitive knowledge of alphabet letters with their newly refined fine-motor skills. Thus, specialization in these two domains results in the ability to learn handwriting.

Plasticity Is a Phenomenon of Brain Development

One of the remarkable aspects of development is the **plasticity** of the human brain that allows alternate neural pathways to be formed to compensate for deficits in other portions of the brain. Damage to a specific area of the brain (e.g., language) often results in another portion of the brain developing the function of the damaged section. An example of this flexibility is seen in infants who are blind or deaf but who acquire necessary developmental skills by focusing on alternate channels of understanding.

Critical Learning Periods Exist in Normal Development

Interactional and developmental theorists contend that critical sensitive periods, during which a child is biologically most ready to learn certain new behaviors, occur throughout human development. When environmental events provide the right conditions for a particularly sensitive period, developmental progress can be maximized. However, when experiences fail to match a child's predisposition for learning, the window of opportunity is missed. Although a child will not necessarily fail to acquire the new skills, learning will take much longer than otherwise possible.

Paired with the theory of "peak" or critical periods of learning is the need to provide diverse learning experiences involving all sensory systems. Many factors can interfere with optimal development. For example, it is now widely recognized that poverty experienced in early childhood has a significant and lasting effect on cognitive aptitude. Impoverishment results in a loss that may be compensated for, but a child's aptitude at birth is never fully regained (Najman et al., 2009). Another example of a missed opportunity is what happens when children have chronic ear infections during a critical period for learning to discriminate sounds used by others in conversations; children with such ear infections may have difficulty acquiring the sounds necessary for speech.

Infant Relationships Are the Key to Cognitive Development

In contrast to some current practices in which parents go to great effort to teach babies complex cognitive skills at an early age (words, numbers, shapes, colors, etc.), the optimal stimulation for cognitive growth is actually the emotional quality of the parent–infant relationship (Lipari, 2000). Neurobehavioral researchers are finding that the emotional quality of relationships directly activates the brain's neural connections, which form a network of neural pathways. These neural structures within areas of the brain form the foundation for higher-level mental functioning such as memory, language, emotion, representation, and states of mind (Reis et al., 2000).

Children Undergo Several Transitions

It is typical for children to undergo stages of **transition** with spurts of growth and development that may be followed by unpredictable behavior or regression. For example, changes in a daily pattern, such as beginning at a new day-care center, may result in behavior problems that are generally short-lived. As children become more inquisitive, more mobile, and more verbal in the latter half of their second year, their behavior also becomes more unpredictable. The resolution of these problems, referred to as **consolidation,** occurs when the disorganized behavior is replaced by more advanced developmental skills. For example, a child may become better behaved when conventional words, a more sophisticated form of communication, replace babbling.

Individual Differences Exist among Children

Children differ in such characteristics as temperament and gender, making each child unique. **Temperament,** or one's adaptation to everyday events, is partially innate and partially learned. Thomas and Chess (1981) concluded that temperament is a relatively constant trait throughout life. Differences in temperament affect the manner in which adults interact with infants and children and often result in a baby being labeled "difficult" or "easy." These responses, in turn, influence the development of a child's temperament. For example, if a cuddly, active, and smiling infant is reinforced by similar adult behaviors, the child is likely to continue being a socially rewarding companion.

Expectations of infants according to gender are obvious, even in newborns, as adults handle and talk to infants differently based on a child's sex (Coltrane, 1998). This social training appears to be powerful, as children (girls first) begin to use gender labels at about 19 months and then subsequently to begin gender-typed play before 2 years of age (Zosuls, Ruble, Tamis-LeMonda, Shrout, Bornstein, & Greulich, 2009). Hines (2011) concluded from recent research that children are influenced prenatally by exposure to testosterone. That is, levels of exposure to testosterone do not determine, but affect, sex differences such as gender identity, sexual orientation, and some sex-related behaviors. Predisposed sex differences are then influenced by early childhood and adolescent hormonal critical periods (Hines, 2011). The results of research on gendered play between parents and children are not surprising. For example, gendered patterns of fathering were found to be different prior to two years of age, with fathers engaging in more physical activities with boys and more literacy activities with girls (Leavell, Tamis-LeMonda, Ruble, Zosuls, & Cabrera, 2012). The interaction of physiological tendency and parental support of gender-specific activities may explain why gender is one of the most dominant determinants of human behavior.

Factors Influencing Development

There is little argument that the developmental achievements of children born into this world are the product of their genetic endowments as well as the capriciousness of the world around them. Although the search to determine the relative degree of these two factors continues, it can be assumed that to some large extent, children's development can be altered by the manipulation (intentional or not) of environmental factors (see Figure 3–4). For example, poverty, maternal income and education, family size, culture, and race are all factors that influence both opportunity and motivation and, consequently, child development. Several factors are known risks for cognitive, social, and language development: mother's mental health, anxiety level, education level, head-of-household status, whether she is in a semiskilled or unskilled occupation, and minority ethnic status; unresponsive mother–child interactions; absent father; many stressful life events; and large household size. When multiple risk factors exist, developmental potential is even more likely to be diminished (Burchinal, Roberts, Hooper, & Zeisel, 2000). The following is a discussion of important factors that affect every child's growth and development.

Family Structure

American families are diverse in structure; many are either in transition or headed by a single parent. The absence of either a dominant female or male adult figure in a child's life influences patterns of development, particularly in social and personal areas. Between 1970 and 2000, the number of children living in two-parent families decreased from 85% to 69%. Much of this change can be attributed to the birth rate of unmarried women, which rose from 5.3% in 1960 to 33.2% in 2000. These data are important because family structure is directly related to family income, which influences children's health. Female-headed families earn only 47% of what is earned by two-parent families (the ratio increases to 65% of the income of two-parent families

Figure 3–4 Pathways Leading from Poverty to Childhood Disabilities

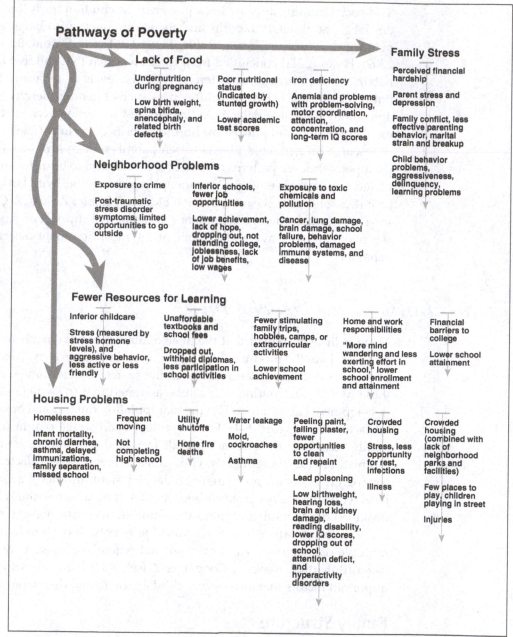

Pathways of Poverty

Lack of Food

Undernutrition during pregnancy

Low birth weight, spina bifida, anencephaly, and related birth defects

Poor nutritional status (indicated by stunted growth)

Lower academic test scores

Iron deficiency

Anemia and problems with problem-solving, motor coordination, attention, concentration, and long-term IQ scores

Family Stress

Perceived financial hardship

Parent stress and depression

Family conflict, less effective parenting behavior, marital strain and breakup

Child behavior problems, aggressiveness, delinquency, learning problems

Neighborhood Problems

Exposure to crime

Post-traumatic stress disorder symptoms, limited opportunities to go outside

Inferior schools, fewer job opportunities

Lower achievement, lack of hope, dropping out, not attending college, joblessness, lack of job benefits, low wages

Exposure to toxic chemicals and pollution

Cancer, lung damage, brain damage, school failure, behavior problems, damaged immune systems, and disease

Fewer Resources for Learning

Inferior childcare

Stress (measured by stress hormone levels), and aggressive behavior, less active or less friendly

Unaffordable textbooks and school fees

Dropped out, withheld diplomas, less participation in school activities

Fewer stimulating family trips, hobbies, camps, or extracurricular activities

Lower school achievement

Home and work responsibilities

"More mind wandering and less exerting effort in school," lower school enrollment and attainment

Financial barriers to college

Lower school attainment

Housing Problems

Homelessness

Infant mortality, chronic diarrhea, asthma, delayed immunizations, family separation, missed school

Frequent moving

Not completing high school

Utility shutoffs

Home fire deaths

Water leakage

Mold, cockroaches

Asthma

Peeling paint, falling plaster, fewer opportunities to clean and repaint

Lead poisoning

Low birthweight, hearing loss, brain and kidney damage, reading disability, lower IQ scores, dropping out of school, attention deficit, and hyperactivity disorders

Crowded housing

Stress, less opportunity for rest, infections

Illness

Crowded housing (combined with lack of neighborhood parks and facilities)

Few places to play, children playing in street

Injuries

Source: From *Wasting America's Future: The Children's Defense Fund Report in the Costs of Child Poverty* (p. 12), by A. Sherman, Boston, MA: Beacon. © 1980.

where one is working), and female-headed families are five times more likely to live in poverty than married-couple families. The reconstitution of divorced families in blended or extended families results in socialization patterns that may affect children's loyalty to others and their values, adaptability, and self-esteem. Research indicates that divorce has a variable influence on children depending on several factors. For example, Fagan (2012) found little difference between the preschool literacy of children of custodial mothers who stayed single and children whose parents did not divorce. However, the children of divorced women who remarried or cohabited scored significantly lower on preschool literacy evaluations than the other groups. On the other hand, Thomas and Woodside (2011) believed that early research on the effects of divorce on children were based on a biased preference for a two-parent family and suggested that many children possess a resiliency that protects them from long-term effects of divorce. This is supported by the contention that divorce itself may be less important to long-term development of children than parental-interaction patterns that lead to divorce (Kim, 2011). In fact, several factors have been identified that may mediate the harmful effects of divorce on children: warm, positive relationships with the mother, consistent and effective behavior management, parental warmth and acceptance, and family cohesion (Vélez, Wolchik, Tein, & Sandler, 2011).

Childcare

Raising children while working full-time places stress on both parents, especially when the working mothers are expected to fulfill all their traditional responsibilities (Schor, 2003). An assumption underlying research comparing maternal versus nonmaternal childcare is that nonmaternal will lead to insecure attachment, yet research has consistently shown that child development is neither positively nor negatively associated with type of childcare per se (Erel, Oberman, & Yirmiya, 2000). The only caveat to these findings was the observation that children placed in childcare after the age of 30 months showed less secure attachment than children placed in childcare prior to 30 months of age (Erel et al., 2000).

The effect of nonmaternal childcare on cognitive development is not clear. For example, Hansen and Hawkes (2009) found that both group childcare and grandmother care in preschool years prepared children well for school. While problem behaviors did not appear to be higher when children attended formal group care, behavioral problems were associated with grandmother care (Hansen & Hawkes, 2009). On the other hand, Bernal (2008) found that full-time maternal employment and formal childcare were associated with lower test scores. Still, Baker and Milligan (2010) studied child outcomes when mothers took advantage of maternity leave entitlements in Canada, increasing time spent with their children by about 50 percent in their children's first year. In this study, this extra maternal care did not significantly improve temperament or social or motor development. Findings suggest that factors other than who is the actual caretaker (e.g., quality of care, maternal age, and education) are more important than mothers' employment status in predicting child development outcomes.

Psychological Factors

The maintenance of a nurturing environment is as important to child development as health care and nutrition. From the first days of life, adults begin to nurture children through breastfeeding, eye contact, smiling, kissing, and vocalizations, which in turn establish an attachment between infant and caregiver referred to as *bonding* (Siegel, 1982). Unlike other species, however, human babies resiliently retain the capability of bonding even if parents miss opportunities in the first days and weeks of life. As infants grow, other psychological factors begin to influence development. Erikson

(1963) wrote that one of the primary tasks of infants in the first year of life was to develop a sense of trust, which comes out of predictable and positive responses of caregivers and siblings. Although responsiveness in parenting early in life is critical to social and cognitive development, it also appears that parents must be vigilant over time (Landry, Swank, Assel, Smith, & Vellet, 2001). Landry and colleagues observed that a failure to consistently provide responsive caregiving resulted in a deceleration in cognitive growth after age 4.

It seems that children not only require secure social attachments; they also may need intermittent solitude as a condition of normal growth (Buchholz, 1997). Buchholz contended that increased emphasis on social interactions may actually deplete opportunities that infants have to self-regulate, organize information, and take a "psychological rest"; this may actually prove harmful if taken to an extreme. The results of research citing the physiological benefits of solitude show improvements in the immune system and general functioning.

Parental style is important to the nurturance of children. Adults who use warm and gentle tones to give directions and provide frequent positive feedback supporting appropriate behaviors develop the strongest levels of attachment (Reis et al., 2000). Child-rearing strategies are also important predictors of problems with social skills. Harsh parenting, in which children do not perceive consistent warmth, may lead to aggression and rejection by peers (Miller, Loeber, & Hipwell, 2009). Intimate partner violence (IPV) is an emerging health crisis. IPV occurs when a nonparent partner who assumes a parenting role handles a child violently and engages in maladaptive parenting practices (Knous-Westfall, Ehrensaft, MacDonell, & Cohen, 2011). Millions of children are exposed to IPV and suffer significant social and cognitive problems. Children who experience *any* IPV are likely to experience disrupted peer relations. More severe IPV is associated with overt aggression including bullying of peers.

Environmental deprivation and environmental chaos can affect social and cognitive development (Kim & Evans, 2011). Kim and Evans (2011) found that chaotic environmental factors, including poverty, interact biologically with certain genes, resulting in more problem behaviors in childhood. When infants and toddlers who were in low-income families and homeless were assessed at 9 months and then at 18 months of age, a significant drop in their motor and cognitive developmental scores was observed. These findings suggest that poverty has a cumulative negative effect on development, increasing proportionately to the length of time children are exposed to related conditions including single parenting, violence, maternal depression, and substance abuse. Significantly, the worldwide economic downturn of the 21st century, referred to as the Great Recession, has had a disproportionate impact on children. Additionally, children of color are more than three times as likely to live in poverty (Oberg, 2011) than Caucasian children. Given the detrimental effect of poverty on child development, we can anticipate the long-term consequences of this international economic crisis on the potential of our youth.

Infants and young children must be given the freedom to explore their environments and to experiment and play with appropriate toys or materials. For decades, it has been recognized that the absence of stimulation or deprivation of experiences negatively affects development (Skeels, 1942, 1966). In Skeels's original research, 25 infants were selected from an overcrowded orphanage; 13 of them were sent to an institution to be cared for by adult women with mental retardation who provided the children with a stimulating and responsive environment. Although initially testing an average of 22 IQ points lower than the 12 infants remaining in the orphanage, a year and a half after placement in the institution, the children raised by women with mental retardation gained an average of 28 IQ points. Meanwhile, the children who remained in the overcrowded orphanage during that same period of time lost an average of 26 IQ points.

In the past decade, more concern has been paid to the rising "stress" exerted on families related to such factors as longer work days and longer commutes to and from work, the need for day care (and unavailability of quality childcare), feelings of isolation, commercial and moral pressure exerted on children by society and the media, the perception of increasing danger in the world, the obligations of caring for multigenerational family members, and the intrusion of television and computers into family life (Schor, 2003). That these stress factors may be related to a sharp increase in pediatric behavioral problems means that early intervention professionals will be best able to assist families in meeting the needs of their children by addressing families as a whole.

Education

Educational opportunities, when of good quality, can compensate for some disadvantages. At the same time, when children are economically disadvantaged, a poor education can serve to exacerbate the negative effects of an inadequate environment. The following list represents some educationally related factors that have been found to differentially influence children's development:

1. Opportunity for preschool educational services, especially for children raised in poverty
2. Educational level of parents
3. Structure and curriculum focus of an educational program
4. Safety in school
5. Opportunity for success and positive experiences in school
6. Consistency of school attendance and mobility
7. Value of children's education to parents
8. Parents' knowledge of the educational system

Evidence is mounting in support of early educational childcare for infants and preschoolers. For example, a longitudinal study of economically disadvantaged minority children compared full-time, high-quality educational program for children from infancy to age 5 to the outcomes of a control group of children that did not receive early education (Campbell, Pungello, Miller, Burchinal, & Ramey, 2001). Those who received early education performed far better on long-term **indexes** of development: Although both groups gradually declined in IQ, the control group had a significantly lower average IQ; children who received early intervention scored significantly higher on measures of math and reading than did those in the control group. The observed cognitive advantages for recipients of early intervention, although continuously dropping for both groups when compared to national averages, persisted into adulthood.

Culture

Although cross-cultural research is in its infancy, it has revealed universality in many aspects of development just as differences have been observed in the rates of that development. For example, infants within the same culture seem to behave similarly, but as a group their behavior might be different from that of children from other cultures (Friedlmeier, Chakkarath, & Schwartz, 2005). In the past, educators tended to evaluate the development of all children according to the norms established with white, middle-income children. Similarly, educational priorities favor the values of the dominant culture. For example, most minority groups highly value cooperative group behavior, whereas Caucasians tend to value independence and competition. More recently, it has been realized that this practice gives undue priority to a single culture while arbitrarily devaluing the practices of other cultures that may differentially affect child development.

Culture interacts with other factors, such as family income, in affecting children's development. Differences have been found between the way low-income African American, white, and Latino fathers parent their sons and daughters (Leavell et al., 2012). African American fathers played and visited the most, whereas both African American and Latino fathers played and visited more than white fathers. Regardless of ethnicity, fathers engaged in approximately the same level of childcare.

Technology

The last half of the 20th century has seen a rise of two major technologies: the television and the computer. While these have become household tools for both adults and children, the long-term influence of these technologies on child development is undetermined. However, the influence of television has been the center of controversy for decades. The potential influence of television cannot be underestimated, as patterns of television watching in early childhood are predictive of patterns in adolescence (Francis, Stancel, Sernulka-George, Broffitt, Levy, & Janz, 2011). Children under the age of 2 are particularly at risk, prompting the American Academy of Pediatrics to discourage exposure to digital media (including background media use by parents) before this young age due to the potentially harmful effects on health and development (Council on Communication and Media, 2011).

Of mounting concern is the established relationship between increased television watching and increased childhood obesity (Crespo & Arbesman, 2003). Of particular concern to parents and child advocates have been the correlational findings linking television programming and commercials to children's

© Brian Price

aggression (Browne & Giachristsis, 2005; Hamilton-Huesmann, Moise-Titus, Podolski, & Eron, 2003), alcohol and tobacco use, increased high-risk behaviors, and accelerated onset of sexual activity (Villani, 2001). Beentjes and VanderVoort (1988) identified a reduction in children's academic capacity when they spent more than 3 hours per day watching television. In fact, watching as few as nine minutes of fast-paced cartoons has an immediate and harmful effect on children's problem-solving ability (Lillard & Peterson, 2011).

Although computer and video games and television are sources of concern when overused for entertainment, the computer and television programs obviously have the potential to be valuable learning tools. A study in the United Kingdom found that 45 percent of children aged 3 and 4 years used computers in their homes and self-selected to spend sustained time on computers during free play in nursery school settings (Mitchell & Dunbar, 2006). Furthermore, their teachers believed that computer play enhanced hand-eye coordination, fostered social development, promoted early literacy skills, and increased concentration. Children as young as 14 or 15 months learn and retain simple actions viewed on video (DeLoache & Korac, 2003), and television may be a tool for providing stories and opportunities for language development for very young children that later enhance their reading comprehension (Panayiota et al., 2006).

IN CONCLUSION

Knowledge and practice in the next few decades will be dramatically influenced by technology changes in ways that we cannot begin to predict. Theories of human development will change more rapidly as technology enables researchers to investigate and solve riddles previously inaccessible to observation. In the past, cognitive, linguistic, and social behaviors were largely explained by guesses about what goes on underneath a person's skin rather than by knowledge of actual neurological or endocrinological processes. Now, we know that the brain, in particular, is at peak capacity for learning during the very period of interest in this text. In addition to nutrition, nurturance and secure relationships with adults stimulate brain growth, which is in turn related to children's social and cognitive development. With increased understanding of the importance of these early years, policymakers must be compelled to invest in bringing educational services to all families of very young children (Oberg, 2011). There is little doubt that comprehensive early childhood education will help to level the field for families across economic lines.

Based on this new knowledge, early childhood educators can help families select and design programs that more reliably influence children's acquisition of desirable behaviors. Concomitantly, professionals will need to learn more about family systems so that we are able to respond sensitively and effectively to families with diverse characteristics. This issue is infinitely more complex and intractable than the mind-boggling changes in technology that we are likely to encounter in the coming decades.

Technology is likely to influence children's development in a more direct way. Increasingly, human activities are interwoven with computers. Computers have and will continue to take over traditional routines of daily life. It is possible that computers will replace such basic activities as reading, teaching, and testing. These changes will not only influence what children need to learn but also whether and how they will learn. That is, if children's early learning experiences vary significantly because of interactions with technology, their neural pathways will become hardwired differently than those of today's youth, who have had different kinds of experiences.

All of these changes will take place without our having gained an understanding of the importance of early experiences. For example, is it necessary for children to learn to read? Even if technology replaces the need for this skill, will the loss of literacy affect future generations' chances of survival? Will the neural pathways used to read be formed in other ways, or will these pathways be replaced by other hardwiring more adapted to the demands of the 21st century and beyond? The risk we have taken—without the consent of children—is that some types of early learning experiences will be critical for survival—but not sustained because of our fascination with technology.

STUDY GUIDE QUESTIONS

1. In what areas of development must educators have knowledge?
2. Briefly explain development during the embryonic stage.
3. Describe development of the fetus throughout the fetal stage.
4. What are the requirements for a viable fetus?
5. Why do different children grow at different rates?
6. Would you expect the same pattern of growth across all children? Explain.
7. List and explain the three universal developmental patterns of growth governing motor development.
8. Why is continual monitoring of physical growth important in the early years of life?
9. What is the function of the cardiovascular system and its relationship to the respiratory system?
10. Why is the gastrointestinal system important to physical growth?
11. Describe the relationship between myelinization and neurological development.
12. How is bone maturation related to growth?
13. How is physical growth measured?
14. Describe a "normal" newborn in the first days of life.
15. Devise your own theory of child development, and be sure to cite theorists described in this chapter that you borrowed from in creating your own theory.
16. According to MacDonald (1992), what does emotional warmth or affection provide for humans? What may result if a child does not experience such affection?
17. In what way is child development sequential and universal?
18. Explain the remarkable plasticity of the human brain.

19. What is the theory of critical sensitive periods of learning?

20. Briefly explain how family configuration and lifestyle as well as childcare influence a child's development.

21. Several factors influence bonding. Name three of these.

22. Several educational factors are believed to influence a child's growth. List five of these factors.

23. Why is it important to evaluate a child's development according to the child's culture rather than according to dominant culture?

4 | Human Development: Birth to Six

© Brian Price

Milestones of Development

Understanding the principles of human development is a prerequisite for interpreting the milestones that mark the developmental progression of infants and young children including those with, or at risk for, developmental disabilities. Maturation across developmental domains is typified by markers or **milestones** that serve to acknowledge the advancement of behavior. For practitioners working with young children with disabilities, this knowledge should be constantly at the ready—available for ongoing assessments of the headway children are making. In the absence of this knowledge, an educator's barometer of normalcy tends to drift. For example, early childhood special educators often admit that when they have an opportunity to observe typically developing children, they are reminded of the severity of their own students' delays. The point is not to highlight individual differences; misinterpreting development can lead to lowered expectations, oversight of potential problems,

inaccuracy in educational programming, and miscommunication with families and other professionals. Because drift is possible, even for well-trained professionals, early childhood professionals should continuously recalibrate by revisiting developmental milestones.

In this chapter, our descriptions in each of five areas of development—motor, cognitive, language, social and emotional, and self-help—are accompanied by little theory. The absence of theory is intentional but is not meant to diminish the importance of theory to the field of early childhood special education. Entire courses, indeed entire disciplines, have been devoted to these theories. This text's purpose, however, is to provide elementary knowledge sets used for making judgments about a child's performance in relation to typical developmental patterns and rates.

Motor Development

Motor development provides the physical basis for movement, posture, and balance, which are integral to acquiring concrete knowledge, producing speech, exploring the environment, carrying out daily self-help activities, and socializing with others. Normal physical development allows children to accomplish organized, purposeful, and efficient movement. In the past, movement development was explained almost solely on the basis of neurological maturation. Biomechanical theory, a systems model, has become prominent, particularly in relation to deviations in motor development (Holt, 2005). Reflecting a more ecological approach than past explanations had, biomechanical theory includes the influence of environment, the task at hand, psychological processes such as motivation and personality, and, finally, the interaction between musculoskeletal and neural maturation. Delayed or dysfunctional motor development can greatly influence when and how well children reach expected milestones in areas other than motor development. Conversely, the physical domain is influenced by overall health and developmental capacity. For example, chronic middle ear infections can disrupt vestibular system functions that control posture and balance. Delays in gross motor skills are characterized by excessive falling, clumsiness, and collisions with objects. Motor delays can also signal later developmental problems, such as learning disabilities, intellectual disabilities and attention deficit disorder (ADD). An attempt to identify early markers of autism spectrum disorder (ASD) has revealed that children with autism as well as Asperger syndrome possess many early (before age 2) delays in several motor development areas (Liu, 2012). By age 5, these motor delays have become more pervasive (Liu, 2012) and delays were found in all 26 motor areas tested in all 44 children observed. Consequently, it is important that early childhood professionals understand motor development, recognize deviations from norms, and know appropriate intervention services that may support a child's individual motor needs.

Gross Motor Development

A review of the principles of physical development provides a way to understand the progress of gross motor development. It has been noted that children's muscle control progresses from head to toe (**cephalo-caudal**), from large movements (**gross**

Motor Development

motor) to small movements (**fine motor**), and from the center of the body toward the extremities (**proximal-distal**). The first of these, head to toe, is most useful in determining which skills one would expect to emerge next based on the present level of maturity.

Head Control   Newborns have very little intentional body control, yet they do move their arms, legs, head, fingers, and toes reflexively. Because newborns are unable to independently support the weight of their heads, caregivers provide these babies substantial head support. Soon, neck muscles develop sufficient strength and tone for the baby to turn the head from side to side while in a **supine** (lying on the back) position and to hold it up in an upright or vertical position. This head control becomes stronger until infants eventually raise their heads off a surface from a supine position and turn them from side to side in a **prone** position. Infants are said to have gained good head control when, as they are tilted side to side and front to back, there is no head lag, and the posture of the head remains upright. A test for head control is the facilitated sit-up. A caregiver places a child supine and, taking the arms, pulls the child to a sitting position. If an infant is able to raise the head independently so that it stays parallel to the trunk, there is no head lag.

Shoulder Control   Although overlap exists in the development of neck and shoulder control, the latter cannot fully develop without first achieving complete head control. At approximately 2 to 3 months of age, infants begin to assist themselves in turning their heads from side to side by propping their chests on their forearms. As muscle control is gained, infants are able to prop themselves higher and for a longer time, eventually pushing up on fully extended arms and hands (proximodistal principle in effect). Prone propping is paralleled by supine use of the arms when infants begin to reach, first a few inches and then with fully extended arms. At this age, infants begin to play with mobiles hung over their beds and to reach for near objects while lying on their tummies. When infants have well-developed shoulder control, they are able to turn themselves from prone to supine and back the other way. Usually, the front-to-back roll emerges first because infants get an assist from their extended arms. However, by the fourth or fifth month, most infants are able to do both well because trunk control is also emerging.

© Denielle M. Miller

Trunk Control   Neonates placed in a sitting position droop from the waist to the head, exhibiting little resistance to gravity. At 2 months, infants can hold the head upright in a sitting position and, at 4 months, can hold the upper body upright but fall over when a caregiver releases support of the waist. By 6 months, most infants are able to sit independently, although they may not be able to catch themselves in a fall because protective extension reflexes are still immature. Strong sitters at 8 months independently get in and out of a sitting position, reach for objects on the floor without falling over, and stay upright when pushed gently in all directions. The last protective reaction to develop is extension to the rear, and even at 8 months, an infant is vulnerable to head injuries from falls backward.

Hip Control   When infants are independently able to get in and out of a sitting position, it is because some hip control has developed. At this time, infants in a prone position begin to crawl by coordinating the arms and legs to move across the floor or other surface. Later, weight bearing at the hips permits infants to resist gravity by raising their heads and lifting their trunks off the floor on their hands and knees (some infants go straight to hands and feet in a "bear crawl"). By coordinating movement of the extremities, infants of 9 to 10 months creep from this elevated position.

Lower Body Control   The final major gross motor stage is upright mobility. Once hip control is fully developed, infants are capable of balance and stability on extended legs. Initially, standing may be possible only when knee joints are hyperextended. By 10 to 12 months, however, most children can stand upright while holding onto a support. This evolves into cruising, or stepping sideways while holding onto furniture or some structure for support. Before long, competent cruisers can be expected to transfer short distances between furniture by taking short steps without holding on. Finally, children begin to take first a few, and then several, independent steps.

Refinement   Once children have learned to walk independently, the remainder of gross motor movement can be considered a refinement of the most critical skills of this domain. In fact, early childhood professionals tend to place relatively less emphasis on this domain (see Table 4–1) and more on cognitive and

Table 4–1   Refinement of Gross Motor Development

Age	Behavior
12 to 18 months	Creeps up and down stairs Runs Throws ball overhand
18 to 24 months	Kicks a ball Walks up stairs alone with both feet on each step
3 years	Rides a tricycle by pedaling with alternating feet Catches a large bounced ball Runs smoothly with changes in speed
4 years	Catches a thrown playground ball against body with arms Walks up and down stairs alternating feet and holding rail Jumps over a string held slightly off the floor
5 years	Skips with alternating feet Rides a bike with training wheels Hits a ball with a bat or stick

© Brian Price

language skills after children have begun to walk well. Refinement includes walking up and down stairs, running, standing on one leg, skipping, jumping, and developing recreation skills. While children could be quite functional in life without most of these skills, a delay in development of gross motor coordination could be an early signal of generalized developmental problems later in life.

While it is more important to know the normal patterns of development than the normal ages at which motor skills emerge, every service provider should have a basic knowledge of the motor "windows of achievement." These are age periods during which 98 percent of children achieve the motor milestones and are considered inclusive of normal variations that account for ethnic and cultural influences (WHO Multicentre, 2006):

- Sitting without support: 3.8 to 9.2 months
- Standing with assistance: 4.8 to 11.4 months
- Hand and knee crawling: 5.2 to 13.5 months
- Walking with assistance: 5.9 to 13.7 months
- Standing alone: 6.9 to 16.9 months
- Walking alone: 8.9 to 17.6 months

Fine Motor Skills

Like gross motor skills, fine motor development follows a predictable pattern. The most relevant principle is gross-to-fine motor skill maturation. For example, you would not expect children to be capable of grasping objects intentionally until they have gained shoulder control and are reaching with some accuracy. It can also be predicted that control of grasping progresses from the palm of the hand to the fingertips (proximo-distal).

Eye Contact and Facial Expression   In conformity with head-to-toe development, fine muscle control of the eyes is one of the first observable fine motor skills to begin developing. Within the first few days of life, neonates may be observed matching maternal eye movement, yet they have difficulty tracking—following moving objects with their eyes—and they lose contact once an object has been moved away from their midline. In just a few weeks, however, infants begin to track objects that are moved gradually from side to side, and eventually, they will track 180 degrees by moving their heads to prevent loss of eye contact. Both range and duration of eye contact are important to mobility, fine motor coordination, and language development.

© Randy Lee Williams

Reaching At birth, reaching and grasping are entirely reflexive. Intentional reaching from a supine position begins at about 2 months, after infants have gained some control at the shoulders. Infants initially reach toward objects with minimal coordination and may bat or swing at an object but do not grasp it. Instead, a predominant flexor pattern holds the hands in a fisted position. By 4 months, infants' reach has become more coordinated, and they unhesitatingly move the arm and hand in the direction of a desired object.

Grasping When reaching has become a refined movement, grasping becomes intentional, now permitting infants to acquire and hold objects. Still, the unintegrated grasp reflex does not permit infants to intentionally release objects. The most primitive grasp is referred to as the *palmar grasp* (see Figure 4–1), in which infants acquire an object by scooping it into the palm with all fingers extended. Obviously, this grasp prevents the manipulation of an object in any precise fashion, and play with the object is unsophisticated. Later, infants are able to pick up and hold an object by opposing the palm with the tips of all fingers. Still, there is no differentiation of finger use. A major milestone is reached when infants are able to grasp by opposing their thumbs with other fingers. This development, the *prehensile grasp*, is a feature unique to humans and other primates. First, the thumb opposes all of the fingers, then the second and third fingers, and finally a fine pincer grasp is achieved.

Handedness Handedness, or the tendency to be more skillful at using one hand or foot than the other, is a reflection of the dominance of one hemisphere of the brain

Figure 4–1 A. Palmar Grasp B. Pincer Grasp

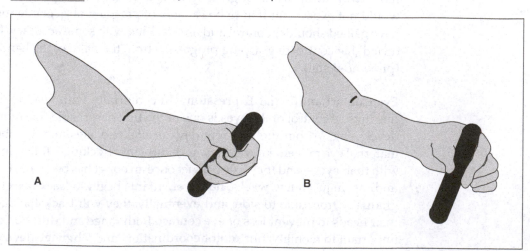

Table 4–2   Refinement of Fine Motor Development

Age	Behavior
12 to 18 months	Holds crayon from radial side of hand Turns pages of a cardboard book Places a peg in a pegboard Builds a tower with two blocks Places a round form in a formboard
18 to 24 months	Imitates vertical and circular stroke Completes puzzle with circle, square, triangle
2 years	Builds tower with several blocks (4–6) Turns door knobs or TV handles by twisting wrist Turns pages one at a time Holds a crayon with thumb and forefinger
3 years	Cuts with scissors on a line Holds pencil with adultlike tripod grasp (resting on third finger) Winds up toys
4 years	Completes puzzle of 3–5 pieces Moves paper and cuts out simple shapes (e.g., triangle) Draws a person with two body parts
5 years	Prints first name Completes 11–15 piece puzzle Copies lowercase letters Colors within lines

over the other. In infancy, most children do not show a preference but use both hands with equal coordination. Later, as children begin to perform more specialized hand movements, the majority show a preference for right-handedness. In spite of beliefs to the contrary, right-handers are not better coordinated than left-handers or children who are "inconsistent" left-handers (Gabbard & Hart, 1995).

Refinement of fine motor abilities is observed throughout the preschool years (see Table 4–2). The gradual refinement is facilitated by increased speed, strength, and coordination of small muscle groups. This ability is closely integrated with cognitive and perceptual development. Infants learn to pick up small objects and use their index finger to point to and probe objects. Toddlers begin to put simple puzzles together and to scribble with a crayon. Later, preschoolers learn to draw, to cut with scissors, and to form objects with clay.

Language Development

One of the most amazing human phenomena is the development of language. In just 3 years' time, infants progress from almost total reflexive responding to the development of adultlike speech. Even in the first few days, however, infants communicate; they send messages that caregivers understand and by their actions show that they also

perceive adult intentions. For most children, this **communication** later conforms to a set of rules that guide how ideas are formed into words and put together in sentences. These symbolic systems, known as **languages,** differ across cultures. Furthermore, language can be communicated in writing, orally through speech, and manually (e.g., American Sign Language). All of these systems have elements in common. Individuals who share a language conform to standardized rules that enable people to communicate quite efficiently. However, humans do not send and receive messages through language alone. Unconventional communication—body language, facial expressions, grunts, laughter, wincing, and so on—all send powerful messages that the listener "reads."

Just as musculoskeletal movement is reflexive at birth, so is the majority of neonatal communication. A newborn communicates basically in two ways—crying and not crying. Within two years, however, a child will have developed all of the basic constructs of human adult language. Several theories attempt to explain the nature of linguistic development. The various theories can be viewed as complementary, contradictory, or supplemental. In fact, our current understanding of language seems to borrow from the most prominent theories. Linguists generally agree on the following principles of language development.

- Humans are born with a certain capacity to acquire language.
- Children acquire language according to a universal pattern, which is observed across children of different languages, cultures, families, and disabilities.
- Children generally develop an understanding of the meanings of concepts before they learn to use the corresponding words. Moreover, children's **receptive language** (words they understand) is almost always more highly developed than children's **expressive language** (words they use).
- Social exchanges are a necessary context for language development.
- Children's language development is facilitated through modeling by adults, repeated practice of sounds and words, and differential reinforcement (i.e., attending to understandable language, not attending to incomprehensible language).

The remainder of this section describes, rather than explains, language development in children from birth to 6 years of age. Interactional theorists describe language as three interrelated components: form, content, and use. The *form* of language refers to its structure: phonology, syntax, and morphemes. Language *content* refers to a child's knowledge of the words and the interrelationship between words. Both receptive and expressive language are considered in language content. Finally, language *use,* or *pragmatics,* is the way in which children communicate in social contexts.

Language Form

Three aspects of language are generally considered when discussing language form. **Phonology** is the study of speech sounds. When considering the linguistic development of infants, the evolution of phonemes (speech sounds) follows a predictable pattern. The rules that govern structural patterns of language utterances and sentence grammar are referred to as **syntax.** Finally, **morphological development** refers to the evolution of word structure and word parts such as prefixes and suffixes.

Phonological Development   The sounds made by neonates are nonspecific crying, grunting, and gurgling. Without training or direction, caregivers are typically able to differentiate types of crying sounds to determine whether an infant is wet, tired, hungry, or otherwise uncomfortable. Infants begin to make vowel sounds within the first few months. Vowel sound production is referred to as **cooing.** Vowels are physically the easiest sounds to make because they require little motor control or use of the articulators (tongue, lips, palate, and teeth).

Infants begin to **babble** by about 4 months of age as they gain increased oral motor control. Babbling is a combination of consonant (C) and vowel (V) sounds (C–V and V–C) and progresses from simple to complex sound production. By the end of the first year, infants' first words begin to appear; many of these are monosyllabic combinations with a consonant and vowel (C–V, "ma" for example) or a vowel and consonant (V–C, "up" for example). Thereafter, consonant sound production progresses along a continuum of easy to hard, relative to oral motor complexity (see Table 4–3).

Children produce words that increase in understandability as initial sounds, ending sounds, and middle sounds of words are put together with precision. The transition to real words is remarkably rapid. Typically, only about 25 percent of infants' language is intelligible at 18 months. By 2 years, when toddlers begin to produce two-word utterances, it is approximately 65 percent intelligible. At 4 years of age, children have acquired most phonetic sounds and are producing almost totally intelligible sentences. When it comes to identifying deficiencies in development of language articulation, some research suggests that our expectations are too high and

Table 4–3   Consonant Development

Age	Emergence	75% Mastery
8 months	d, t, k, m, h	
1 year	g, n, b	
1.6 years	w, s	
2 years	p, s, k, z	
2.5 years	f, ts j, l, r, pw, bw	
3 years	fw, kw, pl, -nts, -nd, -ps, -ts	h, zh, y, w, ng, m, n, p, k, t, b, g, d
3.6 years	dz, sp, st, sn, sl	f
4 years	tw, sk, sm, bl, kl, gl, br, tr, dr, kr, gr	l, sh, ch
5 years	v, fr, sr, pr, fl	j, s, z, r
6 years	skw	v
7 years	spl	
8 years	skr	th as in this
8.5 years		th as in thing

our treatment too weak (Goorhuis-Brouwer & Knijff, 2003). In their study, a large majority of children who had been referred (97 percent of whom were eventually treated) for speech therapy were within normal range in all areas of language development, and after a year of treatment, more than half were still receiving treatment, suggesting that the treatment could not influence the problems to a large extent. The study suggests we should accept a broader range of normal variation in phonetic development and assume a wait-and-see approach in more instances.

Syntax Without direct instruction, children acquire the rules of spoken syntax with surprising accuracy. Ironically, it is not until after children speak that the rules of grammar are specifically taught. Initially, infants rely primarily on one-word utterances, and toward the end of their second year, they rely on successive single-word utterances. Infants do not begin to put words together in phrases until late in their second year. However, this linguistic development represents a major accomplishment in a child's communicative power. Two-word utterances are significant because these telegraphic phrases possess more meaning than either word uttered in isolation. That is, two-word phrases convey the meanings of word A and word B plus the meaning of each word's relationship to the other. Examples of simple two-word phrases used include noun–verb: "baby eat"; verb–noun: "give ball"; and noun–noun: "Daddy ball."

Sentence structure becomes complex in several ways in a child's third year. At about 27 months, children begin to ask questions, although initially only by intonation. Children may ask some "wh-questions" at this time but initially with the verb and subject transposed (e.g., "Where car is going?"). The emergence of wh-questions corresponds to the conceptual knowledge and receptive understanding of these types of questions. "Who," "what," and "where," which have more concrete referents, precede "when," "how," and "why." Queries that require transposition of verbs occur when children have begun to use auxiliary verbs and copulas, or linking words (e.g., "Is the bike outside?"). Tag questions are also complex interrogative forms added on after other question forms have appeared (e.g., "We are having ice cream, aren't we?").

Negative sentences also follow a pattern of increasing complexity as children gradually approximate accurate syntactic rules. To the consternation of adults, negative statements are among the highest frequency utterances made by toddlers. Children first make negative comments by placing a negative marker at the beginning of a sentence. This is followed by placing the negative marker inside the sentence next to the relevant verb but without the use of copulas and auxiliary verbs. Finally, although not until about age 4, children begin to accurately use inflections and negative markers together.

Stage I	No want milk.
Stage II	Kitty no eat candy.
Stage III	I can't fix the bike.

Complex sentences contain at least one independent clause and at least one subordinate or dependent clause. Sentences with more than one independent clause are referred to as **compound sentences.** Both advanced types of sentences combine two or more ideas in a single sentence through the use of conjunctions, relative pronouns, or other linguistic linkages. *And* is the first conjunction to appear and is observed in children as young as 25 months of age, although initially it joins nouns (e.g., "me and Mommy") rather than clauses. **Relative clauses** that modify subjects (e.g., "I like the doll that has the green hair") appear later. By 3 or 4, many children are using compound and complex sentences by adding elements to the beginning or end of kernel sentences. Still later (4 to 13 years of age), children add clauses internally to sentences in a process referred to as **embedding** (e.g., "I saw the girl who is in my class at the park").

Morphological Development

A **morpheme** is defined as the smallest part of a word that possesses meaning. Morphemes that can stand alone with meaning are referred to as *free morphemes*, and those that cannot stand alone are referred to as **bound morphemes.** While a language frequently adds new free morphemes, it rarely adds new bound morphemes. Free morphemes appear first in infants' language as their first words (e.g., bottle, Mommy, ball, cup). Not until much later (beginning at about 24 months) do bound morphemes (inflections) begin to appear (e.g., -ed, -ing, pre-). The latter, along with auxiliary verbs (e.g., can, will), are referred to as *morphological inflections* and emerge according to a predictable pattern that has been consistently documented across time and research studies (Kwon, 2006). Early morphological inflections, appear in the following order: -ing, plurals, prepositions (in/on), and irregular verbs (went, came); possessives, "to be," articles (a, an), and -ed. Eventually, children begin to use the most complex morphological inflections (jumps, does, has), auxiliary words (can, will), and copulas ("It's big"). Knowing this progression can help educators understand morphological mistakes, those that naturally occur because children have not reached higher levels of development, and those that are actual errors because they occur beyond the phase at which the children should have learned to use certain inflections properly. Developmental errors might be met with acceptance and correct modeling to restate the child's phrase, while deviation errors might suggest modeling and asking a child to restate the phrase correctly, or providing purposeful instruction.

An index of the sophistication of children's language is based on the frequency of morphemes in their utterances. **Mean length utterance (MLU)** is calculated by dividing the number of morphemes in an utterance by the number of utterances (at least 50). An MLU of 1.0 is observed when infants are at the one-word-phrase stage. By the time children have MLUs of 3.0 or higher, they are usually incorporating at least some morphological inflections into their phrases. When a child's MLU is higher than 4.0, the score is no longer a valid index of language development.

Morphological development appears to be particularly difficult for children with language impairments. Even children with language delays, however, acquire morphemes in a normal pattern. Although many **late talker** children catch up in later childhood, they often retain minor deficits in morpheme development, particularly those with verb use (Weismer, 2007). Late talkers are those who have limited vocabulary and expressive language but who have relatively normal receptive language and tend to recover expressively by kindergarten (Roos & Weismer, 2008). Distinguishing between children who have actual delays and those who may be late talkers is difficult. In fact, even though late talkers may appear to recover, their overall language proficiency has been found to be significantly lower than typically developing children (Weismer, 2007). Consequently, early language intervention is warranted for all children who have language delays.

Language Content

Content develops along two parameters: receptive and expressive language. The former typically progresses at a more rapid rate but is not necessarily a prerequisite for expressive development. In other words, children sometimes use words in their speech before they understand their meanings. The best example of this rate difference is the word spurt in comprehension that takes place between 15 and 16 months, which precedes an analogous production word spurt 3 to 4 months later. This happens because the cognitive requirements for comprehension are fewer than those needed for production (Casasol & Cohen, 2000).

Receptive Language   Neonates are capable of learning speech in their first days of life. Researchers have long known that the left hemisphere of the brain is more involved in language development than the right. Using this knowledge, Sato and colleagues (2011) measured left-brain activity in neonates, who were just a few days old, when exposed to their native language, nonsense language, and a foreign language. These newborns' metabolic activity in the left side of the brain was significantly higher when they heard their own language spoken naturally than when they listened to the nonsense language or foreign language. Results of this study demonstrated that, even in the first days of life, infants learn to discriminate sounds and are building the neural infrastructure for communication. In fact, infants worldwide have the ability to "hear," if not produce, most, if not all, of the phonetic sounds of all native languages of the world (Kuhl et al., 2006). By adulthood, the ability to hear and produce non-native phonemes is very difficult. Kuhl and colleagues suggest that non-native language perception and articulation skills decline, largely between 6 and 12 months of age, because of the development of a neural commitment to the sounds of an infant's native language. This neural commitment, beginning at around 7 months, appears to be a critical stage in language development that allows infants to progress to more complex language patterns such as words. Those infants who are still able to make undeterred non-native discriminations after 7 months of age tend to develop language at a slower pace, indicating slower brain maturation. Perhaps most importantly, Kuhl, Tsao, and Liu (2003) found that the optimal, if not necessary, vector for efficient phonetic learning is social context, especially when mothers exaggerate speech sounds in talking to their infants.

Within the first few months, a mother might notice that her child will become quiet or pause at the sound of her voice but not at a stranger's voice. Later, when infants develop some head control, they turn their heads toward sounds by sound localization. Infants also begin to identify familiar words as distinct from other words in a sentence by about 7.5 months (Newman, Ratner, Jusczyk, Jusczyk, & Dow, 2006). This skill, known as *segmentation*, is linked to later measures of language competency. It is not until the end of children's first year that they begin to acknowledge specific words. This is evident when children respond differentially to their names. Not surprisingly, one of the first words infants recognize is the word *no*.

By the end of their first year, infants recognize a few high-frequency words and can demonstrate this skill by looking directly at the named objects. One-year-olds are also learning to follow simple commands such as "wave bye-bye" or "give me a kiss." However, these commands are often accompanied by gestures or signals.

The aforementioned gap between comprehension and production is exaggerated from 15 months of age until about the 3rd year of development when the gap narrows again, this time to remain. Still, the first six months of a child's second year represent a turning point in infants' receptive language as they learn to follow simple novel commands that do not have gestures, such as "put the toy on the table" or "give mommy a drink." By 13 months of age, infants begin to understand grammatical morphemes. At 16 months, infants point to body parts on request. Children's understanding of speech is nearly perfect by the end of their second year: They can discriminate accurate and inaccurate phonemes, morphemes, and syntax.

Until the second year, infants' word understanding is referent specific. During their second year, infants begin to categorize concepts by making gradually more sophisticated generalizations. For example, they learn that cats and dogs belong to a category of animals. Later, they learn that even though horses have some of the same characteristics as dogs, they do not belong to the same class. Still, 2-year-olds are bound by literal interpretation of adult language and are unable to solve the figurative meaning behind clichés, metaphors, or analogies. By age 3, young children can both interpret and use figurative speech. A child might be overheard saying about a dog, "Rover is a pig." Anaphoric terms, such as *this, that, it,* and *there,* are concepts children find difficult to master. By 3, though, children are typically able to solve such directions as "put the spoon there." Four-year-olds can understand passive sentences (e.g., "The swing was used by children at the park"), but they use them infrequently in conversation. A 6-year-old is quite good at solving subtle messages in language, such as sarcasm and humor that rely on irony, an ability that occurs especially quickly in children who are gifted (Holt & Willard-Holt, 2009). Because children's language is more often still literal, they might understand transparent or familiar metaphors or idioms, such as "hold your tongue," but even at age 12, children have difficulty decoding opaque idioms such as "smell the roses" (Cain, Towse, & Knight, 2009).

Expressive Language Documenting the development of expressive language is easier than doing the same for receptive language because one does not have to make inferences about the invisible cognitive processes that underlie this form of communication. Although children represent meanings much earlier, their first real words do not generally appear much before their first birthdays. However, intentional pointing emerges earlier, near the end of the first year. It has been found that emergence of pointing and other gestures are related to speech expression and comprehension in later childhood (Capirci & Volterra, 2008). They could be related to an emerging understanding of the relationship between motor development and language development (Iverson, 2010). That is, the extent to which children are able to navigate their environments provides a variety of experiences, which in turn provide content about which to communicate. Children whose mobility is restricted must have the world brought to them, a process that is less efficient and a barrier to language development.

Universally, the first words that infants use represent salient features of their immediate environments. Actions and objects dominate early words, although nouns appear to be more easily learned and more frequently used than verbs (Casasola & Cohen, 2000). This makes sense because objects have a concrete referent whereas actions are not permanent, and their dimensions change with each event. For example, "jumping" can be labeled only when someone jumps, and then the action is gone. Additionally, jumping can be on one foot or two feet, executed by mom or dad, be a few inches or over a high jump, and so on. Words that represent objects that move or are acted on in a variety of different ways (e.g., baby doll) are more frequently used than objects that do not move (e.g., wall).

At 18 months, when infants typically possess a 50-word vocabulary of mostly nominals, their language content begins to change significantly. At this juncture in development, children begin naming many different objects that are less salient and less important. Some have referred to this transition as a *vocabulary spurt,* and it corresponds with a sudden sharp increase in children labeling everything they see. This milestone also seems to be the threshold for combining words into successive single-word and two-word utterances. Finally, at about this stage, a sharp rise in the use of both verbs and adjectives has been observed. Recently, the idea of a singular second-year naming spurt phenomenon has been replaced with a more complete understanding of vocabulary development, which supports a more linear acquisition of words with as many as 17 to 20 "spurts" along the way (Dandurand & Schultz, 2011).

At 2 years, toddlers have acquired a vocabulary of about 300 words. With words paired in telegraphlike sentences, children use only key words (e.g., "baby up" stands in for "the baby is standing up"). A rapid growth in novel **semantic relationships** takes place in children's second year. For example, a child moves from phrases like "Turn da light" at 21 months to "A time to go night-night and push the light" in just four months. Perhaps because of their limited repertoire of words, toddlers commonly engage in **overextension** of words. For example, children might mistakenly refer to all men as "Daddy" because men have physical characteristics similar to their fathers. At the same time, toddlers might alternately look at Dad and his friend Bob when they hear their names, reflecting a lag between language production and cognitive understanding. **Underextension** occurs when categories are defined too narrowly. For example, very young children might use the word *chair* to refer to their high chairs and the dining room chairs but do not include the rocking chair or kitchen stool in this category. It is also common for children to use known words idiosyncratically to fill in for concepts for which they have no words.

Children's expressive language is limited mostly to concrete ideas prior to age 3; children use words for things that they can perceive by seeing, hearing, and touching. These little ones can typically supply a color of an object in answer to the question, "What color is this?" by age 2, although not necessarily accurately. More complex or abstract concepts typically do not appear until around a child's third birthday. For example, *time* and *space* are relative terms, and words used to reflect these concepts begin to appear at about age 4 when concepts such as before, after, next to, in front of, first, and last are observed.

Although a child's vocabulary development is influenced, to some unknown but significant degree, by experiences, there is a pattern of acquisition of words that is fairly predictable. A child typically uses 300 words by 2 years, 1,000 by 3 years,

1,500 by 4 years, more than 2,000 by 5 years, and nearly 3,000 words by age 6. In contrast, a child's receptive vocabulary is approximately 20,000 to 24,000 words by age 6.

It is well known that better acquisition of vocabulary and phonological awareness are associated with children's ability to learn to read. Now, it is becoming apparent that early linguistic skills, including phonologic awareness, size of vocabulary, and color-naming, are also predictive of mathematical acquisition (Sevcik, Romski, & Morris, 2012). However, it does not necessarily follow that teaching colors in early childhood will lead to improved mathematical ability. Knowing that all these prerequisite linguistic skills are related to the integrity of early social play and communicative exchanges between children and adults should give early educators a sense of purpose in providing parents the tools they need to enrich interactions with their children.

Language Use

The final category of language function, language use, is more difficult to define, assess, and plan instruction for than the other categories. This aspect of language refers to the effectiveness of the speaker in establishing and maintaining mutually rewarding interactions with others. Some children have very well developed language form and content but are simply unable to engage others in conversations. Even as adults, some people, for example, can talk and talk but are not desirable conversation partners because they are insensitive to the subtle rules of communication that make interactions mutually rewarding.

Language use comprises three types of behavior. **Speech acts** are the speakers' intentions or purposes for communicating. People communicate to give information, ask questions, make requests, tell a story or entertain, state protests, and show surprise, among other things. When communicating with others, people also make judgments about the listener that allow modifications to the content and style of the communication. These **presuppositions** include, but are not limited to, assessments of social status, educational or developmental level, and the intimacy of relationships. For example, a speaker estimates the level of interest that the listener might have in a particular topic as well as the degree of background knowledge that the listener holds. If these judgments are inaccurate, a speaker could talk over someone's head or, conversely, offend someone by appearing condescending. Finally, conversations have subtle rules, which may vary from culture to culture, that allow humans to converse in a reciprocal manner. **Conversational postulates,** as these rules are called, include skills in initiating conversations, balanced turn taking, questioning, repairing a breakdown in conversation, maintaining interactions, and closing a conversation.

The earliest appearance of language use is in the form of conversational postulates. For example, neonates have been observed engaging in reciprocal turn taking with caregivers in the first days of life. Eye blinking and mouth and tongue movements can become routinized back-and-forth actions between a child and caregiver. However, it will be several more years before these skills become refined. A child of 9 months plays many reciprocal games, demonstrating conversation-like turn taking (e.g., peek-a-boo). This turn taking skill is used primitively in dialogues when a child is 18 to 24 months of age.

During the period when children first begin to use intentional communication, many of their language intentions are nonverbal. For example, a child may point to a favorite doll with several intentions. The child might be making a request to acquire the toy, telling mom that the doll is nice, protesting the removal of the doll, or asking if the doll is hungry. In context, a parent can interpret these limited regulatory requests. Even at this age, these same 1-year-old speakers have been observed altering their communication for their listeners.

By the latter half of their second year, children begin to use language for a variety of new functions that integrate regulatory purposes with interactional skills. At 2 years of age, children have learned that a single utterance can serve more than one function. Because communication has now taken on a social purpose, toddlers need to maintain conversational topics. However, many conversations break down as children appear to flit in and out of them more often than they stay on topic. Limited skills, such as repeating or imitating words or parts of words used in the previous sentence, are used to maintain conversations. Children might fix a topic breakdown by attempting to articulate with increased clarity. By contrast, 4-year-olds are capable of carrying on a conversation for several minutes, discussing the same or related topics. Skills used to fix topic breakdowns at this age include rephrasing sentences, shortening utterances, and expanding sentences.

Three- and 4-year-old children will adapt their communication based on their perceived assessment of the listener's prior knowledge. They may give more or less information based on the extent of previous experiences their listeners are judged to possess. Furthermore, these preschoolers can be observed altering the length of sentences, affect (e.g., facial expression, voice intonation, body language), and language content when interacting with younger children or infants. Although 3-year-olds are able to recall specific details from a story (e.g., "what did you plant in the garden?"), by the time a child is five they are able to offer a narrative when asked an open-ended question such as "What did you do when you were at the garden?" (Hershkowitz, Lamb, Orbach, Katz, & Horowitz, 2012).

Factors Affecting Language Development

Multiple factors can affect the rate and pathology of linguistic acquisition. For example, many developmental disabilities can directly affect language form. Clefts of the lip and palate and oral-structural anomalies associated with Down syndrome influence phonological production. Cerebral palsy may result in reduced respiratory capacity that hampers speech production as well. Other developmental disabilities affect children's rate of learning and slow the acquisition of content and language use. Autism, for example, is linked with aberrations in all areas of language development.

Evidence has established that language delays are highly heritable. For example, genetic mutations of the FOXP2 gene are associated with expressive language processing (Vernes & Fisher, 2011). Stein and colleagues (2011) found that 45 percent of infants with a family history of language impairments had a significant language delay themselves at the same developmental ages.

Although patterns of language development are universal (see Table 4–4), some cultural and sociocultural factors influence the rate of acquisition of language. For example, Spratt and colleagues (2012) found that children who have been neglected

Table 4–4   Milestones of Language Development

Age	Behavior
Birth	Responds to noises (activity stops) Cries frequently Uses vowellike sounds "e" and "a"
1 month	Vocalizes Responds to voices Uses special cry for hunger
4 months	Imitates simple gestures Repeats syllables ("da-da-da") Uses vowel sounds "o" and "u"
8–11 months	Produces consonant sounds in babbling Combines two syllables in vocal babbling ("ba-da") Shows understanding of some words Waves bye-bye Plays peek-a-boo and pat-a-cake
12 months	Says 5–10 words Points to familiar objects when named Expresses wants
18 months	Points to 2–3 pictures named Names familiar objects on request Has intelligible speech 25 percent of time Uses own name in conversation
24 months	Uses plurals Uses two-word phrases Responds to choices Uses utterances that have communicative intents Has intelligible speech 65 percent of time
3 years	Can carry on a conversation Uses four-word sentences Uses present tense and past tense (-ed) verbs Has intelligible speech 80 percent of time
4 years	Says "excuse me" to interrupt conversation Will retell a story read by someone else Carries out instructions with prepositions Participates in group songs Defines words Can tell what simple things are made of
5 years	Knows own birthday, phone number, and parents' names Uses five-word sentences Describes events in the past and future in a logical sequence Answers questions related to spoken content or a spoken story Begins to understand abstract concepts

had cognitive, language, and behavioral delays. Moreover, these researchers found that language abilities in the absence of aggressive-behavior problems are predictive of high IQ scores. Similarly, chaotic family households, specifically those that are disorganized and unstable, predict language delays in early childhood (Vernon-Feagans, Garrett-Peters, Willoughby, & Mills-Koonce, 2011). There has been an irreplaceable loss of oral traditions in American Indian (Markstrom, Whitesell, & Galliher, 2011), African American (Gardner-Neblett, Pungello, & Iruka, 2011), and recent immigrant families; their story telling practices are devalued by the Anglo American school system and obstructed by urban life. The loss of nurturance and social exchange that happens through transmission of family lore is also a loss of critical language stimulation.

Idiosyncrasies in parenting also influence language development. A specialized manner of interaction between mothers and infants is referred to as **motherese**. Motherese facilitates language development through the use of phrases that extend children's expressions (e.g., when a child says, "up" a parent might say "want up"), shortened sentence length and simplified vocabulary, repetitions or rewording, and talking about events within a child's world. Although gender differences do exist in communication with infants, fathers also engage in motherese and alter communication by repeating words, slowing speech rate, reducing proximity to child, animation of gestures and other movements, and heightened enthusiasm (Rutherford & Przednowek, 2011). Untrained though most parents are in effective language communication with very young children, motherese seems to develop naturally by caring adults and is critical to language development. There are many circumstances that interrupt the natural language instruction that takes place during parent–infant interactions. For example, some women who suffer postpartum depression may be insensitive to their infant's communication, and in failing to respond reliably through motherese contribute to delays in language development.

Not surprisingly, qualitative language differences between the way mothers and fathers relate to their infants exist (Kornhaber & Marcos, 2000). Fathers' language tends to be more regulating and contains more action directives aimed at task completion. Mothers, on the other hand, are disposed to be more expressive and play oriented. In turn, infants' language tends to reflect the linguistic content and use of language of the parent to whom they are responding.

Research is increasingly clear that a child's intellectual and social destiny is largely determined prior to entering school. In fact, for children who live in poverty, it may be impossible for educators to undo the effects of early childhood experiences with their parents. Hart and Risley (1995) found that children of university faculty parents far outpaced their same-age peers from poor families in terms of their level of language development. The implication of these findings is that, while all parents have the opportunity to provide rich intellectual experiences required for healthy cognitive development, the failure to do so may lead to deficiencies that present formidable rehabilitation challenges once children reach school age.

For example, pronounced differences in the amount and quality of interactions between parents and their children were documented in monthly observations over a three-year period. Across three income groups, it was found that the more educated the mother, the more she spoke to her children. Welfare, working-class, and professional parents addressed their children an average of 600, 1,200, and 2,000 words per hour, respectively. As a consequence, Hart and Risley estimated that by the time these children reached age 3, the welfare children would have heard 10,000,000 words, working-class children would have heard 20,000,000 words, and professional children would have heard 30,000,000 words.

In addition to the differences in number of words heard, parents of the different groups studied differed in what they talked about to their children. For example, welfare parents made positive comments to their children an average of 6 times per hour, as compared to 15 times per hour for working-class parents and 30 times per hour for professional parents.

These linguistic differences led to significant differences in intellectual accomplishments when children were followed up in the third grade. While performance differences based on socioeconomic status (SES) tended to diminish across time, differences in parental behavior remained a strong predictor of their children's cognitive success.

Hart and Risley (1995) predicted that it would take 40 hours of supplemental care every week from birth on to compensate for the observed differences in parental behavior. While this option is unrealistic, there is clearly a need for better and more parent training, mentorship programs, parental aides, and access to quality childcare.

Children with disabilities who have language delays may require specially structured opportunities to facilitate language development. For example, these children benefit from opportunities to engage in structured play with children whose language is developing normally. These peer models provide their friends more things to talk about, correct models of language structure, and appropriate ways for using language in a social situation (Justice, Petscher, Schatschneider, & Mashburn, 2011). Justice and colleagues (2011) found that the language competencies of peers in preschool classrooms were significantly related to the language development of children with disabilities. In fact, those who enjoyed the greatest benefits of relationships with language-competent peers were children with very low language skills. These findings support the inclusion of children with significant language and cognitive delays in typical preschool classroom where language "instruction" is part of the culture.

Cognitive Development

The process by which human beings learn has been under inquiry and discovery for hundreds of years. The acquisition of knowledge, also known as **cognition,** is a complex phenomenon in which infants, children, and adults are constantly learning about their world. This development allows human beings to learn to reason (both concretely and abstractly), to think logically, and to organize information about their environment in a way that will bring order to their world. Cognitive development is closely tied to the other developmental domains. Failure to follow the normal developmental pathway can result in difficulties in social and emotional development and block the development of communication skills.

The basis of cognitive development is linked to neurological growth and maturation. An explosion of research on the biology of the brain over the past decade has revolutionized the way fetal and infant cognition is viewed (Purpura, 2000). For example, it is now held that even prior to birth, the human fetus is capable of behavioral learning: At between the 36th and 38th weeks of gestation, an infant's movement and heart rate respond to the sound of its mother's voice.

Early experiences are key to neurological development, as the brain goes through a process of "pruning" unnecessary neurons and neural connections based on those experiences (Joseph, 2000). As the brain sheds these neurons, unique and environmentally specific neural pathways create individual cognition. Gradually, a child's perception, selective attention, learning, memory, language, personality, and cognition are sculpted. At the same time, the brain is capable of plasticity and can actually "sprout" and alter neural pathways to adjust to auditory and visual experiences. Repeated exposure to specific stimuli eventually molds the brain to selectively respond to those stimuli, and those pathways that might have responded to less frequently encountered stimuli drop out and die.

The study of cognitive development has resulted in the evolution of many theories about learning and the conceptual frameworks that correlate with those theories. Controversies ensuing over incompatible theories, as well as questions left unanswered, both frustrate and fascinate students. Most theories are based on observations of behaviors that can be related to age, maturity, and environment. Explanations typically hypothesize a link between observed behaviors and unobservable processes. For example, if an infant loses interest in a toy that has dropped off the high chair (the observed behavior: looks away or plays with something new), one can hypothesize that the child has not yet learned that objects still exist when out of the observer's sight (the process–object permanence). All models of cognitive development deal with how humans gather information, process it in both short- and long-term memory, and relate it back in a relevant fashion to be used in determining and executing action.

Theories of Cognition

Jean Piaget is the most well known theorist associated with the **cognitive-developmental approach.** He was originally trained as a biologist and applied many biological principles and methods to the study of human development. Many of the terms he introduced to psychology were drawn directly from biology. Piaget based his earliest theories on careful observation of his own three children. His theory is appreciated because of the ease in adapting constructs of the model to the descriptive observations of infants and their learning processes.

Piaget's model identified four distinct stages of cognitive development that he referred to as *sensorimotor, preoperational, concrete operational,* and *formal operational.* Each stage is characterized by the emergence of new abilities and the reorganization of a child's thinking about the world. Piaget held that the developmental sequence for cognitive skills is largely fixed.

© Estee Aiken

The **sensorimotor stage** of development (birth to age 2) integrates gross and fine motor development with the senses of sight and hearing. This stage consists of simple learning governed by sensations. Primitive reflex activity progresses to repetitive activity and, later, to imitation. In the reflexive stage, repetitive action of the reflexes allows infants to eventually draw associations between their activity and a response. As an example, sucking (initially reflexive) on a nipple produces a milk flow and consequently leads to a feeling of fullness. Later, infants understand (have gained knowledge about) the relationship between the act of sucking and the outcome. Such experiences are used by the developing intellect as a foundation for advancing along a progressive course to the next stage.

This stage is the beginning of voluntary behavior. Deliberate activity begins when an infant learns that certain behaviors can elicit specific responses. Accommodation begins when an infant incorporates and adapts actions with the recognition that certain activities produce a specific response. An infant may begin to cry on hearing the voice of its mother, having learned from previous experience that the general response to crying is the mother picking up and cuddling the infant. This is the beginning of the recognition of sequence and is an early experience with cause and effect.

It is later that both the quality and quantity of activity can be identified. Activities such as grasping progress to shaking (as with a rattle), which produces both movement and noise. Infants learn during this progression that degrees of shaking produce different qualities of sound. Also during this time period, infants learn separateness from other objects in their environment and realize that their environment can be controlled by their own behavior. During this stage, infants demonstrate imitation, object permanence, and attachment, all of which are associated with memory.

Imitation—the repetition of a sound or activity, or both, produced by another individual—implies there has been storage of information in an infant's brain. Studies have consistently shown that infants have the capacity for imitation at birth (Soussignan, Courtial, Canet, Danon-Apter, & Nadel, 2011); observations of even very young infants showed they imitate the facial expressions of caregivers. Moreover, the more opportunities newborns have to imitate, the more accurate they become at matching, which indicates that this presumed innate ability is enhanced by environmental experiences. Careful research on deferred imitation calls into question several of Piaget's assumptions (Jones & Herbert, 2006). First, deferred imitation appears to be contrary to Piaget's assertion that until 18 to 24 months of age infants are cognitively unable to selectively store information and produce an action or word without practice up to 24 hours later; Piaget appears to have drastically underestimated infants' ability. In fact, as early as 6 weeks of age, infants are known to exercise deferred imitation of facial expressions and may perform this cognitive feat in relation to demonstrations with an object by 6 to 9 months of age. Moreover, development of cognitive retention abilities in terms of time span and encoding speed seems to be more of a continuously emerging skill than one of "stage development" as posited by Piaget. Roughly, parents can expect their 6-month-old infant to retain information for up to 24 hours when information is repeated at least six times; by 9 months the number of repetitions needed is only three, and by 12 months, with the same number of repetitions, an infant can be expected to retain the information for up to a week (Jones & Herbert, 2006). It is clear that biology interacts with opportunities to learn in the development of short- and long-term memory.

Object permanence can be described as the demonstration of knowledge that an object exists even though it can no longer be seen. Infants between 4 and 8 months will search for an object if it is at least partially exposed. Infants between 8 months and 1 year of age will seek out an object even if they cannot visualize it at all. For example, when a rattle is placed under a blanket, an 8- to 12-month-old infant recognizes that the rattle still exists and will actively attempt to remove the blanket and expose it. This implies that short-term memory is functioning and that children retain the knowledge of where the rattle is even without seeing it.

Attachment is also a strong indicator of memory in infants. Fear of strangers appears to develop between 6 and 8 months of age and involves recognition memory (Huberty, 2012). This implies that infants draw from an experience base that recognizes the comfort in familiarity and conversely, a lack of trust in the unfamiliar. Whether this is based on sight, smell, or sound remains unclear, but it is obvious that long-term memory is being demonstrated

The last stage of Piaget's sensorimotor development precedes transition to the next level of learning. This stage occurs between 18 months and 2 years of age. Increased gross motor skills and past experience with achievements in behaviors increase an infant's ability to interact with the environment. An increased understanding of object permanence accompanies the initiation of intellectual reasoning. Infants can recognize that an object has singular properties that are separate from the individual possessing the object. For example, they understand that a ball can roll, even if it has not pushed by a person in possession of the ball. Infants at this stage begin to actively engage in manipulating their environment by attempting to remove barriers that keep them from reaching a goal. Toward the end of this period, expressive language skills that increase the ability of young children to successfully interact with their environment are emerging.

Piaget's **preoperational stage** in cognitive development (2–7 years) is characterized by rapid intellectual development. During this period, children view the world only in direct relationship to themselves. They seem to be unable to view a situation from a perspective other than their own, and their thinking processes are generally concrete. They are increasingly able to use language to express ideas and use toys symbolically to replace objects in play (e.g., using a broom as a horse). Finally, children in the preoperational stage begin to understand the relationships between size, time, and weight, and their thought processes are intuitive, or based on just knowing without reasoning.

Although the final stages of Piaget's theory extend beyond early childhood, they are introduced here to show the longitudinal nature of his observations. **Concrete operations** (7–11 years) is the stage of logic. During this period, children can classify, sort, and organize facts about their world to use in problem-solving. They continue to solve problems concretely, based on perception, because most have not yet developed abstract thinking. In looking at the development of memory in children at this stage, the processes of selective attention, strategies used for retention, and the duration of memory must be explored. There is no doubt that age makes a difference in the abilities of children to both attend to learning and remember what has been learned before. During this stage, children also develop the ability to build on past memories and use their current environment for new learning.

Formal operations (11 years to adulthood) is the stage of adaptability, flexibility, and abstraction. During this stage, adolescents can make hypotheses and use them to think in theoretical and philosophical terms. Individuals are aware of the contradictions in life, can analyze them practically, and can act on their conclusions.

Although long-term memory in children varies, use of selective attention processes and strategies improves with age. For example, increasing evidence suggests that an infant's visual habituation, or the ability to focus without distraction, is a useful predictor of cognitive abilities in children (Teubert, Vierhaus, & Lohaus, 2011). Yet, there is little comparison between the ability of children and adults to process information and recall the same information over time, as this ability becomes increasingly more efficient as individuals gather experiences and learn to learn.

Neural maturation is necessary for the development of individual awareness about memory and the relationship of meaning to performance. For example, **metamemory**—which is one's understanding of the strength and limitations of one's own memory—does not begin to appear until about the third grade (Lipko, Dunlosky, Lipowski, & Merriman, 2011). It is not until young adulthood that individuals reach their peak in terms of the capacity to remember and ability to master selective memory, necessary for remembering information that is highly valuable (Castel, Humphreys, Lee, Galván, Bolata, & McCabe, 2011). Yet, by the age of three, preschoolers are beginning to use **metacognitive** (thinking about thinking) strategies; this skill improves when children are given the opportunity to receive instruction related to reflecting about their own thinking (Lai, 2011). For example, children are often asked about the decisions they make during play which result in conflict: "How would you feel if Sally grabbed your toy while you were playing with it?" "What do you think you could do differently next time Sally has a toy you want to play with?" Through this process, children learn how to use available resources to succeed in achieving objectives, which in turn allows them to become more adaptive to their environment (see Table 4-5).

As children age, their cognitive capabilities are typically referred to as *intelligence*. Although many myths surround the construct, intelligence is, in general, the collective ability of children to reason, solve problems, and commit information to memory. The most misleading assumption about intelligence is that it is fixed at birth. In fact, several factors can greatly influence a child's ability. Research indicates a steady rise in the IQ performance from generation to generation. This rise has been attributed to such factors as better nutrition, more schooling, better-educated parents, and more complex environments including "smart" toys and computers. Dweck (2007) has also contributed significant research indicating that mindset contributes to IQ growth. Brinch and Galloway (2012) studied Norwegian children's IQ score trends over five decades and showed that not only is IQ malleable, but early intervention is closely linked to gains in IQ. While generational changes in IQ have significant implications for society, the changes themselves are unrelated to a biological change in human potential. Rather, it is clear that environmental manipulation can greatly enhance cognitive growth.

| Table 4–5 | Milestones of Cognitive Development |

Age	Behavior
1 month	Responds to voices Inspects surroundings
4 months	Shows anticipatory excitement Repeats new behaviors Plays with hands, feet
4–8 months	Repeats new behaviors Finds partially hidden object Indicates continuation of play by repeating movement Touches adult to restart activity Reaches for second object Anticipates trajectory of object Imitates familiar action Finds hidden object Recognizes names of family members
8–12 months	Imitates new action Responds to simple request with gestures (e.g., "point to _____") Uses "tool" to retrieve object Responds to simple verbal request
12–18 months	Enjoys looking at a book Shows understanding of category Places round, and later square, piece in puzzle Imitates "invisible" gesture Matches objects Brings objects from another room on request Identifies at least one body part
18–24 months	Points to pictures named Activates mechanical toys Plays with play dough and paints Matches object to pictures Sorts objects Matches sounds to photos of animals
24–36 months	Understands the concept of one Identifies clothing items for different occasions Engages in simple make-believe play Matches shapes and colors Knows gender Identifies body parts with function Completes 3–4 piece puzzle Begins to understand long and short
3 years	Completes 10 percent of a task with little supervision Counts orally to 3 Draws a circle in imitation Knows most prepositions

Age	Behavior
	Locates big and little
	Sorts by size
4 years	Remains on task for 10 minutes with distractions present
	Knows more and less, many and few
	Matches coins
	Draws a line between two parallel lines
	Places three simple pictures in a sequence
	Locates objects that do not belong
	Determines three ways that objects are similar or different
5 years	Completes 50–75 percent of task
	Determines when a task is done
	Names letters and alphabet sounds
	Counts orally to 10
	Names penny, nickel, and dime
	Relates today, tomorrow, and yesterday to days of the week
	Copies letters and numbers
	Prints own name
	Reads numerals on a clock face
	Names days of the week
	Counts orally to 100
	Draws a 3-to-6-part person

Social-Emotional Development

The emergence of individual emotions and personality is a result of and an influence on dynamic relationships with other human beings and their environment. This social involvement is essential for survival. People need relationships to learn the rules for adapting to community norms that govern living within a society. Social rules, however, are not always constant across settings, culture, or time. Part of social development is learning how to seek the information necessary to learn current rules and recognizing the steps that may be necessary to take when old rules change and new rules are adopted.

It is impossible to separate social and emotional development. For our purposes, we define *social development* as observable behavior; *emotional development* is that which takes place under the skin. In reality, these are interdependent–not independent–phenomena. Furthermore, both influence and are influenced by, and influenced by, and inseparable from language and cognitive development (Bagdi & Vacca, 2006). This interdependence will become clear in the following description of social and emotional development.

Social behavior and emotional maturation depend on interactions with adults and other children. Among other factors, heredity, culture, economics, and the community differentially influence social–emotional development. Developmental delays can occur when infants and young children are seriously deprived of early social nurturance by caregivers. Incredibly, research has also demonstrated that maternal status during gestation is linked to emotional, cognitive, and behavioral problems in children (Van den Bergh, Mulder, Mennes, & Glover, 2005). Thus, a fetus is vulnerable to maternal stress and anxiety, possibly because this stress results in physiological increases in cortisol that cross the placenta and affect hormonal and brain development.

Through nurturance, caregivers reliably provide stimulation to the senses, establishing a mechanism for the development of a trust relationship. This reciprocal confidence in primary caregivers is the first step toward being able to expand and develop other attachment relationships. Mothers who fail to provide support, show high levels of negative emotion, and infrequently engage in emotional dialogue tend to raise children who themselves show low levels of emotional understanding (Edwards, Shipman, & Brown, 2005). When infants experience prolonged subtle forms of emotional deprivation, as in the case of mothers who are depressed, they appear to experience a dampening of their own emotions (Nadel, Soussignan, Canet, Libert, & Gerardin, 2005). In more dramatic cases, infants who do not experience consistency in mothering fail to gain weight regardless of appropriate caloric intake, are lethargic, and do not show a normal developmental progression. Some of these infants may even die if the emotional isolation occurs over a long period of time.

Infants initially require an individual caregiver to provide a relationship in which learning the social rules occurs. Providing the cues for what will be an infant's personality development, this nurturing person (or persons) represents a major influence in early infancy. For example, Kim (2011) found that excessive crying as a result of colic in the first three months often places tremendous stress on infant–mother relationships and can lead to emotional and behavioral regulation disorders by the time babies become toddlers (i.e., tantrums, chronic fussiness, excessive clinginess, sleeping and eating disorders). It is clear, then, that the integrity of caregiver–infant interactions remains one of the most significant influences on social–emotional health throughout a person's life.

Attachment is a central determinant of emotional development in infants and young children. John Bowlby is the most significant theorist of human attachment (Cicchetti & Roisman, 2011). Bowlby's basic assumption was that humans are pre-wired with behavioral systems that enable infants to achieve the goal of establishing secure relations with caregivers, who are expected to protect and provide. The degree of security in that attachment is the basis of emotional maturation. Moreover, a disruption in secure attachment between an adult and an infant may be a direct result of the adult's insensitivity and unresponsiveness to the infant. Emotionally at-risk infants are those who (1) avoid attachment—do not respond differentially to parents or strangers and show no distress when parents leave the room—and (2) refuse attachment—resist exploration to stay close to parents but may resist closeness (i.e., hitting, fussing, crying) when an absent parent returns.

Several environmental factors place parents at risk of being inadequate nurturers of secure attachment: substance abuse, child abuse, underage pregnancy, low socioeconomic status, economic stressors, poverty, infant prematurity, overcrowding, and absent fathers. By comparison, those children whose caregivers foster secure attachments tend to show normal signs of secure maturation: 3-year-olds address attachment problems in a constructive manner, expecting a positive outcome; 4 to 5-year-olds are confident about short separations but show sadness when a separation is stressful;

and 6-year-olds are confident enough about their attachment to introduce stressful, even dangerous, separations into stories (Miljkovitch, Pierrehumbert, Bretherton, & Halfon, 2004). Those whose infancy is characterized by fragile attachment tend to use themes of insecurity in their storytelling later in preschool years: catastrophic events that occur without warning, inability to get help from others, and inability to control behavior or events—examples of perceived lack of control.

Social skills appear at an early age, indicated by an infant's ability to recognize family members. These skills continue to mature throughout a person's life span as different social skills are necessary at different ages. For example, it is acceptable for toddlers to hug family members and acquaintances lavishly, but in adolescence such displays of affection are usually viewed as immature. Normal social development is achieved when an individual exercises the rules of social conduct acceptable for a given age, gender, economic status, and culture.

Human beings are accustomed to receiving rewards for appropriate social behaviors. This is a learned response from early infancy when interactions between infants and significant caregivers include feedback of a physical nature that becomes associated with an activity generally perceived as pleasurable. As an example, infants initially respond physically by body movement and then with vocalization on hearing their caregiver approach, and this activity results in the infants being picked up and cuddled. Infants soon learn which of their behaviors trigger desired responses in caregivers and incorporate these activities into their interactions with other human beings.

Infants also learn to interpret the emotional information caregivers provide. This is a complex skill that develops slowly. For example, infants do not appear to be able to categorize emotions until 7 to 8 months, and even then infants' perceptions of differences in facial expressions do not suggest an understanding of the emotions behind the expressions (Batty & Taylor, 2006). Not until the second year of life do children begin to realize that the emotions of others (i.e., happy, angry) might have specific consequences for themselves.

A transition takes place at about 18 months when toddlers become very mobile. Mothers' responses to infants change from primarily positive to more instructive and prohibitive ("no") (Lipari, 2000). In fact, these interactions are important to neurological development, except when the sequence ends in shame. Episodes in which children go from excitement to sudden deflation (at "no") to recovery in a relatively brief interval stimulate the orbitofrontal portion of the brain (cognition) and the limbic system (emotions) and improve their connectivity to each other. Consequently, an emotional resiliency develops and young children acquire the ability to regulate their emotions and their impulses. On the other hand, predominantly coercive parenting patterns that are characterized by unpredictable, harsh, and inconsistent consequences lead to later social problems and emotional depression (Duckworth & Sabates, 2005).

With the expansion of preschool and day-care services for younger and younger children, the need to understand the emotional development of children between 2 and 4 years of age is increasing. Lev Vygotsky identified age 3 as a critical transition phase or "crisis" in which children begin to struggle with their position with respect to social structures (Hyman, 2011). The most salient description of this transition to higher mental functioning is "defiant behavior," which was organized into seven categories by Vygotsky: negativism, stubbornness, obstinacy, willfulness, protest, devaluation, and despotism (Grendler, 2005). These are tough words for a healthy and natural transition to individuality and autonomy. Keefer (2005) showed that as children progress through this crisis, there is a gradual change in the focus of defiance: 2-year-olds had more conflict with peers while 3-year-olds showed more defiance toward adults.

Two-year-old toddlers show that they understand they can regulate others with their emotional displays by expressing sadness with more intensity and frequency when in the company of their mothers in order to solicit emotional support (Buss & Kiel, 2004). Of the negative emotions—sadness, anger, fear—sadness is the most effective at eliciting positive caregiver responses to help reduce distress (i.e., talk, play, and social interaction). Just so, at this same age (2–3 years), children achieve the ability to attribute emotional outcomes to getting or not getting their desires: Happiness is derived from getting what they want while sadness results from not getting what they want. Two-year-olds are also developing an understanding of morality as good versus less good, and the possession of objects becomes a part of toddlers' "moral space"—akin to the immature moral code of "possession is nine tenths of the law" (Rochat, 2011). By 4 years of age, children still attribute happiness to getting the object of their desires, even when they have broken a social–moral rule (e.g., hurting another child to gain possession of a toy). Gradually, however, children understand that breaking a rule to get what they want can affect emotions in different ways—demonstrating an ability to empathize with victims. More importantly, by age 6 to 7, children are able to attribute positive emotions to willpower or the refusal to break a rule although doing so would lead to a desired outcome (Lagattuta, 2005).

Young children with disabilities are at risk of developing distorted social skills. Because all developmental areas are interlinked, impairment in any one area can significantly alter the ability of infants or children to initiate or respond to interactions in ways that build or maintain social relationships. Physical impairments, such as cerebral palsy, may prohibit postures or gestures that progress to social interactions. Observations of children with visual impairments indicate that their ability to see affects functional play (use of toys or objects as a representation of real objects) but not symbolic play (substituting a toy in form or function by attributing imaginary quality) (Lewis, Norgate, Collis, & Reynolds, 2000). Symbolic play is necessary for language acquisition and both affect children's ability to engage in social play. Caregivers need to learn to read the signals of infants or children with disabilities and use these signals in their interactions with their charges. Teaching families relevant mechanisms to establish relationships with their children is one of the initial responsibilities of an early childhood educator.

Social Play

Play is the medium through which infants and toddlers acquire and execute social relationships. It is within play activities that people behave just to enjoy or amuse themselves. Yet play is also a significant prerequisite for both physical and mental growth and for the acquisition of normal social–emotional maturation. Playing is a form of self-expression and is required in the normal dynamic of growth as a significant part of social development (see Table 4–6). In addition to facilitating language, social play helps children learn sympathy, empathy, problem-solving, creativity, and self-regulation (Schaefer & Drewes, 2011; Wright & Diener, 2012). Differences

Table 4–6	Milestones of Social–Emotional Development

Age	Behavior
1–6 months	Smiles Laughs Discriminates strangers
6–12 months	Lifts arms to mother Shows separation anxiety Cooperates in social games Likes to be in constant sight and hearing of an adult
12–18 months	Displays frequent tantrums Needs and expects routines Shows sense of humor Enjoys being center of attention
18–24 months	Shows jealousy at attention to others Desires control of others Enjoys solitary play
2 years	Is strongly possessive and dependent—clings and whines Engages in parallel play Begins to obey and respect simple rules Takes pride in own achievements and resists help
3 years	Plays games with another person Responds and makes verbal greetings Plays with one or two others
4 years	Volunteers Conforms to group decisions Verbalizes feelings before physical aggression
5 years	Tries again after change or disappointment Sacrifices immediate reward for delayed reward Accepts friendly teasing Cooperates in group games with loose rules Protects other children and animals Offers help to others voluntarily

between boys and girls in emotional maturity and social play have been found (Mathieson & Banerjee, 2011). In the Mathieson and Banerjee research, boys (but not girls) who had greater emotional awareness and verbal abilities tended to engage in interactive peer play, while those with poorer awareness and verbal abilities tended to be disconnected from peer play. Girls (but not boys) who were more capable in interactions with peers and used higher socio-moral reasoning received the highest "likable" peer ratings.

Play is universal and crosses all of the world's physical and social boundaries. Activities that are both fantasy and real constitute play. Play can be individual or collective, can involve a small or large group, and can occur anywhere and at any

© Brian Price

time. Play activities can be divided into three general groups: motor (physical exercise, action toys, etc.), intellectual (mental activities such as card and board games), and sensory (spectator activities, such as track meets, ball games, etc.). Very young children between 2 and 4 years of age generally prefer to engage in motor play activities.

Observations of newborns reveal that they begin to engage in simple play within hours of birth. As mentioned earlier, reciprocal interactions involving facial expressions, eye movements, and sounds begin very early and serve as reinforcers to caregivers, who are drawn to this "playful" little being. Infants' interactions with their environment generally remain within the context of relationships with their primary caregivers. Social-affective play may involve stretching or turning an infant's arms or legs, patting or stroking, and presenting bright objects or introducing sounds to elicit responses, such as cooing. An infant's typical response to social play is pleasure derived from nurturing relationships with familiar people. Thus, play provides a context from which children learn that emotional responses from caregivers can be provoked by smiling, cooing, and other such behaviors. In fact, play is often referred to as *the work* of young children.

Once infants have begun to develop voluntary motor skills, play progresses in ways that help infants acquire new skills. Manipulating objects repetitively brings repeated pleasure that commonly accompanies success. Still, play can produce frustration when attempts to learn new skills are not immediately successful. By the time infants reach 1 year of age, they are able to participate in imitative games. These may include repetitive games, such as pat-a-cake, itsy-bitsy spider, and peek-a-boo. Such games generally involve an infant and an adult, but they are setting the stage for the later initiation of play with other children.

Although these initial social relationships with adults are necessary for the development of social skills, children generally learn many of the rules of social conduct from other children. Peers are less tolerant of deviations from an established standard than are adults who can reason beyond what is obvious. Social play in the preschool years can be categorized into five sequential stages: solitary play, spectator play, parallel play, associative play, and cooperative play. The rate at which an individual child progresses through these stages depends on both the opportunities the child has for interactions and the integrity of the social contacts that are available.

In some cases, children whose families are economically stable may have an advantage because more social contacts are arranged, and these provide the children opportunities for engaging play experiences and may allow for a more rapid progression. For example, in established supervised play groups, parents have the means to take the initiative in providing toys and games that promote peer interactions.

Solitary play involves both isolation and independence. This play experience can involve an individual child within the same physical area as a group of children. Children involved in solitary play are engaged in their own activities and their own group of toys. They enjoy the physical presence of other children but do not speak to the other children, nor do they attempt to decrease the physical distance between play areas. They also show no interest in the activities of other children that differ from their own activities. Young children also engage in solitary play in their own homes while with a caregiver. Although engaging in independent play, a child may frequently move the activity to the vicinity of the caregiver.

Spectator play is also frequently referred to as *onlooker play*. This occurs when a young child observes the play activities of other children but makes no attempt to enter in the activity. This play may involve conversation about the nature of the activity between the observer and child involved.

Parallel play also involves the independent play of children in a group. Children play with toys that are like those of the children around them but of their own choosing and in their own fashion. This play involves children playing beside each other but not with each other. Toddlers frequently engage in parallel play, which is consistent with their world view that objects have properties independent of involvement with each other. Additionally, toddlers' language development is just beginning to allow for verbal expression in a social context.

Associative play occurs between the ages of 3 to 4 years. An individual child plays with other children, engaging in similar or even identical activities. Without adult facilitation, associative play generally lacks organization. Although toys may be shared, each member acts without regard for the group's wishes because no group goal has been established. When an individual child initiates an activity, the entire group typically follows this lead. During this stage, an individual child may make occasional attempts to control both group behavior and group membership. Four-year-olds begin to establish strong preferences for associates and may begin to have a best friend. This friend may change frequently during the course of a play experience, depending on the direction of the play. Hence, children have learned initial strategies to gain power over other children, yet these young children are incapable of wielding power wisely. For example, it is typical of children of this age to be bossy and selfish, to begin to taunt and name call, and to boast and bend the truth a little.

Cooperative play occurs when activities are organized. Children involved in cooperative play are engaged in a goal-directed activity that has been planned by the group to accomplish some defined end. Formal games become important during this stage, and the end goal frequently involves some competition. Group members have designated roles that are generally both assigned and directed by one or two accepted leaders of the group. Even at this age, children develop a great sense of either belonging or not belonging to cooperative playgroups. During this final stage of play development, splits according to gender may occur, with children seeking membership in same-sex groups.

Play enhances skill development in both motor activities and emotions. Active play develops muscle control, cognitive development, and socialization. Through play, children learn about their physical world and its relationship to themselves. Intellectual stimulation is provided in many ways, including manipulating shapes and working with texture, color, and size, as well as through problem-solving, pattern creation, and learning and applying complex organization and rules.

Perhaps most importantly, play is the most effective medium through which children develop language. As early as 18 months, toddlers begin to pretend, demonstrating an awareness of symbolic thought—a prerequisite of language. Children can experiment with abstract thought through fantasy and fabrication within the acceptable context of creativity without being diverted by conformity to a norm of the society. Play becomes less spontaneous and more structured with age, perhaps due to constraints imposed by formal schooling and social expectations.

Because children are not as tolerant of violations of codes within their own play-group, externally initiated codes of behavior for the group facilitate the learning of acceptable social behaviors. Hence, children who are culturally different adjust more easily to new social situations when dramatic play is a part of the curriculum (Howes et al., 2011). Moreover, when early childhood teachers use strategies such as dramatic play to create a positive peer climate, aggression and victimization tend to be lower (Howes et al.). Truth, honesty, fair play, self-control, and leadership skills are learned within the group and provide an important mechanism for teaching the standards of the society and personal accountability for individual actions.

Self-Help Development

Self-help skills include independent feeding, dressing, toileting, and personal responsibility (see Table 4–7). The term **adaptive skills** also refers to the same set of behaviors, and either term may be used by various assessment tools and curriculum packages. The acquisition of skills that enable children to interact independently with their environment is linked closely to both motor development and cognitive skill development. For example, children do not independently use the toilet until they:

1. Have gained sufficient muscle control to stay dry for an hour or two at a time
2. Can move themselves to the toilet
3. Are cognitively aware of the signs of urgency to void
4. Know what action to take to avoid an accident

Independent Eating and Drinking Skills

As in all other areas of development, neonates eat and drink reflexively only, although parents might swear there is some intent involved when a hungry infant wakes them throughout the night and keeps them vigilant during the day with demands to be fed. This aspect of childcare can be exhausting for parents, as infants demand food five to eight times a day, requiring approximately 30 minutes for each feeding.

Although the sucking reflex is present at birth, only infants who are 4 months old suck voluntarily with enthusiasm and vigor. Young infants consume exclusively liquid diets of either breast milk or formula for the first 4 to 6 months. At about this time, infants begin to take some responsibility for eating by holding their bottle. Simultaneously, they tolerate solid pureed foods, although they may remain very passive, not offering to close their lips around the spoon or to push food from the front of the tongue toward the back of their mouth.

Table 4–7   Milestones of Self-Help

Age	Behavior
1–4 months	Coordinates sucking, swallowing, and breathing Recognizes bottle
4–8 months	Swallows strained or pureed foods Feeds self a cracker Holds own bottle
8–12 months	Drinks from held cup Finger feeds Cooperates in dressing
12–18 months	Cooperates in washing and drying Undoes bows and snaps Has regular bowel movements Indicates when wet or soiled Cooperates in dressing
18–24 months	Sits on potty chair Unzips, removes unlaced shoes Washes and dries hands partially Helps with simple household tasks Has apparent food preferences
24–36 months	Delays sleeping by demanding things Understands and stays away from common dangers Undresses with assistance Washes hands and brushes teeth Uses toilet with assistance, has daytime control
4 years old	Takes responsibility for toileting Serves self and helps set table Dresses with supervision Uses spoon and fork well Uses toilet regularly without asking Puts comb and brush in hair Puts shoes on correct feet Knows front from back
5 years old	Drinks from water fountain, serves self, and carries tray Carries liquid in open container without spilling Wipes self after toileting Uses comb and brush, washes face and ears in bath and dries with towel Zips up front opening of clothing Dresses and undresses functionally without being told

A dramatic transition of independence takes place at about 8 months of age. Infants, who now have well-developed fine motor skills, drink from cups with help, feed themselves finger foods (crackers, etc.), and may refuse to drink from their bottles. Very "grown up" now, these infants should be on the same eating schedule as adults and, like adults, enjoying between-meal snacks.

By age 2, toddlers are often independent eaters and drinkers. However, this does not mean that they can eat or drink with grace. Using a spoon, toddlers can feed themselves. However, this level of independence is often paired with independent decision making. It is not uncommon for toddlers to maintain a narrow range of food preferences or to go through stages when they eat very little.

Three-year-olds eat well with a spoon and may be able to use a fork to stab foods. These youngsters display some very sophisticated skills at the table, serving themselves drinks or portions of food. Additionally, vegetables become a food to avoid. Independence in the use of utensils is achieved by 4 years of age. Four-year-olds also enjoy helping prepare meals and are able to make simple meals, such as cereal and toast, independently by age five.

Dressing Skills

The first indication that infants are thinking about dressing skills is when they begin to tug at their feet and incidentally pull off their socks or shoes. At about the same time, at approximately 9 months, significant progress in dressing is made when infants assist by lifting their arms so the caregiver can remove or put on a shirt, stepping into a pair of suspended pants or shoes, and holding still during diapering. Because undressing is easier, toddlers take off jackets, shoes, socks, and unbuttoned pants at about 18 months. Although they try earlier, children have little success in dressing even in articles of clothing that are easy to put on (pants, loose shoes) until they are about 2 years of age. Two-year-olds may learn to fasten large buttons and small front buttons by 3 years of age. Zippers and buckles are more difficult fine motor tasks that may be mastered at age 4 or 5. Usually by the time children are 4, they are able to dress by themselves; although not until age 5 do they recognize and self-correct most dressing errors (putting clothes on backwards or inside out). Complex dressing tasks such as tying shoes and fixing stuck zippers emerge at 5 years of age but may not be mastered until age 6 or 7.

Toileting Skills

Toilet training begins at birth when infants start to gradually gain muscle control. A very young infant is seldom dry, dribbling small quantities of urine almost constantly. Gradually, muscle control permits infants to sustain first brief, and then longer, periods of dryness. By 8 months, infants begin to stay dry for reasonable lengths of time and may communicate their recognition of "wetness" by pulling at their diapers. Parents should not, however, consider toilet training until at least 18 months or later if a child does not stay dry for an hour or more. One sign of sufficient bladder control is when toddlers remain dry during their naps.

Bowel control is more easily achieved than bladder control, as infants begin to have routine bowel movements one or two times a day by 8 months of age. Training for bowel control can begin at 12 months and may be accomplished as early as 18 months. This process is often not completed until age 3, and it is typically accomplished more easily by girls than by boys. By 5 years of age, children can be expected to independently care for all toileting needs including wiping themselves and washing their hands afterward.

Personal Responsibility

From an early age, children can be expected to begin to take responsibility for themselves. Toddlers, for example, can follow directions to pick up their toys, although this behavior might not become habitual until some years later. Two-year-olds will put their coats away regularly when the routine is expected. By 3 years of age, children can take on a variety of responsibilities, such as wiping up spills, helping to clear the table, and placing dirty clothes in a hamper.

Parents should begin brushing an infant's teeth as soon as the primary teeth begin erupting. This can begin by simply using a washcloth to gently clean the newly acquired teeth. As infants gain sufficient fine motor control, parents can ask them to attempt to imitate tooth brushing. Although cleanliness is not the goal, children learn valuable patterns of routine daily care. Bathing and washing are similar responsibilities that can be transferred to young children. By age 4, children should be able to bathe themselves and brush their teeth with acceptable proficiency. While 4-year-olds are unpredictable, 5-year-olds are generally happy to assist in completing jobs around the home. Given chores, children tend to be cooperative and reliable.

IN CONCLUSION

Direct service professionals working with young children with and without disabilities must have a sound knowledge of the sequence and timing of the normal developmental progress. While these professionals cannot be expected to memorize every new advancement, they should have solid general knowledge at the ready. If professionals cannot retrieve such knowledge, they may fail to recognize signs of risk, thereby overlooking an opportunity for screening and subsequent early identification. In addition, because intervention is most efficacious when exercised early, we know that if a chance is missed, it can never be reclaimed with the same level of optimism about the outcome.

Sequencing intervention goals to match normal developmental progression is a time-tested approach to early intervention. Some believe that this progression is both natural and necessary and that a missed stage forever handicaps progression in one or more developmental domains. For example, it has been claimed that a failure to progress normally through every stage of motor development causes deficits in higher-level cognitive functioning. However, for some children whose rate of development is seriously compromised by motor, neurological, or health issues, skipping or avoiding certain stages may be prudent. Judgments such as these are the domain of all early interventionists, who can be guided by research, professional experience, and input from families and other team members.

Normal development is both universal and remarkably constant. In other words, little has changed over centuries in the rate or sequence of human development. However, this stability may change dramatically in the coming decades if not sooner. For example, just as we are beginning to understand the crucial relationship between the richness of social interactions and intellectual and language development, technology is being inserted into the fabric of society and dramatically changing the nature and integrity of social connections. Whether and how technology affects "normal" development is unknown. Perhaps technology will advance our development in important and helpful ways—perhaps not. It is incumbent on professionals to press for research about and understanding of this issue.

An even more dramatic scenario on the horizon is that created by advances in genetic technology. Already, parents may select from a pool of viable embryos those that have the desired traits of their progeny. As a result, the natural selection of gene traits will undoubtedly change—and will influence the overall rate, if not sequence, of human growth. In addition, researchers are learning how to effectively manipulate the human gene code. Large-scale application of genetic engineering *will* rewrite the knowledge base of human development. For now, however, practitioners can rely on the prevailing descriptions of development amassed by parents, researchers, and practitioners as described in this chapter.

STUDY GUIDE QUESTIONS

1. Why should an early childhood practitioner have exceptional knowledge of the milestones of development?
2. Describe the sequence of and age milestones for hip control.
3. Describe the progression of development from reflex to reaching to grasping.
4. Describe the five principles of language development.
5. Explain the three aspects of language considered when discussing form.
6. Briefly outline the general development of phonological skills and sentence structure.
7. What is a morpheme? How do we measure the sophistication of language?
8. Describe the receptive language abilities of a child around the following ages: 1 year, 18 months, 2 years, 3 years, and 6 years.
9. As children begin to develop expressive language, actions and objects dominate their early vocabulary. Explain why this may be so.
10. Describe a child's language use at these ages: neonate, 12 months, 2 years, 3 years, and 6 years.
11. Define *cognition*.
12. Describe the process by which children learn to regulate their environment.
13. Explain how imitation is both a tool and an index of intellectual development.
14. How is the sensorimotor phase of development qualitatively different from the preoperational stage?
15. When and how is caregiver interaction a determinant to the social and emotional evolution of children?
16. What is attachment, and how does it mature over time in secure relationships? What are some indications that an attachment relationship is insecure?
17. How did Vygotsky describe the normal emotional crisis of 2- to 4-year-olds?
18. Describe the emotional give-and-take progression of infants and their caregivers throughout early childhood.
19. Describe the context and importance of play to social–emotional development.

20. Identify the sophistication of children's play behavior in a group according to your knowledge of the following phases of play evolution: solitary, spectator, parallel, associative, cooperative.

21. Give two examples of any infant or toddler behavior demonstrated in a social context and explain how this behavior is an index of social–emotional, cognitive, language, and physical development.

22. List the traditional skills that fall into the domain of self-help.

23. Describe a child's eating and drinking repertoire at the following ages: 4–6 months, 8 months, 2 years, 3 years, 4 years, and 5 years.

24. Describe a child's dressing skills at the following ages: 9 months, 18 months, 2 years, 4 years, and 5+ years.

25. When should training of bowel and bladder begin?

5

Development and Risk During Prenatal, Natal, and Postnatal Stages

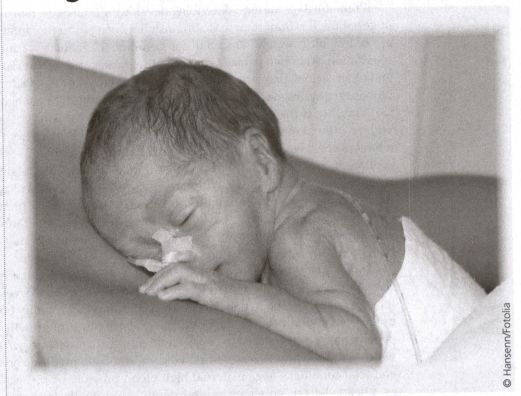

© Hansenn/Fotolia

question 1 study guide

The physical connections between mothers and their infants that exist before pregnancy, during pregnancy, through the labor and delivery process, and in the immediate period after birth can affect the later physical and developmental health of children. **Prenatal** refers to the period before conception through gestation. **Natal** conditions affect the mother or the infant during the labor and delivery process, and **postnatal** conditions affect the mother or the infant following delivery for the first 30 days after birth. A fourth term, **perinatal,** is commonly used to designate a period that actually overlaps all of the preceding periods. Technically though, the perinatal period begins at the 29th week of gestation and ends between the first and fourth weeks after birth. At any time during any of these periods, problems may arise that can compromise the physical or cognitive growth of infants. While knowing the cause or timing of injury seldom guides early childhood professionals as they design intervention plans, this knowledge can be useful to families in understanding their children.

Prenatal Growth and Development

A **term pregnancy** averages approximately 280 days (10 lunar months, or 40 weeks) and terminates in the delivery of a viable fetus that is capable of independent life. Delivery prior to the 37th week of pregnancy is considered to be premature. Viability within the context of current technology exists at about 23 weeks of gestation.

Prematurity is the term describing developing fetuses born prior to the 37th week of gestation. It is important to distinguish between premature infants and those who are of low birth weight, are small for gestational age, or have intrauterine growth retardation. Although babies from all of these categories are at risk due to their size and other factors, premature infants have a unique set of risk factors associated with immature physical development that correspond to gestational age.

Viability is the gestational age at which a fetus can survive outside the womb with or without medical or technological intervention. With current medical practice, a fetus is considered **viable** at a gestational age of more than 23 weeks beyond conception. In fact, the survival of premature infants is directly related to advances in neonatal medical technology. With the improved survival rates of premature infants, it has become possible to identify a normal progression of preterm growth and development. Consequently, researchers have also investigated interventions aimed at improving the quality of survival and assisting families in meeting the needs of their medically fragile premature infants.

While infants born between the 33rd and 36th weeks of gestation have increased risk compared to full-term infants, those born at fewer than 32 weeks are at high risk for significant developmental delays. The corresponding fragility of underdeveloped organ systems, particularly the brain, affects both physical growth and neurological development. Indexes used to project fetal physical growth are gestational age, birth weight, and the presence of additional compromising medical conditions. Maternal and fetal conditions (e.g., maternal high blood pressure or physical anomalies such as a heart defect) can either independently or mutually influence fetal growth. In spite of preexisting conditions, appropriate interventions can alleviate or control high-risk medical conditions while permitting infants to progress along a corrected growth curve established specifically for infants born prematurely. Risk of developmental delays may be further attenuated when mothers respond with sensitivity to infant needs, a strong infant–mother attachment is formed, and infants and parents have access to early intervention (Candelaria, Teti, & Black, 2011).

Effects of Prematurity on Body Systems

Fetuses who will eventually be born prematurely proceed along the same predetermined pattern as that of full-term fetuses until birth interrupts this normal course of development. Although this interruption does not change the normal developmental sequence, it does have an impact on the schedule over which development occurs. That is, premature infants are born with underdeveloped organs, which are not sufficiently capable of meeting the demands of independent life without the support of the mother's womb. The following is an analysis of the particular organ systems that are compromised when infants are born prematurely. Note that all systems, while described in a discrete manner, are essentially linked, and insult to one or more systems affects the development of other systems.

Respiratory System Surfactant is a chemical agent needed for infants' independent breathing that is not produced in sufficient quantity until the 32nd to 33rd week of pregnancy. This chemical prevents the lungs from sticking together during expiration. Without surfactant, the lung surfaces stick together, causing the small air sacs to collapse. The tiny air sacs, called **alveoli,** permit normal exchange of oxygen and carbon dioxide. Collapsed alveoli cause oxygen deficiency, leading to lung disease and, if serious enough, death. Respiratory function can be further compromised by an immature nervous system. Because nerve impulses govern breathing, weak or absent neural stimulation associated with prematurity results in inconsistent patterns of breathing. Consequently, it is common for preterm infants to experience **apnea,** or the cessation of breathing for periods of seconds or minutes.

Cardiovascular System   Blood vessels in premature infants are unusually fragile and break easily. This fragility increases the risk of bleeding into the brain (**intracranial bleeding,** or stroke) or other vital organs. A second condition associated with an immature cardiovascular system is anemia (insufficient availability of red blood cells) because underdeveloped bone marrow is unprepared for the bodies' demand to produce red blood cells. These conditions place additional stress on the young hearts, which are poorly equipped to meet the bodies' demands for oxygen and nutrients.

Neurological System   The younger the fetus, the more serious the probable impact of delivery on a developing neurological system. In particular, the relationship between cardiovascular proficiency and neurological functioning is critical. That is, the more premature the infant, the more likely it is that the blood and oxygen supply to the brain will be compromised. Hence, the brain, which itself is immature and consequently vulnerable to any interruption in the vital oxygen and nutrient supply, can incur permanent damage to its cells. Furthermore, the immature neurological system is incapable of sending or receiving messages efficiently. Thus, the ability of other systems in the body to respond as necessary is decreased, because all systems depend on the nerve network for adequate functioning.

Renal and Gastrointestinal Systems   In addition to being affected by their own immaturity, the kidneys and gastrointestinal systems are seriously affected by compromised cardiovascular and neurological systems. The kidneys are unable to maintain normal sodium and calcium levels or to sufficiently filter waste. The gastrointestinal tract is capable of absorbing nutrients, but the large bowel is too short, so the passage of food is excessively rapid, preventing sufficient absorption and increasing the risk of malnutrition. Interestingly, when the cardiovascular system is weakened (as in prematurity), infants' bodies tend to protect the organs that are the most important to survival. Accordingly, the gastrointestinal system is not considered critical to infants' preservation so blood flow is detoured away from the intestine to provide increased blood to the brain, heart, and kidneys.

Muscular System   Studies have documented the developmental evolution of tone, deep tendon reflexes, pathologic reflexes, and primitive reflexes of infants born between 24- and 32-weeks of gestation. While motor development in full-term infants follows a pattern of upper extremities to lower extremities (cephalo-caudal) and from the center of the body to the extremities (proximal to distal), the preterm developmental progression of tone and reflexes emerges in the opposite directions. **Micropremature infants** born at 23 to 26 weeks of gestation show generalized **flexion** of the lower extremities at birth. These developmental parameters give providers the opportunity to determine whether such infants are following a progressive course typical of gestational age or are experiencing delays.

Skeletal System   A premature infant's inability to adequately coordinate sucking and swallowing, along with gastrointestinal inefficiency, can cause nutrient deficiency. Poor nutrition contributes to bone growth deficiency, which is necessary for linear growth. Most importantly, calcium loss (rickets) in the newly forming bone structures delays both growth and maturation. Height is one of the most critical measures in determining progression according to a normal growth curve in premature infants. In spite of adequate weight gain, infants who fail to grow in height (one should expect 0.5 cm to 1 cm of linear growth per week) deviate from normal expectations.

Integumentary System   The skin in premature infants is extremely fragile due to the ratio of body surface to weight, low storage of brown fats, and poor glycogen supply (Subramanian, Yoon, & Toral, 2001). For a very premature infant, the skin surface provides no protection from heat or water loss and no barrier against infection. These infants are also at risk for the development of yeast infections on the skin surface. Infection can then progress into the bloodstream through breaks in the fragile surface. External heat sources (i.e., isolettes), filtered air, and good hygiene practices are necessary to provide both warmth and protection for these infants.

Indexes of Growth in Premature Infants   As with term infants, weight is an unpredictable measure of both gestational age and maturity. Premature infants who have been under physiological stress during pregnancy exhibit signs of lower birth weight along with less advanced organ function. Because of such inconsistencies in weight, head circumference as a measure of brain growth is used to make growth predictions. **Corrected gestational age** (gestational age versus chronological age) is used to determine whether appropriate growth and development are occurring. This measure is considered to be accurate at least through the first year of life. Prematurity sometimes only affects growth and development during early life. However, prematurity can sometimes produce effects that alter the course of an individual's entire life. When caregivers understand normal progression, they have more opportunities to plan interventions and align resources that promote development to the maximum potential of the affected infant.

Maternal Conditions Affecting Pregnancy Outcomes

Preconception Maternal Conditions

Conditions exist in some women that affect their own health as well as the development and overall health of their fetuses if pregnancy occurs. Actively educating women about these conditions and encouraging them to seek health care and counseling before becoming pregnant is a practice that early educators can adopt. Some of these conditions are diabetes, hypertension, heart disease, drug and alcohol addiction, obesity, age, and some genetic conditions (e.g., cystic fibrosis, phenylke-tonuria [PKU]). Early medical and behavioral interventions significantly reduce the risks to both mothers and infants.

Socioeconomic and environmental factors play an important role in the prevention of prenatal and natal complications. Poverty influences both living conditions and physical conditions that increase the incidence of prematurity. For example, women who suffer sexual abuse have increased stress-related cortisol levels during pregnancy and are at higher risk for low-birth-weight infants and preterm delivery (Bublitz & Stroud, 2012; Gavin, Thompsen, Rue, & Guo, 2012). Limited economic opportunities frequently lead to inadequate prenatal care, poor diet, and increased complications of pregnancy (e.g., pregnancy-induced hypertension), all of which may lead to premature delivery. Consideration of socioeconomic issues prior to becoming pregnant and exploring available resources decrease the incidence of complications of pregnancy.

Prenatal Maternal Conditions

The number of times a woman has been pregnant (**gravida**) and the number of live infants that she has delivered at more than 20-weeks gestation (**parity**) are important factors related to providing prenatal care. That is, the more times a woman has been pregnant, the higher the risk for problems associated with the pregnancy. These problems may include faster labors with quick and uncontrolled deliveries, failure of muscle contraction of the uterus with significant bleeding, and malpositioned placentas. Previous premature delivery is related to the increased probability of a subsequent pregnancy ending in premature delivery and earlier in the gestation period than the previous delivery.

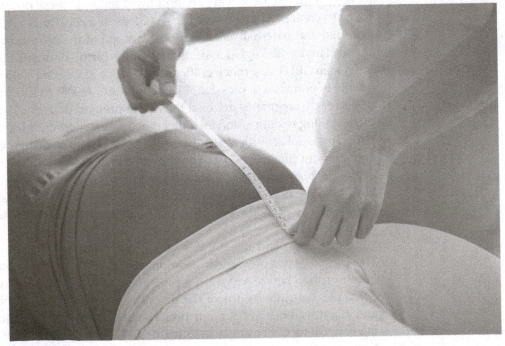

© Ruth Jenkinson/DK Images

Age is an important factor that can be related to the increased incidence of both premature delivery and appearance of physical and genetic abnormalities in the infant. Women younger than 20 or older than 40 have an increased risk of spontaneous abortion, toxemia of pregnancy, premature delivery, and giving birth to babies with congenital abnormalities. Adolescents under 16 years of age have twice as great a risk of premature delivery as women over 18 (National Academies Press, 2006). Often, for a mother whose age may be an issue during pregnancy, especially a young mother, age itself may be less important in terms of outcome than risks that are associated with age. These women frequently have other risk factors present that increase the possibility of pregnancy complications: socioeconomic factors in young women and health problems (preexisting hypertension, diabetes) in older women.

Socioeconomic standing is an important factor in the incidence of premature delivery. Factors associated with differential socioeconomic standing include race, culture, and the availability of adequate shelter, food, money, and social support structures. Studies show that young, single mothers with few support networks have both an increased incidence of unplanned pregnancy (Edin & Tach, 2012) and a higher incidence of premature delivery and low-birth-weight infants (Cheng, Chen, & Liou, 2011). Cheng and colleagues (2011) analyzed socioeconomic characteristics and outcomes for single mothers. These researchers found that more than half the women studied were below poverty level, 77 percent had only a high school education or less, fewer than 20 percent of the pregnancies were planned, 40 percent did not receive quality prenatal care, and 65 percent of the fathers *never* paid childcare expenses.

Increasingly, it is becoming clear that psychological factors can affect pregnancy. Obviously, psychological factors are complicated by other risk factors including maternal health, economics, nutrition, and ingestion of toxins such as drugs and tobacco. Still, researchers are attempting to separate these other contributing factors from psychological factors. One psychological indicator is education level; limited maternal and paternal schooling, perhaps one of the best indicators of social class, is correlated with higher risk of premature birth (Blumenshine, Egerter, Libet, & Braveman, 2011). Another significant risk factor associated with poorer outcomes for infants is perinatal depression. Liu and Odouli (2008) found that maternal depression in early pregnancy doubled the risk of preterm delivery. Psychological stressors often leading to depression include limited interaction with friends, minimal participation in social activities, poor lifestyle choices (such as drinking alcohol every day), and stressful life events (i.e., being involved in accidents, having sexual problems, being a robbery victim). Serious traumatic events are also associated with mental health status, placing women and their babies at risk; post-traumatic stress disorder (PTSD) associated with abuse and homelessness are examples of such traumatic events.

A troubling and inexplicable rise in prematurity has occurred internationally. The United States now rivals developing countries in incidence of preterm births. Poor nutrition before and during pregnancy seems to be a likely contributor to this epidemic. Nutrition is one of the most significant factors associated with maternal and infant well-being. Poor nutritional habits, along with variations in such preexisting conditions as obesity or malnutrition, severely affect a fetus both during gestation and following birth (Bloomfield, 2011). For example, high carbohydrate intake during the first trimester and low dairy intake during the third trimester are associated with poor placental growth (Osmania, 2011). Maternal behaviors that promote malnutrition (e.g., anorexia) result in decreased stores of nutrients for the developing fetus. These infants may be born with **growth retardation** (their weight falls below the 10th percentile and their chest circumference is below the 3rd percentile for gestational age) and may have brain injury due to diminished oxygen and nutrition supply caused by a poorly functioning placenta (Eagles, Lee, Raja, Millar, & Bhattacharya, 2012).

Maternal obesity (20 percent over the standard weight) can also produce both maternal and fetal problems. Infants born to obese mothers may be large, thereby increasing problems with delivery. Maternal obesity may also produce **hypoglycemia** (low blood sugar) in infants and perinatal asphyxia leading to serious fetal and neonatal problems including serious birth defects (e.g., spina bifida), spontaneous abortion, premature delivery, still birth, metabolic instability, and other long-term health problems (Vasudevan, Renfrew, & McGuire, 2011). Pregnant women can be influenced by others in terms of weight gain tendencies during pregnancy; family members encourage women to "eat plenty" because pregnant women are "eating for two." There is some truth to this adage, as adequate maternal nutrition is important, as indicated above. In fact, inadequate weight gain during pregnancy increases the risk of preterm delivery and more than doubles the risk of infant death (Davis & Hofferth, 2012). On the other hand, excessive weight gain during pregnancy is also dangerous, increasing the risks of gestational hypertension and large for gestational age (LGA) fetuses, which complicate birthing (i.e., risk for Caesarian delivery, preeclampsia). Also, the birth weight of LGA fetuses could lead to childhood obesity (Gaillard, Durmus, Hofman, Mackenbach, Steegers, & Jaddoe, 2012). Obese women who actually lose weight during pregnancy improve fetal and perinatal risk factors (Blomberg, 2011). It has been well established that when pregnant women engage in regular cardiovascular exercise, even intense exercise, fetal cardiovascular systems match maternal physiology and the exercise poses no risk (May, 2012).

Maternal infections can play a significant role in fetal outcomes. Both bacterial and viral infections cause a multitude of disabilities for the fetus and neonate. Meningitis, cytomegalovirus, rubella, toxoplasmosis, and numerous other maternal infections and their impacts on newborns are discussed elsewhere in this text. Prenatal education can help prevent many of these infections because it teaches mothers to pay attention to behaviors that place them at risk for contracting an infection.

Chronic diseases in a mother may also have an effect on a fetus. Diseases may include kidney disease, cancer, thyroid disease, Rh sensitization, hypertension, cardiovascular disease, diabetes, genetic disorders (e.g., PKU), respiratory diseases (e.g., cystic fibrosis), neurologic disorders (e.g., multiple sclerosis), infectious diseases (e.g., hepatitis), psychiatric disorders, and intellectual disabilities. Some of these conditions have a known effect on developing fetuses, and taking appropriate preventive measures can decrease risk to the fetuses.

Prenatal care, in which a health-care professional monitors a woman's pregnancy, is statistically the most important factor in decreasing problems associated with any of these maternal conditions. For example, early and consistent care results in an almost eightfold decrease in the incidence of prematurity (Debiec, Paul, Mitchell, & Hetti, 2010). At the same time, lack of prenatal care is one of the most reliable predictors of problems occurring. Many of the conditions discussed in this chapter could be identified and addressed through good prenatal care, thereby reducing risks to mother and infant.

Common Conditions of Gestation

The following conditions are frequently seen during gestation. They lead to the need for advanced intervention for the pregnant woman and account for the majority of premature deliveries. Educating pregnant women through prenatal care to look for signs of complications can decrease the incidence of problems to the fetus. Table 5–1 summarizes these conditions.

Placenta Previa Placenta previa is a condition in which the placenta implants in the bottom segment of the uterus instead of the top segment. The normal site of implantation of a fertilized egg is in the upper half of the uterus. When a placenta previa occurs, the placenta implants over the opening of the cervix. Many pregnant women who have a placenta previa have several episodes of bleeding through the second and third trimesters of the pregnancy. Several factors, including contractions of the uterus, intercourse, and excessive fetal activity, may initiate the onset of sudden and excessive bleeding. This bleeding is generally not painful but can result in a heavy blood loss over a very short period of time and places an unborn infant at high risk for death.

An ultrasound is often conducted after a woman has an episode of bleeding and then seeks care to determine the cause and diagnose the condition. A woman with known placenta previa is placed in the hospital and on bed rest until the length of gestation is sufficient for the fetus to be capable of independent breathing after birth. This ensures that immediate care is available for both the woman and the unborn infant should sudden, excessive bleeding occur from the placenta. A woman who has received consistent care is generally able to carry an infant close to term, and the baby is then delivered by cesarean section.

Table 5–1 Conditions of Gestation

Condition	Characteristics
Placenta previa	The placenta implants in the bottom segment of the uterus instead of the top segment. Requires bed rest until the fetal gestation is sufficient for independent breathing after birth.
Abruptio placenta	The placenta prematurely separates from the wall of the uterus. Causes decreased availability of oxygen and nutrition, decreased blood flow to the fetal brain with decreased tissue perfusion, and even fetal death.
Toxemia of pregnancy	This condition causes an elevation in maternal blood pressure, decrease in urine output, and decrease in the ability of the kidneys to conserve protein and salts, contributing to swelling of the extremities that may advance to the liver and brain. Reduces blood flow to the uterus, and the placenta then begins to shrink in size, causing fetal growth retardation.
Prolapsed or entangled cord	The length of time this condition exists can be a critical factor in determining whether the fetus will asphyxiate *in utero* and die, or blood flow will be resumed at a point at which neurological damage may occur but the fetus will survive the insult.

Abruptio Placenta Abruptio placenta is a condition in which the placenta prematurely separates from the uterine wall before delivery of the fetus. This can occur at any time during gestation and results in varying degrees of separation. The impact on both the mother and the fetus can be significant. Partial separation of the placenta results in vaginal bleeding, which may be light or heavy, and is generally associated with abdominal pain in the mother. The fetus may be affected by decreased blood flow and may respond with either a drop or an increase of the heart rate. This change in blood flow can have a significant impact on an infant's long-term outcomes. Effects include decreased availability of oxygen and nutrition, decreased blood flow to the brain, and even death. Repeated abruptions result in growth retardation along with any of the fetal factors of an acute abruption.

Acute and total abruptio placenta results in fetal death. When the placenta fully separates from the uterine wall, the fetus loses the supply of oxygen and nutrients essential for sustaining life. This condition also has significant maternal effects. Many women who have a total abruption have an increased risk of bleeding from many systems, which could result in maternal death.

Pregnancy-Induced Hypertension and HELLP A major problem associated with pregnancy and delivery is referred to as **pregnancy-induced hypertension (PIH)** or gestational hypertension (high blood pressure); some 6% to 8% of pregnant women develop PIH. This condition presents a variety of symptoms that have variable effects on individual pregnancies. The exact cause of the cluster of symptoms and why they occur during pregnancy remains unknown, although factors that increase an individual's vulnerability to PIH have been identified: diabetes, multiple gestations, and hypertension. The incidence of PIH has increased significantly in the United States, rising from 67 of every 1,000 pregnancies in 1998 to 81 of every 1,000 in 2006 (Kuklina, Ayala, & Callahan, 2009). Women with PIH may experience kidney failure, blood clotting, cardiac episodes, and respiratory distress. Eclampsia and severe preeclampsia are the signature dangers of PIH and represent the leading cause of maternal deaths in the United States (Clark et al., 2008). Although there are no proven means of preventing PIH, consistent, high quality prenatal care can help mitigate the dangers.

For unknown reasons, blood vessel spasms occur in PIH—the vessels alternately expand and contract—resulting in damage to the lining of the vessels. The resulting damage to the veins and to red blood cells passing through these blood vessels signals the body to release platelets. Platelet action in the bloodstream causes clotting over the damaged tissue and cells, increasing the vessel volume and further clogging the flow of blood. Additional stress on the cardiovascular system results when a victim's kidneys react to the loss of red blood cells (hemolysis) by retaining water, further adding to the blood volume. As the volume increases, so does the blood pressure in order to push blood past the damage. This is the hypertension created in PIH. If the pressure continues unabated, the body will signal the kidneys to retain water to make up for the damaged red blood cells, and the vessels themselves "leak" fluid, causing tissue swelling (edema). Decreased blood flow puts additional stress on multiple systems (heart, lungs, brain, kidneys, and liver). These factors can lead to abruptio placenta and eclampsia.

When the liver becomes involved, the risk to mothers and infants increases significantly. This condition is known as **hemolysis, elevated liver, and low platelets**

(HELLP). As mentioned, clotting reduces blood flow and oxygen supply to the body. Lacking oxygen, the liver begins to die, affecting both maternal and fetal vascular systems. Mothers are at risk of liver rupture and damage, abruptio placenta, hypoglycemia, and pancreatitis, among other effects. Infants who survive are at very high risk of intrauterine growth retardation (IUGR) in addition to kidney, cardiovascular, and neurological damage.

Maternal Diabetes   Diabetes in pregnant women can be present prior to the pregnancy or can come about during gestation. Infants of diabetic mothers, regardless of the onset, are at significantly higher risk for natal and postnatal complications.

    Gestational diabetes is a condition of increased blood sugar that is initiated by the pregnancy. It is usually diagnosed during the second trimester through laboratory analysis. Generally controlled through diet, diabetes may occasionally require the use of insulin. Although the condition disappears after delivery, it does appear to be a predictive factor for the development of age-onset diabetes later in the mother's life and increases the risk of maternal diabetes during later pregnancies. Risk factors for congenital diabetes are the same as those that are predictive of later onset diabetes: prepregnancy weight or excessive weight gain during pregnancy (especially associated with high animal fat and cholesterol in the mother's diet), family history of diabetes, non-Caucasian ethnicity, and cigarette smoking (Bowers, Tobias, Yeung, Hu, & Zhang, 2012; Ouzounian et al., 2011; Xiang et al., 2011).

    Preexisting diabetes in a woman who then becomes pregnant raises many issues for maternal care during gestation. The physiological changes that occur in the human body during gestation have a significant effect on a woman's ability to maintain normal control of her diabetic condition. Nutritional factors and insulin needs are inconsistent during the course of the gestation and, in turn, affect the well-being of fetuses. Precise control of diabetes decreases the risk to a fetus, but this control requires a multidisciplinary approach to the pregnancy and a mother who is committed to providing her fetus every opportunity for normal growth and development.

Rh Sensitization   All human beings have a specific blood grouping that is inherited from their parents and whose genetic framework they pass to their children. In some situations, the mother's antigen and that of the unborn fetus are not compatible. When this occurs, the mother produces antibodies against the fetal blood.

    Rh is a blood group or collection of molecules on the red blood cells. Blood groups used to identify a person's blood compatibility include A, B, AB, and O, each of which can be either Rh factor positive or negative. Either the Rh factor is present (Rh+) or absent (Rh–) in an individual's blood system.

    Rh sensitization occurs when a female with a negative blood Rh is exposed to positive blood Rh. This may occur during a blood transfusion or as a result of a pregnancy when the partner has an Rh-positive blood type. Sensitization may occur with any pregnancy, even those that end in miscarriage at a very early gestation. The Rh-positive antigen crosses the placenta, and the maternal response to this foreign protein is to produce antibodies against the perceived invasion. This is a normal response of a healthy immune system.

    The initial pregnancy in which Rh-positive and Rh-negative blood are involved is not affected, but subsequent pregnancies in which the mother now has an activated antibody against Rh-positive blood will be affected if the fetus has Rh-positive blood. The result of fetal exposure to the maternal antibody is profound fetal anemia. If not diagnosed and treated *in utero,* the fetus may die or have problems caused by the anemia.

Progress in medical technology and public awareness has significantly decreased both the occurrence of Rh sensitization and the effects of the process on the development of affected infants. Treatment consists of giving blood transfusions *in utero* or exchanging the fetal blood to prevent the breakdown of the normal blood cells. Either of these interventions supports the affected fetus until the gestation has progressed to viability or the fetus can breathe outside the uterus. Severely affected infants may also require exchange transfusions because of the high levels of bilirubin that build up in the bloodstream as a result of the breakdown of the affected red blood cells. Transfusions are performed to prevent the effects of high bilirubin concentrations on normal brain development. Severe intellectual disabilities and cerebral palsy may occur with very high levels of bilirubin. Prevention of sensitization is now possible with RhoGAM. This vaccine destroys any RH-positive cells that enter the maternal circulation, preventing the mother from producing antibodies that will eventually destroy the blood cells of the unborn fetus.

Premature Rupture of the Membranes   A common condition initiating premature delivery is premature rupture of the membranes. Normally, when this occurs, the bag of waters that surrounds the fetus breaks prior to the 37th week of pregnancy. This may either initiate the onset of uterine contractions and subsequent delivery or place the woman and fetus at risk for infection with the loss of the protective barrier around the infant.

The reasons for premature rupture vary. Although most instances are not explained, an infant who has acquired an infection is thought to initiate the process in many cases. Even with a ruptured sack, the placenta and infant continue to produce fluid, and the woman continues to leak fluid throughout gestation until delivery occurs. Any bacteria (or virus) that may be present in the mother's vaginal tract can find its way into the uterus and come into contact with the fetus. Careful observation of the mother and infant for signs of distress or infection can delay a potential delivery. An infant who experiences a premature loss of the bag of waters is at risk of interruption of normal physical growth related to the alterations in the environment. However, rupture of the membranes tends to speed up the process of maturation of the lungs in a fetus as an infant's self-protective mechanisms sense impending delivery and actually accelerate the maturation process.

Premature Labor   Regular uterine contractions that cause dilatation of the cervix signal the onset of labor. Contractions and dilatation occurring prior to the 37th week of gestation is defined as **premature labor.** While considerable variation exists across sources, it is estimated that as many as 10 percent of all births have episodes related to premature labor. This rate increases when women are at risk due to socioeconomic factors and inadequate prenatal care. That is, women receiving care tend to be educated about the warning symptoms of labor and are more likely to seek help before labor has progressed to the point of making premature delivery unavoidable. Many women have regular uterine contractions prior to delivery. This may result from uterine weight, fetal movement, stress, diet, exercise, and many other factors.

However, unless the cervix changes and moves from a backward to a forward position, premature labor may not be occurring.

One cause of premature labor, an incompetent cervix, is a premature thinning of the lining of the cervix. As a result, the cervix becomes too weak to withstand the pressure of the fetus. Pelvic pressure and spotting may be symptoms of an incompetent cervix, which can result in premature birth or miscarriage. Prior damage to the cervix, such as a biopsy or abortion, can be the cause of incompetency.

In many cases, premature labor can be controlled with medication and bed rest. Careful monitoring of both maternal conditions and the status of the fetus is critical in any situation in which an attempt is made to stop labor. If the labor is progressing and delivery is unavoidable, current technology allows for acceleration of fetal lung maturity with medication (administered within 36–48 hours of delivery), which allows a woman undergoing premature labor to deliver her infant with decreased risk.

Maternal and Infant Natal Complications

Labor is precarious for infants who are expected to pass from the dependent world of dark, warm liquid to a world that is bright, cold, and dry and that requires the ability to both breathe and excrete waste products independently. The physiological adaptations are easier when the labor and delivery process does not place additional stress upon infants.

Labor is the process in which a mother and fetus work together toward the goal of delivery. The uterus provides the contractions that produce pressure on the emerging part of the fetus to dilate the cervix. Dilatation is necessary to provide a passage for the infant from the protective environment of the uterus into the world. Labor requires that both the mother and infant participate to successfully complete the process.

Conditions that negatively influence the ability of either the mother or the fetus to be effective during the labor and delivery process may occur (see Table 5–2). In addition, maternal factors may include an ineffective labor pattern that:

1. Does not produce the uterine pressure necessary for dilatation to occur

2. Has too few uterine contractions

3. Is accompanied by high-risk maternal conditions, such as toxemia of pregnancy

All of these factors place the mother at risk during the labor process. Fetal conditions may also influence the course of the labor and delivery. The normal fetal position for delivery is head down. It is possible, however, for a fetus to present in an abnormal position. The fetus may be breech (bottom first), transverse (sideways), large for gestation, or have congenital defects that prevent proper positioning to occur. The health status of the fetus also influences its ability to withstand labor.

Dysfunctional labor may be improved with the use of medication to increase both the number and strength of uterine contractions. However, if medication is not effective, delivery by cesarean section may be necessary. Medication must be closely monitored to make sure that the fetus can withstand the increased uterine pressure. The shoulders of a large-for-age infant may fail to pass below the mother's pubic bone,

Table 5-2	Maternal/Infant Natal Conditions
Condition	**Characteristics**
Dysfunction of labor and/or delivery	Ineffective labor pattern, too few uterine contractions, or maternal conditions place the mother at risk for abnormal labor process. These may be malposition of the fetus, large size for gestation, and congenital defects that prevent proper positioning.
Prolapsed or entangled cord	The length of time blood flow is obstructed can be a critical factor; the fetus could asphyxiate *in utero* and die, or blood flow will be resumed at a point at which neurological damage may occur but the fetus will survive the insult.
Hypoxic–ischemic brain injury	Hypoxia, decreased oxygen levels, and ischemia—death of the cells and tissue due to decreased blood flow—can occur together or separately. Neurological damage from these conditions generally includes severe intellectual disabilities, intractable seizures, and spasticity.
Meconium aspiration syndrome	The fetus either gasps before delivery (usually from asphyxia) or meconium is aspirated into the trachea and airways with the infant's first breath if its mouth and nose have not been cleared of the amniotic fluid that contains meconium particles. This initiates a state of pneumonia.

which can cause cord compression that, in turn, may lead to asphyxia. Assessment of the maternal pelvis (by examination) and the estimated fetal size (by ultrasound) prior to the onset of labor may prevent a shoulder dislocation. Anticipation of this occurrence may lead health-care providers to surgically deliver the infant.

Prolapsed Cord/Entangled Cord

The umbilical cord is the lifeline by which a fetus is connected to the placenta, which is, in turn, connected to the mother. This structure contains one large blood vessel and two smaller vessels that carry oxygenated blood and nutrients from the placenta to the fetus. The two small vessels return blood with fetal waste products to the fetal side of the placenta, where an exchange takes place across a membrane to the maternal side of the placenta. The cord vessels are protected by both a thick membranous cover outside and a thick jelly-like substance lining on the inside.

If an infant is entangled in its own cord, the fetal heart rate may slightly decrease during a contraction. Occasionally, a fetus may become entangled in the cord during gestation, decreasing blood flow through the cord. The length of time the flow is obstructed can be a critical factor in determining whether the fetus will asphyxiate *in utero* and die or, with the resumption of the blood flow, the fetus will survive. Even though neurologic damage is likely, such infants are born without any outward, physical indications of an *in utero* insult but display obvious and profound symptoms of neurological deficits after delivery. Symptoms of damage may include seizures, abnormalities in muscle tone, and the absence of primitive reflexes.

Prolapse of the umbilical cord   Abnormal positioning of a fetus may cause the umbilical cord to fall from the uterine cavity after the mother's water has broken, causing a **prolapse of the umbilical cord**. The normal position of a fetus for a vaginal delivery should be head down, but when the fetus is breech or transverse, space is available for a cord prolapse. This places a fetus at risk for loss of blood flow due to cord obstruction. The presenting part of the fetus can come to rest on the cord, and blood flow either significantly decreases or stops completely. The fetus then experiences asphyxia, and death occurs rapidly. If prolapse occurs, the emerging part of the fetus must be manually held off the cord, allowing for blood flow, and delivery by cesarean section is performed immediately. Infants who are delivered rapidly can expect normal recovery, but if a prolapsed cord occurs outside the health-care setting, even if the infant survives, significant neurological damage is likely.

Neonatal Conditions

Hypoxic–Ischemic Perinatal Brain Injury

Hypoxia (decreased oxygen levels) and **ischemia** (death of the cells and tissue due to decreased blood flow) can occur together or separately. These conditions account for the largest group of infants with severe, nonprogressive neurological deficits that happen prior to and during delivery. Permanent changes in the neurological structure of the brain matter follow such injuries and result in neurological damage that generally includes severe intellectual disabilities, intractable seizures, and spasticity.

Hypoxic–ischemic brain injury can occur during gestation or during the labor and delivery process. Any situation that causes a decrease in blood flow or oxygen supply or an increased level of carbon dioxide can result in the condition. The cycle is repetitive unless intervention (change of position or supplemental oxygen) increases the blood flow again. Infants do not have the reserves of larger children and adults, and smaller decreases in central blood pressure may severely disrupt blood flow to the brain.

Infants who have experienced either prenatal or natal asphyxia syndrome may have problems with independent respiration and hyperactive responses to the environment. Seizures are often observed between 12 and 72 hours after birth. The earlier the onset of the seizures, the more serious their insults are on an infant's neurological status. Garfinkle and Shevell (2011) followed 62 infants who had experienced neonatal seizures. Of these infants, 37 percent had no long-term developmental problems, 55 percent had one or more serious neurodevelopmental disabilities (i.e., epilepsy, intellectual disability, cerebral palsy), and 8 percent died.

Brain damage from asphyxia can be determined by diagnostic imaging methods such as CT scan or MRI (described in Chapter 6). Death of the brain neurons results in the transformation of brain matter into fibrous tissue. This injured brain matter is ultimately replaced in many areas by cysts, which can be located using scanning methods. Other affected areas of the brain can be identified through the seizure patterns that emerge. Certain seizure patterns are known to evolve from damage to specific brain areas.

Meconium Aspiration Syndrome

Meconium is the accumulation of fetal waste products that collects in the bowel during gestation. The rectum should not relax until after the infant is delivered, but when a fetus experiences asphyxia or is overdue, the muscles of the rectum relax, and the infant passes meconium into the amniotic fluid. This results in a green staining of the fluid, which is generally obvious with rupture of the bag of waters. Even mild asphyxia can initiate the passage of meconium and possibly put the infant at risk for aspiration syndrome. This material contains fetal waste products as well as fetal sludge (skin, hair, cells, etc.), which can be swallowed or absorbed through the intestinal wall.

Meconium aspiration syndrome occurs when a fetus either gasps before delivery (usually from **asphyxia**) or when meconium is aspirated into the trachea and airways with the first breath of the infant whose mouth and nose have not been cleared of the amniotic fluid that contains meconium particles. This aspiration can lead to pneumonia, which may be mild to severe. Multiple physical problems that result from aspiration syndrome can affect the respiratory system, the cardiovascular system, and the neurological system. Permanent neurological dysfunction is common.

A common, but expensive, treatment for infants with severe respiratory distress involves diverting blood from the infant and conducting it through a membrane oxygenator to artificially exchange oxygen and carbon dioxide, warming the blood and returning it to the infant's body. This method, referred to as *extra-corporeal membrane oxygenation* (ECMO), is a heart-lung bypass procedure that greatly increases the chances of survival. However, even with the use of this sophisticated technology, developmental problems occur in approximately 17 percent of survivors (Dargaville, 2012).

Although research is limited, a promising treatment for children with meconium aspiration syndrome and other respiratory disabilities is called high-frequency oscillatory ventilation (HFOV) (Dargaville, 2012). This procedure reduces the risk of lung disease while providing respiratory support to infants with compromised lungs. A failure to respond to HFOV suggests the need to transfer an infant to ECMO therapy, but in clinical trials this was needed in only 5 percent of cases.

Why Does the United States Have Such a High Infant Mortality Rate?

Despite one of the most advanced medical systems and the greatest wealth in the world, the United States seems unable to prevent newborn deaths at the same rates as those of other developed nations. Although infant mortality in the United States dropped from 26 per 1,000 live births in 1960 to 7 per 1,000 in 2004, our country ranks second to last among developed nations. Another blight on the U.S. performance is the obvious racial divide; the Center for Disease Control and Prevention reports that infants born to black mothers were 2.5 times more likely to die than infants

of Caucasian mothers. Although the United States ranks high in the availability of neonatologists and newborn intensive care units (NICUs), nations that have fewer, such as Australia, Canada, and the United Kingdom, continuously outperform our more resource-rich nation in limiting newborn deaths.

Analysts place the blame for poorer newborn performance on the vast disparity in health-care access among racial and economic groups in the United States. In other words, while some people have access to the most and best medical resources in the world, persons of color and those who are poor fare more like those in the poorer nations of the world. Thirty-three percent of all low-birth-weight children in the United States are African American, while only 17 percent of all births were to African American families. The Save the Children organization used 10 measures from the 2007 *State of the World's Mothers Report* to compile an index about mothers. This index included maternal mortality, use of modern contraception, births attended by skilled personnel, adult female literacy, participation of women in national government, infant mortality rate, primary school enrollment rate, safe water availability, anemia in pregnancy, and nutritional wasting in children under 5. The findings of this study revealed that political will was more important than national wealth in determining ratings on this scale. "In countries where mothers do well, children do well."

While the United States underperforms in mother–child support, many nations face even more bleak situations. For instance, Liberia had a mortality rate of 144 per 1,000 in 2005, 20 times higher than that in the United States. In fact, 99 percent of all newborn deaths take place in developing countries—with particularly high rates in countries with a history of armed conflict such as Liberia, Afghanistan, Iraq, Angola, and Sierra Leone. It is believed that three out of four infant deaths could be prevented with simple, low-cost intervention such as antibiotics for pneumonia, sterile blades to cut umbilical cords, and knit caps to keep babies warm. More intensive family planning with modern contraceptives can also reduce the very high rate of infant mortality that results from pregnancies that occur too close together, too frequently, and too late or too early in a mother's life.

Source: From "U.S. Has Second Worst Newborn Death Rate in Modern World, Report Says," by J. Green, 2006. Retrieved July 20, 2007, from *http://www.cnn.com/2006/HEALTH?parenting/05/08/mothers.index/index.html*

Postnatal Conditions

Many of the postnatal complications that infants encounter are the result of prematurity. In addition, infants affected with congenital abnormalities, congenital infections, acute infections, birth trauma, and many other conditions end up in neonatal intensive care units in this country. The following addresses only a few of the conditions that affect these infants. However, the conditions discussed here frequently result in outcomes that place these infants and young children in early intervention programs. Table 5–3 summarizes these postnatal complications.

Prematurity

Prematurity is the condition with the greatest effect on pregnancy outcomes in our society. It is also the single most common cause of sickness and death in infants worldwide. In 2005, an estimated 12.5 percent of all births in the United States were premature (a 33 percent increase over 1981), accounting for 75 percent of all neonatal deaths and 50 percent of all disabilities (National Academies Press, 2006). African American women are one-and-a-half times more likely than women of other races to give birth to premature infants, and those premature infants are more than three times as likely to die due to conditions related to prematurity (Shapiro-Mendoza & Lackritz, 2012). Poverty and maternal behaviors do not explain the disproportionately high percentage of preterm infants born to African American mothers (National Academies Press, 2006). For all births, infection has emerged as the only pathologic process linked definitively as a causal agent to prematurity (Gonclaves, Chaiworapongsa, & Romero, 2002). Infection enters the fetal system through four vectors: vagina to cervix, transplacental, seeding from the peritoneal cavity through the fallopian tube,

Table 5–3	Postnatal Conditions

Condition	Characteristics
Prematurity	Infants delivered before the 37th week of gestation. Two factors impact the prognoses: gestational age and size.
Intraventricular hemorrhages	Bleeding, which may cause brain damage.
Apnea of prematurity	Pauses in breathing due to position or neurological lapses.
Respiratory distress syndrome	Difficulty breathing caused by the absence of, or a deficiency in, the amount of surfactant present in the infant's lungs.
Bronchopulmonary dysplasia	Chronic lung disease of infancy.
Patent ductus arteriosus	Cardiac defect that frequently occurs in the very low-birth-weight and extremely low-birth-weight infant. This condition can result in increased respiratory distress.
Hypothermia	Low core body temperature, which places the infant at risk for other physical problems, such as increased respiratory distress, low blood sugar, and possibly intraventricular hemorrhage.
Retinopathy of prematurity	Overgrowth of connective tissue surrounding blood vessels in retinas of premature infants subjected to excess oxygen. This overgrowth ultimately damages vision.
Anemia	A deficiency in the number of red blood cells available to the infant.
Poor nutrition	Difficulty with sucking, swallowing, and breathing coordination as well as feeding apnea treated with either continuous tube feeding or mild or intermittent tube feedings.
Periventricular leukomalacia	A condition of brain development and function that is related to cerebral blood flow both prior to delivery and during the neonatal period. It most frequently occurs in premature infants; the most frequent and most profound symptom is spastic diplegia.
Failure to thrive	Inability of the infant to maintain or gain sufficient weight for healthy growth and development.

and accidental introduction during invasive procedures such as amniocentesis and fetal blood sampling. Birth defects have also emerged as a significant correlate of prematurity and are twice as common among preterm births and five times more common among very preterm births (24–31 weeks of gestation) (Honein et al., 2009).

Gestational age is a critical factor in determining what problems a particular premature infant may encounter. Pregnancy dating is not a perfect science and cannot determine precisely in which week of gestation a particular infant may be. Technology currently makes survival possible for infants as young as 23 weeks gestation, but these infants have the potential of a multitude of problems that affect them at birth, within the first weeks of life, and possibly into the future. The risk of death or permanent disability increases significantly as birth weight declines. As the March of Dimes (2002) reported, infants born within the normal birth-weight range represent 92.4 percent of babies born in the United States; 7.6 percent are low birth weight, and 1.4 percent weigh less than 1,500 grams (very low, or extremely low, birth weight). Since the late 1990s, innovative and aggressive medical intervention has increased survival rates from 20% to 40% of infants born at 22 to 26 weeks of gestation (<1,000 g infants); developmental delays decreased from 54% to 28%, and severe neurodevelopmental disabilities decreased from 34% to 8% (Zayek, Trimn, Hamms, Peevy, Benjamin, & Eyal, 2011). While risks have by no means been eliminated in ELBW infants, these data suggest that the limits of fetal viability continue to be adjusted as medical invention evolves.

Birth weight and gestational age together are more useful indicators of outcome than gestational age alone. Infants born at less than 2,500 g (5.5 lb) at 38 weeks of gestation are considered to have **low birth weight.** These infants may experience, to varying degrees, many of the problems commonly associated with premature infants: respiratory distress, apnea (breathing pauses), poor temperature control, and nutrition issues. Although survival rates for this group are as high as 95 percent, developmental delays are a concern. Neonatal hypoglycemia may account, in large part, for subsequent risk of cognitive delays in children (Kerstjens, Bocca-Tjeertes, deWinter, Reijneveld, & Bos, 2012).

Infants delivered at less than 1,500 g (3 lb 5 oz) are considered **very low birth weight (VLBW).** Such infants may be both premature and growth retarded. These infants are at risk for respiratory distress, bleeding within the brain and surrounding structures, infections, apnea, nutritional problems, and visual defects. Infants who are considered growth retarded within this context may be at risk for developmental delays due to a history of the placenta's extended inability to supply adequate nutrition to the fetus during the pregnancy. Infants born small for gestational age (SGA) are likely to progress better than VLBW infants who are born appropriate for gestational age (AGA) and better than infants who experience serious neonatal medical complications immediately after birth on long-term neurodevelopmental measures (Marks, Reichman, Lusky, & Zmora, 2006). VLBW infants are also at higher risk for cardiovascular disease, obesity, and diabetes. The incidence of VLBW is low (1.5 percent of live births), yet these infants account for half the infant deaths in the United States; 87 percent of these deaths occur in the first month of life (Lake et al., 2012). Recent research involving birth weight is also providing new insight into neurological functioning. Some researchers (Lampi et al., 2012) have found a link between low birth weight (including VLBW, SGA, and ELBW) and an increased risk of childhood autism, but not Asperger syndrome, which may indicate that prenatal factors affect these two disabilities differently.

Infants delivered at less than 1000 g (2 lb 3 oz) are considered **extremely low birth weight (ELBW).** Survival rates for these very fragile infants have steadily increased over the last 10 years, although 89.2 percent of infants born weighing between 501 g and 750 g at birth either died or suffered major neonatal medical challenges (Horbar et al., 2012). Although technological advances have increased the survival rate of premature infants with decreasing gestational ages, the same cannot be said for the rate of long-term conditions and complications. Of survivors, many require long-term special services that include special education (McGrath & Sullivan, 2011). McGrath and Sullivan (2011) found a decrease in IQ (up to 10 points), as compared to the norm, as the birth weight category became more extreme (i.e., in the order of LBW, VLBW, and ELBW). Early intervention—one of the best predictors of long-term adaptations—is needed for children who are high risk for cerebral palsy, ADHD, broad intellectual disabilities, learning disabilities, behavior disorders, autism, speech and language delays, hearing loss, and visual loss. In one long-term follow-up study, Grunau (2002) found that 48 of 74 extremely low-birth-weight survivors who were neurologically healthy with average broad intelligence had at least one area of learning disability. ELBW infants have the highest risk factors for poor or delayed outcomes. However, infants who escape intraventricular bleeding, chronic lung disease, and adverse environmental factors such as poverty and child abuse have a good chance of surviving with normal cognitive and motor development.

Extremely low-birth-weight infants frequently have some degree of intraventricular bleeding, which may cause brain damage. The effects of the bleeding are variable; deficits include a wide range of developmental delays. Visual and hearing deficits are common with these very immature infants. **Retinopathy of prematurity (ROP)** is a common occurrence caused by the need for long-term oxygen therapy (for apnea of prematurity) and capillary fragility, which may lead to bleeding in the capillaries that supply the retina of the eye. Hearing loss is also common and is related to drug therapy necessary for survival and the neurological impact of bleeding or decreased oxygen.

Infection is a frequent complication for an extremely low-birth-weight infant. The immune system does not become functional for several months after birth, leaving the infant highly vulnerable to any environmental or human bacteria or virus. Many of the infant's common care needs, such as intravenous feedings and airway support, contribute to the baby's risk of developing an infection.

Nutrition is a major complicating factor with extremely low-birth-weight infants. The gastrointestinal tract requires the initiation of oral feedings before maturation can occur. The ability of these infants to tolerate oral feedings is extremely variable. Because of chronic decreased blood flow and lower oxygen levels supplying the system, lung disease places the intestine at risk for perforation. Conversely, lung growth is necessary for healing, and this growth is compromised in the presence of inadequate nutrition. The interventions necessary for providing sufficient calories for growth have an impact on other organs, such as the liver or kidneys. Long-term, intravenous therapy leads to poor liver function. An infant's inability to be fed increases the potential for total system failure that can ultimately lead to death.

Clear ethical questions surround the treatment of ELBW infants. The debate about the human threshold of viability is an important and ongoing one within societies, particularly for medical practitioners, families, and care centers, with the main points for debate focused on long-term morbidity and the social and emotional costs of life support. In 2005, $26.2 billion was spent on medical costs of preterm infants, which is equivalent to $51,600 per infant (National Academies Press, 2006). Markestad and colleagues (2005) looked at outcomes of ELBW infants and found that while survival was up and morbidity down slightly compared to earlier research findings, the amount of resources required to sustain life of infants between 23 and 24 weeks gestation remained extraordinary. With the limits of viability seemingly reached at the same time that the rate of premature births continues to rise, focus has now shifted to prevention of prematurity—the new best way to ensure survival and reduce extreme costs (Masters, 2006). This approach focuses on the "nuts and bolts" of healthy pregnancies: minimizing smoking and drinking, maintaining proper nutrition, preventing infection, eliminating domestic violence, and, when necessary, giving drugs to prevent preterm labor.

Respiratory Distress Syndrome (RDS)

Respiratory distress syndrome (RDS) is a common condition found in premature infants; 50 percent of infants born between 28 and 32 weeks develop it (Pramanik, 2006). It is caused by an absence of, or a deficiency in, the amount of surfactant (a naturally occurring chemical sometimes referred to as *lung soap*) present in infants' lungs. Surfactant increases the surface tension of the lung, allowing the alveoli or tiny air sacs to open and stay open with an infant's respiratory effort. Decreased amounts, or absence, of surfactant cause the air sacs to collapse with expiration. Without sufficient surfactant to lubricate the lung tissue, premature infants are unable to generate enough pressure to reopen the collapsed segments of the lung. This creates a condition in which there is decreased lung surface tissue available for the work of exchanging oxygen for carbon dioxide between the lungs and the blood vessels. A low oxygen state can ultimately result in neurological damage and the advent of stiff lungs that require very high pressures to re-expand the collapsed segments.

Infants suffering from RDS display symptoms of respiratory failure: increased respiratory rate, retraction of the space between the ribs, audible grunting noise when breathing, and a blue-tinged or pale color of the skin in spite of supplemental oxygen. If the symptoms persist without appropriate intervention, infants eventually tire from their efforts and quit breathing. Mechanical ventilation, such as with a respirator or ventilator, is used to treat this condition. Artificial surfactant may decrease the likelihood of chronic lung disease. However, animal-derived surfactant is thought to be more effective because it contains essential proteins (Subramanian et al., 2001). Along with surfactant therapy, the use of antenatal steroids has been found to accelerate lung maturity and allow the use of a gentler ventilation technique—all of which minimize lung damage and have reduced the mortality rate associated with RDS by more than 50 percent in the last decade (Pramanik, 2006).

Mechanical ventilation has certain inherent risks. These include lung damage from increased artificial pressure, tearing of small airways resulting in air leaks between the external lung surface and the rib cage (pneumothorax), bleeding into the lungs from increased pressure, damage to the small capillaries that are part of the circulation pathway (pulmonary hemorrhage), and development of cysts created in the airways from excessive pressure (pulmonary interstitial emphysema), all of which can ultimately lead to chronic lung disease of infancy (bronchopulmonary dysplasia). Gentler ventilation techniques, such as high-frequency ventilation, continuous positive airway pressure (CPAP), and synchronous intermittent mandatory ventilation are three techniques under investigation that attempt to provide supplemental oxygen while reducing damage to infants' lungs (Pramanik, 2006). While oxygenation increases the survival rate of premature infants, those with extreme prematurity frequently acquire chronic lung disease and ROP as a side effect of the treatment itself.

Bronchopulmonary Dysplasia (BPD)

Chronic lung disease of infancy is called **bronchopulmonary dysplasia (BPD)**. It is the condition in which lung injury has occurred during the treatment of premature lung disease. Positive pressure from extensive oxygen use is one of the major causes of BPD. Occasionally, full-term infants who have had meconium aspiration or acute pneumonia from infection may contract BPD, as well. Health-care providers who treat these infants are aware of the potential implication of the treatments but are committed to providing the necessary intervention for acute respiratory failure and then dealing with the effects over the course of the first 2 to 3 years of life. Most ELBW infants also develop BPD, and the majority requires home oxygen therapy through their first year. Aggressive treatment of the accompanying health-care problems allows for the possibility of recovery, and many infants show normal lung function over the course of early childhood.

Infants with BPD show symptoms of respiratory distress including quickened respiratory rate, increased effort in breathing (which may be observed in retraction of the space between the ribs), use of abdominal and neck muscles to breathe, need for supplemental oxygen, and pale or dusky skin color. Additional symptoms may be poor tolerance for activities of daily living and symptoms of cardiac failure, which result from the strain placed on the heart and liver by chronic low oxygen levels and the need to maintain circulation through the injured lungs.

Bronchopulmonary dysplasia can also appear as a cluster of health problems for affected infants. These include, but are not limited to, problems with both acute and chronic infections, cardiovascular problems (including high blood pressure), kidney stones, vitamin and mineral deficiencies (which may result in bone fragility), feeding problems, and poor growth. This combination of factors places these infants at significant risk for developmental delays. Likewise, the longer infants require mechanical oxygenation, the higher the likelihood of cognitive delays. Emotional problems, such as failure to bond, are related to repeated and prolonged hospitalizations and irritability seen in infants with chronic air hunger from lung disease.

Infants experiencing the effects of BPD can recover. Aggressive attention to the infants' nutritional needs (which allows for new lung growth) and their respiratory needs (to prevent further deterioration), as well as medication to control cardiovascular effects, provides the time necessary for healing to occur. In conjunction with the efforts of professionals, early intervention is needed to allow children to develop normally within the constraints of their physical limitations.

Another significant problem associated with this disease is the dramatic impact on family structure. Many of the care needs of these infants may require skilled nursing. This may mean the addition of strangers to the inner family. Family systems that are already stressed may not survive the additional burdens this chronic disease places on individuals.

Patent Ductus Arteriosus (PDA)

Patent ductus arteriosus (PDA) is a cardiac defect that frequently occurs in both VLBW and ELBW infants. Because fetal circulation bypasses the lungs via an opening between the pulmonary artery and aorta, it is critical that this opening spontaneously close at birth. Premature birth, however, may prevent the complete transition to independent functioning, resulting in decreased cardiac output. This condition can result in increased respiratory distress for infants, who may have to be treated with medication or, in some cases, surgery to close this opening at one of the most vulnerable periods, the first week or two of life.

Hyperbilirubinemia

Most infants born at VLBW develop an abnormally high bilirubin level (Subramanian et al., 2001). This high level of dead blood cells is the combined result of an unusually high rate of red blood cell destruction and the inability of the immature liver and kidney to filter these metabolic byproducts from the system. Dangerously high bilirubin counts can result in deafness, intellectual disabilities, cerebral palsy, and death. To treat bilirubin levels, phototherapy is used in which the light from special blue lamps penetrates the skin and breaks down bilirubin into a more water-soluble product. If phototherapy fails, a blood transfusion that replaces up to 90 percent of a neonate's blood may be required.

Neutral Thermoregulation

Low-birth-weight infants do not have the physical or physiological mechanisms to maintain body temperature. Heat loss occurs rapidly in these infants through **convection** (heat loss from the delivery of unwarmed gases such as oxygen), **conduction** (heat loss to unwarmed surfaces such as a mattress), evaporation (heat loss through fluid loss via the skin), and **radiation** (heat dissipated from the body into the air). **Hypothermia** (low core body temperature) places the infant at risk for other physical problems, such as increased respiratory distress, low blood sugar, and, possibly, intraventricular hemorrhage. Caregivers make every effort to preserve body temperature during any interaction with very premature infants.

Temperature regulation may continue to be a problem for infants with chronic diseases. Poor regulatory mechanisms in infants with neurological deficiencies place them at risk for cold stress in what may appear to be a normal environment. Other conditions that may produce temperature instability are those in which there is decreased blood flow to the skin. This may occur in children who have congenital heart defects or acute or chronic infections or in infants who have problems with lung disease.

Intraventricular Hemorrhage (IVH)

The neurological system is one of the most vulnerable in any infant, particularly premature infants. Because the rich capillary beds that lie next to the ventricles of the brain are extremely fragile in premature infants, they are prone to bleeding or leakage when oxygen deprivation leads to rapid changes in blood pressure. Many factors that can influence low-birth-weight infants may result in an **intraventricular hemorrhage (IVH).** Extremes of temperature with rapid fluctuation cause dilatation and constriction of blood vessels, which may cause leakage or rupture of the vessels. Changes in blood pressure affect blood flow in the fragile vessels, also resulting in breakage or leaking. One of the most critical factors leading to IVH is the acid balance of the blood. Infants who are **acidotic** (have high levels of blood acid) are predisposed to fragile vessels, which increase the risk of bleeding. Acid buildup can occur with lung disease (high carbon dioxide levels and decreased oxygen), low blood sugar, infections, and temperature instability, among other conditions.

An inverse relationship exists between an infant's gestational age and the incidence and severity of IVH with the majority of occurrences happening within the first 72 hours of birth (Subramanian et al., 2001). Moreover, infants' area of bleeding, size of the affected area, age, and weight plus many other physical factors determine the amount and potential damage to function that may occur as a result of IVH. Bleeding that is acute and rapid tends to have a more serious impact on the overall stability of infants in the acute phase.

Intraventricular hemorrhages are categorized into four grades. The grade can predict the long-term outcomes for children, although its predictive value is not always accurate. For example, a grade IV bleed frequently results in hydrocephalus, or swelling of the fluid-filled cavities in the brain, which leads to the need for placement of a ventricular peritoneal shunt. Infants with this condition require ongoing developmental follow-up after discharge from the hospital and are at significant risk for serious developmental delays. Injuries to infants who sustain grade I bleeding often resolve without permanent neurological abnormalities. On the other hand, approximately 40 percent of all children with grade III and 90 percent of those with grade IV bleeding develop significant cognitive and/or motor disabilities (Subramanian et al., 2001). A comparison of IQ scores by IVH rating revealed an average IQ of 101 for infants with grade I IVH and a mean IQ score of 67 for infants with grade II or higher IVH rating (Bozzetti, Malguzzi, Paterlini, Colonna, Kullman, & Tagliabue, 2011).

Related to IVH is a second neurological disorder that occurs in premature infants, **periventricular leukomalacia (PVL),** or damage to the white matter of the brain. Also caused by rupturing of the blood vessels in the brain, PVL is associated with the development of cysts or fluid-filled holes, generally on both sides of the brain. ELBW infants with PVL are at risk for spastic cerebral palsy and other developmental disabilities such as cognitive, speech, and visual impairments.

Apnea of Prematurity

Premature infants have a very high incidence of irregular breathing patterns. In fact, 90 percent of infants born at less than 1,000 g suffer apnea of prematurity (AOP) (Hack, Wilson-Costello, & Friedman, 2000). Pauses in breathing are called *episodes of apnea.* These may be apparent at birth for infants who do not require ventilation or may develop over the first few days of life. This apnea results from central nervous system immaturity or even posture in small infants. Many cases may be attributed to a combination of both factors. When breathing pauses occur, an infant's response is generally a decrease in the baseline heart rate. This may be a small decline or a substantial one. Many infants require stimulation by caregivers or, if the apnea is particularly severe, mechanical ventilation.

Initial apnea in the infant may not be severe. When an infant does not self-stimulate (the autoregulatory effect provided by the nervous system), a brief period of nonbreathing can escalate to more profound states of apnea requiring intervention to prevent decreased oxygen to the brain, heart, and kidneys. Failure to appropriately intervene can lead to secondary apnea (respiratory failure or arrest), which is more difficult to reverse. Apnea can lead to the buildup of acid in the blood, placing affected infants at risk for bleeding into the brain.

Several interventions to decrease the incidence of apnea are possible, including continuous external stimulation, such as an oscillating mattress, and medications that stimulate the central nervous system to regulate respiration. These methods may be necessary for the first few months of life until the nervous system has matured sufficiently to maintain consistent regulatory control. Many premature infants are discharged from the hospital with continuous cardiac and respiratory monitoring and medication, provided their caregivers are trained to appropriately respond to apnea events.

Infections

Dangerous infections have several vectors of opportunity in premature infants. As mentioned, the first line of defense to infection—skin—is a target for yeast infection in premature infants. Moreover, stays in intensive care units introduce risk of *streptococci* infections, among other agents of infection. Infants with intravenous tubes and catheters are at greater risk of infection. Therefore, antibiotic and antifungal treatments are usually part of a regimen for premature neonates. The continuing crisis in medicine related to drug-resistant bacterial and fungal strains has resulted in conservative administration of the most powerful antibiotics and antifungal treatments. Such caution is meant to preserve the effectiveness of these reliable treatments for the most dangerous infections.

Retinopathy of Prematurity (ROP)

Because of their size and gestational age, low-birth-weight infants face the possibility of permanent visual damage. The number of ELBW of infants who develop ROP dropped by nearly one-half, to approximately 15 percent between the 1990s and 2007; further risk of structural blindness, or loss of sight in both eyes, is about 1 percent for infants born at <1000 g (Schwarz, Grauel, & Wauer, 2011). The risk of ROP is variable, depending on the ventilation needs of the infant and the need for supplemental oxygen during visual maturation, which takes place between 40 and 44 weeks after conception.

Prolonged exposure of fragile blood vessels in the retina to excessive levels of oxygen constricts and disrupts normal growth of retinal blood vessels. Abnormal new vessels accompanied by fibroblasts that produce scar tissue develop. The new blood vessels are then prone to leakage or rupture and grow outward from the retina into the interior space of the eyeball. In many cases, this overgrowth spontaneously recedes, permitting the retina to develop normally. In other instances, scar tissue continues to spread around the eye. When this scar tissue contracts, it pulls on the retina, causing the retina to detach, eventually leading to blindness.

At one time, ROP in low-birth-weight infants was controlled with the use of less oxygen, but decreased oxygen increased infant mortality rates and created a significantly higher incidence of cerebral palsy. Today, oxygen is administered liberally in an effort to save increasingly smaller premature infants. A mature retina is not affected by increased oxygen use. This is why few full-term infants have ROP. When given supplemental oxygen, premature infants must be closely monitored in order to keep arterial blood oxygen levels within a range that prevents hypoxia while minimizing the risk of eye damage. When deterioration of the retina proceeds rapidly, surgery may be necessary. Cryotherapy, or freezing of the blood vessels, and laser surgery are used to encourage overgrown vessels to recede. If these procedures fail, more invasive eye surgery may be conducted to reduce the contraction on the scar tissue, which causes retinal detachment. Unfortunately, to date, the success rate of such innovative surgical procedures has been limited.

ROP is currently categorized in four stages. In stage 1 and stage 2, damage generally resolves completely without treatment. Some infants with mild ROP that resolves either spontaneously or by laser or cryotherapy surgery undergo regression later in life in the form of strabismus, myopia, ambliopia, glaucoma, or retinal detachment. Stage 3 damage may require laser treatment, and stage 4 damage requires surgery to try to reattach the retina. Most infants who proceed to stage 4 have significant visual defects from this condition in spite of the surgical intervention.

Anemia

Anemia is the condition in which the number of red blood cells available to the infant is deficient. This can result either because of a failure to produce the cells or because cells are used or destroyed faster than they can be replaced. Premature infants may have anemia for both of these reasons.

Because the bone marrow of premature infants is immature, production of red blood cells, which takes place in the marrow, is inhibited until the marrow has matured. In addition to being unable to produce new cells, premature infants are nutritionally deficient, especially in iron, which also leads to decreased blood cell production. Even with supplements in their diets, premature infants often are unable to take in sufficient amounts of oral feedings to meet their iron requirements. Infants may develop symptoms of anemia such as decreased activity, poor feeding, increased apnea, and slowed weight gain. Consequently, premature infants usually require multiple blood transfusions during their initial weeks of life. In many hospitals, parents can request a directed donor. This allows parents and close family members to donate blood to be used by the premature infant, thus decreasing parental anxiety over multiple blood transfusions.

Nutrition

Immediately after birth, neonates must adjust to the loss of nutrition from their mothers and establish balanced glucose levels. Lacking sufficient glycogen stores to make the transition from maternal supplies to self-regulation, premature infants often require a continuous intravenous supply of glycogen to prevent hypoglycemia and its symptoms of seizures, jitteriness, lethargy, and apnea. It was noted earlier that hypoglycemia is the single most dangerous condition for late-term premature (34–38 weeks) infants. It appears that the first six hours after birth are the most critical in terms of stabilizing blood glucose levels (Nadeem, Murray, Boylan, Dempsey, & Ryan, 2011); even though many premature infants require sustained special attention to nutrition for many months, as effective early treatment may be negated if parents are not vigilant. In any case, children whose glucose levels cannot be adequately stabilized are at risk of cognitive delays (Tam et al., 2011). Tabarestani and Ghofrani (2010) described a hypoglycemia syndrome that includes visual impairment, motor impairment, and epilepsy. Excessive loss of body heat and rapid growth compound the risk by demanding very high caloric expenditure. Moreover, feeding is complex because these infants have not developed an instinctive desire to eat. Alterations in either physical or physiological processes that affect eating or digestion place an infant at risk for developing delays. Eating problems also increase the impact of existing disabilities on the course of an infant's life. Adequate fluids and sufficient caloric intake of essential proteins, fats, carbohydrates, vitamins, and minerals are necessary for healthy growth and development.

Term infants are born with primitive reflexes that allow them to initiate sucking and to coordinate breathing and swallowing. These reflexes disappear as maturation occurs, and the act of eating becomes voluntary. Premature infants, depending on gestation, may not have matured to the point of a primitive reflex state. Oral feeding for these infants is not possible. As they mature, these reflexes emerge, and learning to eat becomes possible.

Chronic disease in premature infants has an impact on both their ability to learn to eat orally and to digest food for growth. While disease prevents necessary nutrient intake and digestion, it also increases the need for caloric intake in order to maintain a minimal state of health and for growth to occur. This combination of impacts presented by disease increases the risk that an infant will fail to grow.

Premature infants require a minimum of 120 calories per kilogram (Cal/kg) of body weight each day for growth to occur. Chronic disease increases the daily caloric intake requirement to 150 Cal/kg of body weight for the same growth to occur. Infants should gain approximately 15 g (1/2 oz) to 30 g (1 oz) of weight every day. This allows for the linear growth and brain growth that are critical to a normal developmental progression.

Maintaining electrolyte and fluid balance is difficult as fluid levels are likely to fluctuate dramatically due to treatments, such as radiant warmers, a high proportion of water to other body mass, and because of poorly developed kidney function. Prenatal steroids can be used to help maintain electrolyte balance and prevent neurological, cardiac, respiratory, and other collateral effects (Omar, DeCristofaro, Agarwal, & LaGamma, 2000).

Difficulty with sucking, swallowing, and breathing coordination may necessitate tube feedings. Nonnutritive sucking (as with a pacifier) catalyzes learning and allows nutritive sucking to develop. At the same time, factors such as fatigue, illness, and congenital defects affect the rate and success of learning.

A feeding problem not limited to prematurely born infants is gastroesophageal reflux, or spitting up during or after eating. Infants with developmental delays are at greater risk of more severe and persistent symptoms related to poor coordination of gastrointestinal processes (Borowitz, 2002). While the vomiting is almost never a threat to nutrition, the occurrence can be lessened by appropriate positioning during and after feeding (i.e., with an infant lying down on the stomach or with at least a 30 degree trunk elevation in a supine position), thickening food, increasing the frequency of feedings, or administering medication. Usually when children begin to sit independently, gastroesophageal reflux diminishes.

Occupational therapy may be necessary during the neonatal period to assist in caring for the premature or sick infant who is feeding poorly and not gaining weight. Infants who cannot take in a minimal amount of fluids and calories for normal growth may require multiple interventions to assist in the feeding process. This may involve the placement of a **gastrostomy tube,** or a gastric button through which feedings can be given directly into the stomach, bypassing the esophagus.

Even infants who are receiving primary nutrition through a feeding tube are continually orally stimulated to teach them oral feeding. Once oral feeding begins, mother's breast milk, augmented with additional nutritional supplements, is the best choice to prevent necrotizing of the intestine—a common reaction to premature feeding.

Failure to Thrive

Failure to thrive can be described as the condition of growth failure in infancy and early childhood. Where infants fall on standard growth charts, which provide guidelines for normal growth, determines whether an infant's growth is adequate. Infants and young children who fall at least two standard deviations below the norm over a designated time period (generally 2 months) may suffer from growth failure. The signs of failure to thrive include decreased weight, decreased height, small head size, and any combination of these. This condition may be the result of a multitude of problems that affect the infant, including but not limited to inadequate economic means for adequate food, chronic disease (congenital heart defects, BPD, etc.), genetic disorders, emotional distress, and abuse. Prolonged failure will ultimately affect brain growth, leading to more complex problems.

Failure to thrive may be termed as either **organic** (having a specific physical cause) or as **nonorganic** (not having a specific physical cause). Many physical conditions that result in poor growth can be treated successfully (growth rates rise). These interventions may include increasing caloric intake through dietary changes and medications and the treatment of other physical factors that may affect growth, such as chronic ear infections.

Nonorganic failure to thrive is the more commonly occurring condition. Nonorganic factors that influence an infant's ability to grow normally include economics, ignorance, poor parenting skills, and ongoing family stresses. Feeding problems arise in these situations, resulting in prolonged malnutrition and, if not corrected, may lead to delayed mental development and, in the most severe cases, even death. Many infants with nonorganic failure to thrive appear to lose the will to live during periods of profound depression. This despondency can be mitigated by consistent and nurturing caregivers.

The ability to influence failure to thrive in infancy depends on the age of the infant at its onset, the cause, and the requirements for treatment. The earlier the infant is affected, the poorer the long-term outcome. Kerzner and Milano (2012) described four different types of childhood eating disorders—each with differential implications for effective treatment.

1. *Poor appetite* can occur in those children who are too active to be concerned about eating and those who are apathetic or withdrawn. Weight loss resulting from poor appetite has also been called infantile anorexia, which is not the same as, nor is it treated similarly to, anorexia nervosa. Intervention for active children involves making eating important (e.g., avoiding between meal snacks or drinks), while apathetic and withdrawn children require more aggressive intervention (i.e., temporary replacement of the caregiver) to repair a breakdown in communication between caregivers and infants so the child associates eating with a nurturing relationship.

2. *Highly selective,* or picky, eaters may be irritating, but don't often become so picky that they fail to thrive.

3. *Colic,* or excessive crying, may interrupt eating patterns, though this condition is usually resolved by 3 months and does not usually result in failure to thrive.

4. *Fear of feeding* is the result of a learned aversion to eating and the conditions surrounding eating. This fearfulness is much more challenging than other eating disorders since children have come to understand that eating is miserable. Desensitization requires caregivers to replace any aversive conditions, and in extreme cases, feeding children while they are sleeping. In many cases, children who have developed a fear of feeding may benefit from intervention by feeding teams, which may include behavioral and occupational therapists.

In severe cases of failure to thrive, comprehensive interdisciplinary planning is necessary. Specialized dietary preparations and specialized feeding techniques may be necessary to counteract children's behaviors and their aversion to feeding. Prolonged nutritional deficits place children at risk for learning problems that may affect gross motor skills, expressive language, and social skills.

Intervention for Infants Born Prematurely

Although not all premature infants have the same needs, medical and developmental services are typically needed. The most important factor in improving outcomes for infants who are born prematurely is to keep them healthy in early childhood. These interventions support good health:

- Speech therapy for children with chronic lung disease to promote feeding and language
- Physical and occupational therapy for children with chronic lung disease who have poor exercise tolerance and tire easily
- Home-based therapy to avoid exposing infants with low or poor immunity to risk of infection
- Emotional support for the family, including group meetings
- Aggressive attention to infants' nutritional status
- Regular opthamological examinations for children with prolonged oxygen treatment
- Special adaptations for children with mild or severe ROP to promote sensory integration

Families with children born prematurely undergo tremendous emotional and financial hardship. Educators can expect this stress to be manifest in confusion, anxiety, frustration, guilt, and anger. Due to prolonged neonatal hospital care and the impact of medical and neurological trauma, premature infants often lack the spontaneity and responsiveness of term infants. These factors can interrupt maternal–infant bonding. Professionals can assist parents by being ready to answer questions, encouraging quality interactions between infants and parents, providing a sounding board, and helping find resources for those who want to access resources that might directly or indirectly diffuse some of the stress such families experience. Later in infancy and early childhood, infants with unresolved medical and developmental difficulties are at greater risk for child abuse and failure to thrive (Pramanik, 2006). Therefore, ongoing home visits by social workers and health professionals are advised, especially when professionals have observed a disruption in the parents' attachment during their infants' NICU stays.

In Utero Toxins and Pregnancy Outcomes

Because substance abuse during pregnancy may be associated with many disabling newborn conditions and is entirely preventable, detailed discussion is focused on this topic. Alcohol, drugs, and cigarettes are all considered **teratogens,** agents introduced into the mother's womb that cause either physical or neurological harm to an embryo or fetus. While a range of environmental substances is dangerous, the most common are discussed here.

Fetal Alcohol Syndrome

Although the *in utero* effects of alcohol have been acknowledged for centuries, it was not until the 1970s that the term **fetal alcohol syndrome (FAS)** was officially attached to the constellation of characteristics now considered criteria for this syndrome. Since then, our understanding of FAS has matured thanks to decades of scientific study. The following terms frequently appear in research focused on prenatal alcohol exposure:

- *FAS:* The most severe effects of prenatal exposure to alcohol
- *Fetal alcohol effects:* Includes children who express some, but not all traits of fetal alcohol syndrome
- *Fetal alcohol spectrum disorder (FASD):* A range of effects from prenatal exposure, from those associated with partial fetal alcohol syndrome (pFAS) to those of FAS
- *Alcohol related birth defects:* Includes all children who have known impacts from prenatal exposure to alcohol
- *Prenatal alcohol exposure:* Describes a prenatal period during which fetal development is disrupted by exposure to toxic levels of alcohol
- *pFAS:* Includes children who express some, but not all traits of fetal alcohol syndrome

The scientific community now understands that alcohol consumption during pregnancy results in a range of biological harm to infants, with FAS representing the most extreme end of the gradient. Yet, this understanding has not resulted in a noticeable reduction in FAS. In fact, the incidence of FASD is on the rise in the United States and internationally. At the same time, it is believed that FAS and FASD are grossly underrecognized and underreported. FAS reportedly occurs in 0.5 to 1.5 infants per 1,000 live births (CDC, 2002), making FAS the leading known cause of intellectual disabilities.

Children born with FASD may not be identified at birth, and if FAS is suspected at some later point, the children must be examined by a medical professional to determine whether they have the syndrome. The three primary characteristics of FAS are:

1. Growth deficiency

2. Abnormal facial features

3. Central nervous system dysfunction

Additionally, the physician must find strong evidence of maternal alcohol consumption during pregnancy. If some, but not all, of the characteristics mentioned are present at birth, and if the mother is known to have engaged in heavy drinking during pregnancy, these infants will be labeled children with pFAS. Although this term is not a medical diagnosis, both its cause and effects may be as serious as those of FASD.

Infants with FASD are short for their chronological age and tend to weigh less than average. As these children age, they generally do not catch up physically to their peers. Facial characteristics commonly attributed to FAS include a short, upturned nose, thin upper lip, wide-set eyes, flat midface, epicanthic folds (a skin fold covering the inner corner of the eye), and ear anomalies. The characteristic most reliable for identifying children with FASD is a thin upper lip (Douzgou et al., 2012). All children with FASD have deficits in cognitive abilities, though the degree of intellectual impact varies from severely disabled to low-average intellectual ability. When academic content is concrete (in preschool and early elementary grades), children with FAS and pFAS may do quite well. However, abstract content causes increasing difficulties as children age, and in the middle elementary years the progress of these children tends to plateau, causing them to fall further behind their peers.

The behavioral characteristics of FASD are the most distressing for caregivers. Typical behavior patterns may or may not be associated with neurological damage sustained by vulnerable fetuses. That is, for infants and preschoolers with FASD, postnatal environments are often chaotic and sometimes transient. These chaotic environmental conditions alone could cause the kinds of abnormal developmental behaviors seen in children with FASD. Behaviors that arise from these sorts of environments (not necessarily in all children with FASD) include hyperactivity and impulsivity, language and communication difficulties (especially in social conventions), noncompliance, immaturity, and difficulty in self-regulation, judgment, and decision making (Ryan & Ferguson, 2006).

Children with FASD appear to be unresponsive to subtle kinds of consequences (e.g., praise, redirects) that help other children regulate their behavior. For example, children who are hyperactive tend to get into situations in which they are frustrated and become aggressive, yet it is difficult to isolate consequences that are effective in changing this impulsive behavior. As these children reach adolescence, their negative behavior may become more serious. Children with FASD are more likely than those without FASD to act immaturely, be cruel to others, and lack feelings of guilt or mature judgment, which could lead them to steal and lie (Davis, Desrocher, & Moore, 2011). These behaviors cause significant concern in terms of the children's adaptation to vocational and community settings.

Etiology   The cause of FASD is obvious—alcohol consumption during pregnancy. While the cause is known and entirely preventable, researchers have been relentless in attempting to determine the relationship between factors that interact with alcohol consumption and the range of outcomes that result in FASD. Even though some studies have found that light and even modest alcohol consumption appeared to have no significant damaging effects on infants, researchers are hesitant to recommend *any* safe level. Reluctance is understandable, as the physiological effects of prenatal exposure to alcohol continue to be unpredictable.

While the amount of alcohol necessary to do harm may not be understood, it is known that alcohol consumed during pregnancy crosses the placenta and enters the fetal bloodstream. A fetus's immature liver and neurological systems are less capable of metabolizing the alcohol than a mother's systems. Consequently, the alcohol becomes toxic. Factors, such as gestational timing, duration of alcohol use, and overall maternal health (e.g., age, nutrition, genetics), interact with the amount of alcohol consumed to influence fetal development. Individual women metabolize alcohol differently, with individual capacity varying eightfold (Burd, Blair, & Dropps, 2012). This capacity difference may explain why women who appear to consume the same amount of alcohol during pregnancy can have very different outcomes for their babies.

Musculoskeletal and organ anomalies, intellectual and behavioral deficits, and growth retardation are all thought to be linked to alcohol exposure during the first, second, and third trimesters, respectively (Gardner, 1997). The specific physiology of FASD comes increasingly into focus with advances in brain research. That is, the actual structure of the brain appears to be modified by prenatal exposure to alcohol (Niccols, 2007). Autopsies and brain imaging of individuals diagnosed with FAS found abnormalities in several areas of the brain (basal ganglia, corpus collosum, cerebellum, and hippocampus). In addition to the long-documented incidence of microcephaly, prenatal alcohol exposure is associated with asymmetry in the structure of the corpus collosum, the frontal lobes, and the brain's gray matter. Myelinization of nerve cells—related to the efficiency of neurological function—is also slowed by the toxic effects of prenatal exposure to alcohol.

Maternal drinking patterns explain most of the differences in neurological outcomes for children (May et al., 2011). As expected, higher levels of alcohol consumption correlate with higher incidence of FASD. Other important drinking patterns place women and their children at risk. For example, Walker (2011) studied 50, predominantly single, women seeking pregnancy tests or emergency contraception, to assess their understandings of alcohol's effects and how much they consumed. The younger women in the study had significantly more tolerant attitudes about alcohol consumption and drank significantly more beer than the older participants, drinking at least one time per week at a pace of 1 to 6 beers per drinking encounter. The group also had a very high rate of testing positive for pregnancy, illustrating the known challenge of reducing FASD—women often do not know they are pregnant until well into their pregnancy and may continue drinking during the period when fetuses are most vulnerable to the effects of alcohol. Other studies have found that young women drink in a different pattern than men—by preloading, or quickly consuming, alcohol (3–4 drinks within 2 hours)—a pattern that is particularly dangerous to fetuses and associated with the most severe traits of FAS (May & Gossage, 2011).

The danger from alcohol exposure to neurodevelopment does not end once an infant is born. Many fetuses who had been exposed to alcohol throughout pregnancy actually then go through alcohol withdrawal as neonates (from maternal alcohol consumption immediately prior to birth). Alcohol withdrawal is traumatic for adults, but for vulnerable neonates, the process may exacerbate prenatal damage. Seizures, delirium tremors, and violent agitation associated with subsequent withdrawal may compound the adverse effects of alcohol exposure from binge drinking.

Although the incidence of FASD is relatively high in some ethnic groups due to higher rates of alcoholism (i.e., American Indians and Native Alaskans), the toxic risk of alcohol to a fetus appears to be the same for all women. While FASD does not have a genetic cause, testing is conducted in some cases to rule out chromosomal and other genetic disorders that have similar phenotypic, cognitive, and behavioral characteristics.

Treatment   FASD requires the mobilization of multiple agency resources. For example, families may require alcohol rehabilitation before they can be expected to nurture a child with multiple needs. An early interventionist may be asked to mediate such services as foster care, child protection, mental health, alcohol rehabilitation, public school, public assistance, corrections, and public health. None of these agencies working in isolation is likely to be effective in meeting the many needs of families who have children with FASD. The prospects of children with FASD have been found to improve in stable and nurturing homes of good quality where the household is changed infrequently and the children are not victims of violence.

As one might expect, since FASD can be tied directly to a mother's behavior, these women often experience guilt over their contribution to limiting their children's possibilities. One woman, who drank throughout her pregnancy, said of her son, "There is a lot he wants to do, but I must remind him he's not like other kids; he can work with his hands and build cupboards but not [have a] thinking and writing job. He asks me why I drank so much [while I was expecting him]. I really don't have answers for him" (World Health Organization, 2011, p. 1). Another mother said, "I have lived with my guilt for several years now and I am in a deep depression. I cry a lot every day because I damaged my little girl. I ask myself what kind of mother I am to ruin my own child" (Phung, Wallace, Alexander, & Phung, 2011, p. 1). Professionals working with these families need to find a balance between helping women avoid future prenatal exposure to alcohol and being judgmental about lifestyle decisions. Acting in a way that exacerbates a mother's guilt is a sure way to close the door. On the other hand, when programs with compassionate and informed professionals mentor families with children with FASD by providing education, helping to access resources, and providing advocacy, families can develop self-efficacy (Leenaars, Denys, Henneveld, & Rasmussen, 2011).

The greatest hope for improved outcomes for children with FASD is early intervention (Ryan & Ferguson, 2006). Early intervention for children should center on social language, self-regulatory skills, and sustained attention. Specific suggestions for helping parents of children with FASD (Tanner-Halverson, 1998) include:

1. Foster independence in self-help and play.

2. Give choices and encourage decision making.

3. Establish a limited number of simple rules, and use consistent language to remind children of the rules. For example, "This is your bed; this is where you are supposed to be."

4. Use established routines so children know what to expect—advise them well in advance of changes in routines.

5. Teach new skills in small pieces.

6. Be concrete and teach by showing rather than just telling.

7. Set limits and be consistent in expecting children to follow them by having pre-determined consequences for both following and not following rules.

8. Review rules for getting rewards, and change rewards often.

9. Do not negotiate rules.

10. Redirect behavior rather than threatening.

11. Intervene before behavior escalates, and avoid overstimulating situations.

12. When giving instructions, repeat them and ask the child to repeat them.

Putting all the necessary resources in place for children with FASD is costly. Amendah, Gross, and Bertrand (2011) compared the medical cost alone for children with FAS as compared to children without FAS and found it nine times more expensive to have a child with FAS ($16,782 vs. $1,859 in 2005). In addition to the costly challenges presented by the constellation of developmental problems associated with FASD is the challenge of prevention. Women who place their fetuses at risk by consuming alcohol during pregnancy are themselves often at risk. That is, these women tend to be single, unemployed, on public assistance, lack prenatal care, smoke cigarettes and/or engage in polydrug use, have limited education, and confirm being alcoholics or binge drinkers who drink continuously throughout pregnancy (Cannon, Dominique, O'Leary, Sniezek, & Floyd, 2012). As Cannon and colleagues concluded, this foreboding behavioral pattern should make it possible to identify high-risk women. The benefits of preventative intervention with this population are clear. Further, early intervention professionals can predict that family-centered intervention will likely be both challenging and essential to improving child outcomes.

Prenatal Exposure to Drugs

At the height of the "cocaine baby" media anxiety in the late 1980s, it was suggested that one of the most challenging educational problem of the 21st century would be coping with the after effects of maternal use of recreational drugs during pregnancy. While cocaine use has declined, 50,000 infants are born each year having been exposed to cocaine prenatally (Minnes, Lang, & Singer, 2011). Longitudinal research, conducted with more care and with higher numbers of children, has failed, however, to validate these early dramatic predictions. This is not because drug use has disappeared as a serious social issue or because children who have been prenatally exposed to drugs are in no danger. There is sufficient reason to be concerned about the effects of both prenatal and postnatal exposure to such drugs as tobacco, cocaine, and methamphetamine.

Cocaine/Crack and Methamphetamines The physiology of cocaine (including crack) and methamphetamines on adults and fetuses is similar, although the drugs themselves vary considerably in price, availability, and addictiveness. Crack, the least expensive, is a crystallized form of cocaine (the powder form). Crack provides a more powerful, although shorter-lived, high and is significantly more addictive than either powder cocaine or methamphetamines. Each of these drugs causes blood vessels to constrict, resulting in increased blood pressure. In a pregnant woman, the placenta itself constricts, reducing oxygen flow to the fetus.

Likewise, fetuses directly exposed to cocaine that has crossed the placenta experience "highs" along with associated side effects. Because a fetus is unable to metabolize or break down the drug as easily as its mother, cocaine can stay in the fetal system for up to four times as long as in an adult's system. Primary risks to a fetus include premature birth, placenta previa, abruptio placenta, spontaneous abortion or prematurity, and possible neurological damage. In spite of the apparent risks, it now appears that for most infants, deleterious long-lasting neurological consequences of cocaine or methamphetamine use during pregnancy are either absent or so subtle that they are difficult to detect by common diagnostic procedures (Betancourt et al., 2011; Lewis et al., 2011).

Neonates born to drug-abusing mothers do not always show signs of prenatal exposure, just as some infants born to alcohol abusers do not. However, neonates who do show signs of prenatal exposure have a recognizable constellation of behavioral characteristics. No abnormal attributes in appearance are associated with prenatal cocaine or methamphetamine effects. Neonates who are obviously affected appear to have poorer than normal motor performance and, in responding to their environment, they tend to be less cuddly, more difficult to console, and less alert to environmental stimuli (LaGasse et al., 2011). These withdrawal features may persist for a few days, weeks, or months. Perhaps the most enduring and disturbing behavior is hypersensitivity to stimuli, which in some children remains a serious problem for years.

The long-term, permanent neurological damage to the brain from prenatal exposure to cocaine, once thought to be significant, is now considered to be associated more with polydrug use and smoking or environmental conditions than with crack/cocaine exposure alone (Schempf & Strobino, 2008). Such characteristics include problem behaviors, such as difficulty with habituation, short attention span, hyperactivity, and **attention deficit hyperactivity disorder (ADHD)** (Minnes, Lang, & Singer, 2011). A large longitudinal study of 1,227 children between 1 and 3 years of age found that when birth weight and environmental risks (i.e., quality of caregiving, poverty, maternal education) were controlled for, there was no association between exposure to cocaine and/or opiates and mental, motor, or behavior deficits in children (Messinger et al., 2004). If cocaine does have a long-lasting impact on development, it may be subtle, requiring researchers to carefully parse cognitive subskills to identify links. For example, it may be that cocaine-exposed children experience visual–spatial difficulties, slowing their efficiency in solving spatial maze problems but not their accuracy in these tasks (Schroder, Snyder, Sielski, & Mayes, 2004). Butz and colleagues (2005) also found subtle but significant deficits in preschoolers who were prenatally drug exposed in areas of attention, impulse control, and physiological state regulation (consistency of body temperature, heart rate, and other physical measures).

However, children who are raised in poverty and chaotic environments in general tend to do poorly in social, language, and cognitive development, whether or not they were exposed to cocaine *in utero*. Regardless of the cause, children in both groups may require substantial resources to compensate for their environmental disadvantage. However, children prenatally exposed to cocaine or polydrug use fared well when nurturing mother–infant relationships were established (Motz et al., 2011). Thus, it appears that more important than the drug exposure is the environment in which children are raised.

Bellinghausen (2000) reported on the current drug scene as it relates to childbearing women. While cocaine use by pregnant women has declined over the past decade, there has been an alarming increase in the use of methamphetamines in this same population. In fact, women who, for one reason or another, were unable to "get clean," intentionally switched to methamphetamines during pregnancy, believing its effect to be more benign, if not totally safe. It appears that the most consequential factors related to long-term physical, neurological, and behavioral effects of methamphetamines, like cocaine, are related to a "drug lifestyle." Specifically, women using drugs are less likely to eat well, leading to maternal or fetal malnutrition. Moreover, most methamphetamine users are polydrug users, often combining alcohol, opiates, or other drugs to counter the effects of methamphetamines. Therefore, researchers have not found compelling evidence that methamphetamine use by itself directly affects prenatally exposed infants' long-term behavior significantly.

The sequelae described for cocaine applies to infants who have been prenatally exposed to methamphetamine: low birth weight, SGA, and abnormal behavioral patterns (i.e., excessive crying, jitteriness). It is clear that the mother's behavior is not the only important influence because fathers who use methamphetamines are more likely to be abusive, resulting in an unsafe postnatal environment for mother and child. Again, Bellinghausen (2000) concluded that the best course of action is to provide a nurturing responsive environment—particularly in the first year of life. Some awareness of the potential harm to fetuses may influence drug patterns in pregnant women. For example, a recent longitudinal study of newborns (Buchi, Zone, Langheinric, & Varner, 2003) conducted in Utah between 1990 and 2001 found no significant increases in prenatal exposure to methamphetamine or marijuana and a dramatic decline in cocaine prevalence. This decline runs contrary to an overall rise in methamphetamine use by women of childbearing years in the United States.

Cigarette Smoking Cigarette smoking in North America has declined dramatically in the United States since peak use in the 1950s and 1960s. Yet, smoking continues to be a significant drain on the health and economy of the United States, with 443,000 deaths and nearly $200 billion in direct medical expenses and productivity loss each year (Garrett, Dube, Trosclair, Caraballo, & Pechacek, 2011). Every day, 3,900 teens smoke for the first time; 1,000 of these become daily smokers and most are addicted by the age of 20 (Garrett et al., 2011). Several factors associated with smoking are relevant: low SES, low academic achievement, high-risk sexual behavior, and combined use of drugs and alcohol (Garrett et al.). Although cigarettes contain more than 2,000 active ingredients, nicotine is considered the most harmful.

Tobacco crosses the placenta and causes vasoconstriction of the fetal blood vessels. Subsequent hypoxia or reduction of the oxygen-carrying capacity of the hemoglobin is due to an increase of carbon monoxide, which binds with the hemoglobin. Beginning very early in pregnancy, this process can have a degenerative effect (i.e., tissue death and reduced thickness) on the integrity of the placenta. Several outcomes that increase infant morbidity and mortality have been associated with maternal smoking before or after birth; these include abruptio placenta, placenta previa, still-birth, and premature abruption (Aliyu et al., 2011). The immediate risks of smoking on newborns include preterm delivery, intrauterine growth retardation, and low birth weight. Researchers have consistently found that the more cigarettes women smoke while pregnant the lower the birth weight (Fang, Dukic, Pickett, Wakschlag, & Espy, 2012). However, when mothers stop smoking either before or during pregnancy, the risk of perinatal and postnatal problems declines. In fact, Bailey, McCook, Hodge, and McGrady (2012) found that cessation of smoking may be at least twice as influential to birth weight as quitting illicit drug use. Cigarette smoking has harmful effects throughout pregnancy, though the first trimester may be the most vulnerable (Cornelius, Goldschmidt, DeGenna, & Larkby, 2012), with even moderate smoking (10 cigarettes per day) associated with significant long-term problems.

Prenatal exposure to tobacco is also correlated with a high incidence of lung disease and respiratory illnesses including respiratory distress syndrome and asthma (Harding & Maritz, 2012). In the first 6 months after birth, infants exposed to tobacco smoke *in utero* experienced higher than normal incidences of wheezing, breathing difficulty, and respiratory medical visits (Jedrychowski et al., 2007). Nicotine is a known carcinogen when metabolized during the prenatal period and increases the baby's risk of cancer (Wise, 1998). Moreover, smoking causes a harmful chemical change in breast milk (Bachour, Yafawi, Jaber, Choueiri, & Abdel-Razzak, 2011) as well as reduced breast-milk volume (Almqvist-Tangen, Bergman, Dahlgren, Roswall, & Alm, 2011).

There is also a relationship between the amount mothers smoke and the degree of developmental delays in their babies. In general, children born to heavy smokers tend to do worse on standardized tests of development than infants born to light smokers or nonsmokers (Herrmann, King, & Weitzman, 2008). After following a cohort of children whose mothers smoked during pregnancy for 14 years, researchers found many serious long-term problems associated with this toxic exposure (Cornelius et al., 2012). Behavioral problems included aggression, rule breaking, social problems, distractibility, and attention deficits.

In regard to cigarette smoking, as with other drugs, we should caution that neurologically vulnerable infants may do just as well as uncompromised infants when exposed to a nurturing environment. Nevertheless, it has been impossible to separate the isolated effects from the collateral effects of teratogens. In the meantime, it is most reasonable to assume the worst and recommend against nicotine use during and after pregnancy. As with other prenatal toxins, high-quality, early interventions can mitigate the long-term cognitive risks associated with tobacco exposure (Mezzacappa, Buckner, & Earls, 2011).

Implications for Infants and Children Prenatally Exposed to Drugs

It appears that the drug most harmful to fetuses with known long-term and significant effects is alcohol. There is also little question that cigarette smoking poses a substantial threat to the long-term development of children. Because these drugs cross the placenta—a direct link between mother and infant—women who expose their babies to drugs are blamed and often punished for their actions. Removal of children to foster care is common; a twofold increase in the number of children in foster care between the mid-1980s and mid-1990s was linked to cataloging children as neglected or abused because of maternal drug use. Some consider such removal of children from their biological families a moral obligation of society that is necessary to protect children from the risk of violence and neglect associated with drug-using families (National Association for Families and Addiction Research and Education, 1998). On the other hand, this criminalization of maternal drug use tends to victimize poor, minority women, while foster care becomes a major form of family life for too many minority children. This alleged victimization is clearly a social–ethical concern; however, it is also of practical concern for early intervention specialists' work in very complex social systems, chaotic family lives, and possible adversarial situations between the state and families. Managing the system requires knowledge of the social welfare and child protection systems and of the legal rights of families and children; it also requires careful execution of mediation and professional cooperation skills.

Interestingly, exposure either to a single drug or to polydrug use (and poverty) has similar developmental implications for children. Deficits in social skills and mild to moderate cognitive delays are common to all groups. For early interventionists, these general rules apply:

1. Involve multidisciplinary intervention, including educators, social workers, behavioral specialists, and health-care providers.
2. Establish sustained nurturing relationships with infants and young children.
3. Provide positive, structured, and predictable environments.
4. Avoid highly stimulating environments.
5. Provide direct training of social skills.
6. Adapt tasks to meet individual learning strengths.
7. Carry out functional analysis of serious behavioral problems.
8. Provide concrete, clear, and immediate consequences for both desired and undesired behaviors.
9. Give careful attention to diet and health care.

Caffeine For a long time, research on the prenatal effects of caffeine exposure on fetal development seemed to indicate that no conclusive deleterious effects existed. If anything, the conventional wisdom held that caffeine posed no harm and was even routinely prescribed to stimulate respiratory performance with premature infants. Recently, however, much has been made of new findings that even low levels of caffeine ingestion by pregnant women are associated with a significant increased risk of spontaneous abortions and stillbirths (Weng, Odouli, & Li, 2008; Wisborg, Kesmodel, Henriksen, Olsen, & Secher, 2001). The infants of mothers consuming high levels of caffeine during pregnancy showed signs of distress in the neonatal period: low birthweight, less time in REM sleep, and higher levels of general stress (tremors, jerkiness, and hiccups); moreover, caffeine use was frequently paired with maternal anxiety and depression, smoking, poor prenatal care, less education, and youth (Diego et al., 2008). While there is general agreement that caffeine ingestion during pregnancy should be restricted if not curtailed, there is no agreement on a safe amount. Therefore, pregnant women are advised to limit their intake to no more than 12 oz per day during pregnancy and while breastfeeding.

Chemical Toxic Exposure in the Fetal Environment

While many toxins entering the prenatal environment are avoidable and subsequent threats to development are preventable, the number of chemicals introduced to unborn children that are neither recognized nor avoidable is increasing. There are 83,000 industrial chemicals on the market, more than half of which have never been tested for human effects and 1,400 of which are known to have harmful effects (Madsen & Hitchcock, 2011). More than 100 known toxic chemicals have been found in the bodies of the average citizen in the United States (Madsen & Hitchcock, 2011). Studies conducted to determine the potential harm of synthetic chemicals are typically conducted one chemical at a time. However, as our food, air, and water supplies become increasingly polluted with heavy metals and dangerous compounds, it is clear that the assault on human physiology comes from many chemicals at once. While all humans (and other species) are affected by chemical exposure, it is most damaging to developing fetuses. Research in this area is complicated and still in its infancy.

Emerging understanding of *Bisphenol A* (BPA), used in plastics, has placed this chemical on the research forefront (May, 2011). Plastics are found in every corner of industrialized society; for infants, plastics are used in toys, bedding, diapers, bottles, etc. This chemical has been linked to accelerated puberty in females, obesity, and neurodevelopmental delays (Madsen & Hitchcock, 2011). Based upon a review of research, the alarm sounded by early research regarding BPA may be exaggerated (NIH, 2008). A careful analysis of previous research failed to identify reliable connections between BPA exposure prenatally or neonatally and later behavioral or endocrine disorders (NIH, 2008). However, reviewers at NIH (2008) acknowledged that further research is needed, and in the meantime, cautionary limitation of exposure to plasticized objects is sensible, and BPA-free products are now readily accessible in many stores.

Some chemical compounds used to improve our quality of life are now known to pose a risk to development. Polychlorinated biphenyls (PCBs) are made up of synthetic and organic chemicals and used in hundreds of different commercial and industrial applications. Through their manufacture, use, and disposal, PCBs are common in drinking water and may cause persistent changes in cognitive processing (Hebben, 2004). High levels of perchlorate may reduce iodine levels in breast milk and consequently inhibit thyroid functioning in women, an essential function in the neural development of a fetus (King, 2005).

Heavy metal presence in the environment is also a concern. Lead, mercury, zinc, and other common industrial metals now exist in dangerously high levels in our air, water, and soil. Unsafe amounts are even known to be present in the food we eat. Like many other toxins, these heavy metals can cross the placenta and are known to cause toxic brain injury (Kouris, 2007). While it is well known that lead is poisonous, especially so even at low levels in young children, its relationship to fetal development is less well understood. Although lead levels have been reduced in the past several decades due to decreased lead in fuel emissions, they are nevertheless still unacceptably high in many parts of the developing world. In fact, like prenatal alcohol exposure, there is no threshold below which lead is not toxic—and even small amounts of lead in the bloodstream can have a measurable affects on children's IQs. According to Ronchetti and colleagues (2006), lead toxicity that causes injury to the brain and spinal cord begins as early as the embryonic stage and is particularly dangerous during that stage. Diminished mental acuity later in life is linked to this very early exposure. Where does the lead come from? While lead might be ingested, lead stored in the mother's bones is of greater significance. As fetal calcium requirements rise during pregnancy, calcium is supplied cross-placentally from the maternal skeletal system. Posing no barrier, the placenta allows the calcium–lead transfer from a mother's bones to fetal bones and subsequently to fetal brain tissue.

Mercury, too, passes easily across the placenta. Historically, there have been several cases in which widespread exposure of pregnant women to methyl mercury (generally found in hazardous waste sites) was associated with cerebral palsy, microcephaly, and psychomotor retardation in the women's infants (Davidson, Myers, & Weiss, 2004). One of the major known sources of elemental mercury (used in thermometers, medical instruments, etc.) is through maternal ingestion of seafood and freshwater fish. Damage to the fetal nervous system from mercury is irreversible and long lasting, affecting cognitive functioning later in childhood (Harvard, 2004). For children participating in the Harvard studies and who were affected both prenatally and postnatally by mercury poisoning, exposure was generally at or below minimum levels set by the U.S. Environmental Protection Agency (1 part per billion). Pregnant women exposed to mercury have also been found to have higher rates of spontaneous abortions, stillbirths, and infants born with congenital malformations (Davidson et al.). Because of the dramatic increase in incidence of autism in the past decade, there is great interest in the theory, as yet unproven, that mercury exposure may be linked to this syndrome. Further research is needed to support or refute the contention that genetic mutations are caused by prenatal exposure to mercury (Davidson et al.). Although research points to mercury as an *in utero* neurotoxin, threshold levels for exposure are unknown. Currently, there is no known safe level of exposure to mercury.

IN CONCLUSION

One of the greatest challenges for society over the next decade will be to identify and plan interventions to decrease the impact of prematurity on infants and their families and to influence life choices that affect the health of future children. These plans should include education about prevention of prematurity, assistance to families involved with children with special needs, and interdisciplinary discussion regarding approaches that promote optimal functioning for affected children. Alcohol and substance abuse are two factors that increase the likelihood of premature birth. Most of these highly preventable early births are the consequence of social neglect of women whose lives are challenged by health problems (including depression), poverty, abuse, and poor education. Early childhood professionals who work with children born prematurely or affected by drug abuse will also be working within the context of families who have significant needs. Moreover, medical services are likely to be an ongoing part of the lives of children who are born prematurely. Therefore, a broad understanding of social and health services will be necessary to serve these children and their families well.

STUDY GUIDE QUESTIONS

1. Differentiate between the terms *prenatal, natal, perinatal,* and *postnatal.*

2. Briefly explain how prematurity dangerously affects each of the following systems: respiratory, cardiovascular, muscular, skeletal, integumentary, neurological, and renal/gastrointestinal.

3. List at least 10 maternal prenatal conditions (before and during pregnancy) that affect the outcome of fetal development; include both physiological and psychological conditions.

4. How do the following conditions of pregnancy pose a risk to a fetus: maternal/gestational diabetes, Rh sensitization, and premature rupture of membranes.

5. During labor and delivery itself, several conditions place neonates at risk. Identify and describe them.

6. Explain how hypoxia–ischemia places a newborn at risk for developmental delays.

7. What is meconium, and when does it pose a threat to infants?

8. Distinguish between low, very low, and extremely low birth weight and the effects each has on infants.

9. What is the relationship between RDS and BPD?

10. Explain the heat regulation concerns of premature infants.

11. A major concern of early childhood professionals regarding premature infants is IVH. Explain why this is so.

12. Define *apnea,* and describe its relationship to prematurity.

13. ROP is a common outcome of the treatment of prematurity. Explain why this is so and what is being done to prevent it.

14. What is the relationship between the nutritional needs of premature infants and anemia?

15. Define *failure to thrive,* and explain the difference between organic and nonorganic types.

16. What are the defining characteristics of FAS?

17. Why are children with FAS a challenge to families and professionals?

18. Explain the way in which cocaine and methamphetamines physiologically affect a mother and her fetus.

19. Explain the relationship between possible long-term behaviors associated with cocaine and methamphetamines and their treatment.

20. Summarize the influence of tobacco on fetuses.

21. What risks do PCBs, lead, and mercury pose to a fetus? Where do these teratogens come from, and how do they reach the fetus?

6 | Conditions Affecting Neurological Function

© Jaren Wicklund/Fotolia

Early childhood special educators are often a family's first link to intervention services and, consequently, a first bridge between medical treatment and other professional therapies. It is critical for these educators to have both substantive knowledge and reference information regarding the most common conditions that are associated with neurological damage. Although educators cannot be as intensely trained as medical personnel, they need a basic understanding of medical procedures and conditions in order to communicate effectively with other professionals and with parents.

Early childhood special educators may also find themselves in the role of interpreter for parents and others who need to understand the medical nature of a child's neurological condition in order to plan effective intervention. Educators can refer to this text to refresh their own understanding of a condition as well as to help parents interpret information given by health professionals. Although health professionals are often very direct and thorough, a parent's own ability to "hear" such information can be limited by the normal, initial emotional responses to a child's trauma or poor prognosis. Later, early childhood special educators may be called on to fill in missing information when parents are better able to "hear" and to understand.

This chapter is devoted to conditions that may relate to children's neurological functioning and includes information on diagnostic testing, etiological factors resulting in damage to the nervous system, and characteristics of specific medical conditions common to early childhood special education. The neurological system comprises the central nervous system (brain and spinal cord) and the peripheral nervous system (12 cranial nerves and motor and sensory nerves in the extremities). Neurological impairments can be so subtle that they cannot be detected by medical or educational diagnostic techniques. On the other hand, significant damage to the nervous system can affect functions in all developmental domains including movement, communication, social interaction, and cognitive functioning. Specific permutations of brain damage can also vary. Four children with a similar medical history of prematurity might have any one or all of the following neurological conditions: seizures, cerebral palsy, intellectual disabilities, and attentional deficits. Some forms of damage to the neurological system occur very early in fetal development; other injuries may occur long after birth. Causes of neurological damage include prenatal exposure to toxins, birth trauma, infections, and other factors.

Diagnostic Tools

The first step in clarifying various medical or disabling conditions is medical testing. These tests can be expensive, time-consuming, and frightening for families engaged in the process. A simple understanding of the diagnostic tools involved can help alleviate a parent's concern or lack of understanding. Diagnostic tools involve both invasive procedures, in which a body system must be penetrated, and noninvasive methods, in which the body is not penetrated.

X-Rays

One of the oldest noninvasive tools used to evaluate an individual's condition is the **X-ray,** a form of invisible electromagnetic energy with a short wavelength that bombards a specific area of the body. Because of their very short wavelength, X-rays are able to penetrate most substances, some more easily than others. The density of the tissue and the voltage power used affect the degree to which the X-rays penetrate various tissues. These rays make certain substances fluoresce so that the size, shape, and movement of organs and tissues can be observed. The X-rays themselves are invisible to the human eye but can be captured as an image on a specially coated film. X-rays are useful in detecting foreign bodies and fractures and illuminating radioactive substances that have been introduced to the body. For example, radioactive dye may be injected into a blood vessel, and X-rays can trace its pathway through the body.

Excessive exposure to X-rays, particularly over a short period of time, can pose a serious health hazard. X-rays have the potential to damage living cells, especially those that are dividing rapidly. The risks include damage to bone marrow and other blood-forming organs, damage to genes resulting in genetic or chromosomal mutations (which can be passed to future generations), onset of fetal death or malformation, and development of cataracts. Finally, exposure to X-rays over a long period of time can be carcinogenic. Such damage is avoided by using the lowest possible radiation doses, by using a lead shield to protect tissue that is not of concern, and by avoiding X-rays when there is any possibility of pregnancy.

Computerized Axial Tomography

The **computerized axial tomography** (**CAT, CT,** or **CAT scan**) was developed in 1972 and was proclaimed the most important diagnostic device to be invented since X-rays were first introduced. While operating on similar physical principals as an X-ray (radiology), a CAT scan is 100 times more powerful than its predecessor. To conduct this exam, an individual is placed in a circular chamber and exposed to focused X-rays coming from several planes (e.g., cross-sectional, horizontal). A detector, positioned opposite the X-ray source (scanner), picks up the X-rays, which have been absorbed at different rates depending on the density of the tissue through which they have passed. These measurements are reconstructed using a computer to produce clear, three-dimensional images of body tissue and structure on an oscillating screen. CAT scans are used to distinguish interior body structures such as lesions, bleeding in the brain, hydrocephalus, and tumors (see Figure 6–1). An advantage of CAT scans over X-rays is their ability to

detect structures not visible on conventional tests and their ability to evaluate the targeted body part from many different angles simultaneously. Although more expensive and riskier (increased radiation exposure) than ultrasonography, CAT scans are considerably more accurate in detecting such problems as tumors or abscesses.

Magnetic Resonance Imaging

Magnetic resonance imaging (MRI) is a relatively new technology that is now used widely in diagnosing abnormalities in cardiovascular, orthopedic, and neurological systems. Unlike CAT scans and X-rays, MRI does not rely on radiation, thereby reducing the risks of radiation exposure. Instead, a powerful magnetic force is used to attract ions within cells toward the edges of an organ. An image of those ions reveals whether an anomaly has occurred, for example, the growth of a tumor, torn cartilage, or a fracture.

During imaging, a patient lies very still inside a massive, hollow, cylindrical magnet. Children may be given a powerful sedative or even general anesthetic for the average, half-hour examination. Short bursts of magnetic power are emitted. These cause the hydrogen atoms in the patient's tissues to line up parallel to each other like little magnets. The machine detects this alignment as an image, and a computer processes the information in much the same way as a CAT scan but shows normal and abnormal tissues with more contrast. The test is particularly valuable for studying the brain and spinal cord, identifying tumors, and examining the heart and major blood vessels.

Figure 6–1 A CAT Scan Slice

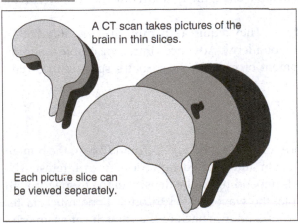

A CT scan takes pictures of the brain in thin slices.

Each picture slice can be viewed separately.

Near-Infrared Spectroscopy

While MRIs are useful diagnostic tools for infants, they are problematic for a number of reasons and not feasible for research. MRIs require severe restriction of head movement for an extended period, and the high intensity sounds introduced preclude language interaction during the procedure. **Near-infrared spectroscopy (NIRS)** is not a new method but has recently been used in research with infants to study vision, memory, and language (Aslin & Mehler, 2005). This technology paired with electroencephalography (EEG) is a more practical tool than MRIs although less precise in imagery because it allows more movement by infants and the potential for interaction between patient and professional during assessment. Like EEGs, NIRS uses a set of probes attached to the scalp to emit near-infrared light and to measure the wavelengths. Like MRIs, NIRS measures neural blood oxygen responses to provide images of the brain. At present, this is an emerging technology that has not been fully evaluated in terms of safety and efficacy but may become the most practical research tool in the future.

Functional Imaging

Although X-rays, CAT scans, and MRIs are useful in analyzing gross anatomical abnormalities, they are not useful in monitoring actual chemical activity. Two relatively new techniques, which have been used largely for research purposes until recently, are capable of measuring this function. **Positron emission tomography (PET)** and **single photon emission computer tomography (SPECT)** are noninvasive techniques that are particularly valuable for evaluating neurological disorders.

PET scanning detects positively charged particles that have been labeled with radioisotopes and injected into the blood. Because of their instability, these substances are taken up in greater concentration by areas of tissue that are more metabolically active, such as tumors. Detectors linked to a computer make a picture of how the radioisotopes are distributed within the body. PET scans can detect brain tumors, locate the origin of epileptic seizures, and examine brain function. Similar to the CAT scan in producing images of the brain in several planes, the PET scan makes a biochemical analysis of metabolism rather than anatomy. PET scanning equipment is expensive to buy and operate, so it is currently available in only a few urban centers, but its contributions are so valuable that its use is likely to become more widespread in the future.

PET and SPECT are safe procedures. They require only minute doses of radiation and carry virtually no risk of toxicity or allergy. Advances in radioisotopic scanning depend on the continuing development of radioactive particles specific to certain tissues.

Ultrasonography

In this noninvasive procedure, high-frequency sound waves (inaudible to the human ear) are passed through a patient's skin and focused on an organ of interest. The sound waves travel at variable speeds depending on the density of the tissue through which they are passing. For example, the waves travel through bone much faster than through muscle. These sound waves bounce back to the transducer as an echo

Table 6–1   Comparison of Diagnostic Tools

Tool	Radiation Risk	Degree of Power	Multiple Analyses	Expense
X-ray	High	Limited	NA	Low
CAT scan	Yes	High	Yes	High
Ultrasound	None	Limited	Yes	Low
MRI	None	High	Yes	Yes
PET/SPECT	Low	High	Yes	Yes
EEG	None	High	Yes	Yes
NIRS	None	Limited	Yes	Yes

and are then amplified. A computer processes these echoes into electrical energy and displays them on a screen for interpretation. The images are displayed in real time, producing motion on a television screen. The images can then be translated into photographs for permanent examination. A distinct advantage of ultrasound over other techniques is the absence of risk incurred by exposure to radiation as in some other diagnostic techniques (see Table 6–1).

Ultrasonography is frequently used during pregnancy to view the uterus and fetus. The technique helps in early pregnancy to establish fetal gestational age, determine whether there is a multiple pregnancy, evaluate fetal viability, identify and confirm fetal abnormalities, and guide amniocentesis. An ultrasound is typically conducted at 20 weeks of gestation in order to evaluate brain growth, major organ development, and, if parents choose, determine the sex of the fetus. Later in pregnancy, ultrasounds may be carried out if the growth rate of the fetus seems slow, fetal movements cease or are excessive, or the mother experiences vaginal bleeding.

In a newborn child, ultrasound can be used to scan the brain to diagnose hydrocephalus, brain tumors, or brain hemorrhage and to determine whether other organs, such as the kidneys, appear normal. A type of ultrasound is also used in echocardiography to investigate disorders of the heart valves. Doppler ultrasound is a modified version of ordinary ultrasound that can look at moving objects such as blood flowing through blood vessels and the fetal heartbeat in pregnancy.

Electroencephalography

Electroencephalography (EEG) is a conventional, noninvasive procedure used to detect normal and abnormal electrical activity within the brain. EEGs detect, amplify, and measure electrical activity on the scalp produced by the brain's neurons. The testing is typically conducted in a small room designed to eliminate electrical interference and distractions. Small electrodes are placed in a definitive pattern on the scalp but do not produce shock or other aversive stimuli. Although the results directly measure only surface activity, changes in electrical patterns effectively represent the activity of deeper structures. These impulses are recorded as brain waves on moving strips of paper.

The EEG diagnostic technique is commonly used to detect the presence of abnormal brain activity that might be related to seizures. Different types of seizures emit differential brain waves. During testing, after an initial baseline is obtained, various forms of stress, such as deep breathing or bright lights, may be introduced in order to elicit brain wave patterns typical of seizure disorders.

EEGs are useful diagnostic tools but are more unreliable than many techniques and should be interpreted with caution. For example, approximately 20 percent of individuals who do not have brain damage have abnormal readings on electroencephalography. On the other hand, a significant portion of individuals with seizures or other kinds of brain damage have unaffected EEGs.

An EEG can also be used to evaluate hearing loss. Sounds are introduced through earphones, and the electrical potentials that are evoked are amplified via EEG and can then be separated from other electrical activity by computers. The resulting record reveals whether the brain has perceived sound.

Neurological Disabilities

The diagnostic tools described previously are widely used to attempt to verify the presence or absence of unusual patterns of neurological functioning in children who have physical, cognitive, behavioral, or language development concerns. As you will see, these tools are often too primitive to provide definitive answers but in many cases are helpful in identifying problems. The remainder of the chapter isolates a variety of relatively high-incidence neurological disabilities that early childhood professionals are likely to encounter.

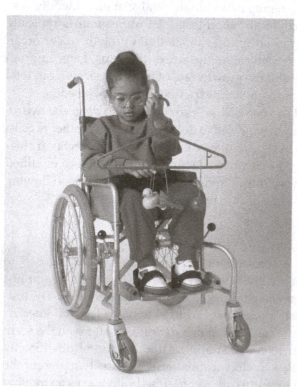

© Susanna Price/DK Images

Cerebral Palsy

Cerebral palsy is the most common of severe disabilities in childhood. It encompasses a broad category of nonprogressive neuromuscular conditions affecting muscle tone, movement, reflexes, and posture. Cerebral palsy results from brain injury sustained during the early stages of development, and although the damage to the brain itself gets no worse during an individual's life, children may develop deformities across time. The original injury to the brain must occur before 16 years of age for the condition to be classified as cerebral palsy.

The incidence of cerebral palsy is 2 in every 1,000 live-born infants and has not changed significantly in decades, although modern medicine has improved the prognosis of premature infants below 2,500 g (5 lbs, 8 oz) (McAdams & Juul, 2011). One reason the rate continues to be high is the success in decreasing the mortality of ever-smaller babies, who do not respond as well as more mature infants to intensive, lifesaving medical treatment. Infants born at very low birth weight are nearly seven times more likely to develop cerebral palsy than children born at normal birth weight (Edwards et al., 2011). As there has been a rise in the rate of premature births in the United States, 20 percent between 1990 and 2005, the birth weight–cerebral palsy connection is relevant to the sustained incidence of cerebral palsy (Kelly, 2011).

It is not just premature birth that causes the disability. Brain damage causing cerebral palsy may occur before, during, or after birth. Neonatal health conditions associated with cerebral palsy are meconium aspiration, anoxia, hypoglycemia, infections such as meningitis or encephalitis, and other conditions leading to neurological damage. Later in childhood, children may incur head injuries or diseases leading to motor involvement that may or may not be labeled cerebral palsy. The physical traits and etiological conditions of persons with cerebral palsy are diverse. In fact, some demographics are more likely to be associated with the incidence of cerebral palsy, including African Americans, women who do not receive prenatal care, mothers with less education, and Hispanics when the mother is younger than 18 (Wu et al., 2011). Again, though, it is clear that risk of cerebral palsy parallels risk factors for low birth weight in the United States. Cerebral palsy is categorized according to the site of cerebral damage, the extent of brain damage, and the parts of the body affected by that damage. Whatever the origin, cerebral palsy causes a functional miscommunication between a person's movement intentions and subsequent motor responses.

Reflexes   One way to describe cerebral palsy is as an interruption of normal reflex development. As an infant's neurological system develops, motor reflexes move from "primitive" to "voluntary." Whereas all infants differ slightly in their rates of development, a significant injury to the brain, either prenatally or postnatally, may impair the normally smooth developmental transitions so much that it causes cerebral palsy. This poor transition is now known to be highly predictive of cerebral palsy when observed both prenatally and postnatally. When observed via ultrasound from about the 10th week of gestation, cramped synchronized general movement, chaotic movement, absent fidgetiness, or abnormal fidgetiness marked infants who would later develop mild to severe cerebral palsy with nearly 100 percent accuracy (Barclay, 2002).

Primitive reflexes are developed *in utero* and are present in the early months of life. They are responsible for involuntary motor responses to specific stimuli. For infants with intact neurological systems, the presentation of a given stimulus, such as a touch to the cheek, is predictably followed by a motor response; in this case, the head turns toward the touch, known as the *rooting reflex*. Primitive reflexes may be a kind of natural "hardwiring" that equips children with basic motor patterns and established neurological pathways. While thought to be useful prenatally (Lacquaniti, Ivanenko, & Zago, 2012), primitive reflexes have limited utility to infants after birth. As they mature, most primitive reflexes are neurologically integrated, giving children control over them. Primitive reflexes gradually disappear and are replaced by postural, or adaptive, reflexes. When this does not happen, persistent primitive reflexes can interfere with a child's development of voluntary movement.

It is generally agreed that reflexes are key to normal motor development. The presence (or absence) of primitive and adaptive reflexes is used to predict developmental potential. Predictable reflex patterns are considered to be "neurodevelopmental markers" and the best index of brain dysfunction, particularly cerebral palsy.

For an optimistic motor outcome, primitive reflexes should appear before 3 months and disappear by 6 months; if they do not disappear by 12 months of age, the outlook for walking is pessimistic. The plantar grasp reflex is particularly significant; when it is weak or absent in early infancy, the plantar grasp reflex is an indicator of spasticity. When the plantar grasp reflex is especially strong and prolonged, this is a red flag for athetoid cerebral palsy and intellectual disabilities (Futagi & Suzuki, 2010). Another sign of potential neurological involvement can be seen even earlier. By the second month, typically developing infants are able to execute movement of joints in isolation, such as the knee, hip, elbow, and shoulder (Kouwaki, Yokochi, Togawa, Kamiya, & Yokochi, 2012). However, infants who have an exaggerated startle response and predominant shoulder rotation typically seen in younger infants are at greater risk for cerebral palsy. Therefore, early childhood educators should be aware of reflex patterns so that noticeable deviations in development can be spotted. Because the objective of subsequent neuromotor intervention is to limit the influence of atypical reflexive development, early identification provides the greatest promise of mediating motor problems.

The **moro reflex** is the most commonly used index of reflexive maturity and is present at birth (see Figure 6–2). When a child's head is suddenly dropped backward, its arms fly back and out in a symmetrical **abduction** (away from body) and **extension** (straightening of the joints); then the child's arms flex and return to the body in **adduction** (toward body), as if to embrace someone. Abnormal neurological maturation is indicated when the moro response:

1. Is absent in the neonatal period

2. Is asymmetrical

3. Persists beyond 3 to 4 months of age

The **asymmetrical tonic neck reflex (ATNR),** also commonly assessed, is sometimes referred to as the fencer's reflex. When a child's head is turned to one side, the extremities of the same side are extended, while the extremities on the opposite side of the body are flexed (bent at the joints) (see Figure 6–3). In a normally developing

Figure 6–2 Typical Moro Reflex

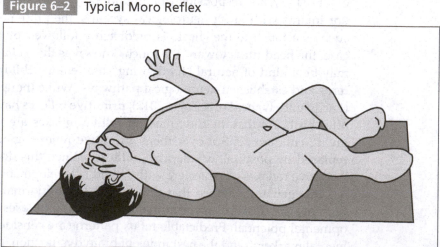

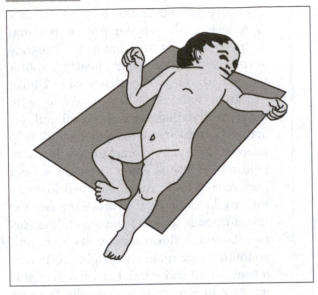

Figure 6–3 Typical Asymmetrical Reflex

infant, execution of the "fencer position" is usually partial or incomplete. On the other hand, when the response is well defined and easily provoked, this is usually a sign of some negative neurological involvement. The ATNR reflex begins to disappear in the first few months. Persistence of ATNR beyond the third month is another signal of possible motor and/or intellectual disability.

Other primitive reflexes seen at birth include the rooting, grasp, startle, and stepping reflexes. The **rooting reflex** occurs when an infant's cheek is lightly stroked. In response, the infant turns its head toward the touch. Stimulating the palm of an infant's hand elicits the grasp reflex, or flexion, of the hand. A **startle reflex** occurs when a sudden noise or movement causes a child to thrust arms outward and then pull them back. It is apparent that if these involuntary responses were to persist, they would interfere with normal motor routines. For example, if the grasp reflex persisted, individuals would never be able to voluntarily release objects once placed in the palm. The disappearance of these reflexes, mostly within the first 4 to 6 months of life, is a necessary transition referred to as **reflex integration**.

Several reflexes could interfere with walking and are typically integrated within the first 6 months. Holding a child in a vertical position so that the feet touch a surface can elicit the **stepping reflex** (see Figure 6–4). This steplike response encourages many parents to inaccurately conclude that their child is precociously ready to begin walking. The **Babinski reflex** is stimulated by stroking the sole of an infant's foot. If this reflex is present, an infant responds by spreading its toes. A third commonly assessed reflex of the lower extremities is the **plantar reflex**. It is observed when pressure applied to the ball of an infant's foot is followed by flexion of the toes around the stimulus, as if to grasp the object.

Primitive reflexes are replaced by adaptive and postural reflexes. If these reflexes do not develop appropriately, a child's motor skills do not progress. The sucking and swallowing reflexes are **adaptive reflexes** that are present at birth, although still immature. These reflexes work in harmony when mature and are usually well developed by 6 months of age. When they are fully developed, a child has good tongue control and lip closure when sucking. These reflexes are paired with the ability to move food from the front to the back of the mouth, to control the path of food to the esophagus (rather than trachea), and to move food down the esophagus to the stomach.

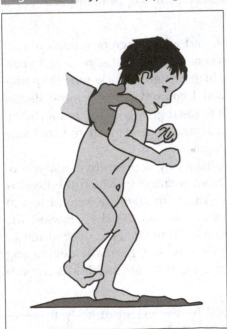

Figure 6–4 Typical Stepping Reflex

Figure 6–5 Typical Parachute Reflex

While much of human movement is voluntary, a significant part of balance is reflexive. The appearance of **postural reflexes** requires the brain to integrate several modalities (sight, hearing, motor movement, etc.) simultaneously. Unlike primitive reflexes, which interfere with movement if persistent, postural reflexes actually supplement movement and help prevent injury. A **parachute reflex** (see Figure 6–5) results when an infant is held horizontally and prone, and then lowered toward the floor. As if to break the fall, the infant extends its arms and legs to the surface. Several reflexes also evolve to permit an infant to maintain an upright position as it learns to sit and stand. Lateral head righting at 2 to 3 months is generally the first postural reflex to appear. An **equilibrium reflex,** which appears at 4 to 6 months of age, is stimulated whenever a child moves or is pushed out of a midline (vertical) position. Resisting gravity, the equilibrium reflex involuntarily causes the body to realign its trunk vertically. Similarly, when an infant's trunk is pushed out of an upright position either to the side, front, or back, the head-righting reflex attempts to hold the head in an upright position. A final and complementary reflex is referred to as **protective extension.** In this case, an infant, pushed out of midline from either a sitting or standing position, reaches out (extension) and attempts to protect itself from falling. Children first learn to protect themselves from falls to the front, then to the sides, and finally to the rear; directional reflexes typically appear, respectively, at 5 to 7 months, 6 to 9 months, and 9 to 12 months.

Muscle Tone Posture, consistency of muscles, and joint range of motion are all affected by muscle tone. A child's muscle tone is generally defined as normal, hypertonic, or hypotonic. An infant with abnormally high or tight muscle tone (**hypertonia**) shows restricted ranges of motion. By contrast, **hypotonia,** or very loose, flaccid tone, is seen in a child who shows little strength to resist gravity or joint movement. Both hypertonicity and hypotonicity are indexes of neurological insult and are likely to result in delayed if not abnormal motor development.

Assessment of muscle tone can be accomplished by comparative analysis of **range of motion.** One test of muscle tone is head rotation in which the head is passively turned toward the infant's shoulder. The *Scarf sign* is a second test of muscle tone. In this test, a child's arm is extended across the chest toward the opposite shoulder. In both cases, the degree to which movement is permitted or prohibited provides an index of neurological maturity: In a normally developing child, the range of motion is neither too loose nor too tight for the child's chronological age.

Affected Site Cerebral palsy can be described by the extent of body involvement (how much of the body is neurologically affected) if one were to imagine it

| Figure 6–6 | Breakdown of Cerebral Palsy by Body Part |

Hemiplegia   Double hemiplegia   Paraplegia   Quadriplegia or Tetraplegia   Diplegia   Monoplegia (any one extremity)   Triplegia (any three extremities)

dissected vertically and horizontally (see Figure 6–6). **Hemiplegia** occurs when one side of the body is affected (double hemiplegia involves both sides, with one side more severely impaired, and the arms more affected than the legs). It is caused by traumatic brain injury to the side of the brain opposite the affected side of the body. In **paraplegia,** only the lower extremities are affected, and in **quadriplegia** (or tetraplegia), all four extremities are involved. Similarly, all four extremities are affected in **diplegia,** but with more involvement of the legs than the trunk and arms. Finally, **monoplegia** and **triplegia** involve one and three extremities, respectively. Both birth weight and timing of injury have been associated with the degree of motor involvement, though these findings have not been consistent. For example, in one study, prematurity was found to be associated with diplegia and quadriplegia, and hemiplegia associated with complications in the neonatal period (Cooke & Abernethy, 2010). In another study, birth weight < 1000 g was associated more with hemiplegia and quadriplegia, while birth weight between 1,500 and 2,499 g (LBW) was linked more to diplegia (Jessen, Mackie, & Jarvis, 1999).

Characteristics of Cerebral Palsy   Although definitions vary, cerebral palsy can generally be classified according to the type of muscle movement or muscle tone abnormality manifested. The most common descriptions of the types indicate the state of muscle tone, the area of injury within the central nervous system, and the quality of muscle control.

Hypertonia occurs when the **pyramidal tract** (the motor cortex and spinal cord) is damaged. Eventually, hypertonia limits joint movement because of shortened muscles and ligaments. If this muscle tightness is severe, children may develop contractures (chronic muscle tightness) that can further lead to deformities of the spine and joint dislocations.

Infants born with cerebral palsy are initially hypotonic, but if their floppiness persists through the first year without the development of other tone problems, generalized hypotonia is diagnosed. Hypotonia is often correlated with cognitive deficit. Hypotonic infants tend to rely on external support and are delayed in the development of motor skills. They also have poor posture and hypermobile joints.

The pyramidal nerve fibers originate in the brain and pass through the spinal cord to attach to motor cells in the body. When cerebral damage occurs outside the pyramidal nerve group, it is said to be **extrapyramidal,** and the resulting condition is called **athetosis,** or **dyskinesia.** Rather than being responsible for initiation of movement, extrapyramidal nerves are responsible for controlling and coordinating posture, tone, and locomotion. Dyskinesia affects approximately 20 percent of all children with cerebral palsy. Athetosis, or variable muscle tone, ranges from rigid to flaccid. Injury, often due to jaundice, is responsible for athetosis, which affects all four extremities. Slow worm-like or writhing movements, more pronounced in children's head and hands, are accentuated when affected children attempt to move and when they become emotional. Children with athetosis may have difficulty sitting, walking, eating, and speaking. Typically, the excessive movement associated with athetosis is not observed until the second year of life, although abnormalities in tone, reflexes, and posture can be diagnosed earlier.

With **ataxic cerebral palsy,** which is very rare, children have difficulty balancing well while walking. The cerebellum is the site of injury in this type of cerebral palsy (McCandless, 2011). Ataxia interferes with coordination in balancing and hand use. Individuals with ataxic cerebral palsy bobble while standing and walking and tend to overshoot a target. They also exaggerate movement in an effort to balance, and the constant effort to stabilize can cause rigid movement.

Spastic cerebral palsy, in which muscle tightens and resists efforts to move, is the most common type of cerebral palsy and results from injury to the pyramidal tract of the brain, usually due to hemorrhaging after premature birth or severe brain damage (perhaps caused by prolonged oxygen deprivation). Spastic movement has been characterized as a "jackknife" response in which joints express hyperresistance to extension or flexion up to a certain threshold, and then resistance is suddenly released. The status of tone may change over time; many children have hypotonia in infancy, which then progresses to spasticity.

All movement, including that of both large and small muscle groups, can be affected by cerebral palsy. The diagnosis of more than one type of cerebral palsy is common with spasticity as in mixed spastic/athetoid quadriplegia (Imms & Dodd, 2010). Early in development, signs of neuromuscular damage include the absence of primitive reflexes or the later failure to integrate these reflexes. Hence, development of head control, crawling, sitting, and walking tends to be delayed.

Severity of Involvement   A diagnosis of cerebral palsy is almost meaningless unless it is also paired with a description of the degree of involvement or the degree to which children are affected motorically. Motor involvement ranges from mild to severe based on the degree to which a child's impairment interferes with independent motor and functional behaviors. Children with mild motor involvement have the greatest mobility and are usually able to meet their physical needs independently. With physical therapy, their mobility and movement can be improved, but without therapy, their motor functioning may degrade. By comparison, children with moderate involvement usually have some motor independence, but typically have significant interference in physical activity due to limitations related to one or more of the following: range of motion, deformities, pain, and perceptual limitations and/or cognitive involvement. Finally, those children who have the greatest motor impact are the most challenged. These children require complete assistance to meet their physical needs because of poor head control, deformities resulting from or related to cerebral palsy, and perceptual and sensory limits that often result in achievement deficits.

Associated Characteristics of Children with Cerebral Palsy   Because cerebral palsy results from damage to the central nervous system, interference with normal movement is almost always accompanied by collateral damage to other biological functions such as hearing and cognition. Furthermore, the motor involvement itself affects functioning in a number of skill areas. For example, self-help skills, such as feeding and dressing, are limited by the degree of motor dysfunction. Kirby and colleagues (2011) found that autism was also associated with cerebral palsy in 8 percent of cases.

Difficulty in feeding children with cerebral palsy, especially those with dystonia, is common. Approximately half of children with cerebral palsy experience serious feeding problems, which are very often accompanied by growth retardation (Karagiozoglou-Lampoudi, Daskalou Vargiami, & Zafeirou, 2012). The most common feeding problems include poor self-feeding, poor swallowing and chewing from oral–motor dysfunction, and inordinately long feeding sessions. Frequent vomiting, dental problems that cause pain and infection, reflux, aspiration, excessive drooling, and poor appetite are all common in cerebral palsy. Diets tend to be restricted in texture and taste; many children are given pureed or powdered foods, which are easy to prepare and feed. Subsequently, children's energy intake and nutritional status are frequently compromised. To assist in monitoring a child's diet, parents should pay attention to several physical characteristics that can indicate to a caretaker that a child might be malnourished, such as failure to gain weight, failure to gain in height (<3rd percentile), and disproportionate weight to height gains (Nützenadel, 2011). Feeding difficulties often begin at birth when a large percentage of infants at risk for cerebral palsy have difficulty sucking during nursing. As children with cerebral palsy age, feeding problems do not diminish. Perhaps because feeding can be so tedious and stressful, important mother–child relationships can become strained. Because of anxiety and exhaustion associated with challenging mealtimes, a mother's behavior may become mechanical, lacking the typical nurturing social interactions associated with feeding. Even though maternal behavior may return to normal levels when feeding is completed, the loss of this valuable opportunity may be significant in terms of social and linguistic development.

The overall growth patterns of children with cerebral palsy are substantially below normal. Although growth measurements are within the normal range by 12 months of age (when corrected for gestational age), many infants have fallen well behind their nondisabled peers in both height and weight. Standard growth charts fail to provide useful information about children with cerebral palsy, because those children tend to be lighter and shorter than the norm, a difference that cannot be accounted for by nutritional limitations alone. Consequently, clinical growth charts, specifically calibrated to children with cerebral palsy (Gross Motor Function Classification System) are more sensitive to deviations in growth patterns and may be able to detect serious nutritional or other health problems early (Brooks, Day, Shavelle, & Strauss, 2011).

Seizure Disorders   Approximately one-third of children with cerebral palsy also have some form of epilepsy (Kirby et al., 2011). Children with spasticity are most likely to experience seizures; those with athetosis are least likely. The most common types of epilepsy observed are **tonic–clonic** and **partial complex** seizures, which will be described in the following section.

Intellectual Disabilities Around one-fourth of children with cerebral palsy have a severe intellectual disability, while another 20% to 50% are found to have learning disabilities (Imms & Dodd, 2010). Accurately assessing the cognitive abilities of children with cerebral palsy is challenging because of the inherent bias of standardized tests, which typically are not normed for children with motor impairments. Taken as a group, however, children with cerebral palsy are more likely to have delayed development in sensorimotor behaviors. This makes sense because these infants and preschoolers are prevented from exploring and interacting with their environments to the same extent as children who have no motor impairment. Some types of cerebral palsy are more likely than others to be associated with intellectual deficits. For example, hemiplegia is rarely associated with cognitive deficits, whereas spastic cerebral palsy is more commonly associated with intellectual delays.

Etiology of Cerebral Palsy It has been maintained that premature birth (prior to 38–40 weeks gestation) and birth complications, such as asphyxia, constitute the major causes of cerebral palsy. On the other hand, many children who experience birth-related problems do not show signs of motor involvement later in childhood. Additionally, approximately half of all children with cerebral palsy are born full term or near term to apparently healthy mothers (Nelson, 2002). Though asphyxia may be a significant factor in most cases of cerebral palsy, it remains that approximately one-third of children with cerebral palsy experienced one or more adverse events related to birth such as cord prolapse, preeclampsia, and birth defects (Gilbert, Jacoby, Xing, Danielsen, & Smith, 2010). Moreover, gestational age is clearly related to the risk of cerebral palsy. Most cases of cerebral palsy are associated with delivery before 39 weeks or after 42 weeks (Moster, Wilcox, Vollset, Markestad, & Lie, 2010). In fact, three-fourths of cases of cerebral palsy occur after 36 weeks gestation. Recent research has focused on prenatal infections as a major potential contributor to cerebral palsy (Gilbert et al., 2010).

Two opposing characteristics of the brain are associated with the long-term prognosis of children who received neurological insult during the fetal or neonatal period. On one hand, the developing brain is especially vulnerable to trauma or physiological disruptions. On the other hand, very young nervous systems are more plastic and may repair or compensate for damage at a rate and effectiveness that cannot be matched by older children and adults. As a consequence, abnormal CAT scans at birth can appear normal with no apparent residual motor or cognitive damage 12 months later.

Extreme prematurity raises the risk of cerebral palsy by a factor of 100 (O'Shea, 2008). Furthermore, low APGAR scores appear to be highly predictive of cerebral palsy (Moster, Lie, & Markestad, 2002). For example, infants with 5-minute APGAR scores from 0 to 3 were found to have an 81-fold increased incidence of cerebral palsy as compared to infants with APGAR scores between 7 and 10. Among very-low-birth-weight children, several factors have been found to correlate with the eventual development of cerebral palsy. Neonates who spend long periods of time on a ventilator, develop widespread infection, have a severe neurological abnormality, or have residual signs of prenatal infection are at greater risk of developing cerebral palsy than infants who do not experience these risk factors (Wilson-Costello et al., 1998).

In addition to birth-related injury, congenital causes are the second largest cause of cerebral palsy, although causation in many cases is based on speculation. There has long been a recognized association between congenital malformations and cerebral palsy, even in cases where the anomaly is unrelated to movement disorders—as in tooth enamel overgrowth or facial anomalies. Because there is still much to learn about factors that may lead to many congenital malformations, the causes of prematurity, and the etiology of cerebral palsy, the interaction between the three are also not clear. It is very possible however, that biological or environmental events affecting prenatal growth may simultaneously increase the risk of all three outcomes, depending upon the timing of these events (Alberman, 2010).

Cerebral palsy can result from neurological damage after birth as well. Infections such as bacterial meningitis and encephalitis, childhood diseases such as chicken pox, and prenatal or natal viruses, including TORCH (see Chapter 8) viruses, can result in fetal and neonatal stroke (Nelson, 2002; Willoughby, 2002). Anoxia, caused by submersion syndrome (water accidents) or near suffocation, is another cause of cerebral palsy; prenatal abnormalities, such as a reduced blood supply to the placenta, cysts, and abnormal brain development, are also associated with it (Nelson). To a small degree, multiple births as well as genetic and metabolic disorders contribute to the incidence of cerebral palsy. Finally, environmental toxins such as prenatal exposure to PCBs, pesticides, smoking, mercury, lead, and alcohol have also been associated with the disability (Saunders & Habgood, 2011; Shepherd, Jepson, Watterson, & Evans, 2012; Winneke, 2011).

However, it is still apparent that a large percentage of cases of cerebral palsy have no known etiology. These cases sometimes result in unfortunate speculation and self-blaming by families. Professionals may inadvertently add to parents' guilt by asking probing questions about prenatal and perinatal history. In most cases, although such information might be interesting, it is of no functional use, and it may be better left unprobed.

© Denielle M. Miller

Treatment of Cerebral Palsy Early intervention for children with cerebral palsy has an objective of restoring brain function lost through neural injury. *Brain plasticity* refers to the ability of brain tissue to change through environmental stimulation and structured learning (Goldstein, 2006). It is known that other centers in the brain can be trained to assume the function normally fulfilled by damaged pathways and centers. While restored areas tend not to be as effective as the original sites, the changes are permanent and can be sharpened with training and experience. Because neural tissue is most plastic in the early years, time spent in rehabilitation during this period has the most promise.

Although many infants and preschoolers with cerebral palsy receive center-based treatment in the form of physical and occupational therapy or special education, parents are usually expected to complete supplementary home programs. Much research has been conducted on the efficacy of home programs, yet there continues to be a general lack of follow-through on the part of parents that does not reflect their overall interest in their children's welfare. Instead, this lack of participation may be due to expectations set by therapists that parents perceive to be unrealistic (Wiart, Ray, Darrah, & Magill-Evans, 2010). Mothers of children with cerebral palsy often experience recurring, permanent sadness associated with their children with cerebral palsy (Masterson, 2010). The chronic sadness that some mothers experience may be associated with a sense of isolation, guilt, frustration, loss of hope, tiredness, financial difficulties, and lack of support. These factors may explain why mothers of children with cerebral palsy report having a poorer quality of life than mothers of children without cerebral palsy (Terra et al., 2011). When mothers are younger they tend to fear for the future of their children; as their children get older, this fear may change to a loss of hope. The following guidelines may help professionals and parents find a balance that is both beneficial for children and possible for caregivers:

- Explore the needs of parents and assist them in developing their own interventions, which should foster their own creativity and reinforce their efficacy as the primary caregivers.

- Provide follow-up, positive support, and feedback related to family solutions and implementation of their own plans.

- Assist parents in developing activities that are consistent with the total family needs and that are realistic.

- Implement collaborative goal selection and treatment plans that are sensitive to a family's daily schedules, and recognize that parents may be unable to follow through as consistently as is recommended.

Research efforts conducted to determine the overall effectiveness of early intervention for infants and preschoolers with cerebral palsy yield modest findings. In a review of various parent intervention programs for example, it was found that every intervention program reported in the literature had positive behavioral outcomes for children with cerebral palsy (Whittingham, Wee, & Boyd, 2011). However, Whittingham and colleagues (2011) cautioned that none of these studies involved rigorous research designs, and so more sophisticated research is needed to provide evidence-based direction for family intervention.

For children with cerebral palsy, management of physical development is a primary focus in early intervention as well as later education. Physical therapists may be the primary or only specialists working with families. Their role is to monitor physical development, detect changes in orthopedic status, and plan and implement specific motor development strategies. It may be necessary for children to wear day and/or night braces, undergo corrective surgery, or be fit for orthopedic equipment such as crutches, a walker, or a wheelchair. The goal of physical development, however, is to facilitate the most functional movement while concurrently working to diminish interfering abnormal movement or reflexes.

The primary focus of physical management is often positioning and handling. Positioning refers to the treatment of postural and reflex abnormalities by careful, symmetrical placement and support of the child's body. Efforts are made to adapt seating and standing equipment to align a child's skeleton in a posture that is as normal as possible and to inhibit the interference of primitive reflexes. Parents and teachers can be trained to use proper positioning techniques, but an occupational or physical therapist should be consulted for the specific needs of an individual child. For example, a child with cerebral palsy who still has a dominant asymmetrical tonic neck reflex (ATNR) would extend the limbs on the side of the body toward which the head is turned and flex the limbs on the opposite side of the body. If a child is allowed to fall into this position much of the time, some muscles of their body would shorten and might cause contractures that would eventually deform the affected bones and joints. Furthermore, the face might be in an awkward position for speech, eating would be difficult, and the child would not be able to bring objects to the midline for functional use with both hands. This child would best be seated in a device adapted to prevent looking to one side, thus inhibiting the ATNR. This might be done by placing blinders on the side of the head so that the child looks straight ahead. Any person feeding or talking would approach from directly in front of the child. Then the limbs could be used at midline in a symmetrical fashion. A child with low muscle tone might be positioned in a standing device that provides a slight forward incline; also, his or her legs might be strapped to support the weak muscles and encourage flexion of the head and arms. This positioning would allow stimulation of the weight-bearing joints and limbs and keep the child upright to interact with other children and adults.

Context-based intervention is an emerging intervention approach for children with cerebral palsy (Darrah et al., 2011). Rather than basing intervention on remediation of motor impairments, children's environments and tasks are manipulated to encourage children to engage in typical program activities in a way that will require movement related to motor objectives. This is a radical shift, particularly for medically based therapists who have been trained to focus on movement-specific tasks. Principles of context-based intervention include having functional goals, collaborating with families, using natural environments, focusing on strength, attention to task and environment rather than remediation, using an innovative approach to movement progression, and providing interdisciplinary support. A child's characteristics and interests provide the starting point for intervention and task characteristics (e.g., size, shape, and use of objects) as well as environmental solutions, such as removal of barriers or provision of resources, all interacting in a dynamic way.

Handling involves preparing a child for movement and positioning. A child who is hypertonic and very stiff may be difficult to dress, for example. If a parent or therapist gently shakes or strokes the child's arms before putting on a shirt, it will be much easier to bend the child's elbow and pull the shirt over as needed. Even soft lighting and music may relax the child's muscle tone in preparation for such an activity. Accurate assessment of an individual child's need for handling is best carried out by an occupational or physical therapist.

In addition to physical therapy, a nutritionist should be involved with families who have a child with compromised nutritional intake. However, some general considerations for all children with oral–motor involvement include frequent short feedings, development of a structured feeding program by a physical and/or occupational therapist, and provision of calorically concentrated food as well as nutritional formula supplements.

Pioneering research into stem cell treatment of neural injury may have promise. Naturally occurring brain chemicals called *chemokines* have been shown to attract

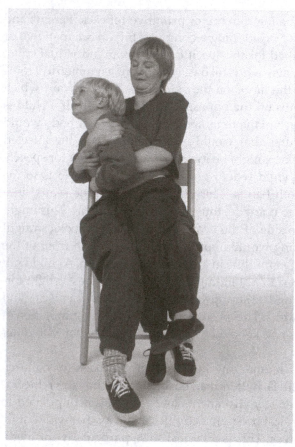

© Andy Crawford/DK Images

stem cells to injured parts of the brain soon after trauma occurs (Ehrenreich, 2004). The challenge is to find out how to make this attraction occur long after damage has occurred, to attract sufficient numbers of stem cells to make a difference, and then to determine whether the stem cells will turn into brain cells that enable recovery of lost function.

Seizures

As many as 1 in 10 people have a **seizure** at least once in a lifetime. In childhood, approximately 2 million Americans experience recurring seizures, a condition known as *epilepsy* (Hingley, 1999). Seizures are the result of abnormal electrical discharges in cerebral neurons. Different types of seizures result from cortical involvement of different regions of the brain. The physiology of seizures, regardless of type, is an imbalance between the usual coordinated efforts of neurons that are excited (activated to perform a function) and those that are inhibited (prevented from activating when not needed). During a seizure, the normal communication between neurons is interrupted by millions of electrical impulses occurring at the same time and that are more intense than usual, resulting in abnormal brain activity, which can usually be detected on an EEG.

Epilepsy is a condition in which seizures are recurrent. Although epilepsy itself is not provoked by external sources (e.g., metabolic disturbances, exposure to poison, or severe insult to the central nervous system), seizures may be caused by such events. All humans have a threshold for seizures beyond which a clinical seizure will occur. The threshold for most individuals is so high that normal life challenges will not push them past these limits. On the other hand, those with multiple daily seizures have very low thresholds as compared to persons who have less frequent seizures. Individual threshold levels are presumed to be both genetically determined and interactive with environmental events. For example, researchers have identified several gene sites associated with seizure thresholds (Shen et al., 2010), and some chromosomal disorders such as Prader-Willi syndrome are linked to seizures (Benson, Maski, Kothare, & Bourgeois, 2010). Physiological events, such as hypoglycemia or serious viral or bacterial infections such as rubella, can also reduce a child's seizure threshold.

Although there are 30 different types of epileptic seizures, they have been grouped into three categories as recognized in the International Classification of Epileptic Seizures: **partial seizures** (those that result from activation of one area of the brain), **generalized seizures** (those that involve activation of the entire brain and affect the whole body), and unclassified seizures. In **simple partial seizures,** individuals may be conscious, whereas **complex partial seizures** impair consciousness.

Table 6–2 Types of Seizures

Type of Seizure	Description
Absence	Sudden interruption of ongoing activity and the assumption of a blank stare for 1 to 15 seconds; usually in people with normal intelligence; good response to therapy, although poor social adaptation and difficulty sustaining attention may be characteristic
Tonic	Rigid muscular contraction, often fixing the limbs in some strained posture
Clonic	Alternate contraction and relaxation of muscles occurring in rapid succession
Tonic–clonic	Rigid muscular contraction followed by the appearance of clonic activity
Myoclonic	Sudden, brief, shocklike muscle contractions, usually in people with normal intelligence, but may be characterized by delays in social development
Temporal lobe (psychomotor)	Repetitive movements such as chewing, lip smacking, rocking; accompanied by bizarre sensations and emotions
Atonic	Sudden reduction in muscle tone, sometimes slumping to the ground
Infantile	Very poor long-term prognosis; mental and neurological damage in more than 80 percent of cases
Febrile	Temporary, tonic–clonic movements resulting from high temperature but not usually requiring medication; terminates when fever is gone

Either of these two **types** of seizures may progress to a partial seizure with secondary generalization in which an individual totally loses consciousness.

Of the seizures just described, generalized seizures are the most commonly discussed in educational literature, and these include the following: **absence** (petit mal), tonic, clonic, tonic–clonic (grand mal), **myoclonic,** and **atonic** seizures (see Table 6–2). During each of these seizures, loss of consciousness occurs.

More than 150 known causes of seizures have been identified, although in 70 percent of individual cases, it is not possible to pinpoint the cause (Hingley, 1999). Most diagnoses are related to factors also associated with other forms of neurological damage. Seizure-associated factors include perinatal trauma, fetal distress, congenital and postnatal infections (e.g., cytomegalovirus, meningitis, and influenza), teratogens, malformations or tumors, head injuries, and chromosomal abnormalities (e.g., juvenile myoclonic epilepsy resulting from an anomaly of the short arm of chromosome 6).

Seizures and intellectual disabilities commonly co-occur; about a third of children with epilepsy also have intellectual disabilities (Chapman et al., 2011). It seems that the risk of seizure disorders is lower for persons with mild intellectual disabilities (15 percent) who do not have cerebral palsy or other types of disabilities than for children with severe or profound disabilities (30%) (Lhatoo & Sander, 2001). Children who have epilepsy without other medical conditions, including more intellectual impairment, resistance to drug treatment of seizures, and other physical disabilities, tend to have a better overall prognosis.

The effects of seizures themselves on cognitive functioning are associated with their type, age of onset, and frequency. Overall, children who experience seizures tend to have diminished attention and cognition (Bhise, Burack, & Mandelbaum, 2009). Generally speaking, the younger a child is at the onset of seizures, the poorer the prognosis (Dunn et al., 2010). Dunn and colleagues also found that children with epilepsy whose parents experienced a high degree of stress and who had a lower level of education experienced more academic difficulty in math, reading, and writing. Children who have seizures are also more likely to have behavior problems than children without epilepsy (Bhise et al., 2009). Furthermore, each seizure has the potential for causing more brain injury due to a depletion of neurological metabolites. Children are most at risk of additional brain injury when seizures are prolonged for 15 minutes or more, a condition referred to as **status epilepticus**.

Approximately 4 percent of children experience breath-holding spells (Olsen, Mathiasen, Rasmussen, & Knudsen, 2010). These are probably not seizures, though one study found that a high percentage of such children had abnormal EEG patterns that were similar to seizures, suggesting a possible link (Hallioglu, Ôzge, Yilgör, Topaloglu, Düzovali, & Canim, 2012). Usually occurring between 6 and 24 months of age, breath-holding tends to disappear completely by age 5. Typically, breath-holding proceeds from a stressful event (e.g., crying or anger) during which the child fails to breathe, eventually causing the child's color to change, which is followed by forceful inspiration. At other times, the breath-holding may be prolonged enough to lead to loss of consciousness, slow pulse, and incontinence. While the condition is generally considered benign, long-term effects have been observed, as some children are more prone to fainting and some have concentration difficulties (Olsen et al., 2010).

The cause of breath-holding episodes is unclear, though there seems to be a higher incidence in families, which suggests a genetic link, and iron deficiency is also common in breath-holders (Hallioglu et al., 2012). Medication, although sometimes prescribed, is generally not necessary, though there is some evidence that iron supplements reduce the frequency of breath-holding (Zehetner, Orr, Buckmaster, Williams, & Wheeler, 2009). To assist parents, professionals should provide reassurance and information. For some children whose temper tantrums precipitate episodes, behavioral intervention may be necessary; but the aim is to change the precipitating behavior, not breath-holding.

Treatment Medical treatment of epilepsy primarily includes the use of several drugs (see Table 6–3). Drugs affect children differently than they do adults. For example, phenobarbital may cause some children to become hyperactive but generally sedates adults. Because of the effect of most antiepileptic drugs, which adversely affect cognitive functioning and memory, some are not recommended for young children; when prescribed, accommodations should be made to prevent secondary problems (Titus & Thio, 2009). Sometimes, a child's seizures do not respond to prescribed medication, but adding a second drug may eliminate or reduce them. The goal of drug treatment is to select the medication that will have the greatest control while causing the fewest side effects and helping the child maintain a good quality of life. This is why many children initially go through a period of "experimentation" to find the right combination of drugs (Hingley, 1999).

Since the 1990s several new antiepileptic drugs (AED) have been introduced. Although most are useful primarily with adults or with children who have very

Table 6–3 Drugs Prescribed for the Treatment of Epilepsy

Generic Drug Name	Common Product Name	Use
Category A: Prescribed to Compensate for Depressed Inhibitory Neuron Functioning		
Barbiturates	Phenobarbital	To provide sedation with generalized seizures
Valproic acid	Depakene	To treat multiple seizure types
Diazepam	Valium	As an adjunct to the treatment of generalized seizure control with other medications
Ethosuximide	Zarontin	To treat petit mal seizures
Vigabatrin	Sabril	To decrease seizures resistant to other therapy by 50 percent (experimental)
Category B: Drugs Used to Counter Hyperactive Excitatory Processes		
Carbamazepine	Tegratol	To stop partial and generalized tonic–clonic seizures
Phenytoin	Dilantin	To stop partial and generalized tonic–clonic seizures (experimental for individuals who are therapy resistant)
Gabapentin	Neurontin	To treat seizures that are therapy resistant
Lamotrigine	Lamictal	To treat seizures that are therapy resistant (experimental)
Paraldehyde	Paral/Paraldehyde	To stop threatening, prolonged seizures

intractable seizure disorders (i.e., Lennox-Gastaut syndrome), experimental applications are in progress for very young children (Nguyen & Spencer, 2003).

However, in 20% to 30% of cases, seizures cannot be controlled through medication, a condition referred to as drug-resistant epilepsy (Blume, 2008). Recent medical advances have made surgery a more viable option for persons with intractable seizures (Nguyen & Spencer, 2003). For example, resective surgery involves removal of abnormal tissue, but if the damage lies in functional cortex areas of the brain, unacceptable deficits could result. Gamma-knife surgery, on the other hand, is less invasive, using focused radiation applied to a single point in the brain; gamma-knife surgery helps over half of treated patients become seizure free and provides significant improvement to those who are not completely cured. Procedures (i.e., video EEG, CAT scans, MRI, and PET) that have helped evaluate potential candidates for surgery, combined with improved surgical techniques, make the procedure safer than in the past. Advanced imagery techniques are also useful in locating previously undetectable lesions (Nguyen & Spencer). In general, surgery is more effective in improving quality of life if done in childhood than if delayed until adulthood.

New developments include a neurocybernetic prosthesis (NCP), which is a surgically implanted device that stimulates the vagus nerve in the side of the neck with an electrical burst lasting about 30 seconds and occurring every 5 minutes throughout the day (Hallbook et al., 2005). Hallbook and colleagues observed an improved quality of life for most of their preschool subjects who had implants; improvements included reduction in the frequency and severity of seizures, improvement in mood and behavior, and no change in cognitive function. Other therapeutic devices are being tested and some have been approved for use outside the United States, but currently only vagus nerve stimulation, which continues to be improved, is used in the United States (Fisher, 2012).

Families of children with seizures can be assisted in several ways. As with other children with disabilities, parents may tend to treat children who experience seizures differently. For example, the potential hazard of having a seizure in traffic, near water, or in other dangerous situations may cause parents to become overcautious. Furthermore, when a seizure happens to occur at the same time as an event such as the enforcement of a family rule, parents may experience guilt and anxiety over future compliance requirements. The social and emotional effect of these family responses may affect sibling and peer relationships. Professionals can offer advice on the importance of consistency in child-rearing practices and normalcy of daily routines. Research indicates that children's overall developmental prognoses are best when the age of onset of epilepsy is later, children have no other medical conditions, EEGs are normal between seizures, and seizures respond to antiepileptic drugs (Nair & Bharucha, 2008). Because seizures are so common in the early childhood special education population, knowledge about seizures helps professionals serve children and families well. At a minimum, professionals should be well versed on the protocol for treating children with generalized clonic–tonic seizures and aware of the symptoms of common types of seizures, regimens and side effects of medication, accommodations for children, and individual seizure threshold levels.

A typical seizure is not a medical emergency, but knowledgeable handing of the situation is important. When a child experiences a generalized tonic–clonic seizure, caregivers should follow these procedures.

- Remain calm. Take time to reassure others that the child will be fine in a few minutes; if appropriate, remind other children of the correct conduct under these circumstances.

- Carefully lower the child to the floor and clear the area of anything that could be harmful.

- Put something flat and soft (e.g., a folded blanket) under the child's head so it will not bang on the floor as the body jerks.

- Let the seizure run its course; it cannot be stopped. Do not try to revive the child and do not interfere with the child's movements.

- Turn the child gently onto one side. This keeps the airway clear and allows saliva to drain away:

  Do not try to force the mouth open.

  Do not try to hold onto the tongue.

  Do not put anything in the mouth.

- When the jerking movements stop, let the child rest while regaining consciousness.

- Breathing may be shallow during the seizure and may even stop briefly. In the unlikely event that breathing does not begin again, check the child's airway for an obstruction and give artificial respiration (remember—no objects in the child's mouth).

- Some children recover quickly after this type of seizure and others require more time. A short period of rest is usually advised. If seizures are routine, caregivers should encourage children and families to maintain daily activities with as little disruption as possible.

Multidisciplinary services indicated for children with seizures and their families include medical assistance, counseling, social skills programming, family support, education, and advocacy. Historically, families were often viewed as needing the assistance of "experts" to help them overcome emotional and psychological trauma and the fear of public attitudes regarding their child's disability. Current efforts are in contrast to this perspective. They focus on the positive aspect of services, which concentrate on the practical, financial, and medical needs of families. This perspective is based on opinions gathered from families who seemed to react sensibly to their children's disabilities and found friends, relatives, and professionals to be sympathetic and helpful.

Attention Deficit Hyperactivity Disorder (ADHD)

The term *attention deficit* has been recognized for at least the last half century. In a 1902 address to the Royal College of Physicians, G. F. Still described 20 children in his clinical practice who were aggressive, defiant, and resistant to discipline; these children were excessively emotional or passionate and showed little self-control. Furthermore, these children were described as impaired in attention and quite over-active. Because ADHD is considered a hidden disorder in which there is no apparent physical anomaly, children are often blamed for their misbehavior and adults expect that they could behave appropriately if they would "just try."

The incidence of ADHD rose dramatically between 1998 and 2009 for school age children, going from 6.9% to 9% (Akinbami, Liu, Pastor, & Reuben, 2011). This rise was seen across genders and races with the exception of Mexican children, where the incidence is consistently lower than it is for other racial or ethnic groups and families with incomes less than 200 percent of the poverty level. For boys, the incidence rose from 9.9% to 12.3%, and for girls, the incidence rose from 3.6% to 5.5%. This rise was also seen in every region of the United States except the West, where the incidence has been consistently lower and stable. Pediatric identification of ADHD is reported to be similar to that found in school age populations in the United States; medical professionals also found a parallel rise in the number of children identified in both age groups (Davis & Williams, 2011).

There is much controversy and disagreement among professionals about the utility and meaning of the term "attention deficit hyperactive disorder." In spite of this disagreement, descriptions of behaviors associated with the condition have remained remarkably consistent since it was first defined in 1902. Although the definition has remained stable, the number of children identified with this disorder has not; the overall incidence of ADHD has increased markedly since the 1980s. Furthermore, increasing numbers of very young children with ADHD are being identified. However, less is known about the characteristics and functioning of preschool age children than of school age children with ADHD. Wilens and colleagues (2002) compared the psychopathology of preschool versus school age children identified with ADHD and found that the younger children's behaviors matched those of the older youth. Both preschoolers and school age children were found to have substantial impairment of social, cognitive, and overall functioning along with clinically significant psychopathology. Finally, preschoolers' manifestations of ADHD symptoms were qualitatively the same as those of school age children. It is no surprise, then, that many preschoolers are now medicated daily with drugs intended to reduce activity levels and improve concentration.

Still, the diagnosis and treatment of preschoolers with ADHD are unreliable. With gaps in services and education for this young group, there is also inconsistency in identification of the condition. Connor (2002) identified three factors that increase the likelihood of diagnosis: (1) when symptoms occur very early and/or are very extreme, (2) when children's symptoms are observed in environments outside the home, and (3) when symptoms outlive the duration of naturally occurring stressors (e.g., trauma, divorce, transition).

Characteristics   Interviews with parents of children with ADHD reveal that symptoms of the disorder manifest even in infancy (Gurevitz, Geva, Varon, & Leitner, 2012). Early signs include squirminess, less interest in cuddling, inability to adjust to change, frequent high-intensity negative moods, irregular sleep patterns (often requiring less sleep), and difficulty in feeding (Ninowski, 2011). Small head circumference in early infancy has also been associated with later diagnosis with ADHD. Predictive behaviors between 9 and 18 months include motor and language delays and difficult temperament (Gurevitz et al.). These symptoms evolve into the behavioral triad defining ADHD: inattention, impulsivity, and hyperactivity. A fourth symptom frequently attached to the triad is poor delay of response or delay aversion. Studies have confirmed that preschoolers who are identified with ADHD also have moderate to high delay aversion, which is higher (when compared to peers with ADHD) in younger preschoolers than in older preschoolers (Pauli-Pott & Becker, 2011).

Inattention manifests itself when children fail to attend to and concentrate on the task at hand. Preschool children with ADHD, more so than other preschoolers, often move from activity to activity, rapidly shifting their attention from one thing to another. If you ask them what they are supposed to be doing, many times they cannot tell you. These children also appear to be distracted by their own thoughts as well as the behaviors of other children and adults. What can be somewhat frustrating and promising is that these children concentrate for longer periods of time in highly enjoyable activities such as going skiing for the first time.

Impulsivity has been viewed as another primary symptom. This can be seen when children with ADHD behave in ways that appear to others as though they do not understand the consequences of their actions. These children get into difficult situations because they respond too soon and make decisions too rapidly. They interrupt conversations, cannot take turns, and interrupt the play of others a great deal of the time. As a consequence, secondary problems erupt in developing self-esteem, interpersonal relationships, and learning.

The third primary symptom of ADHD is *hyperactivity*. This characteristic is the most widely known and easiest to recognize. Most parents and caregivers describe this characteristic as always on the go, constantly in motion, never sitting still, or always fidgeting, talking, or making noise. Children identified as having ADHD have a much poorer prognosis than children without it. The former are more likely to have conduct problems, to be more impulsive, and to be rejected by their peers.

There is much controversy over the clinical definition and diagnostic criteria for ADHD (Kieling & Rohde, 2012). For example, some feel that response aversion should be a part of the definition, as a better description of children with ADHD than impulsivity and attention deficits. Delay aversion more accurately describes children who cannot delay their actions sufficiently and have little tolerance for delay intervals between tasks. This argument is based on a connection to the manner in which language evolved, which assumes that humans gradually developed the skill to delay their response to a signal, message, or event. This ability is said to be part of evolutionary changes in the brain's frontal lobes. Frontal lobe differences can be seen in preschool children who cannot tolerate activity between tasks and activities or who respond too quickly to stimuli. Several secondary characteristics have been associated with ADHD, including poor school performance, learning disabilities, delays in speech and language development, poor problem-solving abilities, and slightly more difficulties in sensory and motor skills.

An emerging theory on ADHD is based upon a reinforcement-learning deficit or deviation. That is, behavior in ADHD can be explained by motivation-related factors in addition to attention-related factors. It is increasingly understood that children with ADHD view rewards differently from children without ADHD. The reinforcement-deficit model has six subcategories, each with a different reinforcement–behavior relationship (Sonuga-Barke, 2011):

1. The brain's response to reinforcement is weak either because the potential for reinforcement is unclear to the child or because typical rewards have limited meaning to the child (e.g., praise, tokens, activities, food, etc., which work as reinforcers for other children, may have no value to some children with ADHD).

2. Children fail to process or learn the relationship between cue-behavior-outcome contingencies. The previous history of reinforcement does not provide a connection to the potential for reinforcement in the future (e.g., just because a child was praised for following instructions does not mean he will understand that following instructions will gain him positive attention if he does so again).

3. Children who are able to understand the cue-behavior-outcome, and who do find reinforcers meaningful, may have difficulty making decisions about reinforcer alternatives (e.g., a child may not be able to make a decision about acting to gain praise or acting to satisfy a desire to play with a toy held by another child).

4. Children with ADHD may be hypersensitive to rewards (including those that may not be seen as rewarding by adults) and impervious to punishment.

5. Children may have an intrinsic reinforcement deficiency where they simply don't find tasks (e.g., academic tasks) to be motivating; therefore, they don't care about the outcome.

6. Children may not have a deficiency as in the categories above; rather, the consequences that children find reinforcing are very different from the kinds of reinforcers other children find meaningful.

Further research is needed to clarify this model and identify which, if any, of these categories apply to different children with ADHD. Knowing how a child processes reinforcement should lead to specific, effective intervention strategies.

Etiology   Considerable research has been conducted to identify the etiology of ADHD. This research has been somewhat inconsistent and conflicting in findings. Although the exact cause of ADHD is unknown, it is generally understood that there are multiple etiologies. Various data-based correlates to increased incidence of ADHD include exposure to toxins (such as lead) in the environment (Braun, Kahn, Froehlich, Auinger, & Lanphear, 2006), differences in the brain's ability to send and receive messages (as a result of low levels of the synaptic neurochemicals dopamine and serotonin), decreased ability to use glucose fast enough to maintain normal thought (Daughton, 2011), and inheritability (Pellow, Solomon, & Barnard, 2011). Other studies have found a twofold to fourfold increase in the incidence of ADHD in children with prenatal exposure to nicotine, but they have not found that postnatal tobacco exposure increases risk (Braun et al., 2006; Linnet et al., 2003). In addition, several theories—ranging from the effects of certain diets to sugar hypersensitivity—have no empirical support but have been with us for some time and continue to appear in the popular press at this writing.

Conduct disorders, the most severe form of ADHD, appear to be related to the quality of a child's home environment. Specifically, marital harmony/discord may be the best predictor of this chronic antisocial behavior (Murray & Myers, 1998). Although children born into low-income families are at higher risk of ADHD, an enriched home environment can significantly improve behavioral outcomes (Ornoy, 2003). Other early childhood environmental factors have also been found to be predictors of ADHD: older mothers, low maternal educational attainment, clustered incidence within families, and family social problems (Gurevitz, 2012). These environmentally associated findings reflect the general opinion of scientists that what is now categorized as a single ailment will eventually prove to be several discrete but related disorders that have different causes and subsequent treatments. For example, it has been suggested that ADHD follows a genetic continuum that includes Tourette syndrome and some learning disabilities (Cavanna, Critchley, Orth, Stern, Young, & Robertson, 2011). While these disabilities can appear independently, they can also overlap in symptoms and outcomes. What is certain is that this disorder starts early in childhood and will follow an individual for the rest of his or her life.

Treatment   There is a wealth of data regarding the effective treatment of infants and children with ADHD. The information available today is clearly more empirically sound and is more accessible to both parents and professionals than was the case in the past. The primary treatment of preference has been, and continues to be, stimulant medication therapy. However, evidence supporting the benefits of drugs for children under the age of 6 is limited (Davis & Williams, 2011). Yet, the rate at which medical professionals prescribed medicines for ADHD in pediatric patients increased by almost 50 percent between 2002 and 2010, whereas, during the same time period, overall prescriptions, including antibiotics, declined for the same population (Chai, Governale, McMahon, Trinidad, Staffa, & Murphy, 2012). The two most common medications prescribed for ADHD have been Cylert (pemoline) and Ritalin (methylphenidate). Even with positive outcomes, the use of medication therapy is not without side effects that caregivers need to monitor (e.g., tics, weight loss, insomnia, stomachaches, anxiety, loss of appetite, headaches, dizziness, nail biting, reduced speech, irritability, nightmares, sadness, and staring).

Nonmedicine alternatives are available for young children with ADHD. One such approach is in-home parent behavioral training (Tutty, Gephart, & Wurzbacher, 2003). As students grow older, behavioral interventions, such as token economies, behavioral contracting, and self-management procedures, alone or in combination with stimulant medication, can be effective at school. Because the home environment is the best predictor of severe social maladaptation, chaotic and fractured families may require intensive support while their children need positive, integrated, educational experiences that allow them to play and work alongside appropriate peer role models. Given the known effectiveness of nondrug interventions paired with concerns about pharmaceutical remedies, the first line of defense is clear. When medication *is* used, Tutty and colleagues found that a combined treatment program of stimulant medication and parent training in behavioral and social skills (as compared to stimulant medication only) improved parents' perceptions of consistency in their disciplinary practices and consequent effectiveness in reducing the overall rate of ADHD-related behavior in their children.

The behavior of a child with ADHD can have a devastating effect on families. Not only are there the predictable daily management problems that require extraordinary supervision, but parents often must deal with marital stress and guilt caused by accusatory suggestions by family, friends, and professionals that the behavior problems are a consequence of misguided parenting. The following quote exemplifies the frustration felt by parents of children with ADHD (Colin, 1997).

> I decide to mention Willie's behavior in school to the pediatrician. "Does every child yell like this?" I ask embarrassed.
>
> The pediatrician tells me not to worry. "Oppositional behavior," he calls it, is common among three-year-olds and should go away on its own. He laughs when I tell him how Willie substituted "old wallpaper" for the offending "stupid idiot."
>
> "He's obviously very creative," the pediatrician says, still smiling.
>
> I stare at him blankly. They never call Willie creative in school. In fact, his teacher rarely says anything positive about him. Why is it so hard for her to appreciate the good things about my son—his sense of humor, his vocabulary, his wonderful singing? (pp. 24–25)

Several excellent texts are available for parents who have children with ADHD. In addition, there is a wealth of information, for teachers and other care providers, about assisting such children. For example, many Internet sites, including parent-specific websites and support networks, provide useful information. The following practical suggestions will prove useful in helping families of children with ADHD:

- Provide constant nurturance through love, support, and kindness.

- Keep undesirable activities (e.g., car travel, shopping) brief.

- Provide immediate (nonviolent) consequences for acting out, to limit repetition of the behavior.

- Limit physical punishment and verbal violence, because this will increase ADHD symptoms.

- Concentrate on teaching social skills rather than on eliminating maladaptive behaviors.
- Give frequent authentic praise for social skills, paying attention, and other behaviors that are incompatible with inappropriate behaviors.
- Use limits where appropriate, but give choices and permit autonomy.
- Limit access to violence on TV, as it is more likely to influence children with ADHD than other children.
- Set behavioral rules and establish clear rewards for following rules.
- Do not try to force children with ADHD to go to sleep, but set routine bedtimes after which children must play quietly and independently until they are ready for sleep.
- Use daily schedules to help young children foresee what they will be doing on a given day and learn self-control.

Much research is needed in the area of preschool diagnosis and treatment of children with ADHD. Although researchers do not yet understand the extent to which preschoolers display symptoms of ADHD and the degree to which some behaviors could be considered typical, professionals are increasingly identifying young children with this disorder and treating them in the same manner they would treat older children (Smith & Corkum, 2007). Because inattention, impulsivity, and hyperactivity are typical of the preschool years, studies have shown that as many as 40 percent of preschoolers show symptoms of ADHD and that most of the time these behaviors are transitory. Of those children being diagnosed in preschool years with ADHD, fewer than half meet criteria for eligibility for special services in elementary school or adolescence (Ninowski, 2011). Giving a child a label early in life can carry unintended consequences in terms of the Pygmalion effect (children will act as they are expected to act). Yet early treatment of behavioral problems is important in teaching adaptive social and preacademic skills. While diagnostic procedures are being honed, a cautionary approach for early childhood professionals would be to limit the risk of overdiagnosis and focus on treating behaviors that may or may not be clinical and may or may not be permanent.

Traumatic Brain Injury

Head injuries, accounting for 40% of fatalities in children ages 1 to 4, are caused by physical assault (abuse) more than 50 percent of the time. Additionally, assault is the cause of 90 percent of cases of **traumatic brain injury (TBI)** among children (Keenan et al., 2003). Each year, about half a million children of ages 0 to 14 suffer TBIs; the rates are highest for children ages 0 to 4 (Langlois, Rutland-Brown, & Thomas, 2005). TBI may also be the result of accidental trauma to the head, such as might occur in a car accident or a fall. Some common accidental causes of TBI in children are falls from shopping carts, walkers, and windows. Keenan and colleagues (2003) found that the greatest risk of inflicted TBI was posed to infants who were under 12 months, male, born to young mothers who were not Euro-American, and part of a multiple birth.

The outcomes and prognoses differ for the two types of head injury, with a better overall health picture for children who suffer noninflicted TBI—not caused by child abuse. Obviously, children with more severe head injuries have the poorest prognosis, though preinjury abilities and family social and behavioral functioning also contribute to the long-term outcomes of children with head injuries (Anderson, Godfrey, Rosenfeld, & Catroppa, 2012). Congress added TBI as a separate disability category under IDEA in 1992, defining it as:

> an acquired injury to the brain caused by an external physical force, resulting in total or partial functional disability or psychosocial impairment, or both, that adversely affects a child's educational performance. The term applies to open and closed head injuries resulting in impairments in one or more areas, such as cognition; language; memory; attention; reasoning; abstract thinking; judgment; problem-solving; sensory, perceptual, and motor abilities; psychosocial behavior; physical functions; information processing; and speech. The term does not apply to brain injuries that are congenital or degenerative, or brain injuries induced by birth trauma. (34 C.F.R., Sec.300.7[6] [12]).

Children whose head injuries result from a blow to the head have a specific type of brain injury that includes lacerations, contusions, and **external hematomas** to the skull, scalp, and brain. However, when a head injury is the result of inertia that involves rapid acceleration followed by rapid deceleration, it is more generalized, as in a concussion and **internal hematomas**. Children with such injuries often make rapid physical recovery and may show no evidence of cognitive processing deficits until several months after the injury. Like seizures, brain injury that results in temporary or permanent disability may not appear on typical diagnostic tests such as MRIs or EEGs. While many children recover fully, others experience long-term effects, which include deficits in personal independence, behavioral and emotional skills, social functioning, basic attention and working memory, speed at processing information, and motor functioning. They may also develop personality disorders. There is no typical profile of a child who has a head injury (Fallows & McCoy, 2011).

The symptoms of TBI generally fall into one of three categories:

- *Physical signs:* nausea, vomiting, dizziness, headache, blurred vision, sleep disturbance, fatigue, lethargy, and other sensory loss

- *Cognitive deficits:* deficits in attention, concentration, perception, memory, speech and language, and executive functions

- *Behavioral changes or alterations in degree of emotional responsivity:* irritability, anger, disinhibition, and emotional lability (regular occurrence of unstable emotional displays)

The severity and manifestations of brain injury depend on the extent and location of damage and may range from mild to severe. The timing of injury may also be important, as one study found that intellectual outcomes of TBI depended on the time at which the injury occurred, in this order, from worst time to best: middle childhood, infancy, preschool, and late childhood (Crowe, Catroppa, Babi Rosenfeld, & Anderson, 2012a). It may be that the neuroplasticity of brains in the preschool years mediates brain damage more than for children in middle childhood. With early and ongoing intervention, symptoms of brain damage may decrease, although there is considerable variability in improvement across children, particularly in infants and preschoolers whose brains are still maturing at a rapid rate. Generally, moderate to severe TBI in infants and toddlers is associated with cognitive deficits and some behavior problems (Crowe, Catroppa, Babi Rosenfeld, & Anderson, 2012b).

Children whose head injury is the result of physical abuse generally follow a pattern of trauma: massive retinal hemorrhages, broken bones (especially ribs), and major head injuries, such as cerebral hematomas, hemorrhages, edema, and stroke (Ewing-Cobb et al., 1998). Generally speaking, children with inflicted TBI are more likely to suffer long-term mental deficiency than are children who suffer accidental TBI, possibly as a result of environmental factors that are associated with child abuse (Ewing-Cobb et al.).

The term *shaken baby syndrome* is used to describe TBI that results from repeated severe shaking of an infant. It is hypothesized that the movement of the brain within the skull can cause serious brain injury in infants (Smith, 2003). However, some question whether the movement alone without rapid deceleration or impact, such as shaking a baby's head against a pillow, is sufficient to cause brain hemorrhage associated with long-term injury. Whatever the mechanism, it is clear that a child can sustain long-term brain damage even when there is no external evidence of harm.

A few general guidelines are available for educators who work with children with TBI, although these suggestions are not appropriate for all variations of the disability:

- Provide repetition and consistency.
- Demonstrate new tasks, state instructions, and provide examples to illustrate ideas and concepts.
- Avoid figurative language.
- Arrange materials and tasks to promote as much independence as possible.
- Lengthen periods of attention to appropriate tasks; provide extra time for task completion.
- Probe skill acquisition frequently and provide repeated practice.
- Build in prompts and teach strategies for memory (picture cues, verbal prompts, etc.).
- Provide breaks to avoid fatigue.
- Reduce unnecessary distractions.

Families of children with TBI are often adversely affected by the stress of chronic behavioral and cognitive changes in their children and the increasingly challenging parental adjustment and parent–child interactions (Smith, 2011). Unlike children whose brain injury is congenital, most of those with TBI and their parents remember how they were before the trauma. As a result, they have a set of emotional and psychological needs that differ from those of other children and parents. The following suggestions support working with families of children with TBI:

- Build a team of professionals including family, child, educators, and rehabilitation specialists.
- Provide behavioral intervention for social and emotional problems.
- Acquire a full assessment of the child across developmental areas.
- Plan intervention that includes a variety of learning methods and materials.
- Conduct frequent assessments (every 30–60 days in the first year postinjury).
- Ensure, if the injury was inflicted, that all appropriate safety net services to child and family are in place.
- Provide substantial support in terms of counseling, instruction, and respite to families.

Close Up

The Promise of Stem Cell Research

Few biomedical advances have captured the imagination or instigated such a heated ethical controversy as investigation of the use of stem cells for the purpose of repairing damaged tissues. It is believed that stem cells have the potential to replace atrophied or lost human cells and restore function affected by many disabling conditions, to be used for studying diseases and normal development, and to be applied to the development of new drugs and gene therapy. Such are the lofty hopes held for a procedure whose potential may never be known due to resistance and restrictive policy based on implicit ethical questions.

Stem cells have two properties: (1) to divide indefinitely, producing a population of identical offspring and (2) on cue, to undergo asymmetric division to produce two different offspring—one like the parent and one with a different set of genetic instructions. The resulting offspring with a different set of genetic instructions eventually becomes a "precursor" cell committed to a specific biological function (differentiated) such as a nerve cell or a muscle cell (Figure 6–7). Differentiated stem cells hold the promise of restoring the function, structure, and capacity of tissue to adapt to physiological conditions. This is known as *cell replacement therapy* or *cell transplantation*. Another use of stem cells is therapeutic cloning, which creates matched human embryonic stem cells by cell nuclear transfer, effectively growing a new stem cell line for every patient. While adult stem cells have some potential, embryonic stem cells have the most diverse morphing potential and are the most abundant, pure, and likely to possess the ability of indefinite proliferation.

During President George W. Bush's administration, federal funds were unavailable in the United States for research using new germ lines of human embryos. Federal guidelines defined life as beginning at the moment of conception. This definition was primarily based on religious beliefs that consider the destruction of human embryos as unacceptable. As a result, American researchers were limited to research on a small line of stem cells and adult stems cells. On the other hand, research in other countries advanced rapidly during this eight-year period. Once elected, President Barack Obama's administration immediately lifted the U.S. ban on embryonic stem cell research. While ethical debate and unreliable policy may slow research, the progress of science cannot be stopped.

Figure 6–7 Differentiated Stem Cell

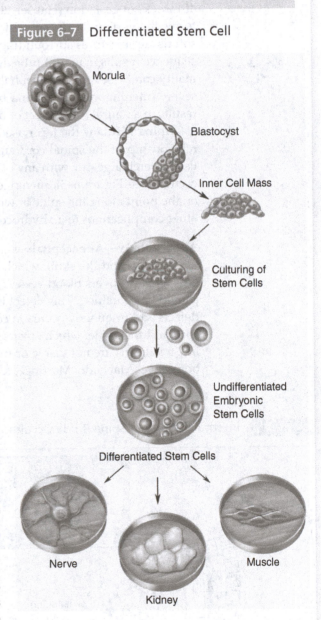

Source: From "Stem Cells: Science, Policy and Ethics," by G. D. Fischbach and R. L. Fischbach, 2004, *The Journal for Clinical Investigation, 114,* 1364–1370.

Congenital Physical Malformations

Neural Tube Defects

The most critical time for development of the nervous system is between the 3rd and 4th weeks of gestation (Hauser, 2003). During this time, the neural groove closes and forms the vertebral column, which houses the spinal cord and is joined to the other soft tissue structures surrounding the nerves. Any disturbance in the developmental sequence results in **neural tube defects** and incomplete closure. The resulting abnormality can be severe (anencephaly), moderately severe (myelomeningocele), or less severe (meningocele and **spina bifida occulta**). Worldwide, 1 in 1,000 conceptions results in a neural tube defect of one kind or another (Boyles et al., 2006).

Spina bifida is the term used to describe an incomplete spinal column and the relationship of the spinal cord and its contents to the defect. The term is frequently used interchangeably with any of the neural tube defects. These include spina bifida occulta (see Figure 6–8), meningocele, and myelomeningocele. Treatment depends on the point along the spine at which the defect is located as well as the existence of other complications (e.g., hydrocephalus or urinary tract involvement).

Anencephaly **Anencephaly** is a congenital malformation in which the brain does not develop and the skull, which normally covers the brain, is absent. A membrane occasionally covers blood vessels that do develop within the cavity where the brain should be contained. This defect is one of the most commonly occurring neural tube defects and frequently occurs in conjunction with other midline defects of the spinal cord and the spine, which covers the cord. Because this defect is incompatible with life, newborns are not viable or treatable and have a life expectancy of 51 minutes if born alive (Machado, Martinez, & Barini, 2012).

Figure 6–8 | Internal Schema of Spina Bifida Occulta

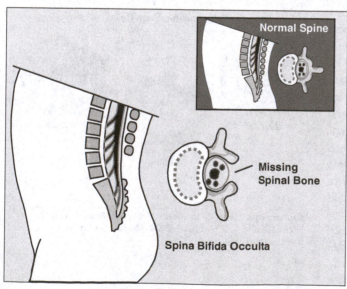

Anencephalic infants are stillborn or die shortly after delivery. Although anencephaly and other neural tube disorders can be spotted via ultrasound, the most definitive diagnosis is made by a laboratory test for maternal or amniotic fluid alpha-fetoprotein (AFP). This protein increases in both the mother's blood stream and in the amniotic fluid when a neural tube defect is present. Genetic counseling is available for families who experience this condition and can be especially valuable when parents are planning future pregnancies. Development of anencephaly occurs between the 23rd and 26th days after conception. No single factor seems to be responsible for the malformation, although a genetic influence may be associated. Environmental factors such as SES have also been linked to this malformation. There may be a gene–nutrient interaction, as an increased risk for babies with neural tube defects, including anencephaly, was discovered when mothers who had the 677TT genotype also had low levels of folate (Lacasaña et al., 2012).

Meningocele   The normal spinal cord is fully protected by bony structures called *vertebrae*. **Meningocele** is a neural tube defect that generally appears in the lumbar area of the vertebrae where the spinal cord is exposed (near the base of the spine). It is a soft tissue mass that is covered by skin and does not contain nerves or nerve roots. The **cerebrospinal fluid (CSF)** and meninges are affected in this defect (see Figure 6–9). Meningoceles occur relatively often with genetic syndromes, suggesting a genetic link to their etiology (Akalan, 2011).

A meningocele is surgically repaired during the first few days of life. There is generally no paralysis or sensory loss, and hydrocephalus rarely occurs. Occasionally, the skin covering the defect breaks down, which increases the risk of infection of the spinal tract. Sometimes nerve roots are trapped within the sac, and this may cause weakness of the legs, but full recovery generally accompanies repair of the defect.

Myelomeningocele   Of all the defects that occur under the heading of spina bifida, myelomeningocele is the most frequent and has the most significant long-term effects. With **myelomeningocele,** both the spinal cord and its covering, the **meninges,** push through the skeletal defect to the surface (see Figure 6–10). As with the other forms of spina bifida, this can occur at any point along the spine. The higher the defect occurs in relationship to the head, the more severe the complications for the infant. Associated problems may include paraplegia, hydrocephalus, incontinence, sexual dysfunction, skeletal deformities, and mental impairment.

There is no known cause for myelomeningocele. Researchers suspect that a combination of factors may be responsible for the occurrence of neural tube defects. These include heredity (women who bear one child with a neural tube disorder are at a significantly higher risk of a similar outcome during subsequent pregnancies), environmental factors such as occupational exposures, socioeconomic status, geographic area (independent of race), and possibly vitamin deficiency (Hauser, 2003). Folic acid, necessary for cell division and tissue growth, has long been considered a factor in the incidence of neural tube defects—although its exact mechanism in relation to this congenital malformation is unknown (Boyles et al., 2006). Mothers whose diets are low in folates are at risk for neural tube incidence, and those who take folic acid supplements *prior to conception* have a reduced risk.

Myelomeningoceles differ in size as well as location. They may be as small as a dime or as large as an apple. The size

Figure 6–9   Internal Schema of Meningocele

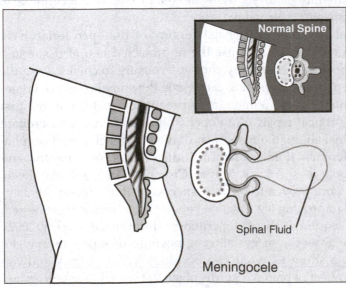

Figure 6–10   Internal Schema of Myelomeningocele

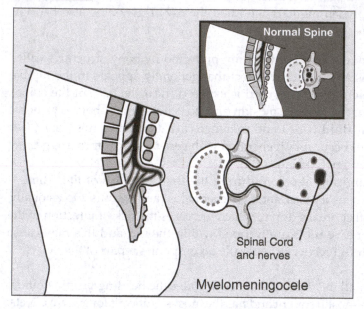

Normal Spine

Spinal Cord
and nerves

Myelomeningocele

of the defect is not always the key to the complications that may arise. Severe neurological involvement may accompany a small defect as well as a large one.

At birth, the defect may be covered with a thin membrane. This is frequently broken during the birth process, and cerebral spinal fluid leaks from the open area, placing the infant at significant risk for meningitis. A broken membrane also increases the need for surgery within the first few days of life. Surgical repair of a myelomeningocele places the contents of the exposed sac into the spinal column and closes the defect. Occasionally, the defect may be so large that it requires a skin graft to cover the open area of the back. Most children who require myelomeningocele surgery also require a cerebral shunt within the first 12 months.

Prior to 1960, most infants affected with myelomeningocele were sent home and managed without the benefit of surgery. Most infants did not survive the first 2 years of life, with the majority dying within the first month. In 1959, the University of Sheffield in Sheffield, England, developed a comprehensive plan for the treatment of affected infants. This plan included repairing the spinal defect within the first few days of life, placing a shunt for hydrocephalus, and establishing a home program including the services of a team of surgeons, physicians, physical therapists, and social workers. The two-year survival rate increased dramatically but presented the community with a whole new set of problems. These included providing services for surviving children who had severe disabilities, degrees of bladder and bowel dysfunction, and lower extremity paralysis. These are the problems that continue to affect children with myelomeningocele today.

Most recently, medical advances in prenatal surgery of the open lesion have improved the prognosis even further. Because the unprotected neural tissue in a fetus is progressively traumatized *in utero* by chronic exposure to chemicals in the amniotic fluid, prenatal repair of the opening can rescue the spinal cord from damage that would occur throughout the remainder of pregnancy. In 1998, in the first reported case of *in utero* surgical repair of an open spina bifida and concomitant placement of a cerebrospinal shunt, the male infant failed to develop hydrocephalus and had met all developmental milestones (including motor) at 6 months, and he developed full use of both legs (Adzick, Sutton, Crombleholme, & Flake, 1998). While this procedure has since proven to be quite successful in reversing the damage to the spinal cord and improving leg function beyond what would be expected, a majority of children still require a ventriculoperitoneal shunt (Fetal Surgery, 2002). Prenatal surgery prior to 26 weeks of gestation is possible to repair the myelomeningocele and to place a shunt to avoid hydrocephaly. When Adzick and colleagues (2011) studied the affect of prenatal versus postnatal surgery for fetuses and infants with myelomengoceles, they stopped the study prior to completion because, although there were significant cognitive and motor benefits for children who received prenatal treatment through surgery compared to those who were surgically treated after delivery, the researchers concluded that risks of premature delivery and possible negative effects on maternal health were too high to continue the study. Surgery, while having great potential to mitigate the effects of neural insult, should be reserved for fetuses at the highest risk for poor outcomes (Simpson & Greene, 2011). At this point, however, prenatal determination of risk cannot be made accurately, suggesting that prenatal surgery should be put off until better diagnostic procedures are developed. A less risky surgery that is experimental but promising with animals is robotic endoscopic surgery.

Common problems experienced by infants and children with a repaired myelomeningocele include genitourinary and orthopedic abnormalities. These problems are anticipated within the neonatal period and realized during infancy and early childhood. Defects in the upper lumbar spine area affect hip flexion and may require children to use a wheelchair, whereas defects in the lower lumbar spine area may allow the child to walk with the aid of braces and crutches. Regardless of the level of the defect, many of these children also have clubfeet that often require casting.

Many affected children have significant problems with the genitourinary system. Because of the nerve involvement in the lumbar spine, the bladder frequently is atonic (without muscle tone); it becomes distended with urine and lacks the nerve impulses required to empty spontaneously. This buildup of urine provides the perfect setting for bacteria to grow, and chronic urinary tract infections place such children at risk for kidney disease. In addition, many of these children lack the nerve impulses for normal bowel control. Rectal muscles lack tone, allowing stool to leak, increasing the opportunity for contamination of the urinary tract with bacteria from feces. These children are also at risk for problems with skin breakdown, both from decreased circulation and decreased sensation below the level of the defect. Consequently, these children have a higher rate of chronic infections. Caregivers must be educated regarding the best method of promoting adequate bladder and bowel function, to decrease the risks of chronic problems. Methods of prevention may include inserting a bladder catheter, teaching the child to place downward pressure on the lower abdomen to empty the bladder, administering antibiotics, or in severe situations, creating an ostomy.

An **ostomy** is an opening made from an internal tube to an external source to allow for passage of urine or stool from the body. The formation of an ostomy is a surgical procedure. A *stoma* is the external opening on the abdomen at the site of the ostomy. The site of the stoma depends on the specific gastrointestinal and genitourinary defects leading to the ostiotomy. The ostomy may be temporary or permanent depending on the condition requiring its creation. Ostomies placed for urine diversion are generally permanent, whereas ostomies created for stool diversion are frequently temporary until staged repairs of abnormalities can be successfully accomplished. A pouch is worn over the external stoma for the collection of urine or stool. This pouch requires careful monitoring to prevent skin irritation from urine or stool. In the absence of other disabilities, children can be taught to monitor and maintain the external pouch. When a child is neither physically nor mentally able, caregivers or even educators must be adept at both monitoring and maintaining the stoma and pouch. Careful monitoring of an ostomy can prevent foul odors, leakage, and skin irritation. This is essential to promoting self-esteem in the children and allowing a normal lifestyle.

Many children with myelomeningocele have average to above average intelligence, depending on the presence of malformations within the brain that correlate with the defect (e.g., Arnold-Chiari malformations). Cases of infants born with myelomeningocele, as well as those with Down syndrome and duodenal atresia, were catalysts for what is known as the "Baby Doe" legislation enacted by the federal government to protect the rights of infants with birth defects. The legislation mandates definitive care for correctable defects and supportive care for problems related to defects that are not correctable but are compatible with life. Health-care providers and educational systems are mandated by law to serve the needs of these children. In spite of the medical, ethical, and educational progress made in recent decades, the issue of viability continues to be disputed. As recently as 2005, a Dutch protocol was proposed as a guide to applying euthanasia laws to newborns with spina bifida (Chervenak, McCullough, & Arabin, 2006). Moreover, when prenatal ultrasounds confirmed the presence of spina bifida between 1996 and 1999, 35 of 38 Dutch families chose abortion rather than carrying the fetus to term. If a medically and ethically advanced society such as the Netherlands continues to grapple with the value of persons with spina bifida, it suggests there is much to be done in the way of advocacy and education. A more subtle implication is the awareness that families with children with spina bifida are likely to experience significant emotional adjustment and need for support in the early childhood years.

Microcephaly

Microcephaly means a very small head and brain. This condition can be either primary or secondary, depending on the reasons for the limited brain growth. Primary microcephaly generally occurs during the first or second **trimester** of pregnancy and can result from genetic malformations, chromosomal abnormalities, or exposure to toxic agents (e.g., radiation, chemicals such as drugs or alcohol, or infections). Secondary microcephaly or acquired microcephaly usually occurs during the last trimester of pregnancy, during the labor and delivery process, or during the period of early infancy. Some of the factors responsible for secondary microcephaly are infections (e.g., TORCH; see Chapter 8), birth trauma (e.g., eclampsia), prenatal exposure to drugs and/or alcohol, maternal conditions (e.g., diabetes, PKU, malnutrition, AIDS, syphilis), and decreased oxygen supply from many different causes (Maria, 2008). Primary or secondary microcephaly may result in only minor developmental delays or in outcomes that range to profound disabilities.

Small head size in infants is usually identified with a head circumference that falls at least two standard deviations below the mean on a standard growth chart for age. Microcephalic head size also tends to be disproportionate to both the weight and the linear growth of a child. Although many chromosomal abnormalities cause small head size, different genes or gene–environment interactions result in varying degrees of disability. Still, many of these conditions are also associated with other physical and developmental disabilities, such as cataracts and skeletal abnormalities.

The most common development of microcephaly after the second trimester of pregnancy is related to hypoxic–ischemic cerebral injury. This generally occurs during the birth process or during the neonatal period and is caused by decreased blood flow to the brain, which in turn decreases oxygen levels (hypoxia) and causes cellular death (ischemia) from lack of oxygen and glucose. Many affected infants are full term and initially have a head circumference that is within normal parameters for height and weight. Conditions that cause hypoxic–ischemic brain dysfunction may be trauma or infection. Development of microcephaly following such events has a major impact on the long-term neurological outcome of an infant. The neurological impairment that occurs generally includes cognitive impairment, cerebral palsy, seizures, and cerebral atrophy (Maria, 2008).

There is no medical treatment for microcephalus. Many of the children with minor impairment show some degree of autism, and many are hyperactive. Both conditions increase the need for carefully planned educational opportunities that address the individual needs of a child and assist parents with the difficult job of raising one with special needs.

Hydrocephalus

Hydrocephalus is a condition in which an excessive amount of cerebrospinal fluid accumulates in the ventricles of the brain. These four ventricles are fluid-filled sacs that occupy space within and around the brain mass. The cerebrospinal fluid bathes the brain and spinal cord, providing both protection and nutrition. Although capillary circulation throughout the brain is the main source of nutrition and allows the elimination of waste products, there is additional diffusion of nutrients from the cerebrospinal fluid to the brain tissue.

Hippocrates was one of the first physicians to describe hydrocephalus. He believed that chronic seizures caused the condition and that treatment should be laxatives, ingesting vegetables, and sneezing. Failure of these treatments would then require surgical intervention that consisted of creating an opening in the skull and extending to the brain material itself, thus relieving pressure. Additional treatment involved the last-hope approach at the time to any disease process—"bloodletting."

Untreated hydrocephalus causes the head to increase in size beyond two standard deviations above the mean on the standard growth chart. Swelling of the ventricles can be caused by an obstruction in the drainage system, an overproduction of spinal fluid, or a failure to reabsorb cerebrospinal fluid into the general circulation. As an example, meningitis may cause swelling that results in blockage of the ventricles (a cause of hydrocephalus) (Kasanmoentalib, Brouwer, van der Ende, & van de Beek, 2010). Alternatively, a blockage of the ventricles and subsequent buildup of fluid may lead to a bacterial buildup that causes meningitis (an effect of hydrocephalus) (van de Beek, Drake, & Tunkel, 2010). When the ventricles fill with excess fluid, they become massively dilated, placing pressure on the brain matter. If left unchecked, the brain structures may become permanently damaged, and intellectual disabilities occur.

Hydrocephalus may also be caused by the presence of a tumor or result from head trauma. Long-term outcomes for infants who are either born with or develop hydrocephalus after birth depend on the cause of the problem, presence of any other neurological problems, and the time frame from onset until a diagnosis is made and treatment is initiated. Early diagnosis and treatment significantly improve the possibilities for normal development and the prevention of intellectual disabilities. Head ultrasounds, CT scans, and MRIs are used to make a definitive diagnosis. The medication Diamox can sometimes aid in controlling the condition without surgical intervention; it pulls excess fluid into the circulatory system where it can be excreted by the kidneys.

Failure to control hydrocephalus medically may ultimately result in the need for surgical intervention in which a temporary or permanent shunt is placed between the ventricles and the abdominal space. Shunting procedures require the surgical placement of a soft, pliable plastic tube between the ventricle and either the heart or the peritoneum (a closed sac lining the abdomen). Generally, the peritoneal cavity is used in children because the surgeon can loop extra catheter tubing into the abdominal space, which allows the children to grow without needing replacement of the system. Most shunts have a small bubble reservoir that is seeded under the skin, usually behind the ear. This reservoir contains a one-way valve that controls the amount of cerebrospinal fluid that can be drained from the ventricle at any one time, depending on the pressure within it. This reservoir also provides a method of checking on the flow of the system; this is especially useful when a shunt failure is suspected. The ease with which the valve can be pumped (gently pushed) aids in evaluating the shunt for free flow of fluid. Symptoms of shunt failure are similar to those of increased pressure from obstruction. This tube must be watched carefully for blockage. Symptoms of tube obstruction include a decreased level of consciousness, vomiting, temperature instability, seizures, and, if the pressure gets high enough, loss of brain mass and even death.

Hydrocephalus may be evident on prenatal ultrasound or completely unexpected at birth. However, an infant affected prior to birth with significant blockage, which has been identified by prenatal testing, may require delivery by cesarean section to attempt to preserve functional brain material and decrease the risk of injury to the mother in attempting to vaginally deliver an infant with a very large head. Many cases of significant prenatal hydrocephalus result in brain wasting from pressure during the developmental process. Surgical intervention in these cases is done not to protect the brain but for comfort for an infant and to assist its family in providing adequate physical and emotional care.

Hydrocephalus frequently occurs with other neural tube defects, such as myelomeningocele. In the latter, initial repair of the spinal defect is the first stage of surgical care, which is then followed by placement of a ventricular/peritoneal shunt in the second stage. Closure of the primary defect (myelomeningocele) causes obstruction of cerebrospinal fluid that results in the need for a shunt.

Hydrocephalus is a lifelong disorder that requires consistent follow-up (Buxton & Punt, 1998). Management of the shunt, observations for function, and awareness of the symptoms of possible infections are requirements of not only the family and care providers but also educators who may be working with these children. Awareness of symptoms that an individual child may display is part of the educational plan.

The cognitive and psychosocial development of children with hydrocephalus varies significantly, depending on its underlying cause. Many children with hydrocephalus have normal intellectual development: Long-term follow-up shows that, on the average, children who received a shunt in their first year of life have average intelligence (median full scale IQ score of 101) (Lindquist, Persson, Fernell, & Uvebrandt, 2011). Frequent shunt infections, plugged shunts, and other malfunctions may affect development of an otherwise normal brain. Early evaluation of possible developmental delays is necessary; many of these children benefit from early childhood developmental stimulation programs. Shunt tubing is versatile and can withstand normal childhood activities. It is essential that children participate as fully as possible in age-appropriate activities so that the illness not be an unnecessary deterrent to full enjoyment of life.

IN CONCLUSION

Children affected with a neurological disability, regardless of the cause, have idiosyncratic responses to their conditions. Continuing research into causes of neurological disabilities, both physical and functional, will provide educators the knowledge base to devise new and innovative approaches to interactions with each child and family. Prevention is the goal, but providing optimal care for affected families is a more realistic short-term objective.

One area in which early childhood professionals must become more knowledgeable is in understanding ADHD and related behavioral disorders. Children with significant management needs cause havoc in preschool programs, and ADHD is increasingly being recognized at younger ages. In fact, this young population of children that tends to be so disruptive is more difficult to manage than older children because their language and cognitive skills are less well developed, and therefore, they are less able to understand rules and their consequences. On the other hand, because the time it takes to remediate behavioral problems is longer than the time the behavior has been in a child's repertoire, very early intervention is optimal. One approach that holds much promise as a method of assessing and identifying effective strategies for preschool children is functional analysis. Using this method, professionals carefully observe and measure the factors that motivate and sustain undesirable behavior. When these factors are identified, systematic attempts are made to alter the conditions that maintain such behaviors. More research, however, is clearly needed. Therefore, future efforts in early childhood special education should be devoted to research in the behavioral management of significant behavior problems, the training of professionals to use such strategies, and, if warranted by the findings, the widespread application of such strategies in early childhood settings.

STUDY GUIDE QUESTIONS

1. Why should early childhood special educators know the etiologies and courses of disabling conditions?
2. What are the medical uses of X-rays? What precautions should be taken when they are used?

3. In what ways do CAT scans provide more information than X-rays?

4. What are the advantages of the MRI over CAT scans and X-rays?

5. Describe how PET scans are performed. What special information do they provide?

6. What kind of information does an EEG provide?

7. What are the primary medical uses of ultrasound?

8. What is cerebral palsy?

9. How has modern medicine maintained the incidence of cerebral palsy?

10. Describe the relationship between primitive reflexes and normal motor development.

11. What is the main difference between primitive reflexes and postural reflexes? How do primitive reflexes interfere with postural reflex development in children with cerebral palsy?

12. Name and describe the primitive reflexes seen at birth.

13. Name and describe three general terms used to describe muscle tone. How do the terms apply to abnormal muscle tone in a child with cerebral palsy?

14. Differentiate each of the following: *hemiplegia, paraplegia, quadriplegia,* and *diplegia*.

15. Briefly describe the characteristics of athetosis, ataxia, and spasticity.

16. Compare and describe cerebral palsy that is severe, moderate, or mild.

17. What nutritional and feeding problems often accompany cerebral palsy?

18. In addition to feeding problems, what other conditions are often present with cerebral palsy?

19. What is meant by *positioning* and *handling?*

20. How are seizures activated?

21. Define *epilepsy.*

22. Describe what is unique about each of the following types of seizures: absence, tonic–clonic, and myoclonic.

23. How do seizures affect cognitive functioning?

24. What should caregivers do to intervene when a child experiences a tonic–clonic seizure?

25. What are the characteristics of ADHD?

26. What are the recommended treatments and precautions for preschoolers with ADHD?

27. Why is it difficult to describe a child with traumatic brain injury? What are some common symptoms of this type of injury?

28. Identify five general recommendations for those who work with children who have traumatic brain injury.

29. Explain the relationship between terms associated with neural tube defects: neural tube defects, spina bifida, myelomeningocele, meningocele, anencephaly, spina bifida occulta.

30. What is *anencephaly*?
31. What are the long-term effects of meningocele, and how is it treated?
32. What is myelomeningocele, and how is it treated?
33. What physical problems are common for children with repaired myelomeningocele?
34. What is microcephaly, and what causes it?
35. What is *hydrocephalus*? How is it controlled?

7 | Inborn Variations of Development

© Denielle M. Miller

When one considers all of the ways in which human development, from embryo to birth, might vary, the fact that so many children are born without apparent disabilities is miraculous. This chapter is devoted to the description of variations in development that originate before birth. These variations do not insinuate devaluation, inferiority, or undesirability of persons born with differences. Rather, the variations in development result in patterns of physical and behavioral characteristics that enable professionals to reliably group children according to similarities. Sometimes specific treatments are implicated when an individual child belongs to a certain group. For example, children with cystic fibrosis usually receive postural drainage treatments because respiratory congestion is always a symptom of the disease. *Usually, however, belonging to a group in itself tells us very little about the specific treatments to be used for a specific child because individual differences are so great.* Furthermore, most treatments are not universally effective for all children with the same characteristics. Anyone who has worked with children who have autism can verify that determining what reinforcers, activities, and instructions work for one child provides little guidance for another child in the same group. This chapter includes an introduction to basic genetics, which helps in understanding the causes of genetic deviations in development. The third section of this chapter is devoted to common disabilities that have no known etiology. It is probable that most of these will eventually be linked to genetics. This chapter intentionally includes more information than will seem necessary for a foundations text, because this text is intended as a reference for later use by early childhood professionals. It is clear from working with parents that as they learn more about their child's disability, they feel more capable. Thus, it is the responsibility of professionals to become as knowledgeable as possible and to be able to help parents seek further information and resources. A caution to professionals relates to the accelerated rate of discovery of the biological causes of, and the treatments for, these and other inborn disabilities. Every day, new discoveries hold the possibility of not only understanding but also curing anomalies that were once believed to be lifelong disorders. So, while this chapter may provide a good beginning, it is no substitute for ongoing attention to research.

The following descriptions are generalizations based on current understanding of groups of children with disabilities that can be categorized. It would be a mistake to assume that one could make specific educational or programmatic recommendations for individual children based on the characteristics and types of treatments described in this chapter. This general information provides a broad beginning point. Beyond that, families and early childhood professionals must define programs based on the unique characteristics of individual children and their families.

Genetics

Genetics is the study of heredity and the variations in the characteristics of organisms, both plant and animal. In humans, genetic research provides information about development and diseases. To understand how individual variability occurs, understanding gene physiology and function in relation to human growth and development is necessary. Treatment and sometimes prevention of disabilities and diseases are made possible by recognizing the role that both genes and the environment play in human development. Not only do genes and the environment have a direct effect on humans, but the interaction between the two is a balanced relationship established through mutual adaptation over eons. Therefore, what affects one also affects the other. An imbalance between the human gene pool and its environment can have unpredictable, even catastrophic, consequences.

Chromosomes are basic genetic units, which stay constant in number within a species and across generations. In a 1911 article printed in the journal *Science*, T. H. Morgan made the first link between genes and chromosomes using saliva from a fruit fly. Chromosomes are made of **deoxyribonucleic acid (DNA)**; an entire set of DNA within organisms is referred to as a species' *genome.* Each human DNA sequence has two parallel strands (one acquired from each parent). The human genome is composed of more than 3 billion of these DNA base pairs. **Genes** are regions of a chromosome made up of molecules that collectively define a particular trait. **Genetic mapping** is the first step in isolating a gene and identifying the individual genes responsible for rare inherited disorders (National Human Genome Research Institute, 2012).

For example, the gene for muscular dystrophy is located on the "p21" region of the X chromosome. The gene is labeled Xp21. By contrast, Prader-Willi syndrome occurs when a region of the 15th chromosome is missing or deleted. The deleted region is called 15q11-13. Only about 2 percent of the human genome is made up of genes; the remainder is composed of uncoded areas with an as-yet-undetermined function. Structural support and the regulation of where, when, and how many proteins are produced are the hypothesized purposes of the uncoded genome, some of which is actually referred to as "junk" DNA.

Genes themselves do not perform moment-to-moment life functions; proteins actually act at the cellular level to cause the dynamic changes in human cells in reaction to tens of thousands of environmental signals from both inside and outside the cells. Large, complex sequences of amino acids make up protein molecules, the constellation of which is referred as a cell's *proteome*. Future research will certainly explore how the structure and function of the proteome relate to health and disease.

The study of genetics has been facilitated by new technologies for study and manipulation at a subcellular level. As a result, the genes responsible for many inherited traits such as Huntington's disease, fragile X syndrome, Duchenne muscular dystrophy, and cystic fibrosis have been isolated. Isolating and identifying genes (genetic mapping), understanding their mutations, and learning about their protein products have increased knowledge about disabilities and diseases. This molecular approach is unlike past approaches to genetics; thus, the term *new genetics* has been applied to it.

The Human Genome Project is an example of new genetics. This international project, which set out to map and sequence the entire genetic code of human chromosomes, concluded in 2003, having identified all of the approximately 20,000 to 25,000 genes in human DNA and determined the sequences of the 3 billion chemical base pairs that make it up (Human Genome Project Information, 2008). The multiple purposes of this project ranged from such esoteric interests as pure scientific curiosity to the discovery of the biological basis for environmental, health, climate, and energy solutions to human problems, to the more pragmatic objectives of discovering cures for genetic disabilities through drug therapy, gene replacement, inactivation of anomalous genes, or other yet-to-be-discovered methods.

Now that the entire human genome has been mapped, it has created fertile ground for generations of future research and application. The Human Genome Project led to the understanding that protein production is the key to human functioning and that the study of protein expression will lead to specific treatments of genetic mutations. The study of protein–genetic mechanics is known as *proteomics*. New drug design, as well as gene therapy, fall under the umbrella of proteomics research and treatment.

Understanding the complexity of the Human Genome Project and its application for families with children with disabilities is an obligation of professionals working with these families (Miller & Martin, 2008). Many families can navigate the new territory with little assistance, but others depend on those who are trained and can readily access information to keep pace with changes in the treatment of, prevention of, counseling for, and financing of care for genetic disorders. Because of the complex bioethical and even political dynamics of the Human Genome Project research, rumors, false hopes, and myths are likely to be as widespread as truth.

While holding great promise, the new knowledge that has accompanied the Human Genome Project has generated some of the most challenging ethical considerations of our time (Iozzio, 2005). Calling modern society "ambivalent" about the progress of genomic medicine, Iozzio posed the obvious question of whether elimination of genetic disability vis-à-vis preconception planning and prenatal diagnosis is either inevitable or desirable. Iozzio warned that by focusing solely on the potential, positive possibilities and ignoring the darker side of genomic medicine, we risk reducing the value of, or even eliminating, people who exhibit undesirable genetic traits. Public dialogue, education, and policies are needed to address the social, legal, and ethical implications resulting from the knowledge provided by the Human Genome Project.

Behavioral genetics represents an evolving category of genetic study. This subdiscipline is so named because researchers seek to identify genes associated with behaviors such as violence, mental illness, and alcoholism. A majority of studies, however, refute the notion that genes, by themselves, cause behavior. Many geneticists warn that research in behavioral genetics should be reviewed critically. It is agreed that the scientific and popular media should emphasize that genes alone rarely determine behavior; rather, genes interact with the environment to cause variations in behavior. At the same time, people with certain genetic makeups are more vulnerable to certain environments and experiences.

Cellular Activity of Genetics

The human body contains more than a billion miles of cells, and an average cell possesses more than a meter of DNA. A nucleic acid compound, DNA carries the chemical coding needed to transmit genetic information from generation to generation. A chromosome is a chain of DNA. Human cells possess a total of 46 chromosomes, or 23 pairs of chromosomes (see Figure 7–1). That is, each member of a chromosome pair has matching genes situated in the same location and arranged in the same sequence as the corresponding member of the pair. Of the 23 chromosomal pairs, 22 are called *autosomes*. The 23rd pair is composed of two **sex chromosomes:** X and Y. The X and the Y chromosome combination determines the gender of an individual— XX in females and XY in males. An **allele** is one of two complementary versions of a gene residing on each of the two chromosomes in a pair. The trait for eye color, for example, is determined by the relationship between the allele for eye color on one chromosome and the allele specifying eye color on the corresponding chromosome. A **homozygote pair** inherits identical alleles for a certain trait, such as two genes for cystic fibrosis. A **heterozygote pair** has two different alleles for a particular trait, such as one normal gene and one gene for cystic fibrosis. **Genotype** refers to the combination of alleles inherited for a particular trait within an individual; **phenotype** refers to the observable expression, or appearance, of the genotype in an individual. For example, the genotype leading to cystic fibrosis is the complement of two cystic fibrosis alleles; the phenotype for this set of alleles is a chronic respiratory and/or digestive disease.

While many disabilities are caused by a single gene or combination of genes, others are the result of a deviation affecting whole chromosomes. When a

| Figure 7-1 | Drawing of the Individual Chromosomes |

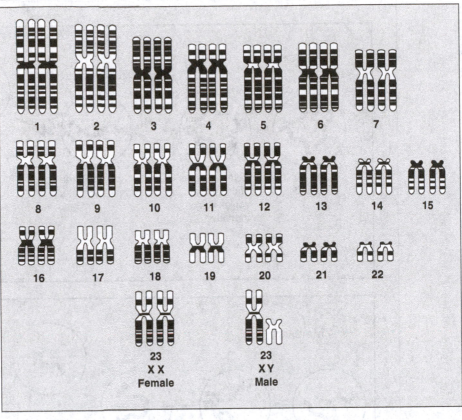

chromosome error is suspected, the number and configuration of chromosomes is analyzed using a **karyotype.** This genetic test examines the whole set of chromosomes in an individual for variations. For example, an analysis of the karyotype is conducted to determine whether a child suspected of having Down syndrome has an extra 21st chromosome or extra chromosomal material that would cause this genetic disorder.

Chromosomal anomalies are usually the result of a deviation from normal cell division. The purpose of cell division is to ensure the growth, development, and repair of an organism. The two types of cell division are mitosis and meiosis (see Figure 7–2). **Mitosis** produces two identical daughter cells, each containing the full set of 46 chromosomes. This occurs in all cell reproduction. After the chromosomes replicate, the cell divides to create two identical cells, as in the regeneration of skin cells. **Meiosis** produces sex cells, called *germ cells,* or **gametes.** Prior to cell division, the chromosome pairs split, with one of each going to the two resultant germ cells. Thus, each germ cell possesses only one-half of the full complement of chromosomes. These cells are involved in reproduction. A sperm is a male gamete, and an ovum is a female gamete. When these cells join during conception, the resultant cell has a full set of chromosomes—one of each chromosome pair from each parent. Abnormalities

Figure 7–2 Comparison of Mitosis and Meiosis of Cells

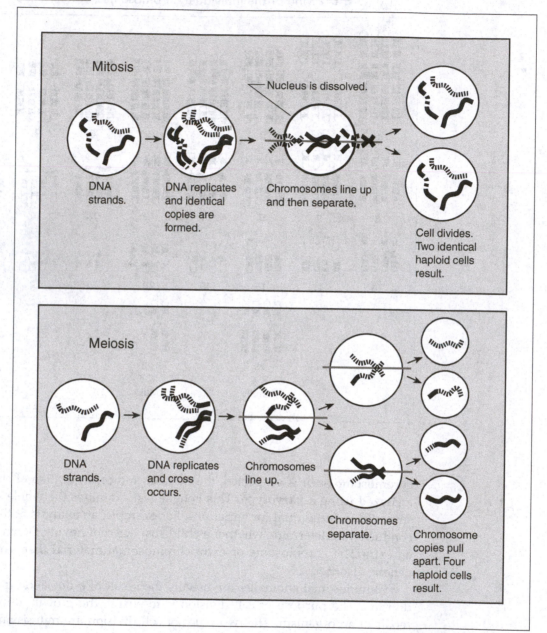

in chromosome number or structure can arise during either mitosis or meiosis. An example of such an abnormality is Down syndrome, in which the 21st chromosome does not divide during maternal meiosis. The two resulting gametes are abnormal, one with no 21st chromosome and one with two 21st chromosomes. The former is not viable, but the latter, when joined with a paternal gamete bearing one 21st chromosome, produces a fertilized egg with three 21st chromosomes; this is known as trisomy 21, or Down syndrome.

Single Gene Disorders

Single gene inheritance is a type of inheritance variation resulting from mutations that may involve one or both genes of a chromosome pair. Examples of single gene disorders are cystic fibrosis, hemophilia, and sickle cell anemia. The occurrence of abnormalities varies. For example, for hemophilia, the occurrence rate is 1 in 5,000 male births with 400 babies born with hemophilia each year (CDC, 2011). By contrast, sickle cell disease occurs once in every 500 live births among African Americans (CDC, 2011).

As a result of the Human Genome Project, an estimated 25,000 protein-encoded genes have been identified; 1,822 are thought to cause single gene diseases, most of which are very rare (Chial, 2008). In several hundred of these diseases, the biochemical defect has been identified, and in many, as mentioned previously, the responsible gene has been isolated. Recently, it has been discovered that many diseases once considered simple single gene disorders actually have a more complex relationship with other genes (Chial). For example, cystic fibrosis is considered a single gene disorder. However, a more thorough understanding of cystic fibrosis reveals that an individual's phenotype may be affected by additional genes within the genome that modulate the severity of the disease.

Single gene disorders are transmitted from one generation to another depending on whether they result from recessive, dominant, or sex linked genes. A **recessive gene** is one whose genetic information is typically overruled by genetic information of a more dominant gene. Usually, it takes two recessive genes, one from each chromosome of a pair, for a recessive trait to be expressed. On the other hand, only one **dominant gene** is typically needed for that gene's trait to be expressed. The terms *recessive* and *dominant* describe only the phenotypic expression, or observable trait; they do not describe what is happening at a molecular or biochemical level. For example, in the case of the inheritance of a single recessive gene, the characteristic trait or traits of such a disorder are usually not expressed. Nevertheless, at the biochemical level, both the dominant and recessive genes are being expressed. **Sex-linked disorders** are transmitted on either the X or Y chromosomes. However, most sex-linked disorders, for example, hemophilia and color blindness, are inherited on the X chromosome.

Recessive-Gene Inheritance   Tay Sachs, phenylketonuria (PKU), cystic fibrosis, and sickle cell anemia are a few of the many recessive, single-gene disorders (see Figure 7–3). As mentioned, a recessive gene is expressed only if it is inherited from both parents. For example, if the recessive gene for sickle cell anemia is inherited from both parents, the child will show signs of the disease. In this case, the offspring has a 25 percent chance of receiving two recessive genes and, consequently, of having the disorder. If just one affected gene is inherited, the person will not show signs of the disease except at the biochemical level. This is because the gene is paired with a dominant gene, which is the one phenotypically expressed. In this case, the person is a **carrier,** and although carriers have no signs or symptoms of the disease, they may transmit the gene to offspring. There is a 50 percent chance of inheriting one gene and becoming a carrier and a 25 percent chance of not inheriting the gene from either parent.

Figure 7–3 Pattern of Inheritance of Autosomal Recessive Genes

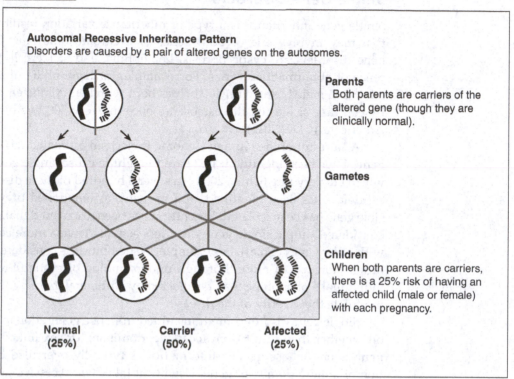

Autosomal Recessive Inheritance Pattern
Disorders are caused by a pair of altered genes on the autosomes.

Parents
Both parents are carriers of the altered gene (though they are clinically normal).

Gametes

Children
When both parents are carriers, there is a 25% risk of having an affected child (male or female) with each pregnancy.

| Normal (25%) | Carrier (50%) | Affected (25%) |

Dominant Gene Inheritance Huntington's disease, familial hypercholesteremia, and some forms of muscular dystrophy are examples of dominant single gene disorders (see Figure 7–4). Dominant genes are phenotypically expressed whenever they appear. Persons having just one of the genes will show signs of the disorder. Therefore, if one parent has the dominant gene and the other parent does not, the offspring has a 50 percent chance of receiving the dominant gene. Early identification of the possession of dominant gene disorders can help parents decide whether or not to prevent the inheritance. At this time, prevention of transmission can occur only when parents decide not to reproduce or, once conception has taken place, to abort a fetus with a genetic disease.

Recessive and dominant traits are not strictly determined by the presence or absence of a normal or abnormal gene. As with most things in nature, heredity is not so simple. If one normal and one mutant gene are present, their combined production of genetic material is what determines the dominant or recessive nature of the trait. For example, if there is enough gene product between the two genes to provide for normal functioning, the mutant gene and its related disorder are overruled and therefore recessive. For example, a hypothetical "syndrome Q" needs 56 units of normal gene product for the syndrome to be expressed. From the mother, who is a carrier of the mutant gene, the fertilized cell receives 10 units of normal gene product and 40 units of mutant Q gene product. From the father, who is not a carrier, the fertilized cell receives 50 units of normal gene product. Because 60 units of normal gene product are present, the offspring of this union will have sufficient gene

Figure 7–4 Pattern of Inheritance of Autosomal Dominant Genes

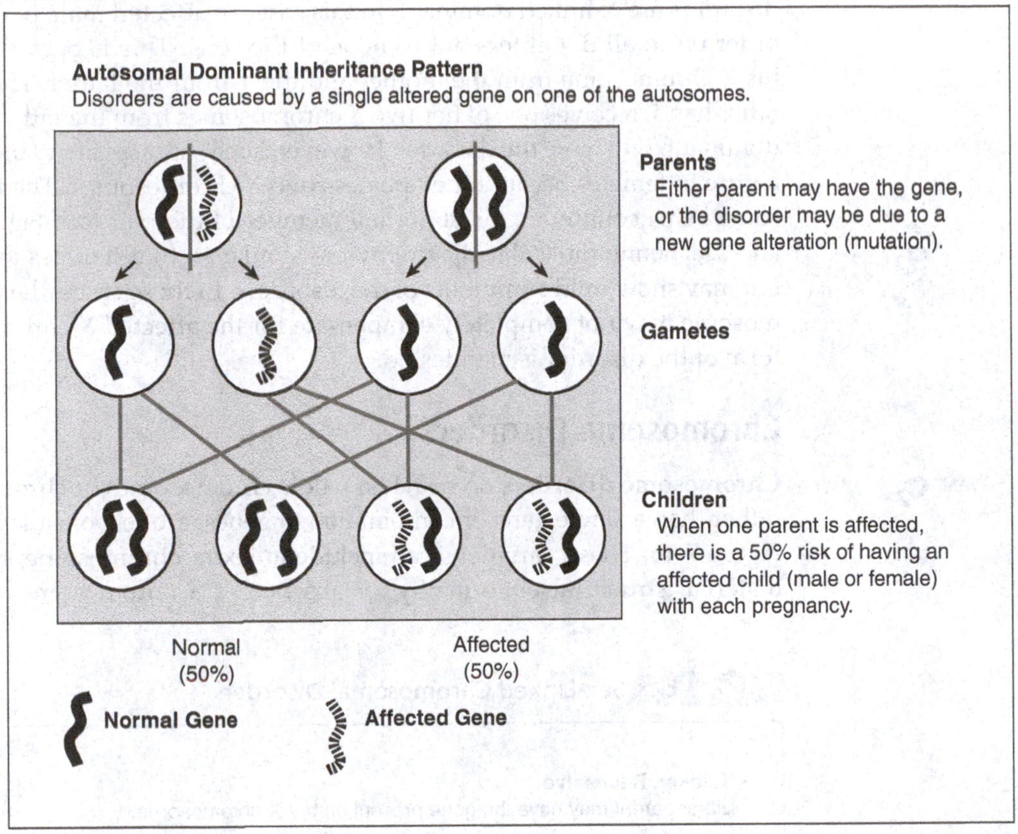

Autosomal Dominant Inheritance Pattern
Disorders are caused by a single altered gene on one of the autosomes.

Parents
Either parent may have the gene, or the disorder may be due to a new gene alteration (mutation).

Gametes

Children
When one parent is affected, there is a 50% risk of having an affected child (male or female) with each pregnancy.

Normal
(50%)

Affected
(50%)

Normal Gene   **Affected Gene**

product for the gene trait to function normally. In this child, the gene for syndrome Q is recessive.

If there is not enough genetic product between the two chromosomes to allow for normal function, the gene and the disorder are said to be dominant. For example, in sickle cell anemia, a recessive gene produces abnormal hemoglobin. If that gene is inherited from each parent, the blood will make abnormal hemoglobin; the person has sickle cell anemia. On the other hand, if one abnormal gene and one normal gene are inherited, the blood will contain some normal and some abnormal hemoglobin. Although both genes are functioning, the person will show no symptoms of the disorder because enough normal hemoglobin is produced to outweigh the effects of the abnormal gene. Such individuals do not have sickle cell anemia, but they are carriers of the recessive gene and can therefore transmit the gene to their children.

Sex-Linked Inheritance Sex-linked disorders have the affected gene on either the X or Y chromosome. Most sex-linked disorders are related to the X chromosome. Hemophilia and Duchenne muscular dystrophy are examples. The incidence of these types of disorders is highest in male offspring. Males inherit X-linked diseases from their mothers, the source of their X chromosome. In males, such diseases are usually more significant because there is no complementary X chromosome. Females with two X chromosomes are usually not affected because the second X chromosome compensates for the recessive gene on the affected X chromosome. Only a few genetic disorders are X-linked dominant. In this case, an affected male parent passes the disorder on to all daughters but to none of the sons. This is because the son receives his X chromosome from the mother and the Y from the father. The daughter, on the other hand, receives one of her two X chromosomes from the father and, because it is dominant, will have the disorder. However, such diseases are usually of a less severe nature in females because they possess two X chromosomes. The normal X chromosome helps counteract the abnormal member of the pair (see Figure 7–5). Fragile X and Duchenne muscular dystrophy are similar in that females are usually carriers but may show mild symptoms of the disorders. In these cases, the unaffected X chromosome may not completely compensate for the affected X chromosome, and some form of the disorder is manifested.

Chromosome Disorders

Chromosome disorders occur when whole chromosomes or chromosome segments, rather than a single gene or combination of genes, are responsible for a problem (see Figure 7–6). These variations can include an extra chromosome, extra chromosome material, structural abnormality, or absence of a chromosome. Turner syndrome

Figure 7–5   Sex-Linked Chromosomal Disorders

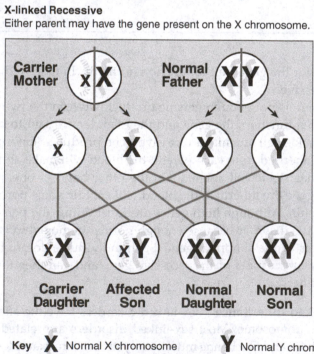

X-linked Recessive
Either parent may have the gene present on the X chromosome.

Carrier Mother   xX

Normal Father   XY

Parents
Since females have two X chromosomes, in order to be affected they must have an altered pair of genes. (Only one X chromosome is altered here.)

Gametes

x   X   X   Y

Children
When a woman has an altered gene on only one X chromosome, she is a carrier (usually not affected), and with a normal father they have a 25% risk of having an altered son.

xX   Carrier Daughter

xY   Affected Son

XX   Normal Daughter

XY   Normal Son

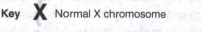 Key   **X** Normal X chromosome   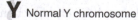 **Y** Normal Y chromosome

X Affected X chromosome

Figure 7–6 Chromosomal Disorders

Some Chromosome Abnormalities

Abnormality	Karyotype	Disorder
Extra #21 chromosome		Down Syndrome (Trisomy 21)
Extra #18 chromosome		Trisomy 18
Extra #13 chromosome		Trisomy 13
Girl with only one X chromosome		Turner Syndrome (45, XO)
Boy with an extra X chromosome		Klinefelter Syndrome (47, XXY)
Long arm of X chromosome is barely attached		Fragile-X Syndrome
Deletion of the short arm of one #5 chromosome		Cri du chat Syndrome
Deletion of part of the long arm of the #15 chromosome		Prader-Willi Syndrome

(discussed later in this chapter) is an example of a chromosome disorder in which one of the two X chromosomes is entirely or partially absent. Chromosome disorders of this nature are fairly common, occurring in 7 of every 1,000 births. It is also estimated that 20 percent of all conceptions and 50 percent of all spontaneous abortions in the first trimester are affected by chromosomal abnormalities. The incidence of chromosomal disorders in the United States has increased over recent decades, partly due to the detection of anomalies that would previously been missed in prenatal genetics testing and partly due to an average increase in maternal age (Jackson, Crider, Rassmussen, Cragan, & Olney, 2011).

Multifactorial Disorders

Multifactorial disorders account for two types of genetic problems: congenital disorders and the predisposition to a disease, usually with onset in adulthood. Congenital disorders account for malformations such as cleft palate, spina bifida, and various heart anomalies. Prenatal environmental factors may also be involved in these disorders. Many diseases do not appear until adulthood. These are exacerbated by a probable genetic predisposition to acquire the disease. A few examples of such disorders currently believed to be affected by genetic predisposition include heart disease, obesity, arthritis, some forms of cancer, and metabolic problems, such as diabetes mellitus. It is also believed that lifestyle moderation, such as diet and exercise, can affect the course of some of these diseases.

Prenatal Testing

Genetic testing and counseling are conducted for people who have questions and concerns about problems that may affect their offspring. In several situations, genetic testing may be warranted: having a family history of genetic disorders, having a child with a genetic disorder, having had two or more miscarriages or a baby who died in infancy, and when parents are of an ethnic origin linked to a specific disorder (e.g., sickle cell anemia is more prevalent among African Americans). Testing is also warranted when first cousins plan to have a child and when a pregnant woman is over age 35.

Analysis of blood samples can detect genetic disorders. Hemophilia, Tay Sachs disease, cystic fibrosis, sickle cell anemia, and Duchenne muscular dystrophy are detected in this way. Blood samples also show whether a person is the carrier of a recessive gene that could be passed on to offspring. Amniocentesis, chorionic villus sampling, and fetal blood sampling from the umbilical cord are prenatal tests that can be used for early detection of abnormalities. Most recently, noninvasive tests have been conducted using a small sample of maternal blood to make prenatal genetic diagnoses (Beals, 2011).

Amniocentesis is a painful and risky procedure that removes fluid from the sac surrounding the fetus. A long, thin needle is inserted through the abdomen to withdraw approximately 4 teaspoons of amniotic fluid. Out of every 100 amniocentesis tests performed, 1.5 spontaneous abortions are likely to occur; the more procedures completed by a health facility, the smaller the risk of fetal death following amniocentesis (Tabor, Vestergaard, & Lidegaard, 2009). Amniocentesis can reveal chromosomal, metabolic, and biochemical disorders. For example, DNA tests can be conducted to detect such problems as cystic fibrosis or sickle cell anemia. Down syndrome is the most common chromosomal problem detected with this procedure. **Chorionic villus sampling (CVS)** is conducted vaginally or abdominally to take a small tissue sample from the chorion, or outer sac that surrounds the fetus. Chorionic villus sampling can be conducted earlier in fetal development than amniocentesis, but the risk to a fetus is higher, with a spontaneous abortion rate of about 2 in 100 tests (Tabor et al.). **Fetal blood sampling** (also called *percutaneous umbilical blood sampling*) can be conducted even earlier than CVS and detects the same problems. A needle is guided into the abdomen and through the uterus to the umbilical cord, from which a blood sample is withdrawn.

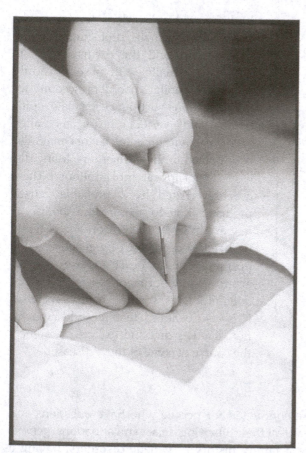

© Eddie Lawrence/DK Images

Other prenatal tests include ultrasound and **alpha-fetoprotein (AFP) screening**. AFP screening is a blood test conducted to detect neural tube disorders, such as malformations of the spinal cord, the spinal column, and the brain. This test, however, produces many false positives because the level of AFP fluctuates during pregnancy. For this reason, AFP testing is usually used as a screening tool leading to further diagnostic tests, such as those already mentioned. **Ultrasound** is used to visualize the fetus and its developing organs. A specific prenatal screening application of ultrasound diagnosis is to evaluate nuchal translucency. An excessive collection of fluid at the back of a fetus's neck is defined as **nuchal translucency,** the presence of which significantly increases the risk of chromosomal abnormalities, genetic syndromes, gene mutations, and heart and skeletal defects. Excess nuchal translucency can also be a variation of normal development. Therefore, follow-up by more sophisticated means is indicated by a positive ultrasound marker. Congenital malformations, such as spina bifida, can be detected using this procedure, as well.

A controversial technology enhanced by the knowledge gained from the Human Genome Project analyzes for genetic defects prior to *in vitro* implantation (Dolan, 2002). Referred to as *preimplantation genetic diagnosis (PGD),* this groundbreaking technique will enable parents to avoid embryos with known disorders—and to choose embryos with the most "desirable" traits. Less controversial are two noninvasive diagnostic procedures being developed that may prove to be highly accurate without the risk of damage to a fetus that accompanies amniocentesis and CVS (Chachkin, 2007). Fetal cells have long been known to circulate in maternal blood. The two procedures in the early stages of clinical use, **maternal serum fetal cell sorting (MSFCS)** and **maternal plasma fetal DNA recovery (MPFDR),** extract fetal cells from maternal blood to prenatally diagnose problems. In addition to being less dangerous, these tests will likely be less expensive and therefore more accessible to all women.

Gene Therapy

Gene therapy has become a tool in the biomedical treatment of inborn anomalies of development. Although still highly experimental, the process has had promising success. Gene therapy may include such treatment (and terminology) as *gene repair, gene replacement, stem cell repair, protein replacement, genetic engineering,* and *enzyme therapy that counteracts genetic errors.* Many of the latest research accomplishments are described in this chapter. Someday, gene therapy may render many of the disabilities included in this book innocuous, if not obsolete. The following are the four general forms of gene therapy:

1. The most common method is to insert a normal gene into a nonspecific location in the genome to replace a gene that is not functioning.

2. A normal gene is inserted into a specific location in the genome, swapping places with the abnormal gene.

3. Using a procedure called *selective reverse mutation,* an abnormal gene is repaired so it can return to its normal functioning.

4. The degree to which a gene is turned on or off is altered to regulate normal functioning.

When a person has diabetes mellitus, the body is unable to produce insulin, resulting in a breakdown in metabolism. Using a gene therapy technique previously described, a normal gene capable of providing the information needed to initiate insulin production would be inserted into a person's cell, the cell propagated, and the new cells injected into the suffering person. These cells would then trigger the individual's body to produce insulin. In this example, the inserted genes are not passed on to the next generation because normal genetic material is not placed in the germ cells.

By contrast, germ line therapy introduces genes into the germ, or sex, cells as well as into the somatic cells. The consequences of this therapy may be profound.

Future generations would be influenced if such therapy is successful, as eliminating certain genes while potentially creating other new abnormalities could compromise the stability of the entire gene pool. For this reason and because it is believed there is a risk of serious ethical abuse, many agree that this type of therapy should not be undertaken even if it could be successful in reversing the effects of a serious genetic defect in some children.

Close Up: Designer Babies

In vitro fertilization (IVF) was the first step in the modern era of genetic engineering. Although the prospect seemed fraught with danger in 1978, it is today rarely questioned as a plausible and ethical option for conception. Fast forward four decades and the prospects now on the horizon have the possibility of changing the very nature of what it means to be human. People may soon be able to change genes to modify longevity, increase intelligence, alter muscle mass, eliminate disease and disabilities, and take advantage of many other "sci-fi-esk" enhancements. While many of the dramatic genetic engineering possibilities are not yet being tested on humans, they are on other species. For example, by inserting the gene that makes a jellyfish fluorescent into mice embryos, glow-in-the-dark rodents have been created. The process is inefficient, however, with many errors, losses, and deformities to show for each "success." Once the process is made safe and efficient, and humans begin engineering the traits of their children, we will have crossed a threshold of no return. Now, procedures for altering the very timetable of evolution are at hand. The power to modify the nature of humanity through biological and technological advances is seductive and may be impossible to resist.

IVF set the path to preimplantation genetic selection (PGS), in which an embryo is microscopically examined for signs of genetic disorder. Knowing the makeup of embryos, families can decide which one, if any, to implant based on the presence or absence of target characteristics such as presence of sickle cell disease or cystic fibrosis. The process can also be used to select embryos of a specific gender—raising the likelihood, if widely used, of altering the gender balance of humanity.

Recently, PGS has been used as a process for tissue matching, where an embryo that matched a child with Diamond Blackfan anemia was implanted to produce a sibling who was to become a tissue donor. The child was cured by transplanted cells from his baby brother's umbilical cord. Now, the nature of IVF has changed from a treatment for infertility to a means of picking and choosing from among embryos as might be done with any other consumer product.

The next step in refining genetic engineering is called "human germline engineering" or "human germline modification." This process goes beyond acceptance or rejection of embryos produced naturally, to actually altering the genes that are carried on the ova and sperm. The term "germline" indicates that traits that are altered are not only changed for the subject embryo, but for all succeeding generations. To accomplish germline modification, the processes of IVF, altering stem cells, gene transfer, and cloning would be are combined. At about 5 days, embryonic stem cells are removed and altered by adding new genes. Once grown successfully, the modified stem cell nucleus is transferred to an enucleated egg cell through cloning techniques. This "constructed embryo" is then implanted into a woman's uterus, producing a genetically modified human.

It does not take much imagination to envision both wild success and unspeakable disaster from such procedures. For example, it is well known that very few genes operate in isolation and that it is difficult to know how a change in one gene will interact with other genes. Moreover, genetic–environmental interactions are not well understood. Therefore, how gene modifications would affect individuals and the rest of the ecosystem cannot be predicted.

Also, there is no universally accepted ideal for winnowing the gene pool down to those genes that would produce the most desirable traits and would result in biological perfection. It is probable that the standards used to determine which traits to eliminate or enhance would be the domain of those with power and money. There are many other considerations and probably not very much time to consider them before the technology for "designer babies" becomes a reality. If there is a need for wide social involvement in discussions regarding the direction of humanity, it should begin now because it is no longer a question of whether it is going to happen but how we want to progress as a species when it does.

Source: From "Designer Babies: Eugenics Repackaged or Consumer Options? The Forces Pushing Humanity Towards Attempts at Self-Motivation, Through Biological and Technological Advances, Are Powerful, Seductive Ones That We Will Be Hard-Pressed to Resist," by Stephen L. Baird, 2007, *Technology Teacher, 66*(7), 12–24.

Genetic Variations in Development

Cystic Fibrosis

Cystic fibrosis (CF) is the most common, fatal, genetic disease in the United States. Approximately 1 in 29 Caucasian Americans is a carrier of the CF gene (Strom et al., 2011). CF affects the **exocrine glands,** which secrete body fluids. In children with CF, the exocrine glands overproduce thick, sticky mucus that eventually clogs the lungs and blocks the functioning of the pancreas. The sweat glands are also affected and produce perspiration containing excessive amounts of sodium.

Characteristics   The excessive thick, sticky mucus produced in the lungs of individuals with CF blocks their airways, interferes with breathing, and eventually results in respiratory failure and death. This mucus further inhibits the pancreas from releasing enzymes to the digestive tract necessary for breaking down foods. Consequently, children with CF are unable to sufficiently metabolize fats and proteins. The sweat glands' tendency to excrete abnormally high amounts of sodium provides the basis for the "sweat test," the primary diagnostic measurement for CF. Because of an excessive release of salt, exposure to fevers and extreme heat are two conditions that can be especially dangerous. Heat can result in further depletion of sodium, which may, in turn, cause confusion, seizures, and other electrolyte imbalance problems.

As a consequence of these physiological disturbances, children with CF have chronic symptoms of persistent coughing, recurrent wheezing and crackles, repeated respiratory infection, excessive appetite, poor weight gain or even weight loss, and frequent or difficult bowel movements (VanDevanter et al., 2008). The progression of CF symptoms varies across individuals with the disease. Some children

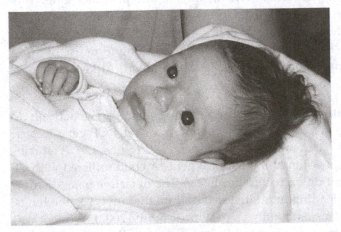

© Estee Aiken

may be affected primarily in the respiratory system; in others, the pancreas and digestive systems might be more significantly affected. No diagnostic tests have yet been devised to predict the course that will be taken in specific patients with CF. In the past, it was very unusual for those affected by CF to live long enough to go to school; most died in infancy. However, with recent treatment advances, life expectancy has improved substantially. Presently, the median life expectancy for persons with CF is 37 (Briescacher, Quittner, Fouayzi, Zhang, & Swensen, 2011). The rate of increase in life expectancy for this disease has an unexpected psychological side effect on persons with this disease. Lori Morris-Hughes described the adjustment she has gone through with progressively improved life expectancies (Schubert & Murphy, 2005). As a young child, she expected to live only until early adolescence; by the time she reached adolescence, her lifetime had been extended to early adulthood, and so on until she reached her mid-thirties. Her entire life has been lived at, near, or past the time when she was expected to die and has been permeated by emotional and physical challenges, including the certainty of early mortality. Now, among the oldest surviving persons with CF, Lori's expression of sadness over a culture that has little patience for those with chronic illness is a poignant reminder to the rest of us that there is much work to be done in the areas of empathy and listening:

> When you reach the expectation and pass it, sometimes people drop their empathy. They figure, hey, she made it to 25, she's a survivor. And they think you're great. But are you kidding? The next five years are probably going to be even worse because there are whole new challenges now that you're not prepared for because you thought you were going to be dead already. (p. 37)

What makes Lori's story especially relevant at this time in history is that advances in medical technology are progressing so fast that the historic life expectancy timelines are certain to continue to extend. For children with CF, sickle cell disease, muscular dystrophy, and other chronic illnesses, every day brings hopeful scientific news and greater optimism about "survival."

Numerous secondary physical complications have emerged concomitant with improved survival of patients with CF. For example, there is an increased incidence of respiratory dysfunctions: lung infections, bloody mucus, and pneumothorax (rupture in the lung, releasing air into the chest cavity). As the life expectancy of patients with CF increases, so does the probability of their developing CF-diabetes and kidney failure associated both with pancreatic insufficiency and long-term use of drugs to treat lung and pancreas deficiencies (Quon, Mayer-Hamblett, Aitken, Smyth, & Goss, 2011).

Etiology   CF results from an autosomal recessive gene transmitted genetically to offspring when both parents are carriers. Carriers inherit a single CF gene located on one of the two number-7 chromosomes. The second chromosome 7 remains unaffected and blocks the expression of the harmful gene. A child afflicted with CF has two CF genes, one present on each chromosome 7. The defective gene disrupts chloride–sodium regulation, leading to multisystem failure that involves the lungs, digestive and endocrine systems, and kidneys (Gaylor & Reilly, 2002). While it was long thought that a single gene was responsible for CF, recent discoveries indicate that the relationship between the gene (CFTR) and other genes is more complex

(Guggino & Stanton, 2006). It may be that the presence of specific additional genes in an individual's genome can affect the activation or severity of symptoms of CF.

Treatment   The diagnosis of CF is usually made by the child's second or third birthday, although for some children, symptoms may go undiagnosed for years. Treatment of CF involves a multidisciplinary approach that addresses the numerous issues likely to arise for both child and family. Professionals likely to be included on the intervention team are a medical director, nurse, physical therapist, clinical pharmacist, respiratory therapist, nutritionist, social service worker, and geneticist, all of whom work together with a patient with CF on long- and short-term treatment goals. Balancing sodium intake is essential for infants and children with CF. Breastfeeding may contribute to sodium depletion, a risk that is increased in high-temperature environments (Guimaraes, Schettino, Camargos, & Penna, 2012). In order to achieve adequate nutrition, a treatment plan for individuals with CF includes a high carbohydrate and protein diet, adequate salt intake, pancreatic enzyme preparations, supplemental doses of fat-soluble vitamins, and adequate fluid intake (Stark, Robinson, Feranchak, & Quinton, 2008). To loosen the mucus in the lungs, a typical treatment plan for individuals with CF includes lung therapies and mucus-thinning drugs as well as antibiotics when necessary. Chronic malnutrition is prevalent in children with CF. Most can compensate for the nutritional deficiency through the consumption of energy-dense foods and pancreatic enzyme supplements. Others require a surgically implanted gastrostomy, which permits nighttime or daytime food infusions. The latter can aid in normal growth and overall health status (Rosenfeld, Casey, Pepe, & Ramsey, 1999). Ninety percent of children and adults with CF die of lung disease or gradual decline of lung function caused by repeated bacterial infection (McCarthy, 1999). Early childhood professionals should be aware that young children with CF should not suppress coughing and may need to be taught to cough expectorant into a tissue. Some children may have to take many pills during the day, requiring adult supervision during the preschool years. Research on drugs that can effectively battle lung infection is ongoing. However, in recent years, due to the spread of panresistant bacteria, respiratory tract infections have become increasingly difficult to treat with antibiotics (White-Williams, 2002).

Although a cure has not been discovered, many promising advances made in the past three decades contribute to an improved quality of life and life expectancy for persons with CF (Jones & Helm, 2009). The Cystic Fibrosis Foundation (2008) summarized the multipronged search for more effective treatments and eventually a cure for this disease:

- *Gene therapy:* This treatment adds normal copies of the gene to cells in an attempt to correct them and ultimately cure the disease.

- *Protein assist/repair:* This therapy is designed to allow sodium and chloride to move properly between the cell lining of the lungs and other organs in an attempt to correct the function of the defective CF protein made by the CF gene.

- *Restore salt transport:* This involves correcting the amount of salt along the lung cell surface to attempt to hydrate the thick mucus in the lungs.

- *Anti-inflammatory drugs:* These may be used to reduce the inflammation in CF lungs.

- *Anti-infective treatment:* To prevent infection, this treatment includes frequent bronchial drainage treatments, aerosol inhalation therapy, antibiotics, and a mist tent employed while the person is sleeping or resting.

- *Lung transplant and lung transplant drugs:* Individuals with CF are primary candidates for lung transplants, usually performed after age 18. Double-lung transplantation has emerged as an increasingly possible and effective choice for persons with CF (White-Williams, 2002). Although lung transplants have improved mortality rates, only a 1-year survival in 30 percent of recipients was reported in 2002 (White-Williams). Moreover, progress in lung transplants has been hampered by lung availability, which declined significantly in the late 1990s. Research on lung transplant drugs is a key battlefront to find a way to improve the chances of successful transplant.

- *Nutritional supplements:* Research is being conducted to develop supplements that will improve the body's ability to fight the effects of CF. Considerable progress has been made in identifying natural supplements to children's diets which co-conspire with medical treatment to improve the health of children with CF.

In the preschool years, children with CF may or may not display symptoms that affect their daily lives. Children who experience medical trauma in the early years may be hindered by frequent absences, physical constraints on activities, and disruptions to normal social interactions (Ashton & Bailey, 2004). Outcomes for children with CF can include anxiety, compulsiveness, impulsivity, arrested emotional development, contrary behavior, and an interruption in the evolution of their sense of self. Observations in early childhood settings provide the following insights (Ashton & Bailey): (1) Parents of children with chronic illnesses such as CF are not as forthcoming as is desirable in providing information to educators, leading to false expectations, denial of support, and underprotectiveness or overprotectiveness, (2) most training programs do not provide educators adequate preparation for accommodating children with chronic illnesses, and (3) educators tend to depersonalize children with chronic illnesses by using labels such as "the cystic fibrosis" and to be skeptical of parental intentions regarding absences and protectiveness. Barriers created by these emotional responses disrupt social and learning opportunities.

Promoting healthy development can be encouraged by fostering normal social relationships, reinforcing self-image, maintaining contact with supporting agencies, continuously supporting children when hospitalized, and emphasizing "typical" child traits whenever appropriate. For example, children with CF can be expected to perform well academically and cognitively, as researchers have shown that frequent absences from school affected GPA, but not standardized test scores (Grieve, Tiuczek, Racine-Gilles, Laxova, Albers, & Farrell, 2011). Even though CF is largely an "invisible disability," failure to understand the emotional and developmental by-products of such a chronic illness can have adverse consequences. Children with the least overt signs of disability, such as those with CF, experience psychological distress that can also go undetected (Grieve et al.; Evans, 2004).

Although the cost of raising a child with CF varies from one family to another, depending on the severity and stage of the disease, covering the costs of prescriptions, medical equipment, nutritional supplements, and hospitalizations can strain family finances, even if the family has adequate insurance coverage (Guimaraes et al., 2012). The social effects of CF on the entire family can also be difficult. Parents, siblings, and the children themselves are emotionally affected. Although families of children with disabilities are as resilient to life's challenges as other families and although new technology offers unprecedented hope for a cure for CF, adjusting to the possible loss of a child or sibling with the disease can begin as early as preschool. Finally, genetic counseling is commonly recommended for those individuals wanting to know if they may be a carrier for certain diseases including CF.

Down Syndrome

Down syndrome was one of the first causes of intellectual disabilities to be categorized as a syndrome. Identified in 1866 by Langdon Down, the syndrome has variously been termed *cretinism, unfinished or ill-finished child,* and *mongolism.* Down referred to the syndrome as a retrogression to the Mongoloid race because children

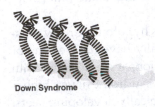

Down Syndrome

and adults resembled persons of this ethnic group in several phenotypic ways (Megarbane, 2009). This name remained common in educational and medical communities until the 1960s when it was replaced with the more dignified label of Down syndrome. The prevalence of Down syndrome is about 1 per 700 live births depending on the mother's age at conception (Megarbane et al., 2009). This incidence makes Down syndrome the second largest genetic cause of intellectual disabilities after fragile X syndrome.

© Denielle M. Miller

Characteristics Although many traits have been associated with Down syndrome, individuals with this disability may have a few or many of the known characteristics. Intellectual disabilities, ranging from mild to severe, are present in almost all individuals with Down syndrome. However, with changing educational practices over the last century, children's educational opportunities combined with innovative teaching methods have greatly improved the cognitive expectations and achievements of children with Down syndrome. The impact of having a child with Down syndrome included with children without disabilities is evidenced in the following letter from a principal to a parent:

I wanted to tell you that I have received many emails from parents requesting that their child be placed in a class with Frankie next year. They write about how positive the experience of last year with Frankie was for their child, and they feel like Frankie is a "good friend" and that their child has "built a relationship" with Frankie. One parent even said they didn't want to request a teacher, they just wanted to request Frankie! It is so heart-warming! (Leanne Sheppard, personal communication)

Very recently, biogenetic research has led to important discoveries regarding the molecular basis of mental deficiency, and it has also led to new hypotheses about correcting for these errors. Hanson and Madison (2007) found a neurological pattern in persons with Down syndrome that is similar to that of persons with fragile X syndrome. That is, brain cells have a very selective flaw that prohibits reaching out and forming connections (synapses) to communicate with other cells. While normal cells do reroute around the "dead-end" cells, the connections are fewer and less complex and are believed to be the basis for intellectual disabilities. Because neural connections are formed early in development, it is possible that finding a way to compensate for the neural breakdown will increase mental capacity.

Phenotypic characteristics include short stature and clubbed short fingers, epicanthal folds (skin at the inner corner of each eye forms a fold, making eyes appear to be slanted), sloping forehead, flat **occipital lobe,** ruddy cheeks, speckled iris, malformed ears, flat nose bridge, upward tilt to nostrils, simian line in the palm (a single deep wrinkle running across the width of the palm), the third toe longer than second, and a gap between the big toe and the next one. A high palate and small oral cavity often lead to tongue protrusion.

One of the most dominant physiological characteristics is hypotonia, or low muscle tone. Consequently, infants with Down syndrome typically have delayed motor and speech development. In addition, many medical conditions are associated with Down syndrome. Along with heart defects, children with this syndrome have a higher incidence of hearing and visual impairments than do their typically developing peers.

Medical conditions also commonly accompany this disability. Neonates often have life-threatening conditions, such as duodenal atresia, in which the small bowel is partially or fully blocked, and patent ductus arteriosis, in which the duct connecting a fetus's blood system to the maternal blood supply does not close automatically after birth. Nearly half of infants born with Down syndrome may have a major heart defect (Freeman et al., 2008). Because of these and other medical conditions, the life expectancy of children with Down syndrome was only 9 to 12 years in the early 20th century. Severe heart problems, depressed immune response, and increased risk of certain kinds of leukemia often lead to premature death. While medical problems do affect the overall life expectancy of persons with Down syndrome, restricted mobility and poor eating patterns of infants are more significant risk factors. Infants who survive their first year now have an average life expectancy of 55, but many live to their 60s and 70s (Glasson, Sullivan, Hussain, Petterson, Montgomery, & Bittles, 2002).

As the life expectancy of individuals with Down syndrome improves, researchers have identified specific areas of premature aging. These differences range from sleep apnea, dementia, premature deterioration of the thyroid function leading to hypothyroidism, and a 15- to 20-fold increased risk of developing leukemia (Solomon, 2002). Compounding the medical problems of persons with Down syndrome is a tendency toward obesity. A higher body mass index and percentage of body fat in persons with Down syndrome compared to their siblings may be the result of increased levels of leptin, a hormone produced by fat cells (Magge, O'Neill, Shults, Stallings, & Stettler, 2008).

Etiology   The discovery of chromosomes quickly led to the identification of genetic anomalies causing Down syndrome. Instead of the normal complement of 23 pairs of chromosomes in each cell (46 total), most individuals with Down syndrome have an extra 21st chromosome and 47 total chromosomes. The three 21st chromosomes, referred to as **trisomy 21,** are always associated with at least a few of the physical or behavioral characteristics described earlier. In addition, two other chromosomal defects can cause Down syndrome:

1. A **translocation** trisomy is the existence of extra chromosomal material that has become attached to another chromosome. The size of the misguided genetic material may vary from a piece of one arm to an entire chromosome. Translocation trisomies are typically genetically transmitted from a carrier parent to an affected child and occur in <5 percent of cases of Down syndrome.

2. In **mosaicism,** a portion of cells have 46 chromosomes and another percentage (usually 10% to 12%) of the cells have the extra 21st chromosome.

The genetic history of each of the three forms of Down syndrome also varies. In typical trisomies, the extra 21st chromosome is associated with **nondisjunction during meiosis** (Figure 7–7). In other words, when cell division takes place to create either an ovum or sperm, there is an incomplete detachment of the 21st pair of chromosomes; in the two newly divided cells, one is left with only 22 chromosomes while the other gains 24. In Down syndrome, the cell with 24 chromosomes (including the extra 21st) combines with a cell (ovum or sperm) with a normal complement of 23 chromosomes. Different causes of Down syndrome, described above, are associated with differences in developmental and physical characteristics. Papavassiliou and colleagues (2009) observed that, on average, children with mosaicism and translocations had fewer physical traits associated with Down syndrome and increased intellectual potential. It appears that there is a direct relationship between the number of cells containing trisomies and the manifestation of physical traits associated with Down syndrome such as cardiac defects.

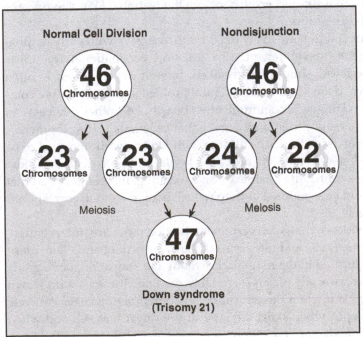

Figure 7–7 Diagram of Cell Division Leading to Down Syndrome

Why some gametes have aberrant cell division, resulting in extra chromosomes, is still unknown. However, for some time, maternal age has been a known factor related to the incidence of Down syndrome. Generally speaking, as women grow older, the chances of conceiving a child with Down syndrome become progressively more likely. Women older than 35 years of age are considered high risk and may generally be advised to undergo prenatal testing, such as amniocentesis, when pregnant. In recent decades, the rate of Down syndrome live births to women younger than 35 has risen relative to the rates of such births to women older than 35 (Egan, Smith, Timms, Bolnick, Campbell, & Benn, 2011). This may be due to higher prenatal screening rates in older women, as 90 percent of parents who receive positive results of fetal chromosomal anomaly choose to terminate the pregnancy. A second factor associated with the incidence of Down syndrome is maternal exposure to low-level radiation over a long period of time. Smoking and the use of oral contraceptives have also been linked to Down syndrome incidence (Solomon, 2002). None of these correlations, however, provides an explanation for nondisjunction, but knowing their relationship to Down syndrome is useful in genetic counseling for women considering pregnancy. As men are increasingly postponing fatherhood, understanding their connection to genetic anomalies has undergone more serious study (Wyrobek et al., 2006). Although no connection has been found between a father's age and Down syndrome, a link has been made with some paternal chromosomal defects and other genetic disorders.

Very recently, the entire 21st chromosome was mapped. In fact, it was the second chromosome to be mapped because it is the smallest and contains the fewest number of genes. This small size—which means it affects the fewest genes—explains why trisomy 21 is one of the only viable human trisomies. It is hoped that this genetic map will help explain which genes are responsible for Down syndrome (Solomon, 2002).

Other Trisomy Disorders   While Down syndrome is the most common live-birth trisomy, other trisomy conceptions are common, and some occur even more frequently than trisomy 21. However, most of these chromosomal anomalies are spontaneously aborted because their characteristics are incompatible with life. Other fetuses may survive the pregnancy but may be stillborn or will likely die within a few days or weeks of birth. Trisomies 13, 16, and 18 are the most common of these chromosomal anomalies.

Treatment   Early intervention for children with Down syndrome should focus on several dimensions. For parents, education regarding the etiology and long-term outcomes is needed. Parents may want to read literature or be put on mailing lists for magazines or newsletters, join support groups, or join the National Down Syndrome Society, a powerful advocacy group.

Intervention goals for children are likely to be comprehensive with early emphasis on motor and language development. Physical and occupational therapists and communication specialists should be involved. Speech development is often impeded by both cognitive delays and oral structural problems. **Augmentative communication** systems (sign language, communication boards, and other devices) can help bridge the social gap, reduce frustration, and enhance language development.

Feeding may also be an issue because children with Down syndrome tend to be underweight in infancy. Later, as toddlers and preschoolers, hypotonicity and slow metabolic rates sometimes contribute to an excessive weight gain. A supervised diet and regular exercise should be scheduled both to reduce body fat and to correspondingly increase energy levels.

There is increasing evidence that, with certain instruction (i.e., early intervention, use of behavior analytic methods, and integration), many preschool and elementary students are able to be educated in the regular classroom and stay at or above grade and age expectancies in some academic areas, notably reading. Students with Down syndrome are most successful when the educational program emphasizes concrete rather than abstract concepts, when skills are taught in a direct manner, and when the students receive frequent and consistent feedback. As children with Down syndrome grow older, their relative intellectual abilities diminish compared to the rate of progress made by typical children. Even so, children with Down syndrome now being served in public schools are accomplishing feats once believed impossible. The potential of such children (indeed all children) is undoubtedly limited by our own boundaries in educational technology.

Boundaries are also being expanded through medical research. For example, infants with Down syndrome have a smaller and less efficient cerebellum and hippocampus. They also have less efficient neural transmitters, which limits their ability to process information, particularly when the processing is related to short-term memory. Recent drug therapy research has shown that cognition and learning improved in rats with trisomies (Wiseman, Alford, Tybulewicz, & Fisher, 2009). As the genetic coding of the 21st chromosome advances, such promising developments in pharmacology hold the promise of favorably treating cognitive and medical conditions associated with Down syndrome.

Fragile X Syndrome

In the past, the higher incidence of intellectual disabilities in males had been explained by social and behavioral gender differences. The identification of fragile X syndrome challenged that assumption. This syndrome was first identified in 1969 when Lubs discovered the genetic abnormality in the X chromosomes of a mother and her son. Now considered the leading genetic cause of intellectual disabilities (Sherman, Pletcher, & Driscoll, 2005), fragile X syndrome occurs in approximately 1 in 3,300 births overall (Hantash et al., 2011). However, this number includes only those individuals with full fragile X. As many as 1 in 178 women may be carriers of fragile X, and 1 in 400 males are carriers. Fragile X is believed to account for 40 percent of the X-related forms of intellectual disabilities and 10 percent of all cases of

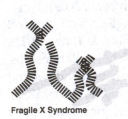

Fragile X Syndrome

intellectual disabilities. Additionally, fragile X may be even more prevalent than these statistics indicate because many carriers who have the anomalous chromosome, but do not have intellectual disabilities, go undiagnosed. Even with such a high prevalence, parents experience widespread knowledge deficits and, more significantly, encounter educators and other professionals that lack interest in family needs (Minnes & Steiner, 2009).

Characteristics Prior to its identification, children with fragile X syndrome were misdiagnosed, as they are even now, with ADHD, autism, nonspecific intellectual disabilities, pervasive developmental disorder, learning disability, and emotional impairment (Schmidt, 1997). These "misreads" suggest the variability and severity of characteristics of this syndrome. The fragile X mutation ranges from partial to full; the full mutation corresponds to more apparent and severe syndrome-related characteristics. These mutations affect both boys and girls, but they affect boys more severely because they have only one X chromosome so the traits are expressed more acutely. The effect on intelligence among females is usually less severe than among males, with only one-third having below-average cognitive abilities. Females who are affected by fragile X generally express either mild to moderate forms of intellectual disability. Only half of those females with a full mutation are recognized as having a disability, although most have some form of learning disability (Turner, Robinson, Wake, Laing, & Partington, 1997). Males, on the other hand, tend to range from borderline to profoundly intellectually disabled (Hessl et al., 2009).

Furthermore, longitudinal documentation indicates a steady deterioration in mental functioning as these children age (Cornish et al., 2008a). Regardless of IQ or gender, fragile X has a specific pattern of learning characteristics. Strengths include good memory for pictures and visual patterns. Consequently, children do well with letter recognition and when directions are presented as pictures. Weaknesses are noted in processing abstract ideas including those related to math, memory, organizing materials, problem-solving, and planning ahead (Hessl et al.)

Even though the most predominant characteristic of fragile X syndrome is intellectual disability, it affects all body systems including the hormonal, neurological, and cardiac functions. Most children with fragile X have a normal appearance at birth (Au & Hagerman, 2013). Prominent physical features are most apparent in postpubertal males. Physical characteristics in adults include short stature, a long face, large ears, prominent forehead, underdevelopment of the midface region, prominent jaw, and enlarged testicles (NICHD). The variability in facial features of females with fragile X makes it difficult to use physical features as an index in diagnosis. Many females with fragile X do experience premature ovarian failure (POF). It is recommended that woman experiencing POF before 40 have testing as part of the evaluation for infertility and prior to in vitro fertilization (Sherman et al., 2005).

As with intelligence, a progressive degeneration of adaptive behavior tends to occur in males with fragile X syndrome (Cornish et al., 2008a). After making steady gains in adaptive behavior until early adolescence, individuals experience a decline in skills. Several behavioral phenomena are associated with the syndrome, although considerable variability exists among individuals with fragile X. Many, including carriers, express psychiatric disorders such as anxiety, mood disorders, social avoidance, and unusual motor (hand flapping and hand biting), speech, and language behaviors (perseveration, echolalia, dysrhythmia, and inappropriate speech) (Bourgeois et al., 2009). Children with fragile X often have other clinical disorders such as ADHD, autism, and tremor/ataxia syndrome (Hagerman et al., 2009).

While much research has been conducted to understand fragile X and its affect on boys, less is known about girls with fragile X (Rinehart, Cornish, & Tonge, 2011). Females may also have social difficulties, including problems with peer relationships, shyness, depression and mood disorders, loneliness, and a tendency to withdraw and act uncomfortable around others (Mazzocco, Baumgardner, Freund, & Reiss, 1998). Although social skills tend to be most affected by the fragile X chromosome, other adaptive behaviors, such as toileting, personal grooming, and domestic responsibilities, appear to be especially well developed relative to intellectual impairment.

Etiology   Fragile X syndrome derives its name from the form of its mutation on the X chromosome. The term "fragile X" is derived from the weak connection of the long arm of the Xq27 gene to the X chromosome, which is held together by an unusually thin strand of DNA. A single defective gene (Fragile X Mental Retardation 1[FMR1]) has been considered responsible. This defective gene fails to produce fragile X protein (FMRP), which is necessary for brain cells to cleanly communicate with each other. A second gene (FMR-4), discovered in 2008, is also related to expression of fragile X syndrome (Khalil, Faghihi, Modarresi, Brothers, & Wahlestedt, 2008). FMR-4 is located in the same fragile region of the X chromosome, and its discovery shows there is still much to be learned about the complex genetic code of fragile X and other inherited syndromes.

Although most prevalent in males, fragile X also affects females, more so than any other X-related chromosome disorder. However, because females possess two X chromosomes, the one intact X chromosome tends to overrule the effects of the fragile X chromosome. There appears to be a selective inactivation of the normal X chromosome in girls with fragile X, which allows the other X chromosome to express itself at the fragile site (Cornish, Turk, & Hagerman, 2008b). By contrast, males have only one X chromosome and are therefore always vulnerable to the defective genetic anomaly.

Fragile X is of a familial nature, transmitted from generation to generation in a unique fashion (Hagerman et al., 2009). The defective chromosome is most commonly transmitted by the mother who may be affected or unaffected; however, it has been noted that unaffected males may transmit the fragile X chromosome to their daughters. Furthermore, genetic studies of families with the fragile X chromosome revealed that as the affected chromosome is transmitted from generation to generation, the incidence of fragile X syndrome increases in frequency and severity (Turner et al., 1997).

The site on the X chromosome responsible for its fragility is normally a region of repeated proteins of 20 to 40 repeats in length. Across generations, this region can slowly increase in length, gradually becoming less stable. When duplicates lengthen past 50 or so, each subsequent generation can suddenly expand rapidly to 200. Two hundred repeats appear to be the threshold for manifestation of symptoms of fragile X and represent a full mutation. Fragile X categorization is separated by the number of protein repeats in the following way (Crawford, 2001):

- *Common:* 6–40 repeats
- *Intermediate:* 41–60 repeats
- *Permutation:* 61–200 repeats
- *Full:* >200–230 repeats

Individuals with the full mutation are considered to be in the disability-causing population in which the symptoms of fragile X are manifested, whereas the permutation mutation range represents the carrier population. The permutation incidence ranges from between 1 in 246 to 468 for females to 1 in 1,000 to 2,000 for males.

The fragile X chromosome travels through families in an unusual manner. A typical family pedigree is one in which all children of female carriers of the syndrome have a 50 percent chance of inheriting the gene from their mothers. Males who are carriers pass the gene to their daughters but obviously not to their sons. When a male carrier passes the abnormal gene to his daughter, the likelihood of intellectual disability is low (Cornish et al., 2008b). On the other hand, in the daughters of females who inherited the abnormal fragile X gene from their carrier fathers, cognitive delays are more common.

Treatment   Fragile X syndrome is rarely detected at birth and may not be identified until school age in affected children with mild disabilities. Health professionals, child study teams, therapists, and educators should be involved in treatment of children with this syndrome. Medical treatment of the syndrome itself is limited; although some doctors have prescribed medication for the various symptoms of fragile X syndrome, such as seizures, mood instability, ADHD, aggression, obsessive-compulsive disorder, and sleep disturbances. After finding success reducing seizures and improving behavior and cognition in animal models of fragile X, drug treatment trials have begun for individuals with fragile X syndrome (Hagerman et al., 2009). In the meantime, the primary treatment for fragile X syndrome is education, with early childhood special education providing the greatest promise for long-term adaptive and intellectual benefits. Because of considerable variability within the population of individuals with fragile X syndrome, educational programs should be designed to fit children's behavioral needs, not the disability itself. It is likely that components of a program would include academic goals, functional skills training, behavioral interventions, physical therapy, occupational therapy, and speech therapy (Hagerman et al., 2009).

Genetic research into a biological cure has had three main foci (FRAXA Research Foundation, 2002). One is gene therapy in which normal genes are injected into brain cells, a technique that has been successful with mice and has great promise for humans. A second is gene repair, which may be possible because the entire normal DNA sequence is present but ill-attached. Although the cell's normal machinery has been "turned off" in fragile X, there may be ways to restore function without introducing new genetic material. A third focus, psychopharmacological research to discover effective and safe medication to treat the symptoms in their infancy, may also prove to be a viable remedy for the defective gene.

In recent groundbreaking research, scientists have been able to correct genetic and physiological errors in mice that were the result of fragile X (Dolen et al., 2007; Lauderborn et al., 2007). Dolen and colleagues described fragile X as a syndrome of excesses: synaptic activity, protein synthesis, memory extinction, body growth, and excitability. It is believed that one type of brain receptor, mGluR5, is responsible for these excesses and that reducing this receptor would reduce the symptoms of fragile X and autism. The target of genetic engineering—and possibly drug therapy, which has the promise of the same effect—is dendritic spines (nubs on the ends of the neurons), which are long, numerous, and spindly, and therefore permit weaker neurological connections in persons with fragile X syndrome. Physiologically, changes in mGluR5 caused spines to become more normal and improved brain development and memory, restored normal growth, and reduced seizures in mice with fragile X (Dolen et al.).

Lauderborn and her colleagues (2007) were also successful in correcting the symptoms of fragile X in mice, in this case by adding a brain-derived protein to the hippocampus region of the brain where memories are formed. The result was a complete restoration of memory-forming capacity. Like the genetic engineering of Dolen and colleagues (2007), the manipulation of this protein by Lauderborn and colleagues had the effect of strengthening the synapses that typically prevent long-term memory development in persons with fragile X. In fact, a consensus is beginning to form among researchers that developmental brain disorders such as fragile X and autism should be classified as "synapsopathies," or disorders of synaptic development and plasticity (Dolen et al.).

Genetic counseling for families with the mutant X chromosome is very important. Because of the unique pattern of transmission and the tendency of the syndrome to be underdiagnosed and silently carried by females, it is important to educate both nuclear and extended families when the syndrome is positively diagnosed. Efforts to develop a newborn detection or screening procedure using blood samples are promising (Saul et al., 2008). When fragile X is identified in infancy, babies may benefit from early intervention, and their families may benefit from genetic counseling.

Duchenne MD

Muscular Dystrophy

Several hereditary, muscle-wasting diseases fall under the category of muscular dystrophy. All forms of muscular dystrophy are characterized by a progressive loss of muscle tissue, which is concurrent with increases in fat and connective tissue and subsequent muscle weakness. The most common form of progressive muscular disease is Duchenne muscular dystrophy (DMD). Approximately 1.3 to 1.8 in every 10,000 males is born with muscular dystrophy (Romitti et al., 2009). A milder but similar disorder, Becker muscular dystrophy, affects approximately 5 out of every 100,000 births, mostly in male children (Joyce, 2011). Although DMD is most severe during the school-age years, its onset is generally early childhood, and it worsens quickly.

Characteristics   The course of DMD follows a fairly predictable pattern. In early childhood (ages 3 to 6), children begin to have weakness during gross motor activities such as running and jumping, and they fall often. The disability is positively identified when children rise from the floor using Gower's maneuver or are unable to get up without using their arms for support. Children tend to waddle when walking and gradually develop scoliosis (spine curvature of the lower back). This misalignment of the body is a primary cause of respiratory disease because the bellows of the lungs are compromised by the posture. As the muscles weaken, **contractures** form in the lower extremities. Chronic pain, especially in the back and legs, is common in children with DMD (Jenson, Abresch, Carter, & McDonald, 2005).

Between the ages of 8 and 12, children with DMD physically deteriorate rapidly and usually are unable to walk by the age of 12. Many children develop some degree of intellectual disability, ranging from mild to moderate, due to the course of the disease. By middle to late adolescence, muscle tissue is almost completely replaced by fat or fibrous tissue. Considerable difficulty breathing and heart disease usually start by age 20, and death usually occurs by age 25, due to respiratory and heart failure (Manzur, Kinali, & Muntoni, 2008). Some individuals live into their 20s and are able to go to college or seek occupations. Becker muscular dystrophy is very similar to Duchenne though it tends to progress much more slowly. Symptoms usually appear in boys between the ages of 5 and 15, and over time walking becomes more difficult; most are unable to walk by age 25 to 30, though in some cases, symptoms don't occur until the third or fourth decade (Joyce, 2011). Individuals with Becker MD may live to be 40 or 50 years of age, but as with Duchenne, their life expectancy is shortened by respiratory and heart disease.

Etiology   Duchenne muscular dystrophy and Becker muscular dystrophy both have X-linked recessive inheritance patterns. Males who receive the affected genes (p21 region of X chromosome) are severely affected, whereas females who carry the gene are either normal or, in about 10 percent of cases, only mildly affected (Bushby et al., 2009). Although females who carry the genetic mutation pass it on to 50 percent of their offspring, the gene responsible for DMD is randomly inactivated in half of the males who receive it. Approximately one-third of all cases of DMD are the result of a new mutation of the Xp21 gene, not the result of family history (Emery, 1998). For these reasons, genetic counseling for Duchenne-type dystrophy is very difficult.

Treatment Although there are no treatments that can stop or reverse the progression of MD, a variety of interventions are available to assist families and keep children independent for as long as possible: Physical therapy, occupational therapy, drug therapy, dietary supplements that include Vitamin D and calcium, diet management to avoid obesity or failure to thrive, surgery, and assisted ventilation are some that are used (Manzur et al., 2008). To ease complications as the disease progresses, surgery for scoliosis can be performed to improve children's comfort, posture, and appearance and provide stability to the back. A more aggressive tendon-transfer operation is sometimes performed to prolong walking for 1 to 3 years, even though lengthening the muscles or tendons eventually makes them weaker. Physical therapy and orthotic braces are necessary to maintain the restored range of motion (Manzur et al., 2008). While seemingly a modest goal, this accomplishment can be very meaningful to children and their families. The following treatment priorities for families are related to maintaining the children's function and comfort and providing emotional support for the families.

1. Provision of a well-balanced diet with adequate fiber to avoid constipation.

2. Discouragement of long periods of bed rest, which can accelerate weakening of the muscles.

3. Encouragement of everyday activities within the child's limits and avoiding of strenuous exercise. Children may be encouraged to walk as long as they can, to slow muscle weakening. Also, when they are no longer ambulatory, they may be encouraged to spend as much time as possible standing with the aid of a standing board. Later, when using a wheelchair, long periods of sitting in the same position should be avoided.

4. Performance of passive range of motion exercises by parents or caretakers to prevent contractures (fixation of joints in a certain position due to lack of movement); the exercises should be demonstrated by a physical therapist.

5. Vigilant anticipation of respiratory problems. Regular pulmonary evaluations should be made even before problems occur to prevent lung damage or serious respiratory disease. Immediate treatment of respiratory infection, including antibiotics, is recommended. Later, when respiratory complications occur, children benefit from postural drainage therapy and, eventually, assisted ventilation.

6. Use of lightweight splints or orthoses can prolong walking.

7. Implementation of an intervention program that addresses all areas of development, including language, social, and cognitive domains.

Experimental research investigating complex treatments for children with muscular dystrophy is occurring in several areas. Gene therapy involves implanting normal muscle cells into the muscles of boys with DMD. So far, the evidence is not sufficient to determine whether such attempts will assist in the recovery of muscle function. Another, perhaps more promising, research line includes "gene insertion," which programs a person's cells to "read" DNA in such a way as to produce the protein deficiency of DMD. "Gene repair" uses a molecular bandage to alter damaged genes and make them functional—a technique that has had some laboratory success for spinal muscular dystrophy (DiMatteo, Callahan, & Kmiec, 2008). Research on stem cells has also been successful in treating mice with DMD. In this research, the muscle-producing stem cells of a DMD carrier were extracted and corrected outside the body using a technique called *exon skipping*. That is, the correction coaxes a gene that contains the error to skip the error and produce an effective (though shortened) dystrophin protein (Aartsma-Rus, Janson, van Ommen, & van Deutekom, 2007). Still other research is investigating the effectiveness of a protein substitute for dystrophin using a protein already produced in the body, *utrophin*. Treatments of specific symptoms of muscular dystrophy also show promise, such as the recent success in the use of Viagra to treat heart problems in mice with DMD (Petrof, 2008). Steroid treatments, specifically *prednisone*, have enjoyed some success in prolonging ambulation, delaying surgery, and even increasing muscle strength in some cases. These and other newly developing procedures bear the promise of finally solving the problem of this devastating disease. In fact, recent recommendations indicate that programs should develop interventions that address lifelong needs of persons with DMD, given their ever increasing life expectancies (Romitti et al., 2009).

For early educators, the goals of intervention for children with muscular dystrophy are very different from those for children with cognitive disabilities, although some boys with Duchenne type dystrophy have some degree of intellectual disability. Intervention plans for these children should be global. Management of muscular function and alignment requires the ongoing participation of a physical therapist. Early interventionists should seek family input in determining educational priorities. Families with children with muscular dystrophy are more likely to experience financial problems, interruption of work and employment, and difficulties coordinating treatment for their child (Ouyang, Grosse, Fox, & Bolen, 2012). Family support and interagency coordination can help families make short- and long-term decisions regarding the education and care of their children.

Phenylketonuria

Phenylketonuria (PKU) is an inherited autosomal, recessive, inborn error of metabolism. Although many other metabolic disorders exist, PKU illustrates well the issues surrounding such errors (see Table 7–1). This error results in the inability of individuals to use the essential amino acid phenylalanine. Buildup of phenylalanine (phe) disrupts **myelinization** of neurons in the brain, destroying both gray and white matter and resulting in intellectual disabilities. Newborns are routinely screened for PKU, and if diagnosed they are treated early so that intelligence is not affected (Bennett, Rinaldo, Wilcken, Pass, Watson, & Wanders, 2012).

Many infants born with PKU are blond with blue eyes and have a fair complexion. Symptoms of untreated cases are vomiting, failure to thrive, irritability, behavior problems, a distinct musty odor of urine and sweat, seizures, and obvious developmental delays by 1 year old (Chetty, Schaffer, & Norton, 2011). Although estimates vary, PKU occurs in about 1 in every 10,000 to 20,000 live births in the United States (Resta, 2012).

Although previous family history is a marker for PKU diagnosis, this defect cannot be detected by prenatal amniocentesis and therefore cannot be diagnosed prior to the delivery of an infant. All newborns between 48 and 72 hours of age are initially screened for phe levels through a simple blood test obtained by sticking the infant's

| Table 7–1 | Metabolic Disturbances | | |

Disability	Characteristics	Cause	Treatment
Hypoglycemia	Decreased glucose for cells. Symptoms of glucose depletion: sweating, poor color, decreased attention, jitteriness, sleepiness/lethargy, seizures.	Metabolic error, other disease processes, genetic defect, stress, nutritional deficiency, infection	High-protein diet, education of all caregivers including educators on symptoms and treatment of hypoglycemia. If untreated, can cause cerebral palsy, intellectual disabilities, failure to thrive.
Galactocemia	Inability to metabolize galactose found in milk produced by mammals; ingested galactose builds up and becomes toxic.	Genetic disorder	Lifelong elimination of galactose completely from diet, use of casein hydrolysate and soybean formulas as milk substitute, education of child and other adults on safe foods. If not treated early, child will need comprehensive early intervention (cognitive, nutritional, visual, etc.). Toxic levels cause intellectual disabilities, failure to thrive, liver disease, cataracts, and if untreated, death.
Hypothyroidism	Inadequate production of thyroid hormone; causes deficiencies in skeletal formations and height, lethargy, abnormal facial features (broad, flat nose, wide-set eyes, coarse features), intellectual disabilities, and motor, language, and visual delays.	Unknown; possibly genetic	Thyroid replacement therapy; with treatment, children score within normal limits. Early intervention for children not treated early. Physical/occupational therapy, nutritionist, visual specialist, and speech/language therapy needed.
Thalassemia	Decreased production of hemoglobin due to insufficient production of amino acid compounds.	Genetic; can occur in conjunction with sickle cell disease	Diet control to reduce the amount of iron; health maintenance in nutrition and feeding; in severe cases, routine blood transfusions. Can cause mild to severe anemia, failure to thrive, poor appetite; can lead to mild or moderate developmental delay, cardiac conditions.

heel. All specimens are sent to a state-sponsored laboratory in order to increase the standardization of results. Results are available within 2 to 3 weeks of birth.

PKU was the first inherited disease that could be successfully treated with diet. The goal of diet therapy is to restrict the oral intake of phe, thereby preventing excess buildup of phe levels in the blood that cause intellectual disabilities; at the same time, a diet adequate for normal growth and development must be provided. The best possible outcomes are derived from initiation of diet therapy within the first 12 to 24 hours after birth to reduce exposure to phenylalanine toxicity (Lin et al., 2011). The first two years are particularly important, as noncompliance during this period can make it very difficult to reestablish blood phe levels (MacDonald, Gokmen-Ozel, & Daly, 2009). Any solid foods that are high in protein (cow's milk, meats, dairy products, etc.) are excluded from the diets of children with PKU. Because protein is essential for normal development, children with PKU receive formulas that are high in protein but contain little or no phenylalanine. It is also important that such children avoid food and drinks that contain aspartame, an artificial sweetener that contains phenylalanine (Anwar & Segal, 2010). Most states within the United States offer assistance to families affected with PKU by providing the dietary supplements essential for normal growth and development. The most commonly used products for infants and children are Lofenalac, a low-phe formula that is used with infants, and Phenyl-Free, a food source that is used with older children.

It was once believed that if treatment was not begun immediately after birth, there would be significant and irreversible brain damage. However, it is now known that there are significant, beneficial effects even when the diet is implemented as late as toddlerhood (Koch et al., 1999). Remaining on a restricted plan through childhood, adolescence, and into adulthood is now the recommended practice. The differences between those who adhered to the PKU diet and those who did not was demonstrated by Koch and colleagues (1999). Late-diagnosed patients had an IQ range of between 44 and 100 at the time of diagnosis and a range of 73 to 108 after going on the PKU diet. The IQ range for all tested persons with PKU (both early and late diagnosis) was 69 to 108, with an average of 82. As adults, late-diagnosed patients who had been most disciplined in adhering to the diet had an average IQ of 82, those who were moderately disciplined averaged an IQ of 77, and those who poorly adhered to the diet had an average IQ of 61.

Recent research holds much promise in the treatment areas of protein cofactor therapy, enzyme substitution, and gene therapy. Oral ingestion of the protein cofactor BH4 has successfully improved the ability of subjects with PKU who were off diet therapy to break down phe levels in their blood (Levi et al., 2007). While the mutated enzyme PAH also had the effect of reducing phe levels in animals, its application for humans is still unknown (Gamez et al., 2007). Finally, gene replacement research, which uses a normal enzyme to repair the mutated enzyme in subjects with PKU, has resulted in only a temporary reduction of phe levels in mice therapy (Ding, Georgiev, & Thony, 2006).

Families with children affected by PKU require counseling and education as well as positive, ongoing reinforcement of dietary goals to be successful in controlling the disease. Success of children and families depends on understanding the diet and the reasons for restrictions, making sure the diet is age-appropriate and adhered to throughout adolescence and into adulthood, and reducing exposure to infections. As children get older, it may become increasingly difficult to adequately monitor their diets. Therefore, the entire family must have a commitment to success.

Sickle Cell Disease

Sickle cell disease (SCD) causes its victims to experience chronic and often painful episodes for which there is currently no cure and only limited treatment, even though SCD is the most common genetic disorder in the United States (Taylor, Stott, Humphreys, Treadwell, & Miaskowski, 2010). Sickle cell disease affects nearly

Sickle Cell

90,000 Americans and disproportionately afflicts persons with African ancestry (Marlowe & Chicella, 2002). Of the total of Americans with the disease, over 80,000 are African American and over 8,000 are Hispanic American (Brousseau, Panepinto, Nimmer, & Hoffman, 2010).

Characteristics   The name of the disorder is derived from its principal characteristic. Abnormal, sickle-shaped red blood cells proliferate and eventually clog the blood vessels (see Figure 7–8), causing less oxygen to be delivered to the body's tissues and eventually causing chronic tissue death (necrosis) in all major organs of the body. The most prominent feature of sickle cell disease is pain (Marlowe & Chicella, 2002). Though usually not constant, the episodic periods of pain are acute and can last from hours to days. These typically last 3 to 14 days, often resulting in expensive and prolonged hospitalizations (Taylor et al., 2010). Sickle cell disease is most associated with these frequent and severely painful episodes referred to as **sickle cell crises**. Pain is most likely to occur in the abdomen, back, extremities, and chest. Several other complications can accompany sickle cell disease: infections, meningitis, spleen dysfunction, enuresis, delayed physical growth, severe anemia, "acute chest syndrome," gallbladder disease, kidney complications, and bone inflammation and decay (Wethers, 2000a). Blood vessel blockages in the brain can result in seizure activity and stroke, even during childhood.

Because sickle cell disease research is limited, few conclusions can be made about its cognitive and behavioral associations. Physiological aspects of sickle cell disease that might eventually compromise an individual's cognitive functioning are (Taylor et al., 2010).

Figure 7–8   The Sickle Cell Process

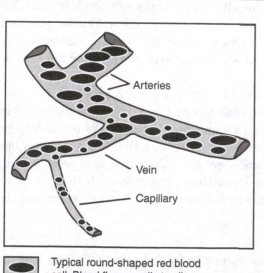

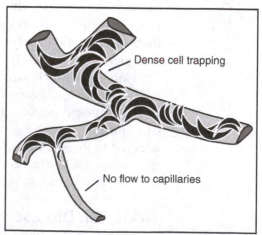

Arteries

Vein

Capillary

Dense cell trapping

No flow to capillaries

Typical round-shaped red blood cell. Blood flows easily to all levels of the circulatory system.

Abnormal sickle-shaped red blood cell. Blood clogs easily and results in pain.

1. Numerous tiny strokes in the central nervous system, specifically the brain
2. Anemia
3. Malnutrition
4. Compromised blood supply to the brain

In spite of these potentially harmful conditions, early research indicated that most children with sickle cell disease had no loss of intelligence or academic performance when compared to peers without sickle cell disease. Recent research shows that individuals who have silent cerebral infarcts (SCI) do have some delays and damage to the brain (DeBaun, 2012). Of those with sickle cell disease, 27 percent have SCI before they are 6 and 37 percent by the time they turn 14 (DeBaun). In one study, 50 percent of preschoolers with sickle cell disease and an average age of 3.5 tested below the age-level cutoff on psychosocial factors (twice the national failure rate) using the *Brigance Preschool Screen II* (Aygun et al., 2010). Research is complicated by variables that, in themselves, could account for academic and social problems, namely, poverty or social class, absenteeism caused by frequent hospitalizations, family structure, and absence of support networks. All of these characteristics are associated with cognitive and social difficulties; they also happen to be disproportionately characteristic of minority populations.

Etiology Sickle cell disease is genetically transferred to the child. The disease is caused by a mutation of genes on the 11th chromosome. In the United States, approximately 10 percent of African Americans are carriers of sickle cell disease, and .3 percent have sickle cell anemia (Ross, 2011). Three types of sickle cell disease are common; a few rare types also occur (Rees, Williams, & Gladwin, 2010). The most severe type, sickle cell anemia, is homozygous and is caused by two abnormal genes on the 11th chromosome. Two other heterozygous (only one 11th chromosome contains the sickle cell anomaly) genotypes (HbSC and HBS-thalassemia) also result in some form of sickle cell disease. HbS beta thalassemia results from a multigene interaction in which different gene combinations produce a gradient in severity of the disease across affected individuals. Therefore, the course of the disease is unpredictable within and across children, with symptoms ranging from very mild to severe (Rees et al.).

Treatment Impressive advances in the treatment of sickle cell have raised the life expectancy from 14 in 1973 to the current ages of 46 and 48 for females and males, respectively (Taylor et al., 2010). At one time, the highest mortality rates from sickle cell disease were in the first five years of life, because of susceptibility to infections, and near adulthood, because of multiple system failure. However, newborn screening and aggressive medical care have dramatically reduced pediatric deaths while increasing the overall life expectancy and quality of life of patients with sickle cell disease (Yanni, Grosse, Yang, & Olney, 2008). Although much progress has been made in the past two decades (Wethers, 2000b), research on sickle cell disease has lagged in spite of the fact that it is twice as prevalent as CF and nine times more common than PKU. Some believe that this disparity in research may be due to the ethnicity of its victims (see Table 7–2). Recently, the goal to improve the life expectancy of people with sickle cell disease has become one of the priorities in the strategic plan set forth by the National Center on Birth Defects and Developmental Disabilities (2011).

| Table 7–2 | Comparison of Screening Paradigms for Tay Sachs Disease and Sickle Cell Disease |

	Tay Sachs Disease	**Sickle Cell Disease**
Ethnicity	Ashkenazi Jews	African Americans
Screening	Voluntary	Compulsory in several states
Effectiveness	65 percent reduction in births from 1970 to 1980	No effect; abandoned in 1980
Education	In all cases, emphasizing lack of blame to carriers	No accompanying education
Screening organization	Community-based plan to conduct screening	National screening funded by federal government; state controlled

Some relatively simple interventions are available for those with sickle cell disease. For example, to prevent infections, it is recommended that children with sickle cell have good medical care, regular checkups, and immunizations (Booth, Inusa, & Obaro, 2010). Meticulous attention to hygiene, cooking food thoroughly, and administration of zinc supplements are further recommendations. Children with sickle cell disease also benefit from taking penicillin as a preventative measure prior to getting infections; this inexpensive treatment is advised for infants by the time they are 3 months of age (Booth et al.). Families are warned that children with sickle cell disease should not get too hot, too cold, or too tired (Kopp-Hoolihan, Van Loan, Mentzer, & Heyman, 1999). Children are often encouraged to take vitamin supplements, although doing so has limited success. Because diet is a concern in children with sickle cell disease, who tend to expend more calories than they take in and possess less body fat than other children, support and planning from a nutritionist should be a part of the intervention plan for children with sickle cell disease.

As with other types of chronic pain, coping with the severe discomfort can be difficult and often involves positive thinking and self-statements. However, for preschoolers, the degree to which such an intervention might work is limited by their cognitive development. Marlowe and Chicella (2002) reported that the pain in those with sickle cell disease is grossly undermedicated, and treatments often fail to adequately control the pain. Because medical providers fear an addiction to opiates, they are reluctant to prescribe sufficient pain medication. In fact, the addiction rate is 1% to 3% for persons with sickle cell disease, whereas the potential for attenuating the excruciating pain of a sickle cell crisis is high. Distrust of medical providers and hoarding of drugs to thwart future episodes are common reactions to improper pain management.

Treatments aimed at prevention of pain are being explored (Marlowe & Chicella, 2002). For example, fetal hemoglobin that is resistant to sickling can prevent the sickle cell sequelae leading to painful episodes. The effectiveness of this treatment depends on successful regulation of dosage and the degree to which a child adheres to the treatment regimen.

All caregivers should be trained to recognize the signs and symptoms of complications related to sickle cell disease and seek immediate medical attention for the following: pain or enlargement of the spleen; temperature elevation; pale skin, lips, or nails; respiratory distress; severe or persistent headaches; and pain or movement problems (Wethers, 2000b). The earliest symptoms are painful swelling of the hands and feet. Caregivers should also consider preventative measures while avoiding overprotectiveness; avoidance of dehydration, overexertion, and exposure to cold are important for children with sickle cell disease.

Advances in research hold promise for persons with sickle cell disease (Wethers, 2000a). Gene therapy is being explored as a means of deactivating the sickle cell gene while increasing the expression of the gene for hemoglobin F. While bone marrow transplantation has the potential to cure the disease, complications include expense, lack of wide availability of the procedure, and difficulty in finding a matching donor. Finally, the use of stem cells derived from cord blood is being investigated as a curative treatment.

Parents of children with sickle cell disease and other chronic illnesses may cope with medical and disciplinary problems differently than parents of healthy children. When there are significant lifestyle disruptions, parents tend to cope by focusing on their child's medical, rather than emotional, needs. Parents also tend to be more aware of effective and less punitive disciplinary practices than parents of healthy children. They tend to use praise and mild punishment, perhaps because of their reluctance to inflict any more pain than necessary on children who already suffer from random and unavoidable pain caused by the disease itself.

Turner Syndrome

Henry Turner first described Turner syndrome in 1938 after identifying similar physical features found in a number of his female patients (Schaefer & Riley, 2004). This disorder results when one of the two X chromosomes is absent (50%–55%), partially absent (12%–20%), mosaic, in which only a portion of the cells has a missing X chromosome (30 percent), or, in rare instances, translocated. In most cases, there is a single X chromosome, and the characteristics of Turner syndrome are more severe than in partial or mosaic cases. The incidence of Turner syndrome occurs in 1 out of 2,000 to 3,500 live births (Morgan, 2007), but 10 percent of all first-trimester miscarriages are caused by Turner syndrome (Morgan).

Turner Syndrome

Characteristics   Girls and women with Turner syndrome are short in stature and fail to develop ovaries. One of the diagnostic characteristics of Turner syndrome is immature development of reproductive organs; most women are infertile. Additionally, webbing of fingers, toes, and/or neck is not uncommon. One-third of individuals with Turner syndrome have heart abnormalities (Morgan, 2007). Strabismus, hearing loss and recurring ear infections, orthodontic and kidney malformations, hip dysplasia, scoliosis, osteoporosis, celiac disease, swelling of the thyroid, obesity, and Type II diabetes are also complications associated with Turner syndrome (Morgan, 2007; Bondy, 2007).

Girls with Turner syndrome have normal intelligence with IQs averaging 90 (Morgan, 2007), though many have normal or superior verbal skills (Bondy, 2007). A distinctive pattern of cognitive functioning has been observed in females with

Turner syndrome. Visual memory and visual-constructional reading and arithmetic abilities tend to be significantly lower than those of typical children. In school, though, children with Turner syndrome tend to have lower academic achievement than their peers (although not significantly lower than siblings), and as adults, they generally attain significantly lower occupational status.

Individuals with Turner syndrome tend to have delayed social maturity, possibly stemming from peer interactions that are disrupted by the odd appearance and unusually short stature of these girls. Difficulty with nonverbal memory and attention may also contribute to social and emotional challenges (Bray, Dunkin, Hong, & Reiss, 2011). Furthermore, girls with Turner syndrome tend to lack subtle social awareness skills, such as being able to "read" facial affect (Mazzocco et al., 1998). Girls with Turner syndrome do seem to have a higher incidence of significant behavior problems, hyperactivity, depression, and loneliness than their peers (Mazzocco et al., 1998).

Etiology   Turner syndrome is not considered to be familial. Therefore, after one child is born with Turner syndrome, subsequent pregnancies do not carry an increased risk of the disorder. Morgan (2007) found that in the first week of fetal development, one X chromosome is inactivated, but in Turner syndrome not all genes from the second chromosome are inactivated. This noninactivated X gene causes the characteristics noted in girls with Turner syndrome. The parent of origin for the Turner syndrome chromosome can be either the father (about a third of cases) or the mother (about two-thirds of cases) (Devernay et al., 2012). Interestingly, most fetuses (98%–99%) with a missing sex chromosome spontaneously abort, as compared to a spontaneous abortion rate of 15 percent for all conceptions (Morgan, 2007). Hence, Turner syndrome has been estimated to represent as much as 1 percent of all conceptions. This disability can often be identified prenatally by ultrasound and confirmed through either amniocentesis or chorionic villus sampling.

The absence or reduction of sex hormones, normally stimulated by both X chromosomes, may adversely affect brain development during fetal growth. The impact of hormone deficiency is thought to be quite specific, resulting in the unique cognitive profile described earlier. That is, Turner syndrome is thought to result from the absence of one or more "Turner" genes rather than the absence of the X chromosome per se (Bondy, 2010). In cases where two normally functioning chromosomes are present, these genes "turn on" the growth production of hormones necessary for healthy fetal development.

Treatment   Early intervention and family support may contravene some of the expected social and cognitive problems associated with Turner syndrome. Preschool intervention might focus on readiness for mathematics and reading skills and opportunities to model and reinforce appropriate social skills. However, because of the type of intellectual deficits described previously, it is very likely that cognitive problems will not surface until children begin academic tasks in school.

When girls with Turner syndrome reach puberty, hormone replacement is usually recommended. The replacement therapy may continue into adulthood and has been shown to increase height by an average of 8 cm (Bondy, Van, Bakalov, & Ho, 2006). In rare cases, spontaneous menstruation begins, and these girls are more likely to be fertile than others.

Syndromes with Unknown Causes

Although the syndromes just described have known etiologies, the origins of a host of other disabling conditions continue to baffle researchers. In fact, a large majority of children have no known cause for their mental anomalies. Environmental deprivations, such as of nutrition, affection, and stimulation, may be the primary cause of most cases of mild to moderate intellectual disabilities. On the other hand, it is likely that those syndromes that are distinctly articulated from others (e.g., autism) have some type of genetic, neurologic, or multifactorial origin. For example, genetic research has recently led to the identification of very common disabilities such as fragile X syndrome as well as more rare anomalies such as Prader-Willi syndrome (see Table 7–3).

Table 7–3 Incidence of Inborn Variations in Development

Disability	Characteristics	Cause	Treatment
Cornelia de Lange syndrome	Facial anomalies (long eyelashes, thin lips, confluent eyebrows, upturned nose, small face), microcephaly, intellectual disabilities (ID), hearing loss, severe language delays (superior language in rare cases), stereotypy sometimes evolving into self-mutilation	Unknown	Family support; speech/language focus, behavioral intervention for stereotypy (self-mutilation usually does not occur until after early childhood), comprehensive early intervention
Prader-Willi syndrome	*Stage I:* Neonatal-hypotonia, weak/absent cry, large head, feeding problems, failure to thrive	Missing portion of long arm of 15th chromosome (15q11–13), paternal in origin (father is carrier)	Family respite care/support groups, early management of insatiable appetite (nutritionist, environmental controls, behavioral self-management), social skills training, exercise programs in early childhood (swim, dance, soccer, etc.)
	Stage II: Childhood—overeating the dominant trait, pear-shaped body, short stature, almond-shaped eyes		
	Stage III: Adolescent—significant behavior problems, mild/moderate ID, good self-help, weak social skills		
Rett syndrome	Normal development (infancy)	Unknown; possibly metabolic	Medication for seizures, physical/occupational therapy, nutritional monitoring for failure to thrive, music therapy to increase movement and social relatedness, family support and collaboration
	Stage I: Onset of developmental deterioration (6–18 months), very intrusive stereotypy begins (i.e., hand wringing)		

Table 7–3 (*continued*)			
Disability	**Characteristics**	**Cause**	**Treatment**
	Stage II: Rapid deterioration for a few weeks to months		
	Stage III: Relative stability with some developmental growth for up to 10 years		
	Stage IV: Regression, sometimes to primitive language and motor state		
Williams syndrome	Failure to thrive; cardiac problems; elfinlike appearance (small chin, large ears, blue iris, wide mouth, wide-set eyes, broad forehead); mild–moderate ID; remarkable verbal proficiency; deficit in nonverbal ability; hypersocial, friendly, talkative, affectionate; later behavior problems; impulsive; hyperactive; self-destructive	Deletion of genes on chromosome 7	Nutritionist, focus on strengthening talents in language and social affability, physical/occupational therapy, later behavioral self-control instruction to manage activity level, parent counseling to avoid guilt when behavior problems arise—reassure parents that this behavior is one of the predictable sequelae of the syndrome

Autism Spectrum Disorder

Prevalence   Although autism spectrum disorders were once considered to be rare (five cases in 10,000 children, depending on the definition used in identification), the identification of children under this umbrella has grown at alarming rates in the past two decades to a rate of 1 of 88 children in the United States (Centers for Disease Control and Prevention, 2012). It has been estimated that the rate of autism diagnosis increased sixfold from 1994 to 2003, not just in the United States but also around the world, and the rate appears to be continuing to increase. Autism providers have been overwhelmed by the number of children and families in need of services (Williams, 2007). Part of this increase has been attributed to changes in definition, which include a broad autism spectrum, and improvement in detection (Hertz-Picciotto et al., 2006). However, an increase of 600 percent cannot all be explained by such changes, and the mystery accompanying this new prevalence awaits a solution. This increase stimulated Congress to pass the Combating Autism Act of 2006 (PL 109-416) authorizing $945 million over five years for autism research, screening, treatment, and education. This act increased federal spending on autism by 50 percent and intensified attention to biomedical research including research on environmental factors. Currently, there is no biomarker that predicts who will develop autism. Despite the large numbers of individuals affected by autism and the increasing rate of incidence, scientists at this time have been unable to determine the cause of autism (Williams). Without knowledge of causative factors, the search for a cure for autism has been severely hampered, and the search for effective treatment has branched out in many directions, with few evidence-based approaches but with many that range from conjecture to malpractice. The search for possible genetic, immunologic, neurologic, or environmental causes for autism is feverish. Unfortunately, unsubstantiated claims regarding the cause and treatment of autism have also multiplied exponentially.

Parents seeking effective treatment for their children with autism must negotiate a minefield of scientific claims and counterclaims. Professionals are often at a loss in terms of how to guide clients through the maze of information and misinformation about treating autism that is disseminated through the Internet, advocacy groups, and publications. In some cases, the recommended treatments place children at greater risk of harm than if they were not treated and seldom result in any improvement in abilities or functioning. Parents and practitioners need as much information as possible to clearly identify evidence-based approaches that are most likely to help a child with autism (Williams, 2007).

Characteristics   There are two categories included in autism spectrum disorder (ASD): autistic disorder (also called "classic" autism) and pervasive developmental disorder not otherwise specified. These classifications are sometimes put under the broader term "pervasive developmental disorders" by some health-care providers. All individuals with ASD fail to develop normal social interactions; have abnormal or no development of language, particularly for communication; and possess a restricted range of interests and behaviors. Symptoms must begin before the age of 3 years, although they are usually present much earlier. About one-third of children with autism develop normally for the first 12 to 18 months and then cease talking, become socially unresponsive, and use objects in repetitive, inappropriate ways. While another common characteristic is unusual sensory sensitivities to taste, touch, and sound, ASD most severely impairs a person's abilities in the areas of language and social relations. About two-thirds of children with autism are identified in infancy when caregivers note such behaviors as disinterest in toys, indifference to caregivers or physical contact, auditory and tactile defensiveness, aberrant sleep patterns, excessive crying, irritability and stiffness, and avoidance of eye contact (Goldsmith, Van Hulle, Arenson, Schreiber, & Gernsbacher, 2006). Because ASD has no biological markers, such symptomatic behaviors are the only way to diagnose autism at present (Barbaro & Dissanayake, 2009). Like many other disabilities, boys are almost five times more likely to be affected with autism than girls, with nearly 1 of every 50 boys being identified (CDC, 2012).

Etiology   Historically, parents (mothers in particular) were blamed for their child's autistic behaviors. It was believed that women who failed to show love and nurturance psychologically impaired their children to such a degree as to cause autism. Thankfully, today, few women are accused of this misguided and harmful assumption.

Currently many studies are being conducted to determine the cause of autism. There seems to be no single cause; rather, a variety of factors—genetic, infectious, neurologic, metabolic, immunologic, and environmental—contribute to it (Grafodatskaya, Chung, Szatmari, & Weksberg, 2010). Sufficient evidence exists for scientists to agree that autism is a neurobiological disorder. Studies have documented irregularities in several regions of the brain and in brain function to support this conclusion. Head circumference, brain size, and brain volume tend to increase rapidly in early childhood in children with autism (Raznahan et al., 2010). Studies of older children with ASD suggest that the differences noted are not "fixed" and may change across the life span (Raznahan et al.). Approximately 22 percent of individuals with autism have seizures or epileptic activity that tends to be associated with significant intellectual disabilities (Bolton, Carcani-Rathwell, Hutton, Goode, Howlin, & Rutter 2011). The results of functional MRIs suggest that individuals with autism may suffer the effects of underconnectivity, in which communication with different parts of the brain is impaired (Just, Cherkassky, Keller, Kana, & Minshew, 2007). Early research found abnormalities in levels of the neurotransmitter serotonin in children with autism (Chugani et al., 1997, 1999; Cook & Leventhal, 1996; Cook et al., 1997), while more recent research indicated that white matter in the brain may also be altered in those with ASD (Barnea-Goraly et al., 2004). Though the intellectual abilities of individuals with ADS vary broadly, the combination of intellectual difficulties and other behavioral and language disabilities often results in profound developmental needs. **Savant** behavior, in which an individual shows extreme aptitude in one area (e.g., music or mathematics) along with autism, is very rare. It is now widely accepted that aberrant brain development resulting in differences in processing information occurs in children with autism (Hertz-Picciotto et al., 2006).

There is also evidence that genetic factors contribute to many cases of autism; although no single gene has been identified and the genetic cause is thought to be polygenic with more than one gene involved (Hertz-Picciotto et al., 2006). Twin and family studies support a genetic component in the development of autism, and the probability that the sibling of an autistic child will have autism is about 2% to 8%, which is a much higher probability than is found in the general population (Muhle, Trentacoste, & Rapin, 2004). In studies of identical twins in which autism was present in one twin, there was up to a 90 percent chance that both children would be affected (Ratajczak, 2011). Some researchers found that relatives of children with autism often exhibit characteristics that are milder and non-pathological but qualitatively consistent with those of children with autism (i.e., lack of emotional responsiveness, oversensitivity, special interest patterns, and oddities in social communication), although other researchers have failed to replicate such findings (Piven et al., 1997).

A new model suggests that autism might also be the result of a spontaneous germ-line mutation. The parent might acquire a genetic mutation for autism and transmit it to his or her offspring at conception. This might explain how parents who have no family history of autism produce a child who has ASD. Autism could be passed on by females or males who do not exhibit symptoms but actually have a high risk (50 percent) of passing autism on to their children even without a family history of the disorder (Zhao et al., 2007). It is, however, unlikely that genes act alone in producing autism. Otherwise, **monozygotic** (identical embryos derived from the splitting of one fertilized egg) twins would always both be equally affected by autism and, in fact, they are not. Even though they are genetically identical, the environment must have affected the twin with autism differently from the twin who was not affected or affected less severely.

Another line of research relates to gene–environment interaction (Szpir, 2006). The growing burden of chemicals in the environment, particularly in industrialized countries, cannot be ignored as a possible connection to neurodevelopmental disorders. That is, children with a genetic tendency toward autism might show no symptoms in the absence of harmful toxins in the environment, such as lead, mercury, manganese, pesticides, polychlorinated biphenyls (PCBs), and polybrominated diphenyl ethers (PBDEs). Yet the presence of such chemicals might weaken the defenses of these same children, amplify neurological damage, and cascade into a clinical syndrome. Although many possible environmental links are being investigated, at this point, the research remains inconclusive, despite the popularity of some suspected agents. For example, overwhelming evidence from multiple, well-designed studies has failed to support any causal connection between vaccines and autism due to either exposure to the measles, mumps, rubella combination or to ethylmercury in the preservative thimerosal; it is likely more dangerous not to vaccinate children (Halsey & Hyman, 2001; Stehr-Green et al., 2003). Few well-controlled studies of diets eliminating gluten (in wheat and other grain products) or casein (in milk products) have been done, leaving this line of research inconclusive (Christison & Ivany, 2006).

Over time, many theories forwarded to explain the origin of ASD have been discredited (as in maternal neglect) or remain invalidated. It is probable that "autism" is the expression of multiple etiologies, some of which may cause autism and others of which may eventually be determined to cause something else. Similarly, some have posited that there may be no such thing as autism; rather many different brain disorders may be expressed similarly enough to fall under the ASD umbrella. Studying these co-occurrences may help researchers pinpoint the genes possibly involved in autism (see Table 7–4).

Table 7–4   Frequency of Secondary Disabilities Associated with Autism

Condition	Percentage
Deafness	20%
IQ above 100	5%
IQ between 70 and 100	20%–30%
Intellectual disabilities	25%–52%
Seizure disorder	33%
Affect isolation	88%
Perceptual inconsistencies (visual/hearing/touch)	80%
Stereotypy/twiddling	82%
Self-injury	65%
Nonverbality	50%
Echolalia	75%
Tuberous sclerosis	6%
Fragile X syndrome	2.1%

Treatment   One of the first steps to treatment is the exclusion of other potential causes of autistic behavior, as other disorders (e.g., otitis media) may have some shared symptoms. Once it has been established that an individual has autism, a life-long condition, substantial resources are required in the course of treatment. Since young children's brains are still forming, receiving early intervention gives children more opportunities for learning and allows them the best chance of developing to their full potential (Rogers & Vismara, 2008). Treatment is likely to be complex, and no single intervention strategy will work with all children. In fact, even for a single child, a strategy that seems to be effective at one point may lose its potency over time or overnight.

Generally, intervention should be directed at maximizing the development of skills that are already present (e.g., converting speech fluency into reciprocal social interactions) while minimizing limiting behavior such as self-stimulation and self-injury. Behavioral intervention involving systematic training has been most effective in teaching new sets of skills while reducing intrusive behavior. However, even those methods are rigorous, slow to show improvement, and difficult to maintain over long periods. Harley, Sikora, and McCoy (2008) recommended that behavior management intervention be focused on increasing social engagement and sustained attention while decreasing aggressive behavior. Families should be supported in working with multidisciplinary personnel, including a communications specialist, early childhood educator, social worker, counselor, respite care worker, and behavioral specialist, if possible. Although one should not presume that a family will need emotional help, some may benefit from ongoing counseling and from ongoing support. In addition, parents should be cautioned when they are investigating costly but questionable dietary, medical, or other unconventional methods that promise a "cure" for their children, as there are no cures at this time.

Because one of the most common deficits of autism is in social adaptation, many educators are aware that the optimal educational environment for children with ASD is an integrated one with peers trained to act as social models. Parents are a necessary part of planning because they can educate both teachers and peers on their child's social and communication repertoire and strategies. Specific target skills for interactions between model peers and children with autism are turn taking, sharing, initiating and maintaining play, asking for help, using conversation skills, and being appropriately affectionate. To facilitate these interactions, communication boards, other augmentative communication systems (i.e., sign language), and various technology tools can be used to mediate conversations. When taught to use visual cues early, children with autism might be able to generalize this skill to picture-reading systems, self-management systems using visual reminders, and language boards used in social interactions.

A great deal of research is being conducted on the effectiveness of early intervention programs for young children with ASD. A recent systematic review was completed and concluded that early and intensive behavioral and developmental intervention delivered over one to two years showed positive outcomes in cognitive performance, language skills, and adaptive behavior (Warren et. al., 2011). According to Dawson and Osterling (1997), six elements are common to effective programs that educate children with autism:

- A curriculum that is focused on increasing attention, imitation, and communication skills
- An environment that is highly structured and supportive
- A classroom schedule that is predictable and teaches skills through natural daily routines, allowing for easier generalization of skills
- A functional and preventative approach to behavior problems, which focuses on teaching relevant skills
- An environment that encourages and plans for family involvement
- The development of a specific plan for successful transitions from preschool to elementary school

In a study designed to test the validity of these elements, Schwartz and Sandall (1998) followed three children with autism from preschool through early elementary school. Each child displayed very different symptoms and functional levels, although all were initially noncompliant or combative. The preschool program used a blend of applied behavioral analysis and family-focused developmental approach with instructional methods that were effective and systematic. Embedding these procedures into a natural integrated preschool classroom, the classes focused on social, communication, and play skills. When followed several years later in elementary school, all three children were thriving in inclusive classrooms with minimal to no special education support. It was concluded that the key to their sustained social and cognitive progress was in controlling noncompliant or violent behavior in the preschool years. Research on effective treatment programs supports the conclusion that early diagnosis and intervention are critical in helping a child manage and minimize the effects of autism. The American Academy of Pediatrics (Johnson & Myers, 2007; Myers & Johnson, 2007) recommended universal screening at the 18- and 24-month well-child pediatric visits. Pediatricians across the nation have been provided with tools for screening all children under the age of 2 for ASD symptoms so that referral for diagnosis and treatment can be made as early as possible. Although the tools used for these screenings are not perfect, using them allows doctors to begin the process and discussion necessary to support parents in understanding early development and obtaining the resources their children may need (Barton, Dumont-Mathieu, & Fein, 2012). Early identification and early behavioral intervention can make substantial differences in the long-term prospects for children with autism (Williams, 2007).

Tourette Syndrome

Like autism, Tourette syndrome is a bewildering and sometimes devastating disability. Until 1972, the syndrome, also referred to as *Gilles de la Tourette syndrome* after the French researcher who identified the disorder in 1885, was thought to be quite rare (50 known recorded cases). At that time, the Tourette Syndrome Association was established by a distraught father of a child with the disability. Now, the syndrome, a condition of the nervous system, is identified in as many as 3 in every 1,000 children ages 6 to 17 (CDC, 2012), and it is estimated to affect up to 1 percent of children internationally (Robertson, 2008). The most obvious characteristic of individuals with this disorder is the expression of tics, which are either purposeless motor movements or irregular vocalizations that have a sudden and unpredictable onset. Although children without the syndrome can exhibit tics, people with Tourette syndrome must have both motor and vocal tics that persist for at least one year (American Psychiatric Association, 2000). The symptoms usually begin to appear between 5 and 10 years of age, and boys are three times more likely than girls to be affected (American Psychiatric Association). The period of most severe tic behavior is about age 10 with nearly half of children becoming tic free by 18 years of age (Leckman et al., 1998). The type and frequency of tics change over time and can appear and disappear, but the condition is considered chronic. Throughout a person's lifetime, tic patterns may vary, and in the early stages of the disorder remissions may occur during which children are symptom free. While tics tend to decrease or disappear entirely for many after adolescence, some continue to have tics into adulthood.

Characteristics   As children age, the intensity and form of Tourette syndrome symptoms change. Because the condition is so misunderstood by educators, children are often undiagnosed for years or may be misdiagnosed as having another disability commonly associated with Tourette syndrome, such as ADD or a learning disability (Bloch & Leckman, 2009). The most common early symptoms are motor tics near the head and neck area such as eye blinking. Motor tics can then become progressively more involved. Eventually, children may have whole body involvement including jumping, kicking, spitting, smelling, squatting, and touching objects or people. Vocal tics may also appear and include humming, clearing the throat, barking, whistling, grunting, or snorting. On rare occasions, people with Tourette syndrome may exhibit echolalia, repeating the words of others, or coprolalia, involuntarily shouting out obscenities. Tics can either be simple, affecting just a few parts of the body, or more complex, involving several parts of the body. Further, tics can sometimes have a pattern such as blinking, shrugging shoulders, and then jumping up. The frequency of tics can vary from a few times when children are tired or tense to 100 times per minute in those most severely affected (Murray, 1997).

Until recently, researchers had not acknowledged an "aura" experienced by many individuals with Tourette syndrome that sends them a message to perform a tic or ritual behavior (Murray, 1997; Kwak, Vuong, & Jankovic, 2003). The inability of the individuals to ignore or defy these messages causes them another form of anxiety. In instances when persons are able to defer performing a tic until a later, more acceptable venue, the self-control may be exerted at great expense (Prestia, 2003). However, while it was once believed that the suppression of a tic would result in a more severe tic at a later point, a phenomenon referred to as a tic rebound, more recent studies support that this is a rare occurrence (Woods, Conelea, & Himle, 2010).

As part of a study by the Centers for Disease Control and Prevention (2009), parents of children with Tourette syndrome were interviewed, and 79 percent reported that their children had at least one additional mental health, behavioral, or developmental condition. Of those children, 64 percent had attention deficit disorder with hyperactivity, 43 percent had oppositional defiant or conduct disorder, 40 percent had anxiety problems, 36 percent had depression, and 28 percent had a developmental delay or difficulty learning. Though some of these additional disorders can be treated successfully while also addressing the symptoms of Tourette syndrome, medical treatment for attentional difficulties may produce the onset of, or exacerbate, the symptoms of Tourette syndrome.

Obsessive-compulsive behavior is commonly associated with Tourette syndrome. The impulse to complete tasks to perfection or to complete certain rituals, such as "evening up," in which actions or materials must be symmetrical, is a unique form of obsessive behavior found in persons with Tourette syndrome. Understandably, individuals may experience excessive fear of expressing their tics or compulsive behaviors in public. In addition to displaying the movement characteristics of Tourette syndrome, afflicted children are particularly vulnerable to psychological distress, including frustration, depression, and anger (Bloch & Leckman, 2009). In fact, because tics are often very unusual, children are frequently ridiculed by their peers and misunderstood by teachers, which results in serious anxiety related to social encounters.

Etiology   Currently, several studies are being done to identify the risk factors and causes of Tourette syndrome, but little is known at this time. Early findings suggest that there is a significant genetic factor; however, prenatal, perinatal, autoimmune, and environmental factors may also contribute (Swain et al., 2007). Research does support that Tourette syndrome is inherited as a dominant gene. Though many genes have been associated with the disorder, no single gene has been identified as the primary cause. It is possible that a combination of factors contribute to the etiology of Tourette syndrome. Currently, neuroimaging is being explored to determine if there are brain abnormalities in people with Tourette syndrome. Initial studies do report differences, such as abnormalities in basal ganglia structures (Kalanithi et al., 2005), but more research is needed.

Treatment   Tourette syndrome can cause heartache for parents as well as children with the disorder. To know that one's child will most likely be ridiculed or mistreated is a lifelong frustration for parents. It is common for youth with Tourette syndrome to be bullied by their peers, which can exacerbate stress and cause tics to increase, leading to internal and external damage (Zinner et al., 2012). It is critical for educators to be aware of this and put preventative practices into place to help children with Tourette syndrome build friendships and gain acceptance from their peers. Children and parents can be comforted by knowing that tics are out of the control of an individual with Tourette syndrome. Informing teachers and parents of other children may also reduce the stigma of tics.

Generally, stress, anxiety, tiredness, and excitement exacerbate the symptoms of Tourette syndrome. Helping families to manage their children's activities to moderate situations that might cause overexcitement, tiredness, and anxiety should be an intervention goal. Tics themselves cause excess "wear and tear" on the joints, organs, and muscles and may cause injury (Prestia, 2003). Relaxing tends to reduce the symptoms. Teaching families and children techniques for motor and emotional relaxation will help children prevent or minimize symptoms. Routines, calm, and removal of obstacles that could cause harm in the event of involuntary jerking or imbalance are ways of attenuating the symptoms of Tourette syndrome.

In the most severe cases, medications may be prescribed, either for the tics or associated diagnoses. While medications do not eliminate tics completely, they can alleviate tics for some children, some of the time. Unfortunately, medications also introduce the risk of side effects, such as lethargy, weight gain, stiff muscles, poor school performance, social withdrawal and depression, as well as a variety of neurological symptoms (Murray, 1997). Sometimes the side effects can be worse than the tics. Consequently, medications should be used only when symptoms are so serious they compromise a child's development (Gilbert, 2006).

Recently, drug alternatives that may be more effective and reduce side effects have been explored. Palminteri and colleagues (2011) found that positive behavior reinforcement in the form of small monetary rewards improved motor development. Interestingly, this was only true of unmedicated individuals with Tourette syndrome, as those taking neuroleptics did not show improvements. Other forms of behavior therapy have also resulted in positive outcomes (Woods, Conelea, & Himle, 2010), although these treatments may be too complex for preschool-age children.

Children with Tourette syndrome can have a successful and positive school experience if educators, school personnel, and families work together. When planning intervention, consideration should be given to providing support for families, educating teachers and peers about Tourette syndrome, supporting children in building friendships with peers, and helping them build the advocacy skills they will need in the future.

Physical Anomalies

Congenital Heart Defects

Congenital heart defects are a problem for a significant number of infants and young children. It is estimated that nearly 1 percent of infants, about 40,000 a year, are born with congenital heart disease, making it the most common type of birth defect in the United States (Hoffman & Kaplan, 2002; Reller et al., 2008). Furthermore, many genetic disorders and other physical abnormalities are accompanied by heart defects, many requiring intervention during the neonatal period. Consequently, 48 percent of deaths caused by congenital heart defect occurred during the first year of life (Gilboa et al., 2010).

Congenital defects are generally categorized into either cyanotic or noncyanotic abnormalities. Categorization depends on the heart's ability to direct blood flow to and from the lungs and then to the general circulation. Situations in which blood bypasses the lungs result in decreased oxygen available to cells and produce a blue-tinged color to the skin known as **cyanosis.** Diagnosis followed by appropriate treatment is the key to decreasing the general, adverse effects of congenital heart defects.

Understanding the differences between fetal circulatory patterns and those required of an infant after birth is useful for understanding how an affected fetus can survive a significant defect through the period of gestation. Fetal circulation consists of parallel circuits. When fetal blood bypasses the lungs, either the right or left ventricle pumps blood directly to the general circulation (see Figure 7–9). The pressure in either ventricle during this period is similar. This parallel structure allows for fetal survival in spite of a variety of significant cardiac defects. Even if one of the ventricles is completely obstructed, the other ventricle can maintain sufficient blood flow with little effort.

The birth process results in a remarkable change in the blood flow pattern of the infant. With the infant's first breath, blood flows into the lungs and the blood flow

Figure 7–9   Fetal Circulatory Patterns

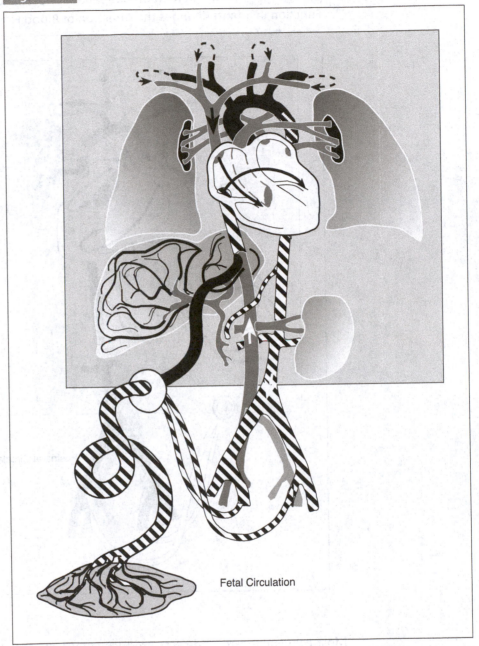

Fetal Circulation

from the placenta ceases (see Figure 7–10). At the same time, an increase in the independent breathing of newborns results in oxygenation of the blood from their own lungs, which, in turn, causes closure of the **ductus venosus** and the narrowing of the **ductus arteriosus.** Finally, changes in **intracardiac** pressures result in the functional closure of the **foramen ovale.** These changes dramatically increase the work of the heart, especially the left ventricle. Because of this demand, many congenital defects produce symptoms that lead to a medical diagnosis of the cardiac defect.

Figure 7–10 Establishment of Independent Heart and Lung Function in Infants Changes the Direction of Blood Flow

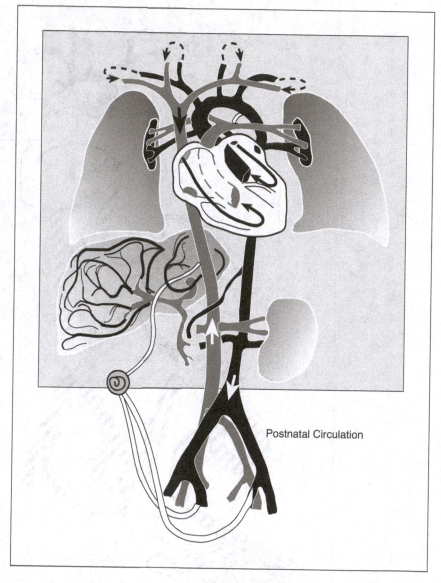

Postnatal Circulation

Most congenital cardiac defects produce symptoms that are diagnosed within the first week of life. Symptoms may include respiratory distress, a heart rate of more than 200 beats per minute, a heart murmur, difficulty with feeding, and failure to gain weight. Many of these may persist into childhood (depending on the defect) with the addition of exercise intolerance, poor physical growth, delayed development, recurrent infections, squatting, clubbing of the fingers and toes, and increased blood pressure. Many children with cardiac defects also have chronic behavior problems, possibly related to repeated hospitalizations.

Certain cardiac defects are known to be associated with specific genetic malformations and maternal conditions. For example, Down syndrome is associated with endocardial cushion defects. Males have an increased risk for coarctation of the aorta, aortic stenosis, and transposition of the great vessels, whereas females have an increased incidence of atrial septal defects. When a mother is diabetic, the risk is high for significant multiple cardiac defects in the fetus. Congenital rubella is associated with narrowing of the pulmonary arteries and patent ductus arteriosus. Lesions associated with prematurity or low birth weight are also found with an increased incidence of both patent ductus arteriosus and ventricular septal defects.

Endocardial cushion defects occur when there is abnormal development of the septa between the atria and the ventricles, which includes a malformed, deficient, or abnormally attached mitral valve. This abnormality results in mixing of oxygenated and nonoxygenated blood between the right and left atria and the right and left ventricles because of incompetent valves. This defect may appear as an isolated cardiac defect but more commonly is associated with other malformations and very frequently with Down syndrome.

Cleft Lip and Cleft Palate

Cleft lip and cleft palate (roof of mouth) are commonly occurring defects. It is estimated that more than 2,500 babies are born each year with a cleft palate, while nearly 4,500 are born with a cleft lip (with or without a cleft palate) (Parker et al., 2010). About 70 percent of cleft lips and/or palates occur as an isolated defect (lip or palate). Approximately 30 percent of children with cleft lip/palate have additional congenital malformations, such as skeletal malformations, intellectual disabilities, cardiovascular problems, gastrointestinal malformations, or facial anomalies (Milerad, Larson, Hagberg, & Ideberg, 1997). A cleft is a division or split that occurs between two tissue planes. Many recognized congenital syndromes have this associated defect (e.g., trisomy 13, 15, or 21). The clefts that appear in either the lip or palate are separate defects, but there may be a relationship between the two because the disruption in normal development occurs during a similar time period in gestational development, between the 5th and 13th weeks of gestation.

Formation of the lip and palate occurs in stages from about the 5th to 12th weeks of gestation. It is during this time that the normal fusion process fails and a cleft occurs. The specific cause for a lip or palate defect is not exactly known but is considered to be multifactorial with known **gene potentiation** and probable environmental interaction. It was recently discovered that a specific gene variant is a major contributor and is associated with a threefold increase in the risk of recurrence in affected families (Vieira, 2008). Other recent findings have shown that women who smoke and those with diabetes diagnosed before pregnancy are at higher risk for having a baby with an orofacial cleft (CDC, 2012). Research has also found some link to alcohol use during pregnancy, poor maternal nutrition, and certain medications (Mossey, Little, Munger, Dixon, & Shaw, 2009).

There are a variety of other suspected contributors to orofacial clefts. Teratogens are thought to be connected to the incidence of clefts. For example, benzodiazepines, drugs prescribed to reduce anxiety, insomnia, or epilepsy in women, are sometimes taken in the first trimester before women realize they are pregnant (Dolovich et al., 1998). Ethnic origins appear to have some relationship to the occurrence of isolated defects. Cleft lip or palate is most common among Native Americans and Asians, whereas African Americans have the lowest incidence. Cleft lip occurs most often among males and cleft palate among females (Redett, 2009).

Clefting of the lip involves a split that affects the lip and gum and may extend upward into the nose. Both cleft lips and palates are classified as unilateral (affecting one side) or bilateral (affecting both sides) and as either complete or incomplete. The occurrence of a cleft lip without a cleft palate decreases the potential difficulties that face affected infants. In cases involving bilateral lip clefts, the defect may be extensive enough to join tissue together at a point behind the gum. In these cases, a section of the lip and gum appears to hang freely from the septum of the nose. The majority of infants with a bilateral cleft lip also have a cleft palate. The impact of such extensive abnormalities on appearance presents significant problems for families. In many cases, the disfigurement is initially so overwhelming that parents experience difficulties in looking past the defect to the infant, and initiation of parent–child bonding is interrupted.

Facial disfigurement (with resulting parental rejection) and feeding difficulties are the two most significant problems that face an infant affected with an isolated cleft lip. Society places a great deal of importance on external appearance, and the face is central to this view. It is vital that health-care providers, extended family members, and other individuals involved in providing service give support during the initial bonding experience of new parents and an infant with a cleft lip. This will allow for every opportunity to get past negative feelings and promote bonding.

Infants with a cleft lip may have difficulty establishing a normal feeding pattern. Interruption in the integrity of the lip produces the challenge of providing optimum nutrition to foster the necessary growth required before surgical repair can be attempted. Feeding devices are available that can use either breast milk or prepared formulas to promote a feeding pattern that is as close to normal as possible. Many infants with an isolated cleft lip can successfully breastfeed. These infants feed using structures within the mouth to express milk from a nipple. Tongue movements assist with this process and, although helpful, the lip is not essential to establish a successful suck. Referral to appropriate experts within the community can provide support for a successful feeding experience for an infant with an isolated defect.

A cleft palate involves a split in the hard or soft palate or, in some cases, both. Infants who are born with a cleft palate experience a wider variety of problems than do those infants born with an isolated cleft lip. These problems include facial deformities, speech impairment, hearing loss, tendency to infections, feeding problems, and learning disabilities that may or may not be related to either speech or hearing problems.

The potential for failure to thrive because of a decreased ability to eat is a significant problem for infants born with a cleft palate. Feeding problems are generally a result of the physical defect but may also be related to other disabilities. Normal sucking requires the tongue and/or the palate to stabilize the nipple and then to suck milk. Cleft palates prevent nipple stabilization and create an abnormal suck. Devices such as extended nipples placed on squeeze bottles, flexible tubing placed next to a breast and connected to a bottle of pumped milk, and standard nipples with enlarged holes are available to assist with feeding. Each defect may require adaptation of feeding devices and techniques. Evaluation by an occupational therapist should be made prior to initial discharge from the hospital after birth and a method of feeding should be devised. This plan includes parental instruction and referral to appropriate resources within the community for ongoing follow-up.

Another significant problem associated with cleft palate is acute and chronic middle ear infection. Acute infection may be a single episode in a susceptible infant that can be cleared with antibiotic treatment. Chronic infection results from a defective opening between the bacteria-laden oral cavity and the Eustachian tubes, which lead to the middle ear space. Surgical repair of the cleft does not significantly decrease the incidence of infection. Therefore, conductive hearing loss from repeated infections is a common occurrence. Although the procedure is controversial, many infants are placed on preventive antibiotic therapy and may even have drain tubes surgically placed through the eardrum in an effort to reduce infection and subsequent hearing loss (Redett, 2009).

Speech delay also frequently accompanies a cleft palate. Sucking is necessary to develop muscles used to make speech physically possible. Alterations in the normal sucking process delay the muscle development. Moreover, the presence of a single cavity (nose and mouth) alters normal sound production. Both the medical condition and the possibility of social isolation decrease the opportunities these infants have for verbal interaction with the adult world, a vital link to the development of speech.

Children with a cleft palate may also experience a disruption in tooth eruption. Dentition is delayed, and in many cases, normal tooth formation may be absent. Early evaluation by a dentist with appropriate referral for orthodontics is part of a team approach that is necessary to meet the total needs of an infant and family.

Hearing loss and speech delay lead to speech-related learning disabilities. These may be influenced by the social isolation that frequently results from the facial disfigurement that is part of this defect. Parents need to work closely with their child to build a positive sense of self and to prepare the child for social situations. In addition, educators sometimes make erroneous assumptions about intelligence in children with facial defects. Parents may need to educate the teachers about cleft lip and palate and work closely with them to insure that children do not become the victims of bullying.

Families of infants who have a cleft palate require a multidisciplinary approach to meet their needs. A treatment team should include the primary care physician, plastic surgeon, public health nurse, speech pathologist, audiologist, dentist, social worker, occupational therapist, and educator. Team collaboration provides for long-term planning to ensure that both the actual and potential needs of infants and families can be met.

Children whose defects have been successfully repaired may continue to experience alterations in social interactions and learning. Persistent problems with articulation and with hypernasality of the voice may lead to ongoing anxiety during group interactions and to low self-esteem. How to avoid stereotyping and identifying personal biases about physical attractiveness are important topics for discussion within the team as it plans services for each infant and family affected by this defect.

IN CONCLUSION

Scientific discoveries such as gene therapy, gene cloning, and genetic selection in fertility are likely to alter the "natural" genetic course of the human species. Many disabilities could go the way of Tay Sachs, becoming eliminated from the gene pool by parental selection. Others, such as sickle cell anemia, could be treated by replacing defective genes with normal genes to prevent the disease. Whether these imminent changes will eventually be healthy for our species or harmful is a question seldom asked. When we get to the point of asking, "Do we want 'this variation' or 'that variation'?" will we be active participants or spectators in a dialogue regarding the ever-expanding knowledge or technology of genetic manipulation?

Much controversy surrounds the practice of using prenatal diagnosis to detect Down syndrome on the grounds that the overriding purpose is to determine whether or not an abortion is needed. The arguments for prenatal screening and selective abortions of affected fetuses include a variety of points, ranging from the benefits to the individual woman and her family to the benefits to society brought by eliminating defective genes in the gene pool. Other arguments focus on reducing the financial burden to society and some even involve the belief that selective abortion is part of preventive medicine. A second issue surrounds the practice in our society of deeming genetic difference as a negative. Many of the arguments previously mentioned, for example, are parts of the mythology surrounding persons with Down syndrome. The thoughts of Pearl S. Buck (1973) regarding her daughter illustrate the belief that lives can be richer, not necessarily worsened, by the membership of persons with disabilities:

> In this world, where cruelty prevails in so many aspects of our lives, I would not add the weight of choice to kill rather than to let live. A retarded child, a handicapped person, brings his own gift to life, even to the life of normal human beings. That gift is comprehended in the lessons of patience, understanding, and mercy, lessons which we all need to relive and to practice with one another, whatever we are.

A study conducted by Meryash (1992) may shed the most light on this issue. When women were asked what factors would influence their decision to abort a child with fragile X syndrome, the most salient answer was a fear that the parents' social lives might be disrupted. It is worth noting that women who were more likely to select abortion were (1) more highly educated, (2) had a better knowledge of fragile X, and (3) had other children with disabilities. Furthermore, the women identified the advice of their physician as an important factor in making a decision to abort. It is concerning that professionals who do not know or work with children with disabilities may be unfairly negative. Genetic researchers might be tempted to move from curing or preventing disorders to enhancing traits. Now, more than ever, this fear is warranted.

STUDY GUIDE QUESTIONS

1. How is individual variability related to treatment and prevention?
2. What is genetics?
3. Describe the basic mechanisms of inheritance. Define the following terms in the course of your answer: (a) *chromosomes*, (b) *genes*, (c) *traits*, (d) *genetic mapping*, (e) *chromosomal region*, (f) *deletion*, (g) *mutation*, (h) *protein product*, (i) *new genetics*, and (j) *human genome*.

4. How do genetic codes and environmental factors interact to cause genetic diseases? How does that interplay effect treatment choices?

5. Describe cellular activity. Define the following terms in the course of your answer: (a) *DNA*, (b) *nucleic acid compound*, (c) *alleles*, (d) *homozygote*, (e) *heterozygotes*, (f) *genotypes*, (g) *phenotypes*, (h) *mitosis*, (i) *meiosis*, (j) *gametes*, and (k) *errors in cell division*.

6. How many chromosomes are there within a cell structure? How many of these are autosomes? What is the 23rd pair?

7. Describe single gene disorders.

8. Discuss the relationship between the following: dominant and recessive traits; male and female sex-linked traits.

9. Define *chromosome disorder*.

10. Define *multifactorial disorder*, and *congenital disorder*.

11. What are the major types of genetic testing, and which genetic diseases can be most readily diagnosed?

12. What is the purpose of gene therapy? What are the social and ethical implications of gene therapy and advanced genetic testing?

13. What roles do the exocrine glands and the pancreas play in the development of the symptoms of cystic fibrosis?

14. What is meant by "secondary physical complications" in cystic fibrosis?

15. What are the primary medical and educational issues facing persons with Down syndrome?

16. Describe the most common characteristics of Down syndrome and the possible degree of variation from child to child.

17. Differentiate between *translocation* and *mosaicism*.

18. Describe the chief characteristics of fragile X syndrome.

19. Briefly describe the etiology and treatment needs of children with fragile X syndrome.

20. Describe the primary characteristics, etiology, and treatment of Duchenne muscular dystrophy.

21. Phenylketonuria (PKU) is an example of a metabolic gene disorder. Using PKU as the model, explain what causes a metabolic disorder, what the consequences are, and how the disorder might be treated now or in the future.

22. What are the traditional and advanced treatment possibilities for persons with PKU?

23. Sickle cell disease is one of the most common genetic disorders. List at least five features of this disorder that distinguish it from Duchenne muscular dystrophy. Now, identify five characteristics that are similar to those of DMD.

24. If you were a person with Turner syndrome, explain five problems you might encounter, how these problems came about, and what solutions you would seek to help resolve these problems.

25. If a parent said to you, "My child has autism," what assumptions would you make about the child, and why would you probably be wrong?

26. What causes autism?

27. What is it about autism that makes this disability especially challenging for parents? For educators?

28. What general recommendations can be made for the treatment of children with autism?

29. How are Tourette syndrome and autism alike? Different?

30. How does fetal heart circulation differ from heart function after birth? What is it about this difference that protects the unborn child?

31. What are the symptoms of congenital cardiac defects?

32. At what point in development is a cleft lip and/or palate formed? What can cause this to happen?

33. Congenital clefts present a wide variety of health problems. What are these problems, and why would we be misguided if we focused only on the physical needs of these children and their families?

8 Sensory Impairments and Infections

© Ruth Jenkinson/DK Images

This chapter is devoted to the effects of bacterial and viral infections on developing fetuses, neonates, and infants. While the symptoms resulting from some invasive organisms are negligible, other infections can cause multiple severe disabilities and even death. Although there are many causes of vision and hearing losses, these and other sensory impairments are often the result of a significant prenatal, neonatal, or early childhood infection.

Hearing Impairments

Hearing is the act of receiving and processing sound vibrations. The auditory mechanisms within the ear transform and transmit these vibrations as a message to the brain allowing humans to discriminate differential sound waves within their environment. A high number of children have degraded or impoverished hearing, which can require them to spend more time and effort to process incoming auditory information, reduce their ability to remember, and impede their ability to communicate. According to the National Institutes of Health (2012), 2 to 3 out of every 1,000 children in the United States are born deaf or hard-of-hearing, and many more lose their hearing during their first three years of life.

Hearing Process

The auditory mechanism is functionally separated into three components: external, middle, and inner ear (see Figure 8–1). The **external ear,** consisting of the auricle, auditory canal, and tympanic membrane, is responsible for collecting sound waves. Physical energy is channeled down the auditory canal where it vibrates the tympanic membrane (eardrum).

The **middle ear** cavity lies beyond the tympanic membrane. Sound vibrations are mechanically transmitted from the tympanic membrane to stimulate, in sequence, three tiny bones: the malleus (hammer), incus (anvil), and stapes (stirrup). The latter is attached to a small opening, referred to as the *oval window,* which leads to the inner ear. The **Eustachian tube** intersects the middle ear to form a continuous passage to the throat. The purpose of the Eustachian tube is to equalize internal and external air pressure on the tympanic membrane. Excessive buildup of pressure within the middle ear can cause the sensitive tympanic membrane to rupture.

Sound waves traveling to the **inner ear** from the vibration of the eardrum and bones of the middle ear are transmitted through the oval window to the **cochlea** (see Figure 8–2). Hair cells, tiny nerve endings within the cochlea, are stimulated by movement of cochlear fluid. The resulting energy (now electrical) is transferred to the temporal area of the brain by way of the eighth cranial nerve, or **auditory nerve.** Contained within the inner ear are the **vestibule** and the three **semicircular canals;**

Figure 8–1   Anatomy of the Ear

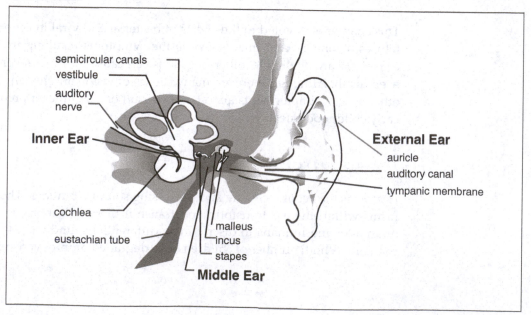

Figure 8–2 Pathway of Sound through Outer, Middle, and Inner Ear

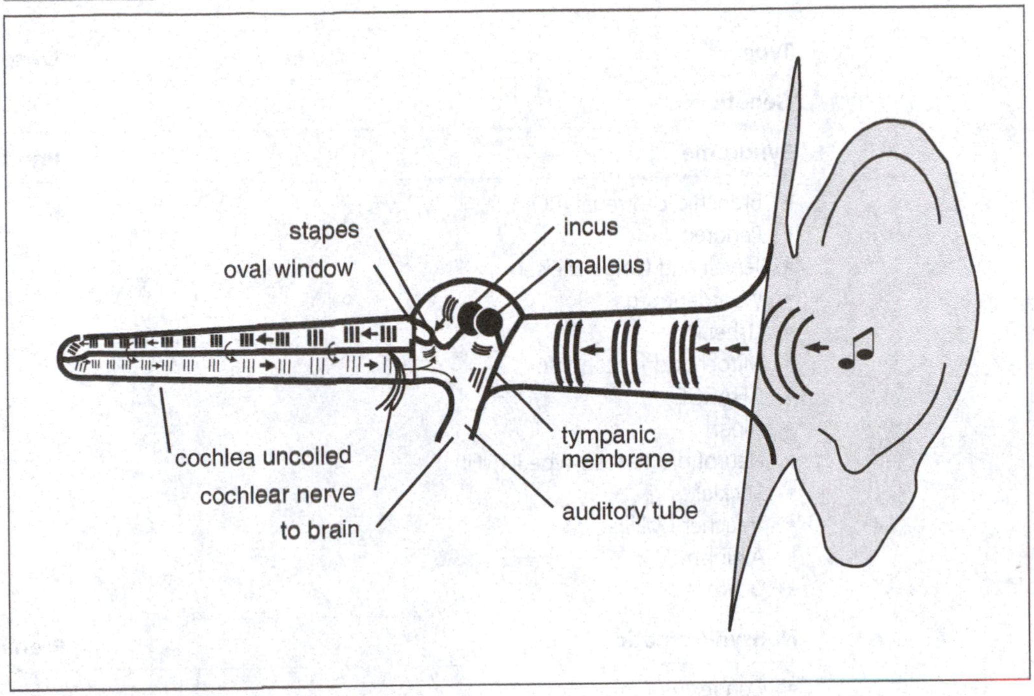

stapes
oval window
incus
malleus

cochlea uncoiled
cochlear nerve
to brain
tympanic membrane
auditory tube

these structures also contain neural hair cells. Movement of these cells, caused by forces of gravity and motion, provides information regarding the body's equilibrium status through the eighth cranial nerve to the brain.

Hearing Loss

Sounds are heard along two dimensions: loudness and pitch. *Pitch* is determined by the frequency of sound waves. Normally, speech sounds range between frequencies of 500 and 2,000 cycles per second. Loudness, or sound intensity, is measured in decibels (dB), and hearing is considered normal when sound is audible at 10 dB. Hearing losses, which range from slight (sound audible at 15–25 dB) to profound (sound audible at more than 90 dB), are the result of a variety of insults to the auditory system.

Approximately 50 percent of hearing losses have no known cause. Unless the cause is known, parents of children with hearing losses should receive genetic counseling, because such a large percentage of these children inherited their disability. The etiology, location, and severity of damage to an ear or ears are variables used in determining immediate and long-range treatment for children with hearing loss (see Table 8–1). A **conductive hearing loss** is one that disrupts mechanical conduction of sound as it is transferred from the outer ear through the middle ear. Although several factors can contribute to a conductive hearing loss, most causes can be treated effectively and efficiently through medical intervention. Furthermore, the degree of hearing loss for most conductive etiologies ranges from mild to moderate.

Otitis media, or middle ear disease, is the most common cause of conductive hearing loss in children. Either viral or bacterial infections cause a buildup of fluid in

Table 8–1 Factors That Cause Risk of Hearing Loss

Type	Onset
Genetic	
Syndrome	**Prenatal**

- Branchio-oto-renal (BOR)
- Pendred
- Jervell and Lange-Nielsen
- Waardenburg
- Usher
- Mitochondrial conditions
- CHARGE
- Alpart
- Neurofibromatosis Type II (NFII)
- Stickler
- Treacher-Collins
- Albinism
- Down

Nonsyndromatic	**Prenatal**

- Connexin 26 mutations

Nongenetic	**Prenatal/Natal**

- Intrauterine infections
- Low birth weight (<1,500 g)
- Lack of oxygen
- Hyperbilirubinemia
- Maternal diabetes
    - TORCH toxoplasmosis
    - Other infections (including syphilis)
    - Rubella (German measles)
    - Cytomegalovirus
    - Herpes
    - Syphilis

Acquired	**After Neonatal**

- Otitis media
- Ototoxic drugs
- Meningitis
- Measles
- Chicken pox
- Encephalitis
- Head trauma
- Neurodegenerative diseases
- Noise-induced hearing loss

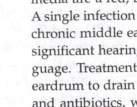

the middle ear and Eustachian tube, reducing mobility of the membranes and bones necessary to adequately transfer sound intensity to the inner ear. Symptoms of otitis media are a red, bulging tympanic membrane, frequent ear pulling, and irritability. A single infection usually results in only temporary and mild hearing loss. However, chronic middle ear disease (serous otitis media) can result in a more persistent and significant hearing loss that might substantially interrupt normal acquisition of language. Treatment of otitis media includes myringotomy (tubes placed through the eardrum to drain fluid), antihistamines (to reduce swelling of the Eustachian tubes), and antibiotics, which generally work with bacterial infections, even though most middle ear infections are viral.

Conductive hearing losses are common in children with a variety of disabilities. For example, children with Down syndrome are at increased risk of middle ear infection for two reasons:

1. A depressed immune response system
2. An anomaly resulting in a more horizontal than normal Eustachian tube, which prevents adequate drainage of the middle ear

Similarly, serous otitis media is quite common in children with cleft palates whose Eustachian tube drainage is hindered by the palate malformation.

Sensorineural hearing losses result from damage to the cochlea or auditory nerve that diminishes the brain's ability to receive sound messages. Genetic inheritance accounts for well over half of known abnormalities that result in serious sensorineural hearing loss. More than 400 known genetic syndromes cause hearing loss; research shows that many of these are the consequence of multiple gene anomalies (Boys Town National Research Hospital, 2009). A third of these cases are the result of a known syndrome, such as Waardenburg syndrome; in addition, a single gene, Connexin 26 (CX26), is responsible for another third of the genetically caused hearing losses. Noise, such as from jet engines, rifle fire, and loud music, can cause sensorineural hearing loss, or *noise-induced deafness*. Unlike conductive hearing losses, sensorineural hearing losses require sound amplification or surgery to improve hearing.

Intrauterine infections also account for a large percentage of serious sensorineural hearing impairments. Toxoplasmosis, maternal rubella contracted during the first trimester, herpes, mumps, syphilis, and cytomegalovirus are all associated with malformations that result in hearing loss. Meningitis, a bacterial infection, is the leading postnatal cause of hearing loss; within the first couple of days, the infection damages the structure of the delicate snail-shaped cochlea.

Neonates and premature infants also are at risk for acquiring hearing losses. For example, asphyxia of infants during delivery may damage the cochlea, resulting in sensorineural hearing loss. High bilirubin levels resulting in severe jaundice

© Denielle M. Miller

may also cause permanent damage to the central nervous system and consequently have an impact on hearing. Other neonatal factors include cerebral hemorrhage, apnea, and, in some cases, the mother's use of antibiotic drugs, which can become toxic.

An uncategorized but very real hearing loss is referred to as a *central auditory processing disorder (CAPD)*. A child who experiences CAPD has difficulty filtering speech messages even though hearing tests reveal normal acoustical sensitivity (Atlantic Coast, 2002). Perceived as sensory overload, messages that lack redundancy (e.g., minimal repetition of content) are particularly difficult for children with CAPD to decode. Like children with other types of hearing losses, those with CAPD benefit from interventions that focus on heightening attentiveness and minimizing interference with communication.

Identification of Hearing Loss

Although the critical period of language development is during the first 3 years of life, nearly 50 percent of infants with hearing loss are not identified until at least their 2nd year. In the past, only high-risk children were screened. Now, 41 states, Guam, and the District of Columbia have statues requiring hearing screening for all infants. The Early Hearing Detection and Intervention data reported to the CDC indicate the number of infants screened has risen from 46.5 percent in 1999 to 97 percent in 2007 (CDC, 2010). Of those infants screened in 2007, 66.4 percent did not pass the screening and were referred for a diagnostic follow-up. Even after parents suspect a hearing loss, the delay is normally one year before children receive formal testing. Early identification of hearing loss enables families and practitioners to plan and implement a remedial program to enhance cognitive and social development. The earlier intervention is started, the more likely the adverse affects on speech, language, social skills, and functional capabilities can be alleviated.

Two tools, which measure brain activity rather than physical responses, are regarded as the most reliable in screening newborns for hearing loss The first, auditory brain stem response (ABS), can be conducted without sedating an infant and is highly accurate. Sounds are presented through earphones while an infant sleeps, and brain responses are measured through electrodes taped to the infant's head. Otoacoustic emissions (OAE) screening is a procedure that is less costly and less complex than other screening methods while still being highly sensitive to hearing loss. In this case, a tiny microscope is placed in the ear canal to detect the movement of cochlear hair cells in the inner ear. Even though a patient being screened must remain still for two to five minutes, this test is particularly useful for infants and young children who may not cooperate with more rigorous procedures. After children are 6 months old, it is possible to conduct behavioral testing in which infants are trained to consistently respond to the emission of a noise. However, this procedure requires well-trained professionals and is less reliable when used with infants who have developmental delays.

Developmental Implications and Resolutions

Children at risk of hearing losses may be identified early when they fail to startle, do not localize sounds, and have delayed acquisition of language milestones. Because of the overlap in symptomatic behaviors, hearing losses are sometimes misdiagnosed as cognitive delays. Yet, there is a relationship between hearing losses and other developmental delays—either by common etiology or because a persistent hearing loss can cause other developmental delays. The developmental domain most directly affected by hearing loss in infancy is language. However, children with hearing losses generally score within the normal intelligence range when tested on nonverbal measures. Though intelligence scores may be normal, children with hearing losses (even in one ear) are 10 times more likely to be held back a year in school as compared to those children with normal hearing (Boys Town National Research Hospital, 2009). Social skills may also be affected because frequent and sustained interpersonal communication is considered an essential component of social interactions. A significant, or even moderate, hearing loss complicates normal communication between infants and their caregivers, and later their peers.

Two factors are related to the interaction between hearing loss and developmental progress. First, because it is estimated that the ability to learn language peaks between ages 2 and 4, it is critical to identify hearing loss early and to provide adaptive intervention at the earliest possible age. Although the brain has functional plasticity, this facility is neither continuous nor limitless. For example, late implantation of cochlear implants has been associated with slower than typical language acquisition (Coene, Schauwers, Gillis, Rooryck, & Bovaerts, 2011). Second, the age of onset and degree of hearing loss influence the degree to which children's language, cognitive abilities, and social skills are affected; as a result, hearing loss sometimes leads to secondary diagnoses. Consequently, early identification and interventions are critical in promoting healthy developmental progress.

Augmentative communication systems should be considered early. Sign language systems, which use hand gestures to communicate, include American Sign Language (ASL), Signing Exact English (SEE-II), and cued speech. ASL is considered a unique language with its own sentence and word structure (syntax and morphology) and is widely used by adults with deafness. This language is the most efficient manual communication system. By contrast, SEE-II resembles spoken and written English in sentence/word structure and usage and may therefore facilitate the acquisition of written language and academic skills. Cued speech is more like spoken language than the other two systems, in that it uses eight hand shapes in four positions to produce a stream of "visual sounds" analogous to the stream of phonemes used in spoken language. The cued hand shapes are paired with lip shapes, to make each sound distinct from the others, making it the visual counterpart of spoken language. Cued speech is not intended as a means of improving spoken language, nor does it depend on speech or voice for communication.

It is important that children with hearing losses not only learn manual sign but also be taught to use residual hearing, speech (lip) reading, and oral speech to communicate. Because most individuals in our society communicate through speech and are not fluent in manual sign, children are better able to communicate with hearing persons if they also learn to supplement sign with conventional language modalities. However, even the most observant and well-trained deaf children do not catch a majority of speech messages when relying only on residual hearing and speech reading. **Total communication** combines manual sign with oral methods of communication and is the most frequently adopted approach.

Several promising computer-based language instruction programs such as *Fast ForWord-Language* have recently been developed (National Institutes of Health, 2008). This particular computer software program uses slow, exaggerated speech to improve a child's ability to process spoken language. Gradually, the speed of speech is accelerated with less exaggeration. Compared to typical language therapy used in public educational settings, substantial improvements in communication abilities were observed as a result of using this program.

Hearing aids, which amplify the sound, are common assistive devices for children with hearing losses. These devices should be fitted at an early age to encourage hearing perception and listening skills necessary for language development. Hearing aids assist, but do not replace, natural hearing abilities. However, significant progress has been made in eliminating irrelevant background noise. Completely-in-the-ear-canal (CIC) aids and the invention of directional microphones allow for more natural amplification. The *Oticon Syncro* is one state-of-the-art hearing aid that mimics the human brain by making as many as 17,000 calculations and adjustments per second. Using artificial intelligence software, the Oticon Syncro uses a multimedia format to improve speech understanding in difficult sound environments such as preschool classrooms, crowded restaurants, busy streets, and so on. Like the human brain, the Oticon Syncro can discriminate between voice and nonvoice sounds, locate sound direction, and assess loudness. The software selects the desirable sounds while screening the unnecessary sounds.

Even with these important developments in technology, young children do not automatically link the sounds heard through amplification to the sounds' sources. Children must be taught to pay attention to sounds, to orient sound sources, and to discriminate between relevant and irrelevant noises. Various amplification devices are available and must be matched specifically to each child's characteristics: age, degree of hearing loss, family environment, and cognitive abilities.

Assisted listening devices (ALDs) are alternatives to the hearing aids that are used in certain situations in which the speaker can be separated from the amplifier. When possible, this separation eliminates much of the background noise that makes it difficult for hearing aid wearers to filter relevant incoming information. Although ALDs cannot replace hearing aids, they can augment the benefit that hearing aids provide and are especially useful if hearing loss is limited to specific environments. Four types of ALD devices are available (Atlantic Coast, 2002):

1. *Hardwire:* In a one-to-one situation, the speaker wears a microphone, which has a thin wire running to a receiver on the person with the hearing loss.

2. *FM:* A radio signal is often used in classrooms of children with hearing losses.

3. *Infrared:* An infrared signal is emitted from a TV or at movies to the person wearing the receiver. This requires a direct line-of-sight from an infrared source to the receiver.

4. *Loop:* A loop of wire is placed around the perimeter of a room and serves as a transmitter by generating an electromagnetic field that can be picked up by a receiver.

Some children with deafness are candidates for cochlear implants. Cochlear implants are electronic devices that can be surgically implanted to transform sound vibrations into nerve impulses for transmission to the brain. Such transmission stimulates nerve cells for children with bilateral sensorineural hearing loss. Children as young as 2 years of age can have a cochlear implant surgically placed. The devices do not restore normal hearing, but when used with speech reading, cochlear implants improve understanding of speech. Each generation of cochlear implants improves the degree of satisfying acoustical information available to patients. To date, however, cochlear implants have not been a panacea. For example, these devices might be of limited use to children with multiple disabilities and those whose hearing loss preceded language acquisition.

When setting up the preschool environment for children with hearing impairments, programs should consider doing the following:

1. Collaborate with and access the services of colleagues who have expertise in working with young children who are deaf or have hearing impairments.

2. Use transdisciplinary teaming to collaborate in assessment and planning. Involve the parent and two or more professionals from different disciplines and with diverse expertise, such as an audiologist, a speech–language pathologist, a psychologist, an educator of the deaf, and so on.

3. Obtain cued language and/or sign language services and interpretation for children who require this to access classroom information.

4. Adapt classrooms by using carpeted floors, acoustical tiles on the ceilings and walls, and visible fire alarm systems.

5. Furnish classes with necessary assistive technological devices such as amplification systems, FM auditory training systems, captioning equipment, computer software designed for children with hearing impairments, and telecommunication devices (TDD) for interacting with parents who are deaf and members of the community of the deaf. Products are continually being designed and improved, so early childhood interventionists must ensure they remain current in this area.

Adapting classrooms for children with hearing impairments and providing necessary assistive technology is expensive and will challenge service providers who are already uncertain of financial resources. Moreover, controversial findings on the relative benefits of integrated versus self-contained programs for children with hearing impairments fail to provide overwhelming support for costly modifications in regular classrooms. Proponents believe that integrated settings improve communication skills and increase social and emotional competency. Opponents argue that hearing peers lack the manual communication skills needed to communicate effectively, and this leads students with hearing impairments to feel isolated and to suffer socially and emotionally. While more study is needed, it does appear that placing students in integrated settings does not harm children with hearing impairments socially as many educators and parents have feared. This conclusion is supported by legal decisions regarding the least restrictive environment for preschoolers with hearing impairments. Etscheidt (2006) found that in a majority of legal decisions, inclusive and natural settings were found to be the most beneficial for students, including the peers of children with deafness. Typically developing peers were viewed as essential language models when the settings included appropriately credentialed staff.

People with deafness differ from people with other disabilities in that they have developed their own social communities of peers and a deaf culture. Segregation of this culture, largely self-selected, has led to controversy that directly affects parents of very young children with deafness. Even those who are deaf sometimes deny membership in the deaf community to those who acquire deafness adventitiously later in life and those who have received cochlear implants. Many deaf people are working to have deaf culture recognized as a distinct cultural and linguistic minority. Contending that inclusion in this community is a source of pride, proponents of the movement shun attempts to bridge the communication gap. This controversy has grown more nuanced with the increase of children and adults receiving cochlear implants. Since members of the deaf community view deafness as part of their cultural identity, they do not consider the hearing loss a disability in need of repair.

Informing and Working with Parents

The birth of a child with deafness can have a profound effect on families (Jackson & Turnbull, 2004). In a comprehensive study of family life, Jackson and Turnbull came to several conclusions. Additional stress on such families was related to such issues as choice of cultural identity for and with their child; sometimes this stress was reported to improve marital relations, and sometimes it was reported to deteriorate such relationships. Communication with family members was often limited by the parents' education level, the size of the group communicating, family members' ability to sign, the degree of hearing loss, and the presence of an interpreter or one-to-one communication partner. Parents of children with deafness ranked their main motives of communication as being those related directly to the issues of deafness (e.g., speech improvement, hearing aid care). Like their relationships with their parents, the relationships that children had with extended family members were defined by family members' ability to sign. For parents of children with deafness to be good learning partners, they needed to adapt to the difficulty of sustaining joint attention through physical, rather than auditory, prompting. Social support could be an important mediator of stress for these parents.

Very early in the life of children with deafness, their parents must make a decision regarding linguistic instruction that will have a lifelong influence on their children in every aspect. Those parents who prefer their children be given every chance to become a part of the hearing world are likely to choose an educational program that emphasizes oral communication or total communication. Other parents might feel that an inclusive setting would result in social and communicative isolation, particularly because communities of deaf individuals are often very active socially and rely on sign language for communication. While manual language does not necessarily preclude integration, its use is usually paired with a philosophy of isolation and specialized educational programs. Other parents, who lack community resources or have limited economic circumstances, feel that they have little choice other than to accept the only services that are offered. Parents must be provided objective information on the implications of different educational choices—and the advocacy skills to negotiate alternative services in areas of restricted options. The National Institute on Deafness and other Communication Disorders (NIDCD, 2011) is one of the most comprehensive resources for parents and educators of children with hearing losses. Through a variety of coordinated programs, NIDCD is engaged in continuing education, research, and dissemination of research and information. Linking parents to this and other helpful resources is made easier through emerging technologies, such as the Internet.

Visual Impairments

Visual acuity is measured by comparing the distance at which a person is able to see an object with clarity to the distance at which a person with average visual acuity (20/20) clearly sees the same object (see Figure 8–3). For example, what a person with 20/70 vision sees clearly only 20 feet away, a person with average visual acuity would be able to see accurately as far away as 70 feet. *Visual impairment* is legally defined as a visual acuity of 20/200 or worse in the better eye, with correction. Additionally, those whose peripheral field of vision is 20 degrees or less are considered legally blind, even though their visual acuity might be normal (see Figure 8–4). **Low vision** is assessed when visual acuity is 20/70 or worse in the better eye, with correction.

While it is thought that legal blindness is a relatively low-incidence disability (1 in 1,000), it is difficult to determine exactly what its prevalence is, as many children with severe visual loss experience one or more other disabilities and are classified under a different disability label. As medical technology advances, very premature and low-birth-weight infants are more able to survive, resulting in an increase in the incidence of children with retinopathy of prematurity. High-risk infants should have their first visual examination 4 to 9 weeks after birth and have follow-up examinations if concerns are noted. If treated, most premature infants have no long-term visual problems (Bustos, 2011). Although reducing visual impairment and blindness is one of the 2010 national health objectives, in 2002 the prevalence remained the same as it had been in 1997, the baseline year (CDC, 2005). The data also indicated

Figure 8–3 Visual Acuity: 20/20 Vision Compared to 20/70 Vision

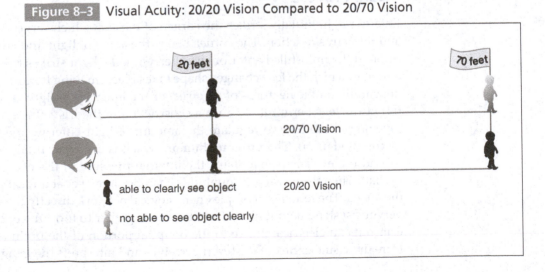

Figure 8–4 Peripheral Vision

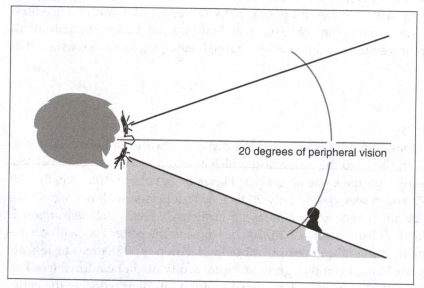

20 degrees of peripheral vision

that children in poverty were nearly twice as likely to be visually impaired as children from more affluent homes (CDC, 2005). Poverty rates for young children continue to increase, and research has demonstrated a relationship between poverty and the incidence of visual impairment. Thus, as poverty continues to increase, it can be projected that the incidence of visual impairments will also increase. The World Health Organization estimates that 90 percent of the world's blind live in the poorest regions of the world (2012). Many causes of these children's visual impairments are considered preventable and could be controlled through vaccinations, vitamins, and available health care (WHO, 2012).

It is believed that newborns have a visual acuity of 20/600 and that children do not develop normal visual acuity until about age 5. This "developmental visual impairment" combined with infants' cognitive immaturity make assessment of mild to moderate visual impairment unreliable before 6 months of age. Even so, early screening results should be interpreted conservatively. More important to children and their families than the clinical certainty of visual disability is the retention of functional visual abilities. That is, parents need to be encouraged to focus on everyday activities that take full advantage of their child's residual vision instead of focusing on their visual deficiencies.

Visual Process

Entering light initially strikes the **cornea** of the eye, which serves both a protective and refractive function. The cornea bends the angle of light and channels that light through the fluid-filled anterior chamber. Once the light strikes the **lens,** accommodation in which the lens changes shape takes place, making it more or less spherical, depending on the nearness of an object or the intensity of light. The elastic properties of the lens permit it to cause a constriction of the iris, which widens the pupil (opening in the eye) to regulate the amount of light entering the vitreous humor (**accommodation**). The **vitreous humor,** which is a second fluid-filled space lying behind the eye's lens, maintains the internal pressure of the eye and shape of the eyeball. The rays passing through this chamber intersect at a focal point on or near the **retina.** The retina is a complex neurological network directly linked to the central nervous system; neural fibers from the retina gather to form the **optic nerve,** which transmits an electrical image to the occipital portion of the brain (see Figure 8–5). Here the visual cortex of the brain perceives and interprets the images. It is relevant

Figure 8–5 Visual Process and Eye Anatomy

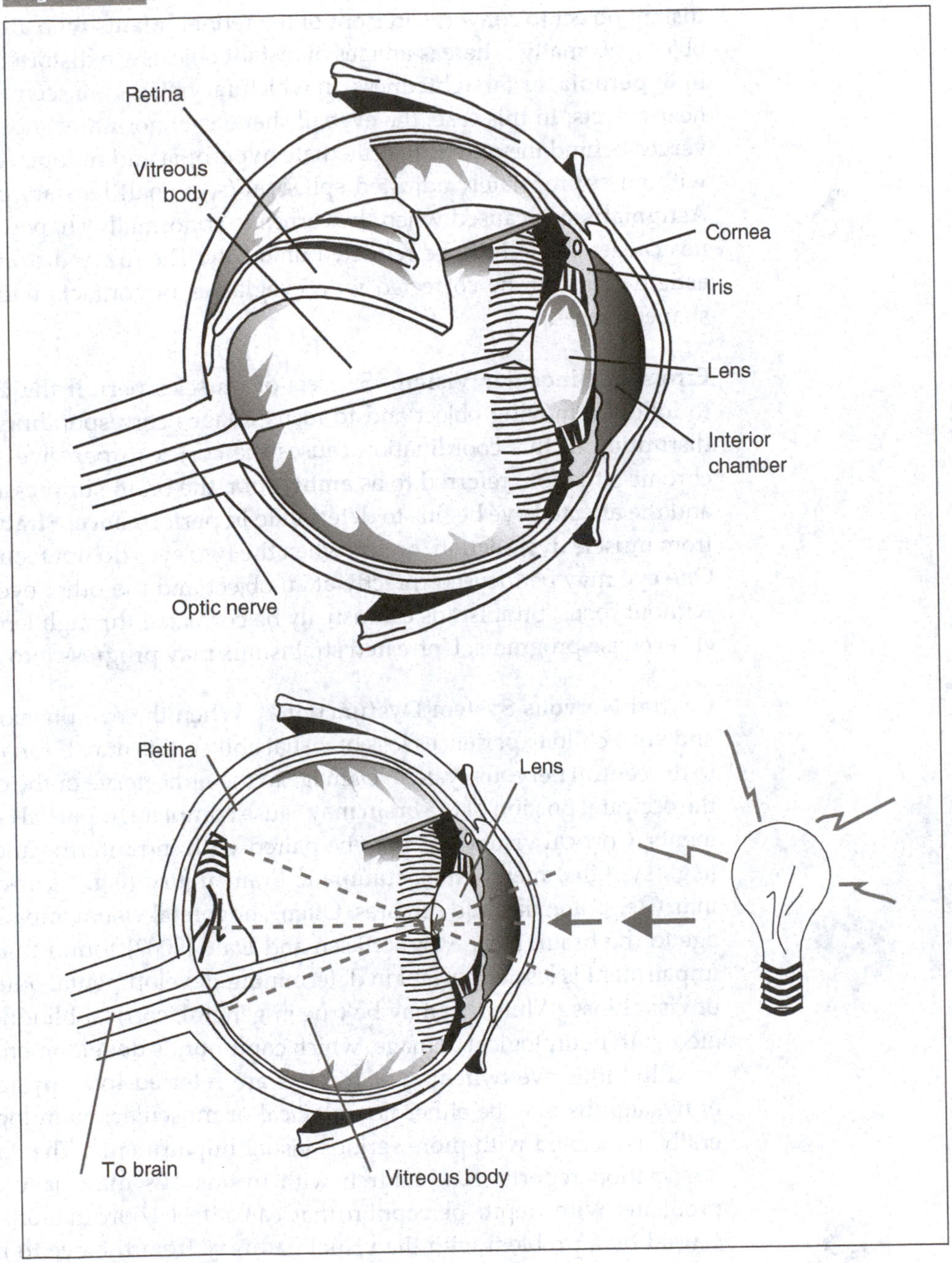
Retina
Vitreous body
Cornea
Iris
Lens
Interior chamber
Optic nerve
Retina
Lens
To brain
Vitreous body

question 10 study guide

that the brain and the eyes emerge from the same embryological mass in fetal development, the neural crest. Consequently, damage of one during fetal development is often associated with damage to the other (Sonksen & Dale, 2002).

Refractive Errors Defects in the curvature of cornea and lens, or abnormal eyeball shape, change the focal point of light rays and are referred to as *refractive errors.* **Myopia,** or nearsightedness, results when the shape of the eyeball is abnormally long (or, less frequently, due to corneal or lens curvature), causing the image of a distant object to converge in front of the retina. Infants who are nearsighted see near objects normally, whereas images of distant objects are distorted. The opposite is true in **hyperopia,** or farsightedness, in which far objects are seen with more acuity than near objects. In this case, the eyeball shape is abnormally short, and the image converges behind the retina. To remediate hyperopia and myopia, eyeglasses or contacts with an appropriately adjusted spherical (sectional) lens are placed before the eye. **Astigmatism** is caused when the cornea is abnormally shaped. An oval-shaped cornea causes the light to be refracted unevenly. The fuzzy distortion that results from astigmatism can be corrected with eyeglasses or contacts with parabolic- or toric-shaped lenses.

Errors in Binocular Vision Six sets of muscles permit the eyes to act in concert to follow a moving object and to focus images correspondingly on both retinas. A disruption in this coordination causes the cortex to perceive a double image. In a chronic situation, referred to as **amblyopia,** the brain suppresses one of the images, and the affected eye begins to deteriorate in performance. **Strabismus,** also resulting from muscle dysfunction, occurs when the two eyes do not focus on the same image. One eye may be focused directly at an object and the other eye is turned elsewhere without focus. Strabismus can usually be corrected through lenses, surgery, or muscle exercise programs. Untreated strabismus may progress into amblyopia.

Central Nervous System Dysfunctions When the eye physiology is not impaired and yet a child experiences loss of visual ability, this may be an indication of damage to the central nervous system. Damage to the optic nerve or the cerebral tissue within the occipital portion of the brain may cause complete or partial cortical visual impairments. Cortical visual loss may be paired with intrauterine and postnatal infection (e.g., syphilis, meningitis), traumatic brain injury (e.g., near-drowning), perinatal injury (e.g., anoxia), and seizures. Often, congenital visual impairments involve damage to the brain. However, Sonksen and Dale (2002) found that the cause of visual impairment is less important in determining developmental outcome than the extent of visual loss. While this may be true in general, cortical blindness is always associated with neurological damage, which compounds developmental challenges.

Rhythmic eye twitching or tremors are referred to as **nystagmus.** The etiology of nystagmus may be either neurological or muscular; neurological causes are generally associated with more serious visual impairments. The American Optometric Association reports that children with nystagmus may have reduced acuity and problems with depth perception that can affect coordination. Nystagmus can be caused by a problem with the visual pathway from the eye to the brain, which can improve throughout childhood but cannot be cured. Surgery to alter the position of the muscles can be performed, though this invasive procedure is rarely used (AOA, 2012).

Just as with other areas of development, visual ability undergoes a normal progression from infancy through the preschool years. Delays in developing visual skills or deviations in the appearance of a child's eyes (e.g., redness, tearing, crusting, droopiness) are indications that intervention may be necessary. A visual specialist can assess vision according to a developmental reference and can recommend training methods for improving visual skills when needed.

Causes of Visual Impairment

© Dave King/DK Images

A large percentage of cases of congenital visual impairments are of genetic origin. For example, albinism and Down syndrome are two genetic syndromes that place children at high risk of visual impairments. Down syndrome is a chromosomal aberration commonly associated with visual disorders such as severe myopia, cataracts, amblyopia, strabismus, glaucoma, and nystagmus. All children with Down syndrome should have regular ophthalmological examinations. Visual impairments accompanying **albinism** are related to a lack of melanin or pigmentosa. The eyes of children with albinism lack color and are extremely sensitive to light, requiring them to wear tinted lenses. Nystagmus is also frequently associated with albinism.

According to the World Health Organization's Vision 2020, the most common cause of congenital visual impairment is exposure to infections, many of which are either preventable or treatable (Gilbert, 2001). Rubella may lead to retinopathy, cataracts, glaucoma, and structural malformations. Cytomegalovirus, toxoplasmosis, herpes simplex, and congenital syphilis are associated with visual impairments ranging from lesions to central nervous system malformations. Researchers are also just beginning to understand the relationship between HIV infection and visual impairments in children. Visual impairments can also result from prenatal exposure to dangerous chemicals (e.g., alcohol) or postnatal exposure (e.g., lead).

Congenital visual impairments are often linked to poor developmental outcomes and, in some cases, to regression and development of autistic-like behaviors (Sonksen & Dale, 2002). Settings in which children learn and develop are complex and require interdependency between behavior, physiology, and environment. An upset in one dimension can cause the others to be interrupted in a cumulative fashion. For example, children with visual impairments may experience difficulty in emotional bonding, fine and gross motor operations, social interactions, formation of language, and so on. These deviations affect neurological pathway development, often leading to further developmental delays. Sonksen and Dale found that while there appeared to be no difference between infants' social responsiveness at 1 year, by 3 years of age, children with profound visual impairment (no perception of form) deviated significantly from those with severe visual impairment (able to see form) and children with no visual impairment. Those with profound visual impairment showed negativistic behavior, lack of social communication, and increased self-stimulation and stereotypical behaviors. It may be that at least part of the reason for this observed regression is due to (1) increased complexity of environmental demands, (2) neurological defects that frequently accompany congenital visual impairment, and/or (3) a failure of caregivers to communicate with children with profound visual impairment on a plane that is meaningful in a sightless world.

A **cataract** is a clouding or opacity of the lens. The location and degree of deviation from transparency caused by a cataract determines the amount of distortion and obstruction of vision. The treatment of cataracts involves surgery to remove and replace the affected lens. Corrective lenses are necessary to compensate for the lens removed in surgery. It should be noted that children born with cataracts which go untreated during infancy will not regain sight, even if the cataracts are removed later. This is because vision processing capabilities in the brain will not develop if not properly used early in life.

Glaucoma is caused by a buildup of pressure in the anterior chamber of the eye. In most cases, the onset of glaucoma is unrecognized until much damage has already been done to peripheral vision. Untreated, glaucoma will cause continued serious visual loss or blindness. However, medical treatment (usually medication) can arrest the otherwise progressive degeneration of vision. Because children with other visual losses often have secondary visual problems, they should be observed throughout childhood for signs of glaucoma (i.e., excessive tiredness, severe headaches, dizziness, loss of field vision, and tearing).

Close Up

Childhood Epidemics of the 21st Century

While infectious diseases continue to be the leading cause of disabilities worldwide, noninfectious factors or gene–environment factors have now taken the lead in causing disease and disabilities in the industrialized world. These new epidemics include diabetes, obesity, and respiratory ailments. It is now known that even very low levels of environmental pollutants (e.g., PCBs, methylmercury) are linked to intellectual impairment, behavioral problems, asthma, and preterm birth. From conception to about 3 years of age, vulnerability to environmental toxins is much higher for young children than for adults, both because of children's immature central nervous systems and their weaker immune systems. Furthermore, significant racial and ethnic differences are found in the probability of disease and disability resulting from pollutants.

A rapid and largely unexplained growth in the rate of childhood **asthma** threatens the health of society. Referred to as the most disabling childhood disease (Lanphear, 2005), asthma has been diagnosed in 1 in 10 children in the United States. Indoor air degraded by tobacco smoke, organic allergens (such as dust mites, mold, animal dander, and cockroaches), and nonorganic allergens (such as carbon monoxide, volatile organic compounds, and pesticides) increase children's risk for allergies, asthma, and other respiratory disabilities. Because people in modern societies spend approximately 90 percent of their time indoors and 66 percent of that time in their home, indoor air quality plays an ever important role in human health. It is possible to mitigate the effects of poor indoor air quality by using home intervention methods such as mechanical ventilation systems, allergen-impermeable bedding, and vacuum cleaners with high-efficiency particulate air (HEPA) filters. It has been estimated that improving indoor air quality in homes and public buildings could reduce asthma symptoms by as much as 10 percent to 30 percent and save $2 billion to $4 billion annually in associated health care costs in the United States.

Obesity and its related counterpart diabetes are two new childhood epidemics related to social changes. While the United States has the highest rate of childhood obesity, the epidemic is a worldwide phenomenon with only Japan avoiding increased rates. The epidemic has multifactored causes relating to an upset in the energy expenditure–energy intake balance. From 1971 to 1974, the incidence of childhood obesity was 5 percent, doubling in the period from 1980 to 1994 and reached nearly 15 percent between 1999 and 2002. Childhood obesity leads to adult obesity. Low-income children and African American children in the United States have had greater increases in their rates of obesity than have other children.

Decreased rates of energy expenditure are due to less physical exercise, more time spent in sedentary activity such as watching television, and urban sprawl that leads to transit by auto rather than walking. Increases in energy intake are related to eating habits that include high-calorie foods and drinks, such as fast foods, soft drinks, juices,

and snacks. A genetic–environmental interaction may also cause some children to be genetically susceptible to particular patterns of calorie intake or expenditure.

The epidemics described here have far-reaching implications for professionals working with very young children. These diseases can exacerbate and even cause behavioral and cognitive problems for children. In addition, the ceiling for the increasing rates of asthma, allergies, and obesity is nowhere in sight. There is a need to consider treatment as well as prevention strategies in an overall approach to these epidemics of the early 21st century.

Sources: "Childhood Obesity: Trends and Causes," by Patricia M. Anderson and Kristin F. Butcher, 2006, *The Future of Children, 16*(1), 19–35; "Origins and Evolution of Children's Environmental Health," by Bruce Lanphear, 2005, *Environmental Health Perspectives, 113,* 24–40; and "Childhood Asthma and Environmental Interventions," by Felicia Wu and Tim K. Takaro, 2006, *Environmental Health Perspectives, 115,* 971–980.

Developmental Implications and Resolutions

Children with visual impairments, particularly those with other disabilities, display unusual patterns of eye contact, yet one of the first intentional acts of infants is eye gaze. Normal language, cognition, and social skill development depend on eye gaze, which sets the occasion for social and language interactions and provides visual memory enabling infants to feel "safe" in exploring their world. To mediate the visual-attentional differences in children with visual impairments, caregivers must develop trusting interpersonal relationships with the children in order to engage routinely in play and social interactions. Play can be enhanced through the use of clear and colorful objects (when relevant) and closely spaced cues to keep children's attention, and by limiting irrelevant sensory information.

Children who are visually impaired usually experience delays in other areas even when they possess normal intelligence. Since most infants who are blind do not use their hands functionally and have difficulty or are reluctant to move around their environment, the development of fine and gross motor skills is generally impeded. This may also lead to stereotypical behaviors such as rocking or postural abnormalities. Because language development depends on imitation of mouth movements as well as nonverbal language cues, children who are visually impaired often experience delays in speech development and conversational abilities. This inability to see nonverbal cues and subtle forms of language may result in self-orientation or social isolation. Children who are blind often develop cognitive skills differently than do sighted children because they use different sensory pathways to understand their world. As a result, children with visual impairments tend to experience delays in understanding object permanence, causal relationships, constancy, classification, and conservation (Strickling, 2010).

One factor affecting the interaction between visual impairments and later functioning is the timing of onset. **Congenital** (born with) blindness and **adventitious** blindness differentially affect the type of intervention a child might need. Because adventitious blindness occurs after a child has had visual experiences, such children are able to "picture" images of their world conceptually, if not visually, after sight is lost.

The primary goal of early intervention is to have children make the best use of their residual vision. Special training is needed to teach infants with blindness to "pay attention." That is, paying attention requires that infants learn to screen out irrelevant sensory stimuli while vigilantly seeking new information. Additionally, to make decisions, infants must learn to use previously gained information in new situations. Very young children can be motivated to use their residual vision if caregivers limit the amount of assistance provided to what is necessary to ensure safety and success. Beyond that, infants and toddlers should be encouraged to explore, to move independently about their environments, and to risk an occasional bump or bruise to increase mobility. Prevention of secondary disabilities requires an interdisciplinary approach that includes giving attention to physical development, language acquisition, and learning social skills. Caregivers can assist in facilitating normal development in other areas by providing enriching experiences, with activities, materials, and interactions that use residual vision as well as tactile, auditory, kinesthetic, and olfactory senses.

Informing and Working with Parents

As with any disability, team members who interact with parents should be considerate enough to present any new information related to visual impairments more than once. It is almost certain that when parents receive a large amount of technical information, especially if this information leads to emotional reactions, they will be unable to focus on the details of the conversation. Team members *need to tailor* the delivery of information to intersect with parents' ability to "hear" and a child's need for services.

Those sharing information should be knowledgeable enough to answer most questions that parents might ask. However, it is worse to give misinformation than to give no information, especially about predictions of how a child's visual abilities will develop or when relaying other developmental prognoses. Whenever possible, vision specialists should assist parents in researching answers to questions and identifying resources. It may also be appropriate and necessary to explain the nature of the visual loss to children themselves. For example, children with congenital blindness may not recognize a deficiency until it is explained to them and they realize how they differ from their peers.

The absence of visual referents that are gained from cumulative visual experiences prevents children with visual impairments from developing conceptual, perceptual, sensory, and body awareness of space and environment. Hence, a primary objective

© Ruth Jenkinson/DK Images

of early intervention should be to teach **orientation** skills, which enable young children with visual impairments to achieve **mobility.** In the 1980s, the orientation and mobility field recognized the benefit of providing services to preschool-age children. Strategies and approaches have been developed to help young children learn to navigate beginning in infancy. Orientation training is necessary to enable young children with visual impairments to gain a sense of position in space. Children are taught to take advantage of other senses, such as touch, smell, and hearing, to augment or replace sight. Mobility training should be coupled with orientation; that is, children need to be taught their location in the room as well as how to move around their environment.

Curriculum specifically designed for infants and toddlers includes precane skills, sensory awareness, trailing (using the back of one's hand to move along a wall and warn against upcoming obstacles), using a sighted guide, and environmental familiarization. Advances in mobility devices for very young children generally consist of modified adult devices, such as shortened long canes (white cane) or devices specially designed for children, such as a push toy that provides both support and protection for a toddler who is blind. Selection of appropriate orientation and mobility adaptations is based on consideration of several factors: a child's motor skills, degree of visual loss, adaptability to change required for continuous accommodation, and need for formal training; concern for the safety of the child and others; the adaptations' cost (which can range from several thousand to just a few dollars) and its need for maintenance; and the availability of technology. Orientation and mobility specialists are available and should be regularly consulted for evaluating, selecting, and adapting mobility devices for specific children. Guide dogs are not an option for infants and toddlers because canines cannot be assigned until children reach age 16. However, preparation in orientation and mobility, even in early childhood, helps prepare children for independent movement and eventual guide dog ownership if needed.

A parent's role in facilitating language in infants who are visually impaired may be particularly difficult. As mentioned, vision is important to nonverbal communication (e.g., gestures, smiling, facial expressions) and to help parent–child dyads communicate about an object of mutual attention. In the absence of these important communication tools, it seems that children who are visually impaired tend to have delayed language development and poor social language skills. The communication of young children with visual impairments tends to be egocentric. Furthermore, parents, teachers, and other adults tend to limit the opportunities of children with visual impairments for meaningful conversation in several ways: by taking many more conversational turns and by using more directives and labeling but also commenting and questioning less than they would with sighted children. Because infants and children who are visually impaired do not spontaneously give the same feedback in conversation as sighted children, it is important to teach parents (and teachers) to share conversational turns equitably, to ask meaningful questions and wait for the answers, and to make relevant comments and expect relevant comments in return about mutual experiences.

Without careful planning and accommodations, students with visual impairments may face a lifetime of disadvantages. Functional visual impairments, or those that require significant accommodations to complete social, domestic, and work-related tasks, result in lifelong financial challenges. Without substantial supports, many professions are closed to persons who are blind. Yet, there are also those who have achieved success at the highest levels in our society. Knowledge of such disadvantages can help educators anticipate likely barriers and act to prevent both blindness and associated secondary disabilities from limiting opportunities. Making adaptations to the environment and thoughtfully planning interactions with children who are visually impaired often mitigate the factors that lead to developmental delays and difficulty in accessing visual learning environments. The following intervention strategies are recommended for children who are blind and visually impaired (Hatten, McWilliam, & Winton, 2002; Palmer, 2011):

1. Collaborate with families and other service providers, respecting diversity and culture, to develop an Individualized Family Services Plan (IFSP) that is based on family and child strengths.

2. Provide families with the materials and resources they need to implement the family-prioritized interventions. These may include access to equipment, supplies, assistive technologies, and information about financial resources.

3. Approach early intervention from a support perspective and ensure that home visits promote functional outcomes for both the child and the family.

4. Develop programs and activities that promote increased independence in all areas of development (cognition, social, language, adaptation, fine motor, gross motor, and self-help) and guard against overprotection.

5. Organize activities around hands-on experiences, using real materials whenever possible, and describe what the child is experiencing, but do not interfere with the play.

6. Allow the child to navigate independently around the environment and provide the family and child opportunities to participate in recreational activities that involve risk-taking, fitness, and social integration.

Infections in Early Childhood

Human beings have been afflicted with both common and complex ailments since the beginning of recorded history. Symptoms such as sore throats, earaches, coughs, and fevers indicate an invasion by biological agents and cause parents of young children to be concerned. The interaction between humans and the microorganisms that cause infections is complex. These **biological agents** cause damage to human cells by either living on cells or causing inflammation of the cells. **Inflammation** is caused by the **toxin** released by a particular **organism**, and that toxin, which acts like a poison to human cells, causes a specific infection. Biological agents may travel throughout the body in the bloodstream or by way of the lymph system. The effect of an infection on a particular individual depends on the agent involved as well as the overall health and age of the individual when exposed.

Infecting agents often affect premature babies, term newborns, infants, and young children differently than older children and mature adults. Reactions among

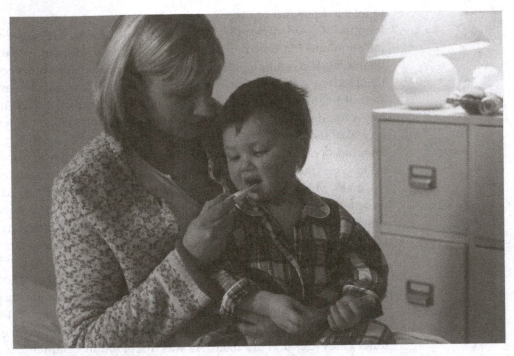

© Ruth Jenkinson/DK Images

very young children may include lowered rather than elevated body temperatures, a decrease instead of an increase in the total white blood cell count, and a more rapid progression of an infecting agent, which produces more significant symptoms. In addition, very young children have immature immune systems and are less capable of dealing with an infection than is an individual with a mature and healthy system. Individuals with compromised immune systems, such as infants with chronic diseases, are also at a much higher risk of being infected. As a result of these factors, neonates, infants, and young children may have more frequent episodes of significant infections that require more extensive interventions. Biological agents that may cause infections in humans include bacteria, viruses, mycoplasmas, fungi, protozoa, rickettsias, and nematodes; bacteria and viruses are the two most common infectious agents.

Bacterial Infections

By adulthood, everyone has experienced an infection. In spite of this, few have actually seen what causes the illness. **Microbes,** or germs, are so small that they can be viewed only through a microscope; **bacteria** are microbes found abundantly in nature. Many bacteria are incapable of causing disease and live in harmony with humans, yet even bacteria that generally are beneficial can cause significant infections in humans under particular circumstances—by becoming **pathogenic** (disease causing).

Pathogenic bacteria create infections that continue to be a significant cause of infant **morbidity** and **mortality** in the United States. Such infections can occur either prior to delivery from an infected mother or shortly after delivery from exposure to infected persons or objects in the environment. An infant's condition can be profoundly affected depending on the particular organism responsible for a specific infection and the time between exposure to infection and initiation of appropriate treatment. For example, infants infected by **group B streptococcus** may show subtle objective symptoms such as mild respiratory distress. However, if these infants are not treated, they deteriorate quickly to the point that death may occur. Medical care providers need to use observable signs along with a maternal history and a review of risk factors when deciding whether to start early and aggressive treatment. Pneumococcal disease is of particular danger to infants and young children with underlying medical conditions such as HIV/AIDS and sickle cell disease (Davis, Misurski, Miller, Bell, & Bapat, 2011). Children in nonfamily child care and/or overcrowded living conditions are at increased risk of acquiring pneumococcal disease due to increased exposure. Moreover, treatment of this disease in early childhood is complicated by the fact that strains of the bacteria that cause it are becoming increasingly penicillin resistant (Davis).

In the United States, children who live in poverty and/or who belong to a minority group (i.e., Hispanic and African American children) are disproportionately at risk for the development of infections. This higher risk correlates with the significantly lower rate of childhood vaccinations among children who are poor and live in inner cities (Cesar et al., 2003). As was discussed in Chapter 5, a direct relationship exists between socioeconomic status and low birth weight as well as the development of both prenatal and postnatal infections. The greater the degree of poverty, the lower an infant's birth weight, and, consequently, the greater the vulnerability to infection (Cesar). Poverty is also linked to many of the maternal conditions that lead to infection, including poor nutrition, environmental injustice (e.g., the location of toxic waste dumps, pollution levels in inner cities, crime), lack of prenatal care, use of drugs, alcohol and/or tobacco, and inadequate attention to chronic diseases, such as hypertension. Appropriate assessment of an infant's physical condition at delivery provides health-care workers the information necessary to determine risk factors that may indicate the presence of a bacterial agent. Keys to effective treatment of an infected infant are awareness of the possibility of infection, assessment of presenting signs and symptoms, and aggressive treatment of any suspected infection in an at-risk infant.

Infants born through infected amniotic fluid or those who acquire a bacterial infection shortly after birth are at high risk for disability or death from the infection. Initial symptoms of an infection include temperature instability, poor feeding, respiratory distress, low blood sugar, and lethargy. Symptoms may also be as subtle as a lack of appropriate response to environmental stimulation. Multiple-physical-systems failure can occur very rapidly in affected newborns. Infants with multiple-system involvement who do not die can experience significant long-term developmental effects, most frequently visual impairment, hearing loss, and intellectual disabilities. Such secondary disabilities may be the result of the infectious process or a result of the treatment used to save an infant's life. Infants experiencing infections at birth or shortly afterward warrant early screening for developmental progress, identification of potential problems, and possible initiation of early intervention programs to provide the greatest opportunity for full development.

Antibiotics are a common treatment for bacterial infections. However, these life saving drugs are a double-edged sword. Overuse of the very antibiotics that have saved countless lives threatens to place humans at even greater health risk. Antibiotics such as penicillin have been effective in destroying bacterial infections such as otitis media, pneumonia, and sinusitis in their human hosts. However, bacteria are incredibly adaptive, and in less than 50 years, almost all common microbes have mutated into antibiotic-resistant strains.

Multiple factors have led to the overuse of antibiotics (Green, 1997). First, the two types of antibiotics, wide spectrum and narrow spectrum, are not always used properly. The former is useful in treating a wide variety of bacteria, whereas the latter is useful in treating very specific bacteria. While wide-spectrum antibiotics are often prescribed for the sake of expedience, their overuse hastens the resistance of bacteria. Second, American families have become overly dependent on antibiotics in order to keep children in school or day care so that parents (both of whom usually work full-time) can avoid taking time off from work to care for sick children. Parents have increasingly put pressure on health-care providers to prescribe antibiotics for children, even when infections are minor or when antibiotic prescriptions are inappropriate (i.e., for viral infections that are unaffected by antibiotics). Third, the congregation of children in day-care centers has hastened the spread of antibiotic-resistant bacteria. Similarly, the American work culture, which places a premium on work productivity, has created "toxic environments," in which people go to work when they are ill, or return to work before they are well, rather than take time off to get well, thereby spreading the disease-resistant bacteria. This practice may further compound the problem because workers may ask physicians for wide-spectrum antibiotics so they can return to work sooner. To prevent antibiotics from losing their effectiveness, several steps need to be taken: (1) medical professionals need to prescribe narrow-spectrum antibiotics, (2) medical professionals need to educate parents (and perhaps physicians) that viral infections do not respond to antibiotics, and (3) parents need to be encouraged to resist repeated dependence on antibiotic prescriptions for mild bacterial infections, even if it means an illness might last longer and possibly delay the person's return to work or school.

Viral Infections

Viruses are the smallest infectious agents and because of their unique properties are more difficult to identify and control than bacteria. Like bacteria, viruses are biological agents but differ from true microorganisms. A virus consists of genetic material, either DNA or RNA, and an enclosing shell of protein. Genetic materials contained in a virus's DNA or RNA make the virus capable of reproducing and attaching itself to susceptible cells. Most viruses attach to and reproduce in specific cells, such as nerve, muscle, and blood cells. Once in a host individual, viruses can survive in an inactive state for extended time periods, but, later, activation and occasional reactivation periods can occur, which cause the disease itself. Other viral infections do not produce recognizable diseases in the infected individual but create a carrier state enabling the person to transfer viruses to others.

Prevention of many dangerous viral diseases has been accomplished largely through the development of **vaccines.** Vaccines consist of either active viral

Figure 8–6   Recommended Immunization Schedule

	Diphtheria, Tetanus, & Pertussis (DTP)	Polio	Measles, Mumps, & Rubella (MMR)	Tetanus Diphtheria	Haemophilus Influenzae Type B (HIb)	Hepatitis B
Birth – 2 weeks						shot
2 months	shot	oral			shot	shot
4 months	shot	oral			shot	
6 months	shot	oral			shot	shot
12–15 months			shot		shot	
15–18 months	shot					
4–6 years	shot	oral	shot			
10–12 years						* shot
14–16 years				shot		

Based on National Standards

* If not done earlier, 3-dose series between 11 and 12 years of age.

immunization delivered by shot

immunization taken orally

replications that have a decreased capability of causing infection and disease or an inactive virus. When introduced into a human being, both activate the immune system to produce **antibodies.** Once established, antibodies prevent an acute infection if the individual is exposed to an active virus. Through a series of childhood immunizations, many common viral diseases such as polio and smallpox have been nearly eliminated or greatly reduced in early childhood (see Figure 8–6). Still, progress is not without setbacks. For example, shortages of vaccines in 2002 were the result of reduction in manufacturing and insufficient stockpiles. Shortages and postponements, like those of 2002, altered recommendations by the Centers for Disease Control (2009) for vaccine use.

Potent drugs are continuously being developed to counteract specific viral agents. The success of these drugs in preventing or controlling viral infections has been variable. When prevention is not possible, antiviral drugs can shorten the duration of some viral diseases. Many serious viral infections with neither vaccination nor cure, such as hepatitis B and HIV, fall into a third category of chronic, though sometimes medically controlled, diseases.

TORCH   Viral infections and many of the common congenital disabilities related to specific agents are frequently discussed under the umbrella of TORCH infections (see Table 8–1). Many professionals add syphilis to this group as a separate entity and refer to the group as the STORCH infections. This text includes syphilis under other infections (O). TORCH stands for toxoplasmosis (T), other infections (O), rubella (R), cytomegalic inclusion virus (C), and herpes (H). Because of the variability in pathology and outcome of these infections, they are usually discussed as independent entities (see Table 8–2).

| Table 8–2 | Characteristics and Outcomes of Congenital Infections | | | | | | |

	Toxoplasmosis	Chicken Pox	Hepatitis B	Syphilis	HIV/AIDS	Rubella	CMV	Herpes
Blindness	X	X		X		X	X	X
Deafness	X	X		X		X	X	X
Retardation	X	X		X		X	X	X
Seizures	X	X		X		X	X	X
Liver effect			X	X	X		X	
Spleen effect			X	X	X		X	
Hydrocephalus	X	X		X			X	X
Microcephaly	X	X		X		X	X	X
Jaundice			X		X		X	
Brain atrophy	X	X		X		X	X	X
Transmittal at birth		X	X	X	X	X		X
Transplacental transmittal	X	X	X	X	X	X	X	?
Shed virus			X	X	X	X	X	X
Hydrops				X				

Toxoplasmosis   Pregnant women must be especially careful to avoid infection by **toxoplasmosis** (*Toxoplasma gondii*), a **protozoan,** acquired by humans from contact with the feces of infected cats or birds or from the ingestion of raw or partially cooked meat, as well as unwashed raw fruits and vegetables (Dalgic, 2008). This infection is discussed in conjunction with TORCH viral infections because the protozoan acts on the cells' RNA and DNA in the same manner as viruses. Likewise, antibodies are developed following acute infections.

A pregnant woman can acquire toxoplasmosis at any stage of pregnancy and can subsequently transmit the virus to her unborn child. However, the protozoan usually remains dormant in adults, except in people with weak immune systems such as those with HIV/AIDS and fetuses with very immature immune responses (Dalgic, 2008). There also appears to be a genetic susceptibility to toxoplasmosis. Maternal infections during either the first or second trimester appear to be most commonly associated with harmful introduction of disease-causing agents that cross the placenta (**transplacental**). This occurs when the agents cross from the maternal side of the placenta to the fetal side, infecting the developing fetus. Unlike other infections that appear to be more dangerous in a very young fetus, toxoplasmosis appears to be most dangerous to a fetus at 36 weeks of gestation, at which point the transmission rate is between 60 percent and 80 percent, as opposed to 1 percent at less than

6 weeks of gestation, a rate of risk that gradually increases throughout pregnancy (Dalgic).

Prevention of toxoplasmosis can be accomplished by educating women of child-bearing age to avoid the ingestion of raw or undercooked meat, changing a cat's litter box, or gardening without gloves. It is also important to recognize that, in rare instances, untreated maternal infections can affect subsequent pregnancies and result in fetal infections and an increased incidence of *in utero* fetal death. Prenatal diagnosis is possible with amniocentesis.

Fetal effects of congenitally acquired toxoplasmosis often include the classic triad of hydrocephaly, cerebral calcification, and **chorioretinitis** (inflammation of the retina and blood vessels that supply the retina with nutrition), which results in visual impairment. Other features commonly associated with congenital toxoplasmosis include microcephaly, deafness, seizures, **encephalitis,** enlargement of the spleen and liver, anemia, jaundice, intellectual disabilities, and cerebral palsy. The infection itself may not always be apparent at birth, and frequently the onset of symptoms is delayed for several months. Treatment of an infected mother may include drug therapy, but most drugs are not effective in treating an infected infant. During a period after birth, antibiotic treatment can reduce parasite damage; however, the window of opportunity is limited by the natural life-cycle transformation of the parasite after which it cannot be penetrated by drugs (Dalgic, 2008). Experimental prenatal treatment of mothers with antiparasitic drugs shows promise of interrupting the disease progression, but the results are not conclusive. Although drugs may be useful in destroying the harmful protozoa, damage already done to the infected infant cannot be reversed.

The prognosis for infants born with congenital toxoplasmosis infection is poor, but many infants who received antibiotic therapy shortly after birth and continued receiving it for 12 months have shown favorable outcomes (McLeod et al., 2006). Although not all children did well with the treatment, the results have shown the importance of diagnosing and treating congenital toxoplasmosis early. Still, toxoplasmosis can have devastating consequences, as many infants die in the first few days of life, and as many as 85 percent of survivors suffer severe intellectual, motor, and sensory disabilities. Children born with toxoplasmosis require long-term care including ongoing assessment for detection of developmental problems and initiation of early intervention programs.

Rubella, also known as *German measles*, generally causes minor illness in otherwise healthy children but is much more of a problem for a pregnant woman. This viral infection has been preventable by immunization since 1969. After an outbreak in the 1990s, the Measles & Rubella Initiative set a goal of eradicating the disease through vaccinations. Consequently, there has been a 74 percent drop in measles-related deaths worldwide between 2000 and 2010. No case of rubella or rubella syndrome has been reported in the United States since 2009 (UNICEF, 2012).

A woman may be susceptible to rubella if she has not previously contracted rubella or has failed to develop sufficient antibodies due to inadequate immunization. An exposed, pregnant woman may pass the infection to her fetus through the placenta. Fetal effects are thought to be the most devastating when the infection occurs during the first trimester, at which time the virus attacks the developing organs and tissues of the embryo; however, evidence suggests that rubella transmitted during the 4th and 5th months of pregnancy also results in fetal infections and significant fetal effects. In the first trimester, a woman who becomes infected has an 80 percent chance of passing the virus to her fetus.

Stillbirth is a common outcome of congenital rubella infection. Other common fetal effects include microcephaly, cataract formation, significant cardiac anomalies, and deafness. Many infants born with congenital infection also show intrauterine growth retardation. Rubella is a progressive disease, and not all the symptoms are present at birth, making it difficult to confirm a diagnosis in the first 3 months. Mortality rates are as high as 80 percent for infants born with congenital rubella syndrome, often due to severe intrauterine growth retardation, microcephaly, and other symptoms of central nervous system disease.

Although as many as 50 percent of infants born with congenital rubella have no apparent symptoms at birth, as these children age, abnormalities begin to manifest, and by the age of 5, most will show effects of the disease (Duszak, 2009). The effects most frequently seen include hearing loss, intellectual disabilities, cardiovascular defects, visual defects, insulin-dependent diabetes, thyroid dysfunction, damage to the central nervous system, and panencephalitis. Consequently, congenital rubella should be viewed as a chronic disease (Duszak, 2009). Other disabilities in childhood associated with congenital rubella include autism, social–emotional disabilities, impulsivity, hyperactivity, and learning disabilities. The long-term outlook for children with congenital rubella is serious, often including multiple disabilities requiring intensive intervention.

Of concern is the finding that infants with no obvious effects at birth can shed large amounts of active virus for up to 18 months, infecting others without caregivers being aware of the condition. Shedding occurs through the infant's urine, stool, and saliva. Individuals coming into contact with shedding infants need to be aware of the infection in order to take appropriate personal precautions to prevent the spread of active virus. Health-care professionals and caregivers who are not adequately immunized or who have not had a previous rubella infection should refrain from contact with an infant with rubella syndrome. Even though rubella has been almost entirely eradicated through early childhood vaccinations, media reports of possible effects of the MMR (measles, mumps, and rubella) immunization have led to a decline in these immunizations (Thomas, Salmon, & King, 1998). This decline will almost certainly lead to an increase in the number of cases of congenital rubella. Individuals in situations in which exposure may occur (e.g., day-care settings or classrooms) should establish whether they have adequate immunity. This can be done through laboratory testing prior to involvement.

For a child with congenital rubella syndrome, treatment recommendations include the following:

1. A neonate born with rubella needs to be isolated from contact with other infants as well as nonimmunized children and adults for up to a year.

2. Assessment of the physical and developmental needs of the affected infant is necessary so appropriate early intervention can be planned.

3. Special attention must be paid to any associated defects, especially cardiac, that place infected infants at a high risk for secondary infections.

4. Attention to nutrition should be vigilant because poor feeding can lead to failure to thrive.

5. Early eye and ear examinations should be performed to determine visual and hearing needs.

6. Referrals to community agencies that provide services for infants with significant disabilities are almost always necessary.

Cytomegalic inclusion virus is the most common congenital viral infection. Approximately 80 percent of adults have antibodies in their blood for human **cytomegalic inclusion viral infection (CMV),** although the causative infection may have produced no noticeable symptoms. The virus is most dangerous when acquired by a woman just prior to pregnancy or during pregnancy; approximately 27,000 new CMV infections in pregnant women occur each year in the United States (Colugnati, Staras, Dollard, & Cannon, 2007). Some of the approximately 0.7 percent of infants born with CMV will have CMV-specific symptoms at birth, and others who were asymptomatic at birth will develop permanent symptoms later in infancy (Dollard, Grosse, & Ross, 2007). Of those who show CMV symptoms at birth, 40 percent to 60 percent, or approximately 8,000, will have permanent abnormalities resulting from CMV (Adler, Nigro, & Pereira, 2007).

This medium-size virus is one of the four herpes viruses seen in humans; the three others are herpes simplex, Varicella-Zoster (chicken pox), and Epstein-Barr. A pregnant woman who becomes infected with CMV through exposure to body fluids or who experiences a reactivation of a past CMV infection can transmit the virus to her unborn child. The risk of transmission is greatest early in gestation. Of the women who become infected during pregnancy, approximately half pass the virus on to their fetuses, and approximately half of those fetuses infected will have symptoms at birth (Adler et al., 2007). Although much more rare, women who have acquired the virus up to 6 months prior to conception may also pass on the infection to the fetus (Adler et al.). Such transmission can have serious consequences, including brain damage. Prevention of CMV infections is a primary goal of research, although no effective prevention or treatment has been established to date; however, research on a vaccination for women to protect fetal exposure is promising (Adler et al.). Those previously uninfected pregnant women who work in childcare settings are at highest risk and should practice hygienic hand washing and other precautions related to exposure to body fluids (Adler et al.).

Prenatal diagnosis of fetal CMV can be accomplished through ultrasound or amniocentesis. Research is currently being conducted on methods to improve the outcome for fetuses through medical treatment of the placenta. One strong hypothesis about how the disease affects fetuses is that the abnormalities related to congenital CMV infection may be directly related to infection of the placenta by the CMV virus (Adler et al., 2007). Damaged by the virus, the placenta's inability to adequately provide oxygen and nutrition to a fetus leads to Intrauterine Growth Retardation (IUGR), which in turn leads to the symptoms described here. If treatment of the placenta can prevent the deprivation of oxygen and nutrients, the symptoms of CMV might be prevented.

The most common symptom of CMV infection is sensorineural hearing loss (Dollard et al., 2007). Other specific congenital anomalies that have been noted in neonates born with congenital CMV infections include microcephaly, deafness, chorioretinitis, optic atrophy, enlarged liver and spleen, platelet destruction, calcifications in solid organs (such as the liver) and the brain, seizures, Dandy-Walker malformations (cystic formations that replace the solid structure of the brain), intrauterine growth retardation, congenital heart defects, and abdominal wall defects. Late onset CMV symptoms tend to be related to less severe morbidity, although the differences are not well studied (Dollard et al.). Neonatal and infant death related to CMV is estimated to be from less than 5 percent to 10 percent of those who are symptomatic at birth.

Current medical treatment for asymptomatic infants is limited. Generally, care is supportive and limited to treating the symptoms presented by an individual infant. **Antiviral** drugs may be used, especially in infants with life-threatening infection who display central nervous system symptoms. However, the adverse effects of these drugs must be carefully considered to determine whether the benefits outweigh the risks. Infants who are born with microcephaly as a result of congenital CMV infections frequently display significant developmental impairment. This finding supports the suggestion that the microcephaly is the result of intrauterine viral encephalitis. Encephalitis frequently results in brain cell death, which causes a halt in brain growth or shrinking of brain tissue.

Although infants born with congenital CMV infection shed live virus throughout their lifetimes, no specific isolation of infected infants or children is required. However, pregnant women should not care for infected children. Because nursing mothers with current infections also shed live virus through their breast milk (although this resolves once the active infection state is over), caregivers who are pregnant can also acquire an infection by handling infected breast milk. To prevent the infection of a pregnant caregiver, it is critical that she knows which adults are possibly infected and which infants and children are affected with congenital disease. Isolating the virus from a urine or saliva sample is the only way to definitively diagnosis a suspected neonatal infection.

Extensive resources may be necessary to meet the developmental needs of infants born with congenital CMV. Assessment of an infant to determine the risk for developmental delay and to identify interventions is essential before initial discharge from the hospital. Reassessment of an infected infant must be done at regular intervals, to determine whether appropriate programs are in place to meet individual and family needs. Visual screening to identify impairments is a high priority. If problems are detected, neurological assessment determines whether visual disturbances are a result of physical or cortical damage and can determine appropriate methods for early intervention.

Developmental impairments related to hearing loss also require monitoring. Children with congenital CMV at birth are more likely to have permanent disabilities, but those infants who present with **asymptomatic** congenital infection appear to be at significant increased risk for late onset hearing loss and should have their hearing tested regularly (CDC, 2010).

Physical and occupational therapy need to be established and undertaken as part of a program of providing service to the entire family unit. Support services should be provided to parents or caregivers; they also need realistic information about an infant's long-term outcome that is based on an individual evaluation.

Herpes Genital **herpes** infections are among the most common venereal diseases in the United States. Approximately 40 million people have herpes. In adults, the virus produces itching, burning, soreness, and small blisters in the genital area. The blisters burst to leave small, painful ulcers that heal within 10 to 21 days. Subsequent attacks tend to occur after sexual intercourse, after sunbathing, or when the affected person is run-down. There is no cure for herpes, and sexual activity should be avoided until the symptoms have disappeared.

Herpes simplex virus types 1 and 2 are closely related and share 50 percent of their basic genetic code. Herpes simplex type 1 is generally associated with oral lesions but can also be present at other body sites. Herpes simplex type 2 is typically associated with genital infection and, as with type 1, can also occur at other body sites. Herpes belongs to a larger group of viruses that have common features; included in this category are CMV, Varicella-Zoster (chicken pox), and Epstein-Barr virus (mononucleosis).

Both primary infections and reactivation of the dormant virus result in the shedding of live virus. This shedding is of critical importance to a pregnant woman because acquisition of the virus during pregnancy may have adverse effects on a fetus. Although transmission is rare, congenital herpes usually occurs when a woman has her first herpes episode during pregnancy; this is because she has not yet produced the disease-fighting antibodies that could help protect the baby during delivery (March of Dimes, 2008).

Although herpes can be acquired in the uterus or right after birth, neonatal infections are usually acquired during passage through an infected birth canal in a normal vaginal delivery. This makes it vital that pregnant women with a history of genital herpes and their health-care providers be certain that no lesions are visible (indicating an active infection) in the birth canal. The presence of lesions or a herpes-positive culture is an indication for delivery by cesarean section.

Women who have a primary herpes type 2 infection during pregnancy may experience more spontaneous abortions and more premature deliveries than those with reactivation of the dormant virus during pregnancy. There have been reports of this virus crossing the placenta, but such cases are rare. In most cases, affected newborns are exposed to the virus shed in the birth canal. Up to half of infants born vaginally when the mother is experiencing her first episode of genital herpes acquire the disease.

Neonates exposed to herpes infection generally do not show any identifiable symptoms at birth. The disease may then take one of three courses. The most favorable outcome occurs when neonates experience a localized disease in which small fluid-filled blisters appear, rupture, crust over, and finally heal. A second possibility is that an infant may develop an infection of the central nervous system (encephalitis). Symptoms of encephalitis may include irritability, vomiting, and the onset of seizures. It is difficult to diagnose very young children, who may also show symptoms of other disorders and then progress rapidly to herpes encephalitis or herpes meningitis (Kimberlin, 2004). A rapid progression of the disease decreases the likelihood of successful treatment. The most dangerous course of the disease, called *disseminated herpes,* affects the internal organs (i.e., liver, lungs, kidney, brain) and, if not treated, is often fatal (Kimberlin).

An estimated 50 percent of untreated neonates who acquire a herpes infection die. Of those who survive, approximately 30 percent have major neurological deficits as a result of the infection (Kimberlin). Structural damage in the brain results from viral destruction of gray and white matter. Hence, normal brain growth will be retarded, producing conditions such as hydrocephalus with frequent seizures, reduction in cortical growth with concurrent visual and hearing impairment, and intellectual disabilities.

An EEG may determine specific focal areas of brain infection in the presence of seizures. Abnormal electrical activity is associated with herpes lesions within the brain. Measuring seizure activity utilizing electroencephalography may be useful in tracking herpes lesions and determining whether the disease has advanced, especially during episodes of reactivation. Antiviral agents have been developed to treat herpes simplex infections in neonates, infants, children, and adults.

Infants who survive systemic herpes infections require developmental assessment and appropriate referrals for services prior to discharge from the hospital. Early intervention planning includes provisions for vision, hearing, and physical and occupational therapy. Caregivers need to be aware that these infants and children can shed active virus from lesions during reactivation phases and should take the appropriate steps to avoid infection. Protection includes covering the lesions so that other children and adults can avoid direct contact with the affected area. Because many children with systemic herpes also have frequent episodes of seizure activity, protective measures (e.g., head gear or removal of dangerous items) may be indicated.

Other Viral Infections   Under the "O," or "Other," category of TORCH are various diseases, many of which are common childhood illnesses, such as chicken pox and mumps. Usually these illnesses cause only temporary problems for an infant. Even when exposed *in utero,* an infant may not experience any long-term effects. However, HIV/AIDS, syphilis, and hepatitis are also among the "Other" diseases, and in almost all cases cause severe disabilities and/or death.

Chicken Pox, Mumps, Measles   Chicken pox is typically a childhood disease, but when a pregnant woman becomes infected, her unborn child is at serious risk because of the infection. **Varicella zoster** (herpes virus varicella, or VZ virus) is a member of the DNA herpes viruses, a cluster of viruses that are genetically linked to Herpes. Primary infections of varicella virus (chicken pox) produce immunity, although late reactivation of dormant virus residing in nerve cells can result in shingles (zoster) in an older child or adult. However, there is no documentation of adverse effects of reactivated virus with the presentation of shingles in a pregnant woman, fetus, or neonate. Susceptible individuals who experience prolonged contact with infected persons are at a very high risk for developing infection. Chicken pox can be prevented through vaccination.

Pregnant, nonimmune women should avoid contact with people known to be infected with chicken pox. Because the virus is so capable of invading and causing infection, most women have acquired immunity through past infection before reaching their childbearing years. Therefore, chicken pox (VZ virus) rarely occurs during pregnancy. Yet, maternal infections can occur at any point during the pregnancy of a nonimmune mother and have a significant effect on the neonate. Although rare, older children who develop infection can experience the same complications from the disease. Developmental disabilities in older children are generally related to the effects of resulting encephalitis.

The more serious neonatal effects of VZ infections result from a maternal infection early in the pregnancy and lead to congenital effects. Congenital varicella zoster syndrome can result in a condition in which the brain stops growing and shrinks; the space remaining within a child's skull becomes occupied by fluid-filled cysts. Microcephaly, chorioretinitis, cataracts, auditory nerve paralysis, and intellectual disabilities with concurrent seizures are all possible consequences. Other frequently occurring effects include limb deformities (most commonly involving one extremity), absence of fingers or toes, and eye abnormalities.

Another childhood disease that presents risks for pregnant women is mumps, a communicable virus causing swelling of one or both of the parotid glands that are located at the junction of the lower jaw and the neck. Currently, mumps is preventable through immunization with the live attenuated mumps virus vaccine, which induces antibody production and protects an individual against acute infection. Acute mumps infections are generally self-limiting, lasting 9 to 14 days, with few complications. In rare cases, the infection damages the nerves in the inner ear and can cause deafness. There do not appear to be any specific congenital malformations associated with maternal mumps. However, infants exposed to mumps infections require early hearing screening and consistent follow-up. As with other infections that may affect hearing, when hearing impairments are identified, inclusion in early intervention programs is necessary to prevent secondary delays in other areas of development.

Measles virus, also called *hard measles,* is a communicable virus, like the mumps virus, that also produces a highly contagious infection. The measles virus is typically spread by droplets of sinus fluids in the air, thus infecting susceptible individuals through the respiratory tract. The measles vaccine, introduced in 1963, has greatly reduced the incidence of epidemic outbreaks of measles in the United States. Underdeveloped countries have not enjoyed the same progress. When access to vaccines and other advances in technology are limited, these countries experience high infection rates with a significantly increased incidence of related morbidity and mortality.

As in the general population, the incidence of measles infections among pregnant women has decreased. Fetal effects from maternal measles appear to be few. Although the incidence of preterm delivery during acute maternal infections has increased, there is no reported evidence of subsequent fetal malformations. The infection rate for measles infections in infants and young children is consistent with the infection rate of the general population. Infants and children who become infected are predisposed to otitis media as a complication. Pneumonia and encephalitis can also occur and are potentially lethal in combination with the measles. A long-term effect of infection includes hearing impairment from ear infections. Viral encephalitis associated with measles can also cause visual impairment and interruption in normal brain growth.

Syphilis is a disease that can produce serious illness when contracted by either adults or children. It is generally considered a sexually transmitted disease but can be acquired by contact with infectious lesions that may be present on the mouth, skin, or other mucous membranes. The virus can also be transmitted to a fetus through transplacental passage. Like herpes, syphilis can be contracted by an infant through contact with a lesion during the birth process.

The disease is caused by a very mobile bacterium. While not identified until 1905, syphilis was known to represent a widespread health problem throughout the world for many centuries. After the discovery of penicillin in the late 1940s, primary and secondary syphilis infections decreased in the United States until 1977, when the incidence of infection began a steady increase until 1990. Since that time, the infection rate has declined among all racial and ethnic groups and in every region of the country except the Northeast. Of the newborn cases reported, a large majority could have been prevented if the mother had received adequate treatment before or during pregnancy for her own infection. Still, women and their medical providers must remain vigilant because the occurrence of syphilis among men has actually been rising since 2000.

A primary infection of syphilis consists of the development of a lesion, also called a **chancre,** at the site of the contact with an infected person. This chancre is generally painless but highly infectious. Multiple chancres may develop with a primary infection. If a primary infection is not detected and appropriately treated with penicillin, it will progress to a secondary, or disseminated, infection. The latter is a **systemic** response to the infection that can have serious effects on many organ systems, especially the kidneys and brain. Individuals treated during the secondary stage may continue to have effects from damage to organ systems that occurred during the active infection. In untreated individuals, syphilis progresses to **tertiary** disease, late syphilis, which manifests itself clinically with severe degeneration of organ systems and leads to significant disabilities.

Pregnancy has no effect on the normal course of syphilis. Pregnant women who acquire an infection require the same diagnosis and treatment course as those individuals who are not pregnant. Furthermore, untreated infection will profoundly affect the outcome of pregnancy because the syphilis bacterium is able to cross the placenta at any time. Asymptomatic infections can occur, making it more important that laboratory testing of all pregnant women take place.

In women with untreated syphilis, congenital syphilis occurs in 40 percent of infants; of these births, death occurs in 20 percent of neonates (CDC, 2010). Although a high percentage of fetuses affected with syphilis do not survive pregnancy, those infants who do are frequently affected with intrauterine growth retardation. Congenital effects from maternal syphilis generally produce significant disabilities. Central nervous system development is altered, resulting in severe intellectual disabilities, visual and hearing impairments, and, frequently, seizures. Normal bone growth is also altered, causing orthopedic malformations and aberrant tooth formation.

Neonatal effects of congenital infection generally consist of enlargement of the liver and spleen, jaundice, and swelling or destruction of the head of the femur, resulting in major orthopedic deformities. Another common finding is moist skin lesions, particularly located over the palms of the hands and the soles of the feet. These lesions are highly infectious, and caution is vital to prevent spread of the infection in a nursery population.

The degree of developmental disabilities for survivors of congenital syphilis infections depends on the gestational age of the fetus when the infection first occurred. Those infants who acquired infection during the first or second trimester of the pregnancy are at highest risk for significant neurological delays and for visual and hearing impairments. Inadequate treatment allows a congenital infection to progress toward tertiary infection, as it does in the adult. The profound developmental delays caused by this progression leave these infants and their families in need of multidisciplinary services.

The goal of treatment is to prevent both primary infections and further progression of the existing disease state. Comprehensive prenatal care allows for diagnostic testing to determine infection and aggressive treatment to prevent fetal involvement and the subsequent significant effects of congenital syphilis infections.

Hepatitis is a viral infection that produces systemic damage to the liver. It is a complex disease involving several subtypes that produce similar symptoms but have different long-term effects. Many children are without symptoms; some may proceed to having severe, overwhelming, and fatal acute infections while others suffer progressive, chronic liver failure with **cirrhosis.** A significant connection exists between hepatitis B in infancy and later development of liver cancer. In developing countries where hepatitis B is endemic, liver cancer is one of the most common forms of cancer (American Liver Foundation, 2001).

Hepatitis A virus (HAV) is generally a mild disease and has been referred to as *infectious hepatitis.* This virus is transmitted through personal contact with food handled by an infected individual. Mainly conveyed by bowel movements, the potential for spreading HAV infection greatly increases as a result of poor personal hygiene, poor sanitation, and overcrowding. Even though 125,000 to 200,000 new cases occur each year, HAV infection in children is rarely fatal though children are at risk of chronic liver disease. HAV does not become chronic and often improves without treatment.

Hepatitis B virus (HBV) is a major health problem throughout the entire world. In the United States, about 40,000 new cases occur each year, but this number has dropped by 80 percent in the last 20 years due to the widespread availability of vaccinations (CDC, 2012) Although the virus does not cross the placenta in all cases of carrier mothers, it does so 6 percent of the time. However, as many as 90 percent of exposed infants acquire the disease as they pass through the birth canal and are exposed to blood or vaginal fluids. Although potentially fatal in infancy, newborns immediately administered hepatitis B immune globulin and the HBV vaccine are effectively protected. Most chronic HBV carriers eventually die from chronic active hepatitis, cirrhosis, or primary liver cancer. The surviving affected infants can potentially transmit hepatitis virus to family members, personal contacts, and health-care providers. These include day-care providers, teachers, and other children involved in the day-care setting.

Hepatitis B virus is a DNA virus that replicates in the liver. It can infect all body fluids, including tears, gastric juices, urine, saliva, and semen. Transmission can occur through puncture wounds, blood transfusions, cuts and abrasions, and by absorption through mucous membranes such as in the mouth or vagina. Screening pregnant women to determine both acute infection and antibody status is critical. Many of those mothers infected with HBV do not have any symptoms. The Centers for Disease Control and Prevention suggests that all pregnant women have prenatal screening and absolutely recommends that women who are in risk categories be screened and followed. Women at high risk include those who:

1. Are of Asian, Pacific Island, or Alaskan Eskimo descent
2. Are Haitian or sub-Saharan African by birth

3. Have acute or chronic liver disease or a history of undiagnosed jaundice

4. Are IV drug users

5. Have personal contacts with HBV carriers

6. Have had multiple episodes of venereal disease or are prostitutes

7. Are sexual partners of hemophiliacs

8. Work in dialysis or renal transplant units

9. Work or live in an institution for persons with intellectual disabilities

10. Are health-care professionals

Laboratory testing identifies women who are carriers or in an acute phase of infection through a blood serum test that identifies a positive hepatitis B surface antigen present on the virus. Individuals with a positive antigen are tested for hepatitis B antigen. This is found only in individuals with a positive serum result, and its presence is associated with active viral replication, which indicates the most highly infective state. During this time, a pregnant mother is at the highest risk of transmitting infection to her fetus. Transmission may occur in as many as 40 percent of cases, and of those infected approximately 25 percent will die of chronic liver disease (CDC, 2012).

The hepatitis B vaccine provides active immunity against the virus and is administered at birth, 1 month, and 6 months of age. Vaccinations can dramatically reduce the incidence of vertical transmission (mother to fetus) but can also reduce the incidence of transmission by other care providers who may contract the infection by providing services. Teachers, day-care providers, health-care workers, social service agency workers, and any other individuals who may have reason to provide service to individuals or families with HBV infections need to strongly consider seeking immunization against the virus. The potential for acquiring HBV virus is significant.

Like hepatitis B, the hepatitis C (HCV) virus can develop into a chronic disease. HCV is also transmitted through bodily fluids and has similar effects on the liver as those of HBV. Unlike HAV and HBV, though, there is no vaccination for HCV. Consequently, if a person has had one type of hepatitis in the past, it is still possible to contract another form later in life. As many as 80 percent of people with HCV show no symptoms and may not even know they are infected. However, even without symptoms, a carrier can pass the virus to others. Children born to mothers with HCV can contract the virus through contact with blood or vaginal fluids, but this is a rare occurrence; only about 4 percent of infants delivered by carrier mothers contract HCV (CDC, 2012).

Human Immunodeficiency Virus/Acquired Immune Deficiency Syndrome   The disease known in our society by the familiar term AIDS is the outcome or clinical manifestation of infection by a virus called the *human immunodeficiency virus (HIV)*. Persons infected with HIV are said to be HIV positive, and in the early stages of the disease, infants are usually asymptomatic, or the symptoms are mild. As the disease progresses, the symptoms worsen. The most severe manifestation of the disease is referred to as *acquired immune deficiency syndrome*, or *AIDS*. Nearly 93 percent of all pediatric AIDS cases are caused by transmission from mother to child during pregnancy, labor and delivery, or breastfeeding. It is estimated that the transmission rate could be lowered to 5 percent if appropriate antiretroviral medications were given to pregnant mothers (WHO, 2010). Compared to adults, children have a shorter incubation period (12 months) between acquisition of HIV and transition to AIDS. In 2009, there were approximately 2.5 million cases of pediatric HIV infection in the world (WHO, 2012). While no known cases were reported before 1982, the World Health Organization now ranks HIV as the 10th leading cause of death (WHO). Though the disease has certainly had a global impact, it has disproportionately affected poor, young, minority women (Stone, 2011).

Most cases of childhood AIDS occur when the virus if transferred from a mother who is HIV positive to her child (1) through the placenta, (2) during childbirth, or (3) through breastfeeding. Although the role of the placenta in transmission of the AIDS virus is unknown, it is believed that the virus transfer occurs either late in pregnancy or during labor. However, only about one-fourth of untreated mothers who are HIV positive transmit the virus to their unborn children. The remaining cases are accounted for by infection through blood products, such as blood transfusions in hemophiliacs, or child sexual abuse. Some infants who are breastfed by women who are HIV positive contract the disease via breast milk. In a sad acknowledgement of conditions elsewhere in the world, women in developing countries are often advised that the benefits of breastfeeding outweigh the risk of infection (Homsy et al., 2010).

Currently, the HIV infection cannot be identified in the nursery population, even though infected children typically display behavioral characteristics such as irritability, inconsolability, poor feeding, and disrupted sleeping patterns that are similar to neonates who are drug exposed. Research has shown that all infants born to mothers who are HIV infected have antibodies to HIV, and there are no known cases of casual transmission of the HIV virus to caregivers in nurseries, day-care settings, or schools. While precaution in handling bodily fluids is the same as it is with children with hepatitis B or C, childcare workers need not be afraid to hug or engage in the human contact that children need.

Because of the relationship between poverty, drug use, and HIV infection, infants and children infected with HIV represent a population already removed from mainstream health care. Furthermore, social and economic factors affecting families increase the likelihood that these children will not receive optimal treatment. Many times, maternal risk behaviors continue after childbirth, reducing the likelihood that infected children will receive the necessary monitoring and interventions that would help their physical and developmental progress. Many of these children are abandoned in health-care facilities or exposed to poor sanitation and overcrowding that speed the progression of the infection. Further, the World Health Organization reported that in 2010 only 25 percent of children from low- and middle-income countries received any HIV treatment (WHO, 2010). While the life expectancy for infants and children with HIV infections continues to improve, the survival rate of children who have contracted HIV, as compared to adults, has not improved as much from new drug treatments.

HIV infection in children is classified according to the rate at which the disease is progressing. In the best case, the disease is static, and infants and children reach developmental milestones even though they tend to start behind and their rate of gain is slower than expected. When the disease is not static, it either has *plateaued* or is *subacute*. In both cases, children tend to lose previously gained abilities, although the loss is more rapid in the subacute form. In 20 percent of cases, infants begin to display symptoms in their first year of life. The life expectancy for these infants is much shorter (4 years) than for the remaining 80 percent of infected children who do not begin to have symptoms until school age or adolescence (Le Doare', Bland, & Newell, 2012). Many children with HIV infection do not reach normal milestones and often show delays in gross-motor and expressive-language skills. As the disease advances, neurologic problems often develop and lead to difficulties in school. Children with HIV often have seizures and symptoms of HIV encephalopathy. Most eventually become sicker as HIV progresses to AIDS and the immune system deteriorates, making these children more susceptible to secondary infections and other ailments. Symptoms include failure to thrive, enlarged lymph nodes, enlarged liver and spleen, enlarged heart, chronic bacterial infections, respiratory infections, diarrhea, and fevers. For unknown reasons, survival times are shorter for children infected prenatally or during the first year of life than for those who contract infection during later childhood and adulthood. *Pneumocystis carinii* pneumonia is the most common complication of the syndrome that affects survival in very young children. Although this very common bacterium is of little danger to those with intact immune systems, it can be very serious for infants and children with HIV or AIDS. The majority of children with AIDS are hospitalized frequently for and most die from pneumonia (Le Doare et al.). **Failure to thrive** is a major problem affecting infants and young children with AIDS. Lactose intolerance and subsequent diarrhea are common findings among the affected pediatric population. Oral lesions due to yeast infections often result from prolonged antibiotic therapy. These lesions are very painful and may cause oral aversion and reduce the child's ability to maintain adequate food intake to support continued health. Consistency in caregivers is important, to develop positive relationships that allow for optimum feeding practices.

Current practice for the care of infants whose mothers are either HIV positive or have AIDS is that of support and observation. These infants are usually not treated with antiviral medications unless symptoms develop. Once the disease progresses and children become HIV positive, medications are initiated in an attempt to slow the progression of the disease. The decision about when to begin treatment is significant because the HIV virus mutates so often that all currently used drugs eventually lose their potency as drug-resistant strains of the virus develop, significantly limiting treatment options (Le Doare' et al., 2012). On the other hand, treatment is most effective if begun when symptoms start to appear.

Many medical centers are experiencing an increasing number of infants being abandoned after delivery by mothers who are HIV positive and are drug abusers, as they are unable to care for their children. Nearly 9 percent of all children who are abandoned in hospitals are AIDS infected; 28 percent of children who have at least one parent who has died of AIDS enter foster care (Chipungu & Bent-Goodley, 2004). Many of these infants experience symptoms related to premature birth or other conditions, including drug addiction, that place them at increased risk for developmental disabilities along with their HIV status. When children are placed in foster care, an opportunity opens up for dealing with the problems these infants experience as a result of the progression of HIV to AIDS.

Advocacy for infants and children affected with both HIV and AIDS is the primary role for those involved with planning care for these children. Because economic disadvantage is closely associated with the prevalence of pediatric HIV, families are likely to benefit from an array of services. Often parents themselves are dealing with the grief, anxiety, and depression associated with AIDS and may have diminished energy for their children (Porter, 2002). Preventing the progression of HIV and AIDS is the goal, but providing a quality of life to those currently affected is also an important task. A multidisciplinary approach to the many problems encountered by this population is essential for establishing a systematic plan for meeting all of the physical, developmental, and emotional needs of these children. An early first step is to assess family resources and priorities. Family-centered interventions that are coordinated across many agencies should be based on a respect for family expectations and goals. "Family" might include nonnuclear members because of the illness or death of one or both parents.

The following are treatment suggestions:

1. Physical therapy for progressive hypertonicity and eventual loss of ambulation
2. Language intervention for loss of ability, especially for expressive and attentional problems
3. Psychological intervention to deal with the stress of living with a terminal illness that has strong social stigmatization
4. The support of a social worker to help the child deal with the probable loss of one or both parents
5. Continuous communication with health-care providers about the child's physical condition

Meningitis and Encephalitis

Both **Meningitis** and encephalitis are infections that involve the central nervous system with particular concentration in the brain. Although the factors causing these infections may occasionally appear to be the same, the implications for treatment depend on the infecting agent. The brain is protected by a fluid-filled sac that surrounds it and the spinal cord. Moreover, the brain matter is intertwined with blood vessels that provide blood flow for the transport of food and oxygen. In a healthy brain, pressure is maintained at a steady state, permitting normal blood flow (see Figure 8–7a).

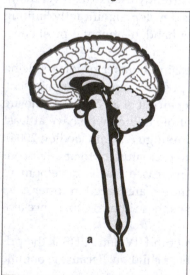

Figure 8–7 (a) Brain with Uninfected Meninges

a

Meningitis Meningitis is a condition in which infection occurs as the result of the entry of bacteria around the surface of the brain, producing inflammation of the **meninges,** the coverings that surround the brain and spinal cord (see Figure 8–7b). The meninges are made up of three membranes (i.e., dura mater, pia mater, arachnoid) that are between the skull and brain and between the vertebral column and the spinal cord. It is in this area that the cerebrospinal fluid flows over the surface of the nervous system. *Cerebrospinal fluid* is a clear, colorless, odorless fluid that resembles water and contains glucose, proteins, salts, and white blood cells. Its function is to protect the nervous system from injury by acting as a shock absorber. It also carries oxygen and nutrition to the nerve cells and takes waste

Figure 8–7 (b) Brain Showing Swollen and Infected Meninges

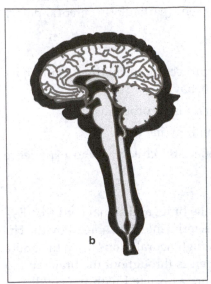

b

products away to be reabsorbed in the circulatory system. Small blood vessels that are part of the skull's lining act as the mechanism for exchange.

Meningitis does not refer to the guilty organism but to the condition that results from a bacterial or viral infection. For example, five pathogens caused more than 80 percent of the cases of bacterial meningitis in the 1970s and 1980s (Thigpen et al., 2011). With the introduction and increase of childhood vaccinations for some of these pathogens, the incidence of bacterial meningitis has significantly decreased for all age groups except children under 2 months of age.

With meningitis, swelling occurs, and some of the surrounding nerve cells degenerate. This swelling and nerve destruction cause the neurological disabilities that follow in 10 to 15 percent of acute cases of meningitis (Kim, 2010). On occasion, the infection may invade the brain matter itself through tears in the meninges. This increases the potential of permanent brain and nerve injury. Acute meningitis may produce significant symptoms in children and lead to death in 10 to 15 percent of the cases (NINDS, 2011).

Immaturity of the immune system in the very young and the compromised immune systems of children with such disabilities as head trauma, spina bifida, and sickle cell anemia place these individuals at greater risk for developing meningitis. Other factors that put children at risk include lack of sleep, secondhand smoke, poverty, close contact with people who are sick, and poor access to health care.

There are about 4,100 cases of bacterial meningitis every year, and approximately 500 of the infected individuals die from the disease (CDC, 2012). Of those who survive, many have some degree of residual effect, ranging from very minor dysfunctions to significant multiple disabilities.

The initial symptoms include sudden onset of fever, vomiting, severe headache, anorexia, increased sensitivity to light, and confusion (CDC, 2012). The diagnosis of meningitis is made through laboratory testing along with a physical examination. A **spinal tap** may reveal cloudy cerebrospinal fluid due to the increased number of white blood cells present in the fluid. Occasionally, the fluid may appear bloody because the tiny blood vessels in the skull's lining break from the increased pressure. Blood and spinal fluid cultures determine which bacterium is responsible for the infection. Powerful antibiotics that would be effective against any of the possible organisms are used until a specific organism is identified.

Survivors of acute bacterial meningitis may have long-term effects generally associated with the central nervous system. Seizures are common and may resist normal anticonvulsant therapy. The intractable nature of the seizures may be the result of specific focal areas of the brain that have been attacked by the disease. Bilateral deafness may occur as a result of pressure placed on the auditory nerve by inflammation of the meninges. Deafness may also be caused by antibiotic therapy needed to eradicate the bacteria. Hydrocephalus frequently occurs because of scar tissue formation in the subarachnoid space that permanently affects the normal fluid pathways for cerebrospinal fluid. Occasionally, brain abscesses that produce symptoms much like those of a brain tumor may develop.

Children with disabilities from meningitis require extensive services. In addition to the effects of the infection already described, many of these children suffer from hyperactivity (as well as seizures), motor involvement (particularly cerebral palsy), and intellectual disabilities.

Treatment considerations should include:

1. Environmental safety measures necessary to protect these children from injury during seizures and during periods of erratic behavior

2. Programs to deal with hearing impairments and visual problems

3. Physical therapy for children with spasticity and/or ataxia.

4. Consideration of the use of a shunt in infants and children who experience hydrocephalus

Encephalitis This disease is an inflammation of the brain and spinal cord (see Figure 8–7c) that may occur as a result of a viral or bacterial infection spread by the circulatory system or from movement of infection through neural **axons** up to the brain. The infecting agent causes inflammation as it disperses throughout the brain and to the meninges. A majority of cases of encephalitis are associated with the childhood viral diseases mentioned earlier in this chapter.

Anyone can develop encephalitis. Because it is transmitted through mosquitoes and ticks, most cases of encephalitis in the United States occur during the spring and summer. Some kinds of viruses that eventually lead to encephalitis selectively attack specific types of neurons (as in polio), while others, such as the herpes virus, establish focal areas of infection that are dispersed throughout the brain. The manner in which dispersion occurs determines the nervous system function following an infection.

Encephalitis can be diagnosed when an individual has symptoms of early onset meningitis, but a spinal tap cannot confirm the presence of bacteria. In other words, ruling out meningitis is one part of the diagnosis of encephalitis because symptoms of the two diseases are so similar. Additional diagnostic findings associated with encephalitis may be a normal white blood cell count and an elevated protein level in the spinal fluid. Early symptoms of this disease include an unsteady gait and seizures with a later onset of a decreased level of consciousness. Medical measures are initiated to prevent further deterioration of the physical condition. Viral cultures may identify agents responsible for acute encephalitis; occasionally a brain biopsy may be necessary to identify the virus producing the illness. Most individuals with viral encephalitis recover without significant long-term effects. Herpes encephalitis is an exception to this rule; all virally induced cases of herpes encephalitis can potentially lead to permanent and significant damage. Also excepted from this rule are infants who are born to virally infected mothers and who have experienced *in utero* viral encephalitis with subsequent interruption in brain growth, who will be born with severe neurological damage.

Effects of encephalitis on central nervous system function may include severe language disorders and muscle weakness or

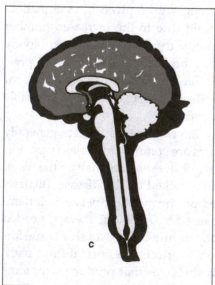

Figure 8–7 (c) Brain Affected by Encephalitis

paralysis on one side of the body. Frequently, focal seizures occur, and EEG findings are sometimes abnormal, indicating the presence of a seizure disorder. Infants and children may experience impairments in vision and hearing, especially with herpes encephalitis. Reactivation of the virus after the initial recovery from the illness may further damage the nervous system. Affected children also have an increased incidence of behavior problems and hyperactivity, requiring environmental precautions to ensure their safety. Depending on the severity of the infection, children may experience intellectual disabilities with all of the adverse affects of developmental delays.

Although neither bacterial nor viral, hookworm is a parasitic invasion that affects 740 million individuals worldwide according to the National Institute of Allergy and Infectious Diseases (2011). Once considered a disease of the tropics as well as the southeastern United States, hookworm disease is now largely controlled in this country but continues to be a major world health concern (NIAID, 2011). The vector for hookworm is soil contaminated with human feces, and it is transmitted through exposure to the skin. Parasitic hookworms attach to the intestinal lining and feed on the intestinal wall, resulting in significant blood loss. Anemia and malnutrition are the most common effects of chronic hookworm infection. Pregnant women suffering from anemia due to hookworm show a compromised fetal environment, iron deficiency, and malnutrition. Intrauterine growth retardation, low birth weight and prematurity, transplacental transmission of the hookworm, and even fetal death can result. In addition to the potential perinatal risk factors mentioned, infected infants who are not treated can also suffer anemia and malnutrition and associated physical and mental developmental problems. Researchers are working to develop a vaccination for hookworm. In the meantime, this social and health issue is one that belongs to the entire world community.

IN CONCLUSION

As children reach preschool and school age, all parents are faced with school placement decisions. These decisions are often more complicated for parents of students with special needs. In the past, most children with blindness and deafness were sent to residential schools for people who are blind or deaf. However, with recent inclusion practices, it seems likely that most children with sensory impairments will be served in general classroom settings even if these children also have other disabilities. Parents need to be aware of placement options, the implications of these options, and some effective strategies to advocate for the choices made for their children. Beginning early with low vision tools (e.g., Braille, large print text, electronic systems), social skills training, and mobility and orientation training can increase the degree of independence and social competence of children with visual impairments in an educational setting. Likewise, techniques that enhance the linguistic and social development of infants and preschoolers with deafness, such as auditory amplification, cochlear implants, use of sign language, and alternative communication methods, should begin as early as possible.

Rapid advancements in electronic and computer technologies will likely continue to open new doors to academic, domestic, and vocational opportunities for persons with visual and hearing impairments. Very young children with visual and/or hearing impairments should be introduced to computer systems. Likewise, team members will be pressed to keep pace with developments in technology that might increase independent functioning while being practical and cost-effective for families.

Procedures for treating many once-untreatable causes of visual and hearing impairment will continue to evolve. Like other forms of early intervention, the cost of remediating loss of vision and hearing may be far less than the costs of long-term specialized intervention for children and families.

Each of the infections described in this chapter may have effects ranging from mild to devastating. The most effective way of decreasing the incidence of infections and their effects on children is through education. Many infections may be prevented by exercising a more cautious approach to living. We can now say that rubella, syphilis, and HIV very rarely affect children born in industrialized countries, but other harmful infections may always be with us, leaving much work to be accomplished in research, advocacy, and education.

STUDY GUIDE QUESTIONS

1. What are the three components of the auditory mechanism and their respective functions?
2. When listening for the mother's voice, is a child attending to pitch or to frequency?
3. List the symptoms of otitis media and describe treatment for the infection.
4. What is the difference between a conductive hearing loss and a sensorineural hearing loss? What are common causes of each type of hearing loss?
5. What developmental domains are most affected by loss of hearing?
6. Name some sign language systems. Which is the most commonly used approach? Explain the debate in favor of and opposed to using manual sign.
7. Is it true that the use of a hearing aid solves all of the problems for an infant with a hearing impairment or deafness? Explain.
8. Explain how the needs of very young children with hearing losses pose challenges different from those associated with other kinds of disabilities.
9. Distinguish between blindness and low vision.
10. Trace how the visual system processes an image to the point that a person understands it.
11. Describe three refractive errors in vision.
12. What are cortical visual impairments?
13. Name and explain two visual errors caused by a disruption in muscle coordination of the eyes.
14. What is likely to happen if cataracts are left untreated in infants?
15. What are the developmental differences between congenital and adventitious blindness?

16. What might be included in programs specifically designed for infants and toddlers with visual impairments? What factors should be considered in selecting appropriate orientation and mobility adaptations?

17. In what ways are children who are visually impaired disproportionately faced with a lifetime of "disadvantage"? How can educators intervene to limit this disadvantage?

18. Define *biological agent*. How do these agents cause damage to human cells? How do they travel throughout the human body?

19. When do pathogenic bacterial infections occur? What circumstances may affect an infant's outcome?

20. Explain the relationship between socioeconomic status, low birth weight, and infection.

21. What are viruses, and how do they differ from bacteria? How has prevention of viral diseases been accomplished?

22. What are the TORCH diseases? Briefly describe the cause, course, symptoms, and outcomes of each.

23. Explain what is meant by "shedding" a live virus. How does shedding occur?

24. List characteristics of women who may be at high risk for contracting hepatitis B virus. Which individuals should most strongly consider immunization against this virus?

25. Why might a child with congenital HIV be found in an early childhood special education setting?

26. Explain the differential causes, courses, symptoms, and outcomes of meningitis and encephalitis. What is the difference between viral meningitis and bacterial meningitis?

9 Discretionary Programs for Infants and Toddlers with Special Needs

Estee Aiken

Early intervention is a term often used to describe special services for very young children, specifically from birth through age 2. However, this simple definition does not do enough to convey the many implications of legally defined services to infants and toddlers. Early intervention is focused on informing and empowering families to access resources and advocate for their children with developmental delays. Goals in education, health care, and social services are incorporated into comprehensive plans for young children and their families. Professionals and parents work in partnership to help these children develop knowledge and skills, with parents often carrying out the planned intervention programs at home. The law also requires intervention services to take place in children's "natural environments," which are defined as "settings that are natural or normal for the children's age peers who have no disabilities" (Wrightslaw, 2012).

In 1986, Congress included early intervention, Part C, in the Individuals with Disabilities Education Act legislation with the purpose of reducing educational costs and improving outcomes for infants and toddlers with special needs by:

- Enhancing children's development
- Minimizing the need for special education services in the future
- Maximizing children's independence
- Enhancing the capacity of families to meet the special needs of their infants and toddlers with disabilities
- Enhancing the capacity of state and local agencies and service providers to identify, evaluate, and meet the needs of all children, particularly minority, low-income, inner-city, and rural children as well as infants and toddlers in foster care

In 2009–2010, the National Early Intervention Longitudinal Study (NEILS) found that infants and toddlers who participated in Part C services showed increased social, motor, and cognitive function, acquired age-appropriate skills, and had the negative impacts of their disabilities reduced (Goode, Diefendorf, & Colgan, 2012). The findings also indicated that 71 percent to 76 percent of the children in Part C demonstrated greater than expected growth in:

- Social relationships with other children and adults
- Knowledge and skills in thinking, reasoning, and problem solving, and early literacy and math skills
- Increased independence in feeding, dressing, self-care, and following health and safety rules
- The crucial role played by the family in optimizing their child's development is recognized and planned for in Part C services. The NEILS report found that 90 percent of families felt that Part C services improved their ability to help their children, 98 percent were confident in caring for their children's basic needs, and 96 percent felt they knew how to help their children learn and develop. It was further reported that 95 percent of families felt that early intervention professionals helped them feel positive about their children's futures, and 96 percent felt they had become better at advocating for the services their children needed. Early intervention also helped parents more effectively recognize, respond to, and support their children's communication attempts, which improved their abilities to communicate effectively (Goode et al., 2011). These improved outcomes have decreased the number of students needing continued special education supports and have helped to reduce educational costs, which were both goals of the legislation (Goode et al., 2011).
- Early intervention for infants and toddlers differs from traditional educational services in several ways; these are important for understanding current practice. First, it is sometimes difficult to diagnose a disability or determine cognitive and language abilities in very young children since they meet developmental milestones at different rates, and children may naturally catch up in the areas showing delays by the time they reach school age. For example, many children are saying their first words by 18 months, but some may be 3 years old before

they speak words. Assessment of cognitive abilities and language sometimes does not accurately predict a child's later performance. Even physical problems may not show up before 6 months of age because time must pass before primitive reflexes disappear. In cases where a specific diagnosis is not possible, a very young child may be identified as developmentally delayed, which indicates a need for special services but ensures that the child is not incorrectly labeled or categorized. Children with developmental delays make up a majority of those served in early intervention programs and generally enter early intervention after 21 months of age (U.S. Department of Education, 2010). On the other hand, those children diagnosed before 12 months of age tended to have complicated and sometimes more severe physical and health issues. The latter made up 12 percent of the children served in early intervention in 2007. A sizable number, 37 percent, had a history of care in a neonatal intensive care unit after birth, and half of those stayed for more than a month (Hebbeler et al., 2001). Of children in early intervention, 26 percent took prescription medication for a chronic condition and 16 percent used a medical device such as a respirator, breathing monitor, or nebulizer. Behavioral challenges, such as failing to pay attention, being easily startled, being very excitable, having sleep problems, and being aggressive with other children, were found in 10 percent to 40 percent of children in early intervention (Hebbeler et al.).

A second aspect of early intervention that differs significantly from services to older children is that the primary responsibility for the care of infants and toddlers usually falls to parents or a consistent caregiver selected by parents. Even a child in commercial day care usually has contact with only a small number of people every day in a familiar and secure environment. It is only reasonable to expect these same people to carry out special interventions and to incorporate them into the **natural routines** of daily life. Parents and caregivers are the mediators of treatment or instruction designed by others. Consequently, it is essential that parents are provided an array of supports including information about the disability, information about services and resources, strategies for intervention, financial assistance, and social and emotional supports (McWilliam & Scott, 2001).

In addition, because so many basic skills are established in the earliest stages of development, intervention may have to address a multitude of domains. Movement, language, self-care, and cognition may be affected in different ways by the same disability and certainly in different ways across different disabilities, requiring assistance from a number of specialists. A child with cerebral palsy, for example, may not learn to sit up, hold a spoon, form words, or put together a simple puzzle without specific accommodations, instruction, or treatment. In many cases, children with disabilities who are identified before age 3 have extensive medical needs as well. Consequently, a team of professionals may be required, to consult with parents or provide treatment to the child. Often these individuals represent different disciplines and even different agencies, so coordinating their services becomes complex. Among the support services that may be provided are speech pathology, audiology, psychological services, physical and occupational therapy, recreation, social work, counseling, medical services, and services from registered dieticians, orientation and mobility specialists, and vision specialists including ophthalmologists and optometrists (Federal Register, 2011).

Finally, very young children are vulnerable to the influence of their surrounding environment. For example, an impoverished home may mean that a child's nutrition is at risk; a lack of transportation may mean that appointments with a therapist are missed; exhausted parents may mean an increased likelihood of abuse or neglect; and overly protective parents may keep children from necessary experiences or from reasonable expectations. A child's prognosis depends greatly on the ability of the parent or parents to provide for and cope with the child's special needs. To best benefit the child, it is critical to assess each family's health and resources and to provide support for their needs.

Thus, early intervention must be designed to be family centered, must carefully coordinate services, and must encourage family empowerment in all aspects of decision making and delivery of services. A child's disability may be defined noncategorically, or a child's disabilities may be more severe and complex and require intensive therapy from a variety of professionals. Moreover, a family's needs may be just as important as the child's. All of these considerations have been critical in shaping the framework of public programs for serving very young children with disabilities.

The Individuals with Disabilities Education Improvement Act (IDEIA): Public Law 108-446

The Individuals with Disabilities Education Improvement Act (IDEIA), Public Law 108-446, was most recently reauthorized in 2004. Originally passed as Public Law 94-142 in 1975 and known for many years as the Individuals with Disabilities Education Act (IDEA), this federal law for educating students with disabilities has evolved through several revisions. The law's passage provided landmark legislation that ensured the free and appropriate education of all children with disabilities. Its impact was primarily on school age children, but the law contained language and funding that encouraged states to further develop services for preschool age children with disabilities. The original Public Law 94-142 linked services to young children with disabilities to public education and brought the field of early childhood special education into public awareness.

Even in its first stages, IDEA recognized the importance of early intervention. IDEA was intended to apply to individuals aged 3 to 21, unless an individual state's law did not allow services to children starting as young as age 3. Financial incentives were built into IDEA to encourage the provision of services to preschoolers; several states took advantage of these incentives.

In 1986, Congress amended IDEA, reauthorizing it under Public Law 99-457. In an action that was surprising to many in early childhood education, P.L. 99-457 extended all of its mandated rights and protections to preschoolers and encouraged states to serve children from birth through age 2 who had disabilities. When the newly revised IDEA was put in place in 1986, fewer than half of the states had mandates for the education of preschoolers with disabilities, but soon all states established such mandates. Almost 400,000 preschool children were served through IDEA programs and funding in the 1990–1991 school year. By IDEA's 25th anniversary in the 2000–2001 school year, over 230,000 infants and toddlers under age 3 were receiving early intervention with the assistance of federal funds, and almost 600,000 children ages 3 to 5 were receiving services (Danaher et al., 2003). With increased efforts to identify children at early ages and the improvement and expansion of services, the number of children receiving intervention continues to increase. In the 2011 child count, it was reported that almost 337,000 infants and toddlers were receiving services (NECTAC, 2012).

At the same time, intensive efforts were initiated to prepare personnel to work with the newborn to 2-year-old population. The unusual degree of caregiver and professional collaboration required meant that training had to be extended to fields beyond special education and early childhood to include mental health, medicine, and the various therapies. In September 2011, the final regulations for early intervention programs under Part C were released, clarifying what constitutes "qualified personnel" and ensuring that related services are provided by competent and skilled individuals (CEC, 2011). The provisions of IDEA did much to encourage the collaboration of parents and community agencies, including schools, in serving infants and toddlers with disabilities. The law made clear that services were the responsibility of an interagency system and resources should be shared. Its emphasis was on delivery of services within the context of the family and in natural settings, which was intended to encourage community-based, culturally sensitive, and family-driven services. In addition, the revised law provided an incentive for states to address the early intervention needs of children who were born at risk for developing later disabilities and delays. Table 9–1 summarizes the landmark legislation on early intervention.

Table 9–1 Landmarks in Early Intervention Services

Year	Description of Legislation
1934	Social Security Act authorized the Maternal and Child Health Bureau with specific attention to "crippled children."
1965	Project Head Start was established to serve 3- and 4-year-olds living in poverty.
1968	Handicapped Children's Early Education Program was established to fund model preschool programs for children with disabilities.
1972	Economic Opportunity Act required Head Start to reserve 10 percent of its enrollment for children with disabilities.
1975	Public Law 94-142, The Education for All Handicapped Children Act, provided funding incentives for programs serving 3- to 5-year-old preschoolers with disabilities.
1986	Public Law 99-457 amended Public Law 94-142 to require services to children age 3 to 5 with disabilities and to provide incentives for programs serving infants and toddlers who were developmentally delayed or at risk of developmental delay. This legislation mandated service coordination.
1990	Head Start Expansion and Quality Improvement Act reauthorized and expanded Head Start programs through 1994.
1997	Public Law 105-17, the 1997 amendments to IDEA, renewed early intervention efforts.
2004	Public Law 108-446, titled the Individuals with Disabilities Education Improvement Act, IDEIA, aligned the law with the No Child Left Behind Act, reduced paperwork requirements, and provided for greater flexibility of funding services for at-risk students.
2011	Final Regulations for Part C were released.

Through its evolution, IDEIA became increasingly developmentally friendly, and early childhood personnel development became closely tied to federally funded demonstration or university programs. Early on, these programs developed early childhood personnel training based on effective instructional procedures for children with severe disabilities (whose needs were similar to those of very young children with disabilities). Several areas of consensus emerged. First, the instructional method of choice in special education was systemic instruction; a structured protocol for intervention was developing. Second, young children at risk for academic failure were also targeted by state programs. Third, the roles of early childhood personnel went beyond instruction and included establishing relationships with families, teaming with other disciplines, and providing services in environments other than classrooms. Finally, attention was being given to younger and younger children; preschool special education was being extended to infants and toddlers.

The multiple factors affecting infants and toddlers with disabilities and their families played a large part in how the IDEIA legislation governing **discretionary programs** for infants and toddlers differs from the laws dealing with preschoolers from ages 3 to 5. The specific mechanisms included in IDEIA that foster successful early intervention include the possibility of noncategorical eligibility, team development of an **individualized family service plan (IFSP),** and designation of a **service coordinator.**

The 1997 revisions placed an emphasis on providing treatment and appropriate education to infants and toddlers in their natural environments. The importance of educating young children with disabilities in settings with nondisabled children was also addressed. For most families, 94 percent in 2010 (NECTAC, 2012), this has meant bringing services to their homes or to a child's day-care setting. For those children with need for more intensive therapies or specialized equipment, justification could be made to provide services in center-based programs for children with disabilities. It also meant that care must be given in planning transition of 3-year-olds into preschool settings. The IDEIA of 2004 revised transition requirements, including provisions related to notification of the local educational agency (LEA) and state educational agency (SEA), timelines, an opt-out policy, a transition conference, and the requirement of an interagency transition plan (Federal Register, 2011). It continues to support the following best practices in early childhood special education and early intervention:

1. State-of-the-art models of appropriate programs and services for young children with disabilities (birth to 5 years) and their families

2. IFSPs to identify and meet the unique needs of each infant and toddler with a disability and of the child's family

3. Effective assessment and teaching practices and related instructional materials for young children and their families

4. National network of professionals dedicated to improving early intervention and preschool education at the state and local levels

5. Collaboration with other federal, state, and local agencies to avoid duplication of efforts in providing early intervention and preschool education

Specific regulations for implementing the IDEIA, Part C, formally describe the appropriate delivery of services for all infants and toddlers who are disabled or at risk for disability and assure the due process rights of these children and their families.

IDEIA Part C Regulations

The federal program for infants and toddlers with disabilities assists states in providing comprehensive programs of early intervention for infants and toddlers with disabilities, ages birth through 2 years, and for their families (NECTAC, 2006). Each participating state must ensure that early intervention will be available to every eligible child and his or her family. The governor of each state designates a lead agency to operate the program and appoints an advisory **Interagency Coordinating Council (ICC)**.

Currently, all states participate, receiving annual funding based on the census figures for the number of children from birth through age 2 in their general populations (NECTAC, 2006). Lead agencies vary by state, as do specific definitions of who is eligible for services. By the end of 2009, almost 343,000 infants and toddlers (about 3 percent of children birth through age 2 in the United States) were directly served under Part C (NECTAC, 2012).

The purpose of Part C of IDEIA is to develop a system that provides early intervention services to children experiencing developmental delays and to encourage states to expand opportunities for children less than 3 years of age who would be at risk of having substantial developmental delay if they did not receive early intervention services. As mentioned earlier, serving these children early has the potential to save society a great deal in resources later on by mitigating more serious problems and to improve the human potential of children at risk. Even though states may provide more expansive services, services must be provided, at a minimum, to infants and toddlers in all states who are under 3 years of age and who need early intervention for one of two reasons: They display a delay in one or more areas of development or there is a diagnosis of a physical or mental condition that has a high probability of resulting in developmental delay. Services must be family directed, and special services such as evaluation, assessment, and planning take place only if a family approves and participates. In addition, the services provided must be based on scientifically based research to the extent that it is practical.

Several factors may influence the extent to which families agree to participate in the special services available. These factors include the nature of a family's concerns about the child, their level of stress and degree of support, family members' beliefs and values, and their education level, prior experience with children, and rapport with those who provide the services. For example, a family may be too emotionally involved in dealing with the child's diagnosis to make long-term plans. Other families may be so overwhelmed by immediate day-to-day survival that they cannot attend to other issues. On the other hand, some families are eager to become involved. It is incumbent upon the service providers to respect the central, active role families play in the care of their child with special needs.

Family-Centered Early Intervention

Ruth Jenkinson/DK Images

Historically, the approach to early intervention was focused on the deficits of the child, and service providers determined the goals of the intervention plan. Parents were encouraged to participate in the activities that professionals planned, and very little thought was given to the impact that families have on their children. Family-centered services have evolved from this original concept to acknowledge the importance of sensitivity to the culture and values of the individual family members, to respect the family's ecology, and to focus on family outcomes in addition to the child outcomes (NECTAC, 2012). In 2007, a national work group supported by the National Early Childhood Technical Assistance Center (NECTAC) was formed to develop a mission statement and principles to support the system of family-centered services. This group identified seven key principles:

- Infants and toddlers learn best through everyday experiences and interactions with familiar people in familiar contexts.

- All families, with the necessary supports and resources, can enhance their children's learning and development.

- The primary role of an early intervention service provider is to work with and support the family members and caregivers in children's lives.

- The early intervention process, from initial contacts through transition out of early intervention services, must be dynamic and individualized to reflect the child's and family members' preferences, learning styles, and cultural beliefs.

- IFSP outcomes must be functional and based on children's and families' needs and family-identified priorities.

- A primary provider, who represents and receives team and community support, is the most appropriate person for addressing the family's priorities, needs, and interests.

- Interventions for young children and family members must be based on explicit principles, validated practices, best available research, and relevant laws and regulations (NECTAC, 2007).

Several elements of the IDEIA, Part C, support a family-centered approach; service coordination and the IFSP are two of the most critical.

Service Coordination

Imagine the family of a child with significant disabilities receiving early intervention services from three different agencies. There is likely to be confusion and frustration about the scheduling of appointments, payment for services, and overlapping information and recommendations for home intervention. The first attempt by Congress to create an early intervention model that was comprehensive also created the need for a new method of managing the various agencies involved in service delivery for infants and toddlers with special needs. Thus a *case manager* role was designated in the IDEIA, and the person assigned that role would assume the responsibility of overseeing the delivery of services to which children and their families are entitled. The law stated that the professional most relevant to the needs of a child and family should serve as that family's case manager. For example, a physical therapist would be the most appropriate case manager for a child with muscular dystrophy, and a speech therapist should serve as the case manager for a child with a cleft lip and palate. Several concerns arose simultaneously with the requirement to provide case managers. Educators and families asked, Who selects the case manager—the family or the agency? Can families serve as their own case manager? How many children should a case manager serve? What are the qualifications of a case manager? Partly as a result of the ensuing debate over such questions, the terminology in the law was changed, so that the case manager became the service coordinator, which reflected a less clinical and more pragmatic approach to delivery of services

When choosing a service coordinator, it is important to find the best match for each family. Several questions should be asked to help determine who would best fit a particular family. The Kentucky Early Intervention Program (2008) suggests teams ask the following questions:

- Is there a person on the team who is close to the family and can respond to its needs most quickly?
- Who has a broad knowledge of the child and family's issues and concerns?
- Who will be working with the family most frequently at this time?
- Who shares the family's culture or communication style?
- Who is knowledgeable about the agency system and plans to stay in the system and in the area for some time?

In the 2011 IDEIA, Part C, regulations, the responsibilities of the service coordinator were clarified. Each infant or toddler with a disability must be provided with a service coordinator who is responsible for coordinating all services across agency lines, serving as the single point of contact, carrying out the seven major components of program delivery, and adhering to federal and state laws. The main responsibilities of a service coordinator are to:

1. Coordinate the evaluations and assessments of the child
2. Facilitate the development, review, and evaluation of individual family service plans
3. Assist families in identifying available service providers
4. Coordinate and monitor the delivery of early intervention services

5. Inform families of their rights, procedural safeguards, and related resources

6. Coordinate the funding sources for early intervention services

7. Facilitate the development of **a transition plan** for moving the child to the next environment

It is not a service coordinator's responsibility to directly provide all services; rather, that person ensures families have access to any needed services. In fact, the primary goal of service coordinators is to foster family empowerment. Strengthening a family's abilities to coordinate their own services promotes human development and helps build the overall capacity of individuals, families, and communities. Moreover, what the families gain from the service coordinator ensures that skills they learn in the family-centric model in early intervention can transfer to a child-centric model in preschool education and beyond.

Service coordinators can empower families by improving their capacity to master a broad range of skills, providing information to increase their understanding of their child's disability, offering choices and encouraging families to make their own decisions about types of services, and showing parents how to access information or perform certain intervention strategies independently. Service coordinators can also improve liaisons and linkages that mobilize social supports within a family's community. Both **primary social supports** (i.e., close family, friends, and neighbors) and **secondary social supports** (e.g., health-care providers, educators, and therapists) can provide a network to support families as caregivers of a child with special needs. Because service coordinators themselves must be careful to honor the privacy of families, they can work to protect families from other sources of unwarranted intrusion. Being careful to avoid paternalism, service coordinators can serve as advocates for family rights. Finally, service coordinators may be able to minimize stress by making essential resources available in a manner that eliminates or reduces unnecessary work or anxiety.

Much has been written about the personal characteristics of a successful service coordinator. Some core traits are a positive proactive attitude, high frustration level, sense of humor, high tolerance to uncertainty, ability to see and celebrate the smallest sign of change, and a strong personal support system.

Service coordinators are most effective when they view each family individually rather than trying to fit all families into a "systems box." Any prior expectations of families are likely to limit relationships with at least some families. Service coordinators must be able to do the following, at a minimum, to support families: assign no blame, no matter what; acknowledge that parents are trying; treat families as the experts on their needs; look at the world from the parents' perspective; set priorities based on family desires; and be sensitive to cultural, environmental, racial, religious, and sexual orientation differences. Service coordinators play a critical role in making sure families are fully informed and understand the procedural safeguards that are assured them in the IFSP process. The service coordinator ensures that families are clear on their options at each step as they develop the IFSP. They can ensure this by:

• Avoiding "legalese" and using family friendly language

• Providing materials written at the family's reading level and in their native language

Estee Aiken

- Breaking lengthy and complex information into brief parts that are relevant to what is being addressed
- Sharing information through face-to-face contact, or providing helpful audio or videotaped materials if needed
- Ensuring that translated materials are accurate and respectfully depict diversity
- Formatting materials to be appealing, attractive, and useful to families
- Making information available in many locations and from different service providers

Interagency Services

When agencies need to coordinate their services to meet the needs of a particular child, it is the lead agency's responsibility to initiate a formal agreement regarding who delivers and pays for early intervention services. Part C funds were not intended to supplant services and funding already provided by public agencies, even though the latter might be contracted to provide services to children identified under Part C. For example, if an interagency agreement is formed with the Public Health Department, which already provides audiological assessment and treatment to the community, then that department, not the lead agency for early intervention, is responsible for the cost of such services.

Ideally, depending on the services provided and the individual situations of families served, various financial arrangements can be made to ensure that no families are denied services for which they are eligible. Sources include local, state, and federal funding through agencies providing services, family cost sharing using a sliding scale, private insurance, and Medicaid. The way in which state and local agencies choose to use these and other state and local services varies according to availability and the priorities of ICCs. Unfortunately, finding agencies that are sufficiently funded to serve all eligible families has remained challenging because of economic realities, limited charitable giving, and restrictive government budgets.

Eligible Children

Unlike the IDEIA regulations for older children, each state is given the responsibility of determining specific eligibility guidelines for early intervention services. In addition to serving children with developmental delays, Congress has permitted and encouraged states to serve children who are at risk of developing a delay later in childhood, defined by the IDEIA as "an individual under 3 years of age who would be at risk of experiencing a substantial developmental delay if early intervention services were not provided" (IDEIA, Section 632[1]). Infants and toddlers with developmental delays and those who are **at risk** must be served by those states receiving Part C funding.

Developmental Delay

Infants and toddlers whose progress in reaching developmental benchmarks is delayed or who have fallen significantly below the age-related norms (25 percent below the norm in most states) in one or more areas have a developmental delay, which may be in communication, physical development, adaptive behavior (feeding, dressing, toileting, etc.), cognition, or social and emotional development. Parent reports and informed clinical opinion are important for determining a child's eligibility because there are limited reliable and valid instruments that are useful with young children.

Infants and toddlers may be identified as developmentally delayed for a variety of reasons. The following are examples, by category, of factors that put children at risk.

- *Established risk.* Children who have a diagnosed physical or mental condition that make later delays in development highly probable have an established risk. Conditions such as Down syndrome, PKU, muscular dystrophy, and sickle cell anemia are examples.

- *Biological/Medical risk.* The term **biological/medical risk** refers to medical conditions that threaten to compromise a child's health, particularly perinatally, and are often predictive of later delays. For example, children born at low birth weight or with intraventricular hemorrhage, chronic lung disease, or failure to thrive are at risk for disabilities and developmental delays but may not have an identified disability or delay.

- *Environmental risk.* An increasing proportion of children in our society grow up in conditions that place them at greater risk for developmental delays. For example, children who live in poverty, whose parents abuse drugs or alcohol, whose primary language is not English, and who are abused live in environments that place them at risk. In 2010, 11 million infants and toddlers under age 3 were living in the United States. Forty-eight percent of these children lived in low-income families, and half of those families were headed by single parents (Addy & Wight, 2012). A disproportionate number of American Indian, Hispanic, African American, and immigrant infants and toddlers lived in poverty—they represented 55 percent of the total number. This group was twice as likely to live in poverty as compared to white and Asian children (Addy & Wight).

The 2010 American Community Survey (ACS) revealed that children represent 24 percent of the population but 34 percent of all people in poverty. Of the children of immigrant parents, 61 percent live in poverty, and 41 percent of children of native-born parents live in low-income families. Eighty-eight percent of children with no employed parents and 69 percent of children with a single parent lived in low-income homes (Addy & Wight). With these staggering numbers and decreasing state budgets, most states are reluctant to serve so many at-risk children and have elected not to offer services to this population. This disinclination is unfortunate because experts agree that children at risk are more vulnerable to the progressive effects of environmental factors and may have problems that grow more serious later on in life. At the same time, it is these same at-risk children who are most amenable to

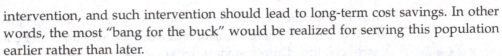

intervention, and such intervention should lead to long-term cost savings. In other words, the most "bang for the buck" would be realized for serving this population earlier rather than later.

In addition to specifying the categories of services that might be provided under Part C, the Act wisely avoiding using labels to identify children served. Rather than assigning infants and toddlers categorical labels, such as "seriously emotionally disturbed" or "mentally retarded," children and their families were simply identified as "eligible," and the act specifies that services are determined and resources allocated according to assessed need. A simple designation of "eligible" avoids the issues of discrimination, testing error, and lowered expectations that are associated with categorical labeling.

Procedural Safeguards

States are required to establish a system that protects the fundamental rights of families and children who are eligible for services under Part C. The intent of **procedural safeguards** is to ensure both that the intended services are not denied to families with eligible children and that an impartial hearing can be requested when families believe their rights are violated. These safeguards are very much like those found under Part B of the IDEIA. Federal law stipulates the following due process rights:

1. *Timely administrative resolution of complaints:* Parents who have disagreements about the delivery and services granted by an early intervention agency have the right to review the child's records, bring forth evidence, and seek a court decision.

2. *Confidentiality:* Parents must give consent before an early intervention agency may share personally identifiable information, even with other agencies serving the child.

3. *Deciding on services:* Parents have the right to accept or decline any early intervention service without losing other services they wish to have.

4. *Right to examine records:* Parents may examine their child's records relating to assessment, screening, eligibility, and the IFSP and may have copies of these records upon request.

5. *Surrogate parent:* When the parents of an infant or toddler cannot be found or the child is a ward of the state, a surrogate parent is assigned to represent the child's best interests in the early intervention process.

6. *Written notice:* A parent has the right to written notice if the early intervention agency proposes to initiate new services, change current services, or refuse services.

7. *Notice in the parents' native language:* Information provided to the parents must be in their native language unless it is clearly not feasible to do this.

8. *Mediation:* Instead of initiating a due process hearing, parents may use a mediator, a third party, to help settle disputes with the agency.

9. *Continuity:* An eligible child can continue to receive services even while a parent's dispute with an agency is being investigated and decided.

It is the obligation of each service provider to ensure that due process rights are made clear to parents. These regulations are complicated and can be intimidating even for early childhood professionals, let alone parents new to this field. Because professionals have the privilege of working more closely with parents in early intervention than with parents of older children, they have the opportunity to enhance families' self-advocacy skills by clarifying the law as much as possible.

Assessment

Services may be delivered to eligible infants, toddlers, and their families after an IFSP—based on assessment information and group input—is completed and approved by the parents. The process of determining eligibility, planning a child's program, implementing the plan, and reviewing progress is similar to that for older children with disabilities (see Figure 9–1).

Unlike the assessment of older children, the evaluation process in early intervention has two distinct but interrelated aspects: child assessment and family assessment. The primary purpose of assessment is to determine eligibility for services and to provide sufficient information for developing the IFSP. Once a child is deemed eligible for services and the IFSP is developed, assessment is necessary to measure progress and evaluate the effectiveness of the services provided. Federal regulations also require that evaluation and assessment are conducted in a nondiscriminatory manner.

IDEIA Guidelines for Assessment

Each lead agency is to adopt nondiscriminatory evaluation and assessment procedures. The public agencies responsible for evaluating children and families are to ensure, at a minimum, that:

1. Tests and other evaluation procedures and materials are administered in the native language of the parents or other modes of communication unless it is clearly not feasible to do so.

2. Any assessment and evaluation procedures and materials used are not racially or culturally discriminatory.

3. No single procedure is used as the sole criterion for determining a child's eligibility.

4. Evaluation and assessments are conducted by qualified personnel.

Four types of assessments are used to evaluate children: psychometric, behavioral, qualitative–developmental, and ecological. A **psychometric approach** is used to compare a child to normal standards of development, intelligence, and achievement, to determine performance discrepancies. That is, does a child's developmental rate keep pace with the usual expectations for typical children of the same age? In a **behavioral assessment,** practitioners examine factors that govern children's behavior under given conditions. With this approach, the goal of assessment is to understand the conditions in a child's setting and how they affect behavior. In other words, the goal is to determine what motivates a child's behavior so that appropriate

Diagram of Identification, Eligibility, Programming, and Review for Early Intervention Services

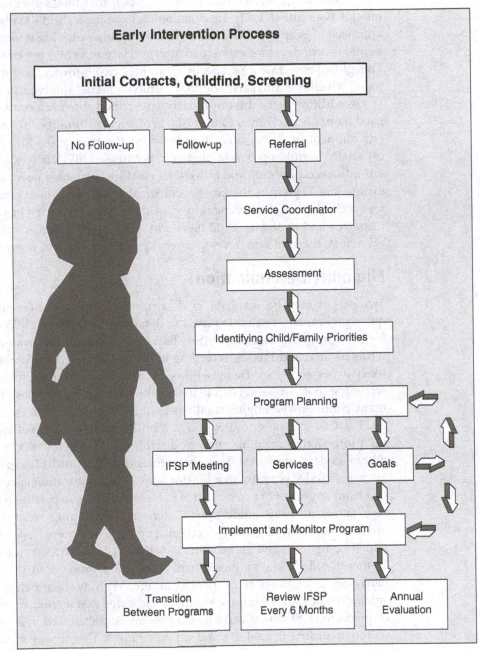

intervention can be planned. An important step in behavioral assessment is to carry out a **functional assessment,** which involves manipulation of those conditions in order to alter the observed behavior. For example, if a child is 18 months old and not attempting to make sounds, observers may discover that the child is placed in a playpen for much of the day at a childcare center and that when she does attempt to communicate, caregivers often overlook her verbalizations. It would be recommended in such a case that caregivers provide multiple opportunities for interaction throughout the day and begin to reinforce the child's verbalizations by imitating or expanding on her communication attempts.

A child's age is irrelevant in an approach that focuses on **qualitative developmental assessment**. Early interventionists examine a child's skills as well as a child's approach to people and tasks. The data they gather provide information about where a child is on a developmental road map and where a child can be expected to go next. This global assessment perspective provides rich information for program development, which is particularly useful in family-centered intervention.

In addition to the three approaches described above, an **ecological assessment** is used by many early interventionists. Ecological evaluations focus on children, their environment, and the interaction between the two, providing information that is especially useful in program planning. Because a child's behavior and development are influenced by multiple factors, all of these variables need to be considered in evaluation. Therefore, the key to ecological evaluations is to comprehensively analyze a child's real environment by considering a wide range of variables, including resources and materials, child behaviors, social relationships, and family and adult behaviors; the goal is to develop a very specific profile and program.

Eligibility Determination

Two stages may be involved in determining eligibility. **Screening** is a relatively quick preliminary evaluation used to determine whether a child should be referred for more in-depth assessment (See Table 9–2). Because full evaluations are costly in terms of time and money, screening helps to identify those children who are most likely to need services. There is, however, a drawback to this efficiency. By definition, screening tools are less accurate than follow-up assessment and, therefore, overlook many children who might actually benefit from special services.

Positive screening results lead to a **multifactored diagnostic evaluation** involving professionals from all relevant disciplines. This evaluation must be completed within 45 days of referral. In early intervention, this **multidisciplinary** team almost always includes parents, an educator, and a communication specialist. The purpose of a team approach to assessment is to have adequate expertise in all program areas.

State regulations guide practitioners in determining what data are needed in order to make an eligibility decision. Formal assessments use standardized tools, which compare a child's behaviors to those of a standard norm. For example, a 10-month-old child's language behaviors are compared to the average language behaviors of children at 10 months of age. With average being the "standard," a significant deviance from the standard indicates that a child may be either delayed or precocious. Standardized assessments are administered in a precise manner and scored according to a set of standard procedures. That is, any variation in giving the test that is not provided for in the testing manual—such as variations in timing, use of materials, or instructions—renders the results unusable for comparative purposes.

Informal assessments may include the use of commercially available or curriculum-referenced tools. Also used are interviews with parents, narrative descriptions of behavior, checklists, and rating scales. These data should be combined with more formal assessment data to make an eligibility determination. If a child is found to be eligible, programs have 45 days from the initial referral to plan and hold an initial IFSP meeting. Services would begin immediately following parental approval of the IFSP.

Table 9–2 Screening Instruments for Identifying Children Who Should Receive Further Testing for Possible Diagnosis and Treatment

Screening Device	Purpose
American Guidance Service (AGS) Early Screening Profiles	Individual screening for children from 2 years to 6 years, 11 months old. Some information gathered by interviews regarding health and home. Children can move from station to station to do tasks related to thinking, language, motor, speech, social, and self-help skills.
Battelle Developmental Inventory Screening Test	Individual screening for children from birth to 8 years old. Information gathered through observation, testing, and interview. Items assess personal–social, adaptive, motor, communicative, and cognitive skills.
Brigance Screens Early Preschool Preschool Screen K & 1 Screen	Individual screens for children from birth through first grade, with different versions administered to children depending on their age. Information includes observations and ratings as well as completion-of-task items. The screens cover language, cognitive, motor, and early academic skills.
Denver II (Revised Denver Developmental Screening Test)	Individually administered to children between birth and 6 years of age. Items cover personal–social, fine motor–adaptive, language, and gross motor skills. Available in English and Spanish.
Developmental Indicators for the Assessment of Learning, 4th ed. (DIAL-4)	A norm-referenced instrument for children between 3 years and 6 years, 11 months old. Items cover motor, concepts, language, self-help, and social development.
First STEP: Screening Test for Evaluating Preschoolers	Individually administered, norm-referenced test for children from 2 years, 9 months, to 6 years, 2 months. It covers cognition, communication, motor, social–emotional, and adaptive behavior. Designed to be a companion to the Miller Assessment for Preschoolers.
Child Development Inventory Screening: Infant Development Early Child Development Preschool Development Child Development Review	Parents respond to questions about their children, and this information can be combined with professional observations. Can be used for children from birth to 5 years old, depending on the screening level used. Is based on the Minnesota Child Development Inventory.
The Temperament and Atypical Behavior Scale (TABS)	Can be used as a screener or an assessment for children from 11 to 71 months. Identifies four categories: detached, hypersensitive/active, underreactive, and dysregulated.
Ages and Stages Questionnaires: Social-Emotional	Uses parent-completed forms for children between 6 and 60 months of age. Addresses self-regulation, compliance, communication, adaptive functioning, autonomy, affect, and interaction with people.

Source: Information from *Assessing Infants and Preschoolers with Special Needs,* 3rd ed., 2004, by M. McLean, M. Wolery, & D. B. Bailey. Upper Saddle River, NJ: Merrill/Pearson Education.

Program Planning

The most efficient assessment process combines eligibility determination with program evaluation. Since assessment and curriculum design are both focused on the developmental level of the child, it is relatively easy in early intervention to use a curriculum-referenced tool to accomplish both purposes. A curriculum-referenced tool is linked to intervention objectives so that the assessment itself is sensitive to relevant behaviors. In early intervention, these tools are generally very practical and measure behaviors in all developmental areas. Some tools are specifically designed

Close Up

Randomized Trial of Intensive Early Intervention for Children with Pervasive Developmental Disorder

After years of debating whether or not early intervention can make significant differences in the later lives of young children with severe developmental delays, several studies using intensive applied behavior analysis (ABA) revealed that important improvements could be achieved. The present study was designed to compare the effectiveness of intensive ABA procedures developed through the UCLA Young Autism Project (Lovaas, 1987), for treating children with pervasive developmental disorders and with autism, to similar treatment implemented by parents trained by UCLA staff.

Children were assigned to either of two treatment groups, an intensive treatment group and a parent treatment group. The intensive treatment group involved 30 hours per week of ABA intervention for each child for 2 to 3 years. Intensive treatment was carried out by teams of four to six therapists and the primary caregiver, who all worked one-to-one, in the child's home, using discrete trial formats that were highly individualized to maximize language, toy play, and self-care. Later in treatment, the children moved into school group settings.

The second half of the children were assigned to a parent treatment group in which parents were trained to use the same ABA treatment approaches used with the intensive treatment group and were given a manual to assist them. Parents were given two training sessions per week, totaling 5 hours per week, in their homes for 3 to 9 months. Parents collaborated with the trainers to select goals for their children, and parent trainers demonstrated ways to work toward these goals. The parent trainers observed parents working with their children and gave them feedback. Throughout the training, children in

this group were also enrolled in special education classes in public schools for 10 to 15 hours per week.

The treatment group who received intensive 30-hour-a-week discrete trial training benefited significantly more than the children in the parent treatment group whose parents carried out treatment. The children in the intensive treatment group scored higher on IQ, visual spatial skills, and language development, although they did not score higher on adaptive behavior in everyday settings. Children in the intensive treatment group were assigned to less restrictive school placements, and a number of these children performed in the average range on academic tests after treatment, while only one child in the parent treatment group scored as well. Children with pervasive developmental delay in the intensive treatment group may have gained even more than children with autism in the same group.

The authors concluded that intensive early intervention can be a powerful treatment; intensive treatment is clearly needed to help preschool children with autism or pervasive developmental delay achieve average functioning. One-to-one training focused on skill building appears to be a necessary prerequisite for children to generalize earlier behaviors to appropriate school behaviors.

Sources: From "Behavioral Treatment and Normal Educational and Intellectual Functioning in Young Autistic Children," by O. I. Lovaas, 1987, *Journal of Consulting and Clinical Psychology, 55*, 3–9; and "Randomized Trial of Intensive Early Intervention for Children with Pervasive Developmental Disorder," by T. Smith, A. D. Groen, and J. W. Wynn, 2000, *American Journal on Mental Retardation, 105*(4), 269–285.

to measure very small steps in learning for children with significant disabilities. Others are closely linked to broad developmental milestones and their associated learning objectives for children with mild disabilities.

Day-to-day assessment provides input for dynamic decision making about the appropriateness of the objectives, intervention strategies, and programming alternatives for a child. Research consistently indicates that regularly scheduled measurement (daily or several times a week) is the most effective way to assess a child's progress on learning objectives. Furthermore, direct observation methods are most useful for daily data collection. Examples of direct data collection include counting the frequency or rate of behaviors (e.g., number of times in a day that child wets), measuring the length of time that a behavior occurs (e.g., duration of independent sitting before falling sideways), and assessing the magnitude of behaviors (e.g., how far a child will reach across the midline to grasp a toy).

Curriculum-based tools are also useful for measuring child progress on outcome objectives specified on IFSPs. Review of each IFSP must take place at least every 6 months because young children can progress so rapidly through developmental stages. A comprehensive reevaluation must be completed at least annually. While it is possible for children to become ineligible for services through rapid development, the at-risk clause of Part C permits agencies to continue services should the families so desire.

Howard Shooter/DK Images

Family Assessment

Development of IFSPs must include statements about family priorities; this means that families need to be assessed to determine their concerns, resources, and priorities. The Part C regulations require assessment, but this does not imply the family needs to be "evaluated" (NECTAC, 2012). Families are especially vulnerable during initial diagnostic stages because they are entering a new arena in which they must rely on the integrity and proficiency of strangers. Therefore, the NECTAC (2012) recommends that parents be invited to share information on a voluntary basis. Assessment for the purpose of defining a family as it relates to care of a child with disabilities is an intrusion into the privacy of families, and it is one to which families of young children without disabilities are not subjected. For these reasons, educators are cautioned to fulfill this legal requirement with wisdom and empathy.

All aspects of a family's conduct that might influence members' ability to meet the needs of the child with disabilities may be considered in the assessment. The IDEIA directed professionals to include a statement of family strengths and weaknesses on the IFSP. Traditionally, social service personnel have used a deficiency model focusing attention on family needs rather than on their strengths. A more proactive way of looking at families, in formulating plans, is to concentrate on their strengths. Toward that end, the 1991 amendments to the IDEIA redirected educators to include a family-directed assessment of family resources, priorities for services, and concerns. Areas of family assessment may include child–parent interactions and assessments in the domestic, educational, vocational, health, financial, and social domains. Again, while it may not be the responsibility of educational service agencies to provide for all of a family's needs, the agencies' responsibility is to help establish linkages between families and corresponding services that will enable each family to meet the needs of their child with special needs more effectively.

One approach to family assessment is a traditional format in which professionals survey parents through a standard protocol during which all parents are asked a set of questions regarding specific skills, interests, and needs. Families might be interviewed or asked to fill out a written survey. Either way, professionals take the risk of offending parents who, although seeking help for their children, find the intrusion into their personal and family circumstances unwarranted. The following real account of a parent whose child was enrolled in a public program for low-income families illustrates the point.

> I wanted my son in an integrated preschool program but was unprepared for the ordeal. The application process included an assessment of my very personal circumstances. I was asked questions related to the adequacy of our housing and food, whether or not I am on welfare or on legal probation, how I discipline my family, and if we use drugs, alcohol, or birth control.

This parent was from a middle-class family and therefore was not accustomed to being treated as if her privacy was less important than the organization's right to ask such questions. It was also apparent that the questions were viewed as perfectly legitimate for families who lived in poverty. While persons who have low incomes are often subjected to intrusive questioning in order to receive other public services, the very implication that a family is deficient could place a barrier between professionals and that family.

Assessment of families for the purpose of identifying the needs of families as opposed to their children's needs could be unintentionally intrusive (see Figure 9–2). Consider, for example, a child who has cerebral palsy. Traditionally, professionals would concentrate on child-centered needs as they pertain to a variety of developmental areas, particularly, motor development. Motor assessment, conducted by a physical therapist, can be viewed as minimally intrusive. When the physical therapist attempts to determine whether family members have the time, resources, or skills to conduct necessary motor development activities at home, the intrusion into family privacy becomes more substantial although perhaps not unreasonable.

Figure 9–2 Relationship between Outcome of Needs Assessment and Level of Intrusiveness

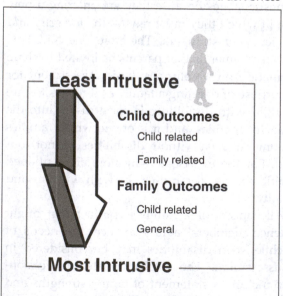

If, for example, a physical therapist working with a child with cerebral palsy concludes that a wheelchair is required, the family might be asked whether it can afford to purchase this child-oriented equipment. Obviously, financial questions can become quite sensitive, but, under the circumstances, they are relevant. The most obvious intrusion and least justifiable questions surround general family needs. For example, the physical therapist, in recognizing that this child is underweight and tends to have chronic upper respiratory infections, might question the family about whether it has enough resources to provide adequate nutrition or health care.

Asking questions regarding employment status, health care insurance, and mealtime habits represents a very delicate assessment issue that should be approached only with the greatest sensitivity. NECTAC (2012) recommended that after building a relationship with the family, professionals gather the information informally through conversations. It is possible that professionals who provide a continuous sounding board and use an IFSP in a dynamic manner will be more effective and have more trusting relationships than those who use a more structured approach.

Individualized Family Service Plan (IFSP) Development

The IFSP is a form of documentation that emphasizes the family-centered intervention highlighted throughout this text. IFSPs are created for infants and toddlers and their families when eligibility for early intervention is established. This legal document is the early intervention analog to an Individualized Educational Program (IEP) used with older students, but it is more holistically conceived than the latter. Reflecting the rate of change in infants and toddlers, IFSPs are reviewed at least every 6 months or more often if needed.

The required components of an IFSP include the following:

1. A statement of a child's developmental status in the areas of communication and physical, social–emotional, cognitive, and adaptive behavior based on the completion of a multidisciplinary assessment.

2. A statement of family priorities, concerns, and resources as they relate to enhancement of their child's development, if the family agrees to its inclusion.

3. A statement of the major outcomes (goals), including preliteracy and language skills, that a child is expected to achieve with the criteria for mastery, timelines for implementation, expected dates of completion, procedures for measuring progress, and modifications or revisions if necessary.

4. A statement of the specific early intervention services that must be provided to meet the child and family outcomes. Included are the frequency, duration, location, and method of delivering these services; the payment arrangements, if necessary; and, when deemed necessary, a specification of "other" services that a family may need but that are not explicitly provided under Part C, and the steps that will be taken to secure those services. While these services may be written into the document, this does not mean that the services must be provided at public expense. Such services might include helping families identify an agency to provide financial assistance, arranging for the child to access medical services, or helping to prepare insurance papers.

5. A statement of the dates when services will be initiated and the anticipated duration of services.

6. The name of the service coordinator, from the profession most immediately relevant to the child's or family's needs, responsible for ensuring that assessment, program planning, program implementation, and transition services and coordination are provided according to the law.

7. A statement of the steps that will be taken to ensure that a child makes a smooth transition from early intervention services to preschool education on reaching age 3. This includes training parents for the legal and programmatic changes expected, procedures to prepare the child for a change in service delivery, confirmation that information about the child has been sent to the LEA or other agency, and a review of program options for the child from his or her third birthday through the remainder of the school year.

Although IFSPs are intended to serve as a blueprint for services and as a legal agreement with families, there was a conscious effort made in developing the IDEIA to avoid some of the pitfalls of legislation regulating the adoption of IEPs in this country. The emphasis is rightly placed on the substance of intervention rather than on paperwork compliance.

Selecting IFSP Family-Centered Outcomes

As in all areas of education, there is an increasing emphasis on planning children's programs that focus on real life and are functional for the family and child. When assisting families in writing IFSP outcomes, it is important to embed them into daily activities and routines. Naturally occurring routines are well suited for the integration of skill domains. For example, bathing can be a context for language, social interaction, motor (fine and gross) execution, and cognitive growth, as well as an obvious avenue for self-help skill development. The point of having outcomes written so that they can fit into daily routines is to increase both their relevance for children and the likelihood that parents will integrate helping their child achieve objectives into their already demanding lives.

The best way to determine family routines is simply to ask parents to describe activities that occur during their typical day: what they do and where they go (Tisot & Thurman, 2002). Families may keep a week-long log of their activities (e.g., looking at books, caring for a pet, eating out, and attending church). Interviews with families can also reveal what behaviors would be important for an infant or toddler in these settings. Families may want to take their young child into new environments where they currently do not feel they can be successful. The team may need to identify what behaviors are needed in that environment in order to include them in the plan.

After reviewing several resources by experts in the field, NECTAC (2007) identified criteria that define high-quality and participation-based IFSP outcomes. Outcomes should be:

- Necessary and functional for the child and family
- Reflective of real-life settings
- Clear, simple, and jargon free

- Not aligned to a specific early intervention service
- Written using active words
- Focused on the positive
- Based on the family's priorities and concerns
- Descriptive of both the child's strengths and needs

Family comfort should also be considered. Some families may have an open-door policy and welcome service delivery in their homes; others may be more private and find their routines disrupted by home services. Service providers should not mistakenly assume that home or local childcare centers are the most natural environments for a particular family (Tisot & Thurman, 2002). The dynamics of a particular family also need to be considered. Financial or emotional stress may be increased—lessening the chance for successful teaching and learning—if a family's options are not available at their preferred setting for services. Setting, though, is less important than what transpires in a location. No matter what the setting may be, the activities must be authentic, functional, and meaningful. The outcome must enhance eligible children's development and learning. Outcomes must also be respectful of the family's values, priorities, and needs. Specialized settings for some children are necessary and appropriate for a child to receive quality services that promote progress and expand future placement options.

McWilliam (2009) developed the Goal Functionality Scale III and identified seven questions teams should ask when evaluating the appropriateness of each IFSP outcome. They are:

- To what extent does the outcome emphasize child participation?
- Is the outcome observable, measurable, and stated specifically?
- Is the outcome necessary or useful for the settings the child participates in?
- Is the criterion identified and documented?
- Have meaningful acquisition criteria been determined and documented?
- Have generalization criteria been determined and documented?
- Has a timeframe for mastery of an outcome been determined and documented?

Several components of IFSPs mimic those of IEPs (which will be described in Chapter 10). However, there are three distinct differences between these documents. First, the identification of a service coordinator described earlier in this chapter is different. Second, the services for which children and their families are eligible include some services unique to infants and toddlers. Finally, IFSPs must include a plan for a child's transition into other programs once the child reaches age 3. While transition plans are also used for school age students, it is only when students with disabilities reach age 14 and are preparing for transition to adulthood that such a plan is required in the IEP. Transitions can be difficult and require careful planning if they are to be successful. Consequently, they play an important part in the IFSP. When children are found eligible for early intervention, assessment of services includes both those that will directly benefit that child and those that will support a child's family. The latter services are intended to indirectly benefit an eligible child by enhancing a family's ability to meet the child's needs. In other words, if a family or family member has a need that is so great it prevents nurturing the child with special needs, the need of that family or family member is as important to address as the child's developmental needs. While this practice makes sense, provision of **tertiary services** to families is both costly and complicated.

Services to infants and toddlers and their families can be provided through a myriad of models and agencies. Although, traditionally, public and private agencies have been centralized in educational facilities, the law permits considerable flexibility in delivery models. It is clear that those who crafted Part C envisioned the coordination of multiple resources; both public and private agencies may be involved when indicated by the needs of families.

Children who are eligible for early intervention may receive the following types of services if appropriate.

1. Assistive technology devices and services
2. Audiology services, sign language, and cued language services
3. Family training, counseling, and home visits
4. Health services deemed necessary to enable infants and toddlers to benefit from the other early intervention services. (These may include clean intermittent catheterization or consultation by health care providers concerning the special medical needs of children eligible for services that will influence the delivery of those services. Specifically, services that are purely medical in nature and surgical services are excluded, as are devices that are used to control or treat a medical condition, as well as medical services such as immunizations.)
5. Medical services only for diagnostic and evaluation purposes
6. Nursing services
7. Nutrition services
8. Occupational therapy
9. Physical therapy
10. Psychological services
11. Service coordination
12. Social work services
13. Special instruction
14. Speech–language therapy
15. Sign language and cued language services
16. Transportation and related costs
17. Vision services including ophthalmology and optometry

This list of services to children is not exhaustive. Other services such as respite care and other family support services should be provided when they are appropriate.

In contrast to the services articulated for children, the law is vague about the kind of services that must be made available to families or family members in order to support them. In theory, families should receive those services that will permit them to adequately meet the needs of their children with disabilities. The law is so broadly stated that professionals worry about the fiscal and logistical nightmare of serving some families who might be very needy. Theoretically, families could receive counseling, drug and alcohol treatment, public assistance, and so forth. However, the services that families might receive could become too expensive and so could not realistically be provided.

Unlike service providers for school age children under special education law, service providers may charge a fee to families of eligible infants and toddlers. However, under no circumstances can there be charges for evaluation and assessment and service coordination. Moreover, guidelines that are established to determine payment may not be used to deny services to children or families who are unable to pay for those services.

A Sample IFSP

A family-centered IFSP should be positive, written with understandable language, and balanced in scope, and it should include specifics. It should not include professional jargon or double-talk. What the family wants must be reflected on the IFSP, and what is written on the IFSP should show up in practice. Figure 9–3 is an example of an IFSP that should be examined part by part.

Figure 9–3 Individualized Family Services Plan

Identifying Information

Child's Name: *Karmen Lynn Burch*   Nickname: *Bitsy*
Date: *10–1–09*

Gender: Male ___ Female *X*   Date of Birth *4–2–06*

Social Security Number: *371–16–5499*

Insurance Type: ___ private (company and policy #) _____
X Medicaid   ___ Champus   ___ none   ___ other

Child's Primary Language: *American Sign Language/English*
Mode of Communication: *Manual Communication*

Initial Referral Date: *9–2–09*
Initial Referral Source: *Jackson County Health Department*

Does the child have a medical diagnosis? *X* Yes   ___ No

If yes, what is diagnosis?   *Bilateral, severe, hearing loss as a result of prenatal rubella infection*

Child's Primary Care Physician: *Glenn Stream, Jackson Clinic South*
Phone: *(517) 499–5228*

Is the child eligible for IDEIA, Part C, services? *X* Yes   ___ No

Parent/Guardian/Surrogate/Caregiver Information

Name: *Barbara Benson, Guardian*   Relationship to the child: *grandmother*
    and
Name: *Laura Burch, Parent*   Relationship to the child: *mother*

Address: *S. 8167 5th St., Apt. #40*   County: *Jackson*
City: *Jackson*   State: *MI*   Zip: *49200*
Telephone: Day: *(517) 554–9191*   (Night): *(517) 554–4252*

(continued)

Figure 9–3 (continued)

Best time to call: *7–9 a.m. and 6–9 p.m.*
Primary language/mode of communication: *English*

Service Coordinator Name: *Cheryl Tully*   Telephone: *(517) 768–2367*
Agency Name: *Michigan Deaf Services*
Address: *8237 Miller Ave.*   City: *Jackson*   State: *MI*   Zip: *49200*

Child's present level of performance

Child strengths:

Bitsy is a happy baby who seldom fusses. Her motor skills are good; she is running, climbing furniture, sleeping in a youth bed, putting together preschool puzzles. She feeds herself and is toilet trained during the daytime (sleeps in diapers). Her inoculations are up to date, vision is average, and though her height and weight are at about the 20th percentile, she appears healthy. Using the Brigance Inventory for Early Development, Bitsy scored at her age level in fine and gross motor and cognition. Bitsy is learning to communicate through American Sign Language and uses about one dozen signs.

Child concerns:

Bitsy was born 4 weeks prematurely, affected by maternal rubella. Her mother was 15 at the time of the birth and had received almost no prenatal care until the 7th month of gestation; father was not identified. Bitsy was treated in the NICU for almost two weeks before she was sent home. She has severe, bilateral hearing loss and does not make any speech sounds. She has very high activity levels and a very short attention span. She scored below the age-1-year level on the Brigance in the areas of receptive and expressive language. She has been fitted for hearing aids but refuses to wear them. Her grandmother and mother have decided against the use of a cochlear implant.

Family Assessment:

Family strengths:

Bitsy's mother, Laura, is attending an alternative high school program that will allow her to complete her degree by next year. She also works full-time as a waitress at the Highland Club, on the 6 p.m. to 2 a.m. shift and helps support Bitsy and Barbara, Bitsy's grandmother. Laura has relinquished Bitsy's guardianship to her mother Barbara. Barbara is on disability because of crippling arthritis. She stays home with Bitsy in the two-bedroom double-wide mobile home they share with Laura. Barbara transports Bitsy to doctor's appointments and to twice-weekly speech and language therapy. Bitsy's maternal uncle, Benjamin, often visits on weekends and brings his 4–year-old daughter and 5-year-old son along as playmates for Bitsy.

Family concerns:

Because of Bitsy's high activity levels and her lack of receptive language she is challenging for her grandmother, Barbara, to control. In addition, Barbara's arthritis periodically flares up, making it physically difficult to care for Bitsy. The family would also like to have Bitsy in an environment where she would have other children to play with and could receive daily instruction in sign language and speech. A priority for the family would be at least a half-time preschool program and afternoon day care for Bitsy while Laura is attending school. There are also concerns about continuing Medicaid services and the paperwork that accompanies it. Barbara and Laura feel they do not know enough sign language to use with Bitsy as she continues to add to what she knows.

Major Outcomes:

We would like to see Bitsy use American Sign Language fluently enough that she can get her wants and needs met and improve her expressive and receptive language to a level expected for her age.

We would like to see Bitsy's attention span increased to age-appropriate levels, so that she can sit and work on an interesting, developmentally appropriate project with an adult or small group of children for up to 10 minutes at a time. This might mean listening to a story, cutting out play dough, or using finger paints.

Figure 9–3 (continued)

We would like to obtain preschool and day-care services appropriate to Bitsy's needs that would provide grandmother with respite during the day while Bitsy's mother is attending high school.

We would like to increase Bitsy's use of her hearing aids so that she wears them on a daily basis.

We would like to enroll Barbara and Laura in weekend sign language instruction so they can add more signs to what they use at home with Bitsy.

For Determining Progress Toward Achieving Measurable Results and Measurable Outcomes, and Whether Modifications or Revisions are Necessary

Measurable Result or Measurable Outcome (including, as appropriate, preliteracy and language skills)	Criteria	Procedures	Timelines
Bitsy will use ASL (receptive and expressive language) at an age-appropriate level	A minimum of 10 new words per week	• Family and teachers will encourage Bitsy to use sign language to get what she wants and needs • Mary, SLP, will work with care providers to demonstrate more ways to encourage Bitsy's language • Family and teachers will try the new strategies with Bitsy	10/5/09–4/2/10
Bitsy will increase her attention span to an age-appropriate level	10 minutes at a time with adult or peer on age-appropriate activity	• Behavioral interventionist will recommend techniques to increase Bitsy's attention span • Family and teachers will try new strategies with Bitsy	10/5/09–4/2/10
Family will obtain preschool services for Bitsy	Enroll Bitsy in Jackson Early Start Center by 10/5/10	• Family will begin enrollment process • Cheryl will send Bitsy's assessment information to school	10/1/09–10/5/09
Bitsy will increase the use of her hearing aids	Daily	• Family will ensure Bitsy has her hearing aids in every day • Teachers will ensure Bitsy keeps her hearing aids in during the school day	10/5/09–4/2/10
Barbara and Laura will increase their sign language skills	A minimum of 20 new words per week	• Barbara and Laura will attend sign language classes each Saturday • Barbara and Laura will use the words they learn each week with Bitsy in the home • Barbara and Laura will set up activities at home during which they can practice their new signs with Bitsy	10/5/09–1/8/10

(continued)

Figure 9–3 (continued)

IFSP Team Meeting Date	Measurable Result or Measurable Outcome	Progress	Modifications or Revisions
March 2010			

Intervention Services Needed:

Early Intervention Service	Beginning Date	Length	Duration	Frequency	Intensity	Method of Delivery	Location
Speech therapy/sign language instruction	10/9/09	30 minutes per day	4/2/10	4 × week	Individual and small group	In the classroom and therapy room	Jackson Early Start Center
Special Education Instruction	10/5/09	3 hours per day	4/2/10	5 days per week	Group setting	Integrated into the classroom	Jackson Early Start Center
Sign Language Instruction	10/5/09	2 hours per week	1/8/10	1 × week		Parent meeting and training	Michigan Deaf Education Assoc. Center
Behavioral interventionist	10/5/09	2 hours per week	4/2/10	Weekly	1 on 1 with family and classroom staff	Training and Consulting	School and Bitsy's home

Continued speech therapy and sign language instruction for Bitsy.

Behavioral intervention planning and consultation with Bitsy's grandmother and mother, as well as with any new caregivers, to motivate increased attending and appropriate behavior.

Instruction in sign language for Bitsy's grandmother, mother, and new caregivers.

Special educational instruction in a group setting.

Strategies, Activities, and Services:
Deborah Tully and Barbara Benson will begin the enrollment process for Bitsy to attend the Jackson Early Start Center, which provides early intervention services in an integrated preschool program. Speech and language therapy will be provided on-site, and the Center's behavioral interventionist will work with the teacher and at home on Bitsy's ability to stay with a task for appropriate lengths of time, to follow simple instructions, and to wear her hearing aids.

Service Initiation and Duration:
Early Start Services will begin 10-5-09 and continue until 4-2-10, at which time Bitsy may begin transition to Head Start or Lynwood Deaf Preschool.

Barbara Benson and Laura Burch will attend parent sessions at the Southern Michigan Deaf Education Association Center in Chelsea, held every Saturday morning. Sign language instruction is provided and childcare for Bitsy is also available at the center. The meetings also provide a parent network for families with deaf children. A deaf adult will act as a mentor and will meet with the family at their home one evening a week to provide additional sign language training and to advise the family on Bitsy's care and education.

Figure 9–3 (continued)

Southern Michigan Deaf Education Association Center meetings will begin 10-5-09 and continue until 1-8-10, at which time the family and service coordinator will discuss the need to continue.

Transition Services:

The service coordinator will arrange for Barbara and Laura to visit two possible preschool programs for Bitsy to attend when she turns 3. One is an integrated Head Start program that provides speech therapy and employs staff who sign. The other is a self-contained preschool program at nearby Lynwood Elementary School that serves only deaf children. Total communication and language instruction is emphasized and all teachers are certified as teachers of the deaf. Transportation for Bitsy will be provided by the local school district.

The service coordinator will be responsible for providing complete records to the receiving program and will identify the main contact person who will follow through with the family.

Evaluation:

The IFSP team will meet again in March, 2010, to discuss progress made on the outcomes identified. We will determine at that time if continued behavioral intervention is needed in the home and if sign language instruction for the family should continue. We will also be prepared to make a final decision on which program Bitsy will transition to.

Service providers:

Type of Service	Person Responsible	Funding Source
Center-based early childhood education	Margaret Devon	Early Start
Family support and sign language instruction	Matthew Liese and Barbara Benson	Michigan Deaf Services
Service coordination	Cheryl Tully	Michigan Deaf Services
Audiology and speech and language assessment	Mary Manix, Jackson Clinic South	Medicare
Medical records and billing to Medicare	Nora Fishback, Jackson Clinic South and Barbara Benson	Jackson Clinic South
Transition services	Cheryl Tully and Laura Burch	Michigan Deaf Services
Medical treatment	Glenn Stream, Jackson Clinic South	Medicaid

This plan was developed by the following IFSP team members:

Name	Title
Barbara Benson	Grandmother/Guardian
Laura Burch	Mother
Cheryl Tully	Service Coordinator
Mary Manix	Speech and Language Specialist
Matthew Liese	Michigan Deaf Services Coordinator
Pamela Kruse	Deaf Education Teacher
Margaret Devon	Early Start Coordinator

At the beginning of the IFSP, identifying information must be included to ensure continued contact and monitoring of progress. This section of the IFSP should include both the name of the child and of the parents or guardians. Sometimes a foster parent or surrogate parent should also be identified because many at-risk children do not reside with their biological parents. Notes describing a parent or guardian's primary language, work and home phone numbers, and best time to call may improve later follow-up. It is also important to note significant extended family or nonrelated kin who may be a significant part of a child's family. Grandparents, live-in partners, step-siblings, and so forth may play an important role in a child's life.

The name of the legally specified service coordinator must be included on the IFSP. It is helpful to the family to include the coordinator's contact information, such as agency address and phone number. It may be wise to spell out the coordinator's responsibilities on the IFSP so that roles and expectations are clear to all involved.

A section of the IFSP is devoted to describing a child's present level of performance. This should include the results of any evaluations, assessments, and observations made about a child. Family input regarding a child's strengths and needs are also recorded in this section. Results from formal evaluations should be indicated as scores, percentiles, age equivalents, and so on, but they also should be summarized in everyday terms that are meaningful to families and other professionals involved. Skill areas include communication, cognition, social–emotional, motor, and adaptive. Physical development, including vision, hearing, and health, are also addressed. Relevant medical information including a birth history should be reported.

A family assessment is important, but, as noted earlier, it can be completed only with a parent's or guardian's consent. Items to consider for this section might be a description of who makes up the immediate family, what the neighborhood or community is like, what friends or relatives are important in supporting the family, what activities the family enjoys doing together, how the child is cared for during the day, and what are the child's typical environments. Checklists might be used to indicate needs for transportation, housing, information on the disability or delay, training, help with insurance or Medicaid or Social Security Insurance (SSI), recreation, child-care, and so on. Parents or caretakers should be given the opportunity to raise their own concerns about a child or the needs of the child's family.

An IFSP must clearly state major outcomes that express what a child's team wants to see happen in the next 6 months. Also addressed are outcomes for the child's family. These outcomes must be related to the assessment information about a child's strengths and weaknesses and should reflect a family's concerns and priorities. The goals must be functional and age appropriate, taking into consideration the context in which the child lives and what skills are needed for that child to be more successful in those settings. For example, perhaps a family priority for the child is to become toilet trained because that will allow access to a regular day-care program. If a young child needs to develop fine motor skills, it makes more sense to work on dressing skills like fastening Velcro than on sorting nuts and bolts. Functional goals make caring for children easier by fostering more independence.

Outcomes should also be realistic because goals that are achievable give families an increased sense of self-efficacy. One way to ensure success is to think of 6-month outcomes as steps needed to reach long-term goals. For example, a family may want a child who is currently nonverbal to speak. The first step toward that goal may be to teach the child to communicate through a picture exchange system in which a picture card is selected to indicate a desire for a snack or a toy. The next time 6-month outcomes are set, the child may be ready to use a communication board or signs to indicate wants. Later, these pictures or signs may be paired with vocalizations, and gradually those vocalizations could be shaped into meaningful words. But the first achievable 6-month step may be using the picture exchange. This task analysis (breaking an ultimate skill into its manageable subskills) should be done with a team so that all members can identify where the outcomes are leading, and all will recognize achievement of intermediate goals as substantive progress. Obviously, one child's 6-month objective may be inappropriate for another child. Knowledge of normal child development coupled with knowledge of patterns of a child's growth rate yield realistic objectives that can be met with reasonable intervention plans.

The IFSP must next indicate the intervention required to reach these outcomes. A series of questions should be considered. (1) What type of service will be devoted to each outcome targeted (for example, home visit, parent education, consultation, speech and language therapy, social work, medical services, transportation)? (2) Who will provide this service and when and where will it take place? A child might be served at home, in family day care, in an outpatient facility, in an early intervention class, or in a hospital, depending on the child's level of need and the intensity of services required. (3) What type of assistive technology or specialized equipment or curriculum is needed to support the intervention? (4) How often each week and for how long during each session will specific therapies or experiences be provided? (5) How will these services be funded? Will private insurance, Medicaid, or family savings be needed? (6) Who will make arrangements for this funding?

An IFSP team must also discuss the settings in which intervention might be provided. When possible and appropriate, team services should be delivered in a child's natural environment, but exceptions may be necessary under certain conditions. Services could be offered in a child's home or care setting. Delivery of services in a community program such as Head Start, in an early intervention classroom, or even in a hospital setting may also be appropriate, if a child's needs are best served in a more structured setting. A child's needs may be such that a center-based program capable of providing intensive therapies is the most appropriate setting. The decision about the service delivery model must be based on what each child needs. A team will indicate the options discussed to determine the most appropriate and natural setting, and will indicate why other sites were rejected. It is also helpful to indicate any special adaptations, transportation, materials, equipment, curriculum, and so on that would be necessary to allow the child to function in the setting selected.

As mentioned, a section of each IFSP must be devoted to plans for eventually transitioning toddlers to preschool special education services provided for children from age 3 on. Transitions might include changes in a child's teacher and other personnel, scheduling, transportation, expectations of children and their families, service delivery models, and educational philosophies. To make a smooth move from early intervention programs to preschool programs, Part C requires that a specific transition plan be developed and included in all IFSPs as children approach age 3. Although planning must take place at least 90 days before a child's third birthday, planning for these transitions should begin as early as possible. Family members, a representative from the child's early intervention program, and a representative of the school district will have a transition conference and write a transition plan that identifies activities that will make the transition as seamless as possible.

Transition plans need to consider a number of factors. Procedures should be identified to help a child adjust to and function in a new setting. A smooth transmission of information about a child (including evaluation and assessment information and copies of IFSPs that have been developed and implemented earlier) to the local educational agency ensures continuity of services. Early childhood educators should work closely with parents to develop a plan to facilitate the child's adaptation to the new environment. The goal of transition planning is to enable a child to be as successful as possible in the future environment. This means anticipating the skills the child and family will need in future preschool settings. Coordination between early intervention programs and preschool programs is also required to ensure that schools receiving young children understand each child's and family's needs and subsequently develop appropriate individualized programs.

The transition plan should answer the following questions:

1. What services are available?
2. Which services are appropriate?
3. What steps must be taken before a child can enter the next program?
4. What skills does the next program require?
5. What additional skills does a child need?
6. What can the current program do to help a child succeed in the next program?
7. What is the next program not able to do to make sure a child succeeds?

Evaluation and monitoring of progress toward outcomes is a requirement of the IFSP, but one that is often overlooked. The team should discuss how the activities planned achieved the desired outcomes and then make any necessary modifications to make the IFSPs more effective. Monitoring progress allows partners who are involved to know what is expected and determine if the intervention is being carried out as planned. Data from evaluations document changes to the child's skill level and provide information that can be used to determine whether the intervention is achieving its stated outcome or if changes need to be made. When developing data collection methods, it is important to keep the needs of the caregiver in mind. Data collection forms should be located close to where the intervention is most likely to occur, easy to understand, and quick and easy to use.

Finally, IFSPs provide a space for all involved to indicate their participation. Team members must include the parents or guardians and early interventionists. The planning might also involve other family members (such as grandparents), individuals invited by the family, specialists knowledgeable in the child's area of disability, medical personnel, and a parent advocate. Note that the latest reauthorization of IDEIA includes an option that allows a child to continue under Part C's IFSP until he or she is eligible to enter kindergarten or elementary school—rather than being transitioned at age 3 to preschool special education under Part B regulations. For the child older than 3, the IFSP must include an educational component that promotes school readiness through early literacy and numeracy skills. Parents must be advised, in writing, of their rights and responsibilities in deciding whether their child will continue with the IFSP or enter a preschool program.

Effective Family-Centered Early Intervention

If early intervention has served its purpose well, both child and family outcomes should be positive. While child outcomes are more clearly measurable, it has been challenging to determine whether families have been well served. Bailey and his colleagues (2005) interviewed families who had participated in Part C and were transitioning into other environments to determine the effectiveness of intervention services in achieving family outcomes. Families were asked if the intervention services had:

- Enabled their family to help their child grow, learn, and develop
- Increased the skills they needed to advocate for services and work with professionals
- Helped them to build a strong support system
- Enhanced their view of the future for their child and family
- Improved their perceived quality of life

More than 95 percent of families felt confident in their ability to help their children develop and learn, work with professionals, and advocate for their children to receive quality services. This number dropped to 62 percent when families were asked about their ability to deal with their children's behavior. Responses were favorable, 93 percent, when asked if they had family and friends to support them, but dropped when asked about supports in the community, with only 36 percent feeling that they were able to participate in community activities. The majority of parents (66 percent) felt positive about their quality of life, and 82 percent were positive about their futures. When asked about the early intervention services they received, families had positive responses, with 82 percent feeling the services had been beneficial (Bailey et al). Although the results of the study were positive, the majority of those who scored their experiences lower were from minority groups, had children with poorer health, and/or were single-adult families, suggesting there are still improvements to be made in meeting the needs of families from diverse backgrounds (Bailey et al).

In general, despite the trauma and disappointment associated with the early diagnosis of a child's disability, early intervention can provide families the support they need to have positive experiences. Unfortunately, this initially positive view can suffer as a child ages because early intervention is often so different philosophically and practically from "the system" operating in public schools. However, early intervention has the potential to greatly influence the way children (especially those with disabilities) learn and how their families are treated. It is incumbent upon all early interventionists to find ways to support positive relationships between families and their children's service providers and to help families build connections within the community. The support provided can have an enormous impact on the child's environment.

Evidence-Based Practice

The involvement of many different professional disciplines in the treatment of very young children with disabilities and delays has contributed to the adoption of evidence-based practice to ensure effective intervention. Evidence-based practice is widely used in medicine and allied disciplines such as occupational therapy, physical therapy, and speech and language therapy. These practices are moving into the early intervention and education fields and are appearing in federal language. Evidence-based practice involves using research-based results in making decisions about the intervention most likely to be beneficial in any individual's circumstances. Early intervention practices should be informed by research in order to help practitioners and parents achieve the best outcomes for children in their care.

Evidence-based practice provides a systematic approach for transferring research information into practice. However, it has caused some tension between researchers and practitioners, as research can sometime conflict with readily accepted practices. Kazdin (2008) encourages all involved to keep focused on improving the quality of intervention for children. When determining which practices should be used for intervention it is important to identify and clearly define the critical outcomes for the child; determine what practices have been found to be the most effective in producing the desired outcomes; articulate the value of both the outcome and the practice; determine what supports the parent and interventionist need, to confidently and precisely use the practice; and determine how to monitor the child's progress in achieving the intended outcome.

Efforts to integrate early childhood research and practices can be found in traditional research reviews, in recommended practice guidelines, and in books devoted to research-based intervention (Dunst et al., 2002). Also, a number of abstraction services, available through Internet subscriptions, can be used to gather and review research. Among these are:

- The Cochrane Library
- PubMed
- MEDLINE
- CINAHL
- HEALTHSTAR
- PsychLIT
- PsychINFO
- ERIC

In addition, the Office of Special Education and Rehabilitation funds Centers for Evidence-Based Practices that develop reviews of research in many areas. The Orelena Hawks Puckett Institute is one of these research-to-practice centers that focuses on early intervention. Evidence, research, and data are becoming a part of the common language of service delivery and important factors in the decision making that goes into prescribing services. However, it is still critical that any review of research findings balances the strengths and limitations of the evidence with the practical realities of care settings. Parents and practitioners have to be able to understand new material and use it correctly. This process can be undermined when resources are limited or when an individual child's circumstances are so unique they do not match those settings in which the research took place. Also, a family's values, preferences, and rights must always be respected, and new, promising innovations should not be disregarded because evidence supporting them is still being gathered. Despite these complexities, evidence-based practice promises continuing progress in developing effective early intervention for all children in need.

IN CONCLUSION

After several decades of implementation, early intervention continues to be a very complex and challenging field. Early intervention involves a variety of service delivery systems, serves a wide range of families and children, requires interagency and interdisciplinary teaming, and varies in implementation from state to state. In addition, children served in early intervention systems must transition into educational settings with very different models when they become preschool age. Despite its challenges, the early intervention system continues to grow. The key responsibilities of meeting the full spectrum of child and family needs requires well-trained professionals who are willing to work in collaborative teams to provide appropriate family-centered services in a variety of environments.

STUDY GUIDE QUESTIONS

1. What does *early intervention* mean?
2. What are the five general principles that guided the IDEIA regulations in regard to early intervention?
3. What are the ideals of good family-centered practices?
4. What kinds of tasks does a skilled service coordinator accomplish?
5. Define and give an example of each of the four eligibility categories under Part C of IDEIA.
6. Name the procedural safeguards meant to protect families and explain the meaning of each in terms of preserving the rights of families.
7. What are the regulations regarding assessment procedures under IDEIA?
8. Why must family assessment be voluntary and carried out with sensitivity?
9. Give an example of strategies you might use to put parents at ease when conducting assessments and gathering background information.
10. Briefly state in your own words what each of the required components of the IFSP includes.
11. Explain the rationale for using natural routines in planning IFSP objectives, and give an example of an objective that involves natural routines.
12. Explain the purpose and legal requirements of transition planning.
13. What does *evidence-based practice* mean?
14. What are the advantages of evidence-based practices?

10 | Mandated Services for Young Children

Brian Price

Many families become frustrated as they move from the Individualized Family Service Plan (IFSP) process, used when their children were infants and toddlers, to the **Individualized Education Program (IEP)** process in place when their children turn 3. Transition from those services provided through infant and toddler programs to **mandated** preschool special education for children from age 3 to 5 means transition to the public school system, which can be very difficult for children with disabilities and their families. While early intervention has adopted a family-centered approach in which services are ensured for both the family and the child, **special education** services to pupils from age 3 to 21 are focused primarily on the student. This shift takes place as planning moves from the IFSP to the IEP. Moving away from intensive family ownership and involvement creates an unwelcome challenge for many parents. Families who have become accustomed to high-quality early intervention services may quickly become disenchanted with special education programs that focus specifically on students and their needs and do not make family-centered planning as much of a priority.

Is the contrast an appropriate one? Certainly such a dramatic paradigm shift is not by intention. In a larger sense, the Individuals with Disabilities Education Improvement Act of 2004 (IDEIA, PL 108-446) validates the role of parents as educational decision makers for their children and encourages collaboration between parents and professionals to a greater extent than any other legislative mandate, court ruling, or public policy. The IDEIA explicitly calls for the active involvement of parents in all aspects of educational programming for their children with disabilities, particularly in assessment and planning. Parents accustomed to family-centered early intervention programs are beginning to demand that such collaborative practices continue throughout their children's education. After all, if family involvement is a good idea when children are very young, it must also be desirable when children get older.

As parents transition into the public school system, it is often difficult for them to find their role within a system that is not always welcoming. Often, the failure of schools to understand the need for embracing and encouraging parent participation results in unsatisfactory levels of communication and collaboration. If professionals dominate the decision-making process and student-centered practices act to exclude family input, the potential for successful family interactions in educational planning and implementation is lost and the principles of the IDEIA are unfulfilled.

A Change of Perspective

Schools that respond to the needs and characteristics of families build positive relationships that increase children's success. Special educators who wish to strengthen their partnerships with parents can take specific steps to do so. Van Haren and Fiedler (2008) suggested 10 ways to increase parent involvement, particularly in the IEP process:

1. Enhance parents' sense of self-efficacy by providing useful information or skills that address current problems. For example, suggest procedures that might hasten toilet training or reduce tantrums at home.

2. Model effective problem solving by working through steps together to define the problem, generate possible solutions, choose a solution to try, implement that solution, and finally evaluate the effectiveness of the solution.

3. Increase coping skills by offering information about community support groups, focusing on a child's positive aspects and strengths, or identifying aspects of family life that can come under the parents' control.

4. Build family competence and capacity by giving them the opportunity to observe their child at school and share information with staff.

5. Offer training and professional development and let parents set their own priorities and evaluate the outcomes.

6. Engage family members in all stages of the IEP process by minimizing jargon, ensuring all staff are in attendance, listening to parent concerns, and following up on decisions.

7. Encourage students to attend the IEP meeting and help them understand the process.

8. Involve families in community collaboration by making them aware of resources and encouraging self-advocacy.

9. Foster optimism and hope about a child's progress and increased independence.

10. Encourage families to envision the child's future and help them articulate ways to reach their children's goals.

Professionals need to understand the strength that families derive from shared decision making and be conscious and understanding of family views. The professionals also need to create parent networks and ensure families and schools are in regular communication, use parent networks, and learn to understand family views and strengths in shared decision making (Pruitt et al., 1998). When Pruitt and her colleagues interviewed 78 families with children in special education, they found almost 27 percent of respondents said they just wanted educators to listen to them. When asked, "What can educators do to be more sensitive to the needs of your family?" one mother responded:

> Taking input from the parents on what works. There are a lot of parents in special ed that don't keep it together. It is an overwhelming experience to have a handicapped child. Sometimes I think parents get written off as being out of line with things. Teachers must remember that there is a lot of value to what the parents say—even though they are hysterical or not rational—because they really do know that child. They may not be coping well right now, but they do know best. (p. 165)

Another 23 percent of the parents interviewed indicated that the quality and quantity of communication between parents and professionals should be improved. The respondents felt professionals should use a more humane demeanor with parents, interact in an honest manner, and treat parents with dignity and respect. A father stated:

> Please don't talk to me like I'm an idiot or assume that I know what you are talking about. Another thing is sometimes I get the feeling that the professionals are talking to each other and not me. It's discouraging. Another thing I might say is that instead of telling me what you are going to do with my daughter, ask my opinion, give me some say in her education and placement. I don't know what all my options are and it's tough. (Pruitt et al., 1998 p. 166)

Other parents' recommendations to professionals included having them provide more information about various disabilities, treating children with respect, and improving the IEP process. A parent suggested:

> Read the IEP. I took my daughter to school before school started, so she would know who her teachers were and could identify them. They hadn't even gotten her IEP, so they really didn't know her. I'm asking, Who would be responsible for adapting her curriculum and keeping track of that? And they're asking me, How much adaptation do you think she'll need? I'm thinking, I don't know; I'm not the teacher! (Pruitt et al., 1998 p. 167)

Although equity can be difficult to achieve, parents and professionals must be equal partners in a team striving for the same goals. The family-centered focus found in early intervention may change as the child enters special education in the school system, but the advantages of family–professional partnerships do not change. Since families have critical information about their individual children and their specific needs, early childhood professionals need to involve them equitably in all aspects of the education process and respect the knowledge they possess. Parent involvement is critical if we want children with and without disabilities to get the most out of their education.

Parent Rights and Responsibilities

Because parent involvement is so essential to the process of planning services for, and providing services to, a child in special education, the IDEIA is quite explicit about those rights. Parents have the right to:

1. Have a free, appropriate public education for their child that is of high quality, at no cost to the family, and designed to meet the unique education needs of the child and the high standards set for public education

2. Request an evaluation if they suspect a child needs special education or related services

3. Be notified, in their native language or mode of communication, whenever the school wants to evaluate their child, change the child's placement, or refuse their request for an evaluation or change in placement

4. Have reasonable efforts made to get their informed consent for initial evaluations, the initial provision of special education and related services, and reevaluations

5. Obtain an independent evaluation if in disagreement with a school's assessment and have that evaluation considered in any decision made regarding services

6. Request a reevaluation if a child's present education program is no longer appropriate or if three years have passed and current information is not sufficient for new decision making

7. Have a child tested in the language he or she knows best, including sign language if appropriate

8. Review all of a child's school records, including teachers' classroom notes

9. Be fully informed of legal rights and due process provided by law at least once a year or at their request and in their native language or mode of communication

10. Participate in the development of an IEP and in making placement decisions and be provided explanations in their native language or mode of communication

11. Request an IEP meeting at any time they feel it is needed

12. Be informed of a child's progress at least as often as parents of children who do not have disabilities

13. Have children educated in the least restrictive environment possible—one that provides all of the supports needed for children to participate with their peers—in a setting that is as close to that of their peers as is possible

14. Participate in voluntary mediation or a due process hearing, if needed, to resolve differences with the school

15. Have services provided to eligible children who have been enrolled in private (including religious) schools or who are being homeschooled

16. Allow access, or refrain from giving access, to a child's public benefits or insurance for use in providing services

17. Be assured that the label of learning disabilities is given only after ruling out a lack of appropriate instruction, limited English proficiency, or other disabilities, and after providing high-quality research-based instruction in the regular classroom

18. Have the right to file a complaint with the school district if they believe their child's rights under the IDEIA have been compromised and to receive assistance from the school or public agency in filing due process complaints

19. Be provided a mandatory "resolution session" before due process is initiated

20. Have two years in which to exercise due process rights after they know or should have known that their child's rights under the IDEIA have been violated

Just as they have certain rights, parents also have responsibilities in regard to their involvement in educational decision making. They:

1. Should work to develop a partnership with their school and to share relevant information and observations that can be helpful in planning their child's program

2. Need to ask for an explanation about any aspects of the program they do not understand, especially about educational or medical jargon

3. Need to review the IEP goals and objectives to be sure they are specific and agreeable

4. Should examine and think about the IEP carefully before signing it

5. Should request periodic reports on their child's progress or suggest changes in the program if their child is not progressing

6. Need to work directly with school personnel to resolve conflicts over assessment, placement, or educational program

7. Have to keep good records so that important information is not lost or forgotten

8. Can, if interested, join a parent organization where they can share their knowledge, experiences, and support. The organized efforts of families have often been the force that brings about needed changes to strengthen services to children.

When the provisions of the IDEIA are fully implemented, both the letter and the spirit of the law are protected. Families and schools can contribute to the process by being mindful that decision making is an ongoing, dynamic, individualized, and collaborative process that must begin with the development of a supportive and mutually respectful relationship between families and professionals. It is imperative that professionals share information about current best practices and give priority to family-initiated goals and objectives. Further, meetings and documents need to be jargon free and fully explained. All options for a range of service settings, and the advantages and disadvantages of each, must be discussed. In short, a true team implements the IDEIA as it applies specifically to each child.

The Individualized Education Program

An IEP spells out where a child is presently at developmentally, where that child should be after intervention, a plan for how to get the child there, when to expect to achieve the objectives of the plan, and how everybody involved will know that the objectives have been achieved (NASET, 2007). In reality, IEP planning and execution has not been consistent with the ideal. The responsibility for ensuring that IEPs support the work of child intervention teams falls on the shoulders of professionals. Bateman and Linden (1998) suggested that early intervention professionals obey these humorously written but seriously conceived "idea commandments":

I. Thou shalt base all eligibility decisions on professional judgment, not on quantitative formulae.

II. Thou shalt open wide the door unto every needed service and placement for each eligible child.

III. Remember thou that categorical delivery of services is an abomination.

IV. Each IEP shall be based solely upon the child's needs. He or she who looks instead to availability of services shall know the inferno.

V. Maketh every IEP in the image of its child. An IEP like unto another is a graven image—despised by all who know the IDEIA.

VI. Place not all children in the same setting, but make available the entire continuum of alternative placements.

VII. Thou shalt not exclude parents from decisions that affect their children.

VIII. Thou shalt not burden parents with the cost of their children's special education and services.

The IEP details a specific plan used by the preschool education team members on a daily basis. IDEIA regulations governing the required elements of an IEP specify that each contain the following components:

1. A statement of the child's **present levels of academic achievement and functional performance** and, for preschoolers, how the disability affects the child's participation in appropriate activities.

2. A statement of measurable academic and functional annual goals, to meet the child's needs educationally and the child's needs resulting from the disability.

3. A statement of short-term **instructional objectives** or benchmarks: This is required only for the 1 percent of children who are significantly cognitively delayed and receive alternative assessments. However, many educators believe short-term objectives are essential stepping stones for reaching goals. Parents can and should request that they be identified.

4. A statement of educational services and related services as well as supplementary aids and services needed, based on, to the extent practicable, peer-reviewed research regarding their effectiveness.

5. The date when services will begin and their duration.

6. A description of the extent to which the child will be included in regular classes.

7. A statement of evaluation procedures for determining how well a child is meeting the annual goals and a schedule for periodic reporting.

8. A statement of individually appropriate accommodations necessary for any required state or district assessments, or a determination that the child should receive an alternate assessment, with justification.

In addition to these components, the IDEIA requires IEP teams to consider the following and address the apparent needs of the child:

1. Behavior strategies and supports for a child whose behavior impedes their own learning and/or the learning of others, including functional assessment and a positive behavioral intervention plan

2. Language needs, if the child has limited English proficiency

3. Communication needs if the child is deaf or hard of hearing

4. Provision of Braille for a child who is blind (unless the team determines it is not appropriate)

5. Need for assistive technology devices

To ensure that an IEP is continuously relevant, it must be reviewed at least once a year by a child's team. In addition, parents, or anyone else on the team, may request a review prior to the annual review date.

An IEP team includes people in several different roles (Wrightslaw, 2008). In addition to the parents who are to be included in placement decisions for their child, teams must include at least one special education teacher and at least one regular education teacher, if the child participates in regular education. A local school district representative who can commit to providing special education services needs to be involved, and that person must also know about the general curriculum and local resources. One of the IEP team members must be able to interpret the instructional implications of evaluation results. Others with knowledge of, or special expertise on, the child's needs, including persons who provide related services, may be invited at the discretion of the parents or the school. When it is appropriate, the child should attend. IDEIA 2004 does allow a team member to be absent from IEP meetings if the parent and the agency agree that that person's attendance is not necessary—either because that member's curriculum area or related service is not being changed or discussed in the meeting or because that member has provided input in writing. In all cases, a child's parent or guardian must consent to the IEP by officially signing it before a service plan is implemented. Formats for IEPs vary widely and may exceed the basic requirements of the law. (A sample IEP is shown in Figure 10–1.)

Present Levels of Academic and Functional Performance

The first step in IEP development is to translate student evaluation results into practical planning information. IEP teams must use current information, state the child's present performance in concise and clear language, and identify specific skills. Teams must consider the child's strengths, the parent's concerns, the results of the initial evaluation or the most recent evaluation, and the child's academic, developmental, and functional needs. Teams draw from standardized test scores, medical records, observations, specialists' reports, and parent input. Crucial questions to be addressed include:

1. What is a student's current level of mastery in each specified skill area?

2. What specifically designed instruction should be provided for each identified skill area?

Areas to be evaluated include speech and language, fine motor, gross motor, sensory, cognitive, social, self-help, and play skills, as well as other skills particular to a

Figure 10–1 Individualized Educational Program

Child's Name: _Jennifer Lovinger_ **Birth date:** _6-19-2006_ **Age:** _38 mos_ **School:** _Pine Valley Preschool (3–5)_

Parents/Guardians: _Lyle & Julia Lovinger_ **Address:** _W. 1125 Post, Pine Valley_ **Telephone:** _328-3520_

Reason for Referral: Jennifer is an adopted child whose mother was addicted to alcohol and cocaine. Evidence of both substances was found in Jennifer's bloodstream at birth. She was premature and seized at delivery. She continued to have tremors for several days as well as increased extension. Jennifer was slow to develop physical skills and lacks age-appropriate self-help skills. She is very active, difficult for the parents to control, and has frequent temper tantrums.

Present Levels of Performance:

Strengths: Jennifer's performance on the test of intelligence fell within the average range expected at this age. She was able to follow directions, imitate line drawings, and complete fine motor tasks. Jennifer is able to place shapes in a box, turn pages of a book, and use a pegboard competently. Her mother reports that Jennifer can turn doorknobs and television and radio dials, and she can manipulate blocks. Jennifer's gross motor skills appear to be at developmentally appropriate levels; she walks, jumps on two feet, and runs with ease. She likes to throw objects and follows them visually. Jennifer sings preschool songs she learned from the television. She has good receptive and expressive language skills. Jennifer has normal hearing and vision.

Areas of Concern: Jennifer's self-help skills are delayed, and she is not cooperative in tasks such as washing hands unless they are done very quickly. Jennifer's toilet training is delayed, and she does not indicate wet or soiled pants. Jennifer still does not hold her own glass when drinking and must be fed with a spoon. She also does not assist in undressing herself. Jennifer has a low frustration tolerance and does not adapt to new situations well. She has tantrums frequently, banging her head and biting herself when upset. Her activity level is high and it is difficult to maintain sustained attention to task. Jennifer does not tolerate sensory stimulation well. She appeared to be tactilely defensive when touched and overreacted to different textures.

Statement of Major Annual Goals:	Specific Educational or Related Support Services Needed to Meet Annual Goals	Person(s) Responsible for Providing Services—Beginning and Ending Dates
1. Establish self-help skills including self-feeding, toileting, and hygiene.	A detailed task analysis for each skill area will be used and Jennifer's entry level to each task identified. A system of graduated guidance will be used within self-help routines in the classroom and at home. Completion of each task and independent completion of any step in a task will be consequated with praise and access to a reinforcing activity.	Occupational therapist, special education teacher, and parent. Initiation of service: 9-6-09 Ending date: 8-15-10
2. Reduce temper tantrums in intensity and frequency (to a rate of no more than once a month).	Jennifer will be differentially reinforced for cooperative behavior and for using appropriate ways to say "no." Each time a temper tantrum occurs, Jennifer will be placed in a chair away from other children and entertaining activities for one minute.	Any classroom staff who are present when these behaviors occur and parents at home. Initiation of service: 9-6-09 Ending date: 8-15-10
3. Increase sustained attention to tasks up to a duration of 15 minutes.	Provide structured one-on-one tutoring for short periods each day, initially with the teacher or paraprofessional, later using peer tutors. Use child-selected high-interest materials and allow Jennifer to switch to various objects or toys, gradually requiring longer contact before switching is possible.	Special education teacher and aide. Initiation of service: 9-6-09 Ending date: 8-15-10

Short Term Objectives

Related Annual Goal	Observable Behavior	Conditions	Criterion	Evaluation and Measurement Procedures—Review Dates
1. (a) Establish self-help skills	Jennifer will unbutton and remove her coat, take off her hat, and hang both in her cubby	with no teacher assistance other than verbal direction at the beginning of class each day and after outdoor play	within three minutes of entering the classroom at least twice each day.	The parent will record completion of the task and time required at entry each morning on a record sheet kept in Jennifer's cubby, and the aide will do the same after outdoor play. Reassess procedure in one month.
1. (b) Establish self-help skills	Jennifer will remove her underpants and urinate in the toilet	when taken to the bathroom after snack, after lunch, and after nap, and at any time she requests to use the toilet	within five minutes of arrival at the bathroom each time she is taken.	The aide will record time and success using a data sheet kept in the bathroom. Review progress in two months.
1. (c) Establish self-help skills	Jennifer will turn on water, use soap, scrub, and dry her hands	with verbal reminders and physical prompting when needed, after toileting and before eating snack and lunch	requiring no more than one physical prompt and two verbal reminders.	The aide will record number of verbal and physical prompts required. Review in two months.
2. (a) Reduce temper tantrums	Jennifer will say "no"	when she does not wish to participate in an activity	without crying, hitting, or running away.	The teacher will observe circle time each day and record the number of invitations to participate given to Jennifer, times "no" is used, and number of times crying, hitting, or running away occurs. Reassess in one month.
2. (b) Reduce temper tantrums	Jennifer will participate	in circle activities when invited to by the teacher	with appropriate singing, talking, or hand movements requested.	The teacher records the number of invitations to participate given to Jennifer, and whether she complied appropriately or not. Review in one month; expand to table activities when possible.

(continued)

Figure 10–1 (continued)

Short Term Objectives

Related Annual Goal	Observable Behavior	Conditions	Criterion	Evaluation and Measurement Procedures—Review Dates
3. (a) Increase sustained attention	Jennifer will manipulate, watch, or listen to a toy	that she has selected while working one-on-one with the teacher, aide, or peer during a 15-minute session,	for three minutes before switching to another toy.	The teacher or aide will use 10-second interval recording to note engagement. Review in one month.
3. (b) Increase sustained attention	Jennifer will sit quietly	during story time	without leaving her seat for three minutes.	Aide will use 10-second interval recording to note quiet sitting.

Recommendations and Justification for Placement:
Jennifer will be integrated into a combination Head Start/School District preschool that primarily serves typical 3- to 5-year-old children from low-income families. This will allow Jennifer to observe appropriate peer models, to have opportunities to learn social and academic skills in preparation for kindergarten, and to engage in age-appropriate activities. A special education teacher is available to work directly with Jennifer and to advise on behavioral and self-help skills. The combination program also offers parent training and support for Jennifer's family.

Date of IEP meeting: August 20, 2010
Persons present—Name/position

Cheryl Howard, Special Education Teacher
Corine Fry, Occupational Therapist
Betty Port, School Psychologist
Pat Lepper, School District Representative
Lyle Lovinger, Father
Julia Lovinger, Mother
Parent Signature

Lyle Lovinger   *Julia Lovinger*

child's disabling condition. Current performance levels should be stated positively so that a child's strengths and resources are examined. If there are delays in any area, the type of intervention recommended for improving that specific skill area should be noted. For example, rather than stating that fine motor skills are not age appropriate, the present levels of performance should identify concretely what a child can do: "Amos can manipulate large puzzle shapes, use a spoon for eating, and stack blocks. He has not yet acquired the skills to fasten buttons and zippers, use a pencil to draw shapes, or lace his shoes, but these skills could be taught directly by his parents with the assistance of an occupational therapist."

Annual Goals and Short-Term Objectives

Annual goals and, when required or requested, short-term objectives should be developed collaboratively by a child's IEP team. They should consider the assessment information gathered to document a child's present level of academic achievement and functional performance as well as the parents' needs and preferences. The National Association of Special Education Teachers (2007) suggests that teams should consider including goals and objectives that have been partially acquired and need to be improved, prerequisite skills for more advanced learning, and those skills that the child is highly motivated to achieve. Goals and objectives that permit a child to participate in daily activities with peers, that allow the child to function more independently in the environment, and that increase opportunities for interactions with nondisabled peers should be considered, as well as skills that would allow participation with peers in the future, such as turn taking and certain classroom behaviors.

An IEP may include specifically developed, short-term instructional objectives. These statements describe the expected outcomes of educational intervention that can be achieved within 12 months and help personnel working with the child stay on the same page and assist the teacher in setting up appropriate daily activities. Good objectives must be clearly defined, must be observable through interactions with the child, must explain the conditions under which the behavior is expected, and must define the criterion according to which the child's performance of the behavior is judged.

An observable behavior is one that can be seen or heard and, therefore, can be measured. "Being kind to others" is a description, not a behavior on which several people could agree. "*Handing a toy* to another child" is a behavior that can be observed and counted and that most people would accept as a demonstration of kindness. Usually, high-quality objectives contain action words that indicate a distinct movement, such as naming, reaching, or stacking. For example, the goal of "joining" in circle activities should be restated as the following behaviors: "*sits in small group, answers questions, sings songs, moves fingers and hands* with the music." Observing and commenting on these behaviors would make it clear that a child is joining in circle activities.

The second key component of a good objective is a description of the conditions under which the behavior is expected. Conditions are situations in which learning is to be demonstrated and might include the materials used, the setting in which a behavior is to occur, and the people to be present when the behavior is performed. Compare these two conditions under which a child is expected to count objects: "Charles will touch and count out loud the number of blocks up to three blocks *that appear one at a time on the computer screen." "*Charles will *stand at the calendar in front of the circle group* and count off each date of the month in order, stopping at today's date." Both are good descriptions of conditions, and, in both cases, Charles is expected to count, but the task of counting under the first set of conditions is probably much easier than under the second set of conditions. The second set implies a much more sophisticated knowledge level and would be influenced by more variables, including the changing number of days in a month, the size of the audience, and the use of numerals rather than semi-concrete images.

Conditions for a behavior may describe the level of assistance or cueing that will be provided, the type of audience that will be present, the mode in which the response will take place, and the type of environmental contingencies present. An example of level of assistance might be: "*Using his crutches,* Tommy will walk with a friend from the school door to the swings" or, at a later time, "Tommy *will use a cane* to walk alone from the school door to the swings." The audience that will be present makes a difference as well. It is one thing for Darette to sing "Itsy Bitsy Spider" to her mother *during bath time,* but another for her to sing "Itsy Bitsy Spider" *on stage* for all of the parents during the spring festival. The mode of performance can also vary; for example, it is important to indicate whether a child will be *drawing, using a computer* keyboard, or *orally telling* a simple story. Finally, the type of contingencies needed to ensure that a particular performance will occur may vary a great deal as well. For instance, Arnold may eat all his soup when he is *given a bite of ice cream* after swallowing each spoonful of soup or when he is *simply praised* after each swallow. All of these factors can have a substantial impact on the quality and strength of a child's overall performance and inform instruction and evaluation.

The criterion for an instructional objective expresses how well a behavior is to be performed to be considered sufficiently learned. Criteria in some cases may be stated as the percentage correct, duration of performance, level of proficiency, topography, intensity, or latency. The following examples illustrate, respectively, each type of criterion. "Katie will turn and make eye contact when her name is called by the teacher *90 percent of the time.*" "Breanna will stay at the art table *for 10 minutes.*" "Jacob will walk using only his wheeled walker for assistance a distance of *20 feet across the classroom.*" "Juan will hold the crayon pinched *between his thumb and first two fingers.*" "Ming will speak in a voice *loud enough to be heard 3 feet away.*" "Amy Jo will remove her coat with assistance, unbuttoning and hanging it in her cubby *within 5 minutes* of entering the classroom."

Performance criteria should identify behavioral levels that are likely to be achieved and naturally reinforced. A child who touches a toy but does not shake it, lift it, listen to it, or in some way manipulate it is not really likely to play with the toy because of its own reinforcing properties. A better criterion for interacting with a toy might be to make it react in some way (rattle, roll, ring, etc.) because it is the toy's properties that will eventually maintain playful behavior.

Criteria should also be set for a high level of proficiency or automaticity that encourages **generalization** and independent functioning. For example, if the criterion for using "please" is "for 20 percent of the times a spoonful of food is offered during feeding," a child is not likely to use this word very often or under new circumstances. On the other hand, if a child is expected to use "please" 90 percent of the times any adult or child offers toys, food, activities, music, or television, that child is likely to maintain use of the word long past training and in new environments. "Please" will become automatic when choices are given and may generalize to become a word used when requesting items or activities before they have been offered.

Guidelines for Developing Good Objectives

In summary, all specific short-term objectives that are developed should be worthwhile. It is perhaps because so many IEPs are written without thought to individual needs or attention to detail that many teachers see IEPs as a waste of time. The initial investment of thought and time in developing a truly individualized IEP pays off in long-term achievements for the teacher, parent, and child. When an IEP team works together to develop a plan designed for the unique needs of the child, it will become a dynamic document that will be used by all. In order to do this, the team should ensure that objectives are appropriate for the child's age and matched to his or her developmental level. For example, 4-year-olds like to put together puzzles, but Sheburra's puzzle may have only two pieces because her level of fine motor skill permits her to only work with two pieces at a time. Objectives should be functional for the environment and help the child become more independent. For example, self-feeding with a spoon allows a child to be more independent and makes dinner less complicated for the family. Further, objectives should include skills that are important for both the parents and other caregivers. Toilet training, for example, is a skill parents of preschoolers and staff in childcare settings both appreciate. It is also important that objectives within the IEP plan be realistic and achievable. For example, a child who can pull on socks is probably ready to learn to pull up pants with an elastic waistband but might not be ready to learn how to button or zip clothing. Lastly, objectives should correspond with the child's stage of learning, mastery, and generalization. A child who has just learned to count to three may need practice counting many different toys, pictures, blocks, and so forth in order to generalize these counting skills to different situations.

Special Education and Related Services

The next step in IEP development is for the intervention team to decide what to teach in order to attain the stated objectives; how to modify or adapt curriculum content, materials, and procedures; and how to arrange the environment to facilitate skill acquisition and generalization. The IDEIA asserts that educational and related services recommended must be supported by strong scientific evidence showing their effectiveness. Services should be aimed at enabling a child to make progress in the general education curriculum and to participate in extracurricular and other nonacademic activities (Greatschools, 2008).

Special education is, by definition, specially designed instruction to reduce or offset the adverse effects of a child's disability. Instruction should include modifications and adaptations that differ significantly from those made for typical students. For example, specially designed instruction might include the use of a communication board to help a child initiate interactions and respond to peers in the classroom, the use of peers to model and reinforce offers to play or share toys, or the use of switch-activated toys as reinforcers for verbalizations. Keeping in mind the importance of designing instruction that is systematic and easily implemented, instruction can be modified according to:

1. Levels of assistance provided

2. The kinds of extrinsic motivation used

3. The arrangement of the environment and materials

4. What opportunities for generalization will be provided

Students should be exposed to routine schedules, methods of instruction, and management strategies. Systematic instruction emphasizes consistency but does not require unnatural and mechanistic instruction. Educational plans should not be so rigid as to rule out regard for the interests and spontaneity of young children.

For example, specially designed instruction often includes providing assistance through prompting. Prompts may be words, gestures, sounds, movements, or picture cues that help a child respond without making errors. Prompts also include models and physical manipulation when necessary. Carefully programmed instructional materials insert and then fade out prompts in such a way that a child can move without error through each lesson.

Specially designed instruction almost always involves "reinforcement-rich" environments in which a child's appropriate responses may be positively **consequated,** making it more likely that the child will repeat the behavior. Many natural reinforcers are available, including smiles, hugs, a favorite toy, or a special game. Arranging the environment to make it easier for children to obtain reinforcement for their efforts increases engagement and the likelihood that skills will be mastered. For example, teaching during natural routines such as lunch, using age-appropriate and interesting materials, and presenting tasks through fun games and activities can naturally reinforce desired behaviors.

Finally, specially designed instruction must address the transfer of skills to other settings, other caregivers, and other appropriate situations. The team must consider how goals will be applied to life beyond the classroom. This generalization of newly mastered skills is ensured only through systematic and naturalistic procedures.

This can be accomplished by using common materials that are applicable to all environments; it also involves using naturally occurring contingencies whenever possible and, when not possible, planning for gradually reducing and eventually eliminating the contrived contingency. Further, professionals can focus on teaching strategies that will help the child in new situations and using a variety of prompts, reinforcers, and corrections. Specially designed instruction may also include related services, which are those supplemental support services that allow children to benefit from their educational experience. For example, a child who uses an electric wheelchair may require special lift-van transportation in order to attend school; a child who requires catheterization may need a nurse or paraprofessional to assist in the mechanics of emptying the bladder; and a mobility specialist may train a child who is visually impaired to use a cane to find the way around the school building in order to move independently from the bus to the classroom.

The provision of services to a wide range of eligible children and their families involves the coordinated efforts of many related personnel that are addressed in the IDEIA. These include, but are not limited to, audiologists, family therapists, nutritionists, nurses, occupational therapists, orientation and mobility specialists, physicians, psychologists, physical therapists, special educators, social workers, speech and language pathologists, and vision specialists. Table 10–1 identifies examples of the related services each professional might provide, as clarified in the IDEIA regulations. All of these personnel concentrate on working with families, addressing child development needs, and coordinating services. In addition, paraprofessionals, under the guidance of a special educator, can work directly with the child on the IEP goals both at home and childcare.

Table 10–1 Related Service Providers Identified in the IDEIA

Professional	Examples of Services Provided
Audiologist	Provide auditory evaluations and training, speech reading, and listening-device orientation and training
Family training	Provide family training, counseling, home visits
Nutritionist	Assess nutritional history, food intake, eating behavior, and feeding skills; provide nutrition information; develop and monitor nutrition and feeding plans
Nurse	Advise parents and caregivers on basic health needs; assess health status; develop health plans; administer medications, treatments, and regimes prescribed by a licensed physician
Occupational therapist	Assess the functional needs of children; enhance sensory function and motor skills; select, design, and build assistive seating and orthotic devices; adapt the environment to promote the acquisition of functional skills
Physical therapist	Screen, evaluate, and assess children to identify movement dysfunction; recommend or build adaptive equipment and mobility devices; recommend and implement environmental modifications; teach handling, positioning, and movement techniques to facilitate motor functioning and posture
Physician	Provide a "medical home," comprehensive medical care, diagnosis, and treatment; instruct parents and caregivers on health care
Psychologist	Assess psychological and behavioral needs and resources; plan and provide psychological and developmental interventions; consult on child development, parent training, and education programs
Sign and cued language interpreters	Teach sign language, cued language, and auditory/oral language; provide transliteration services; provide sign and cued language interpretation
Social worker	Prepare a social/emotional assessment within the family context; make home visits to evaluate living conditions and parent–child interaction patterns; provide counseling; mobilize community resources
Special education teacher	Design the learning environment and activities; plan curriculum, personnel, materials, time, and space; provide families with information, skills, and supports; work with child to enhance development
Speech–language pathologist	Assess and diagnose communication and oral-motor abilities; provide appropriate therapy for oral-motor and communication skills
Vision specialist	Assess visual functioning; provide communication-skills training, orientation and mobility training, and independent living skills training

Least Restrictive Environment

The decision of where a child should be placed cannot be made until after the IEP team, including the parent or parents, identifies the child's needs, goals, and educational and related services (Wrightslaw, 2008). Then the team can consider how these services can be provided in the most appropriate and least restrictive educational setting. The IDEIA makes it clear that children with disabilities should be placed, to the greatest extent appropriate, with peers who are not disabled. Each IEP must include an explanation of the extent to which the child will *not* participate in a regular class with typically developing peers. Children are also entitled to participate in extracurricular activities, so modifications should be made to allow children to take part in a class field trip or after-school program, for example.

In an open letter from the Department of Education (Musgrove, 2012), Melody Musgrove, the director of Special Education Programs, reiterated that children with disabilities should be served in settings that are as similar as possible to those that students would be assigned to if they had no disabilities. Even if the school district does not operate a preschool, the IEP team should try to arrange placements in regular kindergarten classes, public or private preschool programs, community-based childcare facilities, or in the children's homes (Musgrove). A more restrictive environment should be considered only if the nature and severity of the disability is such that education with normal peers could not be achieved with supplementary aids and services.

The IDEIA does not consider placement as just a place, and students with disabilities need to participate in a typical preschool curriculum as much as possible. Several sections of the IDEIA relate to enabling a child to participate and progress in a general curriculum. An IEP must contain a statement of the supplementary aids and services that should be provided on a child's behalf to allow for integration into regular activities in settings such as kindergartens. The law also calls for identifying strategies to deal with special factors, such as behavior problems, that would otherwise prevent a child from participating in the general curriculum with nondisabled peers. Finally, an IEP team must include a regular education teacher if a child is already participating in regular education. Transition planning and supportive services help a child move into less restrictive settings.

The emphasis on preschool integration into natural child settings and regular education programs has presented a considerable challenge to many public school preschool programs. Not all public schools offer programs to nondisabled preschoolers, so innovative administrators must work to develop partnerships with community programs that might serve children with disabilities in integrated settings. At the same time, a continuum of services must be available so that a child who needs more intensive therapies and special education can also be appropriately served. In many cases, public schools have partnered with Head Start; in other instances, they have enrolled normal peers in a school's special education preschool.

There is good reason for the law to require placement in the least restrictive setting as long as appropriate services can be provided. Placing a child with a disability in an environment populated only by other children with disabilities may result in a limited educational experience. Such a setting does not provide typical role models who facilitate learning language, peer interaction, and other functional skills. Furthermore, segregation discourages acceptance by typical peers and adults.

Still, it would be unwise to place children in settings that do not meet their most pressing needs and the preferences of their parents. A preschool setting is not least restrictive if it fails to provide appropriate services and support. Therefore, the concept of least restrictive should *not* be considered equivalent to providing one program for all children. Legislation and litigation uphold the need to provide a variety of possible placement opportunities. Hence, least restrictive environments are best facilitated through a continuum of program options that allow a child to enter the necessary setting and move on to more or less segregated settings when it is deemed appropriate.

For example, a child who is born with a serious medical problem or physical disability may require a longer than normal hospitalization with the extensive involvement of a team of medical personnel. The hospital or residential setting would be considered the most restrictive on a continuum of placement options, but at this point in that child's life, it would be the only appropriate setting for providing the care needed. When the child's health status improves, the hospital is likely to discharge the child to home care, sometimes accompanied by medical equipment, such as a respirator or heart monitor. Often, visiting nurses are assigned to work with the parents and child in the home, and if the child's health continues to be fragile, other early childhood professionals may also provide in-home services.

As the child's strength and stamina increase, placement in a center-based program in which the parents and child can work with therapists and special equipment becomes a reasonable option. Perhaps at first, the child may only attend three mornings a week, and a physical therapist may provide therapy and parent training in a setting where several other families are also present. When the child becomes stronger and has more stable health, placement in a full-time, integrated preschool might allow more normal peer interaction. Typical peers would model and motivate speech and language development and mobility. Eventually, this preschooler might enroll in the neighborhood kindergarten program with consultation from relevant specialists (Table 10–1).

The benefits of children with disabilities being educated with their nondisabled peers are well documented and the strong preference of the IDEIA regulations. A desirable environment is one in which an integrated preschool program is properly structured and children are provided training and reinforcement for interaction. However, preschool settings and their curricula should be scrutinized along several dimensions to determine their appropriateness for a particular child and family. IEP teams must carefully examine the instructional methods used, experiences and activities provided, degree of generalization of skills promoted, physical environment, curricular adaptations, data collection and evaluation, and use of technology when determining if the setting is the most appropriate for the individual child.

To ensure that school systems have an entire range of placements available, the IDEIA requires school districts to provide a continuum of alternative programs. To build and expand their continuum of placements, school districts are encouraged to look at staffing configurations, community collaboration models, and professional development activities (Musgrove, 2012). These give parents and professionals an array of options when determining a child's need for services, and they support the right of the child to be educated with typical peers. As a child reaches school age, teams may want to consider the following options:

1. Direct instruction or consultative services within general education classrooms (such as a regular preschool program)

2. Regular classroom instruction and specialized instruction within a pull-out program

3. Part-time specialized instruction in a special education preschool classroom with some time in the regular preschool or kindergarten

4. Primary instruction in a special education preschool classroom with some inclusion with typical peers

5. Full-time special education preschool and related services within a setting that houses a program that typical children attend

6. Separate public or private special education facility and services

7. Homebound services

8. Public or private residential institution for children with disabilities

9. Hospital services

Although a child's team must always put the emphasis on the least restrictive environment, they must remember that the regular setting is not always the most appropriate setting. If the child with a disability will not receive educational benefits in the regular setting, would receive more significant benefits from a more specialized instructional setting, or would be such a disruptive force in the general education setting that he or she would interfere with the education of the other students, the team must reconsider the placement and look at other options.

The least restrictive and most appropriate setting is one in which critical goals for a child can be achieved. The Sixth Circuit Court's analogy, that a child with a disability is not entitled to a Cadillac education but only to a serviceable Chevrolet, may have given some school personnel the impression that they could provide less than an individual child needed as long as the educational services were in line with those that nondisabled children were receiving. This is not the case, and any child whose disability is so severe that it limits learning in the regular classroom must be given whatever specialized services support that child's educational priorities.

Other Considerations

Instructional Methods

To meet the needs of children with different disabilities, age levels, cultural beliefs, and family values, an early interventionist must be able to use a variety of instructional approaches. However, sometimes educational philosophy dictates which instructional approach is used. A **developmental perspective** is associated with enrichment activities that emphasize a stimulus-rich environment with age-appropriate activities and toys. It encourages play and self-expression. The **behavioral perspective** is associated with direct instructional methods that include a systematic analysis of objectives, sequencing of learning steps, and systematic reinforcement of desired behaviors. Activities and learning tasks in the behavioral perspective are generally **teacher directed.** The **interactional** and **ecological perspectives** place more emphasis on how children and their environments influence each other. These latter perspectives are more often associated with responsive and active-learning techniques, such as milieu teaching, in which the environment is arranged to stimulate a child's interests and behaviors, and the teacher responds to those. They would also be described as **child directed** and emphasize natural events and routines. Still other programs focus on parents as teachers and emphasize parent–child interactions with support systems for families.

An appropriate program for preschool children with disabilities provides a balance of both highly structured (teacher-directed) activities and less structured (child-directed or developmental) activities. Such scheduling allows direct instruction on those skills that provide multiple opportunities for skill acquisition, proficiency, and generalization within natural situations. For example, a specific language curriculum could be used during circle time, and a child with a language disability would be systematically prompted to respond appropriately. During free play, the same child might be encouraged to verbalize about an object or activity that is self-selected.

In addition, generalization is best facilitated if instruction is provided at both the center and home. A center-based program provides opportunities for special instruction and socialization; well-informed parents can intervene by continuing to reinforce specific behaviors during daily routines in a home setting. For example, a child who is learning to fasten clothing may be highly motivated to button a jacket when the whole class is going outside to the playground. The child's teacher uses this opportunity to instruct by providing partial prompts and physical assistance as needed during coat buttoning. At home, the parents may use the same system of partial prompts to help the child learn to button clothing in the morning and then, as a reinforcer, allow the child to play outside for a while before boarding the bus for school.

Experiences and Activities

Because early development occurs primarily within social contexts, intervention programs have a unique opportunity to promote social behaviors between infants and their parents or caregivers and between preschoolers and their peers. Plans should include a range of activities and experiences that promote engagement and active involvement with the environment and that accommodate different ability levels and varied interests.

Consider, for example, Jonathan, a 4-year-old child with autism who is included in a preschool program for other 4- and 5-year-old children. This child is mobile only with the use of a walker, has no expressive or receptive

Denielle M. Miller

Brian Price

language skills, and engages in **self-stimulation.** Most of the children are able to sit quietly during circle time and listen to the teacher read a story. Jonathan turns away from the teacher and flaps his hands and fingers in this situation. Adjusting for this individual child's interests will help Jonathan participate with the group. For example, using concrete objects or a flannel board increases Jonathan's attentiveness, allowing him to hold something in his hands during the story decreases self-stimulation, and letting Jonathan push an appropriate computer key as the story is told allows him to respond. The other children may even prompt Jonathan to keep his hands quiet as they listen to the story. None of these adaptations makes the story less appropriate or less interesting for Jonathan's peers and may, in fact, improve their attention and participation.

Generalization

Generalization of newly acquired behaviors to functional, less structured settings can be a challenge for individuals with disabilities. To make this task less difficult, interventionists should emphasize functional, meaningful behaviors and provide many opportunities for young children to practice skills across settings and with different people and materials. Settings should use natural activities, materials, and routines to promote generalization.

A preschool setting considered as a placement for a child with disabilities should be evaluated according to the preceding factors. For example, are all the children responsible for putting away toys, setting the table for lunch, and dressing themselves for recess (all functional behaviors)? Are the children encouraged to play with each other, to verbalize their needs, to engage in group activities (vital for socialization)? Do children take part in regularly scheduled activities such as hand washing, story time, outdoor play, and snack time (routines)?

The Physical Environment

A quality preschool should provide a safe, warm, inviting, secure, and predictable environment where children with and without disabilities can thrive. A rich and stimulating environment with opportunities for children to develop their personal identities and have control over their physical surroundings should be a part of preschool design. Child-appropriate furniture, personal storage spaces, and an area for escaping overstimulation should be provided. Numerous activity areas should be available for arts and crafts, reading, sand and water play, housekeeping and dramatic play, woodworking, and outdoor exercise.

The Florida Technical Assistance and Training System (NECTAC, 2010) identified 10 elements of a quality environment for children with and without disabilities. The environment should have:

- Furniture arranged to allow for staff supervision
- Appropriate furnishings for young children
- Health and safety procedures that are implemented and on display
- Examples of children's work displayed
- A room free of unnecessary clutter and overwhelming stimulation
- Classroom spaces that are well organized
- Materials accessible to all children
- Evidence that quality language and literacy experiences are being provided
- Staff interacting positively with the children and promoting critical thinking skills
- Materials and activities reflecting diversity
- An outdoor space that is safe and accessible for all children and that includes equipment and materials for a variety of activities

Different areas of a room may be more conducive to specific behaviors and routines or specialized instruction. For example, noisy block play should be located away from language activities where a therapist is working on the production of specific speech sounds. A one-way mirror could be located conveniently so that parents may observe instruction or evaluation without distracting a child. Finally, traffic patterns may have to be arranged to accommodate orthopedic equipment such as standing tables or wheelchairs. It may be necessary to adapt access to playground equipment for some children.

Material Adaptations

To be successful, many children with disabilities need materials that are adapted for them. Regular classroom personnel may need access to specialists and technical assistance or specialized materials to accommodate the children's sensory, motor, health, and other specialized needs. Families may also need these same services readily available. For example, specialized feeding equipment, such as a nonslip plate with a lip to catch food, a built-up spoon handle, and a cutaway cup, might allow a child to self-feed at lunch with other children. Therapy mats and bolsters should be a part of the classroom furnishings so that physical therapy can be provided without removing a child from the classroom. When not used for therapy, the equipment might make a nice obstacle course for all children. A computer with a touch screen could be used to help a child with severely limited movement to demonstrate cognitive skills and for art activities or games with the other children.

Data Collection and Evaluation

A set of procedures for collecting and using data to monitor the effects of program efforts is critical in any preschool program. Data should be systematically collected on a regular basis and used in making daily, ongoing educational decisions. Such data might be collected through direct observation of specific child behaviors, the use of developmental checklists, authentic assessments such as videotapes or audiotapes, or family reporting. Regardless of the method, it is critical that data be linked to a child's goals or program and used to adjust program activities in accordance with changes (or a lack of progress) in a child's development.

For example, a goal for Courtney, a child with Down syndrome, is to increase verbal interactions with peers. Her preschool teacher decides to observe Courtney on the playground and record how often she asks to play with other children during the daily 15 minutes of outdoor play. The teacher quickly discovers that, across a week, Courtney initiated requests to play an average of only once a day, and in every case, the peers failed to accept her as a playmate. The teacher then devises a strategy to verbally prompt and praise such requests and to praise peers who play with Courtney. More data collection shows that requests to play have risen to an average of five per day. Now the teacher can fade out her prompting while continuing to praise interactions with all children.

Assistive Technology

Finally, when determining the appropriateness of a placement setting, one should consider technological interventions that may benefit young children. Technology is ever changing and has given children with disabilities increased opportunities to play, socialize, use language, and manipulate their environments along with their nondisabled peers. For example, some simple electronic switches can be activated with as little as an eye blink or a puff of air to operate toys that teach cause and effect. Augmentative communication devices, such as an electronic board that speaks when a child touches a picture, allow children who have no capacity for speech or signing to interact with others in a variety of settings. Many preschool language programs are now available on personal computers and can be used with groups of children to stimulate language skills.

The IDEIA requires that IEP teams consider what assistive technology is appropriate as a supplementary aid or intervention: Assistive technology is defined as "any item, piece of equipment, or product system, whether acquired commercially off the shelf, modified, or customized, that is used to increase, maintain, or improve functional capabilities of a child with a disability" (CEC, 2011). Assistive technology service is also encouraged. These services can help evaluate needs; purchase or lease devices; select, design, fit, customize, adapt, maintain, or replace devices as needed; train a child or the child's family on using the devices; and train professional staff who work with a child.

Supplementary Aids and Services

Assistive technology is only one part of a continuum of aids and services that students with disabilities may need to benefit from an educational program. The IEP team should discuss aids in terms of several dimensions: physical, instructional, social–behavioral, and collaborative. The physical dimension includes factors such as mobility, room arrangement, lighting, acoustics, and seating. The instructional dimension involves factors related to lesson planning, methodology, and assessment. The social–behavioral dimension relates to services or aids that would reduce disruptive behavior. The collaborative dimension addresses how multiple personnel are coordinated and how time for collaboration is arranged.

In summary, all of these factors—experiences and activities, instructional methods, generalization, physical environment, material adaptations, data collection and evaluation, and technology—should influence the design of a preschool program. If the IEP team focuses on the shared goal of enhancing a child's development and learning, they will create a dynamic document that will benefit all involved. This

The Changing Culture of Childhood: A Perfect Storm

Close Up

Three recent cultural trends that have altered and will continue to alter the nature of childhood in the United States are converging. These trends are (1) the conformity of education to a standardized test-based institution, (2) the replacement of children's spontaneous play by more structured and regulated activity, and (3) the expansion of poverty in the United States and worldwide. Ironically, the observed changes are not new: Educational mistakes of the past related to understanding the nature of learning are being repeated.

The "high-stakes testing movement," which culminated in No Child Left Behind legislation, is fundamentally flawed because it ignores individual differences and assumes a "one-size-fits-all" model. Although little research supports high-stakes testing as a valid educational practice, centuries of study and scholarly work do support individualization. As a result of the latter, emphasis has successfully been placed on individuality, creativity, cooperation, and a balance of academics, arts, and play. Predictably, the No Child Left Behind testing mandate has left chaos in its wake: negative effects on all students, particularly minority and low-income students; daily teaching of and practice on the test itself; severe decrease in students who excel at the highest level; emotional, physical, and intellectual damage to children (wetting their pants, taking their parents' drugs on days of testing, etc.); and high rates of dropping out of school. Among other things, one of the most important aspects of education is creativity in teaching, which values the soul and intellect of both students and teachers. Preschools follow the same model of drilling and prepping for tests instead of teaching the lessons of group cooperation, creative play, and love of literature and art.

At the same time that rigidity is replacing individualization and creativity in schools, children are losing opportunities for spontaneous play. Schools are reducing recess or denying it to children who perform poorly on tests. In the United States, 40,000 schools no longer have play times. Communities have also reduced the space available for children to play outside of school. Cultural changes in leisure activities for children include playing with mass-produced toys and video games, watching television, using cell phones, and so on. There is a growing failure to cultivate the inherent play tendencies of children. The seeds of exploration, artistic passion, creativity, and good health do not germinate when spontaneous play is lost.

Finally, poverty and its effects on families and childhood experiences are factors that will increasingly intertwine with the trends just described. Children's opportunities for exploration and learning are known to be limited when they live in poverty, and parenting practices are known to be generally more limiting when families live in poverty. Since 1999, the number of children living in poverty in the United States and around the world has steadily increased. Along with a diversion of resources to corporations, wars, tax cuts for the wealthy, and natural disasters, there has been a dramatic reduction in resources for social institutions. Education, health insurance, affordable housing, food, and jobs have also been victims of financial diversion. Now, teachers are leaving the profession and schools are cutting programs, jobs, and actual days in service.

The impact of these three converging trends—high-stakes testing, loss of spontaneous play, and poverty—is a destructive force resulting in enormous loss of potential, in children's failures, and in damage to children. It is therefore essential that educators, parents, and all stakeholders (read "all citizens") work together to voice outrage and outright dissent in hopes of restoring thoughtful, creative, interactive learning in our schools, redirecting resources to the essential institutions of civilization, and finding new ways to engage old practices of play in childhood.

Source: Adapted from "The Changing Culture of Childhood: A Perfect Storm," by J. L. Frost, 2007, *Childhood Education, 83*(4), 225–250.

outcome is reached only through the careful planning of instructional objectives, the deliberate selection of special education and related services that support those objectives, and the appropriate placement of the child in the least restrictive setting that will promote involvement and progress.

Susanna Price/DK Images

Challenging Behavior

All young children display inappropriate behavior at one time or another while learning social skills and trying to get their wants and needs met when they have limited communication skills. When these behaviors interfere with children's learning or if they cause harm to themselves or others, the behaviors are considered challenging. Examples of these behaviors include self-injury, negative peer interaction, disruptive behavior, tantrums, and noncompliance. Challenging behavior usually falls into three general categories (Starin, 2011):

- Behavior that produces attention and gets the child a desired item or activity
- Behavior that allows the child to avoid an undesirable item or activity
- Behavior that occurs because of its sensory consequences

Challenging behavior can serve more than one function, which makes it difficult to identify the cause of the behavior and develop appropriate interventions.

The IDEIA requires that appropriate strategies, including positive behavioral interventions and supports, be identified in the IEP. A functional behavioral assessment must be conducted when developing behavioral intervention plans for a student with challenging behavior. A functional assessment assists educators, and others working with a child, to identify the specific cause (function) of the behavior in order to implement the most effective intervention. Failure to identify the specific function of behavior may lead to the implementation of procedures that are ineffective or too restrictive (Starin, 2011). For example, if a child has learned to tantrum so he doesn't have to participate in an activity and is placed in timeout until he stops his tantrum, he has achieved his goal of avoiding the task. The teacher has inadvertently reinforced the child's tantrum, and the child will likely display the behavior again. Completing a functional behavior assessment to determine the function of the behavior can resolve some of these missteps. There are three ways to determine the function of the behavior: interviews and rating scales, systematic observations of the child's behavior, and manipulating different events in the environment to see how the behavior changes (Starin).

Interview and rating scales are usually the first step of the functional assessment. People who know the child best, such as parents, teachers, and others who work with the child when the challenging behaviors occur, should complete interviews. However, research has shown that the reliability of these reports is usually poor, and interventions shouldn't be developed solely on this information (Starin, 2011). A more reliable method is to observe the child's behavior in the natural environment and determine the events that happened before the behavior (antecedent) and the events that followed the problem behavior (consequences). Observations should be completed and analyzed by individuals with specialized training (Starin).

The result of this analysis is a clear definition or description of the behaviors, predictions about the situations in which the behavior might occur and at what times, and identification of the function the behavior serves for the child (i.e., one child might tantrum to escape a demanding situation, whereas another might tantrum to get adult attention).

In addition to meeting the requirements of the IDEIA, completing a functional assessment can be beneficial for everyone who works with the child because it allows the implementation of interventions that teach and reinforce important social skills. Further, it creates a plan so the child will not be punished for making behavior "mistakes." It allows the adults to take preventative actions and make changes to the environment that support the child. The assessment also provides a common language to use when all involved are developing an intervention plan that can be consistently implemented in all environments.

Creating Quality IEPs

While all parties have the same goal of developing an IEP that meets the needs of the student, IEP meetings can be stressful for both parents and educators. Ballero, who writes for Wrightslaw, an advocacy group for parents of children with special needs, identified steps for making IEP meetings better. Written specifically for parents, the suggestions are beneficial for all team members involved in the IEP process. When creating a quality IEP, team members should (Ballero, 2008):

1. Make every attempt to maintain relationships since they are so beneficial for the student.

2. Keep the focus on the child's needs and not the availability of resources.

Brian Price

3. Make sure everyone is comfortable with the assessments that have been completed and, if there are questions or concerns, consider getting an independent evaluation.

4. Design specific, measurable, realistic IEP goals.

5. Work to find a balance between parental expectations and district resources.

6. Always provide "face saving" ways out of a dilemma—have a backup plan and ideas for more than one solution or approach.

7. Always know what your needs are so you can be creative in finding ways to meet those needs.

8. Build comprehensive records and have documentation so the team can look at the facts and work to find viable solutions. This sometimes requires parents to face the reality of their child's disabilities and school districts to examine their flawed policies.

9. Consider the other person's point of view and circumstances—parents should spend time at the school and in the classroom and school personnel should visit the home to see what is happening in that environment.

10. Listen actively, especially to the things you do not want to hear.

11. Encourage everyone to love and value the child for his or her unique characteristics.

12. Have faith that everyone will do their best; understand that differences between members of the team will arise, but that if teams stay committed, they can achieve their goal of a quality individualized plan.

The case manager is in charge of organizing IEP meetings. Several steps can be taken in advance to make the meeting run smoothly. The meeting should be held in a comfortable place and at a time that is mutually agreed upon by parents and personnel working with the child. Meetings should always stay focused on the child and the child's specific needs. Beginning the meeting by focusing on the student's unique qualities and strengths sets the tone for the meeting, and identifying wishes and dreams for the child can keep the team focused on the "big picture" and stop the group from getting caught up in minutia. To build a climate of collaboration, it is helpful to have a picture of the child present and begin the meeting by reviewing the child's strengths. Work samples may also be helpful when looking at the student's present level.

When the team moves toward identifying the specific needs of the student, team members need to be creative, flexible, and innovative. All the student's needs, not just cognitive ones, must be addressed. The team's job is to define a vision for that student, keeping in mind the child's gifts, abilities, and strengths. This vision-defining process starts with listing all of the positives a student may possess, leading the group to interventions best suited for individual needs. Then, the team will focus on identifying specific concerns, brainstorming about how to intervene in areas of need and developing a specific plan of action. Each participant must be invited to express his or her viewpoint on all concerns so that information is complete and decisions are made collaboratively. When stating goals and objectives, the team must assign someone to be responsible for assessing whether the student is actually reaching them.

Along with identifying the special education and related services the child needs, the team should discuss how teachers, other professionals, and paraprofessionals who will be working with the child should be prepared. The team should identify any modifications that will need to be made so the child can participate in the integrated education setting. Members should be aware of their enormous power to arrange for services that are needed, and they should not limit themselves to fitting the child into existing school services if those do not suffice. It is important when stating goals and objectives to remember that someone should be checking to see whether the student actually reaches them.

What are the quality indicators of an exemplary IEP meeting? Consider the following descriptors (Beach Center on Families and Disability, 1999):

- The process is ongoing, dynamic, and individualized.
- Family-initiated goals and objectives are given priority.
- Meetings and documents are jargon free and use clear explanations.
- A mutually respectful relationship exists between families and professionals.
- Families are a part of the collaborative process and share equal decision-making responsibilities.
- Current best practices are discussed and a range of service settings are considered.

Best Practices in Preschool Intervention

A number of early intervention practices that capture the best of what is known about how to serve young preschool children with disabilities have been developed. The team must look at each practice and determine which will be the most effective for each of the students with whom they work. Effective preschools include the following best practices:

1. *Inclusive:* Typical children and children with disabilities are served in the same settings; placement in generic early childhood service sites is supported.

2. *Comprehensive:* A full array of professional services is offered through a transdisciplinary approach that uses direct instruction to teach skills that can be generalized to other settings.

3. *Authentic:* Instruction is stressed across a number of settings, age-appropriate materials and strategies are used, contrived reinforcement and aversive control are avoided, and parents are supported.

4. *Adaptable:* Flexible procedures are employed within noncategorical models; emphasis is on functional behavior rather than its developmental form or sequence.

5. *Family referenced:* The curriculum is validated in reference to the child, family, and community; parents are full partners in decision making.

6. *Evidence based:* The development of skills that are useful in the future is emphasized; transition is carefully planned.

Successful Inclusion

Successful inclusion of children with disabilities requires intentional planning so that students are engaged in age-appropriate groups and activities, follow the same schedule, use the same materials, and participate as fully as possible. Adaptations or assistance should be planned to minimize the differences between children and maximize peer interactions. The least intrusive natural prompts and contingencies that still allow the children to actively participate should be implemented. An example of this would be adjusting the height of an easel and providing a built-up brush so that a child with motor difficulties can paint beside a peer. Another example would be to have the child navigate independently (using a walker, crawling, etc.) to the next activity instead of being carried by an adult.

For inclusion to be successful, a teacher must intentionally orchestrate activities that encourage positive social interactions and facilitate friendships. This can be accomplished by teaching nondisabled peers to initiate play activities, share toys, and respond to their disabled peer's initiations. If the child with disabilities has difficulties talking, teachers must provide some means of communication, such as having the child use signs, gesture, or point to pictures. Nondisabled peers many need to be taught to recognized these communication attempts. When scheduling, teachers can make sure to plan activities that require cooperation, such as bouncing objects with a parachute where everyone holds on to some part of the parachute together to make it go up and down. Giving a child with a disability responsibilities, such as being the line leader or passing out snacks, allows that child to be viewed as competent by his or her peers.

Although it is difficult to admit, the appearance of a child with a disability can limit success with peers. Unpleasant characteristics, such as being dirty, being messy at snack, or wearing diapers, may influence staff and other children negatively. Teaching grooming skills, teaching a child how to use a napkin, and having a private changing area can reduce a child's stigma.

Meaningful inclusion also addresses the goals and objectives identified in a child's IEP. Teachers need to look at basic instructional strategies to ensure students are making progress. They must provide a range of appropriate materials, make sure the child is positioned in a way that allows independent interaction with materials, make plans for releasing support as the child's skills and attention increase, plan multiple opportunities to practice new skills, set up positive and preventative behavior supports, and embed IEP goals into naturally occurring routines and activities in the classroom.

IN CONCLUSION

The purpose of early childhood special education is to provide appropriate intervention services that will ultimately assist all children with disabilities. Four fundamental assumptions support this purpose:

1. Children who have disabilities or are at risk for having disabilities need and have a right to specialized services to enhance their development and the likelihood of success.

2. Families of children with disabilities often experience special needs and stresses.

3. The earlier children's needs are identified and services provided, the more effective these services will be in achieving optimal outcomes.

4. Because of the unique characteristics, needs, and resources of each child and family, an individualized approach to service planning and delivery has to be implemented for each child who qualifies for and is in need of services.

One of the primary goals of special education is to help children with disabilities live a life that is as normal as possible by incorporating them and their families into settings and activities they would participate in if they did not have a disability. Early interventionists understand that it is essential for families to be supported in achieving their goals. Early childhood professionals must serve children in ways that are consistent with family structures, values, needs, and functions. Promotion of child engagement, independence, and mastery across all key domains is essential for the development of the child. When children function successfully in a variety of physical and social environments, generalization is achieved. Early interventionists must also be aware that new disabilities or problems could develop in the future and must work to prevent them.

Beyond the primary goal of meeting the needs of individual children with disabilities, each early childhood professional must also accept responsibility for pursuing goals that will benefit children, and the profession, in the future. The services mandated through the IDEIA are very new in the history of this society and as such must be protected and supported if they are to be maintained. It is important that special educators continue to increase the public's awareness and acceptance of people with disabilities and their need for early intervention. It is essential that special educators continually and consistently attempt to improve the quality of early intervention services through research and evaluation of current interventions. Finally, professionals must be active in communicating best practices and disseminating professional knowledge to others to promote the availability of quality services. Early childhood professionals must advocate not only for the children and families in their direct care but also for future populations that will face the same, if not new, challenges.

Evidence-based practice is now emphasized in treating children with disabilities, and measurable performance outcomes are required. As practitioners come to rely on data-based approaches, an attitude of science becomes essential. Professionals in early intervention have to become adept at understanding research and, at the same time, be skilled in developing positive relationships with families and colleagues, respecting individual and cultural differences and providing appropriate, high-quality, personalized services. Achieving this integration of skills and attitudes is a challenge, but those who work in early intervention have the awesome opportunity to touch a life in its earliest days. This unequalled opportunity comes with tremendous responsibility for providing the best available treatment and education as well as continuous advocacy and support.

STUDY GUIDE QUESTIONS

1. What are some of the important issues related to working with families of preschool children with disabilities?

2. What should professionals do to ease the transition to preschool special education?

3. What are the essential components of an IEP?

4. Generate an original example of a clear statement of present levels of performance.

5. Develop a good objective that describes communication targets for a 4-year-old child with moderate intellectual disabilities. Be sure to include the behavior, conditions, and criterion.

6. What are the critical characteristics of specially designed instruction?

7. Describe how one might ensure the generalization of conversational skills for a 3-year-old child.

8. Describe three specialists who might provide related services to a preschooler (and family) with a hearing impairment. What kinds of support might they provide?

9. Sometimes one setting is least restrictive for one child but not for another. Give an example of a child who is deaf for whom a self-contained preschool program for a child who is hearing impaired might be most appropriate and an example of a child who is deaf for whom it would not be.

10. Briefly describe how a teacher-directed program might be different from a child-directed one. What are possible advantages and disadvantages of each?

11. What is the purpose of a functional behavioral assessment? How might it be carried out?

Glossary

abduction position in which the limbs move outward, away from the body

abruptio placenta separation of placenta from the walls of the uterus prior to delivery

absence seizure momentary interruption of ongoing activity with a brief, blank stare

accommodation (visual) process by which the eye adjusts to focus on near objects

acidotic characterized by high levels of blood acid

active learner humans, as active participants in their environment, affect the direction of their own learning

active listening attentiveness to a speaker on multiple levels: hearing, interpreting, sorting, and analyzing

acute stressors strains on a family that occur as periodic incidents related to a child's disability

adaptive reflexes mature automatic responses such as sucking and swallowing

adaptive skills abilities of self-help, problem solving, responding appropriately to environmental demands

adduction position in which the limbs move in toward the body

adolescent stage time of life starting at about 10 to 16 years of age, depending on physical maturity, and extending to adulthood

adventitious acquired after birth

advocacy favoring and supporting the needs or cause of another

albinism congenital condition characterized by a lack of the pigment that gives color to skin, hair, and eyes

alcohol related birth defects (ARBD) includes all children who have a known impact from prenatal exposure to alcohol

alleles different forms or alternative versions of a gene (with complementary alleles residing on each of the two chromosomes in a pair)

alpha-fetoprotein (AFT) screening examination of a pregnant woman's blood to detect neural tube deficits in her fetus

alveoli tiny air sacs in the lungs that permit normal exchange of oxygen and carbon dioxide

amblyopia dimness of vision not due to organic defect or refractive errors

amniocentesis procedure in which fluid is removed from the sac surrounding the fetus to determine whether it carries a genetic anomaly

amniotic sac membrane that surrounds the fetus and contains fluid that protects it from physical shocks and maintains a constant temperature

anemia condition in which the amount of oxygen-carrying hemoglobin is below normal in the blood

anencephaly congenital malformation in which the brain does not develop, and the skull, which would normally cover the brain, is absent

anomaly abnormality

anoxia deprivation of oxygen to the brain

antibodies proteins produced by the body in response to the presence of an antigen (chemical substance that causes the body to produce specific antibodies) that are capable of combining specifically with the antigen

antiviral description of a group of drugs used to treat infection by a virus

Apgar score index of neonatal wellness measured immediately after birth

apnea breathing pauses due to immature central nervous system

asphyxia loss of consciousness from interruption of breathing as in suffocation or drowning

associative play leisure activity in which individual children participate with other children engaging in similar or even identical activities

asthma a chronic inflammatory disease of the airways

astigmatism visual defect caused by unequal curvatures of the refractile surfaces (cornea, lens) of the eye resulting in light rays not coming to focus at a point on the retina

asymmetrical tonic neck reflex (ATNR) automatic primitive response in which the limbs are extended on the side of the body toward which the head is turned but flexed on the opposite side; also called *fencer's reflex*

asymptomatic showing no symptoms

at risk term used to refer to that class of children who have been exposed to any one of a number of medical or environmental factors that may contribute to later developmental delay

ataxic cerebral palsy cerebral damage that causes difficulty with coordination and balance

athetosis variable muscle tone caused by noncortical cerebral damage producing slow, writhing, and excessive movement

atonic seizure sudden reduction in muscle tone, slumping

attachment emotional bonding to another person

attention deficit hyperactivity disorder (ADHD) combination of characteristics including inattention, impulsivity, and hyperactivity

attitude of science use of parsimony and empirical research to determine what is true

auditory nerve vehicle of transmission of electrical energy from the ear to the temporal area of the brain

augmentative communication way to communicate using appliances or nonspeech systems that enhances a child's natural communication skills

axon nerve cell that carries impulses away from the nerve-cell body; any long nerve-cell fiber

babble combination of consonant and vowel sounds uttered by infants at about 4 months of age as they gain oral-motor control

Babinski reflex response in which stimulation applied to the sole of an infant's foot results in the infant spreading his or her toes

bacteria large group of typically one-celled, microscopic organisms widely distributed in air, water, soil, and the bodies of living plants and animals

behavioral assessment examination of factors that govern children's behavior under conditions such as free play, contingent adult attention, or instructional demands

behavioral perspective instructional approach that uses direct instructional methods that include a systematic analysis of objectives, sequencing of learning steps, and systematic reinforcement of desired behaviors

best practice instructional and collaborative procedures based on current research and knowledge

binding communications habits of oral interaction that generally close or diminish the probability of continued conversation

biological agents microorganisms that cause damage to human cells by either living on cells or by causing inflammation of the cells and that travel throughout the body via the blood stream or lymphatic system

biological/medical risks medical conditions that threaten to compromise a child's health, particularly perinatally; predictive of later delays

Bisphenol A (BPA) chemical compound used in plastics with possible toxic effect on humans

blended families families that include stepchildren and stepparents

bound morphemes morphemes (-ed, -ing, etc.) that alone cannot represent meaning

bronchopulmonary dysplasia (BPD) chronic lung disease resulting from respiratory distress syndrome

cardiovascular system organ system including heart, veins, and arteries

carrier individual who possesses a gene for a trait but does not express the characteristics of the trait

cataract clouding or opacity of the lens of the eye

central auditory processing disorder (CAPD) neurological anomaly preventing accurate processing of auditory speech message

central nervous system (CNS) brain and spinal cord

cephalo-caudal related to the sequence of growth and development of motor skills that is progressively downward from head, to neck, to trunk, to hips, to legs, to feet, to toes

cerebral palsy nonprogressive neuromuscular condition affecting muscle tone, movement, reflexes, and posture

cerebrospinal fluid (CSF) clear, colorless, odorless liquid that resembles water and is produced from blood through secretion and diffusion between the vascular system and the choroid plexuses in the brain; liquid that protects the nervous system from injury by acting as a shock absorber

chancre lesion at the site of contact with a person infected with syphilis

child directed flexible teaching method that follows a child's lead in terms of interests and motivation

chorionic villus sampling (CVS) testing a small tissue sample from the chorion, or outer sac, that surrounds the fetus to determine whether it carries a genetic anomaly

chorioretinitis inflammation of the retina and choroid

chromosome disorders states caused by whole chromosomes or chromosome segments rather than a single gene or combination of genes

chromosomes basic genetic units that stay constant within a species and across generations; for example, a complement of 46 chromosomes or 23 pairs in normal human cells

chronic stressors constant pressures or strains on a family caused by concerns related to a child's disability

cirrhosis interstitial inflammation of an organ, particularly the liver

cochlea portion of the inner ear associated with the reception of sound waves; lies in a cavity in the temporal bone and is shaped like a snail shell

cochlear implant electronic device surgically implanted in the inner ear that simulates neural processing for some with sensorineural hearing loss

cognition thinking, mental processes

cognitive-developmental approach theory about how children learn; recognizes a natural, fixed sequence in which thinking processes emerge

colic excessive or inconsolable crying in infancy thought to be caused by digestive discomfort

collaboration interactive process that enables teams of people with diverse expertise to generate creative solutions to mutually defined problems

collaborative teaming the acts of members of a team who agree to work together collectively to achieve common goals

communication ability of two or more people to send and receive messages; the most necessary skill of both parents and childhood educators

complex sentence sentence that contains at least one independent clause and at least one subordinate or dependent clause

compound sentence sentence that contains at least two independent clauses; combines two or more ideas in a single sentence by using conjunctions, relative pronouns, or other linguistic linkages

computerized axial tomography (CAT or CT) procedure that uses X-Rays to view several planes of the body at one time to produce a three-dimensional image of body tissue

conceptual system set of principles that articulate a body of knowledge

concrete assistance help in acquiring basic needs such as food and housing

concrete operations stages of cognitive development (at ages 7–11 years) when children can use real objects to logically solve problems

conduction heat loss to unwarmed surfaces (such as a mattress) or evaporation (heat loss through fluid loss through skin)

conductive hearing loss disruption of mechanical conduction of sound as it is transferred from the outer ear through the middle ear

congenital present at birth

consensus building guiding groups in decision making based on group agreement

consequate to follow, contingent on a specific behavior

consolidation condition of disorganized behavior that is replaced by more advanced developmental skills

content the meaning of communicated messages

continuum of services a range of therapeutic and educational services and settings from least to most intensive

contractures conditions in which muscles and tendons shorten, causing rigidity and joint immobility

convection heat loss with the delivery of unwarmed gases such as oxygen

conversational postulates subtle communication rules that allow humans to converse in a reciprocal manner (i.e., initiating talking, turn taking, questioning, repairing a breakdown in conversation, maintaining interactions, and closing a conversation)

cooing vowel sound production that requires little motor control or use of the articulators (tongue, lips, palate, and teeth); usually occurs in infants during the perlocutionary stage

cooperative play organized action of children engaged in play activities

cornea transparent epithelium (tissue covering internal and external surfaces) and connective tissue membrane that cover the anterior portion of the eye, which refracts light rays and channels that light through the fluid-filled anterior chamber

corrected gestational age age adjusted to reflect premature delivery

cultural competence knowledge of and respect for diverse beliefs, interpersonal styles, attitudes, and behaviors

culturally sensitive aware of different values and practices of divergent ethnic and cultural groups

cyanosis blue-tinged color to the skin, which can occur when blood bypasses the lungs, resulting in decreased oxygen being available to cells

cystic fibrosis (CF) genetic condition that results in excessive secretion of mucus that blocks lung and pancreas function

cytomegalic inclusion viral infection (CMV) one of the family of herpes viruses that is common and produces few symptoms in adults but can cause malformations and brain damage to an unborn child

demographics statistical characteristics of human populations

dentition development of teeth

deoxyribonucleic acid (DNA) nucleic acid compound that carries the chemical coding needed to transmit genetic information from generation to generation

developmental delays progress in one or more developmental areas that is behind the normal range at which children achieve milestones

developmental guidance act of providing information on age-appropriate behaviors for young children to families and others

developmental milestones major indexes of development identified across developmental areas and across years; used to measure developmental progress

developmental perspective approach that emphasizes using age-appropriate activities and materials

diplegia cerebral palsy affecting all four extremities of the body but with more involvement of the legs than of the trunk and arms

discretionary programs plans or systems allowed but not required by law

dominant gene gene that possesses sufficient genetic information for a characteristic to be expressed when only one allele carries the gene

Down syndrome chromosomal disorder resulting from an extra 21st chromosome and resulting in a range of cognitive, physical, and medical conditions

ductus arteriosus develops through the embryonic liver "with" connects the embryonic lungs and heart

ductus venosus a major blood channel that develops through the embryonic liver

dyskinesia condition caused by noncortical cerebral damage (see *athetosis*)

early childhood special education field of study devoted to serving the developmental needs of infants, toddlers, and preschoolers with, and at risk of, disabilities and their families

early childhood stage time of life from 3 years to 6 years of age

early intervention period of mediation for children from birth to age 3 when services are delivered to infants and toddlers with developmental delays or at-risk conditions

eclampsia pregnancy-induced seizures that are acute and life threatening

ecological approach approach to instruction that focuses on children interacting with their environment by following a child's interests to set the occasion for instruction

ecological approach to assessment evaluation that focuses on children, their environment, and the interaction between the two

electroencephalography (EEG) procedure that measures electrical potentials on the scalp to produce a record of brain activity for analysis

embedding process in which children add internal clauses to sentences (develops at 4 to 13 years of age)

embryonic stage period beginning in the 3rd week of pregnancy, when cell differentiation permits the emergence of the central nervous system and circulatory system; and completed by the 8th week of gestation

emotional support eliciting and listening to a person's needs while encouraging positive attitudes and actions

empirical based on observation and experimentation

empower to improve a person's (or family's) ability to make decisions independently

empowerment encouragement of an individual to rely on self and provision of understandable and practical information that can be used by families

encephalitis inflammation of the brain

epilepsy condition of recurrent seizures

equilibrium reflex involuntary response that causes the body to realign its trunk to a vertical posture after the body moves or is moved out of midline

ethical conduct action that is responsible and respectful of professional rules

ethical standards for conduct accepted professional guidelines for appropriate behavior toward others

ethnocentrism held belief that one's own culture and values are superior to those of others

etiology the cause

Eustachian tube continuous pipe from the middle ear to the throat that acts as a safety tube, equalizing internal and external air pressure on the tympanic membrane

exocrine glands glands, such as salivary or sweat glands, that secrete substances onto an inner surface of an organ or outside the body

exon skipping process of correcting genetic errors by using stem cells to communicate to cells to skip over the gene error

exosystem societal structure of entities such as local and state agencies or advocacy groups that affect a child's life

expressive language coded output message emitted by a child or adult

extension unbending movement of a joint that changes the angle between bones that meet in the joint; the opposite of flexion

external ear part of the ear consisting of the auricle, auditory canal, and tympanic membrane; responsible for collecting sound waves

extrapyramidal outside the pyramidal nerve group; used to refer to noncortical cerebral damage

extremely low birth weight (ELBW) measurement of a newborn of less than 750 g (1 lb 10 oz.) upon delivery

failure to thrive delay in physical and neurological growth in infancy and early childhood due to organic or environmental causes

family first practices that increase the family's power to make their own decisions and act accordingly

family hardiness constellation of three characteristics: (1) control, the ability to influence events, (2) commitment, dedicated and active involvement in events, and (3) challenge, view changes as opportunities for growth and development

fetal alcohol effects (FAE) moderate birth defects caused by prenatal exposure to alcohol

fetal alcohol spectrum disorder (FASD) full range of alcohol-related disabilities derived from maternal consumption of alcohol during pregnancy

fetal alcohol syndrome (FAS) serious birth defects caused by prenatal exposure to alcohol

fetal blood sampling specimen of blood withdrawn from the umbilical cord to determine whether the fetus carries a genetic anomaly

fetal stage period of pregnancy from the 9th week through the 9th month

fine motor movement of small muscles

flexion movement of bending a joint; the opposite of extension

foramen ovale opening between the two upper chambers of the heart that is normal for fetal and neonatal (newborn) circulation but normally closes on its own by 3 months of age

forbearance putting off outcomes—siblings of children with disabilities sometimes put off their own interests in deference to the needs of their brother or sister with special needs

form structure of language that includes articulation and grammar

formal operations the stage of cognitive development (at 11 years and older) when humans develop abstract thinking, which includes classifying and sorting

fragile X syndrome chromosomal disorder resulting from a weak connection of the short arm of an X chromosome to the whole chromosome, with cognitive and behavioral problems ranging from mild to severe

freeing statements remarks that are habits of interaction that encourage expanded dialogue

functional behavioral assessment (FBA) assessment of environmental conditions in order to determine their effects on the observed behavior

functional imaging diagnostic procedures capable of measuring chemical activity

gametes cells involved in reproduction (a sperm is a male gamete, and an ovum is a female gamete). These germ cells have one chromosome from each chromosome pair. When a sperm and ovum join during conception, the resultant cell has a full set of chromosomes

gastrointestinal system part of the digestive system that consists of the mouth, esophagus, stomach, and intestines

gastrostomy tube cylindrical pipe or gastric button through which feedings can be given directly into the stomach, bypassing the esophagus

gene regions of chromosome made up of molecules that define a particular trait

gene potentiation the activation of a gene, usually through environmental influence

gene repair a molecular bandage is used to alter damaged genes and make them functional

gene therapy normal copies of the gene are added to cells in an attempt to correct these cells and ultimately cure the disease

generalization transferral of skills to other settings, other caregivers, and other appropriate situations

generalized seizure uncontrollable muscle movement caused by activation of the entire brain; involves the whole body

genes regions of a chromosome made up of molecules that collectively define a particular trait

genetic mapping process of learning the genetic code of humans by charting the relationships between specific genes and individual chromosomes

genetics the mechanisms of heredity, transmission of biological traits, and the variation of inherited characteristics

genotype combination of alleles inherited for a particular trait. (The genotype can be determined only through cellular testing because the trait determined by the genotype may or may not be expressed.)

gestation period of intrauterine fetal development

gestational diabetes diabetes acquired during pregnancy

glaucoma condition characterized by a buildup of pressure in the anterior chamber of the eye

gravida medical term for a pregnant woman; often used with a number to indicate the number of pregnancies a woman has had (a 3-gravida)

gross motor movement of large muscles

group B streptococcus group of bacteria from the streptococcus family

group process procedure that uses contemplation by a group to determine what actions should be continued and what group behaviors should be changed in order to make collaborative efforts more effective

growth retardation arrested development in which a child is very small for his or her age; weight falls under the 10th percentile

handling therapeutic preparation for movement and positioning

hardwiring neurological process affecting structure of brain and memory when behaviors are repeated many times

heavy metals lead, zinc, mercury

HELLP pregnancy-induced hypertension (PIH) that puts fetus and mother at risk

hematoma bruise or swelling filled with blood

hemiplegia cerebral palsy affecting one side of the body

hepatitis viral infection causing damage to the liver

herpes infection with the herpes simplex virus, causing small, painful blisters on the skin

heterozygote pair condition in which an individual has two different alleles for a particular trait. (For example, a child who receives a normal gene from one parent and a gene for cystic fibrosis from the other parent will not express the disease from this heterozygote pair because the gene for cystic fibrosis is not dominant.)

homozygote pair two identical alleles for a certain trait in an individual. (For example, when the gene for cystic fibrosis is inherited from both mother and father, the alleles form a homozygote pair, and the child will express the disease.)

hydrocephalus abnormal increase of cerebrospinal fluid in the ventricles of the brain, causing the head to increase in size beyond two standard deviations above the mean on the standard growth chart

hyperbilirubinemia abnormally high bilirubin levels in VLBW infants due to immature kidneys; puts infant at significant risk

hyperopia farsightedness; a condition in which parallel light rays come to focus beyond the retina because the refractile system is too weak or the eyeball is flattened

hypertonia high muscle tone that limits joint movement

hypoglycemia condition in which the amount of glucose available for use by cells is decreased

hypothermia low core body temperature

hypotonia state of having low muscle tone that allows excessive joint movement

hypoxia condition in which oxygen flow is decreased

imitation mimic of another's behavior or language

inclusion participation in the same activities as nondisabled peers

index measures of development or achievement, including psychometric measures, academic progress, and measures of social success

Individualized Education Program (IEP) intervention plan developed by a team for a child (age 3–21 years) with a disability; includes a report of current performance, annual goals, instructional objectives, special education and related services to be provided, and an evaluation proposal

Individualized Family Service Plan (IFSP) intervention design developed by a team for an infant or toddler (birth to age 3) who has a disability and for the child's family; includes the identification of strengths and needs, statement of expected outcomes, intervention and support services to be provided, and evaluation proposals for the child and the family

Individuals with Disabilities Education Improvement Act (IDEIA) current federal legislation regarding the education of children with disabilities; provides for a free, appropriate education for all children with disabilities ages 3 to 21 and encourages services to infants and toddlers who are disabled or at risk for developmental delay

infancy time from 30 days to 12 months of age

inflammation redness, swelling, heat, and pain in tissue caused by injury or infection

inner ear fluid-filled chamber located in the temporal bone medial to the middle ear, containing the cochlea, the vestibule, and the semicircular canals

intracardiac inside the heart

instructional objectives expected outcomes of educational intervention within a short-term time frame; should state the observable behavior, conditions, or situations under which the behavior is expected and the criterion for it, or how well the child must perform the behavior

integumentary system skin—the outer barrier of the body that protects against infections and helps regulate heat

interactional perspective approach to instruction that emphasizes structuring the child's learning environment to stimulate interest in active responding

Interagency Coordinating Council (ICC) association of agencies at the federal, state, and local levels that provides administration and service delivery for infants and toddlers with special needs

interdisciplinary combination of expertise from several disciplines for evaluating, planning, and implementing intervention; description of a group whose members perform related tasks independently but interact collaboratively to meet goals

intracranial bleeding bleeding in the brain; stroke

intraventricular hemorrhage (IVH) bleeding in the brain

in utero within the womb

in vitro implantation fertilization of ovum that takes place outside the uterus and then ovum is medically inserted in a woman's uterus to end of definition

ischemia death of cells and tissue due to decreased blood flow and oxygen supply

joint activities play between two or more individuals that involves the same topic, toys, or activity

karyotype analysis of the chromosomal makeup of an individual, including the number of chromosomes and any abnormalities

killer phrases conversational comments that discourage further engagement

kin immediate and extended family

kinship care childcare, housing, and so on provided by members of the immediate or extended family other than the parents

language symbol system by which one expresses and receives messages

late visual bloomers children who, like those with motor, language, and social developmental delays, experience maturational delays in visual ability, appearing to be blind at birth and during their first months of life, but usually developing normal visual ability by 18 months to 3 years of age

least restrictive environment most appropriate setting in which a child with a disability can be with typical peers to the greatest extent possible and still have individual needs met

lens transparent convex structure of the eye just behind the pupil whose curvature can be altered to focus on near or far objects

low birth weight measurement of a newborn of less than 2,800 g (6 lb 3 oz.) at birth

low vision visual acuity at or less than 20/70 in the better eye with correction

macrosystem cultural and legislative and judicial contexts that affect a child; for example, IDEIA legislation

magnetic resonance imaging (MRI) procedure that uses magnetic force to draw ions to the edges of an internal organ to produce an image of normal and abnormal tissues

mandated required by law

maternal plasma fetal DNA recovery (MPFDR) prenatal diagnostic procedure

maternal serum fetal cell sorting (MSFCS) prenatal diagnostic procedure

maturation universally observed sequence of biological changes as one ages; permits the development of psychological functions to evolve

mean length utterance (MLU) index of the sophistication of a child's language determined by measuring the frequency of morphemes in the child's utterances

meconium thick, sticky, greenish-black feces passed by infants during the first day or two after birth

meconium aspiration syndrome disorder that occurs when the dark sticky mucous in the intestine of a fetus is expelled before birth and inhaled as the infant takes its first breaths

meiosis cell division that produces sex cells when chromosomes divide and produce half the complement of 46 chromosomes in each of the resulting gametes

meninges covering of the brain and spinal cord that consists of three layers (arachnoid, dura mater, and pia mater)

meningitis condition in which infection occurs producing inflammation of the meninges, which is the covering that surrounds the brain and spinal cord

meningocele neural tube defect that involves a soft tissue mass covered by skin that does not contain nerves or nerve roots

mesosystem relationship among the microsystems in which a child sometimes spends time; for example, the relationship between teacher and parent

metacognition thinking about, reflecting upon, and understanding one's own mental strategies

metamemory understanding of one's own memory ability

microbes germs that are so small they can be seen only through a microscope

microcephaly condition of a very small head and brain; head circumference that falls at least two standard deviations below the mean for age on a standard growth chart

micropremature infant neonate born at less than 600 g (1 lb 5 oz.) or at less than 25 weeks gestation

microsystem immediate environment in which a child spends the majority of time, for example, the childcare center

middle childhood stage time of life from about 6 to 10 years of age

middle ear small air-filled chamber medial to the tympanic membrane containing three tiny bones: the malleus (hammer), incus (anvil), and stapes (stirrup)

mitosis cell division that produces two identical daughter cells, each containing the full set of 46 chromosomes; occurs in all body cell reproduction in which chromosomes replicate and the cell divides once to create two identical cells, as in the regeneration of skin cells

mobility degree to which an individual is able to move around the environment independently with or without adaptive equipment

monoplegia cerebral palsy affecting one extremity of the body

monozygotic two identical cells deriving from a single fertilized egg

morbidity diseased; pertaining to disease

Moro reflex symmetrical abduction and extension of the arms followed by an adduction when a child's head is suddenly dropped backward (as if the child were embracing something)

morpheme smallest part of a word that possesses meaning

morphological development evolution of word structure and word parts

mortality death rate; the ratio of the total number of deaths to the total population

mosaicism condition that occurs when a portion of cells has 46 chromosomes and another percentage of the cells has a deleted or an extra chromosome

multidisciplinary description of professionals from several different disciplines who work independently but meet to exchange information and to present goals and progress reports

multifactored diagnostic evaluation administration of more than one test to determine the presence of a disability; should be administered in all areas relevant to a child's perceived needs

multifactorial disorder condition that evolves when a genetic predisposition results in a disorder when an individual is exposed to specific environmental conditions

myelin sheath lipid material with protein arranged in layers around many axons to increase efficiency of electrical transmission during neural activity; gives white matter in the brain its color

myelinization production of myelin around an axon

myelomeningocele condition in which both the spinal cord and its covering, the meninges, push through a spinal defect to the surface

myoclonic seizure brief, shocklike muscle contractions

myopia nearsightedness; a condition in which parallel light rays come to focus in front of the retina because the refractile system is too strong or the eyeball is elongated

myringotomy surgically inserting tubes through tympanic membrane to facilitate drainage of fluid

natal pertaining to birth—before, during, and immediately after

natural environments settings in which typical children spend time

natural routines activities that normally take place in the daily events of infants and toddlers and their families

near-infrared spectroscopy (NIRS) an imaging technique using infrared waves to measure brain activity

neonatal time of life from birth to 30 days of age

neonate newborn during the first 4 weeks after birth

neural tube defects disorders in the development, closure, and formation of the neural groove, the vertebral column (which houses the spinal cord), or other soft tissue structures surrounding the nerves

neurological system organ system including the brain, spinal cord, and nerves

neurons cells responsible for receiving and sending messages

noncontingent helping providing assistance without effort or request from the recipient

nondisjunction during meiosis incomplete detachment of the pairs of cells occurring during cell division to create either an ovum or sperm

nonorganic without specific physical cause

normal development sequence of changes across time that is very similar for all children

norms statistically determined age levels for reaching developmental milestones

nuchal translucency application of ultrasound to identify prenatal conditions by measuring fluid at back of fetus' neck

nystagmus rapid involuntary oscillations or tremors of the eyeball; may be horizontal, vertical, or rotary

object permanence understanding that objects continue to exist even when they are out of sight

occipital lobe back section of the head

optic nerve band that transmits the visual image from the eye to the brain

organic of specific physical causation

organism total living form; one individual

orientation conceptual, perceptual, sensory, and body awareness of space and environment

ostomy opening made from an internal tube to an external source, allowing for passage of urine or stool from the body (usually to a collection pouch)

otitis media (middle ear disease) inflammatory disorder of the middle ear; may be acute otitis media or serous otitis media

overextension children's language usage that commonly occurs because of a limited repertoire of words or when categories are defined too broadly; for example, referring to all men as "Daddy"

ovum unfertilized female sex cell; egg

parachute reflex extension of arms and legs toward the surface that results when an infant is held in a horizontal position and prone, and then lowered toward the floor

paraeducator support personnel for educators who are not required to have a terminal college degree

parallel play activity of children who play independently even though they are near other children who are engaged in similar activities

paraphrasing listener's restating the heart of the conversation in order to confirm and clarify what was meant

paraplegia cerebral palsy affecting the lower extremities of the body

parity number of live births delivered by a woman

parsimony adoption of the simplest assumption in formulating a theory or interpreting data

partial complex seizure physical manifestation that commences from one cerebral hemisphere of the brain

partial fetal alcohol syndrome (pFAS) includes children who express some but not all traits of Fetal Alcohol Syndrome

partial seizure seizure resulting from activation of one area of the brain

patent ductus ateriosus (PDA) condition in which the opening between the aorta and the pulmonary artery, which permits blood to bypass the lungs prenatally and normally closes shortly after birth, stays open after birth and diminishes flow from the aorta

pathogenic capable of causing disease

patterning method of treating children with significant disabilities that requires intensive exercises believed to resequence brain patterns and cure children of their disability

perception checks confirmations by a listener who checks his or her perception or understanding of what was said in the course of a conversation in order to open up and clarify the communication

perinatal relating to the period just before or just after birth

periventricular leukomalacia (PVL) condition involving cysts or fluid-filled holes in the brain

personalization provision of comprehensive supports based on individual needs in a manner best suited for a particular child and family

personalize providing comprehensive supports based on individual needs in a manner best suited for a particular child and family

person-first language communication about children and adults with disabilities that specifies personhood before disability, e.g., infant with cerebral palsy

phenotype observable expression, or appearance, of a genetically inherited characteristic in an individual

phonological development progression of speech sounds in humans

phonology study of speech sounds

placenta fleshy mass made up of villi, or projectiles, that insert themselves into the lining of the uterus to nurture a developing fetus

placenta previa condition in which the placenta implants itself near the cervix rather than the top of the uterus

plantar reflex flexion of toes when pressure is put on ball of foot

plasticity in terms of neural function, the quality of being plastic, or capable of being molded

polychlorinated biphenyls (PCBs) potentially damaging agents made up of synthetic and organic chemicals

polydrug combination of drug use including nicotine and alcohol

positioning treating postural and reflex abnormalities by careful, symmetrical placement and support of the body

positron emission tomography (PET) imaging technique used to view tumors, seizures, and so on

postnatal after birth, with reference to the newborn

postural reflexes (adaptive reflexes) involuntary responses that supplement movement while preventing injury

pragmatics the effective use of language in a social context

predictive utility provision of accurate forecasts about what will happen

preeclampsia gestational hypertension occurring after the 20th month that presents a danger to fetus or neonate and mother

preexisting diabetes diabetes that developed prior to pregnancy

preimplantation genetic diagnosis evaluating an egg fertilized in vitro prior to implanting it in the uterus

premature labor labor prior to 37 weeks of gestation

premature rupture of membranes breaking of the membranes of the water sac surrounding the fetus prior to the 37th week of pregnancy

prematurity birth of a developing fetus prior to the 37th week of gestation

prenatal preceding birth

prenatal alcohol exposure (PAE) prenatal exposure to toxic levels of alcohol, which disrupts fetal development

preoperational stage period in which children reason using linguistic input and personal knowledge

present levels of academic achievement and functional performance categories related to the use of current evaluation information to summarize skills and abilities

presuppositions judgments made about the listener in a conversation that allow one to modify the content and style of the communication. (These judgments include assessments of social status, educational or developmental level, closeness of relationships, etc.)

preventive intervention variety of therapeutic services that build interaction skills between parents and their children

primary social supports informal networks comprised of close family, friends, and neighbors who sustain one another

primitive reflexes involuntary motor responses to specific stimuli that interfere with movement if persistent

proactive stance position in which one works to influence others positively about a particular position

procedural safeguards actions to support rights guaranteed to families of children eligible for services under the IDEIA

prolapse of umbilical cord condition that occurs when a baby presses on the umbilical cord during delivery and the blood flow (and oxygen supply) to the baby decreases or stops

promotion furtherance of strategies that support healthy relationships between parents and their children

prone lying on the stomach

protective extension act of reaching out an arm to prevent falling when pushed out of midline, either from a sitting or standing position

proteomics the study of protein production as a result of genetic coding as the key to human functioning

protozoan member of the phylum comprising the simplest forms of the animal kingdom; a unicellular organism

proximal–distal descriptive of the sequence of development that progresses from the center of the body outward toward the extremities

psychometric approach assessment comparing a child to normal standards of development, intelligence, or achievement in order to determine performance discrepancies

psychotherapy professional treatment helping a person understand how past experience has affected current psychological conflicts

Pygmalion effect tendency of traits attributed to a child to come true because they are treated "as if"

pyramidal tract area of the motor cortex and spinal cord

quadriplegia cerebral palsy affecting all four extremities of the body

qualitative–developmental assessment process in which a child's skills and approach to people and tasks are evaluated according to a developmental sequence

radiation heat loss through dissipation from the body into the air

range of motion area of movement for a limb or body part; measured in degrees

range of normalcy area between lower and upper limits of age at which developmental milestones are typically attained

range of reaction the extent to which human development is influenced by environmental factors

receptive language conversation in which the recipient understands the message sent by another individual

recessive gene cell that does not possess sufficient genetic information for the characteristic to be expressed unless the gene is carried on both alleles

refinement sequence of development that progresses from large muscle control to small muscle control

reflex integration coordination of involuntary reflexes to allow for normal motor development

refractive error visual defects caused by abnormal curvature of the cornea, the lens, or the shape of the eyeball that misalign the light rays on the retina and distort vision

reinforcement a change in stimulus, contingent upon a response, that results in an increase in the probability of that response

related services additional support services that allow children to benefit from their educational experiences

relationship building intervention approach that focuses on building relationships between infants and their parents

relative clauses parts of a sentence that identify a thing, for example, "I want a doll *that wets.*"

replicate demonstrate again with the same results

residual vision visual ability remaining to an individual with a visual loss

respiratory distress syndrome (RDS) collapse of alveoli in the lungs due to lack of surfactant production in premature infants

respiratory system organ system including lungs and airways

respite supportive service for families that relieves them temporarily of childcare

retina the innermost layer of the eye; neural layer containing the receptors for light

retinopathy of prematurity (ROP) overgrowth of connective tissue in the eyes due to excess oxygen given to premature infants; oxygenation that causes damage to the blood vessels supplying the retina and, in severe cases, detachment of the retina

Rh sensitization blood type incompatibility of mother and fetus that causes a buildup of antigens in mother's blood

rooting reflex response that occurs when an infant's cheek is lightly stroked and the infant's head turns toward the stimulus

rubella disease caused by a virus that usually produces only mild upper respiratory symptoms and a rash in the infected individual; can cause severe damage to a fetus and can result in spontaneous abortion; commonly called *German measles*

savant individual who shows extreme aptitude in one area (e.g., music or mathematics)

screening relatively quick and preliminary evaluation used to determine whether a child should be referred for more in-depth assessment

secondary social supports formal sources of assistance, such as health-care providers, educators, and therapists, who are usually more temporary than primary social aids

segmentation when infants begin to identify familiar words as distinct from other words

seizure abnormal electrochemical discharge in the brain that causes the body to tremor, lose consciousness, or move in an uncontrollable ways

self-help skills independent abilities including eating, dressing, toileting, and other personal responsibilities

self-stimulation sensory input from personal tactile, visual, auditory, or other physical activity that ignores other people or objects in the environment (such as hand flapping, lip smacking, biting)

semantic relationship combination of two or more words that possess more meaning than any one of the words uttered in isolation

semicircular canals three canals in the temporal bone that lie approximately at right angles to one another, containing receptors for equilibrium, specifically for rotation

sensorimotor stage period of life from birth to age 2; represents children's primitive exploration of their environment during which they attempt to integrate sensory information with their own movement

sensorineural hearing loss auditory disorder that results from damage to the cochlea or auditory nerve

service coordinator person assigned to family of a child with special needs; is responsible for seeing that family and child receive all services for which they are eligible under Part C of the IDEIA

sex chromosomes a pair of chromosomes, usually designated X or Y, that combine to determine the sex and sex-linked characteristics of an individual, with XX resulting in a female and XY resulting in a male

sex-linked disorders conditions transmitted through the parents on a sex chromosome (X or Y) so that it is common for individuals of only one gender to express the disorder

shaken baby syndrome theory about traumatic brain injury that results from frequent severe shaking of an infant

sickle cell crisis frequent and severely painful episode of sickle cell disease

single photon emission computer tomography (SPECT) a diagnostic tool and imaging technique that uses gamma rays to provide a 3D picture of the internal organs, usually presented as cross-sectional slices

socioeconomic relating to income and social factors

solitary play lone activity involving a child with no interaction with others

spastic cerebral palsy cerebral damage that leads to the muscles tightening and resisting efforts to move

special education specially designed instruction that includes adaptations that are significantly different from modifications normally made for typical students and that are necessary to offset or reduce the adverse effects of a child's disability

spectator play when a young child observes the play of others but does not attempt to join them

speech acts verbal intentions of the speaker for purposes for communicating

spina bifida incomplete spinal column and the relationship of the spinal cord and contents to the defect

spina bifida occulta defect in the vertebrae covering the spinal cord with no exposure of the neural membranes or any evidence of nerve tissue in the defect

spinal tap procedure in which a hollow needle is used to draw cerebrospinal fluid from the spinal canal

stage theory response naming and sequential ordering of the complex emotions that are normal during times of grief

startle reflex reaction that occurs when a sudden noise or movement causes a child to throw its arms away from the body and then back toward the midline

status epilepticus prolonged seizure of 15 minutes or more that is a life-threatening condition

stem cells undifferentiated cells that have the potential to divide indefinitely and to assume the function of specific cells (e.g., muscle, neural)

stepping reflex steplike response that occurs when a child is held in a vertical position so that its feet touch a surface

stereotyping making assumptions about others based upon group membership, superficial information, cultural, and/or demographic characteristics

strabismus condition in which the optical axes of the two eyes are not parallel; cross-eyed

supine lying on the back

surfactant chemical agent needed for independent breathing that is not produced in fetuses in sufficient quantity until the 32nd to 33rd week of pregnancy

syntax rules that govern structural patterns of language utterances and sentences

syphilis viral sexually transmitted disease that can be transmitted transplacentally and during birth to the fetus/neonate

systemic pertaining to or affecting the body as a whole

teacher-directed highly structured teaching method planned in advance and guided by the teacher

temperament characteristic of emotional response

teratogen any agent or factor that causes physical defects in a developing embryo

term pregnancy gestational period of at least 38 weeks

tertiary third in order, as in tertiary service delivery in which a professional serves a parent who, in turn, serves a child

tertiary services indirect assistance that benefits children or their families (for example, service providers enabling parents to implement activities to assist in the development of their children)

thermoregulation ability to regulate body temperature

toddler stage time of life from 1 year to 3 years of age

tonic-clonic seizure rigid muscular contraction and rapid alternation of contraction and relaxation of muscles

TORCH cluster of viral diseases that affect a fetus or neonate

total communication combination of manual signing with oral methods of communication

toxemia of pregnancy pregnancy-induced high blood pressure that results in reduced blood flow to the fetus and causes fetal growth retardation

toxin poison

toxoplasmosis protozoan infection acquired by humans from contact with the feces of infected cats or birds or from the ingestion of raw or partially cooked meat; may result in premature delivery or spontaneous abortion

tracking following moving objects with the eyes in several directions (vertically and horizontally)

transdisciplinary model group whose members share roles and combine assessment and treatment tasks so that they may be carried out by one professional

transition change in growth and development that may result in unpredictable behavior or regression

transition plan formal written program that indicates activities and who is responsible for them, so that the child's move from one program to the next is as smooth as possible

transition stressors pressures on a family related to a child's disability that occur at significant milestones in life

translocation existence of extra chromosomal material that has become attached to another chromosome, varying in size from a piece of one arm to an entire chromosome

transplacental having to do with the passing of substances from the maternal to fetal bloodstream, or vice versa, via the placenta

traumatic brain injury (TBI) an intracranial injury that occurs when an outside force causes damage to the brain

trimester period of 3 months, usually pertaining to gestational periods

triplegia cerebral palsy affecting three extremities of the body

trisomy 21 presence of an extra number 21 chromosome, which causes Down syndrome

ultrasonography, or ultrasound procedure that uses high-frequency sound waves to produce an image of an internal organ

umbilical cord supply line that joins the bloodstream of the fetus at the abdomen to the bloodstream of the mother via the uterine lining

underextension language usage by children that occurs when categories are defined too narrowly (for example, using the word *chair* when referring to a high chair or table chair but not including the rocking chair or kitchen stool in the category)

use the purposes and effectiveness of communication in a social situation

vaccines inoculations of either active viral replications with decreased virulence or an inactive virus introduced into a human being to activate the immune system to produce antibodies, preventing an acute infection

varicella zoster virus related to herpes that is responsible for chicken pox and shingles

very low birth weight (VLBW) newborn weight of less than 1,500 g (3 lb 5 oz.)

vestibule small cavity or space at the entrance to a canal, such as that in the inner ear

viable capable of living; age at which the fetus has the potential to live outside of the womb, about 26 to 28 weeks

viruses smallest known types of infectious agent that invade cells, take over, and make copies of themselves

vitreous humor colorless, transparent gel filling the cavity of the eye behind the lens

windows of achievement age periods during which 98% of children achieve the motor milestones

vocabulary spurt sudden sharp increases in number or words children use

X-Rays films taken by invisible electromagnetic energy; allows a view of the size, shape, and movement of organs

References

Chapter 1

Alberto, P. A., & Troutman, A. C. (2009). *Applied behavior analysis for teachers* (8th ed.). Upper Saddle River, NJ: Merrill/Pearson Education.

Allen, S. M., & Hawkins, A. J. (1999). Maternal gatekeeping: Mothers' beliefs and behaviors that inhibit greater father involvement in family work. *Journal of Marriage and Family, 61*(1), 199–212.

Atkins, D. N., & Wilkins, V. M. (2013). Going beyond reading, writing, and arithmetic: The effects of teacher representation on teen pregnancy rates. *Journal of Public Administration Research and Theory.* doi: 10.1093/jopart/mut001.

Atkins-Burnett, S., & Meares, P. A. (2000). Infants and toddlers with disabilities: Relationship-based approaches. *Social Work, 45*(4), 371–379.

Baer, D. M., Wolf, M. M., & Risley, T. R. (1968). Some current dimensions of applied behavior analysis. *Journal of Applied Behavior Analysis, 1,* 91–97.

Balcazar, F. E., Keys, C. B., & Suarez-Balcazar, Y. (2001). Empowering Latinos with disabilities to address issues of independent living and disability rights. *Journal of Prevention & Intervention in the Community, 21*(2), 53–70.

Boe, E. E., & Cook, L. H. (2006). The chronic and increasing shortage of fully certified teachers in special and regular education. *Exceptional Children, 72,* 443–460.

Boser, U. (2011). *Teacher diversity matters: A state-by-state analysis of teachers of color.* Washington, DC: Center for American Progress.

Bricker, D. (2001). The natural environment: A useful construct? *Infants and Young Children, 13*(4), 21–31.

Bronfenbrenner, U. (1986). Ecology of the family as a context for human development. *Developmental Psychology, 22,* 732–752.

Brown-Lyons, M., Robertson, A., & Layzer, J. (2001). *Kith and kin—Informal child care: Highlights from recent research.* New York: The National Center for Children in Poverty.

Children's Defense Fund. (1998). *The state of America's children. Yearbook 1998.* Washington, DC: Author.

Clapton, J., & Fitzgerald, J. (2002). The history of disability: A history of "otherness." *New Renaissance Magazine, 7*(1).

Clark, C. (2007). Childcare. In F. Malti-Douglas (ed.) *Encyclopedia of sex and gender,* vol. 1. Detroit, MI: Macmillan Reference USA, 266–268.

Crockett, J. B., & Kauffman, J. M. (1998). Taking inclusion back to its roots. *Educational Leadership, 56*(2), 74–77.

Diament, M. (2011, July). Lawmakers push for full funding of IDEA. Disabilityscoop: The premier Source for Developmental Disabilities News. From http://www.disabilityscoop/2011/07/22/lawmakers-full-funding-idea/13577.

Dugbatey, K., Croskey, V., Evans, G. R., Narayan, G., & Osamudiamen, O. (2005). Lessons from a primary-prevention program for lead poisoning among inner-city children. *Journal of Environmental Health, 68*(5): 15–20, 26.

Dunst, C., Trivette, C., & Deal, A. (1988). *Enabling and empowering families: Principles and guidelines for practice.* Cambridge, MA: Brookline.

Edelman, M. W. (1991). Ten lessons to help us through the 1990s: The state of America's children. *The measure of our success.* Boston, MA: Beacon Press, 13–15, 19, 20.

Fagan, P., & Coontz, S. (1997). Q: Are single-parent families a major cause of social dysfunction? *Insight on the News, 13*(45): 24–27.

Fenichel, E. (2001). *From neurons to neighborhoods: What's in it for you?* Washington, DC: Zero to Three: National Center for Infants, Toddlers, and Families.

Flanders, S. C., Engelhart, L., Pandina, G. J., & McCracken, J. T. (2007). Direct health care costs for children with Pervasive Developmental Disorders: 1996–2002. *Administrative Policy for Mental Health and Mental Health Services, 34,* 213–220. doi 10.1007/s10488-006-0098-3.

Florsheim, P., Tolan, P., & Gorman-Smith, D. (1998). Family relationships, parenting practices, the availability of male family members, and the behavior of inner-city boys in single-mother and two-parent families. *Child Development, 69*(5), 1437–1447.

Gallagher, D. J. (1998). The scientific knowledge base of special education: Do we know what we think we know? *Exceptional Children, 64*(4), 493–502.

Groark, C. J., Eidelman, S. M., Kazmarek, L., & Maude, S. (2011). *Early childhood intervention:*

Shaping the future with special needs and their families. Santa Barbara, CA: Praeger.

Guo, G. (1998). The timing of the influences of cumulative poverty on children's cognitive ability and achievement. *Social Forces, 77*(1), 257–287.

Guralnick, M. J. (2001). A developmental systems model for early intervention. *Infants and Young Children, 14*(2), 1–14.

Havens, C. A. (2005). Becoming a resilient family: Child disability and the family system. *Access Today: NCA Monographs, 17.*

Heiman, T. (2002). Parents of children with disabilities: Resilience, coping, and future expectations. *Journal of Developmental and Physical Disabilities, 14*(2), 159–171.

Hernandez, D. J. (1995). Changing demographics: Past and future demands for early childhood programs. *The Future of Children, 5*(2), 145–160.

Kelley, P. (1996). Family-centered practice with stepfamilies. *Families in Society, 77*(9), 535–544.

King, M. A., Sims, A., & Osher, D. (2000). How is cultural competence integrated in education. *Center for Effective Collaboration and Practice. http://cecp.air.org/cultural/Q_intgrated.htm Date accessed, 10*(14), 03.

Krausse, M. W. (1991). Theoretical issues in family research. Paper presented at the annual meeting of the American Association on Mental Retardation, Washington, DC (ERIC Document Reproduction Service No. ED 337 923).

Leach, M. T., & Williams, S. A. (2007). The impact of the academic achievement gap on the African American family: A social inequality perspective. *Journal of Human Behavior in the Social Environment, 14*(2/3), 39–59.

Lichter, D. T., Parisi, D., & Taquino, M. C. (2012). The geography of exclusion: Race, segregation, and concentrated poverty. *Social Problems, 59*(3), 364–388.

Matt, M., & Morrison, D. (2008). Choosing advocacy. *Occasional Papers Series 21.* New York: Bank Street College of Education.

McCollum, J. A. (2000). Taking the past along: Reflecting on our identity as a discipline. *Topics in Early Childhood Special Education, 20*(2), 79–86.

McWilliam, R. A. (2010). *Routines-based early intervention.* Baltimore: Paul H. Brooks.

Metzger, J. (2008). Resiliency in children and youth in kinship care and family foster care. *Child Welfare, 87*(6), 115–140.

Mitchell, S. (1995). The next baby boom. *American Demographics, 17,* 22–22.

Montgomery, L. E., Kiely, J. L., & Pappas, G. (1996). The effects of poverty, race, and family structure on U.S. children's health: Data from the NHIS, 1978 through 1980 and 1989 through 1991. *American Journal of Public Health, 86*(10), 1401.

Moore, K. A., Manlove, J., Glei, D. A., & Morrison, D. R. (1998). Nonmarital school-age motherhood: Family, individual, and school characteristics. *Journal of Adolescent Research, 13*(4), 433–457.

National Association for the Education of Young Children. (2011). *Code of ethical conduct.* Washington, DC: Author.

National Association of Child Care Resource and Referral Agencies. (2011). *Public Policy Agenda 112th Congress.* Retrieved June 20, 2012, from http://www.naccrra.org/sites/default/files/default_site_pages/2011/publicpolicyagenda_comp.pdf.

National Center for Education Statistics. (2012). *The Condition of Education 2012.* Retrieved June 13, 2012, from http://nces.ed.gov/pubs2012/2012045_2.pdf.

National Center for Special Education Research (2012). Preschoolers with disabilities: Characteristics, services, and results, 2012. Institute of Educational Sciences. Retrieved from http://ies.ed.gov/ncser/pubs/20063003/sum_a.asp.

National Early Childhood Technical Assistance Center. (2012). *Annual appropriations and number of children under part C of IDEA Federal Fiscal Years 1987–2012.* Retrieved from http://www.nectac.org/partc/partc-datat.asp.

National Research Council and Institute of Medicine. (2000). *From neurons to neighborhoods: The science of early childhood development.* Committee on Integrating the Science of Early Childhood Development. Jack P. Shonkoff and Deborah A. Phillips, eds. Board on Children, Youth, and Families, Commission of Behavioral and Social Sciences and Education. Washington, DC: National Academy Press.

Novella, S. (1996). Psychomotor patterning. *The Connecticut Skeptic, 1*(4), 6.

Nunez, R. C., & Collignon, K. (1997). Creating a community of learning for homeless children. *Educational Leadership, 55*(2), 56–60.

O'Brien, E. M., & Dervarics, C. (2007). *Pre-kindergarten: What the research shows. A Report of the Center for Public Education.* Retrieved from http://www.centerforpubliceducation.org/Main-Menu/Pre-kindergarten/Pre-Kindergarten/Pre-kindergarten-What-the-research-shows.html.

Parker, K., & Wang, W. (2013). Changing views about work. *In Modern Parenthood: Roles of moms and dads converge as they balance work and family. Pew Research Center.* Retrieved from http://www.pewsocialtrends.org/2013/03/14/modern-parenthood-roles-of-moms-and-dads-converge-as-they-balance-work-and-family/2/.

Policy Priorities. (2012). *Washington, DC, Children's Defense Fund*. Retrieved from http://www.childrens defense.org/policy-priorities/.

Shachar, H. & Shmuelevitz, H. (1997). Implementing cooperative learning, teacher collaboration and teachers' sense of efficacy in heterogeneous junior high schools. *Contemporary Educational Psychology*, 22(1), 35–72.

Shelden, L. L., & Rush, D. D. (2001). The ten myths about providing early intervention services in natural environments. *Infants and Young Children*, 14(1), 1–13.

Shelton, D. L. (1998). Downward public health statistics show upbeat trends. *American Medical News*, 41(42), 35.

Skinner, B. F. (1953). *Science and human behavior*. New York: Macmillan.

Slavin, R. E. (1998). Can education reduce social inequity? *Educational Leadership*, 55(4), 6–10.

Smart, J. F., & Smart, D. W. (1997). The racial/ethnic demography of disability. *Journal of Rehabilitation*, 63(4), 9–15.

Smith, B. J. (2000). The federal role in early childhood special education policy in the next century: The responsibility of the individual. *Topics in Early Childhood Special Education*, 20(1), 7–13.

Song, Y., & Lu, H. (2002). *Early childhood poverty: A statistical profile*. National Center for Children in Poverty. Retrieved July 25, 2002, from http://cpmcnet .columbia.edu/dept/nccp/ecp302.html.

Stubblefield, A. (2007). "Beyond the pale": Tainted whiteness, cognitive disability, and eugenic sterilization. *Hypatia: A Journal of Feminist Philosophy*, 22(2), 162–181.

Taylor, R. (1998). Check your cultural competence. *Nursing Management*, 29(8), 30–32.

Turnbull, A., & Turnbull, R. (1997). *Parents, professionals, and exceptionality, A special partnership*. Upper Saddle River, NJ: Merrill/Pearson Education.

U.S. Census Bureau (March, 2001). *Overview of race and Hispanic origin. Census Brief*. Washington, DC: U.S. Department of Commerce.

U.S. Census Bureau (2008). *U.S. POPClock Projection*. Retrieved July 14, 2008, from http://www.census .gov/population/www/popclockus.html.

U.S. Census Bureau (May, 2011). The Hispanic population: 2010. *Census Brief*. Washington, DC: U.S. Department of Commerce.

U.S. Commission on Civil Rights. (2002). *Recommendations for the reauthorization of the Individuals with Disabilities Education Act*. Retrieved July 10, 2002, from http://www.usccr.gov/pubs/idea/ recs.htm.

U.S. Commission on Civil Rights. (2009). *Minorities in special education*. Retrieved June 13, 2012, from http://www.usccr.gov/pubs/MinoritiesinSpecial Education.pdf.

Van Haren, B., & Fiedler, C. (2008). Support and empower families of children with disabilities. *Intervention in School and Clinic*, 43, 231–235.

Ventura, S. J., Curtin, S. C., Abma, J. C., & Henshaw, S. K. (2012). Estimated pregnancy rates and pregnancy outcomes for the United States 1990–2008. *National Vital Statistics Report*, 60(7), 1–21.

Vincent, C. G., Randall, C., Cartledge, G., Tobin, T. J., & Swain-Bradway, J. (2011). Toward a conceptual integration of cultural responsiveness and schoolwide positive behavior supports. *Journal of Positive Behavior Interventions*, 13, 219–229.

Walther-Thomas, C., Korinek, L., McLaughlin, V., & Williams, B. (1996). Improving educational opportunities for students with disabilities who are homeless. *Journal of Children and Poverty*, 2(2), 57–75.

Wetzstein, C. (1998). Teen births decline. *Insight on the News*, 14(44), 40.

Williams, B. F. (Ed.). (2003). *Directions in early intervention and assessment*. Spokane, WA: Spokane Guilds' School.

Williams, B. T., & DeSander, M. K. (1999). Dueling legislation: The impact of incongruent federal statutes on homeless and other special-needs students. *Journal for a Just and Caring Education*, 5(1), 34–50.

Xu, Y. (2007). Empowering culturally diverse families of young children with disabilities: The double ABCX model. *Early Childhood Education Journal*, 34, 431–437.

Chapter 2

Aaron, J., Benz, M. R., & Elliott, T. R. (2012). Evaluating a dynamic process model of wellbeing for parents of children with disabilities: A multi method analysis. *Rehabilitation Psychology*, 57, 61–72.

Anderegg, M. L., Vergason, G. A., & Smith, M. C. (1992). A visual representation of the grief cycle for use by teachers with families of children with disabilities. *Remedial and Special Education*, 13(2), 17–23.

Bailey, D. B., Bruder, M. M., Hebbeler, K., Carta, J., Defosset, M., Greenwood, C. et al. (2006). Recommended outcomes for families of young children with disabilities. *Journal of Early Intervention*, 28, 227–251.

Bauer, A. M., & Shea, T. M. (2003). *Parents and schools: Creating a successful partnership for students with special needs*. Upper Saddle River, NJ: Merrill/Pearson Education.

Bauman, D. C., & Wasserman, K. B. (2010). Empowering fathers of disadvantaged preschoolers to take a more active role in preparing their children for literacy success at school. *Early Childhood Education Journal, 37,* 363–370.

Beach Center on Families and Disability. (2012). After a complex history, family support stands at the crossroads. Retrieved March 3, 2012, from http://www .beachcenter.org/resource_library/beach_re source_detail_page.aspx?intResourceID=2232&Typ e=article.

Belmonte, T. (1996). Developing cross-cultural sensitivity. *Family Childcare Connections, 6*(2), 2–3.

Benzies, K., & Mychasiuk, R. (2009). Fostering family resiliency: A review of the key protective factors. *Child & Family Social Work, 14*(1), 103–114.

Bosch, L. A. (1996). Needs of parents of young children with developmental delay: Implications for social work practice. *Families in Society, 77*(8), 477–487.

Brett, J. (2004). The journey to accepting support: How parents of profoundly disabled children experience support in their lives. *Paediatric Nursing, 16*(8), 14–18.

Brotherson, M. J., & Goldstein, B. (1992). Time as a resource and constraint for parents of young children with disabilities: Implications for early intervention services. *Topics in Early Childhood Special Education, 12,* 508–527.

Brotherson, M. J., Summers, J. A., Naig, L. A., Kyzar, K., Friend, A., Epley, P., Gotto, G. S., & Turnbull, A. P. (2010). Partnership patterns: Addressing emotional needs in early intervention. *Topics in Early Childhood Special Education, 30,* 32–45.

Childress, D. C. (2011). Play behaviors of parents and their young children with disabilities. *Topics in Early Childhood Special Education, 31*(2), 112–120.

Chu, S-Y., & Wu, H-Y. (2012). Development of effective school-family partnerships for students with culturally and linguistically diverse backgrounds: From special education teachers' and Chinese American parents' perspectives. *Scholarlypartnershipsedu, 6*(1), 24–37.

Davern, L. (1996, April). Listening to parents of children with disabilities. *Educational Leadership,* 61–63.

Davis, K., & Gavidia-Payne, S. (2009). The impact of child, family, and professional support characteristics on the quality of life in families of young children with disabilities. *Journal of Intellectual & Developmental Disability, 34,* 153–162.

Dawson, G., Rogers, S., Munson, J., Smith, M., Winter, J., Greenson, J., Donaldson, A., & Varley, J. (2010). Randomized, controlled trial of an intervention for toddlers with autism: The Early Start Denver Model. *Pediatrics, 125,* e17–e23. doi:10.1542/peds. 2009-0958.

Dettmer, P., Dyck, N., & Thurston, L. P. (1999). *Consultation, collaboration, and teamwork* (3rd ed.). Boston: Allyn & Bacon.

Dunst, C. J., & Bruder, M. J. (2002). Valued outcomes of service coordination, early intervention, and natural environments. *Exceptional Children, 68*(3), 361–375.

Dunst, C. J., & Trivette, C. M. (2009). Family-centered helpgiving practices, parent-professional partnerships, and parent, family and child outcomes. In S. Christenson and A. L. Reschly (eds.) *Handbook of school-family partnerships.* New York: Taylor & Francis.

Fraiberg. S. H. (1996). *The magic years: Understanding and handling the problems of early childhood.* (Paperback reissue edition). New York: Fireside.

French, N. K. (2003). Paraeducators in special education programs. *Focus on Exceptional Children, 36*(2), 1–16.

Friend, A. C., Summers, J. A., & Turnbull, A. P. (2009). Impacts of family support in early intervention research. *Education and Training in Developmental Disabilities, 44*(4), 453–470.

Friend, M., & Cook, L. (2009). *Collaboration skills for school professionals* (6th ed.). Columbus: Prentice Hall.

Gonzales-Alvarez, L. I. (1998). A short course in sensitivity training. *Teaching Exceptional Children, 1,* 73–77.

Green, S. E., Barnhill, J., Green, S., Hawken, D. T., Humphrey, L. S., & Sanderson, S. (2011). Creating a village to raise a child: Constructing community in families of children with disabilities. *Research in Social Science and Disability, 6,* 135–155.

Guralnick, M. J. (1998). Effectiveness of early intervention for vulnerable children: A developmental perspective. *American Journal on Mental Retardation, 102*(4), 319–345.

Guralnick, M. J. (2001). A developmental systems model for early intervention. *Infants and Young Children, 14*(2), 1–18.

Hanson, M. J., & Bruder, M. B. (2001). Early intervention: Promises to keep. *Infants and Young Children, 13*(3), 47–58.

Haroutunian-Gordon, S. (1991). *Turning the soul: Teaching through conversation in the high school.* Chicago: University of Chicago Press.

Harry, B. (2002). Trends and issues in serving culturally diverse families of children with disabilities. *The Journal of Special Education, 36*(3), 131–138.

Hartley, S., L., Barker, E. T., Seltzer, M. M., Floyd, F., Greenberg, J., Orsmond, G., & Bolt, D. (2010). The relative risk and timing of divorce in families of children with an autism spectrum disorder. *Journal of Family Psychology, 24*(4), 449–457.

Hatton, C., Emerson, E., Graham, H., Blacher, J., & Llewellyn, G. (2009). Changes in family composition and marital status in families with a child with cognitive delay. *Journal of Applied Research in Intellectual Disabilities, 23*, 14–26.

Hinojosa, J., Bedell, G., Buchholz, E. S., Charles, J., Shigaki, I. S., & Bicchieri, S. M. (2001). Team collaboration: A case study of an early intervention team. *Qualitative Health Research, 11*(2), 206–220.

Kisler, J., & McConachie, H. (2010). Parental reaction to disability. *Paediatrics and Child Health, 20*(7), 309–314.

Klemm, D., & Schimanski, C. (1999). Parent to parent: The crucial connection. *Exceptional Parent, 29*(9), 109–112.

Kresak, K., Gallagher, P., & Rhodes, C. (2009). Siblings of infants and toddlers with disabilities in early intervention. *Topics in Early Childhood Special Education, 29*, 143–154.

Kubler-Ross, E. (1969). *Locus of control: Current trends in theory and research.* Hillsdale, NJ: Lawrence Earlbaum.

Labato, D., Kao, B., Plante, W., Seifer, R., Grullon, E., Cheas, L., & Canino, G. (2011). Psychological and school functioning of Latino siblings of children with intellectual disabilities. *Journal of Child Psychology-Psychiatry, 52*, 696–703.

Mandleco, B., Roper, S., Freeborn, D. S., Ward, E., & Dyches, T. (2012). The experiences of siblings of children with autism. *Registry of Nursing Research and Practice Innovations.* Retrieved May 8, 2013, from http://www.nursinglibrary.org/vhl/handle/10755/211453?mode=full&submit_simple=Show+full+item+record.

Marks, S. U., Schrader, C., & Levine, M. (1999). Para-educator experiences in inclusive settings: Helping, hovering, or holding their own. *Exceptional Children, 65*(3), 315–328.

McCann, D., Bull, R., & Winzenberg, T. (2012). The daily patterns of time use for parents of children with complex needs. *Journal of Child Health Care, 16*, 26–52.

McDonald, E. E., & Hastings, R. P. (2010). Fathers of children with developmental disabilities. In M. E. Lamb (Ed.) *The role of the father in child development.* Hoboken, NJ: Wiley, 486–516.

McWilliam, R. A., & Scott, S. (2001). A support approach to early intervention: A three-part framework. *Infants and Young Children, 13*(4), 55–66.

Milkie, M. A., Kendig, S. M., Nomaguchi, K. M., & Denny, K. E. (2010). Time with children, children's well-being, and work-family balance among employed parents. *Journal of Marriage and Family, 72*, 1329–1343.

Moore, M. L., Howard, V. F., & McLaughlin, T. F. (2002). Siblings of children with disabilities: A review and analysis. *International Journal of Special Education, 17*(1), 49–64.

Morin, R. (2011). The public renders a split verdict on changes in family structure. Pew Research Center. Retrieved May 8, 2013, from http://www.pewsocialtrends.org/2011/02/16/the-public-renders-a-split-verdict-on-changes-in-family-structure/.

Moyson, T., & Roeyers, H. (2011). 'The overall quality of my life as a sibling is all right, but of course, it could always be better.' Quality of life siblings of children with intellectual disability: The siblings' perspectives. *Journal of Intellectual Disability Research, 56*, 87–101.

Neece, C. L., Blacher, J., & Baker, B. L. (2010). Impact on siblings of children with intellectual disability: The role of child behavior problems. *American Journal on Intellectual and Developmental Disabilities, 115*(4), 291–306.

Novak, C. Lingam, R., Coad, J., & Emond, A. (2011). 'Providing more scaffolding': Parenting a child with developmental disorder, a hidden disability. *Child Care Health Development, 16.* doi: 10.1111/j.1365-2214.2011.01302.x

O'Shea, D. J., Williams, A. L., & Sattler, R. O. (1999). Collaboration across special education and general education: Preservice teachers' views. *Journal of Teacher Education, 50*(2), 147–157.

Public Agenda. (2002). *When it's your own child; A report on special education from the families who use it.* New York: Author.

Sawyer, M. G., Bittman, M., LaGreca, A. M., Crettenden, A. D., Borojevic, N., Raghavendra, P., & Russo, R. (2011). Time demands of caring for children with cerebral palsy: What are the implications for maternal mental health? *Developmental Medicine & Child Neurology, 53*(4), 338–343.

Sheppard, D., Mandleco, B., Roper, S. O., Dyches, T., & Freeborn, D. S. (2012). Caregiver burden and family hardiness in families raising a child with a disability. Registry of Nursing Research and Practice Innovations. Retrieved May 13, 2013, from http://hdl.handle.net/10755/211685.

St. John, M., & Pawl, J. H. (2000, February/March). Inclusive interaction in infant-parent psychotherapy. *Zero to Three, 20*(4). Retrieved October 10, 2002, from http://www.zerotothree.org/vol20–4.html.

Stubben, J. D. (2001). Working with and conducting research among American Indian families. *The American Behavioral Scientist, 44*(9), 1466–1481.

Stump, C. S., & Wilson, C. (1996). Collaboration: Making it happen. *Intervention in School & Clinic, 31*(5), 310–313.

Swanson, J., Raab, M., & Dunst, C. J. (2011). Strengthening family capacity to provide young children everyday natural learning opportunities. *Journal of Early Childhood Research, 9,* 66–88.

Trivette, C. M., Dunst, C. J., & Hamby, D. W. (2010). Influences of family-systems intervention practices on parent-child interactions and child development. *Topics in Early Childhood Special Education, 30,* 13–19.

Turnbull, A. P., & Turnbull, H. R. (1996). *Families, professionals, and exceptionality: A special partnership* (3rd ed.). Upper Saddle River, NJ: Merrill/Pearson Education.

Waldman, H. B., & Perlman, S. P. (June, 2008). Homeless children with disabilities: "On any given day, at least 800,000 Americans, including 200,000 children, find themselves without a home." *The Exceptional Parent, 56–57.*

Watson, S. L., Hayes, S. A., & Radford-Paz, E. (2011a). "Diagnose me please!": A review of research about the journey and initial impact of parents seeking a diagnosis of developmental disability for their child. *International Review of Research in Developmental Disabilities, 41,* 31–72.

Watson, S. L., Hayes, S. A., & Radford-Paz, E. (2011b). "Diagnose me please!": A review of research about the journey and initial impact of parents seeking a diagnosis of developmental disability for their child. In R. M. Hodapp (ed.) *International review of research in developmental disabilities.* San Diego, CA: Elsevier, Inc.

Weatherston, D. J. (2000). The infant mental health specialist. *Zero to Three, 21*(22). Retrieved March 5, 2003, from http://www.zerotothree.org/sample.html.

Wehby, G., & Ohsfeldt, R. (2007). The impact of having a young child with disabilities on maternal labor supply by race and marital status. *Journal of Health & Human Services Administration, 30*(3), 327–351.

Wood, M. (1998). Whose job is it anyway? Educational roles in inclusion. *Exceptional Children, 64*(2), 181–195.

Chapter 3

Arzuaga, B. H., & Lee, B. H. (2011). Limits of human viability in the United States: A medicolegal review. *Pediatrics, 128,* 1047–1052. doi: 1-.1542/peds.2011-1689.

Bandura, A. (1971). *Social learning theory.* New York: General Learning Press.

Baker, M., & Milligan, K. (2010). Evidence of maternal leave expansions of the impact of maternal care on early child development. *The Journal of Human Resources, 45,* 1–32.

Beentjes, J. W., & VanderVoort, T. H. (1988). Television's impact on children's reading skills. *Reading Research Quarterly, 23,* 389–413.

Bernal, R. (2008). The effect of maternal employment and child care on children's cognitive development. *International Economic Review, 49,* 1173–1209. doi: 10.111/j.1468-2354.208.00510x.

Bowlby, J. (1958). The nature of the child's tie to his mother. *International Journal of Psychoanalysis, 39,* 350–393.

Bowlby, J. (1960). Grief and mourning in infancy and early childhood. *Psychoanalytic Study of the Child, 15,* 9–52.

Bowlby, J. (1969). *Attachment and loss.* London: The Hogarth Press.

Browne, K., & Hamilton-Giachritsis, C. (2005). The influence of violent media on children and adolescents: A public-health approach. *Lancet, 365*(9460), 702–710.

Buchholz, E. S. (1997, September). Even infants need their solitude. *Brown University Child & Adolescent Behavior Letter, 13*(9), 1–3.

Burchinal, M. R., Roberts, J. E., Hooper, S., & Zeisel, S. A. (2000). Cumulative risk and early cognitive development: A comparison of statistical risk models. *Developmental Psychology, 36,* 793–807.

Campbell, F. A., Pungello, E. P., Miller-Johnson, S., Burchinal, M., & Ramey, C. T. (2001). The development of cognitive and academic abilities: Growth curves from an early childhood education experiment. *Developmental Psychology, 37,* 231–242.

Carmeli, E., Marmur, R., Cohen, A., & Tirosh, E. (2009). Preferred sleep position and gross motor achievement in early infancy. *European Journal of Pediatrics, 168,* 711–715. doi:10.1007/s00431-008-0829-4.

Coltrane, S. (1998). *Gender and families.* Thousand Oaks, CA: Pine Forge Press.

Council on Communications and Media. (2011). Media use by children younger than 2 years. *Pediatrics, 128,* 1040–1045. doi: 10.1542/peds.2011-1753.

Crespo, C. J., & Arbesman, J. (2003). Obesity in the United States. *Physician & Sportsmedicine, 31*(11), 23–28.

DeLoache, J. S., & Korac, N. (2003). Video-based learning by very young children. *Developmental Science, 6*(3), 245–246.

Donahue, S. M., Kleinman, K. P., Gillman, M. W., & Oken, E. (2010). Trends in birth weight and gestational length among singleton term births in the

United States: 1990–2005. *Obstetrics & Gynecology, 115,* 357–364. doi: 10.1097/AOG.0b013e3181cbd5f5.

Erel, O., Oberman, Y., & Yirmiya, N. (2000). Maternal versus nonmaternal care and seven domains of children's development. *Psychological Bulletin, 126,* 727–747.

Erikson, E. H. (1963). *Childhood and society* (2nd ed.). New York: W. W. Norton.

Erikson, E. H. (1968). *Identity, youth and crisis.* New York: Norton.

Erikson, E. H. (1980). *Identity and the life cycle* (2nd ed.). New York: Norton.

Fagan, J. (2012). Effects of divorce and cohabitation dissolution on preschoolers' literacy. *Journal of Family Issues.* doi: 10.1177/0192513X12445164.

Francis, S. L., Stancel, M. J., Sernulka-George, F. D., Broffitt, B., Levy, S. M., & Janz, K. F. (2011). Tracking of TV and video gaming during childhood: Iowa bone development study. *International Journal of Behavioral Nutrition and Physical Activity, 8,* 100. doi: 10.1186/1479-5868-8-100.

Friedlmeier, W., Chakkarath, P., & Schwartz, B. (Eds.) (2005). *Culture and human development: The importance of cross-cultural research to the social sciences.* New York: Psychology Press.

Gesell, A., & Thompson, H. (1934). *Infant behavior: Its genesis and growth.* New York: McGraw-Hill.

Hamilton-Huesmann, L. R., Moise-Titus, J., Podolski, C. L., & Eron, L. D. (2003). Longitudinal relations between children's exposure to TV violence and their aggressive and violent behavior in young adulthood: 1977–1992. *Developmental Psychology, 39,* 201–221.

Hansen, K., & Hawkes, D. (2009). Early childcare and child development. *Journal of Social Policy, 38,* 211–239. doi: 10.1027/S004729480800281X.

Hines, M. (2011). Gender development and the human brain. *Annual Review of Neuroscience, 34,* 69–88. doi: 10.1146/annurev-neuro-061010-113654.

Ismael, S.T. (2007). The cost of war: The children of Iraq. *Journal of Comparative Family Studies, 38,* 337–341.

Kim, H. S. (2011). Consequences of parental divorce for child development. *American Sociological Review, 76,* 487–511. doi: 10.1177/0003122411407748.

Kim, P., & Evans, G. W. (2011). Family resources, genes, and human development. *Biosocial Foundations of Family Processes: National Symposium on Family issues. Part 4,* 221-230. doi: 10.1007/978-1-4419-7361-0_15.

Knous-Westfall, H. M., Ehrensaft, M. K., MacDonell, K. W., & Cohen, P. (2011). Parental intimate partner violence, parenting practices, and adolescent bullying: A prospective study. *Journal of Child and Family Studies.* doi: 10.1007/s10826-011-9528-2.

Landry, S. H., Swank, P. R., Assel, M. A., Smith, K. E., & Vellet, S. (2001). Does early responsive parenting have a special importance for children's development or is consistency across early childhood necessary? *Developmental Psychology, 37,* 387–483.

Leavell,A.S.,Tamis-LeMonda,C.S.,Ruble,D.N.,Zosuls, K. M., & Cabrera, N. J. (2012). African American, White and Latino fathers' activities with their sons and daughters in early childhood. *Behavioral Science, 66,* 53–65. doi: 10.1007/s11199-011-008008.

Lillard, A. S., & Peterson, J. (2011). The immediate impact of different types of television on young children's executive function. *Pediatrics, 128,* 644–649. doi: 10.1542/peds.2010-1919.

Lipari, J. (2000, July/August). Four things you need to know about raising baby. *Psychology Today,* 39–43.

Lung, F., & Shu, B. (2011). Sleeping position and health status of children at six-, eighteen- and thirty-six-month development. *Research in Developmental Disabilities, 32(2),* 713–718.

MacDonald, H. (2002). American Academy of Pediatrics, Committee on Fetus and Newborn. Perinatal care at the threshold of viability. *Pediatrics, 110,* 1024–1027.

MacDonald, K. (1992). Warmth as a developmental construct: An evolutionary analysis. *Child Development, 63,* 753–773.

Miller, S., Loeber,R. & Hipwell, A. (2009). Peer deviance, parenting and disruptive behavior among young girls. *Journal of Abnormal Psychology, 37,* 139–152. doi: 10.1007/s10802-008-9265-1.

Mitchell, D., & Dunbar, C. (2006). Learning and development in the nursery setting: The value of promoting emergent information and communications technology skills. *Child Care in Practice, 12(3),* 241–257.

Najman, J. M., Haytabakhsh, M. R., Heron, M. A., Bor, W., O'Callaghan, M. J, & Williams, G. M. (2009). The impact of episodic and chronic poverty on child cognitive development. *The Journal of Pediatrics, 154(2),* 284–289.

National Center for Health Statistics. (2002a). *Length-for-age percentiles: Boys, birth to 36 months 3rd, 5th, 10th, 25th, 50th, 75th, 90th, 95th, 97th percentiles.* CDC Growth Charts. United States: Author.

National Center for Health Statistics. (2002b). *Length-for-age percentiles: Girls, birth to 36 months 3rd, 5th, 10th, 25th, 50th, 75th, 90th, 95th, 97th percentiles.* CDC Growth Charts. United States: Author.

Oberg, C. N. (2011). The Great Recession's impact on children. *Maternal and Child Health Journal, 15*(5), 553–554. doi: 10.1007/s10995-011-0807-8.

Panayiota, K., Lynch, J. S., van den Broek, P., Espin, C. A., White, M. J., & Kremer, K. E. (2006). Developing successful readers: Building early comprehension skills through television viewing and listening. *Early Childhood Education Journal, 33*(2), 91–98.

Piaget, J. (1963). *The origins of intelligence in children.* New York: W. W. Norton.

Reis, H. T., Collins, W. A., & Berscheid, E. (2000). The relationship context of human behavior and development. *Psychological Bulletin, 126,* 844–872.

Schor, E. L. (2003). Family pediatrics: Report of the Task Force on the Family. *Pediatrics, 111,* 1541–1571.

Siegel, E. (1982). A critical examination of studies of parent-infant bonding. In M. H. Klaus & M. O. Robertson (Eds.), *Birth, interaction, and attachment: A round table.* Skillman, NJ: Johnson & Johnson.

Skeels, H. M. (1942). A study of the differential stimulation on mentally retarded children: A follow-up report. *American Journal of Mental Deficiency, 46,* 340–350.

Skeels, H. M. (1966). Adult status of children with contrasting life experience: A follow-up study. *Monographs of the Society for Research in Child Development, 31*(3).

Skinner, B. F. (1953). *Science and human behavior.* New York: Macmillan.

Skinner, B. F. (1957). *Verbal behavior.* New York: Appleton-Century-Crofts.

Sperhake, J. P., Zimmerman, I., & Püschel, K. (2009). Current recommendations on infants' sleeping position are being followed--and initial results of a population-based sentinel study of risk for SIDS, 1996–2006, in Hamburg, Germany. *International Journal of Legal Medicine, 123,* 41–45. doi: 10.1007/s00414-008-0298-3.

Stoll, B. J., Hansen, N.I., Bell, E. F., Shankaran, S., Laptook, A. R., Walsh, M. C., Hale, E. C., Newman, N. S., et al. (2010). Neonatal outcomes of extremely preterm infants from the NICHD Neonatal Research Network. *Pediatrics, 126*(3), 443–455. doi: 10.1542/peds.2009-2959.

Thomas, A., & Chess, S. (1981). The role of temperament in the contributions of individuals to their own development. In R. M. Lerner & N. A. Busch-Rossnagel (Eds.), *Individuals as producers of their development: A life-span perspective.* New York: Academic Press.

Thomas, D. A., & Woodside, M. (2011). Resilience in adult children of divorce: A multiple case study. *Marriage & Family Review, 47,* 213–234. doi: 10.1080/01494929.2011.586300.

Vélez, C. E., Wolchik, S. A., Tein, J-Y., & Sandler, I. (2011). Protecting children from the consequences of divorce: A longitudinal study of the effects of parenting on children's coping processes. doi: 10.1111/j.1467-8624.2010.01553.x.

Villani, S. (2001). Impact of media on children and adolescents: A 10-year review of the research. *Journal of the American Academy of Child and Adolescent Psychiatry, 40,* 392–401.

Vygotsky, L. S. (1962). *Thought and language.* Cambridge, MA: MIT Press.

Vygotsky, L. S. (1978). *Mind in society.* Cambridge, MA: Harvard University Press.

Zigler, E. F., & Stevenson, M. F. (1993). *Children in a changing world: Developmental and social issues* (2nd ed.). Pacific Grove, CA: Brookes/Cole.

Zosuls, K. M., Ruble, D. N., Tamis-LeMonda, C. S., Shrout, P. E., Bronstein, M. H., & Greulich, F. K. (2009). The acquisition of gender labels in infancy: Implications for gender-typed play. *Developmental Psychology, 45*(3), 688–701. doi: 10.1037/a0014053.

Chapter 4

Bagdi, A., & Vacca, J. (2006). Supporting early childhood social-emotional well being: The building blocks for early learning and school success. *Early Childhood Education Journal, 33,* 145–150.

Batty, M., & Taylor, M. J. (2006). The development of emotional face processing during childhood. *Developmental Science, 9*(2), 207–220.

Brinch, C. N., & Galloway, T. A. (2012). Schooling in adolescence raises IQ scores. *PNAS, 109*(2), 425–430.

Buss, K. A., & Kiel, E. J. (2004). Comparison of sadness, anger, and fear facial expressions when toddlers look at their mothers. *Child Development, 75,* 1761–1773.

Cain, K., Towse, A. S., & Knight, R. S. (2009). The development of idiom comprehension: An investigation of semantic and contextual processing skills. *Journal of Experimental Child Psychology, 102*(3), 280–292. doi: 10.1016/j.bbr.2011.03.031.

Capirci, O., & Volterra, V. (2008). Gesture and speech: The emergence and development of a strong and changing partnership. *Gesture, 8*(1), 22–44. doi:10.1075/gest.8.1.04cap.

Casasola, M., & Cohen, L. B. (2000). Infants' association of linguistic labels with causal actions. *Developmental Psychology, 36,* 155–168.

Castel, A. D., Humphreys, K. L., Lee, S. S., Galván, A., Balota, D. A., & McCabe, D. P. (2011). The development of memory efficiency and value-directed remembering across the life span: A cross-sectional study of memory and selectivity. *Developmental Psychology, 47*(6), 1553–1564. doi: 10:1037/a0025623.

Cicchetti, D., & Roisman, G. I. (2011). *Minnesota symposia on child psychology: The origins and organization of adaptation and maladaptation.* Hoboken, NJ: John Wiley & Sons, Inc.

Dandurant, F., & Schultz, T. R. (2011). A fresh look at vocabulary spurts. In Proceedings of the Cognitive Science Society Meeting. Retrieved July 15, 2012 from http://palm.mindmodeling.org/cogsci2011/papers/0268/paper0268.pdf.

Duckworth, K., & Sabates, R. (2005). Effects of mothers' education on parenting: An investigation across three generations. *London Review of Education, 3*(3), 239–264.

Edwards, A., Shipman, K., & Brown, A. (2005). The socialization of emotional understanding: A comparison of neglectful and nonneglectful mothers and their children. *Child Maltreatment, 10,* 293–304.

Gabbard, C., & Hart, S. (1995). A note on trichotomous classification of handedness and fine-motor performance in children. *Journal of Genetic Psychology, 156,* 97–105.

Gardner-Neblett, N., Pungello, E. P., & Iruka, I. U. (2011). Oral narrative skills: Implications for the reading development of African American children. *Child Development Perspectives.* doi: 10.1111/j.1750-8606.2011.00225x.

Goorhuis-Brouwer, S. M., & Knijff, W. A. (2003). Language disorders in young children: When is speech therapy recommended? *International Journal of Pediatric Otorhinolaryngology, 67,* 525–529.

Grendler, M. (2005). *Learning and instruction: Theory and practice.* Upper Saddle River, NJ: Pearson.

Hart, B., & Risley, T. R. (1995). *Meaningful differences in everyday experiences in young American children.* Toronto: Paul H. Brookes.

Hershkowitz, I., Lamb, M. E., Orbach, Y., Katz, C., & Horowitz, D. (2012). The development of communicative and narrative skills among preschoolers: Lessons from forensic interview about child abuse. *Child Development, 83*(2), 611–622. doi: 10.111/j.1467-8824.2011.01704.

Holt, D. G., & Willard-Holt, C. (2009). An exploration of the relationship between humor and giftedness in students. *Humor, 8*(3), 257–272. doi: 10.1515/humr.1995.8.3.257.

Holt, K. G. (2005). Biomechanical models, motor control theory, and development. *Infant and Child Development, 14,* 523–527.

Howes, C., Guerra, A. W., Fuligni, A., Zucker, E., Lee, L., Obregon, N. B., & Spivak, A. (2011). Classroom dimensions predict early peer interaction when children are diverse in ethnicity, race, and home language. *Early Childhood Research Quarterly, 26*(4), 399-408. doi: 10.1016/jecresq.2011.02.004.

Huberty, T. J. (2012). *Anxiety and depression in children and adolescents: Assessment, intervention, and prevention.* New York: Springer. doi: 10.1007/978-1-4614-3110-7.

Hyman, L. (2011). Vygotsky's crisis: Argument, context, relevance. *Studies in history and philosophy of science Part C: Studies in history and philosophy of biological and biomedical sciences, 43*(2), 473–482. doi: 10.1016/j.shpsc.2011.11.007.

Iverson, J. M. (2010). Developing language in a developing body: The relationship between motor development and language development. *Journal of Child Language, 37*(2), 229–261. doi: 10.1017/S0305000909990432.

Jones, J. H., & Herbert, J. S. (2006). Exploring memory in infancy: Deferred imitation and the development of declarative memory. *Infant and Child Development, 15,* 195–205.

Joseph, R. (2000) Fetal brain behavior and cognitive development. *Developmental Review, 20,* 81–98.

Justice, L. M., Petscher, Y., Schatschneider, C., & Mashburn, A. (2011). Peer effects in preschool classrooms: Is children's language growth associated with their classmates' skills? *Child Development, 82*(6), 1768–1777.

Keefer, L. R. (2005). Defiant behavior in two- and three-year-olds: A Vygotskian approach. *Early Childhood Education Journal, 33,* 105–111.

Kim, J. S. (2011). Excessive crying: Behavioral and emotional regulation disorder in infancy. *Korean Journal of Pediatrics, 54*(6), 229–233. doi: 103345/kip.2011.54.6.229.

Kornhaber, M., & Marcos, H. (2000). Young children's communication with mothers and fathers: Functions and content. *British Journal of Developmental Psychology, 18,* 187–210.

Kuhl, P. K., Steven, E., Hayashi, A., Deguchi, T., Kiritani, S., & Iverson, P. (2006). Infants show facilitation for native language phonetic perception between 6 and 12 months. *Developmental Science, 9*(2), 13–21.

Kuhl, P. K., Tsao, F. M., & Liu, H. M. (2003). Foreign-language experience in infancy: Effects of short-term exposure and social interaction on phonetic learning. *Proceedings of the National Academy of Science, 100,* 9096–9101.

Kwon, E-Y. (2006). The "Natural Order" of morpheme acquisition: A historical survey and discussion of putative determinants. *Teachers College, Columbia University Working Papers in TESOL & Applied Linguistics*, 5.

Lagattuta, K. H. (2005). When you shouldn't do what you want to do: Young children's understanding of desires, rules, and emotions. *Child Development, 76*, 713–733.

Lai, E. R. (2011). *Metacognition: A literature review.* Retrieved July 15, 2012, from http://psychcorp .pearsonassessments.com/hai/images/tmrs/ Metacognition_Literature_Review_Final.pdf.

Lewis, V., Norgate, S., Collis, G., & Reynolds, R. (2000). The consequences of visual impairment for children's symbolic functional play. *British Journal of Developmental Psychology, 18*, 449–464.

Lipari, J. (2000, July/August). Four things you need to know about raising baby. *Psychology Today*, 39–43.

Lipko, A. R, Dunlosky, J., Lipowski, S. L., & Merriman, W. E. (2011). Young children are not underconfident with practice: The benefit of ignoring a fallible memory heuristic (EJ96307). *Journal of Cognition and Development, 13*(2), 174–188.

Liu, T. (2012). Motor milestone development in young children with autism spectrum disorders: An exploratory study. *Educational Psychology in Practice.* doi: 10.1080/02667363.2012.684340.

Markstrom, C. A., Whitesell, N., & Galliher, R. V. (2011). Ethnic identity and mental health among American Indian and Alaska native adolescents. In P. Spicer, P. Garrell, M. C. Sarche, & H. E. Fitzgerald (Eds.) *American Indian and Alaska Native children and mental health: Development, context, prevention, and treatment.* Santa Barbara, CA: Praeger.

Mathieson, K., & Banerjee, R. (2011). Peer play, emotion understanding, and socio-moral explanation: The role of gender. *British Journal of Developmental Psychology, 29*(2), 188–196. doi: 10.1111/j.2044.835X.201 10.02020.x.

Miljkovitch, R., Pierrehumbert, B., Bretherton, I., & Halfon, O. (2004). Associations between parental and child attachment representations. *Attachment & Human Behavior, 6*, 305–325.

Nadel, J., Soussignan, R., Canet, P., Libert, G., & Gerardin, P. (2005). Two-month-old infants of depressed mothers show mild, delayed and persistent change in emotional state after non-contingent interaction. *Infant Behavior & Development, 28*, 418–425.

Newman, R., Ratner, B., Jusczyk, A. M., Jusczyk, P. W., & Dow, K. A. (2006). Infants' early ability to segment the conversational speech signal predicts later language development: A retrospective analysis. *Developmental Psychology, 42*, 643–655.

Purpura, D. P. (2000). Brain research: A view from the top. *Serials Review*, 26(3), 45–50.

Rochat, P. (2011). Possession and morality in early development. *New Directions for Child and Adolescent Development. Special Issues: Origins of Ownership of Property, 132*, 23–38. doi: 10.1002/cd.294.

Roos, E. M., & Weismer, S. E. (2008). Language outcomes of late taking toddlers at preschool and beyond. *Perspectives on Language Learning and Education, 15*, 119–126. doi: 10. 1044/lle15.3.119.

Rutherford, M. D., & Przednowek, M. (2011). Fathers show modifications of infant-directed action similar to that of mothers. *Journal of Experimental Child Psychology, 111*(3), 367–378. doi:10.1016/j. jecp.2011.10.012.

Sato, H., Hirabayashi, Y., Tsubokura, H., Kanai, M., Ashida, T., Konishi, I., Uchida-Ota, M., Konishi,Y., & Maki, A. (2011). Cerebral hemodynamics in newborn infants exposed to speech sounds: A whole-head optical topography study. *Human Brain Mapping.* doi: 10.1002/hbm.21350.

Schaefer, C. E., & Drewes, A. A. (2011). The therapeutic powers of play and play therapy. In C. E. Schaefer (Ed.). *Foundations of play therapy.* Hoboken, NJ: John Wiley & Sons.

Sevcik, R. A., Romski, M., & Morris, R. (2012). Indicators of mathematics skill acquisition in children with mild intellectual disability: Phonological awareness, naming speed, and vocabulary knowledge, *Psychological Theses. Paper 91.* Retrieved July 15, 2012, from: http://digital archive.gsu.edu/ psych_theses/91.

Soussignan, R., Courtial, A., Canet, P., Danon-Apter, G., & Nadel, J. (2011). Human newborns match tongue protrusion of disembodied human and robotic mouths. *Developmental Science, 14*(2), 385–394. doi: 10.111/j.1467-7687.2010.00984.x.

Spratt, E. G., Friedenberg, S., LaRosa, A., DeBellis, M. D., Macias, M.M., Summer, A. P., Hulsey, T. C., Runyan, D. K., & Brady, K. T. (2012). The effects of early neglect on cognitive, language, and behavioral functioning in childhood. *Psychology, 3*(2), 175–182. doi: 10.4236/psych.2012.32026.

Stein, C. M., Lu, Q., Elston, R. C., Freebairn, L. A., Hansen, A. J., Shriberg, L. D., Taylor, G., Lewis, B. A., & Lyengar, S. K. (2011). Heritability estimation for speech-sound traits with developmental trajectories. *Behavioral Genetics, 41*, 184–191. doi: 10.1007/s10519-010-9378-5.

Teubert, M., Vierhaus, M., & Lohaus, A. (2011). Methods for predicting later intelligence during infancy. *Psychologische Rundschau, 62*(2), 70–77. doi: 10.1026/0033-3042/a000068.

Van den Bergh, B. R. H., Mulder, E. J. H., Mennes, M., & Glover, V. (2005). Antenatal maternal anxiety and stress and the neurobehavioral development of the fetus and child: Links and possible mechanisms: A review. *Neuroscience & Biobehavioral Reviews, 29,* 237–258.

Vernes, S. C., & Fischer, S. E. (2011). Functional genomic dissection of speech and language disorders. *Geonomic, Proteomics, and the Nervous System, 2*(3), 253–278. doi: 10.1007/978-1-4419-7197-5_10.

Vernon-Feagans, L., Garrett-Peters, P., Willoughby, M., & Mills-Koonce, R. (2011). Chaos, poverty, and parenting: Predictors of early language development. *Early Childhood Research Quarterly, 27*(3), 339–351. doi: 10.1016/j.ecresq.2011.11.001.

Weismer, E. S. (2007). Typical talkers, late talkers, and children with specific language impairment: A language endowment spectrum? In R. Paul (Ed.), *The influence of developmental perspectives on research and practice in communication disorders: A Festschrift for Robin S. Chapman.* Mahwah, NJ: Erlbaum, 83–102.

World Health Organization Multicentre Growth Reference Study Group. (2006). WHO motor development study: Windows of achievement for six gross motor development milestones. *Acta Paediatrica* (Suppl. 450), 86–95.

Wright, C., & Diener, M. L. (2012). Play, creativity, and socioemotional development: Weaving the threads of influence. In O.N. Saracho (Ed.), *Contemporary perspectives on research in creativity in early childhood education.* Charlotte, NC: Information Age Publishing, Inc.

Chapter 5

Aliyu, M. H., Lynch, O., Wilson, R. E., Alio, A. P., Kristensen, S., Marty, P. J., Whiteman, V. E., & Salihu, H. M. (2011). Association between tobacco use in pregnancy and placenta-associated syndromes: A population-based study. *Archives of Gynecology and Obstetrics, 283*(4), 729–734. doi: 10.1007/s00404-010-1447-8.

Almqvist-Tangen, G., Bergman, S., Dahlgren, J., Roswall, J., & Alm, B. (2011). Factors associated with discontinuation of breastfeeding before 1 month of age. *Acta Paediatrica, 101*(1), 55–60. doi: 10.1111/j.1651-2227.2011.02405.x.

Amendah, D. D., Gross, S. D., & Bertrand, J. (2011). Medical expenditures of children in the United States with fetal alcohol syndrome. *Neurotoxicology and Teratology, 33*(2), 322–324. doi: 10.1016/j.ntt.2010.10.008.

Bachour, P., Yafawi, R., Jaber, F., Choueiri, W., & Abdel-Razzak, Z. (2011). Effects of smoking, mother's age, body mass index, and parity number on lipid, protein, and secretory immunoglobulin A concentrations of human milk. *Breastfeeding Medicine, 7,* 179–188. doi: 10.1029/bfm.2011.0038.

Bailey, B. A., McCook, J. G., Hodge, A., & McGrady, L. (2012). Infant birth outcomes among substance using women: Why quitting smoking during pregnancy is just as important as quitting illicit drug use. *Maternal and Child Health Journal, 16*(2), 414–422. doi: 10.1007/s10995-011-0776-y.

Bellinghausen, P. (2000, April 30). Meth use linked to birth woes. *The Billings Gazette.* Retrieved January 10, 2003, from http://www.manpinc.org/drugnews/v00.n578.a03.html.

Betancourt, L. M., Yang, W., Brodsky, N. L., Gallagher, P. R., Malmud, E. K., Giannetta, J. M., Farah, M. J., & Hurt, H. (2011). Adolescents with and without gestational cocaine exposure: Longitudinal analysis of inhibitory control, memory and receptive language. *Neurotoxicology and Teratology, 33*(1), 36–46. doi: 10.1016/j.ntt.2010.08.004.

Blomberg, M. (2011). Maternal and neonatal outcomes among obese women with weight gain below the New Institute of Medicine recommendations. *Obstetrics & Gynecology, 117*(5), 1065-1070. doi: 10.1097/AOG.0b013e318214f1d1.

Bloomfield, F. H. (2011). How is maternal nutrition related to preterm birth. *Annual Review of Nutrition, 31,* 235–261. doi:10.116/annurev-nutr-072610-145141.

Blumenshine, P. M., Egerter, S. A., Libet, M. L., & Braveman, P. A. (2011). Father's education: An independent marker of risk for preterm birth. *Maternal and Child Health Journal, 15*(1), 60–67. doi: 10.1007/s1095-009-0559-x.

Borowitz, S. M. (2002). Gastroesophageal reflux in infants. Children's Medical Center of the University of Virginia. Retrieved April 10, 2003, from http://med.virginia.edu/cmc/tutorials/reflux/symptoms.htm.

Bowers, K., Tobias, D. K., Yeung, E., Hu, F. B., & Zhang, C. (2012). A prospective study of prepregnancy dietary fat intake and risk of gestational diabetes. *The American Journal of Clinical Nutrition, 95,* 446–453. doi: 10.3945/ajcn.111.026294.

Bozetti, V., Malguzzi, S., Paterlini, G., Colonna, C., Kullmann, G., & Tagliabue, P. E. (2011). Functional outcomes among preterm infants with intraventricular hemorrhage. *Pediatric Research, 70,* 305. doi: 10.1038/pr.2011.530.

Bublitz, M. H., & Stroud, L. R. (2012). Childhood sexual abuse is associated with cortisol awakening response over pregnancy: Preliminary findings. *Psychoneuroendocrinology.* doi: 10.1016/j.psyneuen.1012.01.009.

Buchi, K. F., Zone, S., Langheinrich, K., & Varner, M. W. (2003). Changing prevalence of prenatal substance abuse in Utah. *Obstetrical Gynecology, 102*(1), 27–30.

Burd, L., Blair, J., & Dropps, K. (2011). Prenatal alcohol exposure, blood alcohol concentrations and alcohol elimination rates for the mother, fetus and newborn. *Journal of Perinatology.* doi: 10.1038/jp.2012.57.

Butz, A. M., Pulsifer, M., Belcher, H. M. E., Leppert, M., Donithan, M., & Zeger, S. (2005). Infant head growth and cognitive status at 36 months in children with in-utero drug exposure. *Journal of Child and Adolescent Drug Abuse, 14*(4), 15–39.

Candelaria, M., Teti, D. M., & Black, M. M. (2011). Multi-risk infants: Predicting attachment security from sociodemographic, psychosocial, and health risk among African-American preterm infants. *Journal of Child Psychology and Psychiatry, 52*(8), 870–877. doi: 10.111/j.1469-7610.2011.02361.x.

Cannon, M. J., Dominique, Y., O'Leary, L. A., Sniezek, J. E., & Floyd, R. L. (2012). Characteristics and behaviors of mothers who have a child with fetal alcohol syndrome. *Neurotoxicology and Teratology, 34*(1), 90–95. doi:10.1016/j.ntt.2011.09.010.

CDC. (2002). Fetal alcohol syndrome-Alaska, Arizona, Colorado, and New York, 1995–1997. *MMWR Morbidity and Mortality Weekly, 51*(20), 433–435.

Cheng, C-Y., Chen, Y-J., & Liou, S-R. (2011). Postpartum depression and birth outcomes of single mothers. *Virginia Henderson International Nursing Library.* Retrieved June 15, 2012, from http://hdl.handle.net/10755/169947.

Clark, S. L., Belfort, M. A., Dildy, G. A., Herbst, M. A., Meyers, J. A., & Hankins, G. D. (2008). Maternal death in the 21st century: Causes, prevention, and relationship to cesarean delivery. *American Journal of Obstetrics & Gynecology, 199*(1), 36.31–36.e5. doi: 10.1016/j.ajog.2008.03.007.

Cornelius, M. D., Goldschmidt, L., DeGenna, N. M., & Larkby, C. (2012). Long-term effects of prenatal cigarette smoke exposure on behavioral dysregulation among 14-year old offspring of teenage mothers. *Maternal and Child Health Journal, 16*(3), 694–705. doi: 10.1007/s10995-011-0766-0.

Dargaville, P. A. (2012). Respiratory support in meconium aspiration syndrome: A practical guide. *International Journal of Pediatrics.* doi: 10.1155/2012/965159.

Davidson, P. W., Myers, G. J., & Weiss, B. (2004). Mercury exposure and child development outcomes. *Pediatrics, 113,* 1023–1029.

Davis, K., Desrocher, M., & Moore, T. (2011). Fetal alcohol spectrum disorder: A review of neurodevelopmental findings and interventions. *Journal of Developmental and Physical Disabilities, 23*(2), 143–167. doi: 10.1007/s10882-010-9204-2.

Davis, R. R., & Hofferth, S. L. (2012). The association between inadequate gestational weight gain and infant mortality among U.S. infants born in 2002. *Maternal and Child Health Journal, 16*(1), 119–124. doi: 10.1007/s10995-010-0713-5.

Debiec, K. E., Paul, K. J., Mitchell, C. M., & Hitti, J. E. (2010). Inadequate prenatal care and risk of preterm delivery among adolescents: A retrospective study over 10 years. *American Journal of Obstetrics and Gynecology, 203,* 122e1–122e6. doi: 10.1016/j.ajog.2010.03.001.

Diego, M., Field, T., Hernandez-Reif, M., Vera, Y., Gil, K., & Gonzalez-Garcia, A. (2008). Caffeine use affects pregnancy outcomes. *Journal of Child & Adolescent Substance Abuse, 17*(2), 41–49.

Douzgou, S., Breen, C., Crow, Y. J., Chandler, K., Metcalfe, K., Jones, E., Kerr, B., & Clayton-Smith, J. (2012). Diagnosing fetal alcohol syndrome: New insights from newer genetic technology. *Archives of Diseases in Childhood.* doi: 10.1136/archdischild-2012-302125.

Eagles, J. M., Lee, A. J., Raha, E.A., Millar, H. R., & Bhattacharya, S. (2012). Pregnancy outcomes of women with and without a history of anorexia nervosa. *Psychological Medicine, FirstView,* 1–10. doi: 10.1017/S000332291712000414.

Edin, K., & Tach, L. (2012). Becoming a parent: The social contexts of fertility during young adulthood. *Early Adulthood in a Family Context, 2*(4), 185–207. doi: 10.1007/978-1-4614-1436.

Fang, H., Dukic, V., Pickett, K. E., Wakschlag, L., & Espy, K. A. (2012). Detecting graded exposure effects: A report on an East Boston pregnancy cohort. *Nicotine & Tobacco Research.* doi: 10.1093/ntr/ntr272.

Gaillard, R., Durmus, B., Hofman, A., Mackenbach, J., Steegers, E., & Jaddoe, V. (2012). Risk factors and outcomes of maternal obesity and excessive weight gain during pregnancy. *Pregnancy Hypertension: An International Journal of Women's Cardiovascular Health, 2*(3), 186.

Gardner, J. (1997). Fetal alcohol syndrome—Recognition and intervention. *Maternal and Child Nutrition, 22,* 318–322.

Garfinkle, J., & Shevell, M. I. (2011). Predictors of outcome in term infants with neonatal seizures subsequent to intrapartum asphyxia. *Journal of Child Neurology, 26*(4), 453-459. doi: 10.1177/0883073810382907.

Garrett, B. E., Dube, S. R., Trosclair, A., Caraballo, R. S., & Pechacek, T. F. (2011, January). Cigarette smoking—United States, 1965-2008. *CDC Health Disparities and*

Inequalities Report-United States 2011. Centers for Disease Control and Prevention: MMWR, Supplement/Vol. 60.

Gavin, A. R., Thompsen, E., Rue, T., & Guo, Y. (2012). Maternal early life risk factors for offspring birth weight: Findings from the Add Health study. *Prevention Science, 13*(2), 163–172. doi: 10.1007/s11121-011-0253-2.

Gonclaves, L. F., Chaiworapongsa, T., & Romero, R. (2002). Intrauterine infection and prematurity. *Mental Retardation and Developmental Disabilities Research Review, 8,* 3–13.

Green, J. (2006, May 10) U.S. has second worst newborn death rate in modern world, report says. Retrieved July 20, 2007, from http://www.cnn.com/2006/HEALTH?parenting/05/08/mothers.index/index.html.

Grunau, R. E. (2002). Extremely low birth weight children often have complex learning disabilities. *Archives of Pediatric Adolescent Medicine, 156,* 615–620.

Hack, M, Wilson-Costello, D., & Friedman, H. (2000). Neurodevelopment and predictors of outcomes of children with birth weights of less than 1000 g, 1992–1995. *Archives of Pediatric & Adolescent Medicine, 154,* 725–731.

Harding, R., & Maritz, G. (2012). Maternal and fetal origins of lung disease in adulthood. *Seminars in Fetal and Neonatal Medicine, 17*(2), 67–72. doi: 10.1016/j.siny.2012.01.005.

Harvard School of Public Health. (2004, February). Prenatal exposure to mercury from a maternal diet high in seafood can irreversibly impair certain brain functions in children. Retrieved March 6, 2008, from http://www.hsph.harvard.edu/press/releases/press02062004.html.

Hebben, N. (2004). Commentary on polychlorinated biphenyls (PCBs), toxins and neuropsychological deficits: Good science is the antidote. *Psychology in the Schools, 41,* 681–685.

Herrmann, M., King, K., & Weitzman, M. (2008). Prenatal tobacco smoke and postnatal secondhand smoke exposure and child neurodevelopment. *Current Opinion in Pediatrics, 20*(2), 187–190.

Honein, M. A., Kirby, R. S., Meyer, R. E., Xing, J., Skerrette, N. I., Yuskiv, N., Marengo, L., Petrini, J. R., Davidoff, M. J., Mai, C. T., Druschel, C. M., Viner-Brown, S., & Sever, L. E. (2009). The association between major birth defects and preterm birth. *Maternal and Child Health Journal, 13*(2), 164–175.

Horbar, J. D., Carpenter, J. H., Badger, G. J., Kenny, M.J., Soll, R. F., Morrow, K. A., & Buzas, J. S. (2012).

Mortality and neonatal morbidity among infants 501 to 1500 grams from 2000–2009. *Pediatrics, 129*(6), 1019–1026. doi: 10.1542/peds.2001-3028.

Jedrychowski, W., Glas, A. S., Flak, E., Elzbieta, J. R., Penar, A., Spengler, J., & Perera, F. P. (2007). Increased burden of respiratory disease in the first six months of life due to prenatal environmental tobacco smoke: Krakow Birth Cohort Study. *Early Child Development and Care, 177,* 369–381.

Kerstjens, J. M., Bocca-Tjeertes, I. F., deWinter, A. F., Reijneveld, S. A., & Bos, A. F. (2012). Neonatal morbidities and developmental delay in moderately preterm-born children. *Pediatrics.* doi: 10.1542/peds.2012-0079.

Kerzner, B., & Milano, K. (2012). *Understanding pediatric growth failure.* Abbott Park, IL: Abbott Laboratories, Inc. Retrieved June 15, 2012 from http://www.rd411.com/pdf/March_2012_Kerzner_PDF.pdf.

King, A. G. (2005). Research advances. *Journal of Chemical Education, 82,* 970–971.

Kouris, S. (2007). Update on the role of environmental toxins in neurodevelopmental disabilities. *Exceptional Parent, 37*(2), 49–52.

Kuklina, E. V., Ayala, C., & Callahan, W. M. (2009). Hypertensive disorders and severe obstetric morbidity in the United States. *Obstetrics and Gynecology, 113*(6), 1299–1306. doi: 10.1097/AOG0b013e31381a45b25.

LaGasse, L. L., Wouldes, T., Newman, E., Smith, L. M., Shah, R. Z., Derauf, C., Huestis, M. A., Arria, A. M., Grotta, S. D., Wilcox, T., & Lester, B. M. (2011). Prenatal methamphetamine exposure and neonatal neurobehavioral outcomes in the USA and New Zealand. *Neurotoxicology and Teratology, 33*(1), 166–175. doi:10.1016/j.ntt.2010.06.009.

Lake, E. T., Steiger, D., Horbar, J., Cheung, R., Kenny, M. J. Patrick, T., & Rogowski, J. A. (2012). Association between hospital recognition for nursing excellence and outcomes of very-low-birth-weight infants. *JAMA, 307*(16), 1709–1716. doi: 10.1001/jama.2012.504.

Lampi, K. M., Lehtonen, L., Tran, P. L., Suominen, A., Hehti, V., Banerjee, P. N., Gissler, M., Brown, A. S., & Sourander, A. (2012). Risk of Autism Spectrum Disorder in low birth weight and small for gestational age infants. *The Journal of Pediatrics.* doi: 10.1016/j.jpeds.2012.04.058.

Leenars, L. S., Denys, K., Henneveld, D., & Rasmussen, C. (2011). The impact of fetal alchohol spectrum disorders on families: Evaluation of a family intervention program. *Community Mental Health Journal, Brief Report.* doi: 10.1007/s10597-011-9425-6.

Lewis, B. A.,Minnes, S., Short, E. J., Weishampel, P., Satayathum, S., Min, M. O., Nelson, S., & Singer, L. T. (2011). The effects of prenatal cocaine on language development at 10 years of age. *Neurotoxicology and Teratology, 33*(1), 17–24. doi:10.1016/j.ntt.2010.06.006.

Li, D., Liu, L., & Odouli R. (2008). Presence of depressive symptoms during early pregnancy and the risk of preterm delivery: A prospective cohort study. *Human Reproduction, 24*(1), 146–153. doi: 10.1093/humrep/den342.

Madsen, T., & Hitchcock, E. (2011). Growing up toxic: Chemical exposures and increases in developmental disease. *Maryland PIRG Foundation.* Retrieved June 30, 2012, from http://www.cdn.publicinterest network.org/assets/7bbd6c32b2b40719f78c9c513a b5c41/growing-up-toxic.pdf.

March of Dimes (2002). All birthweight categories: US, 2000. Peristats: An interactive perinatal data source. Retrieved October 10, 2002, from http://peristats .modimes.org/dataviewus.cfm.

Markestad, T., Kaaresen, P. I., Ronnestad, A., Reigstad, H., Lossius, K., Medbo, S., Zanussi, G., Engelund, I. E., Polit, C., Skjaerven, R., & Irgens, L. M. (2005). Early death, morbidity, and need of treatment among extremely premature infants. *Pediatrics, 115,* 1289–1298.

Marks, K., Reichman, B., Lusky, A., & Zmora, E. (2006). Fetal growth and postnatal growth in very-low-birthweight infants. *Acta Paediatrica, 95,* 236–242.

Masters, C. (2006, November). Ahead of their time. *Time, 168*(21), 59–60.

May, L.E. (2012). Maternal exercise throughout gestation and fetal development. *Physiology of Prenatal Exercise and Fetal Development: Spring Briefs in Physiology,* 1–9. doi: 10.1007/978-1-4614-3408-5_1.

May, P. A., & Gossage, J. P. (2011). Maternal risk factors and fetal alcohol spectrum disorders: Not as simple as it might seem. National Institute on Alcohol Abuse and Alcoholism, 34(1). Retrieved June 30, 2012, from http://pubs.niaaa.nih.gov/publications/arh341/15-26.htm.

May, P. A., Tabachnick, B. G., Gossage, J. P., Kalberg, W. O., Marais, A-S., Robinson, L. K., Manning, M., Buckley, D., & Hoyme, H. E. (2011). Maternal risk factors predicting child physical characteristics and dysmorphology in fetal alcohol syndrome and partial fetal alcohol syndrome. *Drug and Alcohol Dependence, 119,* 18–22. doi: 10.1016/j.drugalcdep.2011.05.009.

McGrath, M., & Sullivan, M.C. (2011). School underachievement related to perinatal morbidity in preterm children with various birth weights. Virginia Henderson International Nursing Library. Retrieved from http://hdl.handle.net/10755/163674.

Messinger, D. S., Bauer, C. R., Das, A., Seifer, R., Lester, B. M., Lagasse, L. L., Wright, L. L., Shankaran, S., Bada, H. S., Smeriglio, V. L., Langer, J. C., Beeghly, M., & Poole, W. K. (2004). The maternal lifestyle study: Cognitive, motor, and behavioral outcomes of cocaine-exposed and opiate-exposed infants through three years of age. *Pediatrics, 113,* 1677–1685.

Mezzacappa, E., Buckner, J. C., & Earls, F. (2011). Prenatal cigarette exposure and infant learning stimulation as predictors of cognitive control in childhood. *Developmental Science, 14*(4), 881–891. doi: 10.1111/j.1467-7687.2011.01038.x.

Minnes, S., Lang, A., & Singer, L. (2011). Prenatal tobacco, marijuana, stimulant, and opiate exposure: Outcomes and practice implications. *Addiction Science and Clinical Practice, 6*(1), 57–70.

Motz, M., Espinet, S. D., Jeong, J. J., Major, D., Racine, N., Chamberlin, J., & Pepler, D. J. (2011). The role of the mother-child relationship in developmental outcomes of infants and young children with and without prenatal alcohol exposure. *Journal of Population Therapeutics & Clinical Pharmacology, 18*(3), e545–e563.

Nadeem, M., Murray, D. M., Boylan, G. B., Dempsey, E. M., & Ryan, C. A. (2011). Early blood glucose profile and neurodevelopmental outcome at two years in neonatal hypoxic-ischaemic encephalopathy. *BMC Pediatrics, 11,* 10. doi: 10.1186/1471-2431-11-10.

National Academies Press. (2006). Preterm birth: Causes, consequences, and prevention. Retrieved March 6, 2008, from http://www.nap.edu.

National Association for Families and Addiction Research and Education. (1998). Silent violence: Is prevention a moral obligation? *Pediatrics, 102,* 145–149.

Niccols, A. (2007). Fetal alcohol syndrome and the developing socio-emotional brain. *Brain and Cognition, 65,* 135–142.

NIH. (June, 2008). Peer review report for the draft NTP brief on *Bisphenol A. NTP Board of Scientific Counselors Meeting.* Retrieved April 10, 2009, from http://www .ntp.niehs.nih.gov/ntp/ohat/bisphenol/BPAPeer ReviewReport.pdf.

Omar, S. A., DeCristofaro, J., Agarwal, B. I., & LaGamma, E. F. (2000). Effect of prenatal steroids on potassium balance in extremely low birth weight neonates. *Pediatrics, 106*(3), 561–567.

Osmania, J. (2011). Maternal nutrition in early pregnancy effects placental development. *Medicine and Public Health, 1*(1), 22–29. doi:10.5530/ijmedph.2.2011.6.

Ouzounian, J. G., Hernandez, G. D., Korst, L. M., Montoro, M. M., Battista, L.R., Walden, C. L., & Lee, R. H. (2011). Pre-pregnancy weight and excess weight gain are risk factors for macrosomia in women with gestational diabetes. *Journal of Perinatology, 31,* 717–721. doi: 10.1038/jp.2011.15.

Phung, M. H., Wallace, L., Alexander, J., & Phung, J. (2011). Parenting children with fetal alcohol syndrome disorders (FASD). *WebmedCentral Public Health, 2*(2). Retrieved July 13, 2012, from http://www.webmedcentral.com/article_view1638.

Pramanik, A. (2006). Respiratory distress syndrome. *eMedicine Journal, 2*(7). Retrieved February 14, 2009, from http://emedicine.medscape.com/article/976034.htm.

Ronchetti, R., Van Den Hazel, P., Schoeters, G., Hanke, W., Rennezova, Z., Barreto, M., & Pia Villa, M. (2006). Lead neurotoxicity in children: Is prenatal exposure more important than postnatal exposure? *Acta Paediatrica, 95,* 45–49.

Ryan, S., & Ferguson, D. (2006). The person behind the face of fetal alcohol spectrum disorders: Student experiences, family and professional perspective on FASD. *Rural Special Education Quarterly, 25*(2), 124–142.

Schempf, A. H., & Strobino, D. (2008). Illicit drug use and adverse birth outcomes: Is it drugs or context? *Journal of Urban Health, 85*(6), 858–873. doi: 10.1007/s11524-008-9315-6.

Schroder, M. D., Snyder, P. J., Sielski, I., & Mayes, L. (2004). Impaired performance of children exposed in utero to cocaine on a novel test of visuospatial working memory. *Brain and Cognition, 55,* 409–412.

Schwarz, E. C., Grauel, E. L., & Wauer, R. R. (2011). No increase of incidence of retinopathy of prematurity and improvement of its outcome in a university perinatal centre level III-a prospective observational study from 1978 to 2007. *Klin Monbl Augenheilkd, 228*(3), 208–219.

Shapiro-Mendoza, C. K., & Lackritz, E. M. (2012). Epidemiology of late and moderate preterm birth. *Seminars in Fetal and Neonatal Medicine, 17*(3), 120–125. doi: 10.1016/j.siny.2012.01.007.

Subramanian, K. N. S., Yoon, H., & Toral, J. C. (2001). Extremely low birth weight infant. *eMedicine Journal, 2,* 11–13. Retrieved October 10, 2002, from http://www.emedicine.com/ped/topic2784.htm.

Tabarestani, S., & Ghofrani, M. (2010). Hypoglycemia-occipital syndrome: A specific neurologic syndrome following neonatal hypoglycemia. *Journal of Child Neurology, 26*(2), 152–159. doi: 10.1177/0883073810376245.

Tam, W. Y., Haeusslein, L. A., Bonifacio, S. L., Glass, H. C., Rogers, E. E., Jeremy, R. J., Barkovich, A. J., & Ferriero, D. M. (2011). Hypoglycemia is associated with increased risk for brain injury and adverse neurodevelopmental outcome in neonates at risk for encephalopathy. *The Journal of Pediatrics, 161*(1), 88–93. doi: 10.1016/j.peds.2011.12.047.

Tanner-Halverson, P. (1998). Strategies for parents and caregivers of FAS and FAE children. The National Organization on Fetal Alcohol Syndrome. Retrieved October 10, 2002, from http://www.nofas.org/strategy.

Vasudevan, C., Renfrew, M., & McGuire, W. (2011). Fetal and perinatal consequences of maternal obesity. *ADC Fetal and Neonatal, 96.* doi: 10.1136/adc.2009.170928.

Walker, D. (2011). Preventing fetal alcohol syndrome: Women's attitudes and knowledge about alcohol. *MNRS-Midwest Nursing Research Society.* Retrieved July 1, 2012, from http:///hdl.handle.net/10755/159561.

Weng, X., Odouli, R., & Li, D. K. (2008). Maternal caffeine caffeine consumption during pregnancy and the risk of miscarriage: A prospective cohort study. *American Journal of Obstetrics and Gynecology, 198,* 279–287.

Wisborg, K., Kesmodel, U., Henriksen, T. B., Olsen, S. F., & Secher, N. J. (2001). Exposure to tobacco smoke in utero and the risk of stillbirth and death in the first year of life. *American Journal of Epidemiology, 154,* 322–327.

Wise, J. (1998). Carcinogen in tobacco smoke may be passed to fetus. *British Medical Journal, 317,* 555.

World Health Organization. (2011). Fetal alcohol syndrome: Dashed hopes, damaged lives. *Bulletin of the World Health Organization, 89*(6). doi: 10.2471/BLT.11.020611.

Xiang, A. H., Li, B. H., Black, M. H., Sacks, D. A., Buchanan, T. A., Jacobsen, S. J., & Lawrence, J. M. (2011). Racial and ethnic disparities in diabetes risk after gestational diabetes mellitus. *Diabetologia, 54*(12), 3016–3020. doi: 10.1007/s00125-001-2330-2.

Zayek, M. M., Trimn, R. F., Hamm, C. R., Peevy, K. J., Benjamin, J. T., & Eyal, F. G. (2011). The limit of viability: A single regional unit's experience. *Archives of Pediatric & Adolescent Medicine, 165*(2), 126–133. doi: 10.1001/archpediatrics.2010.285.

Chapter 6

Adzick, N. S., Sutton, L. N., Crombleholme, T. M., & Flake, A. W. (1998). Successful fetal surgery for spina bifida. *Lancet, 352*(9141), 1675–167.

Adzick, N. S., Thom, E. A., Spong, C. Y., Brock, J. W., Burrows, P. K., Johnson, M. P., Howell, L. J., Farrell, J. A., Dabrowiak, M. E., Sutton, L. N., Gupta, N., Tulipan, N. B., D'Alton, M. E., & Farmer, D. L. (2011). A randomized trial of prenatal versus postnatal repair of myelomeningocele. *The New England Journal of Medicine, 364*, 993–1004.

Akalan, N. (2011). Myelomeningocele (open spina bifida)—surgical management. *Advances and Technical Standards in Neurosurgery, 37*(2), 113–141. doi: 10.1007/978-3-7091-0673-0_5.

Akinbami, L. J., Liu, X., Pastor, P. N., & Reuben, C. A. (Aug, 2011). Attention deficit hyperactivity disorder among children aged 5–17 years in the United States, 1998–2009. *NCHS Data Brief, 70*. Retrieved July 3, 2012, from http://198.246.124.20/nchs/data/databriefs/db70.pdf.

Alberman, E. (2010). Congenital malformations and the cerebral palsies—déjà vu, but now what? *Developmental Medicine & Child Neurology, 52*(4), 314–315. doi: 10.1111/j1469-8749.2009.03482.x.

Anderson, V., Godfrey, C., Rosenfeld, J. V., & Catroppa, C. (2012). Predictors of cognitive function and recovery 10 years after traumatic brain injury in young children. *Pediatrics, 129*(2), e254–e261. doi: 10.1542/peds.2011-0311.

Aslin, R. N., & Mehler, J. (2005). Near-infrared spectroscopy for functional studies of brain activity in human infants: Promise, prospects, and challenges. *Journal of Biomedical Optics, 10*(1), 11009–13.

Barclay, L. (2002). General movements in preterm infants predict cerebral palsy. *Archives of Pediatric & Adolescent Medicine, 156*(5), 460–467.

Benson, L. A., Maski, K. P., Kothare, S. V., & Bourgeois, B. F. (2010). New onset epilepsy in Prader-Willi syndrome: Semiology and literature review. *Pediatric Neurology, 43*(4), 297–299.

Bhise, V. V., Burack, G. D., & Mandelbaum, D. E. (2009). Baseline cognition, behavior, and motor skills in children with new-onset, idiopathic epilepsy. *Developmental Medicine and Child Neurology, 52*(1), 22–26. doi: 10.1111/j1469-8749.2009.03404.x.

Blair, E. (2001). Trends in cerebral palsy. *Indian Journal of Pediatrics, 68*, 433–437.

Blume, W. T. (2008). Drug-resistant epilepsy. In J. Engel, T. A. Pedley, and J. Aicardi (Eds.), *Epilepsy: A comprehensive textbook, Volume 1*. New York: Lippincott, Williams & Wilkins.

Boyles, A. L., Billups, A. V., Deak, K. L., Siegel, D. G., Mehltretter, L., Slifer, S. H., Bassuk, A. G., Kessler, J. A., Reed, M. C., Nijhout, H. F., George, T. M., Enterline, D. S., Gilbert, J. R., & Speer, M. C. (2006). Neural tube defects and folate pathway genes: Family-based association tests of gene-gene and gene-environment interactions. *Environmental Health Perspectives, 114*, 1547–1560.

Braun, J. M., Kahn, R. S., Froehlich, T., Auinger, P., & Lanphear, B. P. (2006). Exposures to environmental toxicants and attention deficit hyperactivity disorder in U.S. children. *Environmental Health Perspectives, 114*, 1904–1918.

Brooks, J., Day, S., Shavelle, R., & Strauss, D. (2011). Low weight, morbidity, and mortality in children with cerebral palsy: New clinical growth charts. *Pediatrics, 128*(2), e299–e307. doi: 10.1542/peds.2010-2801.

Buxton, N., & Punt, J. (1998). Failure to follow patients with hydrocephalus shunts can lead to death. *British Journal of Neurosurgery, 12*(5), 399–402.

Cavanna, A. E., Critchley, H. D., Orth, M., Stern, J. S., Young, M-B., & Robertson, M. M. (2011). Dissecting the Gilles de la Tourette spectrum: A factor analytics study on 639 patients. *Journal of Neurology, Neurosurgery & Psychiatry, 82*, 1320–1323. doi: 10.1136/jnnp.2010.225029.

Chai, G., Governale, L., McMahon, A. W., Trinidad, J. P., Staffa, J., & Murphy, D. (2012). Trends of outpatient prescription drug utilization in US children 2002–2010. *Pediatrics, 130*(1), 23–31. doi: 10.142/peds.2011-2879.

Chapman, M., Iddon, P., Atkinson, K., Brodie, C., Mitchell, D., Parvin, G., & Willis, S. (2011). The misdiagnosis of epilepsy in people with intellectual disabilities: A systematic review. *Seizure, 20*(2), 101–106. doi: 10.1016/j.seizure.2010.10.030.

Chervenak, F. A., McCullough, L. B., & Arabin, B. (2006). Why the Groningen Protocol should be rejected. *The Hastings Center Report, 36*(5), 30–33.

Colin, A. (1997). *Willie: Raising and loving a child with attention deficit disorder*. New York: Viking.

Connor, D. F. (2002). Preschool attention deficit hyperactivity disorder: A review of prevalence, diagnosis, neurobiology, and stimulant treatment. *Developmental and Behavioral Pediatrics, 23*, 1–9.

Cooke, R. W. I., & Abernethy, L. J. (2010). The sequelae of neonatal brain injury. *Paediatrics and Child Health. 20*(8), 374–381. doi: 10.1016/j.paed.2010.07.004.

Crowe, L. M., Catroppa, C., Babi, F. E., Rosenfeld, J. V., & Anderson, V. (2012a). Timing of traumatic brain injury in childhood and intellectual outcomes. *Journal of Pediatric Psychology, 37*(7), 745–754. doi: 10.1093/jpepsy/jss070.

Crowe, L. M., Catroppa, C., Babi, F. E., Rosenfeld, J. V., & Anderson, V. (2012b). Intellectual, behavioral, and social outcomes of accidental traumatic brain injury in early childhood. *Pediatrics, 129*(2), e262–e268. doi: 10.1542/peds.2011-0438.

Darrah, J., Pollock, N., Wilson, B., Russell, D. J., Walter, S. D., Rosenbaum, P. & Galuppi, B. (2011). Context therapy: A new intervention approach for children with cerebral palsy. *Developmental Medicine and Child Neurology, 53*(7), 615–620. doi: 10.1111/j.1469-8749.2011.03959.x.

Daughton, J. M. (2011). Conferences scene: The American Academy of Child and Adolescent Psychiatry 57th Annual Meeting. *Neuropsychiatry, 1*(1), 27–29.

Davis, D. W., & Williams, P. G. (2011). Attention deficit/hyperactivity disorder in preschool-age children: Issues and concerns. *Clinical Pediatrics, 50*(2), 144–152. doi: 10.1177/0009922810384722.

Dunn, D. W., Johnson, C. S., Perkins, S. M., Fastenau, P. S., Byars, A. W., deGrauw, T. J., & Austin, J. K. (2010). Academic problems in children with seizures: Relationships with neuropsychological functioning and family variables during the 3 years after onset. *Epilepsy & Behavior, 19*(3), 455–461. doi: 10.1016/j.yebeh.2010.08.023.

Edwards, J., Berube, M., Erlandson K., Haug, S., Johnstone, H., Meagher, M., Sarkodee-Adoo, S., & Zwicker, J. G. (2011). Developmental coordination disorder in school-aged children born very preterm and/or very low birth weight: A systematic review. *Journal of Developmental Behavioral Pediatrics, 32*(9), 678–687. doi: 10.1097/DBP.0b13e31822a396a.

Ehrenreich, H. (2004). A boost for translational neuroscience. *Science, 305,* 184–185.

Ewing-Cobb, L., Kramer, L., Prasad, M., Canales, N. Louis, P. T., Fletcher, J. M., Vollero, H., Landry, H., & Cheung, K. (1998). Neuroimaging, physical and developmental findings after inflicted and noninflicted traumatic brain injury in young children. *Pediatrics, 102,* 30–307.

Fallows, R., & McCoy, K. (2011). Long-term sequelae of cerebellar cognitive affective syndrome: A case presentation. *Archives of Clinical Neuropsychology, 26*(6), 467–470. doi: 10.1093/arclin/acr056.

Fetal Surgery. (2002). Update in obstetrics from SMFM Annual Meeting 2002. Retrieved December 2, 2002, from http://www.medscape.com/viewarticle/424571_3.

Fischbach, G. D., & Fischbach, R. L. (2004). Stem cells: Science, policy and ethics. *The Journal for Clinical Investigation, 114,* 1364–1370.

Fisher, R. S. (2012). Therapeutic devices for epilepsy. *Annals of Neurology, 71*(2), 157–168. doi: 10.1002/ana.22621.

Futagi, Y., & Suzuki, Y. (2010). Neural mechanism and clinical significance of the plantar grasp reflex in infants. *Pediatric Neurology, 43*(2), 81–86. doi: 10.1016/pediatrneurol.2010.04.002.

Gilbert, W. M., Jacoby, B. N., Xing, G., Danielsen, B., & Smith, H. S. (2010). Adverse obstetric events are associated with significant risk of cerebral palsy. *American Journal of Obstetrics and Gynecology, 203*(4), 328e1–328e5. doi: 10.1016/j.ajog.2010.05.013.

Goldstein, M. (2006, October). Cerebral palsy research: What's next? Retrieved June 10, 2008, from http://ucpresearch.org/fact-sheets/confact_whatsnext.php.

Goulden, K. J., Shinnar, S., Koller, H., Katz, M., & Richardson, S. A. (1991). Epilepsy in children with mental retardation: A cohort study. *Epilepsia, 32*(5), 690–697.

Gurevitz, M., Geva, R., Varon, M., & Leitner, Y. (2012). Early markers in infants and toddlers for development of ADHD. *Journal of Attention Disorders.* doi: 10.1177/108054712447858.

Hallbook, T., Lundgren, J., Stjernqvist, K., Blennow, G., Stromblad, L. G., & Rosen, I. (2005). Vagus nerve stimulation in 15 children with therapy resistant epilepsy; its impact on cognition, quality of life, behavior and mood. *Seizure, 14* (7), 504–513.

Hallioglu, O., Ôzge, A., Yilgör, E., Topaloglu, A. K., Düzovali, O., & Canim, A. (2012). Electroencephalographic abnormalities in children with breath-holding. *University of Mersin, School of Medicine.* Retrieved August 1, 2012, from http://tipdergisi.mersin.edu.tr/index.php/MTFD/article/view/31/27.

Hauser, W. A. (2003). Epidemiology of neural tube defects. *Epilepsia, 44* (Suppl. 3), 4–13.

Hingley, A. T. (1999). Epilepsy: Taming the seizures, dispelling the myths. *FDA Consumer, 33*(1), 28–33.

Imms, C. & Dodd, K. (2010). What is cerebral palsy? In K. Dodd & C. Imms (Eds.), *Physiotherapy and occupational therapy for people with cerebral palsy.* Hoboken, NY: John Wiley & Sons.

Jessen, C., Mackie, P., & Jarvis, S. (1999). Epidemiology of cerebral palsy. *Archives of Disability in Child, Fetal, Neonatal Editorial, 80*(2), 158–160.

Karagiozoglou-Lampoudi, T., Daskalou, E., Vargiami, E., & Zafeirou, D. (2012). Identification of feeding risk factors for impaired nutrition status in paediatric patients with cerebral palsy. *Acta Paediatrica, 101*(6). 649–654. doi: 10.111/j.16512227.2010.02641.x.

Kasanmoentalib, E.S., Brouwer, M.C., van der Ende, A., & van de Beek, D. (2010). Hydrocephalus in adults with community-acquired meningitis. *Neurology, 75*(10), 918–923. doi: 10.1212/WNL.0b013e3181f11e10.

Keenan, H. T., Runyan, D. K., Marshall, S. W., Nocera, M. A., Merten, D. F., & Sinal, S. H. (2003). A population-based study of inflicted traumatic brain injury in young children. *JAMA, 290*(5), 621–626.

Kelly, M. M. (2011). Comparison of functional status of 8- to 12-year old children born prematurely: An integrative review of literature. *Journal of Pediatric Nursing, 27*(4), 299–309. doi: 10.1016/j.pedn.2011.03.010.

Kieling, R., & Rohde, L. A. (2012). ADHD in children and adults: Diagnosis and prognosis. *Behavioral Neuroscience of Attention Deficit Hyperactivity Disorder and Its Treatment, 9*, 1–16. doi: 10.1007/7854_2010_115.

Kirby, R. S., Wingate, M. S., Braun, K. V., Doernberg, N. S., Arneson, R. E. B., Mulvihill, B., Durkin, M. S., Fitzgerald, R. T., Maenner, J., Patz, J. A., & Yeargin-Allsopp, M. (2011). Prevalence and functioning of children with cerebral palsy in four areas of the United States in 2006: A report from the autism of developmental disabilities monitoring network. *Research in Developmental Disabilities, 32*(2), 462–469. doi: 10.1016/j.ridd.2010.12.042.

Kouwaki, M., Yokochi, M., Togawa, Y., Kamiya, T., & Yokochi, K. (2012). Spontaneous movements in the supine position of healthy term infants and term infants with our without periventricular leukomalacia. *Brain and Development*. doi: 10.1016/jbraindev.2012.05.005.

Lacasaña, M., Blanco,-Muñoz, J., Borha-Aburto, V. H., Aguilar-Garduño, C., Rodríquez-Barranco, M., Sierra-Ramirez, J. A., Galaviz-Hernandez, C., Gonzalez-Alzaga, B., & Garcia-Cavazos, R. (2012). Effect on risk of anencephaly of gene-nutrient interactions between methylenetetrahydrofolate reductase C677T polymorphism and maternal folate, vitamin B_{12} and homocysteine profile. *Public Health Nutrition, 15*(8), 1419–1428. doi: 10.1017/S136898001100334X.

Lacquaniti, F., Ivanenko, Y. P., & Zago, M. (2012). Development of human locomotion. *Current Opinion in Neurobiology*. doi: 10.1016/j.conb.2012.03.012.

Langlois, J. A., Rutland-Brown, W., & Thomas, K. E. (2005). The incidence of traumatic brain injury among children in the United States: Difference by race. *Journal of Head Trauma Rehabilitation, 20*(3), 229–238.

Lhatoo, S. D., & Sander, J. W. (2001). The epidemiology of epilepsy and learning disability. *Epilepsia, 42*(1), 6–9.

Lindquist, B., Persson, E-K., Fernell, E., & Uvebrant, P. (2011). Very long-term follow-up of cognitive function in adults treated in infancy for hydrocephalus. *Child's Nervous System, 27*(4), 597–601. doi: 10.1007/s00381-010-1311-y.

Linnet, K. M., Dalsgaard, S., Obel, C., Wisborg, K., Henriksen, T. B., Rodriguez, A., Kotimaa, A., Moilanen, I., Thomsen, P. H., Olsen, J., & Jarvelin, M. R. (2003). Maternal lifestyle factors in pregnancy risk of attention deficit hyperactivity disorder and associated behaviors: Review of the current evidence. *American Journal of Psychiatry, 160*, 1028–1040.

Machado, I. N., Martinez, S. D., & Barini, R. (2012). Anencephaly: Do the pregnancy and maternal characteristics impact the pregnancy outcome? *ISRN Obstetrics & Gynecology*. doi: 10.5402/2012/127490.

Maria, B. L. (2008). *Current management in child neurology*. Shelton, CT: People's Medical Publishing House.

Masterson, M. K. (2010). Chronic sorrow in mothers of adult children with cerebral palsy: An exploratory study. *K-State Research Exchange*. Retrieved July 10, 2012, from http://hdl.handle.net/2097/3906.

McAdams, R. M., & Juul, S. E. (2011). Cerebral palsy: Prevalence, predictability, and parental counseling. *NeoReviews, 12*(1), e564–e574. doi: 10.1542/neo.12-10-e564.

McCandless, D. W. (2011). Cerebral Palsy and Counseling. In *Kernicterus* (pp. 209–217). New York: Humana Press.

Medical College Of Georgia (2004, August 18). Stem cell research targets cerebral palsy. *ScienceDaily*. Retrieved May 8, 2013, from http://www.sciencedaily.com-/releases/2004/08/040817075814.htm

Moster, D., Lie, R. T., & Markestad, T. (2002). Joint association of Apgar scores and early neonatal symptoms with minor disabilities at school age. *Archives of Disabled Child, Fetal, & Neonatal Education, 86*(1), 16–21.

Moster, D., Wilcox, A. J., Vollset, S. E., Markstad, T., & Lie, R. T. (2010). Cerebral palsy among term and postterm births. *JAMA, 304*(9), 976–982. doi: 10.1001/jama.2010.1271.

Murray, B. A., & Myers, M. A. (1998). Conduct disorders and the special-education trap. *Education Digest, 63*(8), 48–54.

Nair, G. C., & Bharucha, N. E. (2008). Prognosis of pediatric epilepsy. *Journal of Pediatric Neurosciences, 3*(1), 41–47. doi: 10.4103/1817-1745.40589.

Nelson, K. B. (2002). The epidemiology of cerebral palsy in term infants. *Mental Retardation and Developmental Disabilities, 8*, 146–150.

Nguyen, D. K., & Spencer, S. S. (2003). Recent advances in the treatment of epilepsy. *Archives of Neurology, 60*, 929–935.

Ninowski, J. (March, 2011). What are the earliest signs of ADHD? Retrieved July 15, 2012, from http://www.onehealth.ca/r_alberta_nwt/video_conferences/E110309E-HO.pdf.

Nützenadel, W. (2011). Failure to thrive in childhood. *Deutsches Ärzteblatt International, 108*(38), 642–649. doi: 10.3238/arztebl.2011.0642.

Olsen, A. L., Mathiasen, R., Rasmussen, N. H., & Knudsen, F. U. (2010). Long-term prognosis for children with breath-holding spells. *Danish Medical Bulletin, 57*(11), A4217.

Ornoy, A. (2003). The impact of intrauterine exposure versus postnatal environment in neurodevelopmental toxicity: Long-term neurobehavioral studies in children at risk for developmental disorders. *Toxicology Letters, 140–141*, 171–181.

O'Shea, M. (2008, Feb). Cerebral palsy. *Seminar in Perinatology, 32*(1), 35–41.

Pauli-Pott, U., & Becker, K. (2011). Neuropsychological basic deficits in preschoolers at risk for ADHD: A meta-analysis. *Clinical Psychology Review, 31*(4), 626–637. doi: 10.1016/j.cpr.2011.02.005.

Pellow, J., Solomon, E. M., & Barnard, C.N. (2011). Complementary and alternative medical therapies for children with attention-deficit/hyperactivity disorder (ADHD). *Alternative Medicine Review, 16*(4), 323–337.

Public Health Reports (1998). Please, more folate. *Public Health Reports, 113*(4), 293.

Quinn, P. O. (1997). *Attention deficit disorder: Diagnosis and treatment from infancy to adulthood.* New York: Brunner/Mazel.

Saunders, N., & Habgood, M. (2011). Understanding barrier mechanisms in the developing brain to aid therapy for the dysfunctional brain. *Future Neurology, 6*(2), 187–199. doi:10.217/fnl.10.84.

Shen, J., Gilmore, E. C., Marshall, C. A., Haddadin, M., Reynolds, J. J., Eyaid, W., Bodell, A., Barry, B., Gleason, D., Allen, K., Ganesh, V. S., Chang, B. S., Grix, A., Hill, R. S., Topcu, M., Caldecott, K. W., Barkovich, A. J., & Walsh, C. A. (2010). Mutations in PNKP cause microcephaly, seizures and defects in DNA repair. *Nature Genetics, 42*, 245–249. doi: 10.1038/ng.526.

Shepherd, A., Jepson, R., Watterson, A., & Evans, M. M. (2012). Risk perceptions of environmental hazards and human reproduction: A community-based survey. *ISRN Public Health.* doi: 10.5402/2012/748080.

Simpson, J. L., & Greene, M. F. (2011). Fetal surgery for myelomeningocele? *The New England Journal of Medicine, 364*, 1076–1077.

Smith, A. (2011). Parent perceptions of traumatic brain injury and rehabilitation in children. *Virginia Henderson International Nursing Library.* Retrieved May 15, 2012, from http://hdl.handle.net/10755/180658.

Smith, J. (2003). Shaken baby syndrome. *Orthopedic Nurse, 22*(3), 204–205.

Smith, K. G., & Corkum, P. (2007). Systematic review of measures used to diagnose attention-deficit/hyperactivity disorder in research on preschool children. *Topics in Early Childhood Special Education, 27*(3), 164–173.

Sonuga-Barke, E. J. S. (2011). Editorial: ADHD as a reinforcement disorder—moving from general effects to identify (six) specific models to test. *The Journal of Child Psychology and Psychiatry, 52*(9), 917-918. doi: 10.1111/j.1469-7610.2011.02444.x.

Terra, V. C., Cysneiros, R. M., Schwartzman, J. S., Teixeira, M. C., Arida, R. M., Cavalheiro, E. A., Scorza, F. A., & de Albuquerque, M. (2011). Mothers of children with cerebral palsy with or without epilepsy: A quality of life perspective. *Disability and Rehabilitation, 33*(5), 384–388.

Titus, J. B., & Thio, L. L. (2009). The effects of antiepileptic drugs on classroom behavior. *Psychology in the Schools, 46*(9), 885–891. doi: 10.1002/pits.20428.

Tutty, S., Gephart, H., & Wurzbacher, K. (2003). Enhancing behavioral and social skill functioning in children newly diagnosed with attention-deficit hyperactivity disorder in a pediatric setting. *Journal of Developmental and Behavioral Pediatrics, 24*(1), 51–57.

Van de Beek, D., Drake, J. M., & Tunkel, A., R. (2010). Nosocomial bacterial meningitis. *The New England Journal of Medicine, 362*, 146–154.

Whittingham, K., Wee, D., & Boyd, R. (2011). Systematic review of the efficacy of parenting interventions for children with cerebral palsy. *Child: Care, Health and Development, 37*(4), 475–483. doi: 10.1111/j.1365-2214.2011.01212.x.

Wiart, L., Ray, L., Darrah, J., & Magill-Evans, J. (2010). Parents' perspectives on occupational and physical therapy goals for children with cerebral palsy. *Disability and Rehabilitation, 32*(3), 248–258.

Wilens, T. E., Biederman, J., Brown, S., Tanguay, S., Monuteaux, M. C., Blake, C., & Spencer, T. J. (2002). Psychiatric comorbidity and functioning in clinically referred preschool children and school-age youths with ADHD. *Journal of the American Acadamy of Child & Adolescent Psychiatry, 41*(3), 262–268.

Willoughby, R. E. (2002). Maternal infections are depressing. *Pediatrics, 110*(4), 832–833.

Wilson-Costello, D. Borawski, E., Friedman, H., Redline, R., Fanaroff, A. A., & Hack, M. (1998). Perinatal correlates of cerebral palsy and other neurologic impairment among very low birth weight children. *Pediatrics, 102*, 315–323.

Winneke, G. (2011). Developmental aspects of environmental neurotoxicology: Lessons from lead and polychlorintated biphenyls. *Journal of the Neurological Sciences, 308,* 9–15. doi:10.1016/j.jns.2011.05.020.

Wu, Y. W., Xing, G., Fuentes-Afflick, E., Danielson, B., Smith, L. H., & Gilbert, W. M. (2011). Racial, ethnic, and socioeconomic disparities in the prevalence of cerebral palsy. *Pediatrics, 127*(3), e674–e681. doi: 10.1542/peds.2010-1656.

Zehetner, A. A., Orr, N., Buckmaster, A., Williams, K., & Wheeler, D. M. (2009). Iron supplements for breath-holding attacks in children. *The Cochrane Library.* doi: 10.1002/14651858.CD008132.pub2.

Chapter 7

Aartsma-Rus, A., Janson, A. A. M., van Ommen, G. J. B., & van Deutekom, J. (2007). Antisense-induced exon skipping for duplications in Duchenne muscular dystrophy. *BMC Medical Genetic, 8,* 43–50.

American Psychiatric Association. (2000). *Diagnostic and statistical manual of mental disorders* (4th ed., text rev.). Washington, DC: Author.

Anwar, A. R., & Segal, S. P. (2010). Inherited metabolic disorders and nutrition genomics: Choosing the wrong parents. *Nutrition Guide for Physicians,* 361–368. doi: 10.1007/978-1-60327-431-9_31.

Ashton, J., & Bailey, J. (2004). Slipping through the policy cracks: Children with chronic illness in early childhood settings. *Australian Journal of Early Childhood, 29*(1), 50–62.

Au, J., & Hagerman, R. (2013). Fragile X–associated disorders. In *Neuroscience in the 21st century* (pp. 2391–2410). New York: Springer.

Aygun, B., Parker, J., Freeman, M. B., Stephens, A. L., Smeltzer, M. P., Wu, S., Hankins, J. S., & Wang, W. C. (2010). Neurocognitive screening with the Brigance Preschool screen-II in 3-year-old children with sickle cell disease. *Pediatric Blood & Cancer, 56*(4), 620–624. doi: 10.1002/pbc.22833.

Baird, S. L. (2007). Designer babies: Eugenics repackaged or consumer options? The forces pushing humanity towards attempts at self-motivation, through biological and technological advances, are powerful, seductive ones that we will be hard-pressed to resist. *Technology Teacher, 66*(7), 12–24.

Barbaro, J., & Dissanayake, C. (2009). Autism spectrum disorders in infancy and toddlerhood: A review of the evidence on early signs, early identification tools and early diagnosis. *Journal of Developmental & Behavioral Pediatrics, 30,* 447–459.

Barnea-Goraly, N., Kwon, H., Menon, V., Eliez, S., Lotspeich, L., & Reiss, A. L., (2004). White matter structure in autism: Preliminary evidence from diffusion tensor imaging. *Biological Psychiatry, 55*(3), 323–326.

Barton, M.L., Dumont-Mathieu, T., & Fein, D. (2012). Screening young children for autism spectrum disorders in primary practice. *Journal of Autism and Developmental Disorders, 42,* 1165–1174. doi 10.1007/s10803-011-1343-5.

Beals, J.K. (2011). Noninvasive prenatal genetic diagnosis raises clinical, ethical challenges. *Medscape Medical News.* Retrieved August 11, 2012 from http://www.medscape.com/viewarticle/735979.

Bennett, M. J., Rinaldo, P., Wilcken, B., Pass, K. A., Watson, M. S., & Wanders, R. J. A. (2012). Newborn screening for metabolic disorders: How are we doing and where are we going? *Clinical Chemistry, 58*(2), 324–331. doi: 10.1373/clinchem.2011.171215.

Bloch, M. H., & Leckman, J. F. (2009). Clinical course of Tourette syndrome. *Journal of Psychosomatic Research, 67,* 497–501.

Bolton, P. F., Carcani-Rathwell, I., Hutton, J., Goode, S., Howlin, P., & Rutter, M. (2011). Epilepsy in autism: Features and correlates. *The British Journal of Psychiatry, 198*(4), 289–294.

Bondy, C. (2007). Turner syndrome. *National Institute of Child Health and Human Development.* National Institutes of Health-Eunice Kennedy Shriver. Retrieved August 12, 2012, from http://www.nichd.nih.gov/health/topics/Turner_Syndrome.cfm.

Bondy, C. A. (2010). Turner syndrome. In D. T. Carrell, & C. M. Peterson (Eds.), *Reproductive endocrinology and infertility: Integrating modern clinical and laboratory practices.* New York: Springer.

Bondy, C. A., Van, P. L., Bakalov, V. K., & Ho., V. B. (2006). Growth hormone treatment and aortic dimensions in Turner syndrome. *Journal of Clinical Endocrinology & Metabolism, 91,* 1785–1788.

Booth, C., Inusa, B., & Obaro, S. K. (2010). Infection in sickle cell disease: A review. *International Journal of Infectious Diseases, 14,* e2–e12.

Bourgeois, J., Coffey, S., Rivera, S. M., Hessl, D., Gane, L. W., Tassone, F., Greco, C., Finucane, B., Nelson, L., Berry-Kravis, E., Grigsby, J., Hagerman, P. J., & Hagerman, R. J. (2009). Fragile X permutation disorders—Expanding the psychiatric perspective. *Journal of Clinical Psychiatry, 70*(6), 852–862. doi: 10.4088/JCP.08m04476.

Bray, S., Dunkin B., Hong, D. S., & Reiss, A. L. (2011). Reduced functional connectivity during working memory in Turner syndrome. *Cerebral Cortex, 21*(11), 2471–2481. doi: 10.1093/cercor/bhr017.

Bray, S., Hirt, M., Booil, J., Hall, S., Lightbody, A., Walter, E., & Reiss, A. (2011). Aberrant frontal lobe maturation in adolescents with fragile X syndrome is related to delayed cognitive maturation. *Biological Psychiatry, 70*(9), 852–858.

Briesacher, B. A., Quittner, A. L., Fouayzi, H., Zhang, J., & Swensen, A. (2011). Nationwide trends in medical care costs of privately insured patients with cystic fibrosis (CF), 2001–2007. *Pediatric Pulmonology, 46*(8), 770–776. doi: 10.1002/ppul.21441.

Brousseau, D. C., Panepinto, J. A., Nimmer, M., & Hoffman, R. C. (2010). The number of people with sickle-cell disease in the United States: National and state estimates. *American Journal of Hematology, 85*(1), 77–78.

Buck, P. S. (1973). *The child who never grew.* New York: Day.

Bushby, K., Finkel, R., Birnkrant, D. J., Case, L. E., Clemens, P. R., Cripe, L., Kaul, A., Kinnett, K., McDonald, C., Pandya, S., Poysky, J., Shapiro, F., Tomezsko, J., & Constantin, C. (2009). Diagnosis and management of Duchenne muscular dystrophy, part 1: Diagnosis, and pharmacological and psychosocial management. *Lancet Neurology, 9*(1), 77–93.

Centers for Disease Control and Prevention (CDC). (2009). Prevalence of diagnosed Tourette syndrome in persons aged 6–17 years—United States, 2007. *MMWR Morbidity & Mortality Weekly Report, 58*(21), 581–585.

Centers for Disease Control and Prevention. (2012). *CDC estimates 1 in 88 children in the United States has been identified as having an autism spectrum disorder.* Retrieved August 13, 2012, from http://www.cdc.gov/media/releases/2012/p0329_autism_disorder.html.

Centers for Disease Control and Prevention. (2012). Prevalence of autistic spectrum disorders—Autism and Developmental Disabilities Monitoring Network, 14 sites, United States, 2008. *61*(SS03), 1–19.

Chachkin, C. J. (2007). What potent blood: Non-invasive prenatal genetic diagnosis and the transformation of modern maternal care. *American Journal of Law and Medicine, 33*, 9–53.

Chetty, S. P., Shaffer, B. L., & Norton, M. E. (2011). Management of pregnancy in women with genetic disorders: Part 2: Inborn errors of metabolism, cystic fibrosis, neurofibromatosis type 1, and Turner syndrome in pregnancy. *Obstetrical and Gynecological Survey, 66*(12), 765–776. doi: 10.1097/OGX.0b013e31823cdd7d.

Chial, H. (2008). Mendelian genetics: Patterns of inheritance and single-gene disorders. (*Nature Education, 1*(1), 1–5.

Christison, G.W., & Ivany, K. (2006). Elimination diets in autism spectrum disorders: Any wheat amidst the chaff? *Journal of Developmental and Behavioral Pediatrics, 27*(2, Suppl): S162–S171.

Chugani, D. C., Muzik, O., Rothermel, R., Behan, M., Chakraborty, P., Mangner, T., da Silva, E. A., & Chugani, H. T. (1997). Altered serotonin synthesis in the dentatothalamacortical pathway in autistic boys. *Annals of Neurology, 42,* 666.

Cook, E. H., Courchesne, R., Lord, C., Cox, N. J., Yan, S., Lincoln, A., Haas, R., Courchesne, E., & Leventhal, B. L. (1997). Evidence of linkage between the serotonin transporter and autistic disorder. *Molecular Psychiatry, 2,* 247–250.

Cook, E. H., & Leventhal, B. L. (1996). The serotonin system in autism. *Current Opinion in Pediatrics, 8,* 348–354.

Cornish, K. M., Li, L., Kogan, C. S., Jacquemont, S., Turk, J., Dalton, A., Hagerman, R. J., & Hagerman, P. J. (2008a). Age-dependent cognitive changes in carriers of the fragile X syndrome. *Cortex, 44*(6), 628–636. doi: 10.1016/j.cortex.2006.11.002.

Cornish, K., Turk, J., & Hagerman, R. (2008b). The fragile X continuum: New advances and perspectives. *Journal of Intellectual Disability Research, 52*(6), 469–482. doi: 10.1111/j.1365-2788.2008.01056.x.

Crawford, D. C. (2001). *FMR1 and the fragile X syndrome.* Human Genome Epidemiology Network: CDC. Retrieved October 2, 2002, from http://www.cdc.gov/genomics/hugenet/factsheets/FS_FragileX.htm.

Cystic Fibrosis Foundation. (2008). *Research milestones.* Retrieved June 6, 2008, from http://www.cff.org/research/ResearchMilestones/index.cfm.

Dawson, G., & Osterling, J. (1997). Early intervention in autism: Effectiveness and common elements of current approaches. In M. Guralnik (Ed.), *The effectiveness of early intervention: Second generation research* (pp. 307–326). Baltimore, MD: Brookes Publishing.

DeBaun, M.R., Armstrong, F.D., McKinstry, R.C., Ware, R.E., Vichinsky, E., & Kirham, F.J. (2012). *Silent cerebral infarcts: A review on a prevalent and progressive cause of neurologic injury in sickle cell anemia. Blood* 119(20), 4587–4596. Retrieved August 12, 2012 from http://bloodjournal.hematologylibrary.org/content/119/20/4587.full.html.

Devernay, M., Bolca, D., Kerdjana, L., Aboura, A., Gerard, B., Tabet, A., Benzacken, B., Ecosse, E., Coste, J., & Carel, J. (2012). Parental origin of the X-chromosome does not influence growth hormone treatment effect in Turner syndrome. *The Journal of Clinical Endocrinology & Metabolism, 97*(7), e1241–e1248.

DiMatteo, D., Callahan, S., & Kmiec, E. B. (2008). Genetic conversion of an *SMN2* gene to *SMN1*: A novel approach to the treatment of spinal muscular atrophy. *Experimental Cell Research, 314,* 878–886.

Ding, Z., Georgiev, P., & Thony, B. (2006). Administration-route and gender-independent long-term therapeutic correction of phenylketonuria (PKU) in a mouse model by recombinant adeno-associated virus 8 pseudotyped vector-mediated gene transfer. *Gene Therapy, 13,* 587–595.

Dolan, S. (2002). Preimplantation genetic diagnosis (PGD): Success and controversy. *Report from the Annual Clinical Genetics meeting.* Retrieved October 10, 2002, from http://www.medscape.com/viewarticle/432290_2.

Dolen, G., Osterweil, E. Shankaranarayana, R., Smith, G. B., Auerbach, B. D., Chattarji, S., & Bear, M. F. (2007). Correction of fragile X syndrome in mice. *Neuron, 56,* 955–962.

Dolovich, L. R., Addis, A., Vaillancourt, J. M. R., Power, J. D. B., Koren, G., & Einarson, T. R. (1998). Benzodiazepine use in pregnancy and major malformations or oral cleft: Meta-analysis of cohort and case-control studies. *BMJ 317,* 839–843.

Egan, J. F., Smith, K., Timms, D., Bolnick, J. M., Campbell, W. A., & Benn, P. A. (2011). Demographic differences in Down syndrome livebirths in the US from 1989 to 2006. *Prenatal Diagnosis, 31*(4), 389–394. doi: 10.1002/pd.2702.

Emery, A. E. H. (1998). The muscular dystrophies. *British Medical Journal, 317,* 991–996.

Evans, T. (2004). A multidimensional assessment of children with chronic physical conditions. *Health and Social Work, 29*(3), 245–250.

FRAXA Research Foundation. (2002, July). *Are there any treatments available?* Retrieved December 2, 2003, from http://fraxa.org/html/about_treatment.htm.

Freeman, S. B., Bean, L. H., Allen, E. G., Tinker, S. W., Locke, A. E., Druschel, C., Hobbs, C. A., Romitti, P. A., Royle, M. H., Torfs, C. P., Dooley, K. J., & Sherman, S. L. (2008). Ethnicity, sex, and the incidence of congenital heart defects: A report from the National Down Syndrome Project. *Genetics in Medicine, 10,* 173–180. doi: 10.1097/GIM.0b013e3181634867.

Gamez, A., Wang, L., Sarkissian, C. N., Wendt, D., Fitzpatrick, P., Lemontt, J. F., Scriver, C. R., & Stevens, R. C. (2007). Structure-based epitope and PEGylation sites mapping of phenylalanine ammonia-lyase for enzyme substitution treatment of phenylketonuria. *Molecular and Genetic Biology, 91,* 325–334.

Gaylor, A. S., & Reilly, J. C. (2002). Therapy with macrolides in patients with cystic fibrosis. *Pharmacotherapy, 22*(2), 227–239.

Gilbert, D. (2006). Treatment of children and adolescents with tics and Tourette syndrome. *Journal of Child Neurology, 2*(1), 690–700.

Gilboa, S.M., Salemi, J.L., Nembhard, W.N., Fixler, D.E., & Correa, A. (2010). Mortality resulting from congenital heart disease among children and adults in the United States, 1999–2006, *Circulation. Journal of the American Heart Association, 122,* 2254–2263. doi: 10.1161/CIRCULATIONAHA.110.947002.

Glasson, E. J., Sullivan, S. G., Hussain, R., Petterson, B. A., Montgomery, P. D., & Bittles, A. H. (2002). The changing survival profile of people with Down's syndrome: Implications for genetic counseling. *Clinical Genetics, 62,* 390–363.

Goldsmith, H. H., Van Hulle, C. A., Arneson, C. L., Schreiber, J. E., & Gernsbacher, M. A. (2006). A population-based twin study of parentally reported tactile and auditory defensiveness in young children. *Journal of Abnormal Child Psychology, 34*(3), 378–392.

Gordon, D. (2011). Fragile X research into fragile X syndrome, a common inherited cause of intellectual disability is starting to generate treatments. *Neurology Now, 7*(5), 37, 45–49.

Grafodatskaya, D., Chung, B., Szatmari, P., & Weksberg, R. (2010). Autism spectrum disorders and epigenetics. *Journal of the American Academy of Child & Adolescent Psychiatry, 49*(8), 794–809.

Grieve, A. J., Tiuczek, A., Racine-Gilles, C.N., Laxova, A., & Albers, C. A., & Farrell, P. M. (2011). Associations between academic achievement and psychosocial variables in adolescents with cystic fibrosis. *Journal of School Health, 81,* 713–720. doi: 10.111/j.1746.1561.2001.00648.

Guggino, W. G., & Stanton, B. A. (2006). New insights into cystic fibrosis: Molecular switches that regulate CFTR. *Nature Reviews Molecular Cell Biology, 7,* 426–436.

Guimaraes, E. V., Schettino, G. C. M., Camargos, P. A. M., & Penna, F. J. (2012). Prevalence of hyponatremia at diagnosis and factors associated with the longitudinal variations in serum sodium levels in infants with cystic fibrosis. *The Journal of Pediatrics, 161*(2), 285–0289.

Hagerman, R. J., Berry-Kravis, E., Kaufmann, W. E., Ono, M. Y., Tartaglia, N., Lachiewicz, A., Kronk, R., Delahunty, C., Hessle, D., Visootsak, J., Picker, J., Gane, L., & Tranfaglia, M. (2009). Advances in the treatment of fragile X syndrome. *Pediatrics, 123*(1), 378–390. doi: 10.1542/peds.2008-0317.

Halsey, N. A., & Hyman, S. L. (2001). Measles mumps-rubella vaccine and autistic spectrum disorder: Report from the New Challenges in Childhood

Immunizations Conference convened in Oak Brook, Illinois, June 12–13, 2000. *Pediatrics, 107*(5), e84. Retrieved November 10, 2007, from http://www.pediatrics.org/cgo/content/full/107/5/e84#Ful.

Hanson, J. E., & Madison, D. V. (2007). Presynaptic *Fmr1* genotype influences the degree of synaptic connectivity in a mosaic mouse model of fragile X syndrome. *Journal of Neuroscience, 27*, 4014–4018.

Hantash, F. M., Goos, D. M., Crossley, B., Anderson, B., Zhang, K., Sun, W., & Strom, C. M. (2011). *FMR1* permutation carrier frequency in patients undergoing routine population-based carrier screening: Insights into the prevalence of fragile X syndrome, fragile X-associated tremor ataxia/syndrome, and fragile X-associated primary ovarian insufficiency in the United States. *Genetics in Medicine, 13*, 39–45. doi: 10.1097/GIM.0b'3e3181fa9fad.

Hartley, S.L., Sikora, D.M., and McCoy, R. (2008). Prevalence and risk factors of maladaptive behaviour in young children with autistic disorder. *Journal of Intellectual Disabilities Research, 52*(10), 819–829. doi:10.1111/j.1365-2788.2008.01065.x.

Hertz-Picciotto, I., Croen, I. A., Hansen, R., Jones, C. R., van de Water, J., & Pessah, I. N. (2006). The CHARGE study: An epidemiologic investigation of genetic and environmental factors contributing to autism. *Environmental and Health Perspectives, 114*, 1111–11125.

Hessl, D., Nguyen, D. V., Green, C., Chavez, A., Tassone, F., Hagerman, R. J., Senturk, D., Schneider, A., Lightbody, A., Reiss, A. L., & Hall, S. (2009). A solution to limitations of cognitive testing in children with intellectual disabilities: The case of fragile X syndrome. *Journal of Neurodevelopmental Disorders, 1*(1), 33–45. doi: 10.1007/s11689-008-9001-8.

Hoffman, J. L., & Kaplan, S. (2002). The incidence of congenital heart disease. *Journal of the American College of Cardiology, 39*(12), 1890–1900.

Human Genome Project Information. (2008). *Human Genome Project progress*. Retrieved March 25, 2008, from http://www.ornl.gov/sci/techresources/Human_Genome/home.shtml.

Iozzio, M. J. (2005). Genetic anomaly or genetic diversity: Thinking in the key of disability on the Human Genome. *Theological Studies, 66*, 862–875.

Jackson, J. M., Crider, K. S., Rasmussen, S. A., Cragan, J. D., & Olney, R. S. (2011). Trends in cytogenetic testing and identification of chromosomal abnormalities among pregnancies and children with birth defects, metropolitan Atlanta, 1968–2005. *American Journal of Medical Genetics, 158*(1), 116–123. doi: 10.1002/ajmg.a.34385.

Jenson, M., Abresch, R. T., Carter, G. T., & McDonald, C. M. (2005). Chronic pain in persons with neuromuscular disease. *Archives of Physical Medicine and Rehabilitation, 86*, 1155–1163.

Johnson, C. P., & Myers, S. M. (2007). Identification and evaluation of children with autism spectrum disorders. *Pediatrics, 120*(5), 1183–1215.

Jones, A. M., & Helm, J. M. (2009). Emerging treatments in cystic fibrosis. *Drugs, 69*(14), 1903–1910.

Joyce, N. C. (2011). Muscular dystrophy: Becker. In M. Nelson (Ed.). *Pediatrics*. New York: Demos Medical Publishing.

Just, M. A., Cherkassky, V. L., Keller, T. A., Kana, R. K., & Minshew, N. J. (2007). Functional and anatomical cortical underconnectivity in autism: Evidence from an fMRI study of an executive function task and corpus callosum morphometry. *Cerebral Cortex, 17*(4), 951–961.

Kalanithi, P. S. A., Zheng, W., Kataoka, Y., DiFiglia, M., Grantz, H., Sapter, C. B., Schwartz, M. L., Leckman, J. F., & Vaccarino, F. M. (2005). Altered parvalbumin-positive neuron distribution in basal ganglia of individuals with Tourette syndrome. *Proceedings of the National Academy of Sciences, 102*(37), 13307–13312.

Khalil, A. M., Faghihi, M. A., Modarresi, F., Brothers, S. P., & Wahlestedt, C. (2008). A novel RNA transcript with antiapoptotic function is silenced in fragile X syndrome. *Public Library of Science ONE, 3*(1), e1486.

Koch, R., Moseley, K., Ning, J., Romstad, A., Guldberg, P., & Guttler, F. (1999). Long-term beneficial effects of the phenylalanine-restricted diet in late-diagnosed individuals with phenylketonuria. *Molecular Genetics and Metabolism, 67*(2), 148–155.

Kopp-Hoolihan, L. E., Van Loan, M. D., Mentzer, W. C., & Heyman, M. B. (1999). Elevated resting energy expenditure with sickle cell anemia. *Journal of the American Dietetic Association, 99* (2) 195–199.

Kwak, C., Vuong, K. D., & Jankovic, J. (2003). Premonitory sensory phenomenon in Tourette's syndrome. *Movement Disorders, 18*, 1530–1533.

Lauderborn, J. C., Rex, C. S., Kramer, E., Chen, L. Y., Pandyarajan, V., Lynch, G., & Gall, C. M. (2007). Brain-derived neurotrophic factor rescues synaptic plasticity in a mouse model of fragile X syndrome. *Journal of Neuroscience, 27*, 10685–10694.

Leckman, J. F., Zhang, H., Vitale, Al, Lahnin, F., Lynch, K., Bondi, C., & Peterson, B. S. (1998). Course of tic severity in Tourette syndrome: The first two decades. *Pediatrics, 102*, 14–19.

Levi, L., Milanowski, A., Chakrapani, A., Cleary, M., Lee, P., Trefz, F. K., Whitley, C. B., Feillet, F.,

Feigenbaum, A. S., Bebchuk, J. D., Christ-Schmidt, H., & Dorenbaum, A. (2007). Efficacy of sapropterin dihydrochloride (tetrahydrobiopterin, 6R-BH4) for reduction of phenylalanine concentration in patients with phenylketonuria: A phase III randomised placebo-controlled study. *Lancet, 370,* 504–510.

Lin, H. J., Kwong, A. M., Carter, J. M., Ferreira, B. F., Austin, M. F., Devarajan, A. K., Coleman, R. J., Feuchtbaum, L. B., Lorey, F., & Jonas, A. J. (2011). Extremely high phenylalanine levels in a newborn on parenteral nutrition: Phenylketonuria in the neontal intensive care unit. *Journal of Perinatology, 31,* 507–510. doi: 10.1038/jp.2010.207.

MacDonald, A., Gokmen-Ozel, H., & Daly, A. (2009). Changing dietary practices in phyenylketonuria. *The Turkish Journal of Pediatrics, 41,* 409–415.

Magge, S. N., O'Neill, K. L., Shults, J., Stallings, V. A., & Stettler, N. (2008). Leptin levels among prepubertal children with Down syndrome compared with their siblings. *Journal of Pediatrics, 152,* 321–326.

Manzur, A. Y., Kinali, M., & Muntoni, F. (2008). Update on the management of Duchenne muscular dystrophy. *Archives of Disease in Children, 93*(11), 986–990. doi: 10.1136/adc.2007.118141.

Marlowe, K. F., & Chicella, M. F. (2002). Treatment of sickle cell pain. *Pharmacotherapy, 22*(4), 484–491.

Mayo Clinic. (2011). *Turner syndrome.* Retrieved August 12, 2012, from http://www.mayoclinic.com/health/turner-syndrome/DS01017.

Mazzocco, M. M. M., Baumgardner, T., Freund, L. S., & Reiss, A. L. (1998). Social functioning among girls with fragile X or Turner syndrome and their sisters. *Journal of Autism and Developmental Disorders, 28*(6), 509–517.

McCarthy, M. (1999). Inhaled antibiotics effective for cystic fibrosis. *The Lancet, 353*(9148), 215.

Megarbane, A., Ravel, A., Mircher, C., Sturtz, F., Grattau, Y., Rethore, M., Delabar, J., & Mobley, W. C. (2009). The 50th anniversary of the discovery of trisomy 21: The past, present and future of research and treatment of Down syndrome. *Genetics in Medicine, 11,* 611–616. doi: 10.1097/GIM.0b013e3181be34c.

Meryash, D. L. (1992). *Characteristics of fragile X relatives with different attitudes toward terminating an affected pregnancy. American Journal of Mental Retardation, 96,* 528–535.

Milerad, J., Larson, O., Hagberg, C., & Ideberg, M. (1997). Associated malformations in infants with cleft lip and palate: A prospective, population-based study. *Pediatrics, 100*(2) 180–186.

Miller, V. L., & Martin, A. M. (2008). *The Human Genome Project: Implications for families. Health and Social Work, 33*(1), 73–80.

Minnes, P., & Steiner, K. (2009). Parent views on enhancing the quality of health care for their children with fragile X syndrome, autism or Down syndrome. *Child: Care, Health and Development, 35*(2), 250–256. doi: 10.111/j.1365-2214.2008.00931.x.

Morgan, T. (2007). Turner syndrome: Diagnosis and management. *American Family Physician, 76*(3). 405–417.

Mossey, P. A., Little, J., Munger, R. G., Dixon, M. J., & Shaw, W. C. (2009). Cleft lip and palate. *Lancet (London, England), 374*(9703), 1773–1785.

Muhle, R., Trentacoste, S. V., & Rapin, I. (2004). The genetics of autism. *Pediatrics. 113* (5), 472–486.

Murray, J. B. (1997). Psychophysiological aspects of Tourette's syndrome. *J Psychology 131,* 615–626.

Myers, S. M., & Johnson, C. P. (2007). Management of children with autism spectrum disorders. *Pediatrics, 120*(5), 1162–1182.

National Human Genome Research Institute. (2012). *Genetic Mapping.* Retrieved August 7, 2012, from http://www.genome.gov/10000715.

Ouyang, L., Grosse, S. D., Fox, M. H., & Bolen, J. (2012). A national profile of health care and family impacts of children with muscular dystrophy and special health care needs in the United States. *Journal of Child Neurology, 27*(5), 569–576. doi: 10.1177/088307381140719.

Palminteri, S., Lebreton, M., Worbe, Y., Hartmann, A., Lehéricy, S., Vidailhet, M., Grabli, D., & Pessiglione, M. (2011). Dopamine-dependent reinforcement of motor skill learning: Evidence from Gilles de la Tourette syndrome. *Brain, 134*(8), 2287–2301.

Papavassiliou, P., York, T. P., Gursoy, N., Hill, G., Nicely, L. V., Sundaram, U., McClain, A., Aggen, S. H., Eaves, L., Riley, B., & Jackson-Cook, C. (2009). The phenotype of persons having mosaicism for trisomy 21/Down syndrome reflects the percentage of trisomic cells present in different tissues. *American Journal of Medical Genetics, 149A*(4), 573–583. doi: 10.1002/ajmg.a.32729.

Parker, S. E., Mai, C. T., Canfield, M. A., Rickard, R., Wang, Y., Meyer, R. E., Anderson, P., Mason, C. A., Collins, J. S., Kirby, R. S., & Correa, A. (2010). Updated national birth prevalence estimates for selected birth defects in the United States, 2004–2006. *Birth Defects Research Part A: Clinical and Molecular Teratology, 88*(12), 1008–1016.

Petrof, B. (2008, May 12). New approach to protect the hearts of patients with muscular dystrophy.

Proceedings of the National Academy of Sciences. *Montreal, QC: National Academy of Sciences.*

Prestia, K. (2003). Tourette syndrome: Characteristics and treatments. *Intervention in School & Clinic, 39*(2), 67–71.

Priven, J., Palmer, P., Jacobi, D., Childress, D., & Arndt, S. (1997). Broader autism phenotype: Evidence from a family history study of multiple-incidence autism families. *American Journal of Psychiatry, 154*(2) 185–190.

Quon, B. S., Mayer-Hamblett, N., Aitken, M. L., Smyth, A. R., & Goss, C. H. (2011). Risk factors for chronic kidney disease in adults with cystic fibrosis. *American Journal of Respiratory and Critical Care Medicine, 184*(10), 1147–1152. doi:10.1164/rccm201105-0932OC.

Ratajczak, H. V. (2011). Theoretical aspects of autism: Causes-A review. *Journal of Immunotoxicology, 8*(1), 68–79.

Raznahan, A., Toro, R., Daly, E., Robertson, D., Murphy, C., Deeley, Q., Bolton, P. F., Paus, T., & Murphy, D. G. M. (2010). Cortical anatomy in autism spectrum disorder: An in vivo MRI study on the effect of age. *Cerebral Cortex, 20*(6) 1332–1340.

Rees, D. C., Williams, T. N., & Gladwin, M. T. (2010). Sickle cell disease. *The Lancet, 376,* 2018–2031.

Reller, M. D., Strickland, M. J., Riehle-Colarusso, T., Mahle, W. T., & Correa, A. (2008). Prevalence of congenital heart defects in Atlanta, 1998–2005. *Journal of Pediatrics, 15,* 807–813.

Resta, R. (2012). Generation n+1: Projected numbers of babies born to women with PKKU compared to babies with PKU in the United States in 2009. *American Journal of Medical Genetics, 158A,* 1118–1123. doi: 10.1002/ajmg.a.35312.

Rinehart, N. J., Cornish, K. M., & Tonge, B. J. (2011). Gender differences in neurodevelopmental disorders: Autism and fragile X syndrome. *Current Topics in Behavioral Neurosciences, 8,* 209–229. doi: 10.1007/7854_2010_96.

Robertson, M. M. (2008). The prevalence and epidemiology of Gilles de la Tourette syndrome Part 1: The epidemiological and prevalence studies. *Journal of Psychosomatic Research, 65,* 461–472.

Rogers, S. J., & Vismara, L. A. (2008). Evidence-based comprehensive treatments for early autism. *Journal of Clinical Child and Adolescent Psychology, 37*(1), 8–38.

Romitti, P., Puzhankara, S., Mathews, K., Zamba, G., Cunniff, C., Andrews, J., Matthews, D., Miller, J. K., Druschel, C., Fox, D., Pandya, S., Ciafaloni, E., Adams, M., Mandel, D., Ouyang, L., Constantin, C., & Costa, P. (2009). Prevalence of Duchenne/Becker muscular dystrophy among males aged 5–24 years—

four states, 2007. *Journal of Morbidity and Mortality Weekly Report, 58*(40), 1119–1122.

Rosenfeld, M., Casey, S., Pepe, M., & Ramsey, B. W. (1999). Nutritional effects of long-term gastrostomy feedings in children with cystic fibrosis. *Journal of the American Dietetic Association, 99*(2), 191–194.

Ross, L. F. (2011). Carrier detection in newborns: Should it be discovered? Should it be disclosed? Lessons from sickle cell anemia and cystic fibrosis screening in the United States. In B. M. Knoppers (Ed.), *Genomics and public health: Legal and socio-ethical perspectives.* Boston: Martinus Nijhoff Publishers.

Saul, R. A., Friez, M., Eaves, K., Stapleton, G. A., Collins, J. S., Schwartz, C. E., & Stevenson, R. E. (2008). *Genetics in Medicine, 10,* 714–719. doi: 10.1097/GIM.0b013e3181862a76.

Schaefer, G. B., & Riley, H. D. (2004). A tribute to Henry H. Turner, MD (1892–1970). *The Endocrinologist, 14*(4), 179–184.

Schmidt, M. (1997). Fragile X syndrome: Diagnosis, treatment and research. *Journal of the American Medical Association, 277,* 1169.

Schubert, J. D., & Murphy, M. (2005). The struggle to breathe: Living at life expectancy with cystic fibrosis. *Oral History Review, 32* (1), 35–50.

Schwartz, I. S., & Sandall, S. R. (1998). Outcomes for children with autism: Three case studies. *Topics in Early Childhood Special Education, 18,* 132–144.

Sherman, S., Pletcher, B. A., & Driscoll, D. A. (2005). Fragile X syndrome: Diagnostic and carrier testing. *Genetics in Medicine, 7,* 584–587.

Solomon, L. (2002, July). Researchers seek answers to Down syndrome. *WebMD Medical News.* Retrieved December 2, 2003, from http://www.content.health./article/3608.1134.

Stark, L. J., Robinson, K. A., Feranchak, A. P., & Quinton, H. (2008). Evidence based practice recommendations for nutrition-related management of children and adults with cystic fibrosis and pancreatic insufficiency: Results of a systematic review. *Journal of the American Dietetic Association, 108*(5), 832–839. doi: 10.1016/j.jada.2008.02.020.

Stehr-Green, P., Tull, P., Steltfeid, M., Mortenson, P. B., & Simpson, D. (2003). Autism and thimerosal-containing vaccines: Lack of consistent evidence for an association. *American Journal of Preventive Medicine, 25,* 101–106.

Strategic Plan - Sickle Cell Disease (2011). *Centers for Disease Control and Prevention (CDC) – National Center on Birth Defects and Developmental Disabilities (NCBDDD).* Retrieved 8/1/12, from http://www.cdc.gov/ncbddd/AboutUs/sicklecell.html.

Strom, C. M., Crossley, B., Buller-Buerckle, A., Jarvis, M., Quan, F., Peng, M., Muralidharan, K., Pratt, V., Redman, B., & Sun, W. (2011). Cystic fibrosis testing 8 years on: Lessons learned from carrier screening and sequencing analysis. *Genetics in Medicine, 13,* 166–172. doi: 10.1097/GIM.0b013e3181fa24c4.

Swain, J. E., Scahill, L., Lombroso, P. J., King, R. A., & Leckman, J. F. (2007). Tourette syndrome and tic disorders: A decade of progress. *Journal of the American Academy of Child and Adolescent Psychiatry, 46*(8), 947–968.

Szpir, M. (2006). New thinking on neurodevelopment. *Environmental Health Perspectives, 114*(2), 100–117.

Tabor, A., Vestergaard, C. H. F., & Lidegaard, O. (2009). Fetal loss rate after chorionic villus sampling and amniocentesis: An 11-year national registry study. *Ultrasound in Obstetrics & Gynecology, 34,* 19–24. doi: 10.1002/uog.6377.

Taylor, L. V., Stotts, N. A., Humphreys, J., Treadwell, M. J., & Miaskowski, C. (2010). A review of the literature on the multiple dimensions of chronic pain in adults with sickle cell disease. *Journal of Pain Symptom Management, 40*(3), 416–435. doi: 1026/j.painsymman.2009.12.027.

Turner, G., Robinson, H., Wake, S., Laing, S., & Partington, M. (1997). Case finding for the fragile X syndrome and its consequences. *BMJ, 315*(7117), 1223–1226.

Turner Syndrome Society. (2012). *What is Turner syndrome?* Retrieved August 12, 2012, from http://www.turnersyndrome.org/learn-about-ts/what-ts.

VanDevanter, D. R., Rasouliyan, L., Murphy, T. M., Morgan, W. J., Ren, C. L., Konstan, M. W., & Wagener, J. S. (2008). Trends in the clinical characteristics of the U. S. cystic fibrosis patient population from 1995–2005. *Pediatric Pulmonology, 43*(8), 739–744. doi: 10.1002/ppul.20830.

Vieira, A. R. (2008). Unraveling human cleft lip and palate research. *Jounal of Dental Research, 87,* 119–125.

Warren, Z., McPheeters, M.L., Sathe, N., Foss-Feig, J.H., Glasser, A., & Veenstra-VanderWeele, J. (2011). A systematic review of early intensive intervention for autism spectrum disorders. *Pediatrics, 127,* e1303. doi: 10.1542/peds.2011-0426. Retrieved August 14, 2012, from http://www.pediatricsdigest.mobi/content/127/5/e1303.full.pdf.

Wethers, D. L. (2000a). Sickle cell disease in childhood: Part II. Diagnosis and treatment of major complication and recent advances in treatment. *American Family Physician, 62,* 1309–1314.

Wethers, D. L. (2000b). Sickle cell disease in childhood: Part I. Laboratory diagnosis, pathophysiology and health maintenance. *American Family Physician, 62,* 1013–28.

White-Williams, C. (2002). Lung transplantation. *Medscape.,* Retrieved December 2, 2003, from http://www.medscape.com/viewarticle/436545.

Williams, B. F. (Fall, 2007). The stakes are high: Every moment precious in fight against autism. *Whitworth Today.* Retrieved June 24, 2008, from http://www.whitworth.edu/Administration/Institutional Advancement/UniversityCommunications/WhitworthToday/2007_Fall/FacultyFocus.htm.

Wiseman, F. K., Alford, K. A., Tybulewicz, V. L. J., & Fisher, E. M. C. (2009). Down syndrome—recent progress and future prospects. *Human Molecular Genetics, 18*(R1), 75–83. doi: 10.1093/hmg/ddp010.

Woods, D. W., Conelea, C. A., & Himle, M. B. (2010). Behavior therapy for Tourette's disorder: Utilization in a community sample and an emerging are of practice for psychologists. *Professional Psychology: Research and Practice, 41*(6), 518–525.

Wyrobek, A. J., Eskenazi, B., Young, S., Arnheim, N., Tiemann-Boege, I., & Jabs, E. W. (2006). Advancing age has differential effects on DNA damage, chromatin integrity, gene mutations, and aneuploidies in sperm. *Proceedings of the National Academy of Science, 103,* 9601–9606.

Yanni, E., Grosse, S. D., Yang, Q., & Olney, R. S. (2008). Trends in pediatric sickle cell disease-related mortality in the United States 1983–2002. *Journal of Pediatrics, 154*(4), 541–545.

Zhao, X., Leotta, A., Kustanovich, V., Lajonchere, C., Geschwind, D. H., Law, K. Law, P., Qiu, S., Lord, C., Sebat, J., Ye, K., & Wigler, M. (2007). A unified gene tic theory for sporadic and inherited autism. *Proceedings of the National Academy of Sciences of the United States of America, 104*(31), 12831–12836.

Zinner, S. H., Conelea, C. A., Glew, G. M., Woods, D. W., & Budman, C. L. (2012). Peer victimization in youth with Tourette syndrome and other chronic tic disorders. *Child Psychiatry Human Development, 43,* 124–136. doi 10.1007/s10578-011-0249-y.

Chapter 8

Adler, S. P., Nigro, G., & Pereira, L. (2007, February). Recent advances in the prevention and treatment of congenital cytomegalovirus infections. *Seminars in Perinatology.* Bethesda, MD: National Institutes of Health.

American Optometric Association. (2012) *Nystagmus.* Retrieved July 18, 2012 from http://www.aoa.org/x9763.xml.

Anderson, P. M., & Butcher, K. F. (2006). Childhood obesity: Trends and causes. *Future of Children, 16*(1), 19–35.

Atlantic Coast Ear Specialists. (2002, July). *Central auditory processing disorders.* Retrieved July 30, 2002, from http://www.earaces.com/CAPD.htm.

Boys Town National Research Hospital (2009). *About hearing loss: Genetics and deafness—current progress in finding genes involved in hearing impairment.* Retrieved July 18, 2012, from http://www.boystown hospital.org/hearing/info/genetics/syndromes/current.asp.

Bustos, D. (2011). *Retinopathy of prematurity.* National Center for Biotechnology Information. Retrieved July 20, 2012, from http://www.ncbi.nim.nih.gov/pubmedhealth/PMH0002585.

Centers for Disease Control. (2005, May). Visual impairment and use of eye-care services and protective eyewear among children—United States 2002. *MMWR Weekly, 54*(17), 425–429. Retrieved fromhttp://www.cdc.gov/mmwr/preview/mmwr html/mm5417a2.htm.

Centers for Disease Control and Prevention. (2009, February). *Current vaccine shortages.* CDC: National Immunization Program. Retrieved February 19, 2009, from http://www.cdc.gov/nip/news/short ages/default.htm.

Centers for Disease Control and Prevention. (2010, December). *Congenital CMV infection.* Retrieved July 27, 2012, from http://www.cdc.gov/cmv/congential-infection.

Centers for Disease Control and Prevention. (2012, January). *Genital herpes.* CDC Fact Sheet. Retrieved July 27, 2012, from http://www.cdc.gov/std/Herpes/STDFact-Herpes.htm.

Centers for Disease Control and Prevention. (2012, June). *Perinatal transmission.* Hepatitits B Information for Health Professionals. Retrieved July 30, 2012, from http://www.cdc.gov/hepatitis/HBV/Perinatalxmtn.htm.

Cesar, G. V., Wagstaff, A., Schellenberg, J. A., Gwatkin, D., Claeson, M., & Habicht, J. P. (2003). Applying an equity lens to child health and mortality: More of the same is not enough. *The Lancet, 362*(9379), 233–241.

Chipungu, S. S., & Bent-Goodley, T. B. (2004). Meeting the challenges of contemporary foster care. *Future of Children, 14,* 74–84.

Coene, M., Schauwers, K., Gillis, S., Rooryck, J., & Govaerts, P. J. (2011). Genetic predisposition and sensory development: Evidence from cochlear implanted children. *Language & Cognitive Processes, 26*(8), 1083–1101. doi: 10.1080/01690965.2010.520540.

Colugnati, F., Staras, S., Dollard, S. C., & Cannon, M. J. (2007). Incidence of cytomegalovirus infection among the general population and pregnant women in the United States. *BMC Infectious Diseases, 7,* 71–81.

Dalgic, N. (2008). Congenital toxoplasmosis gondii infection. *Marmara Medical Journal, 21*(1), 89–101.

Davis, K. L., Misurski, D., Miller, J. M., Bell, T. J., & Bapat, B. (2011). Cost of acute hospitalization and post-discharge follow-up care for meningococcal disease in the US. *Human Vaccines, 7*(1), 96–101.

Dollard, S. C., Grosse, S. D., & Ross, D. S. (2007). New estimates of the prevalence of neurological and sensory sequelae and mortality associated with congenital cytomegalovirus infection. *Review of Medical Virology, 17,* 355–363.

Duszak, R.S. (2009). Congenital rubella syndrome-major review. *Journal of the American Optometric Association, 80*(1), 36–43.

Etscheidt, S. (2006). Least restrictive and natural environments for young children with disabilities: A legal analysis of issues. *Education, 26,* 167–180.

Green, M. (1997). Appropriate principles in the use of antibiotics in children. *Clinical Pediatrics, 36,* 207–209.

Hatton, D., McWilliam, R. A., & Winton, P. J. (2002, November). Infants and toddlers with visual impairments: Suggestions for early interventionists. *ERIC Digest, E636,* EDO-EC-02-14, http://ericec.org.

Homsy, J., Moore, D., Barasa, A., Were, W., Likicho, C., Waiswa, B., Downing, R., Malamba, S., Tappero, J., & Mermin, J. (2010). Breastfeeding, mother-to-child HIV transmission, and mortality among infants born to HIV-infected women on highly active anti-retroviral therapy in rural Uganda. *JAIDS Journal of Acquired Immune Deficiency Syndromes, 53*(1), 28–35.

Jackson, C. W., & Turnbull, A. (2004). Impact of deafness on family life: A review of the literature. *Topics in Early Childhood Special Education, 24,* 15–28.

Kim, K. S. (2010). Acute bacterial meningitis in infants and children. *Lancet Infectious Diseases, 10*(1), 32.

Kimberlin, D. (2004). Herpes simplex virus, meningitis and encephalitis in neonates. *Herpes.* Retrieved July 15, 2012, from http://www.ncbi.nim.nih.gov/pubmed/15319092.

Lanphear, B. (2005). Origins and evolution of children's environmental health. *Environmental Health Perspectives, 113,* 24–40.

March of Dimes. (2001). Infections that threaten a healthy birth. *2001 March of Dimes research report.* Retrieved September 10, 2002, from http://www.marchofdimes.com.

March of Dimes. (2008). Genital herpes. *Pregnancy Complications*. Retrieved July 20, 2012, from http://www.marchofdimes.com/pregnancy/complications_herpes.html.

McLeod, R., Boyer, K., Karrison, T., Kasza, K., Swisher, C., Roizen, N., Jalbrzikowski, J., Danis, B., Stein, M., Pfiffner, L., Suth, A., Noble, G., Withers, S., Perkins, J., Cameron, A. W., Weissbourd, M., Humphries, M., Holfels, E., Rabiah, P., Meyers, S., Kipp, M., Gupta, S., Mieler, W., Abdulsalam, A., Zhang, H., McAuley, J., Marcinak, J., Heydemann, P., Mets, M., Hopkins, J., Patel, D., Mojatahedi, S., Bardo, D., Mack, D., Kirisits, M., Chamot, D., Mui, E., Remington, J., Thisted, R., Stein, L., Latkany, P., & Meier, P. and the Toxoplosmosis Study Group (2006). Outcome of treatment for congenital toxoplasmosis, 1981–2004: The national collaborative Chicago-based, congenital toxoplasmosis study. *Clinical Infectious Diseases, 42*(10), 1383–1394.

National Institute of Allergy and Infectious Diseases. (2008, September). HIV infection in infants and children. *Health & Research A to Z*. Retrieved July 24, 2012, from http://niaid.nih.gov/TOPICS/HIVAIDS/UNDERSTANDING/POPULATION%20SPECIFIC%20INFORMATION/Pages/children.aspx.

National Institute of Allergy and Infectious Diseases. (2011). Hookworm disease. *Health & Research A to Z*. Retrieved July 25, 2012, from http://www.niaid.nih.gov/topics/hookworm/Pages/Default.aspx.

National Institutes of Health. (2008, January). Study shows variety of approaches help children overcome auditory processing and language problems. *National Institute on deafness and other communication disorders*. Bethesda, MD: National Institutes of Health.

National Institute on Deafness and Other Communication Disorders (2013). Retrieved May 8, 2013, from http://www.nidcd.nih.gov/Pages/default.aspx.

Palmer, P. (2011). *Environmental adaptations for preschool classrooms serving children who are blind or visually impaired*. Path to Literacy. Retrieved June 20, 2012, from http://www.pathstoliteracy.org/environmental-adaptations-preschool-classrooms-serving-children-who-are-blind-or-visually-impaired.

Porter, V. (2002). Angels on the web: Helping children and their families cope with AIDS. *Medscape Infectious Diseases, 4*(1). Retrieved July 9, 2003, from http://www.medscape.com/viewarticle/433150.

Sonksen, P. M., & Dale, N. (2002). Visual impairment in infancy: Impact on neurodevelopmental and neurobiological processes. *Developmental Medicine & Child Neurology, 44*, 782–791.

Steele, R. W. (2001). 2001 American Academy of Pediatrics National Conference and Exhibition: Pediatric infectious disease highlights. *Medscape Pediatrics, 3*(2). Retrieved June 20, 2012, from http://www.medscape.com/viewarticle/415038.

Stone, V. E. (2011). HIV/AIDS in women and racial/ethnic minorities in U.S. *Current Infectious Disease Report*. DOI 10.1007/s11908-011-0226-4.

Strickling. C. (2010). *Impact of visual impairment on development*. Texas School for the Blind and Visually Impaired. Retrieved July 20, 2012, from http://www.tsbvi.edu/infants/3293-the-impact-of-visual-impairment-on-development.

Thigpen, M., Whitney, C., Messonier, N., Zell, E., Lynfield, R., Hadler, J., & Schuchat, A. (2011). Bacterial meningitis in the United States, 1998–2007. *New England Journal of Medicine, 364*, 2016–2025. doi: 10.1056/NEJMoa1005384.

UNICEF. (2012). The measles & rubella initiative welcomes world health assembly commitment to measles and rubella elimination goals. Retrieved June 20, 2012, from http://www.unicef.org/media/media/62517.html.

World Health Organization. (2010). Antiretroviral drugs for treating pregnant women and preventing HIV infections in infants. Geneva, Switzerland: World Health Organization. Retrieved from http://whqlibdoc.who.int/publications/2010/9789241599818_eng.pdf.

World Health Organization. (2010b). Antiviral therapy for HIV infection in infants and children: Towards universal access. Executive Summary. Retrieved from http://www.who.int/hiv/pub/paediatric/paedprelim-summary.pdf.

World Health Organization. (2012, June). Visual impairment and blindness. World Health Organization Media Center Fact Sheet No. 282. Retrieved from http://www.who.int/mediacentre/factsheets/fs282/en/.

Wu, F., & Takaro, T. K. (2006). Childhood asthma and environmental interventions. *Environmental Health Perspectives, 115*, 971–980.

Chapter 9

Addy, S., & Wight, V. R. (2012). Fact sheet—Basic facts about low-income children, 2010—Children under age 3. *National Center for Children in Poverty*. Retrieved May 15, 2012, from http://nccp.org/publications/pub_1056.html.

Bailey, D. B., Hebbeler, K., Spiker, D., Scarborough, A., Mallik, S., & Nelson, L. (2005). Early intervention, family impact. *Pediatrics, 116*(6), 1346–1352.

Council for Exceptional Children, Division of Early Childhood, IDEA Infant and Toddler Coordinators Association. (2011). Individuals with Disabilities Education Act Part C: Early intervention program for infants and toddlers with disabilities.

Final regulations side-by-side comparison. Retrieved July 15, 2012, from http://www.cec.sped.org/Content/NavigationMenu/PolicyAdvocacy/IDEAResources/Celebrating_25_Years_of_Early_Childhood_Programs/PartCRegsSideBySideFULL.pdf.

Danaher, J., Kraus, R., Armijo, C., & Hipps, C. (Eds.). (2003). Section 619 profile (12th ed.). Chapel Hill: The University of North Carolina, FPG Child Development Institute, National Early Childhood Technical Assistance Center. Retrieved July 1, 2012, from http://www.nectac.org/~pdfs/sec619_2003.pdf.

Dunst, C. J., Trivette, C. M., & Cutspec, P. A. (2002). Toward an operational definition of evidence-based practices. *Centerscope, 1*(1), 1–10.

Goode, S, Diefendorf, M., & Colgan, S. (2011). *The importance of early intervention for infants and toddlers with disabilities and their families.* National Early Childhood Technical Assistance Center. Retrieved July 26, 2012, from http://www.nectac.org/~pdfs/pubs/importanceofearlyintervention.pdf.

Goode, S, Diefendorf, M., & Colgan, S. (2012). *The outcomes of early intervention for infants and toddlers with disabilities and their families.* National Early Childhood Technical Assistance Center. Retrieved May 25, 2012, from http://www.nectac.org/~pdfs/pubs/outcomesofearlyintervention.pdf.

Hebbeler, K., Wagner, M., Spiker, D., Scarborough, A., Simmeonson, R., & Collier, M. (2001). *National Early Intervention Longitudinal Study: A first look at the characteristics of children and families entering early intervention services.* SRI International. Retrieved September 9, 2002, from http://www.sri.com/neils/reports/html.

Individuals with Disabilities Education Improvement Act, H. R. 1350, 108th Congress (2004), Section 632[1].

Kazdin, A. (2008). Evidence-based treatment and practice, new opportunities to bridge clinical research and practice, enhance the knowledge base, and improve patient care. *American Psychologist, 63*(3), 146–159.

Kentucky Early Intervention Program. (2008). *Individual Family Service Plan.* Retrieved April 15, 2012, from http://chfs.ky.gov/NR/rdonlyres/7963E44F-5B14-47DC-A0D2-BFD0E9547372/138731/Section-VIIFSP108.pdf.

Lovaas, O. I. (1987). Behavioral treatment and normal educational and intellectual functioning in young autistic children. *Journal of Consulting and Clinical Psychology, 55,* 3–9.

Lucas A., Hurth, J., & Kasprzak, C. (2010). Essential elements of high performing, high quality Part C systems. *The National Early Childhood Technical Assistance Center. No. 25.* Retrieved August 1, 2012, from http://www.nectac.org/~pdfs/pubs/nnotes25.pdf.

McLean, M., Wolery, M., & Bailey, D. B. (2004). *Assessing infants and preschoolers with special needs.* Upper Saddle River, NJ: Merrill/Pearson Education.

McWilliam, R.A. (2009). Goal functionality scale III. *Siskin Children's Institute.* Retrieved July 10, 2012, from http://www.nectac.org/~pdfs/topics/families/GoalFunctionalityScaleIII_2_.pdf.

McWilliam, R. A., & Scott, S. (2001). A support approach to early intervention: A three-part framework. *Infants and Young Children, 13*(4), 55–66.

National Early Childhood Technical Assistance Center. (2006). Part C updates. Retrieved February 22, 2007, from http://www.nectac.org/pubs/titlelist.asp.

National Early Childhood Technical Assistance Center. (2012). *Family assessment: Gather information from families.* Retrieved July 20, 2012, from http://www.nectac.org/topics/families/famassess.asp.

National Early Childhood Technical Assistance Center (NECTAC) Workgroup on Principles and Practices in Natural Environments (November, 2007). Agreed upon mission and key principles for providing early intervention services in natural environments. *OSEP TA Community of Practice-Part C Settings.* Retrieved July 15, 2012, from http://www.nectac.org/topics/natenv/natenv.asp.

Smith, T., Groen, A. D., & Wynn, J. W. (2000). *American Journal on Mental Retardation, 105*(4), 269–285.

Tisot, C. M., & Thurman, K. S. (2002). Using behavior setting theory to define natural settings: A family-centered approach. *Infants and Young Children, 14*(3), 65–71.

U.S. Department of Education. (2010). *Twenty-ninth annual report to Congress on the implementation of the Individuals with Disabilities Education Act, 2007.* Washington, DC: Author.

Wrightslaw. (2012). *Early intervention (Part C of IDEA).* Retrieved May 10, 2012, from http://www.wrightslaw.com/info/ei.index.htm.

Chapter 10

Bollero, J. (2008). 8 steps to better IEP meetings: Play hearts, not poker. *Wrightslaw.* Retrieved August 1, 2012, from http://www.wrightslaw.com/info/iep.index.htm.

Beach Center on Families and Disability. (1999). *Quality indicators of exemplary IFSP/IEP development.* Retrieved September 9, 1999, from http://www.lsi.ukans.edu/Beach/html/9i.htm.

Council for Exceptional Children (CEC), Division of Early Childhood (DEC), IDEA Infant and Toddler Coordinators Association (ITCA). (2011). *Individuals* with Disabilities Education Act Part C: Early intervention program for infants and toddlers with disabilities. Final regulations: Side-by-side comparison. Retrieved July 15, 2012, from http://www.cec.sped.org/Content/NavigationMenu/PolicyAdvocacy/IDEAResources/Celebrating_25_Years_of_Early_Childhood_Programs/PartCRegsSideBySideFULL.pdf.

Frost, J. L. (2007). The changing culture of childhood: A perfect storm. *Childhood Education, 83*(4), 225–250.

Greatschools. (2008). IDEA 2004 close up: The Individualized Education Program (IEP). Retrieved June 18, 2008, from http://www.schwablearning.org/articles.aspx?r=978#contents.

Musgrove, M. (2012). *Open letter.* United States Department of Education-Office of Special Education and Rehabilitative Services. Retrieved July 24, 2012, from http://www2.ed.gov/policy/speced/guid/idea/memosdcltrs/preschoollre22912.pdf.

National Association of Special Education Teachers (NASET). (2007). *Determining measurable annual goals in an IEP.* Retrieved July 31, 2012, from http://www.naset.org/760.0.html.

Starin, S. (2011). *Functional behavioral assessments: What, why, when, where, and who?* Wrightslaw. Retrieved July 31, 2012, from http://www.wrightslaw.com/info/discipl.fab.starin.htm.

Van Haren, B., & Fiedler, C. R. (2008). Support and empower families of children with disabilities. *Intervention in School and Clinic, 43*(4), 231–235.

Wrightslaw. (2008). *IDEA 2004.* Retrieved June 18, 2008, from http://www.wrightslaw.com/idea/index.htm.

Author Index

Dube, S. R., 183
Duckworth, K., 137
Dugbatey, K., 22
Dukic, V., 184
Dumont-Mathieu, T., 273
Dunbar, C., 107
Dunkin, B., 266
Dunlosky, J., 133
Dunn, D. W., 208
Dunst, C. J., 7, 27, 28, 43, 57, 79, 362
Durmus, B., 155
Duszak, R. S., 311
Düzovali, O., 208
Dyches, T., 48, 54

Eagles, J. M., 155
Earls, F., 184
Edelman, M. W., 39
Edin, K., 154
Edwards, A., 136
Edwards, J., 195
Egan, J. F., 251
Egerter, S. A., 154
Ehrenreich, H., 206
Ehrensaft, M. K., 104
Eidelman, S. M., 14
Elliott, T. R., 53
Emerson, E., 47
Emery, A. E. H., 257
Emond, A., 65
Engelhart, L., 28
Erel, O., 103
Erikson, E., 94–95, 103–104
Eron, L. D., 107
Espy, K. A., 184
Etscheidt, S. K., 293
Evans, G. R., 22
Evans, G. W., 104
Evans, M. M., 203
Ewing-Cobb, L., 218
Eyal, F. G., 166

Fagan, J., 102–103
Fagan, P., 22
Faghihi, M. A., 254
Fallows, R., 217
Fang, H., 184
Farrell, P. M., 247
Federal Register, 331, 334
Fein, D., 273
Fenichel, E., 11
Feranchak, A. P., 247
Ferguson, D., 178, 180
Fernell, E., 227
Fetal Surgery, 222
Fiedler, C. R., 25, 26, 366

Fischbach, G. D., 219
Fischbach, R. L., 219
Fischer, S. E., 126
Fisher, E. M. C., 253
Fisher, R. S., 210
Fitzgerald, J., 14
Flake, A. W., 222
Flanders, S. C., 28
Florsheim, P., 23
Floyd, R., 181
Fouayzi, H., 246
Fox, M. H., 259
Fraiberg, S. H., 45
Francis, S. L., 106
FRAXA Research Foundation, 256
Freeborn, D. S., 48, 54
Freeman, S. B., 250
French, N. K., 44
Freud, S., 94
Freund, I. S., 254
Friedlmeier, W., 106
Friedman, H., 171
Friend, A. C., 43
Friend, M., 43, 74, 75
Froehlich, T., 214
Frost, J. L., 387
Futagi, Y., 196

Gabbard, C., 117
Gaillard, R., 155
Gallagher, D. J., 6
Gallagher, P., 49
Galliher, R. V., 128
Galloway, T. A., 133
Galván, A., 133
Gamez, A., 261
Gardner, J., 179
Gardner-Neblett, N., 128
Garrett, B. E., 183
Garrett-Peters, P., 128
Gavidia-Payne, S., 57
Gavin, A. R., 153
Gaylor, A. S., 246
Georgiev, P., 261
Gephart, H., 215
Gerardin, P., 136
Gernsbacher, M. A., 269
Gesell, A., 95
Geva, R., 212
Ghofrani, M., 173
Gilbert, D., 276
Gilbert, W. M., 202
Gilboa, S. M., 276
Gillis, S., 291
Gillman, M. W., 93
Gladwin, M. T., 263

Glasson, E. J., 250
Glei, D. A., 23
Glover, V., 136
Godfrey, C., 217
Gokmen-Ozel, H., 261
Goldschmidt, L., 184
Goldsmith, H. H., 269
Goldstein, B., 65–66
Goldstein, M., 203
Gonclaves, L. F., 164
Gonzales-Alvarez, L. I., 68
Goode, S., 270, 330
Goorhuis-Brouwer, S. M., 120
Gorman-Smith, D., 23
Goss, C. H., 246
Gossage, J. P., 179
Govaerts, P. J., 291
Governale, L., 214
Grafodatskaya, D., 269
Graham, H., 47
Grauel, E. L., 172
Greatschools, 377
Green, J., 164
Green, S., 50
Green, S. E., 50
Greene, M. F., 223
Grendler, M., 138
Greulich, F. K., 101
Grieve, A. J., 248
Groark, C. J., 14
Groen, A. D., 346
Grosse, S. D., 259, 263, 312
Grunau, R. E., 167
Guggino, W. G., 247
Guimaraes, E. V., 247, 249
Guo, G., 21
Guo, Y., 153
Guralnick, M. J., 15, 72, 77, 78, 79
Gurevitz, M., 212

Habgood, M., 203
Hack, M., 171
Hagberg, C., 279
Hagerman, R., 254, 255, 256
Halfon, O., 137
Hallbook, T., 210
Hallioglu, O., 208
Halsey, N. A., 271
Hamby, D. W., 43
Hamilton-Giachritsis, C., 107
Hamilton-Huesmann, L. R., 107
Hamm, C. R., 166
Hansen, K., 103
Hanson, J. E., 249
Hanson, M. J., 79
Hantash, F. M., 253

Subject Index